Springer Textbooks in Law

Springer Textbooks in Law compiles high-quality educational content aimed at undergraduate and graduate students in all areas of law. All self-contained volumes are authored by accomplished academics and suitable for use in class as well as individual study. Many of them include chapter abstracts, definitions of technical terms, cases and self-assessment exercises, as well as recommended reading sections. This series is an invaluable resource for students and lecturers alike and spans the full range of topics in international and European law, including fundamentals of law and comparative law. Special attention is paid to current and emerging topics such as IT law, intellectual property, human rights as well as dispute resolution, mediation, arbitration – and many more.

Dragica Vujadinović • Mareike Fröhlich •
Thomas Giegerich
Editors

Gender-Competent Legal Education

Assistant Editor: Julia Jungfleisch

Springer

Editors
Dragica Vujadinović
Faculty of Law
University of Belgrade
Belgrade, Serbia

Mareike Fröhlich
Europa-Institut
Saarland University
Saarbrücken, Germany

Thomas Giegerich
Europa-Institut
Saarland University
Saarbrücken, Germany

This work was supported by University of Belgrade, Universidad de Cádiz, Libera Università Maria Ss. Assunta, University of Örebrö - The Centre for Violence Studies (CVS), Europa-Institut der Universität des Saarlandes.

This project has been funded with support from the European Commission. This communication reflects the views only of the author, and the Commission cannot be held responsible for any use which may be made of the information contained therein.

ISSN 2509-999X ISSN 2510-0009 (electronic)
Springer Textbooks in Law
ISBN 978-3-031-14359-5 ISBN 978-3-031-14360-1 (eBook)
https://doi.org/10.1007/978-3-031-14360-1

This Springer imprint is published by the registered company Springer Nature Switzerland AG
The registered company address is: Gewerbestrasse 11, 6330 Cham, Switzerland

Foreword

I am delighted to be invited to write the foreword for this important book, which was produced as part of the Master's Study Program Law and Gender (LAWGEM) project of the LUMSA University, Örebro University, Saarland University, the University of Cadiz, and the University of Belgrade, which is my alma mater.

Gender equality is an important component of European legal value system, and one of the leading principles of international human rights protection, at universal and European level. It is of particular importance that the jurisprudence of the ECtHR is resolute in protecting equality of the sexes, preventing the unequal treatment of men and women (*Karlheinz Schmidt v Germany*) in all aspects of life, as well as regarding sexual life of both sexes (*Carvalho Pinto de Sousa Morais v. Portugal*), condemning domestic violence and insisting on state's duty to prevent, investigate, and prosecute acts of domestic violence (*Volodina v. Russia, Opuz v. Turkey*), securing reproductive autonomy (*Tysiąc v. Poland*), condemning bullying at workplace (*Špadijer v. Montenegro*), protecting from discrimination by refusing employment-related benefit to pregnant woman (*Jurčić v. Croatia*), etc.

In the spirit of a living instrument doctrine, the Court interprets the European Convention on Human Rights and the Protocols thereof in the light of present day conditions, which has great importance for the issues regarding gender equality, as well as those aspects of the human rights protection that were not explicitly included in the text of the Convention 72 years ago. In that sense, the Court has strengthened the protection of rights of transsexual persons over the years, beginning with the finding of a state obligation in the sense of "the need for appropriate legal measures should therefore be kept under review having regard particularly to scientific and societal developments" in *Rees v. UK* (para 47), over the *Goodwin v. UK,* where the Court decided that the respondent Government "can no longer claim that the matter falls within their margin of appreciation" (para 93), requiring the states to ensure legal recognition to the gender re-assignment; to recent decisions such as *A.M. and Others v. Russia*, in which the Court pointed out the rights of transsexual parents and the prohibition of discrimination.

Still, we live in the societies and work for the institutions that are not organized in terms of full respect of gender equality principle. Even at the ECtHR the figures are negatively illustrative: number of female judges is far from equal with the number of male colleagues. Also, the pending applications concerning gender equality and gender identity show the constant, if not growing, importance of gender competent lawyers and judges.

Taking part of women in decision-making processes, as equally as men, is necessary for the realization of the international rule of law, as well as it is evident in respect of the political participation of all groups of a society, meaning the representatives of both minorities and majority. In particular, this is important for the states in transition towards modern democracy and their full compliance with the requirements of the rule of law.

The gender perspective not only plays an important role in the work of the ECtHR, but also in any other legal profession and all areas of law, which makes it all the more important that students are taught to have an understanding of it. At this stage, it is crucial to educate young people and, by doing so, to contribute to developing the culture of human rights, where equality and prohibition of discrimination are the pillars.

This book provides students and professionals with a first insight into gender perspective in law at the international, European, and national levels. It is an important reading as it enables its readers to learn the necessary basics, while preparing them to become gender competent legal professionals.

Because of all this, I am glad to have the opportunity to support this project, convinced that it will tremendously contribute to development of legal culture and, consequently, to more gender-sensitive judgments.

European Court of Human Rights
Strasbourg, France

Ivana Jelić

Acknowledgement

LAWGEM
Master`s Study Program
Law and Gender

Co-funded by the
Erasmus+ Programme
of the European Union

With support of

UCA Universidad de Cádiz

EUROPA-INSTITUT
SAARLAND UNIVERSITY
INTERNATIONAL LAW SCHOOL

LUMSA UNIVERSITÀ

ÖREBRO UNIVERSITY

Contents

List of Contributors

María Acale Sánchez University of Cadiz, Faculty of Law, International Public, Criminal and Procedural Law, Jerez de la Frontera, Spain

Rigmor Argren Örebro University, School of Law, Psychology and Social work, Örebro, Sweden

Teresa Pontón Aricha University of Cadiz, Faculty of Law, Jerez de la Frontera, Spain

Ivana Barać University of Belgrade, Faculty of Law, Civil Law, Belgrade, Serbia

María Angustias Benito Benítez Labour and Social Security Law, University of Cadiz, Faculty of Law, Cadiz, Spain

Eva Bermúdez Figueroa University of Cadiz, Faculty of Social Sciences and Communication, Department of General Economics, Area of Sociology, Jerez de la Frontera, Spain

Amalia Blandino University of Cadiz, Faculty of Law, Private Law, Cadiz, Spain

Gabriele Carapezza Figlia LUMSA, Faculty of Law, Palermo, Italy

Marco Cedro LUMSA, Palermo, Italy

Letizia Coppo LUMSA, Faculty of Law, Palermo, Italy

Francesca Costanza LUMSA University Rome, Department of Law, Palermo, Italy

Beatriz Cruz University of Cadiz, Faculty of Law, International Public, Criminal and Procedural Law, Jerez de la Frontera, Spain

Valerija Dabetić University of Belgrade Faculty of Law, Sociology of Law, Belgrade, Serbia

Snežana Dabić Nikićević University of Belgrade, Faculty of Law, Civil Law, Belgrade, Serbia

Marko Davinić University of Belgrade, Faculty of Law, Belgrade, Serbia

Antonio Álvarez del Cuvillo Department of Labour and Social Security Law, University of Cádiz, Cádiz, Spain

Una Divac University of Belgrade, Faculty of Law, Belgrade, Serbia

Katarina Dolović Bojić University of Belgrade, Faculty of Law, Civil Law, Belgrade, Serbia

Marco Evola LUMSA, Department of Law, Palermo, Italy

Maurilio Felici LUMSA University, Department of Law, Palermo, Italy

Giampaolo Frezza LUMSA, Faculty of Law, Palermo, Italy

Mareike Fröhlich Europa-Institut, Saarland University, Saarbrucken, Germany
Saarland University, Faculty of Law, Europa-Institut, Saarbrücken, Germany

Thomas Giegerich Europa-Institut, Saarland University, Saarbrucken, Germany

Manuela Ortega Gil University of Cadiz, Faculty of Law, General Economics, Cadiz, Spain

Vanesa Hervías Parejo Area of Social Work and Social Services, Department of Labour and Social Security Law, University of Cadiz, Faculty of Labour Sciences, Cádiz, Spain

Pietro Lo Iacono LUMSA University, Department of Law, Palermo, Italy

Tatjana Jevremović Petrović University of Belgrade, Faculty of Law, Civil Law Department, Belgrade, Serbia

Julia Jungfleisch Saarland University, Faculty of Law, Saarbrücken, Germany

Ljubinka Kovačević University of Belgrade, Faculty of Law, Belgrade, Serbia

Eleonor Kristoffersson Örebro University, School of Law, Psychology and Social Work, Örebro, Sweden

Nina Kršljanin University of Belgrade Faculty of Law, Belgrade, Serbia

Ivana Krstić University of Belgrade, Faculty of Law, Belgrade, Serbia

Jelena Lepetić University of Belgrade, Faculty of Law, Civil Law Department, Belgrade, Serbia

Lydia Bares Lopez University of Cadiz, Faculty of Law, General Economics, Cadiz, Spain

Natalija Lukić University of Belgrade, Faculty of Law, Criminal Law, Belgrade, Serbia

Fabio Macioce LUMSA, Philosophy of Law, Rome, Italy

Tanasije Marinković University of Belgrade, Faculty of Law, Belgrade, Serbia

Ivana Marković University of Belgrade, Faculty of Law, Criminal Law, Belgrade, Serbia

M^{a}. Isabel Ribes Moreno University of Cadiz, School of Labour Sciences, Cadiz, Spain

Uros Novaković University of Belgrade, Faculty of Law, Private Law, Belgrade, Serbia

Thais Guerrero Padrón University of Cadiz, School of Labour Sciences, Cadiz, Spain

Fuensanta Rabadán University of Cadiz, Faculty of Law, Private Law, Cadiz, Spain

Branko Radulović Economics and Economics Analysis of Law, University of Belgrade, Faculty of Law, Belgrade, Serbia

Carmen Jover Ramírez Labour and Social Security Law, University of Cadiz, Faculty of Law, Cadiz, Spain

Zara Saeidzadeh Örebro University, School of Humanities, Education and Social Sciences, Örebro, Sweden

Vojislav Stanimirović University of Belgrade Faculty of Law, Belgrade, Serbia

Susanne Strand Örebro University, School of Law, Psychology and Social Work, Örebro, Sweden

Sofia Strid School of Humanities, Education and Social Sciences, Unit of Gender Studies and Sociology, Örebro University, Örebro, Sweden
Department of Sociology and Work Science, Gothenburg University, Gothenburg, Sweden

Dragica Vujadinović Faculty of Law, University of Belgrade, Belgrade, Serbia

Raquel Pastor Yuste University of Cádiz, Faculty of Law, Department of General Economic, Area of Sociology, Jerez de la Frontera, Spain

Lidija Živković University of Belgrade, Faculty of Law, Belgrade, Serbia

Introduction

1

Dragica Vujadinović, Mareike Fröhlich, and Thomas Giegerich

One of the key findings of the July 2022 Global Gender Gap Report of the World Economic Forum is this: "At the current rate of progress, it will take 132 years to reach full parity."[1]

This textbook *Gender Competent Legal Knowledge* explains the legal mechanisms available for accelerating that process and is the result of joint work of authors from five European universities—Lumsa University (Italy), Cadiz University (Spain), Orebro University (Sweden), Saarland University (Germany), and Belgrade University (Serbia) which also acted as coordinator. These institutions have been working together since 2019 on the Erasmus+ project entitled *New Quality in Education for Gender Equality – Strategic Partnership for the Development of Master's Study program "Law and* Gender"—*LAWGEM*. One of the main intellectual outputs of the LAWGEM project is the publication of this textbook, which reflects all relevant fields of legal education of the curriculum for the master's study program "Law and Gender". This book will not only be used in this master program, but will also equally be highly relevant for any effort to study law in a systemic and gender-competent way.

Male dominated law and legal knowledge has almost completely characterized the whole of pre-modern history inasmuch as the patriarchy represented the axis of social relations in both the private and public spheres. Indeed, modern and even contemporary law still have embedded elements of patriarchal heritage, even in the

[1] Global Gender Gap Report of the World Economic Forum, p. 5, available at https://www3.weforum.org/docs/WEF_GGGR_2022.pdf.

D. Vujadinović
Faculty of Law, University of Belgrade, Belgrade, Serbia
e-mail: dragicav@ius.bg.ac.rs

M. Fröhlich (✉) · T. Giegerich
Europa-Institut, Saarland University, Saarbrucken, Germany
e-mail: m.froehlich@europainstitut.de; giegerich@europainstitut.de

D. Vujadinović et al. (eds.), *Gender-Competent Legal Education*, Springer Textbooks in Law, https://doi.org/10.1007/978-3-031-14360-1_1

secular modern legal systems of Western developed countries, either within the content of legislation or in its implementation and interpretation. This is true across different legal systems to a greater or lesser extent, although the secular modern legal systems of the Western developed countries have made great advances in terms of gender equality in law. The traditional understanding of law has always been self-evidently dominated by men, but modern law and its understanding has itself also been more or less male-streamed. It has become necessary to overcome the given maskulinity of the legal thought. This necessity emerges as a logical consequence, as well as practical demand based on civilizational shifts brought about through modern political revolutions and the gradual development of consciousness of the centrality of dignity of each person, universal equality of all individuals. Along with gender-based equality, this has also meant the necessity of recognition of differences among individuals belonging to sexual minority groups.

Gender inequality and heteronomous social relations within the patriarchal matrix still represent something uncontestable for many men and even women, including many legal scholars and practitioners of law of all genders. The mainstream of the legal theory, knowledge, and practice has been male-streamed even in contemporary times. However, the shift in historical consciousness (in Hegel's words) towards building an emancipatory, gender-equal matrix has been an unstoppable process; although this does not mean that the mentioned process cannot be halted or slowed down here and there. Generally speaking, if this emancipatory matrix had been allowed to evolve only spontaneously, it would have been a rather slow process, while the patriarchal heritage has remained stubbornly present, changing its modalities in order not only to survive but also to attempt to maintain or even increase its domination. Boosting emancipatory processes through various institutional, collective, and personal mechanisms is necessary, and it is especially productive and useful if done within legal and higher education. Male-dominant or male-streamed legal knowledge, education, and practice should be transformed into gender-mainstreamed and gender competent knowledge, education, and practice.

In contemporary legal and political orders, gender mainstreaming of law has been of the utmost importance for overcoming a deep and persistent embeddedness of power relations and gender-based heteronomous social relations. Consequently, complementary and, equally important, the gender mainstreaming of legal education—to which this book aims to contribute—serves for a gradual elimination of the mentioned male dominance and power relations from legal education and higher education as a whole.

The textbook *Gender Competent Legal Knowledge* represent a pioneering and unique intellectual attempt towards a systemic gender mainstreaming of legal education and higher education in general. The title of the textbook implies that the chapters and the textbook as a whole intend to reconsider from gender equality perspective all relevant fields of law and other fields of multidisciplinary knowledge closely related to law. The term "gender-competent" is used to accentuate the reconsideration of different fields of legal knowledge from the point of gender equality approach and with offering relevant and convincing arguments in that regard. It is addressed to all students and learners worldwide, with an attempt to raise their gender awareness in mainstream legal knowledge. The intention is to invite scholars to broaden their views and to open their minds for theoretical, methodological and pedagogical approaches which prioritize gender equality over allegedly neutral concepts, which however contain heteronormative power relations, male domination and female subordination.

Regarding the legal background, public international law and supranational EU law are playing ever more important roles in a globalized world. This has also raised the importance of introducing gender competency in making, interpreting, applying and adjudicating international and supranational law as well as teaching and learning it. While we have come a long way regarding *de jure* and *de facto* equality of women in international and supranational law, a huge gap between promise or theory and reality or practice remains there, too. Narrowing that gap is not easy because the backlash against (international) human rights in the name of "national autonomy" and "traditional values" which we are currently witnessing is often specifically directed against the rights of women and non-binary persons. We need more gender sensitivity in the making and enforcement of inter-/supranational as well as national law, and for that, gender-sensitive legal education needs to be intensified. On the other hand, we must spread the word that the gender-equality standards of international and supranational law are often more advanced than those in national legal systems and that they can and should be used as benchmarks for further progress on the ground.

The famous documents initiating the human rights revolution in the late eighteenth century were formulated by men and proclaimed the human rights of men[2]—to such an extent that Olympe de Gouges felt compelled to add her own declaration of the rights of women in 1791.[3] The situation is different with the United Nations Charter of 1945 that brought about the human rights revolution at the international level by transforming the human rights protection from the *domaine réservé* of individual sovereign States to a matter of concern for the international community as a whole. The Charter immediately adopted the notion of equal rights of women. Underlining the "dignity and worth of the human person" and the "equal rights of men and women" in its Preamble, the Charter went on by declaring in Art. 1 (3) that "[t]o achieve international co-operation . . . in promoting and encouraging respect for human rights and fundamental freedoms for all without distinction as to . . . sex" was one of the purposes of the United Nations. The Charter obliges the United Nations to promote "universal respect for, and observance of, human rights and fundamental freedoms for all without distinction as to . . . sex" in Art. 55 lit. c and in Art. 56, "[a]ll Members pledge themselves to take joint and separate action in cooperation with the

[2] See the U.S. Declaration of Independence of 4 July 1776: "We hold these truths to be self-evident, that all men are created equal, that they are endowed by their Creator with certain unalienable Rights . . ."; Déclaration des droits de l'homme et du citoyen of 26 August 1789 by the French National Assembly.

[3] Déclaration des droits de la femme et de la citoyenne, available at https://gallica.bnf.fr/ark:/12148/bpt6k426138/f10.item. See also Mary Wollstonecraft, A Vindication of the Rights of Woman (originally published in 1792).

Organization for the achievement of the purposes set forth in Article 55." In 1948, the UN General Assembly proclaimed the Universal Declaration of Human Rights in gender-neutral terms, underlining the equal rights of men and women and the prohibition of discrimination based on sex.[4] The Declaration had been drafted by the UN Human Rights Commission chaired by Eleanor Roosevelt.[5]

This was a good start in theory and it was somewhat belatedly followed by the two International Covenants of 1966, general human rights treaties prohibiting discrimination on ground of sex and obliging States Parties to ensure equal rights of men and women.[6] But in practice UN Member States had to admit the obvious in 1979—that "extensive discrimination against women continues to exist", so that a gender-specific Convention on the Elimination of All Forms of Discrimination against Women (CEDAW) was needed.[7] As a matter of fact, stereotyped roles for "superior" men and "inferior" women have long been deeply entrenched in the cultural and religious traditions of many societies. Thus, while CEDAW is one of the most widely accepted of the nine core human rights treaties at UN level, it is also the one riddled with the greatest number of far-reaching and impermissible reservations by States. These States obviously fear the effective realisation of women's rights and the creation of substantive equality with men because that inevitably requires "a change in the traditional role of men as well as the role of women in society and in the family", as the preamble of CEDAW expressly and rightly states. Moreover, CEDAW's implementation mechanism (a mere State reporting system) is weaker than the implementation mechanisms of other core human rights treaties, not least because the treaty body (Committee on the Elimination of Discrimination against Women) is limited to one annual meeting period of normally not more than two weeks to consider the reports submitted by the States.[8] The 1999 Optional Protocol to CEDAW that introduced an individual complaint mechanism has so far been ratified by only sixty percent of the States Parties of CEDAW.[9]

The unpleasant truth is that despite all these efforts, "extensive discrimination against women continues to exist" even more than forty years after the entry into force of CEDAW in 1981. In these forty years we have even witnessed barbarous acts against Bosnian, Yezidi, Rohingya and many other women which have outraged the conscience of humankind and led to the inclusion of gender-specific offences in

[4]UN General Assembly Resolution 217 A (III), available at https://www.un.org/sites/un2.un.org/files/udhr.pdf.

[5]Mary Ann Glendon, A World Made New: Eleanor Roosevelt and the Universal Declaration of Human Rights (2001).

[6]Arts. 2 (1), 3 and 26 of the International Covenant on Civil and Political Rights (UNTS vol. 999, p. 171); Arts. 2 (2), 3 of the International Covenant on Economic, Social and Cultural Rights (UNTS vol. 993, p. 3).

[7]UNTS vol. 1249, p. 13. The quotation is taken from the preamble of CEDAW.

[8]Art. 20 (1) CEDAW. A 1995 attempt to revise that provision by eliminating the two-week limit has still not entered into force.

[9]UNTS vol. 2131, p. 83.

the code of crimes under international law, specifically as variants of crimes against humanity and war crimes.[10] Obviously, one cannot in a few decades change attitudes that have hardened for centuries if not millennia. But at least we have widespread agreement today that the gender gap in the effective realisation of global human rights constitutes a serious problem which needs to be solved in order to consummate the human rights revolution and ensure freedom, justice and peace in the world. In other words, there already is a high degree of gender-sensitive problem awareness and it is growing. Thus, international public opinion is closely watching the fate of women's rights in Afghanistan after the takeover by the Taliban. But we definitely need to accelerate the frustratingly slow pace of closing that gender gap—and for that purpose also make determined use of the instruments of international and supranational law at our disposal. That presupposes not only gender-competent legal education in general, but gender-competent education in international and supranational law in particular.

On the regional levels, only Africa has an equivalent to CEDAW—the Protocol to the African Charter on Human and Peoples' Rights on the Rights of Women in Africa of 2003.[11] In the Americas and in Europe, we only find special treaties on the prevention and elimination of violence against women: The Inter-American Convention on the Prevention, Punishment and Eradication of Violence against Women (Convention of Belém do Pará) of 1994[12] and the Council of Europe Convention on Preventing and Combating Violence against Women and Domestic Violence (Istanbul Convention) of 2011. In Asia, there is no gender-specific human rights treaty.[13] The Arab region, which straddles Africa and Asia, has not brought forth any gender-specific treaty, but the Arab Charter on Human Rights of 2008 addresses the obligation to eliminate discrimination on grounds of sex and guarantee "effective equality" between men and women as well as the need to protect women from all forms of violence or abuse in family relations.[14] But on the regional level, all is not well either: Turkey that had been proud to be among the first States to sign the Istanbul Convention in 2011 denounced it in March 2021, although the number of women killed there, mostly by (former) male partners or family members continues to rise. The good news is that this move provoked heavy criticism both inside and outside Turkey and that deliberations in Poland to leave the Convention as well have

[10] See Arts. 7 (1) lit. g and h, 8 (2) lit. b (xxii), lit. e (vi) of the Rome Statute of the International Criminal Court of 1998 (UNTS vol. 2187, No. 38544).

[11] Available at https://au.int/sites/default/files/treaties/37077-treaty-charter_on_rights_of_women_in_africa.pdf.

[12] Available at http://www.oas.org/juridico/english/treaties/a-61.html.

[13] There is a Declaration of the Advancement of Women in the ASEAN Region of 1988, available at https://asean.org/declaration-of-the-advancement-of-women-in-the-asean-region-bangkok-thailand-5-july-1988/, and a Declaration on the Elimination of Violence against Women in the ASEAN Region of 2012, available at https://asean.org/declaration-on-the-elimination-of-violence-against-women-in-the-asean-region-3/.

[14] Arts. 3, 33 (2). Available at https://digitallibrary.un.org/record/551368.

not been pursued any further. This is an encouraging sign of gender-sensitivity in transnational public opinion.

In supranational law, the equality between women and men does not only feature prominently among the values of the European Union set forth in Art. 2 TEU as well as the Charter of Fundamental Rights,[15] but the EU is outright charged with combatting discrimination and promoting equality between women and men.[16] The EU has fulfilled this obligation to a considerable extent by enacting various Directives.[17] More specifically, Member States are obliged under Art. 157 (1) TFEU to "ensure that the principle of equal pay for male and female workers for equal work is applied". That obligation was already included in Art. 119 of the original Treaty establishing the European Economic Community of 1957 and the European Court of Justice determined forty-five years ago that the supranational principle of equal pay was directly applicable, giving underpaid women an actionable entitlement also *vis-à-vis* private employers.[18] It also partakes in the primacy of supranational law over the law of the Member States.[19] Yet, there still is a significant gender pay gap in many Member States and thus a gap between promise and reality regarding equal rights of women in the EU, too.

Another EU-specific example for the gap between promise and reality regarding equal rights for women is the delay in the ratification of the Istanbul Convention which the EU signed already in 2017. Only 21 Member States have become parties to the Convention so far, the other six have only signed it because in the national ratification processes objections based on traditional conceptions of the family were raised. Apart from the question on what TFEU-articles the Council decision to authorise the conclusion of the Istanbul Convention on behalf of the Union should be based, the problem is whether the Council can adopt that decision before all the Member States have ratified the Convention. The European Parliament requested an opinion from the Court of Justice of the European Union pursuant to Art. 218 (11) TFEU on these questions which was given on 6 October 2021.[20] The Court decided that it was within the discretion of the Council whether or not to wait until all the Member States had ratified. In any event, the ratification of the Istanbul Convention by the EU (and the closing of the gap between promise and reality) has not yet been accomplished.

A third such gap is currently about to open up: Commission President von der Leyen announced in her State of the Union Address on 15 September 2021 that by

[15] Arts. 21 (1), 23.

[16] Art. 3 (3) (2) TEU. See also Arts. 8, 10, 19 (1) TFEU.

[17] The most important one is the Directive 2006/54/EC of 5 July 2006 on the implementation of the principle of equal opportunities and equal treatment of men and women in matters of employment and occupation (recast), OJ 2006 L 204, p. 23.

[18] ECJ, judgment of 8 April 1976, Case 43/75, ECR 1976, 455 (Defrenne II).

[19] Declaration (No. 17) concerning primacy in the Annex to the Final Act of the Intergovernmental Conference of Lisbon of 13 December 2007 (OJ 2016 C 202, p. 344).

[20] Opinion Procedure 1/19.

the end of the year, the Commission would propose a law to combat violence against women.[21] On 8 March 2022, the Commission published its Proposal for a Directive of the European Parliament and of the Council on combating violence against women and domestic violence.[22] The Commission proposes the EU legislature use powers pursuant to Art. 82 (2) and Art. 83 (1) TFEU which would permit the Council to decide by qualified majority within the ordinary legislative procedure.[23] But Art. 82 (3) and Art. 83 (3) TFEU both give every Member States veto power to shield "fundamental aspects of its criminal justice system". It is quite likely that at least one of the six Member States that have so far refused to ratify the Istanbul Convention will use its veto to derail the proposal. On the other hand, the fact that the Commission President has made such an announcement on this important occasion, investing political capital on a gender issue, shows that she expects a political profit. She obviously believes that the amount of gender awareness and sensitivity has grown considerably throughout the EU.

This overview of international and supranational developments demonstrates that the gap between promise and reality regarding equal rights for women is still significant also at those levels. But at the same time it reveals that international and supranational law have the potential to improve the situation of women by helping to overcome national obstacles and resistance. International and supranational law can lead the way by performing a role-model function, because these areas of the law are further detached from the cultural and religious traditions of individual societies that often prevent progress. On the other hand, that detachment inevitably lowers the legitimacy of international and supranational solutions. In order to prevent a backlash, one must avoid the impression that solutions are imposed from above. Rather, it is a matter of persuasion by opening up new and broader perspectives to as many people as possible. It should be made clear that by discriminating women societies waste talents and suffer a competitive disadvantage.

This textbook is intended to make a contribution to these efforts. Without gender-competent legal knowledge there will be no gender equality—neither in law nor in real life. Since lawyers are also multipliers for raising gender awareness and sensitivity in the society at large, teaching them gender competency will have a real impact.

The chapters of this book articulate scientific analyses of all legal fields of knowledge related to the positive civil, public, international, criminal law, European Union Law, as well as to the legal-economic, legal-historical, theoretical-legal fields of legal education. Metaphorically speaking, the mainstream interpretation of the mentioned fields of legal education and knowledge production will be "deconstructed" and "reconstructed" from a gender-sensitive point of view. Visibility of the female half of the population will have to be accomplished by first

[21] Available at https://ec.europa.eu/commission/presscorner/detail/en/SPEECH_21_4701.

[22] COM(2022) 105 final, available at https://eur-lex.europa.eu/legal-content/EN/TXT/PDF/?uri=CELEX:52022PC0105&from=EN.

[23] Art. 289, 294 TFEU read together with Art. 16 (3) TEU.

demonstrating how pre-modern law defined women in a discriminatory manner, and how modern law also made women invisible in the concepts of universal rights of men and citizens, i.e., identified the notion of legal universality and equality with the male population. It will show how women had to fight from the eighteenth century onwards to become visible in the law and get equal voting and education rights. And finally, in general, how gender equality has been framed in different dimensions and fields of law and legal education, including both women's rights as well as rights of non-binary persons (who, although they have received some justifiable visibility and importance in the public realm also must be promoted in the frame of human rights protections).

This textbook will certainly stimulate its users, but also the broader legal public to continue reconsidering the law and specific fields of interest within it from a gender perspective. The educators have passed through an innovative learning process: they have been educating themselves about gender-competent approaches, in order to be capable to impart new quality knowledge to their students and colleagues. That is how the spiral of progressive gender mainstreaming of legal education will be conducted and promoted. Structural conservatism linked to legal education will be questioned and the overcoming of the male stream *status quo* will be taken up by a growing number of law professors and professionals. Gender-mainstreaming of the legal education implies and demands building and enhancing this chain of mutually interconnected processes of learning/teaching/studying in favor of gender equality.

This textbook is intended to make a contribution to these efforts. Without gender-competent legal knowledge there will be no gender equality—neither in law nor in real life. Since lawyers are also multipliers for raising gender awareness and sensitivity in the society at large, teaching them gender competency will have a real impact.

In aiming to achieve the gender-competent reconstruction of legal knowledge in particular fields and do so in a systematic, consistent way with regard to all relevant fields of law, this project set itself a pioneering task. It could be characterized as an innovation: (1) in a factual sense, as it is the first attempt at a systemic reconstruction of legal knowledge from a gender equality perspective; and (2) in an essential sense, due to its intent to reconstruct legal education from within. Trying to reconsider law across all its disciplines in a way that goes beyond the mainstream/male stream matrix, indeed to reform legal knowledge systematically from within, that same matrix has been itself revolutionized. Doing that by studying the extra-curricular feminist legal literature has meant letting feminist critical legal thought enter mainstream knowledge and change it. This endeavor has been complementary and complying with critical legal studies. However, instead of standing apart and trying to impact mainstream legal knowledge from the outside, the authors sought to equip themselves with insights from critical legal studies in order to reconsider and transform from within their fields of research and teaching. To reiterate, this revolutionary attempt contributes in a final instance to the systematic gender-mainstreaming of legal knowledge.

Academic scholars from universities across five different countries were involved in writing this book. Such successful teamwork gives the text a specific quality and is an unprecedented academic phenomenon. Working at different universities (primarily at faculties of law), researchers accepted to investigate and study feminist critical legal and political literature, reconsidering from a gender perspective their various fields of academic research and teaching.

The research and teaching project that produced this book represents an extremely exciting, innovative, and challenging academic undertaking. Individual academics of different educational backgrounds, very different religious, political, cultural, social, historical heritage, and independently of possible binary or non-binary gender orientation, who had not known each other before—readily took up a huge effort, with a common and unique aim to reconsider and deconstruct legal knowledge (as well as that of the disciplines close to it) in order to articulate a gender-competent understanding of the law and related disciplines and reconstruct them accordingly. These intellectuals managed, in spite of all their differences, limitations, and obstacles, to establish a culture of dialogue, readiness to share research and writing duties, to open their minds to new insights and the potential to overcome their own gender-based biases. Accordingly, the chapters have been built as the real team work results.

All chapters are an in-depth attempt to deconstruct and reconstruct specific relevant fields of legal education from a gender perspective. Sometimes the notion of "woman" still features as the paradigmatic subject, rather than the notion of "gender;" other times, the notion of "gender" is considered mostly in a binary way and primarily in a heteronormative sense. This is problematic when faced with the diversity of lives women lead and considering the changing notions of "man" and masculinity, as well as that of "gender," and indeed, when witnessing the impact changes to family law, inheritance law, criminal law, tax law etc., have had on the heteronormative order.

Some authors and chapters have kept the binary gender construction, others have moved towards conceiving issues surrounding the identities of a third gender and transgender persons. These differences in levels of understandings are not a failure or drawback of the book, but rather reflect the different stages and states of affairs in knowledge and mindsets of the authors involved, thus also generally reflecting existing differences in that regard among the contemporary intellectual, political, and legal public.

It could be said that the scope of these texts surpasses their inner quality; indeed, they do because they seek to stimulate and provoke further academic attempts at ever better and richer results of systemic gender-competent legal knowledge.

In essence the textbook is structured in three major parts which deal with the gender perspective in different contexts. The first part "Gender in a general context" focusses mainly on explanatory contributions which help to understand the following chapters in a better way. The second part organises all chapters in the context of the public sphere—differentiating the European and international level from the national one. It analysis the gender perspective in the field of administration, planning and politics. It also includes criminal law issues as part of the public life. In contrast to this, the last part deals with the private dimension of the gender perspective, especially in private life, economy and business as well as in the world of labour.

In detail, the first chapters want to set the ground for a gender-competent legal knowledge. Therefore the chapter on "Gender Issues in Comparative Legal History" gives a historical overview of gender issues and the domination of the patriarchal system in the Western legal systems from the antiquity to modern times. The different feminist political and legal theories have been introduced and critically analysed in the chapter "Feminist political and legal theories", which also considers the necessity of reconsidering "old" political and legal concepts from the feminist perspective and introducing the "new" ones, which better inform the political and legal knowledge about gender equality importance and content. The chapter "Gender and structural inequalities from a socio-legal perspective" focus on structural gender inequalities in private and public social spheres, especially education production, labour market and media, by deconstructing the gender binary system. The important role of gender in the judicial decision-making in the context of the composition of the bench has been analysed in the chapter "Feminist Judgements" which also highlights a few projects to overcome the effects. The general part of the textbook has been rounded up by the chapter "Gender Research and Feminist Methodologies" which deals with ontological and epistemological approaches of methodology and explains how to conduct research with a gender equality perspective.

The chapters on "Human Rights Law through the lens of the Gender Perspective" and "The Evolving Recognition of Gender in International and European Law" explain the international and European framework for gender protection and mainstreaming. The first addresses the different aspects in Human Rights Law and discusses among others the prohibition of gender-based violence, slavery and human trafficking, the freedom of religion as well as women's access to justice and education. The second one explains the different legal sources for fighting gender-based discrimination and gender mainstreaming and put special emphasis on the UN Charter, the Convention on the Elimination of All Forms of Discrimination Against Women as well as the Charter of Fundamental Rights of the European Union and the European Convention on Human Rights.

The national public perspective, promoted also by international instruments, will be examined in the chapter on "Gender Equality Aspects of Public Law". The chapter deals prominently with the underrepresentation of women in governmental and state institutions and introduces a multi-layered approach of gender empowerment to raise the impact on public policies. The role of governments to secure the social welfare of citizens and gender equality has been addressed in the chapter "Gender Perspective of Social Security Law". This chapter introduces especially cases where discrimination due to the different nature and roles of women and men takes place. Gender equality in the public expenditure management as well as the national taxation laws have been analysed in the chapter "Gender Equitable Taxation". It tries to point various ways of gender discrimination in taxing affairs within a household, at the workplace and within the broader economy denying the principle of fairness. The role of public engagement is reflected in the chapter "Public Policies on Gender Equality" which introduces different ways to support gender mainstreaming and impact assessment of public policies. In the aftermath, key gender sensitive policies in different sectors are elaborated.

The general and special part of criminal law, which deals with gender discrimination and gender-based crimes, is explained in the chapter "Gender Competent Criminal Law". It focusses mainly on the Istanbul Convention but also examines the general theories of criminal law in the light of gender equality. The chapter "Gender Perspective of Victimization, Crime and Penal Policy" shows the criminological perspective regarding the relationship of crime and gender. Data is evaluated to explain the ethological background, the awareness for gender victimization and the penal policy of courts facing different genders.

In the last part of the textbook the chapters deal with gender issues in the private law context. The main overview of gender discrimination in private law is found in the chapter "Gender Equalities in the different fields of Private Law". The focus is on property regulations, freedom of contracts and tort liability. The context of family law is analysed in the chapter "Gender Competent Family Law", and there is firstly explained the genesys of the family throughout the history and up to multiple forms of family and social relations within families of today. It then examines the interplay of rights and responsibilities of partners, parents and children and its impact on gender equality, including also marital contracts. Finally, it also addresses the important topic of domestic violence. Gender discrimination as being widely spread in labour relationships has been elaborated in the chapter "Labour Law and Gender". The chapter covers different relevant dimensions, like as protection against gender-based discrimination by the employer, women empowerment and gender-based discrimination during the hiring process. The economical aspects of gender issues are dealt with in the chapter "Integrating Gender Equality in Economics and Management". The theory of feminist economics is explained, taking into account gender indicators, gender parity, gender equality and gender mainstreaming. The managerial and innovative side of economics are also examined in the light of gender. The last chapter "Gender, Business and the Law" deals with gender aspects in the business and economic world. It explains not only the impact of gender diversity in company boards or in dispute resolution boards, but also how women's economic empowerment is supported by various initiatives. One main actor is the European Union, although the EU internal market has not had much impact on gender equality, but recent trade agreements follow a gender-mainstreaming approach which opens new possibilities for women.

All chapters end with some questions which allow the reader to control if they understood how the traditional parts of laws have an impact on gender equality. The questions also ensure that the reader can evaluate themselves if they can apply the knowledge to different new situations. This methodological-pedagogical approach attempts to enable the reader to get a comprehensive overview which combines theoretical and practical knowledge.

This would not have been possible without the authors of the chapters. We would like to express our gratitude to them for their excellent contributions and wonderful collaboration. In addition, we would like to thank Judge Ivana of the ECtHR for her introductory words and support in the LAWGEM project and beyond. Moreover, we would like to express our sincere thanks to our Assistant Editor Julia Jungfleisch. Her support was essential for the realization of this book. We would also like to thank the research and student assistants at Thomas Giegerich's chair Anna Kothe, Nana Pazmann, Annika Blaschke, Merle Arndt for their impressive reviewing and editing work as well as Catriona Laidlaw, Joshua Eve and Archina Sivarajpillai for the proof-reading.

We hope that this textbook will contribute to highlighting gender perspectives in all fields of law and also to taking them into account in legal assessments. We hope that all readers will enjoy and gain insight from studying the individual contributions.

Part I

Gender in a General Context

Gender Issues in Comparative Legal History 2

Una Divac, Maurilio Felici, Nina Kršljanin, Pietro Lo Iacono, and Vojislav Stanimirović

Contents

Authors are listed in alphabetical order. The Sect. 2.1 and 2.5 are written by Vojislav Stanimirović and Una Divac, Una Divac authored Sect. 2.2.4. Maurilio Felici authored Sect. 2.3.5; Sects. 2.3.6 and 2.4.5 are written by Pietro Lo Iacono. The Sects.2.3.1, 2.3.3, 2.4.2–2.4.4, 2.4.6 and the questions have been prepared by Nina Kršljanin, and Vojislav Stanimirović authored Sects. 2.2.1–2.2.3, 2.3.2, 2.3.4–2.3.5 and 2.4.1.

U. Divac · N. Kršljanin (✉) · V. Stanimirović
University of Belgrade Faculty of Law, Belgrade, Serbia
e-mail: una.divac@ius.bg.ac.rs; nina.krsljanin@ius.bg.ac.rs

M. Felici · P. L. Iacono
LUMSA University Department of Law, Palermo, Italy
e-mail: m.felici@lumsa.it; p.loiacono@lumsa.it

D. Vujadinović et al. (eds.), *Gender-Competent Legal Education*, Springer Textbooks in Law, https://doi.org/10.1007/978-3-031-14360-1_2

Abstract

This chapter analyses the key gender issues throughout comparative legal history, from the Antiquity to the contemporary era. A wide array of subjects will be briefly touched upon, such as the traditional roles of men and women and their legal recognition, the legal status of women, the patriarchal patterns and the trends of their change, the interaction of religion and law in these areas. These various subjects all portray a millennia-long domination of the patriarchal system and the long and arduous struggle for gender equality. The text is mainly concerned with the Western legal systems, broadly speaking—European, Near-Eastern and American—showcasing individual legal systems in the Antiquity and Middle Ages, where differences during these times were greater, but focusing instead on key issues and areas of law in the Modern era, where convergence and common tendencies become more pronounced. By understanding these issues in their historical context, readers will gain valuable knowledge of the historical background of the current status of gender relations in the main legal systems of the world.

2.1 Introduction

During the second half of the twentieth century, the alluring myth of the initial rule of matriarchy was dispelled. It was impossible to reach a general and definite conclusion that women were the dominant sex in the earliest stages of human history, when the only available evidence were the sporadic instances of matrilineality and matrifocality in a handful of cultures. Unfortunately, the patriarchal patterns have been dominating the history of gender relations for thousands of years, skilfully changing their form and tailoring the structure of marriage, family, and society, which enabled them to survive until today. From its emergence in the middle stage of barbarianism—according to Morgan—patriarchy bloomed and persisted, finding its support in customs, religion, and laws, all created by men.[1]

For this exact reason, researching gender relations throughout history up to the modernity has been, in its essence, a one-way road. The main focus has always been placed on the male perception of the female sex and the roles which men gave women in society and family, and not on the ways in which both sexes shaped and

[1] Bolger (2013); Lerner (1986).

influenced each other.[2] Even in Ancient Egypt, the civilisation which was a sole bright spot in the Antiquity and Middle Ages when it came to the position and treatment of women, a queen as powerful as Hatshepsut had to don male clothes and wear a ceremonial beard in order to resemble a male pharaoh. Above that, her heir and stepson Tuthmose III, ordered the destruction of every one of her representations and mentions of her name.[3] The history of mankind is actually a chronicle of male supremacy, written by a male hand. Therefore, it is not surprising that the Trojan war was not attributed to Achaean voracity and greed, but to Helen's infidelity and defence of male honour. Delilah was not a patriot, but an evil traitor. Cleopatra was not a skilful and powerful queen of Egypt, but a seductress and the mistress of Julius Caesar and Mark Antony. Theodora was not an intelligent Byzantine empress who used her wits to protect her husband, but a woman of the lowest class who used her spells to cloud Justinian's mind and occupy a place which did not belong to her. Joan of Arc, a woman of great bravery and unwavering faith, whose agency was pivotal to the outcome of the Hundred Years' War, went down in history as a witch who was burned at a stake simply because she dared to wear a pair of trousers. Catherine the Great, a prominent empress who picked the reformation process up where Peter I left off and rebuilt Russia, was depicted as a lustful and insatiable ruler. Cynicism attributed to Marie Antoinette's 'Let them eat cake' was presented as the cause of the French Revolution, and not the existing socio-economic issues.

The second characteristic of the history of gender relations is that it is, above all, a representation of the gender relations among the higher class. The surviving sources usually tell nothing of the poor, although it is not difficult to assume that the position of lower-class women was quite bad. Especially because of the intersectionality and multiple discrimination that they endured.

Another important characteristic is that researching gender relations must have an interdisciplinary approach. Patriarchal matrix can be revealed only when legal history bands together with ethnology, anthropology, sociology, archaeology, and other social science disciplines. That is the only way to paint a comprehensive picture of patriarchy and all of its forms, and discover effective weapons to overpower it. This battle has been fought for thousands of years and it must not and will not be lost. The chapters in this textbook are dedicated to that cause.

In the Antiquity, all civilisations, with the exception of Egypt, removed their women from public life and confined them within their homes. Neither Greece nor Rome changed that. On the contrary—Ancient Athens, the cradle of democracy, granted equality only to Athenian men, but never Athenian women. Women were always second-class citizens.

In criminal law, women were severely punished, but barely offered any protection. In private law, their position was constantly inferior, with slight differences between the states: some awarded women partial legal capacity, but some kept them completely legally incapacitated.

[2] Clay et al. (2009); Jones et al. (2011); Meade and Wiesner-Hanks (2004).

[3] Cooney (2014).

An almighty male head of the family dominated family law and sometimes even had the power to decide over life or death of his family members. Additionally, everything revolved around sons. They inherited not only the material goods, but also the spiritual family legacy. Sons continued the family line and maintained the cult of—primarily—male ancestors. Undesirable as a daughter, oppressed as a wife, living in the shadow of her father, brothers, husband and in-laws, a woman sometimes managed to gain fragments of legal capacity only as a widow.

In marriage law, there were three usual, but quite undignified ways of securing a wife: through purchase, kidnapping or an agreement which included a dowry. The outcome was always the same: the husband gained complete power over his wife, and sometimes certain aspects of that power extended into the arms of his relatives (e.g., levirate). Women were usually denied the right to inherit, especially when it came to immovable property, and most of the time the only property they could "inherit" was their own dowry.

In property law and law of obligation, women were considered to be unreliable business partners, thanks to the male prejudice that women were superficial and error-prone. For that same reason, women were often unable to be witnesses. In some legal systems, seen in Sharia law, it went a step further. Witness statements of two women were considered of equal value as a statement of a single man.

The Middle Ages seem to have slightly improved the position of women, however not for reasons that have anything to do with achieving gender equality. The main motivation behind such changes stemmed from the religions' and churches' own interests and calculations. During this period, Christianity had an important role: the church occasionally improved the position of women—when it was in its interest (e.g. improving women's property rights as women frequently bequeathed their property to the church), but mostly it had a great role in reproducing patriarchy. In Byzantine and even in post-classical Rome, under the influence of Christianity, child protection was bettered and women's inheritance rights were broadened, however women still remained in the shadows. Germanic peoples heavily relied on their customs, codified in *Leges barbarorum* when transitioning from their pre-state societies to kingdoms after the fall of the Western Roman Empire. Women enjoyed great protection under criminal law and were somewhat respected, but their position in family, inheritance and marriage law was not improved. The Near East was generally unsympathetic to women, but their treatment in Pre-Islamic Arabia was especially brutal. While spreading the new religion, Muhammad became aware that both men and women were needed in order for Islam to prevail. For that exact reason, the Qur'an changed the position of women for the better. Unfortunately, those same verses that brought women some kind of liberation in seventh century AD, became their ball and chain in modern times. In other places, like Medieval England, the position of women remained unfavourable for a very long time.

The Modern Era, which started with great industrial and political revolutions, was the first one to carry the essential historical changes in the political, economic, social and cultural spaces. This enabled the later emergence of the emancipatory tendencies regarding the position of women and gender relations. However, the historical changes which the Modern Era brought were quite controversial. For example, the Industrial Revolution finally introduced women into the public sphere, creating new job positions for them, but primarily because there was a great need for a cheap workforce.[4] The Age of Revolution did not result in the realisation of women's revolutionary demands and its outcome was not very beneficial to women. The Puritan Revolution worsened the position of women and the great French Revolution completely bypassed them, blatantly ignoring their desire to contribute, as well as their expectations to be the equal subject of "the rights of the man and of the citizen". Notwithstanding, Modernity is the first era in human history which started to essentially scrutinise patriarchy. Consequently, it enabled the beginning of a long struggle for overcoming the patriarchy and establishing gender equality.

Learning Goals
With the help of this chapter, the students should:

- have a basic understanding of the key gender issues throughout comparative legal history;
- be able to perceive the historical background of the current status of gender relations in the main legal systems of the world (both the achieved improvement and those issues where there is more left to be gained), and
- be able to understand/envisage the most appropriate solutions (historically and culturally speaking) to issues still open in the twenty-first century.

2.2 The Antiquity

Urbanisation, emergence of the first states, the invention of the writing system, increasing conflicts between the communities—all of these factors were responsible for the worsening of the position of women. Patriarchy had already set its roots in tradition, customs and religion, but now it made a grand entrance through the first law codes written by male hand. All of the cuneiform law codes, Hebrew commandments of the Old Testament, the Laws of Manu in India, laws of Ancient Greece and *ius civile* provide clear evidence of that.

2.2.1 Egypt

Isolated from the rest of the world by a desert, Ancient Egypt managed to develop peacefully. Stability and lack of conflicts were the main reasons why patriarchy had not reached its full extent. Order was maintained by the pharaoh, under the watchful

[4] Gerhard et al. (2016).

eye of the goddess Ma'at, a metaphysical representation of justice and cosmical balance (manifested through the 'right way of living' on Earth). In Egyptian mythology, the loving relationship between Osiris and Isis became a role model for all spouses.[5] Great respect for the family and the intergenerational hierarchy were the main conservative elements in Egyptian society. Just as the pharaoh took care of his people, parents took care of their family. That is why they were deeply respected and protected—the only known cruelty of the Egyptian law was the punishment for patricide.

On the other hand, patriarchy manifested in two spheres. Firstly, women penetrated the public sphere and became rulers with great difficulty. Women pharaohs were rare—some of the most notable were Hatshepsut and Cleopatra.[6] That being said, women could take on any other profession, just like men. Secondly, the belief in the afterlife and the cult of the ancestors led to the glorification of the firstborn son, who had an advantage over his siblings in the Inheritance Law. Apart from this, differences between the sexes and genders were minor.

Unfortunately, no laws have been preserved, only a few individual legal texts which cannot offer a more detailed account of the legal system. What is certain is that women had full legal capacity—they could own property and after a divorce, one-third of marital property went to the wife. Women could marry and divorce by free will, they could conclude contracts and go into court by themselves. In inheritance law, sisters were equal to brothers (with the exception of the firstborn son). Also, women could freely dispose of their property mortis causa (e.g. the will of a certain Naunakhte).[7]

In criminal law, no difference was noted between the sexes. Some Greek writers had very disputable claims about Egyptian society, like Diodorus Siculus who mentioned that women's noses were cut off as the punishment for adultery.[8] However, there is no trace of such practice in the Egyptian sources and the usual way of resolving this situation was initiating divorce.[9]

The appearance of eunuchs in the court could be interpreted as the first manifestation of transgender relations, but one has to keep in mind that becoming a eunuch was not a voluntary act.[10]

2.2.2 Mesopotamia

Things were completely different in Mesopotamia, whose grounds were not so tame and hospitable. Although almost every cuneiform law code stressed the intention of

[5] Wilkinson (2017).

[6] Cooney (2018); Graves-Brown (2010).

[7] Robins (1993); Stanimirović (2006); Tyldesley (1995); Graves-Brown (2010).

[8] Robins (1993); Stanimirović (2006); Tyldesley (1995); Graves-Brown (2010).

[9] Robins (1993).

[10] Depauw (2003); Wilfong (2010).

the ruler to bring justice and protection to the most vulnerable members of the society, patriarchy was deeply rooted and men were valued more than women.

The first law codes of humanity show exactly how men perceived women. They were already at that moment characterised as sinful, lustful, reckless and dangerous to men. Women's rights were heavily limited, so it comes as no surprise that Middle Assyrian laws are also known as the 'Women's Mirror'—the laws were a reflection of how women were supposed to behave.[11]

A father, as the head of the family, exercised great power over its members. He could surrender them into peonage and send his daughter to a temple (where sometimes she would engage in religious prostitution). If a child ever attempted to hit him, they would lose their arm. Incest between a mother and a son was punished severely, unlike the one committed between a father and a daughter.[12]

Women had limited legal capacity. Marriages were arranged between the groom and the father of the bride. As for the marriage gifts, there was *tirhatu* (pre-marital gift), *sheriktu* (dowry) and *nudunu* (marital gift).

▶ **Definitions** *Tirhatu* was a sum of money which was given by the future groom to the future bride's father, as a promise that the marriage would happen. If the future groom backed out of the arrangement, he would lose the money; if the future bride's father married her off to someone else, he would have to return double the amount of *tirhatu* to the misled groom. *Sheriktu* was the property which a father gave to his daughter when she was getting married as an element of financial security, and it was the only part of her father's property she would inherit and officially own in case of his death. *Nudunu* was a gift which a wife would receive from her husband during their marriage, but it officially became her property only when the husband died. (*The Code of Hammurabi* art. 159–184)

In inheritance law, the only property a woman could own were *sheriktu*, *nudunu,* and also a part of her father's property in one specific case: when a father would surrender his daughter to a temple, she had the right to inherit one-third of the share her brother would receive. However, a wife could sometimes lose her *sheriktu* and *nudunu* when her husband initiated a divorce. Also, he had the right in certain instances to turn his ex-wife into his slave, who then had to serve him and his new wife. The right to initiate a divorce was rarely given to a woman—only in certain extreme cases. Infidelity and various sexual liberties were allowed to men, but strictly forbidden to women under the threat of a death sentence. Her 'purity' was tested in a trial by water.[13]

Patriarchal patterns are especially noticeable in criminal law. One of the most brutal sanctions—impaling, was reserved for a woman who murdered her husband because of another man. Such punishment was not imposed if the roles were

[11] Stol (2016); Roth (1997); Peled (2020).

[12] Budin (2008).

[13] Stol (2016); Chavalas (2014); Stanimirović (2006); Westbrook (2003a, b).

reversed. In the law code of Ur-Nammu, raping a newlywed woman was punished not because of sexual violence, but because her husband was deprived of personally taking her virginity. Many other provisions of the law are focused only on female culprits.[14]

2.2.3 Jewish People of the Old Testament

Not even the two most important monotheistic religions of Antiquity treated women well. The Bible laid down a path of their discrimination and removed them from the public life, creating an 'ideal woman' who was servile, humble and unconditionally obedient to her father or husband.[15]

There is a great contradiction in the Old Testament regarding the attitude towards women. There are passages which claim that God created men and women simultaneously in his image, but there are also mentions that Eve was created from Adam's rib. On one hand, the Old Testament created religious patterns for subduing women and enabled the transmission of patriarchal relations from generation to generation. The first sin, which was attributed to Eve, was used as an excuse to portray women as reckless, superficial, treacherous, prone to sin and of weak character. These same arguments were also used to justify the existence of polygyny in Jewish society.[16]

On the other hand, Jewish people could not exist without women, so there is a passage in the Old Testament which says: 'When people began to multiply on the face of the ground, and daughters were born to them, the sons of God saw that they were fair; and they took wives for themselves of all that they chose' (The Book of Genesis 6.1–6.2). Even the wisest of them all, King Solomon, fell from God's grace due to his love of women. Also, there are many representations of strong, brave and clever women. There is a mention of a female judge in the old Hebrew state—a woman named Deborah who was an oracle.[17] As family was deeply valued, the Old Testament offered equal protection to both parents, but did so in a calculating manner in order to secure the enforcement of patriarchal patterns by both mother and father. Spiritual legacy was extremely important, so unsurprisingly sons were greatly valued, as they continued the bloodline. For that same reason, the institution of levirate was created.[18]

▶ **Definition** Levirate was a custom which dictated that when a man died childless, his brother was obliged to marry his widow. Their first-born son would be considered as a son and heir of the deceased brother, not the living one (the biological father). (*Deuteronomy* 25.5–10.)

[14]Tetlow (2004).

[15]Harris (1984).

[16]Heger (2014); Peled (2020).

[17]Deen (1955).

[18]Weisberg (2009); Marsman (2003).

In everything else, relations between the sexes were regulated in the same way as in other Near Eastern societies.[19] It is obvious that in many of its segments, the Old Testament followed the tone of its cuneiform predecessors.

2.2.4 Ancient Greece

In the most important Doric polis, Sparta, patriarchy was deeply ingrained into the state politics and goals. Being war-oriented, it was in constant need of strong, obedient and brave men, which directly shaped the idea that men were of key importance for the polis. Women were valued only within the role which was reserved for them: they had to become mothers—preferably to boys, as many times as possible.

Excessive females and handicapped male babies were instantly killed after birth. Marriage served only for the purpose of producing healthy boys and therefore, unsurprisingly, was polyandrous. Wives were allowed to commit adultery, however two conditions had to be met: firstly, her lover had to be stronger than her husband and secondly, the purpose of the affair had to be in creating offspring ('the stronger the father—the stronger the child' logic was applied). It is obvious that unfaithfulness was allowed for women only because it served the needs of the polis.[20]

Both boys and girls were removed from their mothers at a very young age and were placed into the *agoge* system where strict discipline and physical toughness were encouraged. Mothers were expected to accept this and to willingly participate in the enforcement of the patriarchal patterns, which were hidden behind the motives of patriotism and honour.[21]

Example

> The famous sentence which mothers used to say to their departing sons is a perfect example: *'Come back with your shield or on it!'*, meaning: return from war victorious or die honourably. (Plutarch *Moralia* 241) ◄

If there were no sons, the bloodline could be continued through a daughter-heiress. Until the end of the fifth century BC, a daughter was nothing more than a means to create a true heir to her father by marrying someone from the group of her closer male relatives. Only in the next century did daughters become true heirs of their fathers and could own land.[22]

[19] Hecht (2002); Peled (2020); Matthews et al. (1998).

[20] Pomeroy (1994, 2002); MacDowell (1986); Lacey (1968).

[21] Pomeroy (1994, 2002); MacDowell (1986).

[22] Pomeroy (2002); MacDowell (1986).

Minoan civilisation, based on the preserved artifacts, valued women. Indicative of it is the fact that they worshiped the Snake Goddesses, mother and daughter, often connected to fertility and the Sacred Feminine.[23] However, that changed with the arrival of the Doric tribe on Crete.

In a more peaceful polis they created, Gortyn, women had more rights than in any other Greek polis. However, in the oldest preserved law code of Europe—the Gortyn law code, significant influence of conservative Doric values is noticeable.

Women had limited legal capacity: they could possess movable property and were the sole beneficiary of the *donatio mortis causa* in the amount of 100 staters. On the other hand, indifference towards women is visible in the II column of the law code, where the only crimes mentioned were rape and adultery, for which the punishment was pecuniary and its amount depended on the social status of the victim/adulteress. The Gortyn daughter-heiress never received the right to own her father's property, like the Spartan did.[24]

The most important Ionic polis, Athens, famous for its democracy and cultural heritage, was undoubtedly the least favourable in Ancient Greece, regarding the treatment of women. One of many examples of it is seen in the title of the famous Aristophanes' comedies—'*Women in Parliament*'.

Unmarried Athenian men were forbidden from becoming state officials, so that was the main motivation behind getting married. Women were completely excluded from the public sphere and confined within their homes as mothers, wives and housekeepers. They couldn't show up in court, in marketplaces they needed to have an escort and there was a special state official whose task was to monitor women's behaviour in public.[25]

Women had no legal capacity and throughout their whole lives they had a *kyrios* (guardian). Until marriage that was the role of their father (or the closest male relative of age, if the father had died) and after that was their husband. They could not own or inherit anything: the position of the Athenian *epikleros* (heiress) was similar to the one in Gortyn, however the first had absolutely no choice in whom to marry—it *had* to be her closest living male relative, while in Gortyn she could choose from a wider group of men.[26]

Women's infidelity was severely punished, unlike men's who had an array of women for their entertainment (*pornai*—street workers, *pallake*—concubines, *hetairai*—elite prostitutes). The only women who had access to education were the *hetairai,* highly cultured courtesans who had to relinquish the idea of having a family in order to gain knowledge.[27] Also, homosexual relations between Athenian men were not uncommon.[28]

---

[23] Marinatos (1993).

[24] Avramović (2020); Gagarin and Cohen (2005).

[25] Katz (1992); MacDowell (1978); MacLachlan (2012); Just (1989); Todd (1995).

[26] Schaps (1981); Pomeroy (1994); Lacey (1968); Harrison (1968); Golden (2015); Foxhall (1989).

[27] Pomeroy (1994); Tetlow (2005); Gilhuly (2008); Katz (1992); Winkler (1990).

[28] Dover (1989).

It is interesting how Egyptian and Greek law became intertwined during Hellenism, which directly reflected on the position of women. In Greece, women gained limited legal capacity, thanks to the influence of Egyptian law. In comparison, the position of the Egyptian women became slightly worse and some new, until then unthinkable rights of the *kyrios* appeared, like the right to renounce his new-born.[29]

2.2.5 Ancient Rome

A synthetic frame on Roman women's condition, starts from the patriarchal setting of society and the existence of a class hierarchy that prevents us from talking about a single idealised type of woman.[30]

Rome was intimately founded on the benevolent relationship with the land, which conditioned the very structure of the family. There is also a problem of availability of legal sources, suggesting a wider consideration for the imperial age.[31]

It can be said that women certainly followed a path of emancipation.[32] Firstly, within the family, and later outside the *domus.* Often behind the scenes, public offices were formally interdicted to *mulieres.*[33] But, it was a matter of levels: compared to Greek women, Roman ones were granted better dignity and legal status.[34]

The whole is condensed into two famous statements by Papinian and Gaius, well-known Roman jurists. Papinian affirmed (D. 1.5.9): "There are many points in our law in which the condition of females is inferior to that of males".[35]

This is an undeniable truth, but it should be read in its context.[36] The traits of this *deterior condicio* must certainly be identified in the awe that the wife had, due to the respect to her husband.[37] Educated in the values of modesty, humility and confidentiality, Roman women generally married very young, mostly to a man chosen by the family.[38]

Latin terms *patrimonium* and *matrimonium* actually hide the truth of a distant world. The main task of the matron was to manage the household, to generate and educate children, as *mos maiorum* prescribed. Marriage originally envisaged a

[29] Pomeroy (1990, 1994).

[30] Peppe (2016), pp. 27 ff.

[31] Giunti (2012); Pölönen (2016), pp. 8 ff.

[32] Vigneron and Gerkens (2000).

[33] Evans Grubbs (2002).

[34] Dixon (2001), pp. 74 ff.

[35] [transl. by A. Watson, *The Digest of Justinian*, IV, Philadelphia 1998].

[36] Lamberti (2014).

[37] Mercogliano (2001).

[38] Treggiari (1991), pp. 34 ff.

woman's submission to the *manus*, the marital power: but around II century BC *sine manu* unions became absolutely prevalent.[39]

From an archaic age, Roman women had the right to inherit part of their father's assets, just as Roman men did. It matters little whether control was expressed through *patria potestas*, *manus* or *tutela* and, therefore, that was exercised by a father, a husband or a legal guardian.

Physical frailty or fickleness of the soul[40] were falsely charged to women in order to justify surveillance on their activities. But when the agnatic family finally faded out, the fresh energies and entrepreneurial skills of women were established. Thus the mask of hypocrisy falls and legal science recorded these transformations. Gaius frankly admitted (Gai. 1.190): "But why women of full age should continue in wardship there appears to be no valid reason."[41]

Formally, the juridical concept of *tutela mulierum* survived. However, from the first century BC the whole system appeared widely outdated.

In the context of his reform of family law - summarised in the *lex Iulia et Papia* - Augustus recognises the *ius liberorum* to women, which allows exemption from *tutela* who has at least two or three children. A few years later, emperor Claudius abolished the agnatic guardianship on women.

Incidentally, with the crisis of the Roman Republic, new female models entered society. Roman women, at least those belonging to higher social classes, received a school education and examples were not lacking (such as Cornelia and Pompeia).

Among the most educated and cultured women who went down in history, some were capable of animating cultural circles and promoting trends with their ideas.[42] We should not only think of the Augustae, who often inspired the good government of emperors.

Of course, these are women who actively participated in what has been called the "Roman paradox",[43] in the sense of attributing to Roman women the care and diffusion of male morality and patriarchal tradition, through social behaviour.

In short, the complexity of the various female figures does not allow for a single and unitary portrait. Even the world of cults confirms this datum, with the particularities relating to the college of Vestals. Being a Vestal was certainly a hard burden and an honour at the same time, but it permitted an autonomous management of sometimes large personal assets.[44]

[39] Gardner (1986), pp. 259 ff.

[40] Quadrato (2001).

[41] [transl. by Ed. Poste, Gai Institutiones, 4th ed., Oxford 1904].

[42] Hemelrijk (1999), pp. 20 ff.

[43] Cantarella (1996).

[44] Ortu (2018).

2.3 Middle Ages

Early Medieval law slightly improved the position of women, but not because of the sudden enlightenment of the Medieval people or the emancipation of women. Instead, it was due to specific reasons which mostly had to do with the interests of the church and religion. Byzantium inherited post-classical Roman law, which improved the position of women under the influence of Christianity. This was especially in the segment of marriage, inheritance, and property law, however, more in the interest of the children than women. Shariah law also improved the position of women to a certain extent, as they were much needed for the expansion of Islam. The Germanic peoples managed to preserve their customary law which was relatively benevolent to women. Still, many legal systems of this era, even those which emerged in the later years like the common law in England, together with the existing religious systems, continued to protect patriarchy and give advantage to men.

2.3.1 Byzantine Law

According to Ostrogorsky, Byzantium developed on the basis of "Roman political concepts, Greek culture and the Christian faith".[45] Yet the gender hierarchy was less strict and the legal position of women was better than in both classical Rome and Greece, although the overall patriarchal structure remained. Women had full legal capacity like men. The dowry belonged to the wife, although the husband had usufruct on it. A husband usually gave his wife a marriage gift (*hypobolon*), which belonged to her after his death, if they were childless. If they had children, she had to share equally with them and usufruct on the rest.[46]

While court and army roles were closed for women, some women became ruling empresses.[47] Women could not be priests, but convents, some founded and organised by prominent women, could have a high degree of autonomy.[48]

A pronounced dichotomy existed in sex-related crimes. Adultery of either spouse was a ground for divorce, but only an adulterous wife and her lover could be criminally prosecuted: they were to be whipped, shorn and their noses cut off. A rapist was to suffer the same penalty, while the abduction of a woman could be punishable by death.[49]

A category distinct enough to be worth calling a 'third gender' were eunuchs, mostly castrated on purpose at a young age to make them suitable for court service, since they could not conquer the throne (the Emperor had to be perfect in body), had

[45] Ostrogorsky (1968), p. 27.

[46] Von Lingenthal (1892), pp. 55–207; Buckler (1936); Laiou (1981).

[47] Garland (2002); Herrin (2013).

[48] Garland (2016).

[49] Von Lingenthal (1892), pp. 341–345; Laiou (1998).

no progeny to conspire for, and could safely serve in the women's quarters. They could rise to prominent positions in the court, the army and the Church (they could even be patriarchs—heads of the Orthodox Church), but they were not considered fully men. They could not marry and until Leo VI, could not even adopt children.[50]

2.3.2 The First Arabian Caliphates

In the infidel Arabia, divided by tribal chauvinism, one common denominator was an extremely bad position of women. In a society where polygyny existed, women were acquired by purchase or kidnapping, had no legal capacity and were inherited as a part of their fathers' or husbands' property.

The prophet Muhammad and the Qur'an understood the significance of women for the victory of Islam, so they improved their position in the beginning of the seventh century. Although still needing to submit to their fathers or husbands, women slowly stepped out of the shadows.[51] They could appear in court, but as witnesses they were only half as worthy as men. This idea that one man is as worthy as two women got transferred into the inheritance law: if they were descendants of the same degree, a man's inheritance share was twice as big as the woman's. However, it should be noted that women could inherit both movable and immovable property, which was then unimaginable in Western Europe.[52]

Polygyny was limited to four wives, but only if the husband could provide for each one of them with separate lodging, be it a house or a private room. Men had the traditional role of the protector and provider. It was a matter of family honour that he financially supported his wife, in accordance with the reputation and the social status of her native family.

Excursus

This is why there is no dowry in Islam, only *mahr.* This marriage gift used to be a bride price in the pre-Islamic times, but after the introduction of Islam it became an obligatory marriage gift. The groom gave it to the bride and it also represented an obstacle to a one-sided divorce initiated by the husband, because only then he would have to pay the bride its full amount.[53] ◄

In marriage, wives were submitted to their husbands to such an extent that the Qur'an compares them to their husbands' fields.[54]

[50] Guilland (1943); Ringrose (2007); Tougher (2008).

[51] Heger (2014).

[52] Nasir (2009); Russell and Abdullah Al-Ma'a Mun (2008).

[53] Stanimirović (2006); Voorhoeve (2012).

[54] Tucker (2008).

In criminal law, the Qur'an lists adultery among the only five felonies which were punishable by Allah himself (*hudud*). Adultery was at first punishable by one hundred lashes, but later with stoning, just like in old Jewish society. Another felony mentioned in the Qur'an was the false accusation of adultery.[55]

2.3.3 Eastern Europe (Slavic Laws)

Some Slavic countries (such as Russia, Serbia and Bulgaria) were culturally, religiously and legally influenced by the Eastern Roman Empire and a part of the "Byzantine Commonwealth."[56] Other Slavs were more influenced by the Catholic faith and Western cultural traditions. Yet a core of common customary law was visible in Slavic countries and the position of women within it was fairly positive by medieval standards, though women were still subservient to men.

Before Slavs accepted Christianity, polygyny was likely present but not widespread. Customs such as a bride-price or bride kidnapping were also present, and divorce initiated by both sides was easy. Some sources (e.g. the sixth century *Strategikon*) document a widow's suicide after her husband's death—likely voluntary, yet supported by custom. Christianity brought monogamy and gradually fought against customs that were contrary to its teaching, with mixed success.[57]

Women mostly had full legal capacity and could own property,[58] while their husbands had only usufruct on their dowry. But dowries were usually not too valuable (at least in the more numerous lower classes), and a woman with no property was very dependent on her husband. Males mostly had priority in inheritance, though regimes varied. Further, women were expected to gain financial security in marriage: in Russian law, a nobleman was even fined if his adult daughter wasn't married.[59]

Crimes such as rape and abduction were punished severely, but so was a woman's adultery. Estate differences were also pronounced: e.g. the Serbian Dušan's Code (1349, amended in 1354) punished a noblewoman's liaison with a servant with the severance of arms and nose to both parties: the same penalty as for a man's rape of a woman of his own station. However, a nobleman's rape of a commoner would likely be punished only by the slitting of the nose, according to transplanted rules of Byzantine law. This shows that such crimes were primarily seen as insults to the man's (husband's or father's) honour. An emphasis on male honour was also

[55] Hamzić (2016).

[56] Obolensky (1971).

[57] Kadlec (1924), pp. 78–82; Levin (1989), pp. 79–135; Пушкарева (1989), pp. 70–85.

[58] E.g., only two contracts of sale survive from medieval Serbia, but in both the sellers are women (Šarkić (2001), pp. 567–569).

[59] Stanimirović (2006); Taranovski (2002), pp. 512–516; Margetić (1996), pp. 246–252; Щапов (1970).

apparent in some other crimes, such as the insult of pulling one's beard (a symbol of masculinity), which was also severely punished.[60]

Example

Sex crimes in the Code of Stefan Dušan (1349).[61]

Art. 53: "And if any lord takes a noblewoman by force, let both his hands be cut off and his nose be slit. But if a commoner takes a noblewoman by force, let him be hanged. And if he takes his own equal by force, let both his hands be cut off and his nose slit."

Art. 54: "And if a noblewoman commits fornication with her man, let the hands of both be cut off and their noses slit." ◄

Women could also appear in various roles before courts: e.g. Czech law allowed a woman to take part in trial by combat, under special conditions; in Serbian law, women could be jurors.[62]

2.3.4 Western Europe (Germanic Laws)

Germanic tribes applied the law on the basis of the principle of personality, which was one of the reasons why each tribe protected their customary law. These customs were preserved from the pre-state period, throughout Antiquity, until the early Middle Ages, when they were codified as *Leges Barbarorum* by the rulers of the first Germanic states.[63] With the exception of Langobards,[64] every other tribe managed to avoid the influence of Roman law, which continued to be an important source of law among the conquered Gallo-Roman people.

Although the role of the male protector was prominent, women had a certain number of rights and even fought shoulder to shoulder with men in some tribes.[65] Firstly, women enjoyed great protection under criminal law. Every touch (on the finger, hand or elbow of a woman) was punished. For murdering a woman who could not bear children, the punishment was blood money (*Wergeld*), as well as for the murder of a free Frank. For murdering a woman who was of childbearing age, the punishment was fixed on 600 solids, which was also the punishment for murdering the Frankish courtiers. Finally, for the murder of a pregnant woman, the punishment

[60] Levin (1989), pp. 160–246; Kršljanin (2021); Solovjev (1928), p. 193.

[61] Translation from Old Serbian: Burr (1949), p. 208, slightly modified.

[62] Kuklík (2015), p. 24; Solovjev (1939).

[63] Gibbon (2000); Todd (1992); Brunner (1880).

[64] Drew (1973).

[65] Tacitus *Germania* 18.

was fixed on 800 solids. Some Germanic legal systems even penalised insulting a woman.[66]

Women were under the power (*mundium*) of men their whole lives: first their fathers and later their husbands. Marriage was arranged between the groom and the father of the bride. During the conclusion of the marriage, the father would transfer his *mundium* to his son-in-law, who in return gave a symbolic gift to the bride. The most important Germanic marriage gift was the 'morning gift' (*Morgengabe*), which reached one-quarter of the husband's property in Langobard society. It was given to the bride the morning after the wedding night, if her chastity was proven. However, if it was not proven, the disgraced bride would have to return to her family and various methods of public humiliation of the bride and her family were available.[67]

In inheritance law, daughters were considered as heirs even when they had living brothers, however it seems like they could inherit only the movable property.[68]

2.3.5 England (Common Law)

The English common law was uniformed thanks to the work of the King's Courts. When the Roman law was banished from the isle, by the Statute of Merton from 1236, the common law developed into one of the rare autochthonous legal systems in the late Middle Ages.[69] Although the church's efforts were somewhat helpful, women still had a very low position in England—especially the married ones.

Example

Apart from the dowry, the common law also recognised another form of special women's property—paraphernal property. The ecclesiastical courts contributed especially to its establishment by separating the wife's property from the husbands during a divorce from bed and board.[70] ◀

With marriage, women lost their legal capacity and their husbands gained total control over them. All matters related to marriage, with the exception of the marital property issues, fell under the jurisdiction of the church. One thing where the Church and the common law were in agreement: '*The husband and wife are one, and that one is the husband!*' (*William Blackstone*). He made decisions about everything. Women needed their husbands' permission in order to appear in court. Additionally, husbands personally punished their wives for every offense at their own discretion.[71]

[66] *Lex Salica* titles XX, XXIV and XXX.

[67] Drew (1991); Oman (1919).

[68] Drew (1991); Kandić (1969).

[69] Baker (2005); Hale (2002); Stanojević (1980).

[70] Basch (1982); Stone (1990); Stone (1993).

[71] Leyser (1995); Jones (2006); Karras (1996).

Upper classes of the English society, just like the upper classes of other societies, used their daughters to arrange political marriages, get closer to influential families or to gain allies. In marriage, all spousal property was in the husband's hands. Also, a dowry (at first called *maritagium*, and from the fourteenth century dowry), belonged to the husband through the institution of courtesy. The only thing that guaranteed the wife some kind of a future was her widow's share (dower), in case she outlived her husband. Dower was first mentioned (as well as dowry) in the Doomsday Book. A widow gained legal capacity on the basis of the dower. Yet she could still not dispose of the immovable property in her hands, but had to take care of it and leave it to her sons or other male heirs.[72]

2.3.6 Gender within the Christian Church(es)

An analysis of the complex topic of law and gender in Christian churches must start with an examination of Jesus Christ's teachings. Jesus did not discriminate against women. In fact, he always showed great respect for them, choosing them as interlocutors or witnesses, or indicating them as a model of authentic faith.[73] The Gospels clearly tell us that some women were Jesus' followers and supported his mission,[74] both materially and spiritually. Equality between men and women is proclaimed by the Apostle Paul in a famous passage of his Letter to the Galatians: "There is neither Jew nor Greek, there is neither slave nor free person, there is not *male and female* [italics ours]; for you are all one in Christ Jesus".[75] His appreciation of female identity did not only concern family life, with regard to which he claimed the will of the wife was on the same level as the will of the husband because without it the marriage could not arise,[76] but also the public organisation of the ecclesiastical community. Women had three roles in particular: widow, virgin and deaconess. The most important role was certainly that of deaconess. This is a bit of a mysterious title, because it is not totally clear what the nature and functions of deaconesses were. However, in the Eastern Church, they performed some important tasks, such as to handle other women, carry out some tasks which would have been imprudent to entrust to men visit sick women, anoint neophytes' bodies during the christening and to supervise women's behaviour during the holy Mass.[77]

The situation was totally different in the Western Church, where there is no trace of this role, even in the first centuries of Christianity. Some councils actually forbade

[72] Stanimirović (2006); Jewell (1996); Broomhall (2015).

[73] *Matthew* 15.21-28, 26.13, 28.1-10; *Mark* 5.27-34, 14.9, 16.1-8; *Luke* 7.37-47, 10.38-42, 24.1-11; *John* 4.7-29, 20.11-18.

[74] *Matthew* 27.55-61; *Mark* 15.40-41; *Luke* 8.2-3, 23.49 and 55-56.

[75] *Galatians* 3.28.

[76] *Ephesians* 5.22-24.

[77] *The Didascalia Apostolorum in English* (translated from Syriac by Gibson (1903)).

the ordination of deaconesses, deeming this ritual heretical, for instance, the Council of Nimes and the First Council of Orange.

This hostility against deaconesses was probably caused by the fear that they could carry out some of the tasks typical of clerics and be included in the clergy. In that period the Church absolutely ruled out women being able to receive the sacred order.

The role of deaconess therefore only survived in the Eastern Churches, gradually losing its relevance until it vanished between the eighth and ninth century AD.

Once the deaconess had disappeared and the tasks of widows and virgins had become focused on in prayers and charity, the original equality between men and women was gradually forgotten partly because of the influence of cultural and social backgrounds. In addition to some discriminatory elements, this influence was contained in the New Testament and in Patristics.[78]

The idea of the inferiority of women to men was confirmed and exacerbated in subsequent rules of canon law, especially during the so-called Classical Age (twelfth–sixteenth century), in which the *Corpus Iuris Canonici* took shape.[79] The Catholic Church excluded women from every ecclesiastical position about administration of sacraments and acts of worship. Their incapacity to receive the sacred order was reaffirmed: they were not able to serve at the altar or allowed to move close to the altar. Similar restrictions concerned the public functions of women. They were not able to teach, preach, proclaim the Gospel and neither to take the floor in public.

According to canon law, there were other incapacities affecting women: they could not testify at trials, with the only exception of matrimonial causes, nor file a complaint. Inside the family, the woman had to be submissive to her husband, who was her chief.

2.4 Modernity

The Modern Era brought many changes in the field of women's emancipation and gender equality. It marked the beginning of the steady deconstruction of the male-dominated society. The Industrial Revolution and the political revolutions of the eighteenth and nineteenth century were the main initiators of change, as they included women in the economic production and encouraged them to fight for their rights.[80] Also, the First and Second World War had a great, yet paradoxical role in the history of human rights. On the one hand, they brought massive destruction and devastation and on the other hand they helped women in their fight for equality. These wars enabled women to give their patriotic contribution to their countries, both by fighting in combat and taking men's places in the production back

[78] *1 Corinthians* 1.8-9, 11.5-10, 14.34-35; *1 Timothy* 2.11-14.

[79] The so-called *Corpus Iuris Canonici* is a set of compilations of the canon law. It was used as the main repository of law until the *Code of Canon Law* of 1917.

[80] Vujadinović (2015).

home. This made them more visible in the public sphere and softened the public attitude towards their attempts to be politically recognised.

The second half of the twentieth century was marked by the rise of numerous feminist movements which further emphasised the necessity of introducing full gender equality and nurturing women's self-awareness. Many feminist authors emerged during this period and contributed greatly to the fight for women's rights and recognition (Betty Friedan, Simone de Beauvoir, Kate Millett and many, many others). The shift in the international law also happened, where after several centuries of using the term "men's rights" to describe human rights, the expression was finally abandoned in favour of the neutral term "human rights," which now included women's rights as well (as seen in The Universal Declaration of Human Rights).[81] The fight for women's political and citizens' rights, right to education and labour rights was lengthy and hard. It was finally recognised in international law during the end of the twentieth century, when a legal framework for the protection of women's rights was established. In the twenty-first century, legislation is being reviewed under the feminist lens, and "gender mainstreaming, e.g., the so-called "state feminism" has taken central stage."[82]

2.4.1 Gender and Civil Law

The great bourgeois revolutions marked the end of the absolute monarchies, feudalism and legal particularism. Unfortunately, this victory failed to bring changes within the family structure or improve the position of women. Regardless of women's patriotic contributions, they were excluded from the new democracy and denied political rights. Puritans confined women even more, and such a rigorous attitude would travel across the ocean and reach Northern America with the first settlers—the Salem witch trials are the perfect example.[83] However, what the political revolutions, the American Declaration of Independence and the French Declaration of the Rights of the Man and of the Citizen brought into the historical arena was this very revolutionary idea of universal equality. This would be recognised by women as the basis for their emancipation. Thus, inspired them to fearlessly fight for their rights and to strive for their own recognition.

The first modern law codes were expected to right these wrongs. Nevertheless, it would take an additional one and a half centuries to finally introduce provisions of gender equality into the democratic constitutions and contemporary civil law. The French *Code Civil* of 1804 was chronologically the first modern law code. It was created under the influence of the School of Natural Law and incorporated both Roman law and French customary law. It was indeed a magnificent codification, except for the provisions of family law, marriage law, property and inheritance law

[81] Vujadinović (2015); Offen (2011).

[82] Vujadinović (2015).

[83] Gerhard et al. (2016); see also the subsection on Criminal law.

which regulated the position of women. They maintained strong elements of patriarchy, mostly due to the great influence of the extremely conservative Napoléon Bonaparte.

Example

"The husband owes protection to his wife, the wife obedience to her husband. The wife is obliged to live with her husband and to follow him to every place where he may judge it convenient to reside: the husband is obliged to receive her, and to furnish her with every thing necessary for the wants of life, according to his means and station. The wife cannot plead in her own name, without the authority of her husband, even though she should be a public trader, a non-communicant, or separate in property."[84] ◄

Women had only partial legal capacity and if married, they were under the total power of their husbands, just like in Medieval England. They were heavily discriminated against in inheritance law. Full adoption and consensual divorce were introduced only because Napoléon needed them: he wanted to divorce his first wife, Joséphine, because they did not have any children. Marital property was regulated as a communion of goods under the control of the husband. However, the law code allowed the spouses to use a marriage contract to make different property arrangements.[85]

The Civil Code of Austria from 1811 (ABGB) partially improved the position of women in accordance with the Germanic tradition. The separation of property regime in marriage shows that women had legal capacity. A husband had a usufruct on his wife's property and a wife had the right to deal with all legal business regarding the household. Also, a husband had a responsibility to financially support his wife in accordance with her social status. Under the pressure from the Catholic church, divorce and separation from bed and board was not allowed. On the other hand, sons and daughters were equalised under inheritance law, which was unthinkable in many less developed societies in the nineteenth century.[86]

Excursus

Sometimes, regulations on these subjects underwent unusual changes. For example, Serbia used the ABGB as a model for its own Civil Code of 1844. However, under the pressure of customs, traditions and patriarchy, changed its marriage, family and inheritance law provisions to better serve the needs of traditional Serbia. Regulations of a joint family (*zadruga*) were added, as it was typical for the Serbian society, women were made more inferior (especially married women

[84] Code Napoléon, title V ch. VI art. 213–215, translated from the original by A barrister of the Inner Temple, William Bening, Law bookseller (1827).

[85] Lobingier (1918); Crabites (1927); Herchenroder (1938).

[86] Baeck (1972); Berger (2010); Frohnecke (2001).

who were equated with minors, squanderers and mentally disabled), women were also denied inheritance, and dowry became optional, unlike in ABGB where it was obligatory.[87] On the other hand, the Turkish Civil Code of 1926, created during the effort to modernise and westernise Turkish law, adopted a large part of the Swiss Civil Code of 1912. In marriage law, civil marriage was introduced, polygyny abolished, and the husband's right to divorce his wife by a simple statement, originating in shariah law (*talak*) was replaced by a list of causes for divorce available to both spouses. However, these reforms were very slow to reach the rural population, the majority of which continued to live according to old customs.[88] These are just two of many interesting examples of Alan Watson's theory of legal transplants – a theory which claims that most changes in most legal systems occur as a result of borrowing legal solutions from one system to another, and the choice of the system to borrow from is often a result of convenience and coincidence.[89] ◀

In England, despite the growing dissatisfaction with the treatment of women and many written works dealing with this topic, like those of John Stuart Mill and Harriet Taylor Mill, things changed only at the end of the nineteenth century. The *Married Women's Property Act* of 1882 was enforced, which radically improved the position of women, as married women were finally given the right to own property and dispose of it in their own right. This launched England to the very top of the list of countries which greatly contributed to the emancipation of women. Similar processes took place in the USA, Canada, Australia and New Zealand.[90]

2.4.2 Gender in Front of the Courts

Until well into the twentieth century, procedural law more or less copied the gender hierarchy of private law. While women generally could be parties or witnesses in a trial, wherever a married woman's legal capacity was reduced (a prevalent case), so was her procedural capacity. In some countries, even women who had full (material) legal capacity, still needed to be represented by a man in court. Women were mostly accepted as witnesses, but frequently considered to be less credible than men. Where a jury system existed, only men were initially jurors, with women being reluctantly admitted to jury service around the turn of the twentieth century Though in practice, their participation was often avoided, under various pretexts.[91]

---

[87] Avramović (2017); Polojac et al. (2015); Stanimirović (2006).

[88] Oguz (2005).

[89] Watson (1974).

[90] Birks (2001); Mendelson and Crawford (2000); Szreter (2002); Pinchbeck (2014); Stanimirović (2006).

[91] Röwekamp (2020); Rodriguez (1999); Crosby (2017).

From the mid-nineteenth century and in greater numbers from the early twentieth century, women gained access to legal education and the practice of law. The first women lawyers faced both formal obstacles and informal problems in practice. Many universities did not accept women, or only accepted a small quota of female students, thus making the criteria for their acceptance markedly higher. As in other professions, female graduates were often not expected to practice, as it was thought they had entered university to find a good husband there—or they were expected to give up their career and devote themselves solely to the house and family upon marriage. Access to the bar was often restricted, with women first not being accepted at all (some had to go to court to demand access), and later only in front of lower courts. Setbacks also happened in some countries. Furthermore, as law was seen to embody mostly male values, clients were frequently sceptical of female attorneys, believing them to be less intellectually capable or less aggressive than men. Even such superficial issues as "unbusinesslike" (feminine) clothing could lead to a loss of a client. For these reasons, many of the first women lawyers were members of their country's women's rights movements, fighting for equal access to the legal profession, equal standing in civil law matters and female suffrage.[92] They often specialised in giving legal counsel to other women, including free legal aid for the poor, thus raising awareness of the importance of law in women's lives. It is argued that female lawyers saw helping others and improving the system as goals more important than self-promotion and profit.[93]

Entry to the judicial function was even slower, and the percentage of women judges stayed disproportionately low (compared to the overall number of female lawyers) for a long time. Appointments to higher courts were all the rarer, with supreme and constitutional courts opening their doors to women only in the late twentieth century.[94] The appointment of female judges has been a particularly sensitive subject in Muslim countries, as many Islamic scholars argue that it violates *shariah* because of women's inherent intellectual deficiencies. Further, feminist initiatives are often seen as unwelcome intrusions of the west. Other issues, such as the general patriarchal outlook of large numbers of the population or mandatory gender segregation in public spaces must also be taken into account. Thus, advancement has been much slower in these countries, with some Islamic countries appointing their first female judges only in the twenty-first century.[95]

[92]International organizations also played an important role, particularly the International Federation Women in Legal and Juridical Careers (founded in 1928) and the International Federation of Women Lawyers (founded in 1944).

[93]Mossman (2006); Kimble and Röwekamp (2016) (and papers within), Kimble and Röwekamp (2018). It is worth noting that women were accepted to the medical profession much more easily, as it could be justified as an extension of a woman's natural nurturing role, as well as by the needs of female patients' modesty.

[94]Cook (1984); Kenney (2008).

[95]Sonneveld and Lindbekk (2017).

2.4.3 Gender and Criminal Law

Throughout history, men were widely considered to be more violent and more prone to criminality. But this did not mean the treatment of women was necessarily milder: on the contrary, women who committed violent crimes were often viewed as monsters or madwomen.[96] Women also, being physically weaker, frequently employed different means of achieving the same criminal goal: e murder by poisoning was considered a typically female crime.[97] Still, the gender profiling of some crimes merits attention.

While men were more often involved in violent crime (for both biological and social reasons), the criminalisation of duelling created a purely male crime, as duels used to be a purely male activity. Private vendettas, where they were still a living custom, were also almost certain to be executed by men.[98]

Crimes against civil, military or clerical service were *de facto* male offences until women gained entry to those professions. A different, but also notable, aspect of this patriarchal outlook is the fact that few women held important positions in criminal organisations.[99]

A typically male crime, of course, was rape. As in pre-modern times, only a man was foreseen as a perpetrator, and frequently (though not always) only a woman as a victim. A gender-neutral definition of rape appeared only in the late twentieth century and is still absent from many legislations. Many misguided notions about anatomy and sexuality, carried over from the Middle Ages—such as the belief that conception could not occur if the woman had not consented to intercourse—lowered the conviction rate for rape for a long time; matters of class and status also played an important role.[100]

Homosexuality was also widely punishable until the mid-twentieth century, though usually only male homosexual acts were illegal: lesbianism was mostly overlooked by legislators.[101] On the other hand, adultery was still dominantly a female crime. While most legislations punished a woman for any intercourse with a man other than her husband, a man's adultery was either not a crime, or was punishable only if he kept his mistress in the family home. The contemporary era brought about a decriminalisation of adultery in the Western world, but it is still punishable in many Muslim countries.[102]

Accusations of witchcraft, where still extant, were mostly directed against women, frequently single or barren ones. Officially, they were considered weaker

[96] Lombroso and Ferrero (2004); Zedner (1991).

[97] Jones (2009); Martin (2007), pp. 123–154.

[98] Frevert (1999); Boehm (1984).

[99] Pizzini-Gambetta (1999).

[100] Walker (1998), Vigarello (2001). Naturally, most rapists *are* men and most victims women, but the relative rarity of other combinations led to such cases not being criminalized.

[101] Han and O'Mahoney (2018).

[102] Weinstein (1986), pp. 216–238.

than men in resisting the Devil's temptations. Unofficially, women living on the margins of society and not fulfilling their stereotypical roles as wives and mothers were more likely to attract the negative attention of all-male witch-hunters.[103]

Excursus

The first witch trials in Northern America were documented in the end of seventeenth century, in the city of Salem in the puritan colony of Massachusetts, as a transatlantic continuation of the European witch-hunt fervour which emerged in the fifteenth century. ◄

Two more typically female crimes were abortion (which was illegal worldwide until the twentieth century) and infanticide. Both were frequently caused by a patriarchal double standard in which an extramarital pregnancy brought shame and sometimes even legal sanction upon a woman (more than the man, even when he was known), and efficient means of contraception were scarcely available.[104] Penalties for infanticide varied greatly. Some legislations counted it as murder (even a severe case of murder) and some, from the nineteenth century on, adopted a theory that blamed a temporary postpartum disorder, thus prescribed lighter penalties. Where special regulations for infanticide existed, it was usually defined as the killing of a (newborn) infant by its mother, making it an exclusively female crime. if the father or a third party killed the child, they would be tried for ordinary murder.[105]

Another complex subject was prostitution. Whether it was criminalised or legally regulated, depended both on country and period, with many countries changing their attitudes back and forth over the centuries. Naturally, prostitutes were mostly women and their clients men, while both men and women appeared in the roles of procurers or owners of brothels. Where prostitution was illegal, both legal sanctions and social stigma were usually significantly higher for the prostitute than for the client.[106]

When men and women were convicted of the same or similar crimes, penal policies usually favoured women. Women could also postpone execution or corporal punishment, or sometimes even have those penalties exchanged for milder ones, if they were pregnant when convicted. The modern conception of prisons included sex-segregation, but the harshest prison regimes were usually reserved for men, believed both to deserve and be able to endure harsher punishment and were more likely to attempt to escape.[107]

[103] Durrant (2007).

[104] Though abortions were also used by married women who already had many children and could not support more.

[105] Milner (2000), Kilday (2013), Lewis (2016).

[106] Gibson (1986), Bartley (2000), Laite (2012).

[107] Rafter (1985), King (1999).

2.4.4 Gender, Public Law and Democracy

Just as public functions in the Antiquity and Middle Ages were an exclusively male domain, they continued to be that way for the greater part of Modernity. Even in those monarchies where a woman could inherit the throne, women could not vote, be elected or hold a high public office. The Enlightenment and the French Revolution brought the idea of natural rights of Man to the fore, but that "Man" was mostly a white male, and not every human being. Olympe de Gouges, advocate of women's rights and the author of the Declaration of Rights of Women and (Female) Citizens, was executed in 1793. Further, men who advocated women's rights, such as Marquis de Condorcet, fared no better.[108]

Example

"Habit can so familiarise men with violations of their natural rights that those who have lost them neither think of protesting nor believe they are unjustly treated.

Some of these violations even escaped the notice of the philosophers and legislators who enthusiastically established the rights common to all members of the human race, and made these the sole basis of political institutions.

Surely they were all violating the principle of equal rights by debarring women from citizenship rights, and thereby calmly depriving half of the human race of the right to participate in the formation of the laws. Could there be any stronger evidence of the power of habit over enlightened men than the picture of them invoking the principle of equal rights for three or four hundred men who had been deprived of equal rights by an absurd prejudice, and yet forgetting it with regard to 12 million women?"

Marquis de Condorcet, "On the emancipation of women. On giving women the right of citizenship (1790)".[109] ◄

The 19th and early twentieth century saw the rise of strong feminist and suffragist movements in many countries, headed by such figures like the Mills (John Stuart and Harriet) and the Pankhurst family in England, Elisabeth Cady Stanton, Susan B. Antony or Alice Paul in the USA, Kate Sheppard in New Zealand, Mathilde and Fredrik Bajer in Denmark or Mathilde Hidalgo de Procel in Ecuador, to name but a few.[110]

Many suffrage movements in the west were linked to anti-slavery or temperance (anti-alcohol) movements, attracting some supporters, but alienating others. Elsewhere, connections between feminism and socialism intensified with time: Auguste Bebel's book *Women and Socialism* propagated equality before the law (while still

[108] Landes (1988), Beckstrand (2009); Offen (2011), Vujadinović (2019).

[109] Lukes and Urbinati (2012), p. 156.

[110] van Wingerden (1999), Nym Mayhall (2003); Chapman Catt and Shuler (1923); Baker (2002); Adams (2014).

assuming that many women would opt for the role of mother and housewife), reaching beyond Germany to fame in Eastern Europe; the revolutionary Alexandra Kollontai became the leading feminist in Russia/USSR.[111] But throughout the world common male responses to female suffrage campaigns included ridicule, pointing out women's intellectual inferiority or the un-femininity of politics (this echoed even by many women),[112] or using the struggle as a political bargaining chip, while more extreme campaigners often faced criminal prosecution.

Female suffrage on a local level, or votes by noblewomen or female property owners existed previously in many countries. Some federal component states in USA and Australia granted women suffrage in the nineteenth century. and some small island communities[113] were organised on a basis of gender equality.[114] But the first independent country to enfranchise women (all, including Maori) was New Zealand in 1893. Australia followed in 1902, but only for white women: Aboriginal women only if they already could vote in their states. Over 20 countries enfranchised women during or shortly after WWI—mostly European, but also Canada and USA (though black women soon lost the vote in many states and did not fully regain it until the 1960s). A second wave took place after WWII and decolonisation, with women in over 100 countries gaining suffrage. The last European countries to grant it were Liechtenstein (in 1984) and Switzerland (where women gained suffrage on a federal level in 1970, but the last canton do grant it on a cantonal level, Appenzell Innerrhoden, did so in 1990). The last overall was Saudi Arabia, where women gained the right to vote in municipal elections in 2015.[115]

Most feminist authors believe that the fight of suffrage movements led to this victory,[116] some claim the impetus came from wars or national liberation movements[117] and some credit the changed perception of women's roles.[118] The truth likely lies somewhere in between: the movements brought out the question of female suffrage and public service and gradually changed the views of the public, while wartime or national struggles accelerated the process in some countries.

Passive suffrage usually was not far behind active suffrage on paper, but in practice, despite eligibility, women continued to occupy a small percentage of parliament seats and government functions. Some countries have adopted positive

[111] Bebel (1904); Roelofs (2018).

[112] Bush (2007).

[113] E.g. Pitcairn Island, Rarotonga (Markoff 2003, pp. 102–103; Adams 2014, pp. 24–27).

[114] As Markoff (2003), p. 90 claims, "Women's suffrage was pioneered in lesser places in the geography of wealth and power and then advanced to more central locations."

[115] Grimshaw (1988), Oldfield (1992); Adams (2014); Karolak and Guta (2020).

[116] E.g. DuBois (1998).

[117] Adams (2014).

[118] McCammon et al. (2001).

discrimination measures, but their fairness is sometimes disputed: this question remains open for the twenty-first century.[119]

2.4.5 Religion, Law and Gender in a Secularising World

After the so-called classical age, canon law regarding women, continued without any big changes until the twentieth century. In 1917, the first code of canon law was promulgated. Unfortunately, women's inferiority was recognised by the code, which limited their legal influence and capacity, describing them as frail creatures, emotionally fragile, intellectually deficient, in need of protection and unable to perform executive roles. The code affirmed that women were not able to receive the sacred order, they were not allowed to move close to the altar, inside religious buildings they had to sit separately from men, they had to veil their heads and they had to dress demurely.[120] Regarding teaching, women were not allowed to preach or take the floor in public.[121] Moreover, the charters of ecclesiastical universities made it very difficult for women to study the sacred sciences and graduate.

Turning to the power of governance, the few forms of participation that were allowed for the lay male believers remained closed to women. For instance, they were not able to be a diocesan administrator (the person who rules the diocese while the episcopal see is vacant), a member of the board of directors of the diocese, or a canon lawyer.[122]

Regarding the family, the code of 1917 established the supremacy of the husband over his wife both in their relationship with each other and with their children.[123] Ultimately, the code reaffirmed all the directives about women's inferiority contained in the *Corpus Iuris Canonici*.

In the second half of the twentieth century, the huge movement aimed at promoting the emancipation of women, inspired the Catholic Church to completely change its attitude to the female sex.

The new code of canon law for the Latin Catholic Church, promulgated in 1983, has recognised the equality of every kind of person and consequently has banned sex discrimination. The difference between the sexes is not relevant, for instance, in relation to marriage: "Each spouse has an equal obligation and right to whatever pertains to the partnership of conjugal life" (can. 1135). This equality concerns both the relationship between husband and wife and the relationship between parents and children.

This absolute equality between men and women also includes the three public functions of the Catholic Church, the teaching function (*munus docendi*), the

[119] Swiss (2009), Wängnerud (2009).

[120] The *Code of Canon Law* of 1917, cann. 813, § 3, 968, § 1, 1262, §§ 1–2.

[121] The *Code of Canon Law* of 1917, cann. 1327, § 2, and 1342, § 2.

[122] The *Code of Canon Law* of 1917, cann. 1520, § 1, and 1521, § 1.

[123] The *Code of Canon Law* of 1917, e.g., cann. 756, § 2, and 1112.

sanctifying function (*munus sanctificandi*) and the power of governance (*munus regendi*). Regarding the teaching function, women have the right to attend the ecclesiastical universities and receive a higher knowledge of catholic doctrine. They can be catechists, missionaries and university lecturers in sacred science.[124] They can also preach, with the sole exception of the homily, during the Mass.[125]

Moving on to the sanctifying function, women can access religious buildings without any restrictions, including service at the altar.[126] The active role of women also includes cooperation with parish priests, as ministers of exposition or reposition of the Most Holy Eucharist, or distributing it. Recently, women have been permitted to perform durably the role of lector and acolyte.[127]

Finally, lay women can take part in the power of governance, in the same way as lay men. By and large, women are able to hold every ecclesiastical office, which does not require the sacred order (for instance, legates of the Roman Pontiff or judges in a canon court).[128]

In relation to this sacrament, we must highlight that the code and some statements by the Popes and the Congregation for the Doctrine of the Faith, have reaffirmed that one of the prerequisites of becoming a member of the clergy is to be a male.[129] The prohibition against ordaining women certainly concerns the episcopate and the presbyterate, but leaves an opening about the diaconate, referring to additional in-depth analysis for a definitive solution. Unfortunately, it has been impossible to clarify the question about the position of deaconesses in the first century and consequently, to establish whether it would be possible to restore this particular role. In August 2016, Pope Francis established a Commission (half of whose members were women) to look at the problem, but it was unable to reach a definite conclusion. As a result, in April 2019, the Pope appointed a new Commission, which has been examining this topic once again.

In recent years, some voices have been calling for the reinstatement of the female diaconate. These requests have never been accepted, and the recent Post-Synodal Apostolic Exhortation "Querida Amazonia" by Pope Francis reaffirmed that women

[124]The *Code of Canon Law* of 1983, cann. 211, 217, 229, §§ 2 and 3, 774, § 1, 784 and 785, § 1.

[125]The *Code of Canon Law* of 1983, cann. 230, § 3, and 767, § 1.

[126]The *Code of Canon Law* of 1983, cann. 213 and 214.

[127]Francis, *Spiritus Domini* (2021, 10th January), in www.vatican.va; the *Code of Canon Law* of 1983, can. 230, § 1, as modified by *Spiritus Domini* ("Lay persons who possess the age and qualifications established by decree of the conference of bishops can be admitted on a stable basis through the prescribed liturgical rite to the ministries of lector and acolyte. Nevertheless, the conferral of these ministries does not grant them the right to obtain support or remuneration from the Church").

[128]The *Code of Canon Law* of 1983, cann. 129, § 2, and 274, § 1.

[129]Cfr. the Code of Canon Law of 1983; John Paul II, Apostolic Letter *Ordinatio sacerdotalis* (1994, 22 May) in www.vatican.va; Congregation for the Doctrine of the Faith *Responsum ad propositum dubium concerning the teaching contained in "ordinatio sacerdotalis"* (1995, 28 October), *ibidem*; Id., *General decree regarding the delict of attempted sacred ordination of a woman* (2007 19th December), *ibidem*.

cannot become clerics. However, it did specify that they should have access to positions that do not entail Holy Orders,[130] including ecclesial services.

Turning to other Christian churches, during the Modern Age, the Protestant denominations developed their legal systems, which were less complete than canon law because in the Reformation there was a very strong contrast between law and Gospel. The former was typical of the State and the latter was typical of religion. As a result, some matters, like marriage, remained under the rules of the State.[131] However, it is also possible to analyse the relationship between law and gender in the Protestant denominations, especially with regard to the priestly calling. Since the beginning of Protestantism, the three kinds of calling, deacon, pastor and bishop, have been accessible to women. The first ministry fulfilled by women was the diaconate. Some denominations decided to revalue the praxis of the primitive church, conferring some functions regarding charity and teaching to some women: the deaconesses. The first examples of Protestant deaconesses were Germany in 1836 and France in 1841. The Anglican Church had some deaconesses in 1861 and the Methodist Church in 1888.[132]

In the nineteenth century a debate started about the possibility of having women as pastors or bishops. Quaker communities affirmed this, based on the principle that "souls do not have a sex". In 1821, American Quakers officially recognised a woman as a pastor.[133]

In Europe, at the beginning of the twentieth century, the so-called congregationalist denominations of the United Kingdom had the first female pastors. Other Protestant churches, especially the more structured ones, arrived at this result later and more gradually. In the 50s and 60s in Germany, France and Scandinavia, Protestantism accepted female pastors. The pattern in the Anglican Church was different, and the first female pastors were ordained outside the United Kingdom, in Hong Kong, the USA, Canada, New Zealand, Kenya and Uganda. Only in 1992 did the English Anglican Church reach a decision about this subject and there is still no unanimity about this point in the Anglican Community. Most Pentecostal denominations preferred (and prefer) to only award women the diaconate.

Later, several denominations made it lawful to ordain women bishops. The first female bishop was an American Methodist, in 1980, followed, 2 years later, by a woman belonging to the Reformed Church of Alsace Lorraine.

Sometimes, a strange phenomenon occurs, because the function of parish priest or of bishop are jointly assigned to a married couple. For instance, in the first years of the twenty-first century in Nuremberg, in Germany, the role of Lutheran bishop was taken on by a husband and wife.[134]

---

[130] Cfr. Francis, *Post-synodal apostolic exhortation "Querida Amazonia"* (2020, 2th February), nn. 99–103, in www.vatican.va.

[131] Witte (2002).

[132] Witte (2002); Long (2008).

[133] Green (1996); Long (2008).

[134] Long (2008).

The Orthodox Churches have been living an historical path very similar to the Catholic Church's one.[135] In the past they experienced a very deep contradiction between the theological data, the equality of men and women and the influence of conservative society. Gregory from Nazianzo highlighted that males and females have the same Creator, the same law, the same death and the same resurrection. Moreover, some women were called "isapastoloi", that is "like the Apostles", because they had a fundamental place in the spread of Christianity. At the same time, the Orthodox society marginalised women inside a household role, putting them under the rule of men (fathers, brothers or husbands).

Nowadays, the Orthodox Churches have left the idea of women's inferiority but only partially. Furthermore, they only hold men to be the true members of the clergy. Recently (since the second half of the twentieth century), some sectors of public opinion have been asking for the reintroduction of the female diaconate.[136] The Orthodox Greek Church decided, in 2004, to approve the request. However, there is not a general decision binding all the Orthodox Churches: the Pan-Orthodox Council, which happened in Crete (17–26 June 2016), did not face the question about the deaconesses.

2.4.6 Gender, Race and Colonialism

No overview of historical relations of law and gender can be complete without addressing racial issues and the grim legacy of colonialism all over the globe. By subjecting many countries to imperialist rule and turning their inhabitants into slaves (or, later, cheap workforce) to be exported, colonial powers created the cruel myth of lower races, which deeply impacted the lives of both men and women.

Colonial powers frequently enforced native patriarchal laws and customs because it suited their needs. But even when they sought to reform them, this caused two new problems. Seen as "invaders' interventions", the reforms were frequently opposed in order to preserve indigenous traditions—e.g., the practice of *sati* in India (a wife's suicide on the husband's funeral pyre) rose in frequency after the British forbade it. Even when reforms were successful, they were lauded as successes of civilised white colonisers saving backward natives, enforcing this harmful stereotype. Naturally, while male conquerors argued about women, these women's own voices were rarely heard.[137]

In some areas, the traditional social structure and customs, while patriarchal in their particular modality, differed from the model known to white colonisers. In many African or Native American traditions, for example, women played an active role in agriculture, commerce, social life and even politics (although male and female activities were often separate and the male superior). Not attempting to

[135] Kalaitzidis (2016).

[136] Salapatas (2015); Kalaitzidis (2016).

[137] Spivak (2010); Banerjee-Dube (2014), pp. 93–99.

understand local traditions, colonisers imposed legal, economic and social reforms that shifted this structure towards the western type of patriarchy and worsened the position of women.[138] For example, in colonial Nigeria, the British bureaucracy, used to the European division of gender roles, focused their measures for improving agriculture solely on men as cash crop farmers, ignoring the fact that in traditional Nigerian farming practices, male and female activities usually complemented each other. Only men were drawn into educational programmes for modernising agriculture, although women played an important role in Igbo agriculture.[139]

As invaders' power allowed them to set their own standards to conquered societies, white colonisers were projected as ideals of civilised masculinity, and native men as either effeminate, often 'boys' compared to white men, or savage and bestial. White ladies were delicately feminine, while dark-skinned women were seen as sly and promiscuous. Far from being 'just' social stereotypes, these views frequently impacted both legislation and verdicts, ranging from attitudes towards sexual violence to labour conditions and wages.[140]

Of the colonial powers themselves, this issue was particularly expressed in the US due to widespread slavery and later segregation. While the female suffrage movement was born of the antislavery movement, middle-class white women have long ignored the plight of black women (and even working-class white women), dismissing many issues important to them (racism, lynching, unequal access to education and job opportunities, as not being real women's issues. A good example can be seen in the fight for reproductive rights, where white women focused only on access to contraception and abortion, while others were frequently subjected to forceful sterilisations. Black men were, on the other hand, frequently depicted as more prone to crime and violence, especially through the myth of the black rapist. Segregation, systematic disenfranchisement and lynchings, that authorities turned a blind eye on, were the reality of the US black population for a long time. While direct legal discrimination has been abolished, negative stereotypes and indirect discrimination live on, often with disastrous consequences.[141]

As non-white women felt excluded from the feminist movement, and their burning issues were ignored by its white leaders, this gave rise to a critique of feminism, and new movements such as *womanism* or *black feminism* evolved.[142]

[138] Korieh (2010); Osborn (2011); Jagodinsky (2016); Chuku (2018).

[139] Korieh (2010), pp. 97–111.

[140] Sinha (1995); Harris-Perry (2011), Fjelde Tjelle (2013).

[141] Davis (2011), Freedman (2002), pp. 73–94, Wing (2003); Breines (2006).

[142] See chapter on Feminist Theories in this book.

2.5 Conclusion

Thousands of years of written sources speak of the dominance of patriarchy and countless manifestations of patriarchal patterns. Written law has, from the beginning, followed the beaten path so devotedly paved by ancient customs and religions. Men persistently and consistently guarded their privileges woven into the tradition of primitive societies, leaving no room for manoeuvre in the struggle for the emancipation of women and gender equality. Both the Antiquity and the Middle Ages removed women from public life. It was a world of visible men and invisible women. In every branch of the law, women have been discriminated against, and certain concessions to women have been made for a million reasons, but not as an expression of awareness of the ubiquitous injustice against them. Monotheistic religions mostly made the already difficult situation worse, being immune to any form of change. Catholicism during the Inquisition and Modern Radical Islam are perhaps the most vivid examples.

The first real advances were made in the Modern Era, although patriarchy was still putting up a vigorous fight. The first codifications slowly improved the position of women, primarily in Civil Law), but it is only after the Second World War that the Civil Law[143]—especially the Family Law,[144] and the Criminal Law[145] greatly improved the gender equality on the basis of two key moments. First, the establishment of the constitutional democracies in the developed Western countries as the role model for the rule of law. Second, the shift in the focus of International Law towards human rights,[146] followed by transferring the centrality of the human rights (and gradually also the women's rights) into the national legislations. Despite the positive legal changes in favour of the universal human rights and women's rights in the Public Law, and also against gender discrimination in Civil Law, the full implementation of gender equality is yet to be achieved in the private and public life of every country. Although there was more advancement in Western democracies. The struggle for women's rights and gender equality bore its first fruits in the last century, universal female right to vote has been achieved, but the fight for the gender equality has not yet been won, especially when taking into account all the various existing grounds of discrimination within the societies and within the global context. The modern contradictions between patriarchy and the methods of overcoming it, both in law and everyday life, differ globally depending on the economic, cultural and political conditions. Not only are there differences between countries, but there are also great divisions within the countries themselves. As such, there are also various modalities of multisectional discrimination of different minorities and women. During the twentieth century, the human rights revolution

[143] See chapter on Private Law in this book

[144] See chapter on Family law in this book.

[145] See chapter on Criminal Law in this book.

[146] See the chapters on EU and International Law, as well as the chapter on Human Rights in this book.

and the question of minority rights has been emerging ever since the 1970s, encompassing gradually and increasingly the rights of the LGBTQIA+ community. The common factor for all the above-mentioned contexts and movements for recognition, is the necessity of the continuous struggle for overcoming the discriminatory nature of patriarchy and for preventing its potential revival. In other words, the fight for widening the space of human rights protection/liberation/emancipation both in the private and public life, in developed and underdeveloped countries, locally and globally.

The awareness of the necessity of change is growing. In the twenty-first century it is crucial to create the mechanisms which will overcome the persistent logic of patriarchy faster and more efficiently. Further, these mechanisms will reach gender equality, and for the sake of the advancement of gender equality, prevent the current rising regressive trends of repatriarchalisation and re-traditionalisation. The past experiences are there to learn from and not to repeat the same mistakes.

Questions

1. How did gender influence an individual's legal status in the legal systems of the Antiquity? What are the common characteristics? Is any legal system an exception to this rule, and why?
2. How did legal recognition of gender differences change in the Middle Ages? What was the role of religion in this period—was it a force of change or stagnation? What were the positive and negative sides of religious influence on law and gender?
3. In which area of law did the legal status of women and gender discrimination improve first in the Modern era, and why? Which area do you feel was the slowest to change, and why?
4. What were the main reasons and manners of limiting the legal capacity of women throughout history? How much do you think this affected their everyday life?
5. Why did males have precedence over females in inheritance in most legal systems? How did economic and cultural reasons combine to cause this discriminatory regime, and what contributed to achieving gender equality in this area?
6. What were the most prominent reasons for the different treatment of male and female offenders and victims in criminal law throughout history? Do you think they were justified, and to what extent?
7. Why do you think men frequently dominated government and state law, even in societies where the position of women in private law was fairly good? Which factors contributed to the realisation for the need of female suffrage and other forms of participation in the state government?
8. Which factors other than gender itself could influence (or work together with) gender discrimination throughout history? Which of them do you

(continued)

consider to be the strongest and why? Which have been mostly eliminated in the modern world and which are still present?
9. How did the legal position of individuals who do not conform to gender archetypes and stereotypes (eunuchs, homosexuals, transgender people etc.) change throughout history? What does this tell us of the law's treatment of gender issues?
10. Do you see any parallels with today's law in what you've learned about the historical development of the influence of gender on one's legal status? Which of the problems shown in the historical outline do you believe to be still present in contemporary legal systems?

References

Adams J (2014) Women and the vote: a world history. Oxford University Press, Oxford
Avramović S (2017) The Serbian Civil Code of 1844: a Battleground of Legal Traditions. In: Simon T (ed) Konflikt und Koexistenz. Die Rechtsordnungen im 19. und 20. Jahrhundert, Bd. II – Serbien Bosnien-Herzegowina, Albanien. Max-Planck-Institut für europäische Rechtsgeschichte, Frankfurt am Main, pp 379–482
Avramović S (2020) Rano grčko parvo i Gortinski zakonik. Pravni fakultet Univerziteta u Beogradu, Beograd
Baeck PL (1972) The general civil code of Austria. Oceana Pubns, New York
Baker JH (2005) An introduction to English legal history. Oxford University Press, Oxford
Baker JH (2002) Votes for women: the struggle for suffrage revisited. Oxford University Press, Oxford
Banerjee-Dube I (2014) A history of modern India. Cambridge University Press, Cambridge
Bartley P (2000) Prostitution: prevention and reform in England, 1860–1914. Routledge, New York/London
Basch N (1982) In the eyes of the law- women, marriage and property in nineteenth century New York. Cornell University Press, Ithaca
Bebel A (1904) Woman under socialism (trans: De Leon D). Labor News Press, New York
Beckstrand L (2009) Deviant women of the French revolution and the rise of feminism. Farleigh Dickinson University Press, New Jersey
Berger E (2010) Österreich Allgemeines Bürgerliches Gesetzbuch (ABGB). Eine europäische Privatrechtskodifikation. III – Das ABGB außerhalb Österreich. Duncker & Humblot, Berlin
Birks P (2001) English private law. Oxford University Press, Oxford
Boehm C (1984) Blood revenge: the enactment and management of conflict in Montenegro and other tribal societies. University of Pennsylvania Press, Philadelphia
Bolger D (2013) A companion to gender prehistory. A John Wiley & Sons, Inc. Publication, Chichester
Breines W (2006) The trouble between us: an uneasy history of white and black women in the feminist movement. Oxford University Press, Oxford
Broomhall S (2015) Authority, gender and emotions in late medieval and early modern England. Palgrave Macmillan, New York
Brunner H (1880) Zur Rechtsgeschichte der römischen und germanischen Urkunde. Wiedemann, Berlin
Buckler G (1936) Women in byzantine law about 1100 AD. Byzantion 11:391–416

Budin SL (2008) The myth of sacred prostitution in antiquity. Cambridge University Press, Cambridge

Burr M (1949) The code of Stephan Dušan: tsar and autocrat of the Serbs and Greeks. Slavonic East Eur Rev 28:198–217

Bush J (2007) Women against the vote: female anti-suffragism in Britain. Oxford University Press, Oxford

Cantarella E (1996) Il paradosso romano: la donna tra diritto e cultura. In: Medici G, Teresa M (eds) *Orientamenti civilistici e canonistici sulla condizione della donna*. Edizioni scientifiche italiane, Napoli, p 13ff

Chapman Catt C, Shuler NR (1923) Woman suffrage and politics: the inner story of the suffrage movement. Charles Scribner's Sons, New York

Chavalas MW (2014) Women in the ancient near east. Routledge, London

Chuku G (2018) Colonialism and African womanhood. In: Shanguhyia MS, Falola T (eds) The Palgrave handbook of African colonial and postcolonial history. Palgrave Macmillan, New York, pp 171–211

Clay C, Paul C, Senecal C (2009) Envisioning women in world history. McGraw-Hill Higher Education, New York

Cook BB (1984) Women judges: a preface to their history. Golden Gate Univ Law Rev 14:573–610

Cooney K (2014) The woman who would be King. Crown Publishing Group, New York

Cooney K (2018) When women ruled the world. National Geographic, Washington

Crabites P (1927) Napoleon Bonaparte and the code Napoleon. Am Bar Assoc J 13:439–444

Crosby K (2017) Keeping women off the jury in 1920s England and Wales. Leg Stud 37:695–717

Davis AY (2011) Women, race, & class. Vintage Books, New York

Deen E (1955) All the women of the bible. Harper & Row Publishers-Harper Collins Publishers Inc, New York

Depauw M (2003) Notes on transgressing gender boundaries in ancient Egypt. Zeitschrift für Ägyptische Sprache und Alterumskunde 130:49–59

Dixon S (2001) Reading Roman women. Sources, genres and real life. Bristol Classical Press, London

Dover KJ (1989) Greek homosexuality. Harvard University Press, Cambridge

Drew KF (1973) The Lombard laws. University of Pennsylvania Press, Philadelphia

Drew KF (1991) The Laws of the salic franks. University of Pennsylvania Press, Philadelphia

DuBois EC (1998) Woman suffrage & women's rights. New York University Press, New York

Durrant JB (2007) Witchcraft, gender and society in early modern Germany. Brill, Leiden/Boston

Evans Grubbs J (2002) Women and the law in the Roman empire. A sourcebook on marriage, divorce and widowhood. Routledge, London

Fjelde Tjelle K (2013) Missionary masculinity, 1870–1930 the Norwegian missionaries in South-East Africa. Palgrave Macmillan, London

Foxhall L (1989) Household, gender and property in classical Athens. Class Q 39:22–44

Freedman E (2002) No turning back: the history of feminism and the future of women. Ballantine Books, New York

Frevert U (1999) Male crime in nineteenth-century Germany: dueling. In: Arnot ML, Usborne C (eds) Gender and crime in modern Europe. UCL Press, London, pp 173–188

Frohnecke E (2001) Die Rolle des ABGB in Gesetzgebung und Rechtswissenschaft des 19. Jahrhundertss. LIT, Münster

Gagarin M, Cohen DJ (2005) Cambridge companion to ancient Greek law. Cambridge University Press, Cambridge

Gardner JF (1986) Women in Roman law and society. Routledge, London

Garland L (2002) Byzantine empresses: women and power in Byzantium AD 527–1204. Routledge, London

Garland L (2016) Till death do us part?' Family life in byzantine monasteries. In: Neil B, Garland L (eds) Questions of gender in byzantine society. Routledge, London, pp 29–56

Gerhard U, Meunier V, Rundell E (2016) Civil law and gender in nineteenth-century Europe. Clio Women Gender Hist 43:250–275

Gibbon E (2000) The history of the decline and fall of the Roman empire. Penguin Books Limited, London

Gibson M (1986) Prostitution and the state in Italy, 1860–1915. Ohio State University Press, Columbus

Gilhuly K (2008) The feminine matrix of sex and gender in classical Athens. Cambridge University Press, Cambridge

Giunti P (2012) Il ruolo sociale della donna romana di età imperiale: tra discriminazione e riconoscimento. Index 40:342–379

Golden M (2015) Children and childhood in classical Athens. Johns Hopkins University Press, Baltimore

Graves-Brown C (2010) Dancing for Hathor – women in ancient Egypt. Continuum, London/New York

Green EE (1996) Perché la donna pastore. Il volto femminile del ministero nelle Chiese. Claudiana, Torino

Grimshaw P (1988) Women's suffrage in New Zealand. Oxford University Press, Oxford

Guilland R (1943) Les eunuques dans l'empire byzantin. Etude de titulature et de prosopographie byzantines. Revue des études byzantines 1:197–238

Hale M (2002) The history of the common law in England. University of Chicago Press, Chicago

Hamzić V (2016) Sexual and gender diversity in the Muslim world. I. B. Tauris & Co. Ltd, London/New York

Han E, O'Mahoney J (2018) British colonialism and the criminalization of homosexuality: Queens, crime and empire. Routledge, London

Harris K (1984) Sex, ideology and religion. Barnes & Noble Books, New Jersey

Harrison ARW (1968) The law of Athens: the family and property. Clarendon Press, Oxford

Harris-Perry MV (2011) Sister citizen: shame, stereotypes, and Black women in America. Yale University Press, New Haven/London

Hecht NS, Jackson BS et al (2002) An introduction to the history and sources of Jewish law. Oxford University Press Inc, Oxford

Heger P (2014) Women in the Bible, Quran and early rabbinic literature. Brill, Leiden/Boston

Hemelrijk EA (1999) Matrona Docta. Educated women in the Roman élite from Cornelia to Julia Domna. Routledge, London

Herchenroder MFP (1938) The capacity of married women in French law. J Comp Legis Int Law 20:196–203

Herrin J (2013) Unrivalled influence: women and empire in Byzantium. Princeton University Press, New Jersey

Jagodinsky K (2016) Legal codes and talking trees: indigenous Women's sovereignty in the Sonoran and Puget Sound Borderlands 1854–1946. Yale University Press, New Haven/London

Jewell HM (1996) Women in Medieval England. Manchester University Press, Manchester

Jones A (2009) Women who kill. The Feminist Press at CUNY, New York

Jones J, Grear A et al (2011) Gender, sexualities and law. Routledge, London

Jones K (2006) Gender and petty crime in late medieval England – the local courts in Kent, 1460–1560. The Boydell Press, Woodbridge

Just R (1989) Women in Athenian law and life. Routledge, London

Kadlec K (1924) Prvobitno slovensko pravo pre X veka. Preveo i dopunio Taranovski. Geca Kon, Beograd

Kalaitzidis P (2016) Nel mondo ma non del mondo. Sfide e tentazioni della Chiesa nel mondo contemporaneo. Edizioni Qiqajon, Magnano (BI)

Kandić L (1969) Salijski zakon i društveni odnosi u Franačkoj u doba Merovinga. Anali Pravnog fakulteta 1:53–61

Karolak M, Guta H (2020) Saudi women as decision makers: analyzing the media portrayal of female political participation in Saudi Arabia. Hawwa 18:75–95

Karras RM (1996) Common women: prostitution and sexuality in medieval England (studies in the history of sexuality). Oxford University Press, Oxford

Katz M (1992) Ideology and 'The Status of Women' in ancient Greece. Hist Theory 31:70–97

Kenney SJ (2008) Gender on the agenda: how the paucity of women judges became an issue. J Polit 70:717–735

Kilday A-M (2013) A history of infanticide in Britain, c. 1600 to the present. Palgrave Macmillan, London

Kimble SL, Röwekamp M (2016) New perspectives on European Women's legal history. Routledge, London

Kimble SL, Röwekamp M (2018) Exclusion and inclusion in the legal professions: negotiating gender in central and east Central Europe, 1887–1945. Acta Poloniae Historica 117:51–93

King P (1999) Gender, crime and justice in late eighteenth- and early nineteenth-century England. In: Arnot ML, Usborne C (eds) Gender and crime in modern Europe. UCL Press, London, pp 44–74

Korieh CJ (2010) The land has changed: history, society and gender in colonial eastern Nigeria. University of Calgary Press, Calgary

Kršljanin N (2021) Legal regulation of sex crimes in medieval Serbia and the Mediterranean communes under its rule. In: Domingues LZ, Caravaggi L, Paoletti GM (eds) Women and violence in the late medieval Mediterranean, ca. 1100–1500. Routledge, London, pp 101–120

Kuklík J (2015) Czech law in historical contexts. Karolinum Press, Prague

Lacey WK (1968) The family in classical Greece. Thames and Hudson Ltd, London

Laiou AE (1981) The role of women in byzantine society in XVI. Jahrbuch der Osterreichischen Byzantinistik Wien 31:233–260

Laiou AE (1998) She, consent and coercion in Byzantium. In: Laiou AE (ed) Consent and coercion to sex and marriage in ancient and medieval societies. Dumbarton Oaks Research Library & Collection, Washington DC, pp 109–221

Laite J (2012) Common prostitutes and ordinary citizens: commercial sex in London, 1885–1960. Palgrave Macmillan, London

Lamberti F (2014) Donne romane fra Idealtypus e realtà sociale. Quaderni Lupiensi di Storia e Diritto 4:61–84

Landes JB (1988) Women and the public sphere in the age of the French revolution. Cornell University Press, Ithaca/London

Lerner G (1986) The creation of patriarchy. Oxford University Press, Oxford

Levin E (1989) Sex and Society in the World of the orthodox Slavs, 900–1700. Cornell University Press, Ithaca/London

Lewis MB (2016) Infanticide and abortion in early modern Germany. Routledge, London

Leyser H (1995) Medieval women: a social history of women in England 450–1500. St. Martin's Press, New York

Lobingier CS (1918) Napoleon and his code. Harv Law Revies 32:114–134

Lombroso C, Ferrero G (2004) Criminal woman, the prostitute, and the Normal woman. (trans: Gibson M, Hahn Rafter N). Duke University Press, Durham

Long G (2008) Ordinamenti giuridici delle Chiese protestanti. il Mulino, Bologna

Lukes S, Urbinati N (2012) Condorcet: political writings. Cambridge University Press, Cambridge

MacDowell DD (1978) The law in classical Athens. Thames and Hudson Ltd, London

MacDowell DD (1986) Spartan law. Scottish Academic Press, Edinburgh

MacLachlan B (2012) Women in Ancient Greece. Continuum International Publishing Group, London/New York

Margetić L (1996) Hrvatsko srednjovjekovno obiteljsko i nasljedno pravo. Narodne novine, Zagreb

Marinatos N (1993) Minoan religion: ritual, image and symbol. University of South Carolina Press, Columbia

Markoff J (2003) Margins, centers, and democracy: the paradigmatic history of Women's suffrage. Signs J Women Cult Soc 29:85–116

Marsman HJ (2003) Women in Ugarit & Israel: their social & religious position in the context of the ancient near east. Brill, Leiden/Boston

Martin R (2007) Women, murder, and equity in early modern England. Routledge, London

Matthews VH, Levinson BM, Frymer-Kensky T (1998) Gender and law in the Hebrew bible and the ancient near east. Sheffield Academic Press, Sheffield

McCammon HJ, Campbell KE, Granberg EM, Mowery C (2001) How movements win: gendered opportunity structures and US women's suffrage movements, 1866 to 1919. Am Sociol Rev 66: 49–70

Meade TA, Wiesner-Hanks ME (2004) A companion to gender history. Blackwell Publishing Ltd, Oxford

Mendelson S, Crawford P (2000) Women in early modern England 1550–1720. Oxford University Press, Oxford

Mercogliano F (2001) Deterior est condicio feminarum.... Index 29:209–220

Milner LS (2000) Hardness of heart/hardness of life: the stain of human infanticide. University Press of America, Lanham/New York/Oxford

Mossman MJ (2006) The first women lawyers: a comparative study of gender; law and the legal professions. Hart Publishing, London

Nasir JJ (2009) The status of women under Islamic law and modern Islamic legislation. Brill, Leiden/Boston

Nym Mayhall LE (2003) The militant suffrage movement: citizenship and resistance in Britain, 1860–1930. Oxford University Press, Oxford

Obolensky D (1971) The byzantine commonwealth: Eastern Europe, 500–1453. Praeger, New York

Offen K (2011) Feminism and the republic. In: Berenson E, Duclert V, Prochasson C (eds) The French Republic – history, values, debates. Cornell University Press, Ithaca and London, pp 289–299

Oguz A (2005) The role of comparative law in the development of Turkish civil law. Pace Int Law Rev 17:373–386

Oldfield A (1992) Woman suffrage in Australia: a gift or a struggle? Cambridge University Press, Cambridge

Oman C (1919) The dark ages 476–918. Rivingtons, London

Ortu R (2018) Condizione giuridica e ruolo sociale delle vestali in età imperiale. Sandhi Edizioni, Cagliari

Osborn EL (2011) Our new husbands are here: households, gender, and politics in a West African state from the slave trade to colonial rule. Ohio University Press, Columbus

Ostrogorsky G (1968) History of the Byzantine state (trans: Hussey J). Basil Blackwell, Oxford

Peled I (2020) Law and gender in the ancient near east and the Hebrew bible. Routledge, London

Peppe L (2016) Civis Romana. Forme giuridiche e modelli sociali dell'appartenenza e dell'identità femminili in Roma antica. Edizioni Griffo, Lecce

Pinchbeck I (2014) Women workers and the industrial revolution 1750–1850. Routledge, London

Pizzini-Gambetta V (1999) Gender norms in the Sicilian Mafia, 1945–86. In: Arnot ML, Usborne C (eds) Gender and crime in modern Europe. UCL Press, London, pp 257–276

Polojac M, Mirković Z, Đurđević M (2015) Srpski građanski zakonik: 170 godina. Pravni fakultet Univerziteta u Beogradu, Beograd

Pölönen J (2016) Framing 'Law and Society' in the Roman world. In: du Plessis PJ, Ando C, Tuori K (eds) The Oxford handbook of Roman law and society. Oxford University Press, Oxford, pp 8–22

Pomeroy BS (1990) Women in Hellenistic Egypt. Wayne State University Press, Detroit

Pomeroy BS (1994) Goddesses, whores, wives, & slaves. Pimlico, London

Pomeroy BS (2002) Spartan women. Oxford University Press, Oxford

Quadrato R (2001) Infirmitas sexus' e 'levitas animi': il sesso "debole" nel linguaggio dei giuristi romani. In: Scientia iuris' e linguaggio nel sistema giuridico romano. Atti del Convegno di Studi

Sassari (22–23 novembre 1996). Pubblicazioni dell'Università degli studi di Sassari, Milano, pp 155–194
Rafter NH (1985) Gender, prisons, and prison history. Soc Sci Hist 9:233–247
Ringrose KM (2007) The perfect servant: eunuchs and the social construction of gender in Byzantium. University of Chicago Press, Chicago
Robins G (1993) Women in Ancient Egypt. British Museum Press, London
Rodriguez CM (1999) Clearing the smoke-filled room: women jurors and the disruption of an old-boys' network in nineteenth-century America. Yale Law J 108:1805–1844
Roelofs J (2018) Alexandra Kollontai: socialist feminism in theory and practice. Int Crit Thought 8: 166–175
Roth MT (1997) Law collections from Mesopotamia and Asia minor. Scholars Press, Atlanta
Röwekamp M (2020) In: Collin P (ed) Frauen vor und im Gericht. In Konfliktlösung im 19. und 20. Jahrhundert, Handbuch zur Geschichte der Konfliktlösung in Europa 4. Springer, Berlin, pp 99–109
Russell AD, Abdullah Al-Ma'a Mun S (2008) Muslim law: an historical introduction to the law of inheritance. Routledge, London
Salapatas D (2015) The role of women in the orthodox church. Orthodoxes Forum 29:177–194
Šarkić S (2001) Nekoliko napomena o pravnom položaju žena u srednjevekovnom srpskom pravu. Pravni život 9:565–572
Schaps DM (1981) Economic rights of women in ancient Greece. Edinburgh University Press, Edinburgh
Sinha M (1995) Colonial masculinity: the 'manly Englishman' and the 'effeminate Bengali' in the late 19th century. Manchester University Press, Manchester
Solovjev AV (1928) Zakonodavstvo Stefana Dušana, cara Srba i Grka. Skopsko naučno društvo, Skoplje
Solovjev AV (1939) Žene kao porotnici u Dušanovom zakoniku. Arhiv za pravne i društvene nauke 1:403–407
Sonneveld N, Lindbekk M (2017) Introduction: a historical overview of gender and judicial authority in the Muslim World. In: Sonneveld N, Lindbekk M (eds) Women judges in the Muslim world: a comparative study of discourse and practice. Brill, Leiden/Boston, pp 1–19
Spivak GC (2010) Can the subaltern speak? In: Morris R (ed) Can the subaltern speak?: reflections on the history of an idea. Columbia University Press, New York, pp 21–78
Stanimirović V (2006) Brak i bračna davanja u istoriji. Pravni fakultet Univerziteta u Beogradu, Beograd
Stanojević O (1980) Osnovi precedentnog prava. Pravni fakultet Univerziteta u Beogradu, Beograd
Stol M (2016) Women in the ancient near east. Walter de Gruyter Inc, Boston/Berlin
Stone L (1990) Road to divorce: England 1530–1987. Oxford University Press, Oxford
Stone L (1993) Broken lives: separation and divorce in England, 1660–1857. Oxford University Press, Oxford
Swiss L (2009) Decoupling values from action: an event-history analysis of the election of women to parliament in the developing world, 1945—90. Int J Comp Sociol 50:69–95
Szreter S (2002) Fertility, class, and gender in Britain, 1860–1940. Cambridge University Press, Cambridge
Taranovski T (2002) Istorija srpskog prava u Nemanjićkoj državi. Lirika, Beograd
Tetlow EM (2004) Women, crime, and punishment in ancient law and society vol. 1: the ancient near east. The Continuum International Publishing Group Inc, New York
Tetlow EM (2005) Women, crime, and punishment in ancient law and society vol. 2: the ancient Greece. The Continuum International Publishing Group Inc., New York
Todd M (1992) The early Germans. Blacwell Publishing, Hoboken
Todd S (1995) The shape of Athenian law. Clarendon Press, Oxford
Tougher S (2008) The eunuch in Byzantine history and society. Routledge, London
Treggiari S (1991) Roman marriage. Iusti coniuges from the time of Cicero to the time of Ulpian. Calrendon Press of Oxford University Press, New York

Tucker JE (2008) Women, family, and gender in Islamic law. Cambridge University Press, Cambridge
Tyldesley JA (1995) Daughters of Isis: women of ancient Egypt. Penguin Books, London
Van Wingerden SA (1999) The Women's suffrage movement in Britain, 1866–1928. Palgrave Macmillan, London
Vigarello G (2001) A history of rape: sexual violence in France from the 16th to the 20th century (trans: Birrell J). Polity, Cambridge/Oxford
Vigneron R, Gerkens J-F (2000) The emancipation of women in ancient Rome. RIDA 47:107–121
Von Lingenthal KEZ (1892) Geschichte des griechisch-römischen Rechts. Weidmannsche Buchhandlung, Berlin
Voorhoeve M (2012) Family law in Islam: divorce, marriage and women in the Muslim world. I. B. Tauris & Co. Ltd, London/New York
Vujadinović D (2015) Gender mainstreaming in law and legal education. Annals FLB Belgrade Law Rev 3:56–74
Vujadinović D (2019) Rod i pravna regulativa. In: Vujadinović D, Stanimirović V (eds) Studije roda. Univerzitet u Beogradu – Pravni fakultet, Beograd, pp 97–115
Walker G (1998) Rereading rape and sexual violence in early modern England. Gend Hist 10:1–25
Wängnerud L (2009) Women in parliaments: descriptive and substantive representation. Annu Rev Polit Sci 12:51–69
Watson A (1974) Legal transplants: an approach to comparative law. University Press of Virginia, Virginia
Weinstein JD (1986) Adultery, law, and the state: a history. Hast Law J 38:195–238
Weisberg DE (2009) Levirate marriage and the family in ancient Judaism. Brandeis University Press, Waltham
Westbrook R (2003a) A history of ancient near eastern law, vol 1. Brill, Leiden/Boston
Westbrook R (2003b) A history of ancient near eastern law, vol 2. Brill, Leiden/Boston
Wilfong TG (2010) Gender in Ancient Egypt. In: Wendrich W (ed) Egyptian archaeology. Wiley-Blackwell, West Sussex, pp 164–179
Wilkinson RH (2017) The complete gods and goddesses of ancient Egypt. Thames & Hudson, London
Wing AK (2003) Critical race feminism: a reader. New York University Press, New York
Winkler JJ (1990) The constraints of desire – the anthropology of sex and gender in ancient Greece. Routledge, London
Witte J Jr (2002) Law and protestantism: the legal teachings of the Lutheran reformation. Cambridge University Press, Cambridge
Zedner L (1991) Women, crime, and penal responses: a historical account. Crime Justice 14:307–362
Пушкарева НЛ (1989) Женщины Древней Руси. Мысль, Москва
Щапов ЯН (1970) Брак и семья в Древней Руси. Вопросы истории 10:216–219

Further Reading

Ågren M (2016) Making a living, making a difference: gender and work in early modern European society. Oxford University Press, Oxford
Arjava A (1998) Women and law in late antiquity. Clarendon Press, Oxford
Bennett JM (2006) History matters: patriarchy and the challenge of feminism. University of Pennsylvania Press, Philadelphia
Bosworth M, Flavin J (2007) Race, gender, and punishment: from colonialism to the war on terror. Rutgers University Press, New Jersey
Brundage JA (1987) Law, sex, and Christian Society in medieval Europe. The University of Chicago Press, Chicago

Cremer AC (2020) Gender, law and material culture: immobile property and mobile goods in early modern Europe. Routledge, London

Gottschalk K (2013) Gender difference in European legal cultures. Historical perspectives. Dedicated to Heide Wunder on the occasion of her 70th birthday. Franz Steiner Verlag, Stuttgart

Hawley R, Levick B (1995) Women in antiquity: new assessments. Routledge, London

Hufton O (1992) Women and the limits of citizenship in in the French revolution. University of Toronto Press, Toronto

Jacobsen G, Wunder H (2015) East meets west. A gendered view of legal traditions. Kiel, Solivagus

Kapparis K (2021) Women in the law courts of classical Athens. Edinburgh University Press, Edinburgh

Kingston-Mann E (2018) Women, land rights and rural development: how much land does a woman need? Routledge, London

Meder S, Mecke C-E. Family law in early women's rights debates. De Gruyter, Cologne

Moore LR (2019) Women before the court: law and patriarchy in the Anglo-American world, 1600–1800. Manchester University Press, Manchester

Murray M (1995) The law of the father?: patriarchy in the transition from feudalism to capitalism. Routledge, London

Norgren J (2018) Stories from trailblazing women lawyers. New York University Press, New York

Wagner R, Sally. (2019) The women's suffrage movement. Penguin Books, London

Rodriguez Ruiz B, Marín RR (2012) The struggle for female suffrage in Europe: voting to become citizens. Brill, Leiden/Boston

Ruggiero G (1985) The boundaries of Eros: sex crime and sexuality in renaissance Venice. Oxford University Press, Oxford

Schandevyl E (2014) Women in law and lawmaking in nineteenth and twentieth-century Europe. Ashgate Publishing House, Farnham

Feminist Political and Legal Theories 3

Antonio Álvarez del Cuvillo, Fabio Macioce, and Sofia Strid

Contents

Authors are listed in alphabetical order. Antonio Álvarez del Cuvillo has written Sect. 3.1 and 3.2; Sofia Strid has written Sect. 3.3 and Fabio Macioce has written Sect. 3.4 and 3.5. The authors would like to thank Mareike Fröhlich, Thomas Giegerich, Julia Ricarda Jungfleisch and Dragica Vujadinović for their valuable comments and engagement with the chapter. Antonio Álvarez would like to thank Fabio Macioce, Asunción Aragón and Sofia Strid for the comments on his section. The contents of this chapter are based on the syllabus for the course Feminist Political and Legal Theories, by Dragica Vujadinović, Miodrag Jovanović, Tanasije Marinković, Bojan Spaić, Antonio Álvarez del Cuvillo, Asunción Aragón, Fabio Macioce, Sofia Strid and Zara Saeidzadeh.

A. Álvarez. del Cuvillo (✉)
Department of Labour and Social Security Law, University of Cádiz, Cádiz, Spain
e-mail: antonio.alvarez@uca.es

F. Macioce
LUMSA, Philosophy of Law, Rome, Italy
e-mail: f.macioce@lumsa.it

S. Strid
School of Humanities, Education and Social Sciences, Unit of Gender Studies and Sociology, Örebro University, Örebro, Sweden

Department of Sociology and Work Science, Gothenburg University, Gothenburg, Sweden
e-mail: sofia.strid@gu.se

D. Vujadinović et al. (eds.), *Gender-Competent Legal Education*, Springer Textbooks in Law, https://doi.org/10.1007/978-3-031-14360-1_3

Abstract

This chapter presents an overview of feminist legal and political thought, aiming at discussing the different perspectives within feminist thought. In the first part, basic concepts in feminist thought such as gender, patriarchy, and feminism are explained, and a brief overview of the historical evolution of feminist movements is provided. The other two sections focus in greater detail on political and legal theories, respectively, including a critical analysis of the influence of patriarchy on mainstream legal and political discourses. The chapter will further provide a description of how classical concepts of political or legal tradition have been reconsidered from a feminist point of view, and a short presentation of the most important issues at stake in both these fields.

3.1 Introduction

This chapter will present an overview of what is usually called, *feminist jurisprudence*, that is to say, feminist legal theory. As legal theory is deeply intertwined with political theory, especially with regard to the critical analysis of the law, we have seen fit to include the latter in the study.

This text provides a basic theoretical framework, which is necessary to apply gender mainstreaming to the different branches of law. While other chapters of the book are mainly focused on empirical material, such as positive law or court decisions, this chapter focuses on theories and ideas. Before beginning to analyse legislation and cases, it is necessary to go in depth into various fundamental issues; the concept of gender, the relevance, the purpose of gender mainstreaming and the different approaches or methodologies that can be adopted. Besides this theoretical chapter, the chapter on Sociology of Law in Gender Perspective as well as to a certain extent the chapter Gender Issues in the Comparative Legal History deal with the most relevant concepts and phenomena, but by placing them in a social-political or historical-political context instead of this mostly theoretical one.

This chapter is mainly focused on feminist theories, and the basic distinction between women and men. LGBTQIA+ and other non-binary aspects are addressed with more detail in the Sociology of Law chapter.

In this brief summary of feminist legal and political theories, this chapter tried to acknowledge the great diversity of perspectives that exists within feminist thought, including debates that have taken place about some essential problems. In that context, the reader is advised to maintain a critical attitude, not only toward the dominant legal discourse but also toward feminist theories themselves and, of course, toward the views adopted by the authors of this chapter.

The contents are divided into three main sections. First, the chapter explains certain basic concepts in feminist thought such as *gender*, *patriarchy*, and *feminism*. In this section, the chapter explores the historical evolution of the feminist movement and the different types of feminism. The other two sections refer to political and legal theories, respectively, following a similar structure, which includes a critical analysis of the influence of patriarchy on mainstream discourse, a reconsideration of the classical concepts of political or legal theory from a feminist point of view, and a short presentation of the most important issues in each field.

3.2 Gender, Patriarchy and Feminism

3.2.1 Patriarchy and Gender

It is usually accepted that, from a biological or reproductive point of view, the human species has two sexes, because there are two types of gametes.[1] Commonly, there are anatomical, morphological and physiological disparities between *females* and *males*, many of which are easily noticeable by human perception. For that reason, in every society, perceived sex is used to delimit two social groups, women and men. Invariably, this distinction has economic, social, political and cultural relevance.

Binary opposition between women and men is ubiquitous as a cultural mechanism, however it is neither absolute nor continuous. Throughout history, there have been many variations and interpretations of gender and sex. Further, there are cultures or societies that currently recognise additional gender categories that incorporate individuals who do not fit with specific contemporary or traditional gender roles; e.g. third and further genders. Nevertheless, these categories presuppose the binary distinction, in order to be intelligible: for instance, in Zapotec cultures a *muxe* would be a person assigned 'male' at birth that assumes social roles normally attributed to 'females'. Even the 'non binary' category itself implies that there is a binary distinction in society.

This differentiation between men and women is not neutral from the perspective of power or dignity. Indeed, in all known human societies there is some type of male dominance that implies significant inequalities in symbolic status, economic functions, political power, freedom of choice, life opportunities and access to society's resources. These inequalities are structural and systemic because they are not related to isolated behaviours, but firmly interwoven in society's patterns, rules,

[1] This idea does not imply necessarily that every individual could be objectively classified in one of the sexes, as we will see later. In this sense, the binary distinction between the sexes is widely challenged in the academic literature. Also, there are some authors who argue that sex, and not just gender, could be a social construct, which we will discuss in this section.

and the structures of power. Therefore, in every society there is a system of male domination; a set of representations, beliefs, values and practices that tends to maintain and reproduce women's subordination. In Feminist Theory, this structure of power which generates systemic inequalities between women and men is usually called *patriarchy*. The subsections will delve into the notion of patriarchy in Sects. 3.3.1 (political theories) and 3.4.1 (legal theories).

Every domination system presents itself as an objective reality stemming from the natural order of things. In all societies, the subordinate position of women has been historically considered inherent to the biological distinction between the sexes. For instance, in Western culture, until very recently, the greatest male philosophers and thinkers explicitly legitimized male dominance on the basis of divine will, natural order, or pure reason.

Consequently, the political aim of women's emancipation necessarily requires denaturalising women's subordinate position in the social structure, dissociating it from anatomical differences or metaphysical essences. This strategy is present in the eighteenth century in the discourse of Mary Wollstonecraft, who highlighted the importance of education in women's subjugation, but is particularly well expressed in the mid-twentieth century by Simone de Beauvoir in her famous quote, "One is not born, but rather becomes a woman".[2]

Throughout the twentieth century, beginning with Margaret Mead's classical anthropological work,[3] social scientists have gathered a good deal of evidence that proves the features, personality traits, characteristics, values and social roles attributed to women vary widely across history and cultures, and thus they are not linked to biological differences. Although women have almost always held a subordinate position, the social expectations attributed to them are not the same from one society to another.

Since the late 1970s, the category *gender* has been used in feminist theory and the social sciences to depict this critical differentiation between sex as a biological reality and the contingent social and cultural patterns attributed to each sex. In the 1950s and 1960s, the term had evolved from grammar to psychiatry and psychoanalysis, in reference to individuals' *gender identity*. In contrast, the anthropologist Gayle Rubin coined the term to designate a social structure (the *sex-gender system*), defined as "the set of arrangements by which a society transforms biological sexuality into products of human activity".[4] Hence, we could define *gender* as determined social roles and expectations, even as the set of stereotypes, prejudices and cognitive biases that different societies and cultures attribute to each biological sex, that are not a necessary consequence of physiological differences between men and women. In conclusion, whereas sex is biological and relatively objective, gender is a social construct.[5]

---

[2] de Beauvoir (1949), p. 285.

[3] Mead (1935).

[4] Rubin (1975).

[5] Fletcher (2002), p. 9.

Some authors have suggested that perhaps even the category *sex* could be a social construct.[6] This claim is very controversial as biologists use the label as a scientific category to represent an objective reality that supposedly exists, regardless of human representations, related to the phenomenon of sexual reproduction that characterises most living species, including humans. Of course, all linguistic categories are social constructions, however this assertion in particular could be interpreted as a relativistic denial of the current scientific consensus about human biology.[7] Furthermore, from the perspective of social sciences, the deconstruction of sex could dilute the importance of the sex/gender distinction, which has been useful for understanding how social differences are produced on the basis of an individual's perceived sex. On the other hand, the hypothesis of sex as a social construction could help us to be aware that, in many cases, when we are talking about biological sex in social discourse or in legal reasoning, we are in fact attributing social, cultural, or legal significance to the perceived sexual attributes of a person. In that sense, perhaps we are referring to gender instead of pure biological sex.

In this context, it is useful to differentiate between *gender identity* and *gender*. Gender identity is the self-conception that a person has of being a man, a woman, both, or neither. Most people are *cisgender*, i.e., they identify themselves with the sex assigned at birth. Some people are labelled as *transgender*, identifying as members of either the opposite gender category or outside the binary classification. While gender identity is a purely subjective experience, gender is a social, intersubjective phenomenon that normally operates regardless of the individual's self-identification. Gender expectations, roles and stereotypes linked to the social category of *women* or *men* will be applied to every person socially perceived as *female* or *male*, even if they do not identify themselves as such or if their chromosomal sex does not match their phenotypical *feminine* or *masculine* features.

Example

Gender-fluid people that are socially-perceived as women because of their physical appearance could be victims of sexual harassment or sexist discrimination at work, regardless of their personal self-identification as non-binary people. ◀

Gender has a direct connection with patriarchy; the subordination of women and the inequalities of power are supported by a set of psychological dispositions, cultural values, social roles and expectations, that tend to reproduce systemic inequalities. In other words, gender patterns form the basis of symbolic violence, sex discrimination, and gender violence.

Symbolic violence occurs when the cognitive schemes available to women for perceiving themselves and their social relationships with men are "the embodied

[6] Butler (1990), pp. 8–10. See also the "Sociology of Law and Gender Equality" Chapter in this book (subsection 1.1).

[7] Marinov (2020).

form of the relation of domination".[8] In that context, social inequalities or the conditions that reproduce such inequalities are internalised, naturalised, or accepted by its victims. When symbolic violence is not sufficient for maintaining the subjugation of women, discriminatory practices, including gender violence, come into play.[9] Of course, these practices are sustained by gender stereotypes and prejudices. Therefore, discrimination and gender violence could be described, not only as consequences of the system of masculine domination, but also as mechanisms that contribute to perpetuating it.

Due to its links with the reproduction of patriarchy, gender is usually considered an oppressive and alienating force in feminist literature; for some authors, the final aim of feminism would be to create a genderless society in which sexual anatomy was irrelevant,[10] although this is not a unanimous opinion. For instance, gender difference is appreciated by cultural feminism, and self-perceived gender identity could be relevant for personality development. Gender patterns could also be detrimental to men in some way, since they are imposed on the individual regardless of their preferences or personal needs. In this way, Bourdieu states that male privilege is a trap since it gives every man the duty to "assert his manliness in all circumstances".[11]

Gender is not the only factor that determines social position, discrimination, and privilege. In fact, it interacts with other personal characteristics, including, but not limited to, social class, race or ethnic origin, age, disability, sexual orientation and gender identity. Experience modulated by the intersection of different categories or social circumstances is not merely the sum of these categories.[12] In that context, *intersectionality* is the analytical perspective that takes into account the combination of different aspects of people in order to understand their position in the social structure.

3.2.2 Feminism

Feminism is a philosophical and political movement aimed at ending women's oppression,[13] encompassing both theory and activism. Since patriarchy is characterized by systematic inequalities, the basic goal of feminism is to achieve equality between women and men.[14]

[8] Bourdieu (2002), p. 35.
[9] Millet (1969), p. 43.
[10] Rubin (1975).
[11] Bourdieu (2002), p. 50.
[12] Crenshaw (1989), p. 140.
[13] Mikolla (2008).
[14] Lorber (2010).

3.2.2.1 History of Feminism

Throughout history and across cultures, people have advocated for women's rights and against misogyny, or have defended women's capability to do certain things that were not considered appropriate in the context of patriarchy. This kind of discourse could be called *protofeminism*, since modern feminism, as an organized movement, appeared in the late nineteenth century in Europe and North America.

This movement has its ideological roots in the philosophical principles of the Enlightenment of the seventeenth and eighteenth centuries, even though in that period masculine domination was not challenged by most authors.[15] In the late eighteenth century, the declarations of rights resulting from the bourgeois revolutions in the United States and France proclaimed that all "men" were born free and equal; this did not imply the inclusion of women, proletarians or ethnic minorities. In fact, the subordination of women in the public and private spheres was considered natural and implicit in the social order regardless of formal proclamation of the principle of equality. Trying to criticize this contradiction, the revolutionary Olympe de Gouges wrote a pamphlet titled "Declaration of the Rights of Woman and of the Female Citizen" (Déclaration des droits de la femme et de la citoyenne) in 1791, in imitation of the 1789 "Declaration of the Rights of Man and of the Citizen". In 1792, Mary Wollstonecraft published a protofeminist essay "A Vindication of the Rights of the Woman: With Strictures on Political and Moral Subjects" in Britain and later, in the nineteenth century, authors like Harriet Taylor Mill and her husband, John Stuart Mill, published dissertations which advocated for women's equality, specially concerning education and politics.

The history of the feminist movement is usually divided into *waves*, characterized by the main objectives pursued in each historical period. Of course, this distinction is a simplification and should not be considered absolute. There is a great deal of diversity regarding the objectives pursued in each wave, and at the same time, there are many overlaps between them.[16]

- The *first wave* is identified with the suffrage movement from the late nineteenth century to the first decades of the twentieth century. It is usually considered that the suffrage movement was born at the Seneca Falls Convention, in the state of New York in 1848. Later, in the 1860s it expanded to the United Kingdom and to other countries thereafter.

Besides women's suffrage, which was clearly the main goal,[17] the feminist movement in this period was focused on women's access to higher education and other basic civil rights that nowadays are taken for granted, like the right to own property.[18]

- The *second wave* is usually related to the feminist movement in the 1960s and 1970s, although some authors consider it began with the publication of Simone de

[15]Bryson (1992), p. 18.

[16]Hewitt (2010).

[17]Bryson (1992), p. 87.

[18]Lorber(2010), p. 1.

Beauvoir's essay, *The Second Sex,* in 1949.[19] This new impetus of the feminist movement had its roots in the failure of the promises of independency and fulfilment that the dominant liberal ideology of this time granted to women.[20] Formal equality had essentially been achieved in the United States and other countries, nevertheless, gender inequalities were pervasive. In this period, the feminist movement was mainly divided into two main currents.[21] On the one hand, many efforts were made to fight discriminatory practices in the public sphere, especially discrimination in the labour market and sexual harassment at the workplace. On the other hand, a new emphasis was placed on analysing personal, sexual and family life from a radical feminist perspective. In this regard, the most famous feminist slogan of this era was "the personal is political", which is explored in the following sections.

- The *third wave* is considered to have begun in the 1990s. This stage was characterized by an increase of the diversity of perspectives within feminism. Even though the other waves were not monolithic, criticism was raised concerning the overrepresentation of the interests and views of white, middle-class, professional, cisgender and heterosexual women in high-income countries in the previous configuration of the feminist movement. A new focus was placed on intersectional feminism that drew on the connection between gender, class, race and other personal characteristics. Movements like transfeminism or postmodern feminism have even questioned the meaning or the significance of basic concepts of feminist theory like women, gender or even sex.

- Some authors identify a *fourth wave* of feminism, from 2012–2013 to the present day, that implies a new impetus in the movement. This is mainly concerned with diverse online/offline forms of gender violence (domestic violence, rape culture, sexual harassment), body shaming and women's representation in the media and Internet.[22] Online activism and social media are particularly important in this wave, providing rapid global dissemination to initiatives, such as the #MeToo movement. Intersectionality is still highly relevant in the fourth wave, perhaps even more so than in the third wave.

3.2.2.2 Types of Feminism

Feminism is very diverse. In fact, it could be considered not as a single movement or ideology, rather as a set of different social movements and theories that share the same basic goal of defeating the systemic oppression of women. Feminist theories vary and often contradict or complement each other due to epistemological, ideological, or strategic differences. Such a plurality gives rise to many heated debates regarding concrete practical issues, such as the regulation of prostitution or the inclusion of trans women. A classification of theories could allow a better understanding of this complexity, however it should be approached with caution due to the

[19] *Ibid.*, p. 3.

[20] Bryson (1992), p. 159.

[21] Legates (2001), pp. 347–364.

[22] Munro (2013), pp. 22–25; Negar, Kharazmi (2019), pp. 129–146.

diversity within each type of feminism, and there being many combinations of these different approaches, both in theory and in practice.

The most common classification distinguishes liberal feminism, Marxist feminism, radical feminism, cultural feminism and postmodern feminism as different types.[23] In the last decades, ecofeminism has also become popular.

- *Liberal feminism* agrees with political liberalism, and for that reason, it claims the basic values of freedom and equality should be applied to women as well as to men. Women should enjoy the same legal and political rights as men, since they are rational beings. [24] However, they are sometimes excluded from the public sphere (employment, politics and legal field) without proper justification, given that they are equally capable to fulfil these roles. In that context, the main concern of the liberal feminist is fighting discrimination without challenging the dominant ideology, the liberal democracy, the meritocratic principle or the market economy.[25]
- *Marxist feminism* relates women's oppression to the social relations of production that cover basic human needs in all societies. Although classical Marxism is indeed concerned with women's subordination, this topic has usually been subsumed under class oppression,[26] which implies that gender relations have often been ignored or marginalised in classical studies.[27] However, subsequent studies in the last decades have used Marxist analysis to address the situation of women as a central political issue.[28] It should be remembered that, in Marxist theory, the material basis of society is constituted not only by the production of material goods, but also by the reproduction of human life. In that vein, the subjugation of women would be related to the division of productive and reproductive labour that implies some kind of appropriation of the domestic and reproductive work of women. Marxist feminism is also called *Socialist feminism*, although some Socialist theories are not particularly linked with Marxist methodology.
- *Radical feminism* focuses on the unequal power relationships between men and women, embedded in the core structure of the society and supported by law.[29] Whereas in *liberal feminism*, women's exclusion from formal institutions is the main cause of gender inequality, in radical feminism, it is a consequence of the deeper structures of male domination.[30] Patriarchy is seen as the most ancient and

[23] Barnett (1998), pp. 121–204; Bryson (1992), pp. 2–7; Lorber (2010), pp. 9–13.

[24] *Ibid.*, p. 2.

[25] Barnett (1998), pp. 124–134.

[26] *Ibid.*, p. 137; Bryson (1992), p. 3.

[27] Barnett (1998), pp. 137–138.

[28] Bryson (1992), pp. 232–260.

[29] Barnett (1998), pp. 14, 163–164.

[30] Bryson (1992), p. 194.

pervasive system of domination[31] and it is firmly attached to society, not only in the public sphere, but also in family life and private relationships. Therefore, women's liberation is not only achieved through legal reform, but also through awareness of the systematic relations of domination in everyday life. Hence, the slogan of second wave feminism, quoted above, "the personal is political".

- *Cultural feminism* (or *difference feminism*) highlights and celebrates physical and psychological differences between women and men,[32] such as female sexuality, attitudes considered to be feminine or the experience of motherhood. As seen above, feminist theories and movements usually tend to emphasise substantial equality between women and men, denaturalising gendered expectations about the essence of masculinity or femininity. Conversely, cultural feminism values and appreciates women's experiences and feminine attitudes, detaching them from the social position of inferiority that women historically have suffered. In some cases, it implies that "womanly" attributes like emotional sensitivity, nurturance and cooperation, are valued over attitudes related to masculinity such as competitiveness or aggressiveness.[33] Some cultural feminists consider that there is an actual feminine essence, derived from biological facts, however not all of them are essentialist. Indeed, it is possible to recognize that gender patterns are contingent, and, at the same time, to have a positive understanding of the real experiences and values developed by women in gendered societies.
- *Postmodern feminism* is characterized by a general mistrust of the pursuit of objectivity, certainty or ultimate truths.[34] It denies the universal validity of global explanations and meta-narratives[35] and embraces complexity, uncertainty, particularities and diversity of perspectives. As this chapter has mentioned earlier, basic concepts relevant in feminist theory like sex, gender, women or feminism itself are often criticised, questioned, or deconstructed. Postmodernism is also related with *queer theory*, a critical academic discourse that claims gender identity and sexual orientation are fluid and variable rather than fixed and discrete, thus undermining the boundaries between the sexes, the genders and the sexual orientation categories.[36]
- *Ecofeminism:* explores the connections between patriarchy, exploitation of nature and all forms of violence.[37] Therefore, it blends feminism and environmentalism, and sometimes, pacifism too.[38] There are different approaches to ecofeminism

[31] *Ibid.*, 2.

[32] Barnett (1998), p. 143.

[33] Lorber (2010), p. 11.

[34] Bryson (1992), pp. 5–6.

[35] Barnett (1998), p. 18.

[36] Lorber (2010), p. 13.

[37] Mies and Shiva (1993), pp. 13–16.

[38] "Ecofeminism [. . .] grew out of various social movements — the feminist, peace and the ecology movements [. . .] We see the devastation of the earth and her beings by the corporate warriors, and the threat of nuclear annihilation by the military warriors, as feminist concerns", *Ibid.*, pp. 13–14.

(for instance, cultural ecofeminism, radical ecofeminism, socialist ecofeminism)[39] and some branches are interested in spirituality or religion, whereas others are not.[40]

3.3 Feminist Political Theory

3.3.1 Patriarchy in Feminist Political Theory: An Overview

If we focus on political theories, the concept of patriarchy, as well as the many terms used to denote the contested concept, has a long history: it has been used by feminists like Virginia Woolf, the Fabian Women's Group and Vera Bitten.[41] The concept itself goes back much further, being at the core of feminist political theory, either as the explanans or the explanandum, until relatively recently.[42]

Patriarchy can be conceptualised as a system or systems producing and reproducing gendered and intersectional inequalities, and men's power and women's subordination. It is a system of social, political and economic structures and practices, in which men as a group/category govern, oppress and exploit women as a group/category.[43] The concept refers to both the greater aggregate social, economic, and political power men as a group have over women as a group and over further genders as a group, and to the power hierarchies between both individual men and between groups of men.[44] Patriarchy is simultaneously structural and ideological, a hierarchical organisation of social institutions and social relations: "structurally, the patriarchy is a hierarchical organization of social institutions and social relationships that allows men to maintain positions of power, privilege, and leadership in society. As an ideology, the patriarchy rationalizes itself. This means that it provides ways of creating acceptance of subordination not only by those who benefit from such actions but also by those who are placed in such subordinate positions by society".[45]

---

[39] Lorenzen and Eaton (2002), p. 1.

[40] "[. . .] some tried to revive or recreate a goddess-based religion; spirituality was defined as the Goddess. Some call it the female principle, inhabiting and permeating all things — this spirituality is understood in a less 'spiritual', that is, less idealistic way [. . .] Many women, particularly those who combine their critique of capitalism with a critique of patriarchy and still cling to some kind of 'materialist' concept of history, do not easily accept spiritual ecofeminism", Mies and Shiva (1993), pp. 17–18..

[41] Beechey (1979), pp. 66–82.

[42] DeKeseredy (2020), pp. 621–638.

[43] Walby (1990); Hunnicutt (2009), pp. 533–573; Bryson (1999), pp. 311–324.

[44] Strid and Hearn (2021); DeKeseredy (2021).

[45] DeKeseredy (2021), p. 3; See e.g., Sheila Rowbotham who confirms this statement with the notion of "interiorization of subordination/slavery", meaning that women traditionally have interiorized and accepted subordination (Rowbotham (1979), p. 402).

Whether advanced as an analytical tool or the focus of substantial critique, the concept of patriarchy has formed a constant feature of feminist academic and activist work. Politically, feminists have used the concept in the search for an explanation of experiences and feelings of oppression and subordination, and in the desire to transform these into political practices. Analytically, patriarchy has been used to address and explore the basis of women's subordination and to analyse the variations of the basis/bases. In feminist theory emerging in the 1960s, patriarchy became a crucial framework for explaining the persistence of gender inequality at a systemic level.[46] The concept was used by Millet in the seminal book *Sexual Politics* published in 1969 to refer to male domination and to the power relationships by which men dominate women,[47] and the year after by Firestone in *The Dialectic of Sex* to capture the "sexual class system", which she argues predates and runs deeper than any other form of oppression.[48] A few years thereafter, Mitchell used patriarchy in *Psychoanalysis and Feminism* (1974), to analyse the effects of kinship systems where men exchange women, and of fathers' symbolic power in those systems on the psychology of women.[49] Hartmann used it to define men's power over women and to analyse the relationship between men's power over women and capitalism.[50] In Eisenstein's defence of liberal feminism, patriarchy was used to describe the sexual hierarchy manifested in the many roles of women within the family, e.g. as mother, domestic labourer and consumer.[51] To Jónasdóttir, patriarchy is a historically specific form of men's exploitation of women in formally equal and developed democracies, captured by the concept of love power,[52] to mention a few.[53]

Feminist theories of patriarchy, or feminist theorising patriarchy, include the attempts to formulate a coherent theory of the basis, or rather bases, of the subordination and oppression of women. These include Millet's aforementioned deployment of sexuality,[54] Hartmann's use of capitalism,[55] and additional bases of oppression, including biology;[56] sexuality;[57] the domestic mode of production;[58] kinship pattern;[59] biological reproduction and the care of dependent children;[60]

[46] Bryson (1999).
[47] Millett (1969).
[48] Firestone (1970).
[49] Mitchell (1974).
[50] Hartmann (1979), pp. 1–33.
[51] Eisenstein (1981).
[52] Jónasdóttir (1991).
[53] Beechey (1979), pp. 66–82.
[54] Millett (1969).
[55] Hartmann (1979), pp. 1–33.
[56] Firestone (1970).
[57] MacKinnon (1982), pp. 515–544; MacKinnon (1983), pp. 635–658.
[58] Delphy (1977); Delphy (1984).
[59] Weinbaum (1978).
[60] O'Brien (1981).

reproduction more generally;[61] and sex/affective production (the production of sexuality, bonding, and affection as the core processes of society).[62]

While noting the variety of theoretical approaches and attributed bases to patriarchy, it is also clear that the exact form, in terms of structures, processes and actions, that patriarchies take varies across societies and cultures, and varies historically. There is a vast literature on historical analyses on patriarchy, or patriarchies, ranging from Elshtain's classic expositions of the patriarchal line from God(s), to monarch/emperor, to fathers and to other men[63] through to historical change from private or domestic patriarchy to public or modern patriarchy.[64] These latter historicizations of patriarchy can be seen in part as a response to some (feminist) critiques of broadbrush and overgeneralized analyses of patriarchy.[65] Such broad historical accounts have sometimes been complemented by attention to the historical diversification of structures and domains within different societal forms of patriarchy, in which violence exists alongside other domains, for example, sexuality, work/capitalism, family/procreation, civil society, polity, culture/ideology/discourse.[66] There have been further developments of a strong class take on patriarchy and of 'patriarchy-capitalism'.[67] More recently, there has been further engagement of patriarchy with neoliberalism, as, for example, in Campbell's (2014) coining of 'neoliberal neopatriarchy'[68] and globalization, postcolonialism, and processes of transnationalization, as in 'global patriarchy',[69] 'trans(national)patriarchies',[70] 'postcolonial patriarchy',[71] various transitional forms of patriarchy,[72] 'racialized patriarchy' and the inherent racism of patriarchy.[73] Hence, there is wide variation in the meaning and use of both term and concept.[74]

The debates about the usefulness of patriarchy as a concept are often arguments about ontology, methodology or politics, and the usefulness in understanding and enabling the analysis of various relations, processes and sites/domains as structure. Hence, the concept of patriarchy offers an axis for understanding female

[61] Hearn (1987); Vogel (1983).

[62] Ferguson (1989); Ferguson and Folbre (1981), pp. 313–318.

[63] Elshtain (1981).

[64] Brown (1981), pp. 239–268; Dworkin (1981); Walby (1990); Hearn (1992).

[65] Rowbotham (1979), pp. 970–971.

[66] Hearn (1987); Hearn (1992); Walby (1986, 1990).

[67] Messerschmidt (1988).

[68] Campbell (2014).

[69] Parekh and Wilcox (2020), https://plato.stanford.edu/entries/feminism-globalization/, last accessed 5 October 2021.

[70] Hearn (2015).

[71] Newbigin (2010), pp. 121–144; Kaur Hundle (2019), pp. 37–52.

[72] Bosch-Vilarrubias (2014), pp. 205–217; Kocabicak (2020).

[73] Ortner (2014), pp. 530–549; Ortner (2020).

[74] We are indebted to unpublished work by the author and Jeff Hearn, Örebro University, for this paragraph.

subordination throughout premodern history. However, the logic of patriarchy without the logic of emancipation embedded in modernity (connected with political revolutions, industrial revolution, emerging of mass education, and the suffragette and feminist movements) cannot serve as the analytical tool for understanding contradictory status of gender relations in modernity. The conclusion is, then, that it is not enough to use only the logic of patriarchy in the context of modernity, rather the dialectic of patriarchy and emancipation from patriarchy must be used as the methodological axis and analytical tool for understanding gender relations in modernity and contemporaneity.[75]

3.3.2 Central Concepts of Political Thought Reconsidered

Feminist political theory challenges some of the most established and taken for granted concepts in the history of political thought, including public and private, equality/inequality, freedom, justice, citizenship and democracy—to mention a few. This subsection first considers the central role of *the political*, deriving from the second wave feminist argument regarding the interrelation of the private and public, personal and political. This concept and its consequences are central to feminism, feminist theory and feminist political theory, laying the foundations for how we can think politically whilst challenge prevailing patriarchies, labelled gender orders (as used by R.W. Connell), gender systems (as used by Yvonne Hirdman) and gender regimes (introduced by Sylvia Walby).[76] It then introduces the concepts of equality/inequality, freedom, justice, citizenship and democracy, including the feminist critique of them (?).

For most of its history, political theory has ignored women and women's experiences. Consequently, most of the history of feminist political theory has attempted to remedy this. The inclusion of women, women of colour, women of different social classes, women of different sexualities, women of differently abled bodies and ages and so forth has been a key achievement for feminist political theory over the past 60 years. A second key achievement for feminist political theory, and an ongoing unifying commitment, is the expansion of the boundaries and enlargement of the scope of the political sphere.[77] The political argument, turned into famous slogan, of the student movement and second wave feminist movement of the late 1960s, "the personal is political", which was mentioned in the first section, points towards this expansion. The core of the argument is that politics takes place in the personal, in the private, in women's everyday experiences of subordination and inequality, and what happens in the personal, private sphere, in women's everyday life, has political importance. The political argument underlines the interrelations

---

[75]We are indebted to Professor Dragica Vujadinovic, Belgrade University, for this analysis and paragraph.

[76]Hirdman (1990).

[77]Tucker (2011), pp. 1033–1036.

between personal experience and the larger social and political structures, thereby challenging both the nuclear family and family values.[78] Further, the expression "the personal is political" emphasised that issues that were considered women's personal issues were in fact political issues and in need of political intervention to generate change. Such issues included: sex(uality), reproduction and birth control, childcare and housework, bodily integrity and intimate partner violence. Finally, "the personal is political" connects to the idea of a global sisterhood, a perception that women share common needs or interests irrespective of ethnicity, race, class, culture, marital status, sexuality and (dis)ability, although the specific content of that shared commonality has long been debated.[79]

The distinction between private and public, personal and political, has been pivotal and one of the "grand dichotomies" in western political theory and thought.[80] Since Aristotle, the 'political' has been constructed as the realm of reason and rationality. It was in the political sphere that social and cultural institutions could be questioned and changed, a place for reasoned and rational discussion and deliberation. However, as feminist political theorists Jane Mansbridge[81] and Susan Moller Okin[82] write, when Aristotle defined politics as the affairs of the polis, he simultaneously defined the household, the home and the private as other, as the non-political, thereby as a realm that could neither be questioned nor changed.[83] The influence of Aristotle, often considered next to Plato as a founding figure of political philosophy whose writings constitute canon literature in political philosophy and political theory, on western political thought and its consequences for the position of women and women's rights cannot be overestimated. Aristotle's definition of the polis as public, distinct from the private, set the boundaries of political thought and intervention up until, and in part including, the twentieth century, thereby excluding much of women's lives and experiences from political questioning and state interventions. It further excludes women (and others, e.g. enslaved men, non-athenians) from citizenship: to Aristotle, citizenship was linked from public participation, to involvement in politics. For example, the division of private and public, where state interventions are considered illegitimate in the private, has long term and serious, sometimes deadly, consequences for women victims/survivors of men's violence: as will be discussed in the Sect. 3.4, devoted to legal feminism, such a distinction effectively sanctioned and legitimised marital rape, sexual violence,

---

[78] McCann and Kim (2013).

[79] Geoghegan and Wilford (2014), pp. 179–120. For an early debate about the shared interests or needs of women, see Jónasdóttir (1991); Diamond and Hartsock (1981); Sapiro (1981); Mansbridge (1999); Philips (1995); Young (1997).

[80] Squires (2018), https://doi.org/10.7765/9781526137562.00015, last accessed 5 October 2021.

Catharine MacKinnon adopts one of the most directly hostile stances in relation to the public/private distinction itself, arguing that the idea of a private realm is 'a means of subordinating women's collective needs to the imperatives of male supremacy': MacKinnon (1989), p. 188.

[81] Mansbridge and Okin (1994).

[82] Okin (1978).

[83] Spelman (1983), pp. 17–30.

forced marriage, female genital mutilation and other forms of violence against women. These were considered for a long time as private matters, sacred in the realm of the family—and by no means a matter for the polis or democracy itself.

Feminist political theorists showed, in their critique, that what had been considered the private realm was saturated with unequal power relations: the household was, as shown by Susan Moller Okin, structured by gender hierarchies, domination and inequalities.[84] The hierarchies of the household and its effect on women's capacity to participate in the public led to an argument that the very distinction fuelled the domination of women by men. The sexual division of labour in the household led Carol Pateman to conclude that the "Sexual Contract" between women and men preceded the "Social Contract" between equal and independent men, as introduced by Hobbes, Locke and Rousseau.[85] Drawing on the notion of the social contract Pateman, and others (e.g. Iris Marion Young, Sheyla Benhabib, Ruth Lister and Rian Voet), developed a key critique of the concept of citizenship and illustrated how it was gendered: the history of the concept and practice of citizenship is built on an abstract gendered subject who is male, white, and able-bodied, hence excluding women, minority groups and marginalised groups. Citizenship is therefore constructed around men, male and masculinity, and rests on the separation/dichotomy of public and private – on patriarchy. Women can only access it by resolving the so-called Wollstonecraft's dilemma, which presents two alternatives: "either women become (like) men and so full citizen, or they continue at women's work, which is no value for citizenship."[86] To Young, the solution lies not in resolving Wollstonecraft's dilemma, but in a model of a heterogeneous public, which situates women as a group among other marginalised groups, such as ethnic minorities, the poor, and the aged. According to Young, these groups are prevented from participation in the public arena,—preventing from exercising ones citizenship, due to the liberal emphasis on homogeneity, impartiality, and normative rationality.[87] Instead of highlighting similarity and sameness, Young emphasises group difference.

The basis of women's access to full citizenship hence draws attention to issues of sameness and difference, and the concept of equality in feminist political theory. At its core, feminist theory (and feminism) theorises political, economic and social equality between sexes and genders—albeit that different feminist theories and movements have different visions of what equality means and what strategies to deploy to achieve it. Gender equality can first, be categorised as either a *vision* and a goal in its own right, or as a *strategy* and a means to some other goal, for example economic development in contemporary capitalism. Gender equality has been defined in three ways: (i) sameness, (ii) difference, and (iii) transformation. Sameness, here, means that since men and women are fundamentally the same, they should be treated equally. Hence, equality means equal treatment. This leads to

[84] Okin (1978).

[85] Pateman (1988).

[86] Pateman (1988), p. 197.

[87] Young (1989).

understanding equality as equal opportunity and resonates with a liberal feminist vision of equality. Difference, here, means the equal valuation of different contributions: men and women are fundamentally different and may contribute differently, however those contributions should not be valued differently. The transformation approach to gender equality does not focus on the extent to which men and women are the same or not, but rather on the social, political and economic systems and forces that enable, or not, change. Instead of comparing contributions, the focus is on the transformation of structures that can cause change, and transform gender equality.[88]

The centrality of the private/public dichotomy in political thought and the feminist challenge of these boundaries have consequences for our thinking and understanding of further central concepts, not only democracy, citizenship and equality as outlined above, but the very notions of freedom and justice that develop from this distinction (see Sect. 3.4.2 below).

3.3.3 Central Feminist Political Issues

Feminist political theory concerns not only women or gender, rather, a range of topics and concerns including: power relations and how these are gendered; and how they intersect with class, disability, ethnicity, gender identity, nation, race, religion, sexual orientation, and masculinity. Feminist political theory questions the seemingly natural and natural objects, including the self, the family, and sexuality, thereby questioning the power relations embedded in these seemingly natural institutions. Feminist political theory offers a critique of the history of political philosophy; its norms and theories, and is inherently diverse, plural and characterised by its rejection of essentialism, as "a notion that social categories are unchangeable with essences that map onto given characteristics and inequalities".[89] Following on from the logic of the section on feminist political theory, starting in patriarchy and continuing with the notion of "the personal as political", issues of central concern in this subsection are violence, pornography, prostitution and (hetero)sexuality. Other key central feminist issues, such as the division of labour, gender and economics etc., are discussed in the chapters on Labour Law and Gender and Economics in this textbook.

There is a long tradition of feminist and intersectional research on men's violence against women.[90] Violence is key to understanding social inequality and gender relations: men's violence against women is often understood as both cause and consequence of unequal power relations between men and women.[91] Feminist

[88] Strid (2020).

[89] Tucker (2011), pp. 1033–1036.

[90] Brownmiller (1975); Kelly (1988); Walby (1990); see also Chapter on Gender and Human Rights as well as the chapter on criminal law in this book.

[91] UN (1993); Strid and Hearn (2021).

understandings of violence against women are not limited to use or threats of physical force, but also include sexual, psychological, verbal, and economic forms of violence and financial abuse, as well as coercion, control, harmful traditional practices, and in online/offline contexts.

The UN Secretary General's widely cited definition of gender-based violence against women goes beyond physical injury, defining it as:

► **Definition** "violence that is directed against a woman because she is a woman, or violence that affects women disproportionally. It includes acts that inflict physical, mental or sexual harm or suffering, threats of such acts, coercion and other deprivations of liberty".[92]

Further, and contrary to conventional psychology and criminology, feminist and intersectional analyses of violence make visible how violence is being directed from the relatively powerful to the relatively powerless.[93]

Such feminist definition and understanding of violence links sexual violence with prostitution/sex work and pornography. This is a central issue and debate in feminism, dubbed the 'sex wars' or the 'porn wars' in the late 1970s and 1980s, it continually influences and positions contemporary feminist theory.[94] The differences spanned across various issues related to sexuality, sexual activities, and sex, including pornography, erotica, prostitution, LGBTQIA+ and the role of transgender women. Feminists such as Andrea Dworkin and Catherine MacKinnon are positioned on the critical side, declaring that pornography and prostitution were exploitation and violence rather than sexual preference or orientation. In contrast, Ellen Willis and Gayle Rubin declared these issues to be a matter of preference and choice. Some commentators have announced the sex wars as the end of the second wave and beginning of the third wave feminism.[95] Although contested, sex and sexual violence tend to be pictured as two radically different phenomena.[96] In contrast to this, contemporary feminist researchers have highlighted that it is often unclear where to draw the line between just sex and sexual violence. Notions of 'grey zones' and debates around consent have arisen, not least after the feminist campaigns and social movements #talkaboutit and #metoo.[97] They have pointed out that, in so far as (hetero)sexual scripts are organized in line with a gendered logic that has much in common with the dynamics of sexual violence, "[m]any rapes merely extend traditional heterosexual exchanges, in which masculine pursuit and female reticence are familiar and formalized".[98] Catharine MacKinnon famously took this

[92]UN (2006), p. 16.

[93]Morell (1981); Faludi (1992); Strid and Hearn (2021).

[94]Duggan and Hunter (1995).

[95]Duggan and Hunter (1995).

[96]Gunnarsson and Strid (2021).

[97]Walby et al. (2015); Chandra and Erlingsdóttir (2020).

[98]Gilbert and Webster (1982), p. 74.

insight to its logical extreme, virtually erasing the distinction between (heterosexual) sex and violence. MacKinnon's disturbing question still resonates: If sexual and gendered reality is socially constructed in a way that eroticizes male power and female submission, how can we possibly distinguish sex from violence? In a less reductionist form, the observation that normative (hetero)sexuality is infused with violent dynamics has been articulated as a *continuum* of sexual violence, whereby "'typical' and 'aberrant' male behaviour shade into one another".[99] Other central feminist issues are discussed towards the end of this chapter.

3.4 Feminist Legal Theory

3.4.1 Patriarchy in Legal Thought and Legal Practice: An Overview

When considering the legal aspects of feminism, the effects of patriarchy in law are pervasive and well-established. As Luce Irigaray clearly highlights, "Their [men's] discourses, their values, their dreams and their desires have the force of law, everywhere and in all things. Everywhere and in all things, they define women's function and social role, and the sexual identity they are, or are not, to have".[100] Accordingly, it is not surprising that feminism has devoted a wide range of studies to the analysis of the influence of patriarchy and patriarchal norms on the conditions of women, extending to those who do not conform to these male, heterosexual, and cis-gender norms. And since, as has already been argued, patriarchy is not merely a form of social organisation in which males are the head of the family, rather where the whole of society is governed by male rules, male hierarchies, male desires, and gendered social structures. Feminist legal scholars have focused on the intersection of gender and law, contemporaneously discussing strategies to correct gender injustice, exploitation, or restriction. In this vein, feminist scholars have analysed legal systems and institutions starting from the recognition of their intrinsic patriarchal structure, which creates a subtle duality between men, who are the "Subject", and women, who are the "Other".[101] In relation to law, this pervasive dualism produces oppression and the invisibility of women, creating difficulties in making their voices heard and acted upon: all this, behind a veil of objectivity and neutrality that hides the orientation of law towards the needs and goals of male subjects.

In a 1992 essay, the British sociologist Carol Smart identifies three phases of feminist positions on law. These phases are linked to the three "waves" of feminism, which have been analysed in the subsection devoted to the history of feminism (Sect. 3.2.2.1). Although they are not reducible to them: "the first stage is epitomized by the phrase 'law is sexist', the second by the phrase 'law is male', the third by the phrase

[99] Kelly (1988), p. 75.

[100] Irigaray (1991), p. 78.

[101] de Beauvoir (1949), p. 16.

'law is gendered'.".[102] Therefore, starting from the recognition of such a patriarchal orientation of law, the first phase feminist legal scholarship focused on the consequences of patriarchy in terms of exclusion of women from public life, what some scholars labelled as the *male monopoly* of law.[103] In this phase, those positions which criticise the law prevail because it is not (as it claims to be) objective, rational, and impartial. Rather, by distinguishing between men and women, the law discriminates against women by distributing fewer resources to them, denying them equal opportunities, and refusing to recognise the offences against them. Consequently, the debate on patriarchy takes the form of the quest for equality in the professions as well as in politics, attempting to remove existing rules that operated to the detriment of women, without criticising the basic assumptions of the legal system itself (its consideration of subjects as gender-neutral individuals, holding gender-neutral rights).[104]

It is in the second phase that legal feminism explicitly addresses the male orientation of law; feminist legal scholars criticize the impartiality and objectivity of legal systems, uncovering the male standards and assumptions that permeate these concepts. MacKinnon, for instance, argues that ideals such as objectivity and neutrality, which are typical of Western legal culture, are actually masculine values that have been taken as universal values. Thus, with respect to the approach "the law is male", this means that when a woman stands before the law, the law applies fundamentally masculine criteria.[105] Similarly, feminist legal scholars highlight the male standards underlying criteria such as the "reasonable person", and how these standards mask male construct and male standards, thereby consolidating male dominance. Analyses thus focus more on the societal structure which is the legal systems' background, than on specific rules that unequally affect women. Within these perspectives, both radical and Marxist feminists argue that inequalities arise from the gendered structure of the whole of society (rather than from single *bad* laws), and that the relationship between the sexes is determined and shaped by the oppression of women by men, in addition to the structure of privilege and oppression.[106]

The third phase does not simply question the gendered structure of society and legal systems, but the role of law itself, adopting postmodernist philosophies and deconstructionist approaches. In this third phase, the condition of women is analysed with greater attention to the local dimension and specific context. The critique of the effects of patriarchy on the condition of women is carried out without referring to mono-causal theories; the impossibility of reducing the condition of women to a single set of factors is emphasised, and the possibility of highlighting 'essential' elements useful in defining the condition of women is denied, highlighting instead

[102] Smart (1992), p. 30.

[103] Naffine (1990), p. 2.

[104] Sachs and Wilson (1978).

[105] MacKinnon (1978), pp. 116, 122.

[106] MacKinnon (1989).

the importance of factors such as class, race and age. As some scholars have pointed out,[107] the deconstructionist approach tends to question certain assumptions of previous feminist theories, and in particular the implicitly white, heterosexual, and middle-class point of view that underpin these theories. What is criticised, as highlighted in the Sect. 3.2.2.2 on the "types" of feminism, are not the conclusions reached by these theories, instead the very claim to be able to elaborate a theory of patriarchy that is adequate for all women regardless of race and class differences, and the ethnocentrism of some theories of women's oppression in non-Western cultures. More generally, any theory which fails to attend to the diversity of women's condition is criticised, claiming that in order to understand the many different forms that patriarchy can take, the importance of contextual analyses, of subjective narratives, and of individual experiences must be stressed. Therefore, the substantial irreducibility of the experience of women of colour to that of white women is reaffirmed, including the impossibility of talking about patriarchy and the oppression of 'women' in general, and the need to include different experiences and points of view in the debate.[108] At the same time, lesbian feminists point out that patriarchy and oppression, as theorised by prevailing theories, presuppose an underlying heterosexual binarism, which neglects the condition of lesbian women and their needs.[109] In the same vein, postmodernist theories deconstruct the very concepts of gender and sex, and the binarism (man-woman, subject-other, oppressed-oppressor) that they presuppose. The results of this approach, while significant in philosophical terms, have nevertheless been criticised politically, and in relation to their ability to affect the legal structures and institutions that are the source of inequality and oppression. As Bordo points out,[110] the postmodernist critique risks delegitimising feminism as a theory, so as to make the claim of rights and opportunities more difficult: in other words, even though convincing on a theoretical level, the post-modernist approach risks neglecting the everyday difficulties that women encounter on a legal and political level.

3.4.2 Central Concepts of Legal Thought Reconsidered

Since law determines the fundamental values of a society, and codifies what is (allegedly) universal and objective, legal feminism is aimed at unmasking the systemic prejudices on which the law is based, which condition not only the subjects charged with applying the law, but also the life of every individual. In order to fulfil this task, feminist scholars reconsidered and renamed personal experiences and legal concepts, applying methodologies such as conceptual analysis and normative critique. The work of MacKinnon has been pivotal, as already seen in Sect. 3.3.3, in

[107] Smart (1989); Currie (1992).

[108] Harris (1990); Spelman (1990).

[109] Cain (1988).

[110] Bordo (1990), p. 136.

renaming sexual harassment, pornography and rape from the point of view of those who suffer these offences, and in conceiving this point of view as collective.[111] Even if she has been accused of blindness to the differences between women, and a totalising view of the 'domination' of men over women, her use of legal concepts nonetheless enhances both their practical and symbolic implications. Similarly, Olsen reflected on a series of oppositional pairs that emerge in the liberal tradition, such as active/passive, rational/irrational, objective/subjective, thought/feeling, reason/emotion, power/sensibility, culture/nature etc. As already observed in the Sect. 3.3.2, while the first terms of these pairs have been traditionally associated with the masculine, and within the world of law, the second have been linked with the feminine. As a consequence, not only have women's traits generally been stereotyped and regarded as alien to law, but women's access to and influence in law have been limited.[112] On this basis, the sexualisation of law can either be rejected as such, claiming the full capacity of women to be rational, active, etc., and use the law for their own ends, or it can be rejected in its hierarchical structure, claiming the importance of "feminine" values and their importance in law. A third approach, which Olsen calls 'androgyny', tends to highlight how both character groups are present in both men and women, and to problematize their very content and boundaries. In other words, feminist approaches to legal studies have been characterised by the assumption of a gender perspective (aimed at unmasking the alleged neutrality of law); by a critical orientation (oriented towards the promotion and emancipation of women through legal norms); and by a desire to reframe the relationship between theory and practice (in order to eschew abstractions in legal interpretations and offer effective solutions to real-life needs).

One of the concepts that has long attracted the attention of feminist legal scholars is certainly that of equality, and the relationship between equality and difference. In considering the conceptual relationship between equality and difference, the reformulation of these concepts in the search for an equality that may be realised through the enhancement of differences, as well as the consequences in terms of political and legal choices, have long occupied feminist literature. The principle of procedural justice articulated by Aristotle that like cases should be treated alike, and different cases differently in proportion to their differences, has been taken as a critical starting point, in considering what equality requires against a patriarchal legal background. This notion of equality, although apparently neutral and objective, has proved problematic for women because of the circumstances in which women are not like men (such as sexuality, reproduction), and of their different social, political, and economic background. Therefore, the concept of equality has been crucial in eighteenth and nineteenth century to promote the idea that women (as any human being) are by nature free, equal, and endowed with the same inalienable rights as man, thereby challenging their inferior legal status. In contrast, feminists challenged the concept of equality by arguing that equality takes man as the standard

[111] MacKinnon (1983).

[112] Olsen (1990), p. 205.

(equal *to whom*?), presuming that men and women should be similarly situated in society, contemporaneously ignoring both the differences between the sexes and those amongst women themselves. Consequently, with regard to the equality/diversity pair, feminists not only elaborated subtle analyses on the alternative between formal and substantive equality, they further expanded the concept in terms of equality of opportunity, equality of results or outcome, equality of condition, equality of power, and social equivalence[113] but also argued for an intersectional approach in order to better acknowledge the way in which race, class, gender and other systemic oppressions work together.[114]

The debate over the pair equality/difference aimed, among other things, at unravelling the biases and male basic assumptions that underlie the traditional legal understanding of equality, thus advocating for a reconsideration. Feminist scholars stressed that when women are compared to men in order to assess whether they have been treated equally or not, the outcome may be the pathologisation of women themselves; such an approach uses the male as a comparator. In doing so, this normalizes *his* experiences, measuring women's experiences against male standards.

Example

In the debate on policies related to pregnancy and motherhood of women workers, it is affirmed that maternity protection regulations serve to protect women and to shift the costs of reproduction (in terms of career, time, opportunities) onto society. However, many feminists believe that this kind of legislation favourable to working mothers tends to brand women as 'problematic' and reinforces the idea that only mothers should take care of children.[115] In Italy, for example, maternity leave is only granted—albeit extensively consisting of a minimum of 5 months—to women. If, from a formal point of view, this guarantees job protection, from a substantial point of view this tends to disadvantage women at the time of recruitment, and in income levels. It may represent women as 'costly' from the employer's point of view, compared to their male colleagues. ◀

In this vein, some feminists argued for a reconsideration of the equality/difference dilemma outside the logic of hierarchy. Such logic, as highlighted by Mackinnon, stems from the overlapping of biological difference and societal gender hierarchy, whilst hiding underlying asymmetries of power and systems of domination.[116] Equality, in her view, should be understood as a counter-balancing force, a way to reshape power asymmetries between groups and individuals, dismantling the

[113] Hunter (2008).

[114] Crenshaw (1989).

[115] Finley (1986).

[116] MacKinnon (1991).

domination of some (historically, men) over others. What is at stake, as highlighted in Sect. 3.3.2, is not merely an asymmetrical and detrimental *treatment*, rather an asymmetrical *distribution of power*: equality, in this perspective, is almost a function of empowerment. Therefore, as in legal analyses, the discussion on equality goes beyond the alternative between what is "same" and what is "different": it requires that male domination be uncovered and balanced, by constructing a legal standard that takes the perspective of women and their possibilities to act in society into account. MacKinnon's works on sexual harassment of working women[117] and violent pornography[118] have been pioneering in this regard.

A second, fundamental goal of feminist jurisprudence has been the pair oppression/discrimination, in order to oppose and reform barriers to women's participation in the public sphere, with specific regard to legal structures that put disproportionate burdens on women. Accordingly, MacKinnon's analyses on male domination urged feminist legal scholars to focus on the legal structures of oppression, rather than on specific rights-related discriminations. In contrast from discrimination, oppression is produced in a systemic way; it operates through social, political and economic systems that simultaneously limit women's opportunities and penalise them in different but inevitable ways. With an instructive metaphor, Frye describes oppression as "a birdcage". "If you look very closely at just one wire, you cannot see the other wires. If your conception of what is before you is determined by this myopic focus, you could look at that one wire, up and down the length of it, and be unable to see why a bird would not just fly around the wire (. . .) it is only when you step back, stop looking at the wires one by one, microscopically, and take a macroscopic view of the whole cage, that you can see why the bird does not go anywhere; and then you will see it in a moment".[119] Additionally, oppression targets groups rather than individuals. Unlike discrimination, which can affect individuals as well as groups, oppression primarily involves groups. Individuals are consequently affected by oppression because they belong to a group; legal, social and cultural norms, institutional mechanisms, practices and habits, symbols and mechanisms of mass communication. Each of these forces can represent a vehicle for oppression, from a structural perspective, regardless of individual conditions and resources.[120]

One of these sources of women oppression, and a third central focus of feminist critique over the years, has been the distinction between the public and private spheres. The political relevance of this distinction has been already discussed in Sect. 3.3.2. Focusing on the legal consequences, it is possible to highlight the assumption of a clear-cut distinction between the public and the private realm entails the idea that personal relations are a site of legal non-intervention, a sphere where individuals are sovereigns, and a boundary which the law cannot (normally) cross. Accordingly, feminist scholars attempted to overcome the distinction itself,

[117] MacKinnon (1979).
[118] MacKinnon (1985).
[119] Frye (1983), p. 3.
[120] Young (1990), p. 41.

criticising ideologies that assign men and women to different spheres on the basis of their natural characteristics, inevitably confining women to positions of inferiority, and hiding abuses and oppression from judicial scrutiny and redress.[121] Contemporaneously, other scholars insisted that it should be preserved, both to protect women's interests in matters like child custody and reproductive freedom, and to protect a site of women's empowerment against discrimination, especially for non-white women.[122] For that reason, some scholars attempted to reconsider the distinction, highlighting the relations between the domestic sphere with both the state, the official-economy of paid employment, and the arenas of public discourse.[123] Others argued for a different rethinking of both the private and the public sphere, by drawing attention to the many aspects of family life that, in spite of the rhetoric of privacy, are in fact hedged with legal regulation, such as marriage, divorce, child custody, and social welfare rules. The fact that even if state's regulation may be less relevant, there are non-state power and non-state bodies at work, which are linked with each other.[124] In more recent times, feminist legal scholars argued for a deconstruction of such a hierarchically ordered dichotomy, rejecting any either/or analysis: for instance, struggles for the integration of same sex relationships into marriage had the effect of both proposing different definitions of marital relations and the notion of spouses, and gaining access for gay and lesbian people within the public realm, thereby reconsidering the public/private divide rather than abolishing it.

The understanding of the public sphere as the realm of reason, required in order to take part in public debates and linked to an alleged standard of objectivity, prompted feminist scholars to scrutinize the concepts of reason and reasonableness, with specific regard to their legal use. If knowledge and rational argumentations claim objectivity, the rational/objective standards in both civil and criminal law, the so called "reasonable person", if not explicitly "reasonable men", are modelled around a person who is both gendered (as a male), and specified in terms of class, ethnicity, and more. Feminists' analyses focused on these biased legal standards, both to unveil and to reconsider them. In this perspective, the reasonable-unreasonable dichotomy and the objective-subjective dichotomy are criticised as working together when objective standards are implemented to determinate reasonableness, and reasonableness is used to better understand objectivity. This overlap underlies court jurisprudence and its patriarchal power structures; as long as the courts maintain the appearance of rational and objective actors and hide their biased positioning. As Noddings exclaimed, law has long used a "reasonable man" standard to evaluate human actions, for instance in criminal trials. Even if in recent years it has been renamed the "reasonable person" standard, such a change was developed in a

[121] Weintraub (1997), p. 28.

[122] Hooks (1990).

[123] Fraser (1997), p. 70.

[124] Lacey (1993).

masculine and patriarchal culture, still reflecting its values.[125] From Criminal Law to Tort Law, extending to other areas of legal systems, the reasonable person worked to answer relevant questions (did the defendant exercise reasonable care? Did the person comply with a reasonable standard of fair dealing? etc.) by using a gendered perspective, both because it arose from a male culture, and because it has been enforced by courts that are still largely made up of men. In other words, the 'reasonable person' represents a community ideal of reasonable behaviour, which dismisses gender, age, and intellectual ability as relevant subjective characteristics to a court's evaluations. Consequently, not only are standards of behaviour set, which entire subpopulations (not just women) tend not to exhibit, but society's majoritarian prejudices concerning normalcy are used to draw the picture of such a 'standard' person (male, heterosexual, white, able-bodied, etc.).

Example

In sexual harassment law and battered women's self-defence cases, as well as in rape law, the standard of the "reasonable person" implicitly requires women to conform to a certain image and to certain modes of conduct, for their experiences to be legally recognised as crime. Otherwise, to the extent that their behaviour does not match what could be expected of a reasonable person, largely conditioned by male biases and ideals, they are blamed for provoking or seducing men, thereby disempowering the female victims. For instance, a "reasonable" victim is expected to cry, to try to escape, not to be dressed provocatively, to denounce immediately, etc.[. . .] She is expected to correspond to an abstract ideal of a victim, elaborated in a patriarchal culture. These stereotypes can affect judges' understanding of who is a victim and who is not, can influence their views about the credibility of witnesses, and permit irrelevant or prejudicial evidence to be admitted.[126] ◀

The reasonable person standard has been reconsidered by feminist scholars to include the experiences of both women and other excluded groups. A first strategy has been that of proposing the "reasonable woman" standard, which requires thinking from the perspective of a woman's reaction in a given situation, rather than that of the standard/average man. However, since the interpretation of the standard is left to white, male judges, such a different standard may merely represent a change in language with no positive consequence, perpetuating stereotyped representations of women themselves.[127] A second strategy has been to reformulate reasonableness, in both an intersectional and contextual perspective, which focus on the person's experiences and needs, avoiding the stereotypes imposed by any

[125] Noddings (1990), p. 65.

[126] Karen Tayag Vertido v The Philippines (18/08), CEDAW/C/46/D/18/2008 (2010).

[127] Cahn (1991–1992), p. 1434.

particular theoretical standard.[128] With specific regard to rape, sexual harassment, or domestic violence cases, extending to cases concerning employment discrimination, the victim's perspective must be taken into account, requiring that she exposes her feelings in a non-judgmental and unbiased environment.

3.4.3 Central Feminist Legal Issues

It is possible to argue that feminist analysis of law "is, negatively, an analysis of how some or all women have been excluded from the design of the legal system or the application of law, and positively, a normative argument about how, if at all, women's inclusion can be accomplished".[129] Thus, while in the 1970s the main objective of feminist legal scholarship was to affirm equality of treatment among men and women in all legally relevant purposes, by the 1980s feminist legal scholars focused on the analysis of structures and systems that undermined the inclusion of women in any areas, extending to practices and norms that prevented substantive equality. Within this framework, scholars addressed specific challenges and topics, by taking the 'dilemma of difference' into account, i.e. recognising that women's disadvantage might be reinforced both by ignoring the difference and by acknowledging it. If measures are taken to compensate the disadvantage, stereotypes are acknowledged that perpetuate the disadvantage; if no measure is undertaken, and women are not stereotyped, they do entirely bear the cost of the disadvantage.[130] In this phase, scholars argued that such a dilemma arises on a biased premise, which implies that the status quo is natural and good, and that only specific differences are to be addressed: however, women are *different* only if men are taken as the standard, and women need special rules only because the rules they are confronted with have been formulated by and for men.

A first issue that has been crucial in feminist legal scholarship, and clearly illustrates this evolution, is the economic subordination of women. Within this field, specific questions and topics came to the fore: among the many, the equality of opportunity in access to the public sphere and in the labour market has been considered. Restrictions on women's participation in certain professions, such as the judiciary, the military, and many others, have been the target of feminist scholars in a first phase, with the aim of opposing barriers that bolstered a second-class citizenship for women. However, even if these struggles led to an increase in female participation in the workforce, substantial disparities remained. Not only women were largely confined to certain 'female' occupations (nursing, teaching, secretarial, etc.) with lower wages and fewer career prospects, when they entered traditionally 'male' fields (law, medicine, business, etc.) their treatment remained disproportionally

[128] Minow (1990).

[129] Réaume (1996), p. 273.

[130] Minow (1987).

worse.[131] Therefore, feminists focused on the analysis of rules and practices that adversely affect women, so as to generate inequalities at a substantial level. A first challenge concerned the application of supposedly objective rules, and the pressure of unrecognized biases (for instance, in recruitment procedures, or in workers' evaluation). Secondly, a reconsideration of norms that ruled workplaces by assuming the 'male breadwinner' with no care burden as a standard, has been deemed necessary: norms concerning flexible work schedule or part time work, as well as affirmative actions, have been proposed as corrective measures. Thus, whilst, legal scholars argued that cases of discrimination in the labour force are rooted in both cultural beliefs and gender stereotypes (which may affect women, as well as LGBTQIA+ people, people of colour, immigrants, etc.), and organizational structures, policies, and practices. In contrast, feminist scholars highlighted the biased premise of these arguments: the so-called 'culture of domesticity' underpinning the workplace, within which the perfect worker is available to work overtime, and to travel, without being restricted by personal and familial responsibilities (since *his* personal life depends on the unpaid work of a woman/wife). Therefore, some feminists argued it is not only necessary to challenge the current organisation of the workload and the masculine standards operating in the workplace, family norms and entitlements. This can be done either by recognizing the value of parental care, in order not to leave women impoverished and constantly dependent due to their domestic work, or by suggesting alternative models of family and marriage as a legal institution.[132]

A second group of topics in the legal feminist agenda concerned the status of the female body, sexual relations, self-determination of women over it, and in more general terms the regulation of sex and sexuality: pornography, reproductive rights, domestic violence, sexual harassment, and rape, to name only a few issues, figure centrally in feminist legal theory. The political relevance of these topics has been discussed in Sect. 3.3.3. Paying specific attention to legal consequences, feminist scholars analysed these against the background of the patriarchal social structure which leads to the stereotyped construction of the woman as the 'good' battered wife, the 'bad' mother, the 'real' rape victim.[133] Such a culture coerces women and penalises them for corresponding to the image invoked by law, as well as for failing to correspond to it. Until recently (twentieth century) women did not properly own their bodies, not having a voice, legally, in decisions concerning reproduction, sex, intimate relationships, and without protection from harms inflicted by their intimate partners (husbands, lovers, as well as employers). To be more precise, it is the very nature of harm that was disputed within a male culture which considered these actions as either inevitable or justifiable. Therefore, a crucial task for legal feminism has been to explore the ways in which law fails to protect women from abuses and violence. Even if all Western states recognize spousal rape and physical violence

[131] Estrich (2001).

[132] Fineman (2004).

[133] Smart (1992), p. 37.

occurring within marriage as crimes today, both are sometimes considered as less serious than violence occurring outside of marriage. All these crimes have been analysed by feminists starting from different perspectives (cultural feminists, race theorists, dominance feminists) and with different approaches, however a common theme was identified being the biased regulation of these crimes. Feminist scholars highlighted that interpretations of both the force and lack of consent required a woman to offer the "utmost resistance" or "reasonable resistance", thereby making the verbal resistance, crying, begging, saying "no", not enough to manifest the lack of consent. In a parallel way feminist scholars focused on domestic violence, and what is now labelled as femicide. On one view, they deemed the law to be inadequate to protect against being coerced into sexual intimacy, as elements of these crimes are still vague if not favourable to the defendant. Contrarily, feminists highlighted the extent to which social attitudes about sex, and intimate relationships are pervasively biased to favour male dominance, holding necessary reforms back. For instance, scholars who analysed pornography[134] tended to see it as a reinforcement of the patriarchal culture and of male dominance that results in rape, harassment, and violence. Contemporaneously, it is important to emphasise that reflections on domestic abuse have been discussed from an intersectional perspective: while initially the 'battered woman' was perceived as essentially white and involved in heterosexual relationships, subsequent studies focused on the intersection of race, class, ethnicity, language, and sexual orientation, highlighting the difficulties faced by gay men or lesbians to defend themselves from violence and abuse.

Another area of interest was certainly that of reproductive rights, on the assumption that if a woman is not free with regard to self-determination over her own body and sexuality, she is not free at all. While abortion has certainly been one of the first and most significant issues debated by legal feminism, other issues arose in the following decades. The debate on abortion, which has been heightened and thoughtful inside and outside feminism, raised moral, religious, philosophical and legal issues. Among these, it has been questioned whether the best foundation on which to base a right to terminate pregnancy is privacy or equality.

Example

Norma McCorvey, known in her lawsuit under the pseudonym "Jane Roe", was born in Louisiana in 1947. At the age of 16, she married a violent man with whom she had two daughters. While pregnant with her third child, Norma began her lawsuit to assert her right to an abortion. The US Supreme Court was asked whether the Federal Constitution recognises a right to abortion even in the absence of health problems of the woman, the foetus and any other circumstances other than the woman's free choice. In a landmark decision[135] (made by a majority of 7 judges in favour and 2 against), the Supreme Court based the

[134] MacKinnon (1993); Dworkin (1981).

[135] Roe v. Wade, 410 U.S. 113 (1973).

right to abortion on the fundamental right of privacy, interpreted as "broad enough to encompass a woman's decision whether or not to terminate her pregnancy", thereby fuelling the criticisms concerning the state's abdication of women and its unaccountability for the disadvantages shouldered by women as a group.[136] If abortion belongs to the private realm, state interference is avoided, however the state does not have to support these private choices with public funds or institutions. ◄

Alternative solutions have been adopted across the world, depending on the political circumstances and cultural traditions of the different countries, the availability of a more or less extensive welfare state, and other political factors (across the European Union, 24 countries have legalized abortion on a woman's request or broad social grounds, and two[137] allow it on social and economic grounds. More restrictive regulations are emerging in Poland, where abortion is now allowed only on grounds of woman's health, incest or rape,[138] and Malta is the only EU country were abortion is illegal. Other limitations are present in several EU Member States, including mandatory waiting periods for abortion on request, mandatory counselling or information prior to abortion, and refusals of care on grounds of conscience and religion). It is worth noting, however, that while non-feminist arguments about abortion mainly focused on the morality and/or legality of performing abortions, feminist scholars also considered other questions, which are deemed relevant in overcoming the oppression of women and in meeting their needs. Among the many, questions were posed concerning the accessibility and delivery of abortion services, the legitimacy of unnecessary and burdensome conditions on abortion providers, doctors' conscientious objection, as well as many other measures aimed at restricting access or availability of abortion procedures. These are only some of the issues debated.

The debate on abortion did not exhaust the issues raised in the field of reproductive rights; the rise in medical technologies was accompanied by both an increased medicalisation of reproductive issues, and increased regulation of this field, where women's rights to exercise control over their bodies are placed in competition with the claims of others (the state, the husband, the unborn, etc.). The availability and safety of means of contraception, the management of pregnancy and childbirth, sterilisation (both its positive side, as a right to self-determination, and its negative side, as in cases of sterilisation programs performed on minority groups and on mentally incompetent adults), the use and misuse of caesarean sections, are only a few issues debated by legal feminists. Recently, questions concerning surrogacy have been debated within and outside feminist scholarship, often engaging arguments similar to those already proposed in the debate concerning prostitution

[136] MacKinnon (1991), p. 1311.

[137] UK and Finland.

[138] The 1993 Polish law allowed abortion also in cases of severe foetal disabilities; on 2020 the Constitutional Tribunal declared this exception allowing legal abortion unconstitutional.

and the commodification of the female body. Proponents of surrogacy argue that surrogate mothers, if allowed to use their reproductive capacity by entering into these contracts, may increase their income and improve their education, in addition to helping others by transforming procreative labour into a market asset. Opponents highlight the conditions of exploitation and poverty in which surrogate mothers find themselves, and interpret these choices as the result of oppression and subordination by others, rather than a sign of freedom.[139]

Postmodern feminism approached these and other issues through both a criticism of the false essentialism of classical approaches, and a more nuanced analysis of subjectivity and power relations. The postmodern critique of the idea of the subject, labelled by Susan Bordo as "feminist skepticism" about gender,[140] accuses the latter of being a totalising fiction. In this vein, multiculturalists complained that Western feminists excluded and ignored non-Western women and their worldviews, thereby rejecting any all-embracing assumption on woman's identity and patriarchy. While from a Western perspective the decision of a Muslim woman to wear a hijab may represent an internalization of patriarchy, from a non-Western point of view it might denote the rejection of the equation between "uncovering" and "liberating" women inflicted by Western patriarchal culture.[141] Contemporaneously, lesbian and gay theorists highlighted the links between heterosexism and sexism—in addition to the marginalisation of their perspective by the mainstream feminist movement, and the peculiar challenges they face, from a legal point of view.[142] These include; the right to assume more childcare responsibilities, to obtain custody of their children, and not to be excluded by employment rights that are granted to straight women. Additionally, gay and lesbian theorists argued that sexual orientation meets the standards established (in the US) by Supreme Court jurisprudence for suspect classification and should receive strict scrutiny under the Fourteenth Amendment equal protection analysis. Similarly, other challenges arose from queer and postmodern theories, which questioned the dominant binarism in law.[143] From the registration of gender on official documents, to marriage laws and anti-discrimination laws, legal systems still tend to identify people according to a twofold distinction between men and women. Therefore, transgender and intersex people raised questions concerning the right not to be identified by law as either male or female, and argued for the legal recognition of multiple identities, extending to the abolition of sex as a relevant legal category.[144] Even if feminist scholarship seemed to be generally sympathetic towards these claims, by refusing a biologically determined model of

[139] Hewitson (2014).

[140] Bordo (1990), p. 619.

[141] Al-Hibri (1997), p. 4.

[142] Rich (2007).

[143] Sharpe (2002).

[144] Creighton and Minto (2001); Council of the European Union (2013), Guidelines to Promote and Protect the Enjoyment of All Human Rights by Lesbian, Gay, Bisexual, Transgender and Intersex (LGBTI) Persons.

gender and sexuality, some authors emphasized that such a fragmentation of human identity into multiple frames risks undermining feminist claims and the struggle against the oppression of women. Further, the self-determination of gender identity is at odds with the definition of feminist political goals and its political community.[145]

3.5 Conclusion

The aim of this chapter was to present an overview of feminism, with a specific focus on legal and political challenges. Therefore, the chapter provided a basic theoretical framework, which is necessary to explore feminist analyses of the different branches of law, as well as related political questions.

The chapter did not offer to the reader a unitary definition of feminism, not even in its legal or political applications. Rather, feminism has been presented in its internal complexity, and its multifaceted understanding. Even if feminist theories aimed at ending women's oppression, encompassing both theory and activism, they should be considered a set of different social movements and theories that share the same basic goal of defeating the systemic oppression of women, rather than a single movement or ideology. Consequently, the chapter presented the "types" of feminism, and its "waves", highlighting the multiple combinations of these different approaches, both in theory and in practice.

The chapter discussed many of the typical themes of feminist reflection, and in particular, focused on those that are most relevant from a political and legal point of view. Of particular relevance here have been the analysis of the binary opposition between women and men, the distinction between sex and gender, and the notion of patriarchy. All these notions and categories are interwoven with inequalities in symbolic status, political power, life opportunities and access to society's resources, within a system of rules, values and practices that tend to maintain and reproduce women's subordination, thereby being pivotal for any attempt of legal and political emancipation of women.

Specific topics and concepts have also been discussed in the second and third part of the chapter. This section was devoted to the analysis of how feminist political theory explored fundamental concepts of Western political thought, including the distinction between public and private realm, equality, freedom, citizenship and democracy, specifically considering the interrelation of the private and public, personal and political. Moreover, this chapter argued that feminist political thought not only unravelled unequal power relations behind these concepts and distinctions but also struggled for the inclusion of women, women of colour, women of different social classes, women of different sexualities, women of differently-abled bodies and ages within the political realm, gaining women's access to full citizenship and enabling social change. Specific attention has been further devoted to the issues of

[145] Raymond (1979).

violence, pornography, prostitution and (hetero)sexuality, interpreting them as both cause and consequence of unequal power relations between men and women.

The final part of this chapter has been dedicated to the analysis of legal feminism, once again starting from the notion of patriarchy and the consequences that this social and cultural structure has on the law. This section highlights the consequences of patriarchy in terms of exclusion of women from public life (epitomized by the phrase 'law is sexist'), the false impartiality and objectivity of legal systems, which covers the male standards and assumptions that permeate legal concepts (epitomized by the phrase 'law is male'), and the importance for legal theories of contextual analyses, subjective narratives, and individual experiences, criticising the binarism man-woman, subject-other, oppressed-oppressor (epitomized by the phrase 'law is gendered'). The application of these theoretical approaches to legal discussions and analyses are manifold: among the many, the chapter offered a discussion of traditional policies and rules aimed at promoting equality (and their male biases), the male standards behind the concepts of reason and reasonableness, with specific regard to their legal use, the status of the female body and self-determination of women over it, and in more general terms the legal regulation of sex and sexuality.

This chapter has many limitations. First, it does not explore all the relevant issues, and not all those that are analysed are analysed with the necessary depth. Second, it focuses on the European and US context, and largely neglects non-Western cultures and legal systems. Third, it does not delve into the historical, cultural and political context in which feminist claims and reflections were elaborated. These limitations depend, of course, on the limits of space as well as on the expertise of the authors; but above all, they depend on the aim of the chapter itself, which, as said, was to offer an overview of the theoretical and philosophical assumptions of legal feminism, whose specific aspects will be discussed in the following chapters of this book.

However, there is a common thread throughout the chapter: it is the idea that, first, we live in a world where women's oppression is still at stake, not only because the vast majority of women across the world lack basic rights and legal protection, rather, even in Western countries major inequalities remain. Second, we live in a world that is still, largely, male. As de Beauvoir argued, the construction of society, of language, of law, all rests on male assumptions and male standards, thereby relegating the women to a condition of otherness and exceptionality (or deficiency). Women's priorities, feelings, and practices are marginalised as 'different' and neglected as inferior, in a dichotomous conception of gender and identities that hierarchically assign rights, roles, and behaviours. Exploring this assumption was, from different perspectives, the aim of the chapter. Challenging this structure, and rethinking society and law from a different, non-male perspective, is the ever-present challenge of all feminism, and legal feminism in particular.

Questions

1. In your view, what are the advantages and the disadvantages of the distinction between sex and gender? Do you believe that it is useful at the present time? Do you think that sex is really binary in human biology?
2. Do you consider that fourth-wave feminism has emerged?
3. Do you think that the different schools or branches of feminism are complementary or contradictory? Justify your answer.
4. What is the difference between the three phases of legal feminism, which have been labelled as law is sexist', 'law is male', and 'law is gendered'? In what sense the second phase addresses the "male orientation of law"?
5. Describe the origins and implications of the slogan "the personal is political", and use it to justify the state's intervention in the family.
6. What are the three notions of gender equality, and how does each relate to different feminist waves and feminist political theories?
7. What are the arguments for the exclusion/inclusion of women and marginalized groups in the concept of citizenship?
8. Why, according to many scholars, does the "reasonable person" standard work to answer relevant legal questions through the use of a gendered perspective? What alternative strategies have been proposed in order to reconsider such a standard?
9. Why many feminists criticised the decision of the US Supreme Court to recognise the right to abortion on the basis of the right to privacy?
10. Why legal scholars argue that cases of discrimination in the labour force are rooted not only in cultural beliefs and gender stereotypes, but also in organizational structures? Can you provide some example?

References

Al-Hibri A (1997) Islam, law, and custom: redefining Muslim Women's rights. Am Univ J Int Law and Policy 12:1–44

Barnett H (1998) Introduction to feminist jurisprudence. Cavendish Publishing Limited, London/ Sydney

Beechey V (1979) On patriarchy. Fem Rev 3:66–82

Bordo S (1990) Feminism postmodernism and gender-scepticism. In: Nicholson L (ed) Feminism/ Postmodernism. Routledge, London, pp 133–156

Bosch-Vilarrubias M (2014) Transitory masculinities in post-9/11 Arab American literature written by women. In: Carabí À, Armengol JM (eds) Alternative masculinities for a changing world. Palgrave Macmillan, New York, pp 205–216

Bourdieu P (2002 [originally published in French in 1998]) Masculine domination. Stanford University Press, Stanford

Brown C (1981) Mothers, fathers and children: from private to public patriarchy. In: Sargent L (ed) Women and revolution: the unhappy marriage of Marxism and feminism. South End Press, Boston, pp 239–268

Brownmiller S (1975) Against our will: men, women and rape. Simon and Schuster, New York

Bryson V (1992) Feminist political theory: an introduction. The MacMillan Press Ltd, Houndmills/Basingstoke/Hampshire/London
Bryson V (1999) Patriarchy: a concept too useful to lose. Contemp Polit 5:311–324
Butler J (2007 [originally published in 1990]) Gender trouble. Routledge, London
Cahn NR (1991–1992) Looseness of legal language: the reasonable woman standard in theory and in practice. Cornell Law Rev 77:1398–1446
Cain PA (1988) Feminist jurisprudence: grounding the theories. Berkeley Women's Law J 4:191–214
Campbell B (2014) End of equality. Seagull, London
Chandra G, Erlingsdóttir I (2020) The Routledge handbook of the politics of the #MeToo movement. Routledge, London
Creighton S, Minto C (2001) Managing intersex: most vaginal surgery in childhood should be deferred. BMJ 323:1264–1265
Crenshaw K (1989) Demarginalizing the intersection of race and sex: a black feminist critique of antidiscrimination doctrine, feminist theory and antiracist politics. Univ Chic Leg Forum 1:139–168
Currie DH (1992) Feminist encounters with postmodernism: exploring the impasse of debates on patriarchy and law. Can J Women Law 5.1:63–86
De Beauvoir S (1949) Le deuxieme sexe. Gallimard, Paris
DeKeseredy WS (2020) Bringing feminist sociological analyses of patriarchy back to the forefront of the study of woman abuse. Violence Against Women 27:621–638
DeKeseredy WS (2021) Woman abuse in rural places. Routledge, London
Delphy C (1977) The main enemy: a materialist analysis of Women's oppression. WRRC, London
Delphy C (1984) Close to home: a materialist analysis of Women's oppression. Hutchinson, London
Diamond I, Hartsock N (1981) Beyond interests in politics: a comment on Virginia Sapiro's "when are interests interesting? The problem of political representation of women". Am Polit Sci Rev 75:717–721
Duggan L, Hunter ND (1995) Sex wars: sexual dissent and political culture. Routledge, London
Dworkin A (1981) Right wing women. The politics of domesticated females. Women's Press, London
Eisenstein Z (1981) The radical future of Liberal feminism. Longman, New York
Elshtain JB (1981) Public man, private woman: women in social and political thought. Princeton University Press, Princeton
Estrich S (2001) Sex and power. Riverhead Books, New York
Faludi S (1992) Backlash: the undeclared war against women. Crown, New York
Ferguson A (1989) Blood at the root. Pandora, London
Ferguson A, Folbre N (1981) The unhappy marriage of patriarchy and capitalism. In: Sargent L (ed) Women and revolution: the unhappy marriage of Marxism and feminism. South End Press, Boston, pp 313–318
Fineman MA (2004) The autonomy Myth. The New Press, New York
Finley LM (1986) Transcending equality theory: a way out of the maternity and the workplace debate. Columbia Law Rev 86(6):1118–1182
Firestone S (1970) The dialectic of sex. Jonathan Cape, London
Fletcher R (2002) Feminist legal theory. In: Banakar R, Travers M (eds) An introduction to law and social theory. Hart Publishing, London
Fraser N (1997) Justice Interruptus. Routledge, London
Frye M (1983) The politics of reality: essays in feminist theory. The Crossing Press, New York
Geoghegan V, Wilford R (2014) Political ideologies: an introduction. Routledge, London
Gilbert L, Webster P (1982) Bound by love: the sweet trap of daughterhood. Beacon Press, Boston
Gunnarsson L, Strid S (2021) Varieties of sugar dating in Sweden: content, compensation, motivations. Oxford University Press, Oxford
Harris AP (1990) Race and essentialism in feminist legal theory. Stanford Law Rev 42:581–616

Hartmann H (1979) The unhappy marriage of Marxism and feminism: towards a more progressive union. Capital Class 8:1–33
Hearn J (1987) The gender of oppression. St Martin's, New York
Hearn J (1992) Men in the public eye. Routledge, London
Hearn J (2015) Men of the world: genders, globalizations, transnational times. SAGE Publications, London
Hewitson G (2014) The commodified womb and neoliberal families. Rev Radical Polit Econ 46(4): 489–495
Hewitt N (2010) Introduction. In: Hewitt N (ed) No permanent waves: recasting histories of US feminism. Rutgers University Press, New Brunswick/New Jersey/London, pp 1–14
Hirdman Y (1990) The gender system: theoretical reflections on the social subordination of women. Maktutredningen, Uppsala
Hooks B (1990) Yearning: race, gender, and cultural politics. South End Press, Boston
Hundle AK (2019) Postcolonial patriarchal nativism, domestic violence and transnational feminist research in contemporary Uganda. Fem Rev 121:37–52
Hunnicutt G (2009) Varieties of patriarchy and violence against women: resurrecting "patriarchy" as a theoretical tool. Violence Against Women 15:553–573
Hunter R (2008) Rethinking equality projects in law: feminist challenges. Bloomsbury Publishing, London
Irigaray L (1991) The bodily encounter with the mother. In: Whitford M (ed) The Irigaray Reader. Blackwell Publishers, Cambridge, pp 167–181
Jónasdóttir AG (1991) Love power and political interests: towards a theory of patriarchy in contemporary Western societies. Göteborg Studies in Political Science, Göteborg
Kelly L (1988) Surviving sexual violence. University of Minnesota Press, Minnesota
Kocabicak E (2020) Why property matters? New varieties of domestic patriarchy in Turkey. Social Politics: International Studies in Gender, State & Society. https://www.researchgate.net/publication/344071569_Why_Property_Matters_New_Varieties_of_Domestic_Patriarchy_in_Turkey
Lacey N (1993) Theory into practice - pornography and the public/private dichotomy. J Law Soc 20(1):93–113
Legates M (2001) In their time: a history of feminism in Western society. Routledge, London
Lorber J (2010) Gender inequality: feminist theories and politics. Oxford University Press, Oxford
Lorenzen LA, Eaton H (2002) Ecofeminism: an Overview. https://skat.ihmc.us/rid=1174588237625_665601541_9501/ecofeminism.pdf
MacKinnon C (1978) Feminism unmodified. Harvard University Press, Cambridge
MacKinnon C (1979) Sexual harassment of working women: a case of sex discrimination. Yale University Press, New Haven
MacKinnon (1982) Feminism, marxism, method and the state: an agenda for theory
MacKinnon C (1983) Feminism, marxism, method, and the state: an agenda for theory. Signs J Women Cult Soc 8(4):635–658
MacKinnon C (1985) Pornography, civil rights, and speech. Harv Civil Rights –Civil Liber Law Rev 20(1):1–70
MacKinnon C (1989) Toward a feminist theory of the state. Harvard University Press, Cambridge
MacKinnon C (1991) Reflections on sex equality under law. Yale Law J 100:1281–1328
MacKinnon C (1993) Only words. Harvard University Press, Cambridge
Mansbridge J (1999) Should blacks represent blacks and women represent women? A contingent "Yes". J Polit 61:628–657
Mansbridge JJ, Okin SM (1994) Feminism. Edward Elgar Publishing, Cheltenham/Northampton
Marinov G (2020) In humans, sex is binary and immutable. Acad Quest 33:279–288
McCann C, Kim S-K (2013) Feminist theory reader: local and global perspectives. Routledge, London
Mead M (1935) Sex and temperament in three savage societies. William Morrow & Co, New York

Messerschmidt J (1988) Capitalism, patriarchy and crime: toward a socialist criminology. Rowman & Littlefield, Lanham

Mies M, Shiva V (1993) Ecofeminism. Zed Books Ltd, New York

Mikolla M (2008) Feminist perspectives on sex and gender. https://plato.stanford.edu/entries/feminism-gender/

Millet K (2000 [originally published in 1969]) Sexual politics. University of Illinois Press, Urbana/Chicago

Millett K (1969) Sexual politics. Granada, New York

Minow M (1987) Foreword: justice engendered. Harv Law Rev 101:10–95

Minow M (1990) Words and the door to the land of change: law, language, and family violence. Vanderblit Law Rev 43:1665–1699

Mitchell J (1974) Psychoanalysis and feminism. Vintage Books, New York

Morell C (1981) 'Black Friday' and violence against women in the suffragette movement. Women's Research and Resource Centre, London

Munro E (2013) Feminism: a fourth wave? Political insight. Polit Stud Assoc UK 4:22–25

Naffine N (1990) Law and the sexes: explorations in feminist jurisprudence. Allen & Unwin, Sidney

Negar S, Kharazmi ZN (2019) The fourth wave of feminism and the lack of social realism in cyberspace. J Cybersp Stud 3:129–146

Newbigin E (2010) A post-colonial patriarchy? Representing family in the Indian nation-state. Mod Asian Stud 44:121–144

Noddings N (1990) Feminist fears in ethics. J Soc Philos 21(2–3):59–65

O'Brien M (1981) The politics of reproduction. Routledge & Kagan Paul, London

Okin SM (1978) Women in Western political thought. Princeton University Press, Princeton

Olsen F (1990) Feminism and critical legal theory: an American perspective. Int J Sociol Law 18(2): 199–215

Ortner SB (2014) Too soon for post-feminism: the ongoing life of patriarchy in neoliberal America. Hist Anthropol 25:530–549

Ortner SB (2020) Racializing patriarchy: lessons from police brutality. In: Fenstermaker S, Stewart AJ (eds) Gender, considered. Genders and sexualities in the social sciences. Palgrave Macmillan, New York, pp 137–163

Parekh S, Wilcox S (2020) Feminist perspectives on globalization. https://plato.stanford.edu/entries/feminism-globalization/

Pateman C (1988) The sexual contract. Stanford University Press, Redwood City

Philips A (1995) The politics of presence. Oxford University Press, Oxford

Raymond J (1979) The transsexual empire. The Women's Press, London

Réaume DG (1996) What's distinctive about feminist analysis of law. Legal Theory 2:265–299

Rich A (2007) Compulsory heterosexuality and lesbian existence. Routledge, London

Rowbotham S (1979) The trouble with patriarchy. New Statesman 98:970–971

Rubin G (1975) The traffic in women: notes on the 'Political Economy of Sex'. In: Reiter R (ed) Toward and anthropology of women, vol XX. Monthly Review Press, New York

Sachs A, Wilson JH (1978) Sexism and the law: a study of male beliefs and legal bias in Britain and the United States. Martin Robertson, Oxford

Sapiro V (1981) Research frontier essay: when are interests interesting? The problem of political representation of women. Am Polit Sci Rev 75:701–716

Sharpe AN (2002) Transgender jurisprudence: dysphoric bodies of law. Cavendish Publishing, London

Smart C (1989) Feminism and the power of law. Routledge and Kegan Paul, London

Smart C (1992) The woman of legal discourse. Soc Leg Stud 1(1):29–44

Spelman E (1983) Aristotle and the politicization of the soul. In: Harding SG, Hintikka MB (eds) Discovering reality: feminist perspectives on epistemology, metaphysics, methodology, and philosophy of science. Kluwer Academic Publishers, Amsterdam, pp 17–30

Spelman E (1990) Inessential woman: problems of exclusion in feminist thought. The Women's Press, London

Squires J (2018) Public and Private. Political concepts. https://www.manchesteropenhive.com/view/9781526137562/9781526137562.00015.xml. Accessed 27 Sept 2021

Strid S (2020) Jämställdhet under angrepp: En feministisk analys av våldsamt motstånd online. Tidsskrift for kjønnsforskning 44(4):269–284

Strid S, Hearn J (2021) Violence and patriarchy. In: Kurtz LR (ed) Encyclopedia of violence, peace, and conflict, vol XX. Academic, Cambridge

Tucker E (2011) Feminist political theory. In: Gibbons M (ed) The encyclopedia of political thought. Wiley Blackwell, New York, pp 1033–1036

UN (1993) Declaration on the elimination of violence against women. https://www.ohchr.org/

UN General Assembly (2006) In-depth study on all forms of violence against women: report of the secretary general. A/61/122/Add.1. https://www.un.org/womenwatch/daw/vaw/v-sgstudy.htm

Vogel L (1983) Marxism and the oppression of women. Toward a unitary theory. Pluto, London

Walby S (1986) Patriarchy at work. Polity, Cambridge

Walby S (1990) Theorizing patriarchy. Basil Blackwell, Cambridge

Walby S, Olive P, Towers J et al (2015) Stopping rape: towards a comprehensive policy. Policy Press, Bristol

Weinbaum B (1978) The curious courtship of Women's liberation and socialism. South End Press, Boston

Weintraub J (1997) The theory and politics of the public/private distinction. In: Weintraub J, Kumar K (eds) Public and private in thought and practice: perspectives on a grand dichotomy. University of Chicago Press, Chicago, pp 1–42

Young IM (1989) Polity and group difference: a critique of the ideal of universal citizenship. Ethics 99:250–274

Young IM (1990) Justice and the politics of difference. Princeton University Press, Princeton

Young IM (1997) Intersecting voices: dilemmas of gender, political philosophy, and policy. Princeton University Press, Princeton

Gender and Structural Inequalities from a Socio-Legal Perspective

4

Eva Bermúdez Figueroa, Valerija Dabetić, Raquel Pastor Yuste, and Zara Saeidzadeh

Contents

Authors are listed in alphabetical order. Eva Bermúdez Figueroa authored Sect. 4.4 and 4.5, Raquel Pastor Yuste wrote Sect. 4.7, Valerija Dabetić was responsible for Sect. 4.6 and Zara Saeidzadeh authored Sect. 4.1, 4.2 as well as 4.8.

E. Bermúdez Figueroa (✉)
University of Cadiz, Faculty of Social Sciences and Communication, Department of General Economics, Area of Sociology, Jerez de la Frontera, Spain
e-mail: eva.bermudez@uca.es

V. Dabetić
University of Belgrade Faculty of Law, Sociology of Law, Belgrade, Serbia
e-mail: valerija.dabetic@ius.bg.ac.rs

R. Pastor Yuste
University of Cádiz, Faculty of Law, Department of General Economic, Area of Sociology, Jerez de la Frontera, Spain
e-mail: raquel.pastor@uca.es

Z. Saeidzadeh
Örebro University, School of Humanities, Education and Social Sciences, Örebro, Sweden
e-mail: zara.saeidzadeh@oru.se

D. Vujadinović et al. (eds.), *Gender-Competent Legal Education*, Springer Textbooks in Law, https://doi.org/10.1007/978-3-031-14360-1_4

Abstract

This chapter critically analyses different socio-legal phenomena through a feminist prism on gender. With an aim to promote gender equality, it addresses the problems of structural gender inequalities in both private and public social spheres. Outlining the political, economic and ideological connection between laws and specific social contexts, it uncovers (hidden) effects of social reproduction and construction of gender and sexuality. Deconstructing the gender binary system and provoking a heterosexual matrix, it shows how traditional, patriarchal gender roles determine and establish the social position in the structure of society. Dealing with the gender (in)sensitive education, production, and reinforcement of gender inequalities in the labour market, and media (re)presentation of gender and symbolic violence, it shows how widely accepted values and gender roles shape, and ultimately define, the access to social resources, professional positions and social status. Limiting research to only some areas of this broad socio-legal thematic, this chapter addresses some policies for overcoming structural inequalities based on gender.

4.1 Introduction

This chapter aims to address and contribute to the understanding of some key concepts and contexts, explaining the implications and causal factors of gender inequality. In this sense, this chapter hopes to contribute to a better understanding of the specific legal chapters that will be presented hereafter. It will discuss institutionalised gender inequalities within the educational systems, labour market, politics, and media, among others. These main concepts and topics on gender and their implications in everyday life, will shed light on how gender inequalities operate. In turn, it will lead to a better comprehension of the structural gender determinants of law, and their application in the law disciplines throughout the subsequent chapters.

The key concepts and points that will be covered in this chapter are: social reproduction of gender and sexuality; gendered power relations in law and society; gender regimes of inequality; structural inequalities; gender socialization; gender segregation; gender representation; hegemonic masculinity; rape culture; structural violence, and global patriarchal legacies.

Learning Goals

- The first learning objective of this chapter is to address feminists' critical analysis of the gender binary system to convey how gender binary understanding, and the patriarchal nature of society and law affect gendered social relations and a variety of diverse genders and sexualities within social structures; family, education, labour market, media and the political sphere. Despite legal recognition, social norms tend to exclude social practices related to gender and sexuality. Thus, this chapter critically analyses how gender relations and sexual stereotypes, together with gender roles, determine and shape the fundamental constituent structures of society.
- The second learning objective of this chapter is to reflect on the poststructuralist way of understanding power; that power is widely dispersed and operates discursively. Feminists' approaches to socio-legal studies have been concerned to highlight and challenge the implications of gendered power relations in law and society. Hence, the chapter deals with structural inequalities embedded in private and public spaces. These result in lesser life opportunities for women, and other traditionally subordinated identities, at the micro, meso and macro levels of the fundamental constituent structures of society.
- The third objective of this chapter is to learn about the ways feminist sociolegal scholars have problematised the exercise of structural violence against women, and other subaltern identities, through an intersectional perspective within law and society. Structural inequalities within gender systems generate multiple forms of structural violence at different levels of society in various facets of their lives. Such inequalities ultimately shape people's lives in private and public spheres, online- and offline. This chapter discusses gender analysis of structural inequalities in organizations, focusing on legal and economic systems, health, labour market, media and political representation.

4.2 Feminist Socio-Legal Perspectives on Gender

This part of the chapter introduces feminist critical views on gender, and gender relations, from a socio-legal perspective. The section starts with explaining feminist understandings of sex and gender within the process of social reproduction. Then, it reflects on the construction of gender at interplay with law and society. Moreover, it problematises the heteronormative nature of the law and focuses on the constitution of laws in relation to gender and sexuality, drawing on same- sex relations and trans identity. The second section discusses the power and politics of gender through examining gender regimes and gender equality policies; emphasising the politics of recognition within law and society. The third section deals with an intersectional approach to legal protection that involves gender identity, sexual orientation, age, dis (ability) and poverty.

4.2.1 Social Reproduction and Construction of Gender and Sexuality

Social reproduction refers to a process by which a social system reproduces itself. It is a complex network of social processes and human relations that produce the conditions of existence for people under a capitalist society. Organisation of care, sexuality and gender roles are central to social reproduction which are affected by family, market, community, and the state. Critical to gender essentialism and natural attitude towards gender, feminist theories were developed in the mid twentieth century arguing that gender is a social construction as opposed to sex that is biology. However, influenced by poststructuralism in the 1990s, feminists deconstructed the distinction between sex and gender, arguing that gender is a produce of social discourse.[1] Thus, social gender differences are not caused only by bodily differences. Based on this notion, sexuality is not a direct expression of gender, as such a perspective ignores variations within female and male sexuality. The relationship between gender and sexuality is complex, dynamic and fluid. It is therefore specific to certain localities and historical periods.[2]

4.2.1.1 Gender Binary System of Law and Its Transformations

"Gender binary system" refers to a social system that assigns gender to people based on dichotomies of male and female sexes. "Law as a social system of society is based on the binary code of male and female, lawful/unlawful, and consists of "institutionalization of normative expectations", which are in fact legal rules."[3] Gender social normativity laws have social preconditions which affect society. At the same time, interactions among socio-cultural practices within a legal system create what Eugen

[1] Butler (1990).

[2] Richardson (2007), pp. 457–474.

[3] Rottleuthner (1989), p. 275.

Ehrlich calls 'living law'. This means that law is a product of society, including non-state actors, which can have authority if they are created to preserve social control.[4]

4.2.1.1.1 Family within Binary System and Its Transformation

The binary system has been primarily expressed in the nuclear family, established in modernity as the dominant form of family. Patriarchal social roles and relations have been reproduced through this dominant family pattern until 1970s. However, the nuclear family with father, mother and one or two children also represented at that same time the most vital form and the motor of changes within family life, towards modern values and ways of life. The nuclear family, the binary family model and related institution of marriage, have been legally affirmed in Family law and Constitutions of Western countries as the paradigmatic model.

As already implied, changes in family relations started happening in the last decades of the twentieth century with a rising resistance towards its patriarchal manifestations (mass rise of divorces was one of the consequences), on one hand, and under the impact of the human rights revolution in international and national legislations, on another.

Culturally, politically and from the point of everyday life, the mentioned changes in understanding justifiable family social roles and marriage, started happening in dominant trends. These trends could be summed up as putting into question the patriarchal character of a nuclear family; demonstrating the inter-relation of this patriarchal structure and mindset, with family violence and all forms of gender-based violence, striving for more just family relations. These changes begam emerging due to the sudden, significant access of women to labour market. This provided women with autonomy they did not have previously. Still, the patriarchal family system continues to assign women all the care-related activities, including children and the elderly, together with home tasks. Changes in international and domestic law and human rights in general, progressively put a focus on women rights. This was reinforced by the increasing importance in the public domain of feminist movements (private is political) and multiculturalism (recognition of differences, including differences based on sex and gender). These changes can be linked to a significant rise of education, employment, participation in public life of women, as well as to changing cultural patterns in favour of more partnership, like relations among spouses, and affirmation of individual dignity and autonomous personality of both women and children. These changes in the system of values and awareness regarding the importance of gender equality, affected progressively, not only female but also male persons. It further influenced rising trends of democratic political culture and emerging more democratic pedagogic approaches in educational systems in the last decades of the twentieth century.

Struggle for the recognition of differences based on sex, gender and minority rights led in the context of the aforementioned human rights revolution, towards gradual

[4] Banakar (2008).

changes in Western legal systems and constitutions at the beginning of twenty-first century; in favour of recognizing different types of family and even marriage.

All these phenomena have resulted in gradual, though radical, changes in legal and political articulations of categories of family and marriage. Changes have been happening within the system of family and marriage towards their transforming into equitable gender relations and partially, moving away from the patriarchal model of these relations. Even more radical change has been on the legal and political agenda, in the case of extending categories of family and/or marriage towards same sex marriage and trans gender people.

However, consensus does not exist; many controversies and struggles *pro at contra* recognition of rights of gay, lesbian or transgender people have been articulated in the public space, as well as within individual and collective mindsets. What, however, is misused by the extreme right nowadays is that identifying the family with the traditional (nuclear) family, has been clearly refused by the proponents of gender equality. Partnership, like relations within the binary family system, have become the new trend in the cultural, political and legal pattern[5] for the so-called advanced democracies (however not all of them)., There is a significant difference between official law, social facts and everyday life (see e.g. Poland or Hungary governments today and their homophobic or anti-abortion positions).

4.2.1.2 Gender Non-Binary System

Different social and legal systems have recognized a variety of gender identities. Legal recognition of non-binary, trans and queer gender identities are clear proof of understanding gender as a social construct, and disproof of determining gender based on biology. Simply put, genders are not limited to women and men. Binary gender categories have been the dominant social construction throughout history and legal affirmation in the social/cultural construct as the paradigmatic one. However, there are also genders that do not fit into the binary distinction. A third gender or variations of gender identities exist by which people identify themselves. Gender is a social practice that is relational, plural and material with different historical trajectories.[6] It is not the cultural norms that express bodily differences. It is rather the society that addresses bodies and deals with bodies differently. In other words, gender concerns the way human beings deal with bodies, and the consequences of that dealing in everyday life.[7] When a person's gender is determined based on their genitalia, the cultural practices and social relations restrain and define their existence as to female and male. This leads normally to the primacy of heterosexual male in respect to power and privilege, and to the subalternity of women and any other sexual identity.

4.2.1.2.1 Same Sex Marriage

The law's heteronormative nature has been challenged by social practices of sexual orientation. Deconstructing the heterosexual matrix through social struggles has

---

[5]Vujanovic (2016).

[6]Connell (2005).

[7]Connell (2011).

been adopted to advocate for decriminalisation of same sex relations in laws. Based on equality and liberation discourse, such struggles started to become successful in some parts of the world in the 1950s. Legalisation of same sex relations has changed social attitudes towards non-heterosexual people. Nevertheless, despite some society's resistance around the world, same sex relationship is still considered illegal and subject to legal punishments. in multiple countries in South Asia, the Middle East and North and East Africa. As of today, twenty-eight jurisdictions around the world have legalised same sex marriage, whilst various others have recognized civil partnership.[8] However, it should be noted that the cultural and legal dimensions of same sex cohabitation/marriage are closely intertwined. In a contradictory way in some societies, despite the legal recognition of same sex cohabitation/marriage, social norms might exclude social practices related to same sex relations. Due to religious ideologies and laws' rigid heteronormativity, the legal recognition of non-heterosexual reproduction, parenthood and kinship remain to be a social struggle in many countries.[9]

4.2.1.3 Gender Transition and Legal Recognition

Multiple configurations of social practices and relations result in gender embodiments; a social process through which a person embodies the gender they identify with, which transcends gender binarism. Trans people identify themselves differently from the gender assigned to them at birth by which they "disrupt and denaturalize psychosocial understanding of gender that is rooted in physical material of the body".[10] Hence, trans and gender transition is about crossing the boundaries and mobilizing categories. Trans people might or might not undergo gender reassignment.

The law's limited knowledge and understanding of trans amounts to misrecognition of trans people as full members of society. Legal recognition refers to "the official recognition of person's gender identity including gender marker and names in public registries".[11] Feminist researchers have shown the struggle of trans people against state institutions for recognition of their subjectivities and experiences.[12] The process of gender transition happens through severe contradictions in personal and social life, and yet the law's denial and misrecognition make it harder for people.

---

[8] Hamilton and La Diega (2020).

[9] Lasio et al. (2019), pp. 501–512.

[10] Stryker and Whittle (2006).

[11] European Commission, Legal gender recognition in the EU - The journeys of trans people towards full equality, https://ec.europa.eu/info/sites/default/files/legal_gender_recognition_in_the_eu_the_journeys_of_trans_people_towards_full_equality_sept_en.pdf.

[12] See Namaste (2000); Hines (2010), pp. 101–119.

4.2.2 Power and Gender Politics

Power as a dimension of gender has been central to feminists' concept of patriarchy; the idea of men as dominant sex, as in the analysis of rape manifesting men's assertion of power over women. Later feminist theorists realized that patriarchal power is not only due to men's direct control over women. It is rather the structure that is patriarchal. Therefore, the state, at the structural level, became the target of analysis through which the unequal power relations are reinforced. For example, court procedure in rape cases effectively place the complainant rather than the defendant on trial.[13] Furthermore, the patriarchal structure of family resembles the authoritarian state order in controlling private and public domain. However, feminists, gay and trans theorists have gradually adopted the poststructuralist approach which understands power as being widely dispersed, and as something that is discursively embedded in society. Therefore, gender power relations are contested through engagement with a differentiated set of institutions which hold power. Thus, the state as a heterogeneous entity is not the sole and unitary power structure, but the state's agencies' discourses and practices is the product of patriarchal and political conjuncture.[14] Law as an institution of power constitutes gender and gender identities, based on gender essentialism and gender fundamentalism as permeated by the society and social process. This is challenged by feminist legal scholars who focused mainly in women's inequality due to patriarchal justice system. Feminist approaches to socio-legal studies have been concerned to highlight and challenge the implications of gendered power relations in law and society, primarily affecting women opportunities.[15]

Social struggle for change in gender and gender relations is a simple definition of gender politics.[16] For example, the struggle against gender-based violence is a central feature of gender politics. Feminism has been the most important part of gender politics through activism, research, and theories. However, gay liberation and trans movements in the EU and US have had their own politics. Men as smaller proportion of gender equality supporters have been part of gender politics around the world.

4.2.2.1 Gender Regimes of (in)Equality

Gender regimes are the ways through which gender relations are shaped in specific systems.

▶ **Definition** Gender regimes refer to "the continuing configuration of gender relations that structures the gender practices of its participants".[17]

[13]MacKinnon (1983), pp. 635–658.

[14]Cooper (1993), p. 257.

[15]Fletcher (2002), pp. 135–154.

[16]Connell and Pears (2015).

[17]Connell (2006b), pp. 435–452.

Gender regimes manifest gender relations in gender occupational cultures, labour hierarchies, and gender division of labour.

▶ **Definition** Joan Acker defines inequality regimes as the "loosely interrelated practices, processes, actions, and meanings that result in and maintain class, gender, and racial inequalities within particular organizations".[18]

Inequality regimes became a main performing feature of the organizations, institutions, political parties, trade unions, administration, NGOs, etc., that base their practices on the model of a white heterosexual man as the universal model of "human being". This is further used as a universal pattern for bureaucracy. Many authors criticize the theoretical neutrality of bureaucracy based in this pattern, as will be seen below, in relation to the definition of hegemonic masculinity. This is one of the reasons for gender relations taking shape in different domains of economy, polity, violence, and civil society, that engender multiple forms of inequalities. Struggles over the forms of gender regimes are a very important part of feminist politics.

4.2.2.2 Socio-Legal Recognition of Citizenship Status

Recognition is a matter of accepting and promoting people's social status rather than their belonging to an identity group. Citizenship status recognition in the classical Marshall's concept, is related to political, social and economic rights. It means recognizing every citizen as full members of society, who have equal rights of participation in social life and enjoy redistribution of wealth and political presentation.[19] The ultimate aim of recognition is 'parity participation'. According to Nancy Fraser, misrecognition means 'institutionalized relations of social subordination'.[20] Institutionalised misrecognition in the form of law, policies and professional practices results in rendering some members of society inferior to others, as historical and traditionally occurs with women, ethnic groups, lower class people or non-heteronormative identities. Therefore, it is necessary to overcome this subordination by providing full participation in society through the real recognition of their status and needs. Subordination results in their status being inferior in society, marginalises their being, and overlooks their social and legal needs; ultimately subjecting them to violence and discrimination.

4.2.2.3 Gender Equality Policy

We live in an era of gender change. Gender and gender relations are not fixed but in flux. Gender equality policies are an attempt to gender change.[21] The main steering mechanism for gender equality policy is the state, state agencies and institutions

[18] Acker (2006), pp. 441–464.

[19] Fraser (2000), p. 107.

[20] Fraser (2001), pp. 1–13.

[21] Connell (2011).

which not only regulate the lives of women representing the half of the society, but also men and other gender variant people. In this sense it is relevant to mention the gender mainstreaming in European Union equality policies introduced in the political agenda since the 1990s, to improve the equal opportunities between men and women. This is despite a lack of implementation in many countries. Equal opportunity in factual level reforms within law and policies have had an impact on the public sector: breaking down gendered roles; trying to disrupt gender hierarchies and gender division of labour, and restructuring private and public spheres (even if there is still a long way to gender equality). Furthermore, women's participation in politics has brought about social and political changes which have helped transformation of society; enabled by feminist struggle and progress in international and domestic law, education, family relations, cultural settings and boosted by feminist movements.

4.2.3 Intersectionality and Legal Protection

The analysis of intersectionality has often focused on the intersection of sets of social relations. Kimberlé Crenshaw's work in the realm of law showed how race and gender work together to create hybrid forms of bias that law does not recognize. Scholars of law started to write about this approach as intersectionality critique in the early 1990s.[22] Intersectionality scholarship has since found a strong presence in academia, emphasizing the ways in which gender and class intersect with minorities and marginalized experiences. In turn these intersect with class, race, sexuality, nationality, ethnicity, religion, age and (dis)ability, which are often rendered invisible.[23] Legal protection should occur in the face of intersecting grounds of inequalities, such as race, class, ethnicity, age, disability, poverty, sexual identity, and other social subordinating categories producing inequalities. Moreover, legal protection should realize the significance of the relations of inequalities rather than reducing and conflating inequalities into one ground. For example, discrimination against immigrants should emphasize the sex, race, age and sexuality of immigrant people rather than merely immigrant subjects.

4.2.3.1 Gender Identity and Sexual Orientation

Gender is a social construction of sex, and gender and sexuality should not be examined distinctively; it is not possible to examine gender without sexuality as the two are inseparable. The grounds of inequalities based on gender and sexuality should realise the significance of other inequality grounds including class, age, and disability to name but a few. Over the past few decades, LGBTQIA+ legal rights have been addressed by scholars and activists across a variety of issues such as marriage, employment, medical care, military service and access to public places

[22] See for example, Conaghan (2008).

[23] Bartlett (2020).

such as bathrooms. Despite the improvement of legal protection from discrimination against LGBTQIA+ groups, it is still a challenge for many legal systems on how to respond to non-binary identities embracing different sexualities.

4.2.3.2 Age, Disability, and Poverty

Delving into categories of privilege or subordination in intersectionality analysis, poverty, age and disability, are the grounds on which structural inequalities intensify, together with gender inequalities. UN data affirms that 70% of people living in poverty in the world are women and little girls[24] (a higher number for risk of poverty and exclusion). It is important to note that having a disability and reaching an advanced age represent more physical and mental impairments, resulting in specific social inequalities and discriminations. The link between disability and poverty has received the attention of researchers in the recent decades. The gendered lens, however, needs more attention. For example, research has shown that women with disabilities are less likely to manage their lives in comparison with men;[25] "Disabled women particularly with intellectual impairment are victims of sexual crimes, but their offenders tend to be regarded in more lenient way when judgment is passed. Feminist research in many parts of the world have suggested that women with disabilities are more prone to experience social oppression and domestic violence because of their gender and disabled state".[26] Moreover, the factor of low-income status or poverty contributes to gendered injustices within law and society.

Example

The case of *I.G. and Others v. Slovakia* filed in 2012 at the European Court of Human Rights[27] sought justice for three Roma women who had been sterilised without their consent during childbirth. This case of forced sterilisation is a clear example of structural violence against Roma women based on different underlying factors; their gender, race, ethnicity, religion and poverty.

Based on the European Convention, the court found Slovakia in violation of the right to freedom from torture and inhuman treatment (article 3) and also in violation of the right to private and family life (article 8).The court awarded compensations to the applicants. ◀

[24] Chant (2015).

[25] Moodley and Graham (2015), pp. 24–33.

[26] Mays (2006), pp. 147–158.

[27] European Court of Human Rights, I.G. and Others v. Slovakia, https://www.refworld.org/cases,ECHR,50a289e22.html.

4.3 Feminist Socio-Legal Perspectives on Structural Violence in Family and Private Life

This part of the chapter introduces structural violence, with a specific focus on laws and policies that shape people's lives in the private and public sphere. The first section focuses on structural violence through examining rape against women in forms of statutory rape, extending to marital rape and forced marriage. Thereafter, it examines the social and legal aspects of intimate partner violence, followed by an explanation of how economic violence interacts with the labour market and family household. The second section discusses structural inequalities within medical systems, examining the effects of laws in society and socio-cultural practices that amount to legal discrimination. Thus, it explains the existing inequalities within laws and social practices that forbid women or other subaltern identities from the rights to safe sex, reproductive health, women's rights to legal abortion and access to care.

4.3.1 Structural Inequalities and Structural Violence

Social systems create situations where people are being oppressed, suppressed or deprived of their basic needs. All this happens in various domains such as the family unit, the economy and health; creating what is called structural violence.

► **Definition** Structural inequalities refer to unequal relations, rights and opportunities that are systemically rooted in the normal operations of dominant social institutions such as law, economy, healthcare and media. Laws and policies construct structural forms of inequality based on sex, gender and sexuality, class, race, ethnicity, age and disability.

One of the most evident forms of direct violence exerted against women and children worldwide is defined in the United Nations' Declaration on the Elimination of Violence towards Women. This defines violence against women as "Any act of gender-based violence that results in or is likely to result in physical, sexual or psychological harm or suffering to women [or girls], including threats of such acts, coercion or arbitrary deprivation of liberty" (1993, Article 1).[28] In this sense, statistics of this kind of violence worldwide are overwhelming and relate to phenomena such as sexual violence; rape; intimate partner violence; prostitution and trafficking; forced marriage; honour based-crimes; sexual exploitation; genital mutilation; sexual harassment and stalking.[29]

[28]Declaration on the Elimination of Violence towards Women, UN General Assembly, 20 December 1993.

[29]For UN data in Violence towards women and girls information, access https://unstats.un.org/unsd/gender/vaw/.

The structures that create unfair social and economic positions can themselves be seen as a systemic form of unequal power and domination, prevailing the model of men power over women and subordinated-considered collectives. Accordingly, structural inequalities within gender systems expose women and subordinated-considered collectives to multiple forms of structural violence at different levels of society, in various facets of life. Johan Galtung coined the term structural violence within peace research, that investigates the cause of violence with regards to war, to refer to the harm that is built into the structure as a result of inequality in power relations.[30] According to this notion of structural violence, everything that prevents people from developing their capabilities counts as violence.

Example

Some examples of structural inequalities, and structural violence, within laws and policies include: those that do not recognize sexual rape among men or rape in marriage; that permit marriage of woman or girls under the age of 18, and that mete out death sentences for juveniles. ◄

The following subsections will elaborate on various forms of structural inequalities within law and society.

4.3.1.1 Rape: Statutory Rape and Marital Rape and Child Marriage

Rape as gender-based sexual violence is pervasive and occurs against all genders and different sexualities. However, women and girls continue to represent the majority of rape victims while perpetrators are usually male.[31] Sexual intercourse with a person who is below the age of consent, whether or not the sexual act is against the person's will, is defined as statutory rape. Marital rape or spousal rape occurs when the spouse does not consent to sexual intercourse. Child marriage entails both statutory rape and marital rape as it entails coerced sexual intercourse with an underage girl. Feminist scholars have stressed the social structures that underpin rape; [32] feminist theories and activism have contributed a great deal to legal culture by expanding society's perception and legal recognition of what constitutes rape. This has been extended to encompass marital rape and forced marriage, along with the injuries perpetrated to the victims, historically these have demonstrated patriarchal control over women's bodies. Forced marriage is a way through which men use women as objects of transactions for their own benefits. Feminist discussions on forced marriage are linked to hegemonic masculinity and compulsory heterosexuality, especially in homophobic legal systems supported by conservative religious structures.[33]

---

[30] Galtung (1969), pp. 167–191.

[31] UN Women (2020).

[32] Buchwald et al. (1993).

[33] Rich (1980); Rich (2003), pp. 11–48.

4.3.1.2 Intimate Partner Violence

Intimate Partner Violence is defined as any pattern of assaultive and coercive behaviour, including physical, sexual, psychological and economic coercion, used by adults and adolescents against their intimate partners without their consent, and which results in shame, fear and helplessness[34] Apart from being known as a major public health problem, IPV is a clear example of structural violence. Feminist theories have challenged understanding of IPV over the years by arguing it is not a private or family matter. Rather, it is a deeply embedded social problem. Furthermore, patriarchal social structures, including unequal power relations, are the primary causes of IPV that occur in both heterosexual and homosexual relationships. Intimate partner violence is prevalent among gender and sexually diverse people and is usually perpetrated by men. As a result, feminists advocate for making changes, not only in in the laws and policies of institutions, but also changes in gender practices imbued with unequal power relations to combat IPV.

Example

For example, socio-legal scholars have advocated for law reforms in the area of gender-based violence to recognize offences perpetrated by partners and ex-partners as a result of coercive control that have serious effects on the victim (see for example, section 7: Serious Crime Act 2015, the UK).[35] ◀

4.3.1.3 Economic Violence: Exploitation in Labour Market and Family Household

Economic violence is a form of structural inequality that includes any act or behaviour that causes economic harm, such as: restriction or limited access to financial resources (funds and credits); employment, and the labour market; economic decision making besides unpaid work, and discriminatory laws on inheritance. Economic violence results in growing poverty and undermines educational development for the victims. Due to patriarchal structure and capitalism, women and girls are the main victims of economic violence, in addition to physical violence, sexual exploitation and trafficking.[36] In this sense, structural economic violence is worldwide, assuming that 70% of the world's 1.3 billion poor are women.[37] Factors of race, class, nationality, sexuality, age, religion and disability exacerbate economic violence.

From a political point of view, family policies on balancing work and family life are usually addressed to women; increasing the labour gap in hours worked

[34] Glossary of definitions of rape, femicide and intimate partner violence, EIGE, European Institute for Gender Equality (2017).

[35] Walklate et al. (2018), pp. 115–131.

[36] Fawole (2008), pp. 167–177.

[37] ILO (2020).

(regarding part time jobs, for instance), or the majority of monoparental families are headed by women, particularly those families in risk of poverty.[38] Therefore, family and welfare policies are criticized for perpetuating women's economic vulnerability by contributing to the construction of women as dependent entities; often living on a thin aid from the state.[39] Therefore, gender equality policies should encourage the collective support of all family members, instead of falling predominantly on women (fostering man co-responsibility).

Economic violence is a common form of intimate partner violence, resulting in severe sexual, physical and psychological consequence for the victims. The attitudes, beliefs and practices that perpetuate economic violence are often deeply entrenched with cultural, social and legal norms of society on gender and power. In heterosexual households, men hold power in allocation of resources such as food, education, and health care. Moreover, economic violence is exercised by male members of households through coercive control, economic exploitative behaviour and employment sabotage.[40] Feminists and practitioners discuss economic violence as a major form of men's IPV against women, usually hidden. Economic abuse takes away women's independence and autonomy. Rendering them insecure, dependent, inferior, and oppressed.[41]

Under the framework of gender equality, legal reforms have taken shape to combat such gender-based violence by means of problematising gendered division of labour, women's unequal pay and employment discrimination as violation of women's integrity. These issues will be covered later in this chapter.

4.3.2 Structural Inequalities in Medical System

One of the major forms of structural inequalities occurs in the health care and medical system. "Structural domination arises when social processes put large groups of people under systemic threat of domination or deprivation of the means to develop and exercise their capacities while at the same time this process enables others to dominate and have more opportunities to exercises capacities available to them".[42] In the medical system, women and women's bodies are often made inferior, subject to neglect, pathologisation and subordination. For example, menstruation, menopause or depressions are taken as a feminine disease linked to social stereotypes. Moreover, specific illnesses suffered mainly by women such as fibromyalgia, and endometriosis are often disregarded by the medical system. The

[38] Ibidem.

[39] Aguado (2018).

[40] Postmus et al. (2011), pp. 411–430.

[41] Lindskog (2020).

[42] Young (2011).

universal model for medical research and practice prioritizes men's health related issues over women's health and wellbeing.[43]

4.3.2.1 Sexual and Reproductive Health

Physical, mental, and social well-being in all matters relating to the reproductive system are about sexual and reproductive health. This implies people have the ability and freedom to decide on a safe and healthy sex life.[44] In order to be healthy, both sexually and reproductively, women require access to accurate information and services that can help them to have appropriate means of health care. This includes information regarding safe sex, hygienic menstruation and safe pregnancy (vital also for trans people).[45] Traditionally, or in many countries with restrictive women's rights today, women have been denied such access. The obstacles to sexual and reproductive health rights are entrenched with factors such as class or poverty, race, ethnicity, (dis)ability, sexual identity, and age. This is the case of many poor, racialized, or disabled women sterilized en masse by some states or administrations (Roma women in Europe, native women in all America, etc.).[46] Together, the concept of obstetric violence involves the structural violence exerted by the medical system against women throughout pregnancy, birth and perinatal period. This resembles the violation of the right to body, abuse, and mistreatment.[47]

4.3.2.2 Abortion

Providing public health benefits for abortion represents a significant component of supporting women's sexual and reproductive health rights. Abortion is a deliberate termination of pregnancy due to the process started spontaneously, or "deliberate termination of an unintended pregnancy that threatens the life or health of the pregnant woman including her social and mental well-being".[48] Unintended pregnancies occur as a result of forgetting to take the pills failing to use condom, or stealthing as a result of forced sexual intercourse. This applies to many poor pregnant women or girls forced to give birth around the world today; social and economic inequalities affect preventing unintended pregnancies. One of the main claims of feminism has been the legalisation of abortion based on women's free choice of family forming and bodily autonomy. Women's active participation in society is recognized through their choice of having children. The right to abortion is approached as a basic human right, protected under international human rights law. Nevertheless, there are still many countries that strictly penalise abortion for women

---

[43] Etienne (2019).

[44] United Nations Population Fund, Sexual & Reproductive Health. https://www.unfpa.org/sexual-reproductive-health.

[45] Glasier et al. (2006), pp. 1595–1607.

[46] United Nations Population Fund, Sexual & Reproductive Health, https://www.unfpa.org/sexual-reproductive-health.

[47] Please see chapter on Human Rights.

[48] European Institute for Gender, Abortion, https://eige.europa.eu/thesaurus/terms/1040.

with severe punishment in some parts of Europe, Central and South America and Asia. For example, the socio-political struggle to legalise abortion in Poland has focused on the rights of women to self-determination and the social construction of womanhood.[49] (See chapter on Family Law and Human Rights).

4.3.2.3 Access to Health Care

Since the 1970s, feminist legal scholars have argued that access to health care is a feminist issue; a matter of gender equality. The role of law as a tool to promote health care quality and patient safety is a dominant discourse. Independently, poverty is the main obstacle to access health care worldwide. However, the gender hierarchies and gendered practices between doctors and patients affect access to care. Women and other genders are denied access to health care under different legal systems because of their sexuality, age, economic situation and/or disability.

Example

Trans people are usually denied access to health care and medical treatment related to gender transition. This often involves hormonal therapy, surgical treatments and/or other medical procedures and treatments. ◀

Denial of, or severely limited access to, such medical care by refusal of coverage or lack of knowledge among health care professionals may have detrimental effects on well-being of trans people.

4.4 Gender (in)Sensitive Education: Differential Socialisation and Educational Systems

Educational systems are often a fundamental structure of society in terms of reproducing and perpetuating inequalities, especially gender inequalities. In examining the educational path, it will be analysed how gender inequalities are deeply imbricated, both in the structures of the professional educational system, and in the differential socialisation for boys and girls through the hidden curriculum and heteronormative gender models presented as valid throughout academic life. These models reproduce, and result in, weaker opportunities for women and those who do not conform to the patterns of the hegemonic masculinity characteristic of social organisations, [50] especially in the labour market.

[49] Nowicka (2007), pp. 167–196.
[50] Connell (2006a), pp. 837–849.

4.4.1 Gender (in)Sensitive Education: Gender Differential Socialisation, the Hidden Curriculum, and the Consequences for Life and the Labour Market

Socialisation is the process through which people adopt and integrate themselves into the community in which they are born. It is a process that goes beyond mere learning; it is the internalisation, assimilation, and apprehension of behavioural patterns, traits, norms, customs, and ways of thinking. This integration and assimilation is so intense and profound that it becomes part of our personal identity without our being aware of it.

Differential gender socialisation, or gendered socialisation, involves the assumption and internalisation by the members of a community of the roles, stereotypes, beliefs, customs, and norms for each sex that are considered appropriate by the community or the wider society. It thus becomes an adaptive process that will provide the person with the ability to live in and fully integrate into a society, identifying with the roles, gender expectations, rewards, and social valuations that the society reserves for his or her biological sex. The fundamental process begins with primary socialisation in the first years of life with the family, the school, and, to a lesser extent, a group of equals or peers. These influences act as fundamental and determining agents in this first stage. Thus, the educational system is a primordial element in the analysis of gender. Educational systems have two contradictory social functions; social continuity and social change. As a social institution, education is responsible for perpetuating patterns for the successful integration of individuals into society. Contemporaneously, it is a recipient and promoter of social change. Education and educational systems can innovate and open social mechanisms that promote gender equality through equal opportunities. However, despite institutional efforts at the European and global levels, numerous critical theories show the fundamental role educational systems play in the production and social reproduction of the symbolic order of gender and, therefore, the survival of power relations and the privilege of one sex over the other. In addition, educational systems function as a stratifying element from an intersectional perspective; perpetuating ethnicity, social class, sexual orientation or identity, and functional diversity, among other variables. This is reflected in theories of social reproduction, resistance, correspondence and the hidden curriculum.[51] These theories are based on manifestations reproducing the privileges of one part of the population and the consequent disadvantages of others. The hidden curriculum is manifested in a series of values, codes, norms, ideas, assumptions, myths, discourses, concepts, beliefs, power relations, and roles. Gendered and sexist textual and symbolic resources are transmitted at school in the form of organisation, management, and control of the school system; in the work and routines of the classroom, and in educational and social practices and

[51] As represented by Louis Althusser, Samuel Bowels and Herber Gintis; Pierre Bourdieu and Jean Claude Passeron; Henry Giroux; Apple and Lundgren.

interactions. Inevitably, this will lead to an exact reflection in the labour market, as will be examined below.

4.4.1.1 Primary Socialisation: Family, Day-Care, and Elementary School

Primary socialisation takes place in the first years of childhood. This process has the most significant impact on people. The fundamental agents responsible are mainly the family and the educational institutions in childhood: the day-care centre; nursery, and elementary school. The fundamental guidelines in this educational stage occur in an environment in which the child's emotional involvement with the adults in charge of education is indispensable. It is essential for the children to be enveloped within the group; a cheerful acceptance and stimulation of their actions and behaviours is required. Correspondingly, they will inhibit certain behaviours if the stimuli are negative. Learning and interaction occur through imitative patterns of behaviour perceived and evaluated as positive by the child, as these will mark their integration into the group. Family models of behaviour will be internalised, and primary references in terms of social gender roles will be assumed and understood; their personality is constructed without a distinction between external and innate constructed elements. This process will give rise to personal identity.

The phenomena that develop from this assimilation process from a micro-sociological perspective, and that determine gender identity, are marked by two fundamental social processes: (a) normalisation, or the tendency of people to remain within the limits of what their social group considers regular or habitual, assimilating their behaviour to others, especially those with whom they have to identify; and (b) social control, where the group rejects or penalises certain behaviours and attitudes that are outside the social expectations of each sex, reinforcing others that are habitual and seen as desirable by the group. Gender differentiation, therefore, occurs from the beginning of life with the expectations generated by a baby's sex, determining familial and environmental attitudes.[52] At this stage, both socialisation and learning take place both through play, and in a playful environment. This is generally linked to an essential emotional and affective load on the part of the adults in charge who, are usually women at this stage of the educational system. The imprint of primary socialisation will mark the future development of the person throughout her or his life.

4.4.1.2 Secondary Socialisation: Secondary Education and its Consequences

In secondary socialisation, and especially during adolescence, peer groups exert the most significant influence on the individual. This is despite the importance of other agents of socialisation such as the educational system, the media, religion, and other

[52]This phenomenon can be explained through a brief experiment (Girl toys vs. boy toys: The experiment - BBC Stories) on how adults, without knowing a baby's sex, but based on their clothing, unconsciously offer traditional toys sexually differentiated according to their belief that the child is a boy or a girl. The experiment can be viewed at https://www.bbc.com/news/av/magazine-40942691.

organisations. However, despite the need for a more in-depth analysis of peer relations, some characteristic elements of the gender gap in education must be briefly mentioned.

The fundamental axes of differential gender socialisation are constituted by general social trends. Boys are encouraged to learn the development of physical skills, mechanics, science, and technology. The fields are generally oriented toward an intellectual dimension, with considerations of employment and social success. Little importance is given to learning related to stereotypical female roles. In contrast, the social norm of learning for girls revolves around the development of the affective aspect and care for others. Less attention is paid to science and technology, with incursions into traditionally male roles being considered unsuitable. This binarism in social roles, which entails different social considerations and implies a lower valuation of the role associated with women, is one of the essential determinants of the presence and distribution of gender inequality in the labour market.

4.4.1.3 Educational Systems: Schools, Secondary Education, and Universities

The gender gap in education is evident. The distribution of students tends to be equal in European countries, in kindergarten and elementary school, but not at the global level. A brief analysis of the distribution of teachers confirms that more than 90% of teachers in early childhood education are women.[53] In most countries, the initial educational stages are less well paid and have a lower level of social consideration, with some exceptions such as the Nordic countries, especially Sweden or Finland. As primary education is socially identified with a more emotional teaching job, it is inevitably related to gender stereotypes and roles associated as a feminine task. However, by moving through the educational system it can be found that secondary education, in certain aspects, tends to be more egalitarian in terms of the teaching staff, even though there is still a female majority in the case of European countries. In vocational training, the gender bias tends to be very marked, even more so than at university.

Concerning universities, the enrolment statistics this chapter looked at in depth, both at the European and global level, show that women accumulate in branches of knowledge related to social studies, care, and administration-related professions. In this sense, the axes of gender socialisation bear fruit in women's choices of careers, commonly comprising nursing, teaching, social work, pedagogy, psychology, and administration. In contrast, it can be argued that men are primarily concentrated in engineering and technical careers, being more highly valued socially and better paid. Despite incorporating women into STEM careers (Science, Technology, Engineering and Mathematics), and some already at an equal split between men and women, there is no correspondence between the student body and the teaching staff, which is mainly male. Furthermore, female graduates have a lower level of labour market

[53] Eurostat (2019).

insertion in their sectors than their male counterparts. This is despite the fact that women tend to have a higher level of success throughout their academic life and, conversely, boys tend to have higher rates of school failure (European Commission 2018).

4.5 Labour Market: Reproduction and Reinforcement of Inequities

The analysis of the patterns of women's inclusion in the labour market provides a global approach to the position of women in society. The possibilities of entering the labour market and retaining a job determine life and family opportunities; defining class, position, and status in the social structure. This section will explore the conditions and characteristics of female employment and its inescapable relationship with gender roles and stereotypes, through the sexual division of labour. It will analyse the lack of labour policies for the reconciliation of family life, which continue to be oriented towards women, with little involvement of men. This is despite institutional efforts in most EU countries, and consequently, this lack determines women's employment. We will conclude by analysing the good practices and employment policies adopted by the so-called welfare states to reduce this evident gender gap.

4.5.1 Gender and Intersectionality in the Labour Market[54]

As explained in the previous section, differential gender socialisation has direct consequences for people's life opportunities insofar as it determines the possibility of studying, the choice of academic itineraries, and, therefore, their subsequent life conditions marked by access to, and permanence in, the labour market. The labour market is not only biased in this sense by gender.[55]

The socio-labour problems affecting women in the labour market are closely linked to the sexual division of labour, and gender stereotypes and roles. In the industrial and modern era, this division consolidates and spreads throughout the social body as other constituents of the economic system, identified as growth and progress. The capitalist organisation of industrial work, together with the development of patriarchal social relations in the nuclear family, reinforced by the state and by religion,[56] shape the public sphere and the private sphere. This can be identified

[54]These explanations about the factors that produce and reinforce gender inequalities in the labour market, will help to understand and contextualize the chapter on Labour Law.

[55]Although these are global phenomena, given the enormous variability among countries in the statistical data on employment and gender, as well as the limited length of this chapter, only general trends will be mentioned without going into quantitative details, with some exceptions that can be verified by the statistical resources and reports corresponding to the institutions and organizations referred to in the previous note (ILO, OECD, EIGE, UN, Eurostat, etc.).

[56]Hartmann (1981), pp. 366–394.

with the labour market and the home, respectively, separate, and unconnected entities. This identification of work as productive work (visible, socially considered, in the market, and remunerated) has had, and continues to have, an evident gender bias. It essentially ignores the private sphere by ignoring the traditional space of women: reproductive work; the care of the home; the elderly, and minors (invisible, not socially considered, outside the market, and unpaid). This separation obviates the inescapable relationship between the two spheres; it renders invisible, and undervalues, the relevance of physical and symbolic reproductive work. Such work, in turn replenishes the labour force. This is a determining and essential factor in understanding the unequal social valuation of work related to traditional male and female roles. The direct incidence of the sexual division of labour, manifested in the assumption by women of traditional domestic and child-rearing tasks, generates a significant difference in life opportunities; fundamentally those related to women's access, promotion, and permanence in the labour market.

Although women have significantly joined the labour market in EU countries in the years since World War II, combined with a trend towards legal protection against discrimination based on sex, ethnicity, ability, social class, and other conditions, the reality is that we are far from achieving real equality despite the progress made in this area. Indirect discrimination, more subtle and less overt, is ultimately responsible for most of the gender gap in the labour market; "Discrimination occurring where an apparently neutral provision, criterion or practise would put persons of one sex at a particular disadvantage compared with persons of the other sex, unless that provision, criterion or practice is objectively justified by a legitimate aim, and the means for achieving that aim are appropriate and necessary"(gender issue(s) | European Institute for Gender Equality s. f.). Even though the principle of equal pay for work of equal value has been enshrined in the European Treaties (Article 157 TFEU) since 1957, in many cases, depending on the country, women earn less than men for doing jobs of equal value. Despite improvement, progress is extremely slow in the European Union, with the gap only decreasing by 1% over the last 7 years.[57] Next, we move on to quote very briefly the gender characteristics of the labour market, defining the fundamental obstacles women face in access, permanence, and promotion at work.

4.5.1.1 Gender Pay Gap: Job Segregation, Wage Gap, Glass Ceiling, Sticky Floor, Undervaluation of Women's Work

Wage gap:

► **Definition** The *wage gap* is defined as 'the difference between female and male employees' average gross hourly earnings. (...) Gross earnings are wages or salaries paid directly to an employee before income tax and social security contributions are deducted'.[58]

[57] Boll and Lagemann (2018).

[58] European Commission (2014), p. 3.

Wage gap in the EU typically refers to an unadjusted wage gap, as it does not consider all the factors that affect it; differences in education, type of work, experience in the labour market, and hours worked. Among the most critical determinants of the wage gap are occupational or horizontal segregation and part-time work, typically a female work feature. According to data from the European Employment Institute, the estimate for all countries is 16% among employees.[59]

Occupational/horizontal segregation:

▶ **Definition** This is the accumulation of the same sex in professions and occupational sectors, usually related to stereotypical characteristics of traditional male or female roles and related to unequal social valuation to the detriment of women.

According to EU data, 30% of the wage gap is a consequence of the overrepresentation of women in relatively lower-paid sectors, such as education and the health sector (in their lowest positions) as well as care-related professions. Higher-paid sectors such as science, technology, engineering, and mathematics (STEM), are occupied mainly by men.

Vertical segregation: Glass ceilings and sticky floors.

The first metaphor alludes to an invisible barrier, or ceiling, that prevents upward mobility. As we move up the career ladder, we find fewer women in positions of power and decision-making.[60] Fewer than 10% of CEOs in large companies are women. The profession with the most notable differences in hourly wages in the EU are managers; women earn 23% less than men.[61] This phenomenon is not only a fact of the labour market; in any organisation, it is hard to find an equal proportion of women and men in positions of power and decision-making areas, surprisingly even in feminised labour sectors. The other metaphor that defines women's employment is the sticky floor.

▶ **Definition** Women's employment is understood as the accumulation of women in labour positions corresponding to lower levels in the labour hierarchy; in subordinate positions corresponding to lower salaries and poor working conditions (cleaning, home assistance, etc.).

Both phenomena, the glass ceiling and the sticky floor, are directly related to the undervaluation of women's work and skills.

Undervaluation of female work and skills:

---

[59] For deeper detail, consult the reports on gender gap in the UE Gender pay gap among employees in the EU (EIGE 2014) Gender pay gap in EU countries based on SES (2014) Christina Boll, Andreas Lagemann.

[60] Acker (2009); Beghini et al. (2019); Billing (2011); EIGE (2014).

[61] EIGE (2014).

The undervaluation of female work comes hand in hand with the sexual division of labour previously explained; Joan Acker's concept of inequality regimes[62] and Raewyn Connell's concept of hegemonic masculinity.[63] Their theories explain how the white heterosexual male model constitutes the ideal on which organisations are built. The educational system, companies and the state are imbued by this supposedly neutral model, assuming women's identity, and any other type of identity, to be subordinate.[64]

Some of the causes of the undervaluation of female labour and occupational segregation are related to the social construction of the value of different occupations, professions and jobs.[65] The authors summarise the influences linked to the social construction of the value of work as visibility, valuation, vocation, added value and variance. *Visibility* refers to the difficulty of detecting women's capabilities due to the aggregation in large and undifferentiated salary tables. *Valuation* refers to the frequent male structure on which classification and salary structures are based. *Vocation* stands out, directly related to women's skills derived from the supposedly feminine essence, understood as mother and caregiver is usually treated as natural and directly linked to low wages. *Value-added* corresponds to the greater possibility of finding men in high value-added jobs or labour-intensive occupations than women. Finally, and of particular relevance, *variance* in the norm of work patterns and work itineraries differentiated between men and women, that lead to women's work occupying a sphere not comparable to that of men.

All these obstacles can be addressed in the specific labour market analyses found in statistics on employment and its characteristics, collected both by the national statistical institutes of each country, and national and international institutions at the global level.[66]

4.5.2 Reconciliation of Work and Family Life

According to the literature and reports from European institutions, conclusions regarding the reconciliation of work and family life[67] are clear; women spend fewer hours in paid work than men on average, but more hours in unpaid work. Statistics on time use (UNSD, OECD, EU, ILO, among others) show how the structuring of time spent caring for the elderly and children is usually significantly

[62] Acker (2006).

[63] Connell and Messerschmidt (2005).

[64] Acker (2006); Connell (2016).

[65] Bettio y Verashchagina (2009).

[66] Bettio and Verashchagina (2009); European Trade Union Confederation (2014); Kirton and Guillaume (2017); Mullins and Saldivar (2015); Rubery and Hebson (2018).

[67] EIGE (2014); Franzway and Fonow (2011); Mikucka (2008); Prieto and Pérez De Guzmán (2013); Rubery et al. (1998).

unbalanced; women are responsible for most of this care.[68] Overall, women work more hours per week than men.[69] One of the most significant obstacles women face in the labour market and in social participation is the double (family and work) or triple workload (if we talk about women trade unionists). Women trade unionists are further underrepresented in trade union organisations, reflecting their absence from positions of power and decision-making in the labour market. If trade union organisations are in charge of defending labour rights, and women are not represented and/or present in collective bargaining, they will hardly manage to defend their labour interests.[70]

Policies encouraged by the EU try to foster co-responsibility for care through parental leave, appropriate provision of childcare services, and encouraging company policies regarding flexible work arrangements.[71] However, because work-life balance policies have generally been oriented toward facilitating the development of women's work activity, they can reproduce these labour inequalities and generate effects that, although positive in the short term, provide extensive negative results in the long term, particularly when combined with the patriarchal culture of female care orientation.. The possibility of a leave of absence to care for dependents with job reservation, the reduction of the working day to care for minors and other reconciliation measures mean, in the short term, the maintenance of women in the active labour market, even though the attendant salary reduction may not guarantee economic sufficiency. This directly results in a greater risk of poverty for women; it implies the continuation of the employment relationship without economic remuneration.

The positive nature of these measures, in an immediate sense, contributes to the maintenance and reinforcement of a pattern of behaviour that has a double effect on retirement income.[72] Throughout their working lives, women spend less time contributing through paid work than men and have more interruptions in the intermediate periods. In such periods they tend to receive fewer unemployment benefits and consequently their contributions are reduced. Therefore, women have more unstable employment trajectories (maternity leave, leave of absence for caregiving, part-time jobs, etc.) and lower contributions than men in general. Combined with the fact that women tend to be grouped in lower salary categories and in predominantly feminised occupations, where salaries are lower than those of their counterparts in masculinised professions, it is possible to conclude that the labour market generates a system of inequality for women's retirement, not just their current employment. This has special significance; it penalises women in the form of smaller pensions. In conjunction with less time contributed, this results in a widening of the

---

[68] EIGE (2014).

[69] Chatzitheochari (2012); Prieto and Pérez De Guzmán (2013).

[70] Bermúdez-Figueroa and Roca (2019); Kirton (2005, 2013).

[71] Hubbard et al. (2008).

[72] Cebrián López (2015).

gender gap and of the deterioration of women's conditions in a period of greater vulnerability, old age.

A demand from a large part of society is to encourage men to adopt conciliatory measures to facilitate a work-life balance. Despite their existence, men make very little use of such policies, as reflected in the statistics of international organisations such as the European Union Labour Force Survey.[73] In this scenario, using this type of measure to reconcile work and the need for family care, women's employment would not exclusively be penalised, rather it would be distributed more equitably. Likewise, this gender gap would cease to be a reason for rigidity and inefficiency in the labour market, which, if only from the simple perspective of human resources, is losing a large mass of trained workers with excellent work potential. The social and labour benefits they could contribute would undoubtedly lead to a fairer and more egalitarian society. This would minimise asymmetrical relations and their negative consequences for half of society, while involving men in family care, a public good. This is the basis on which measures to extend paternity leave in various European countries that have equalised maternity and paternity leave are based. This has created positive effects for women's employment, satisfaction at the level of men and women and primary reinforcement of the pro-natalist policies, necessary in most European countries to face the ageing of the population.

4.5.3 Unprotected Employment: Domestic Workers, Informal Care, Informal Employment

Domestic employment, whether formal or informal, is one of the most invisible labour sectors and enjoys minimal social protection, especially considering its role in the underground economy and the unreliability of the data on this employment at the official level. It is in many ways a feminised sector, and one that statistically reflects the care and household work done by a precarious workforce and subjected, in numerous cases, to abuses of all kinds enhanced by this invisibility. We must reflect on the outsourcing in households of paid domestic work, which is often informal work and not in the visible and legalised labour market. It implies that, in order to balance work and family life for higher income and/or higher class women, there is another lower class woman assuming their burden of care. Women with more impoverished lives and fewer social opportunities, in many cases migrants, carry out work that is essential for life and the functioning of the labour market. They do so without a contract, without social security contributions, they are paid well below minimum wage, undervalued, and often in abusive conditions. This workforce is mainly made up of women who migrate to other countries or continents to take on these reproductive activities in the global care chain. The discourse of critical international organisations related to migration, gender, and development have focused on the issue of transnational families and mothers as a problem and, to a

[73] EPIC (2013).

much lesser extent, as a contribution. This has not been the case for transnational fathers. Migrant men have played a leading role in migrations research due to the traditional patterns of mobilities in general; they frequently leave their families in a higher proportion than women, depending on the countries involved. However, men are not examined in their fatherhood as women are and have been less frequently studied in the academic field. This illustrates the gender bias of the academy in the election of the subject on research.[74]

4.6 Symbolic Representation of Gender

This part of the chapter deals with the role of mass media in creating, promoting and maintaining symbolic representation of gender. By using ideology-coloured language and promoting gender stereotypes in the public sphere, mass media are often seen as important actors in maintaining male dominance and sustaining traditional, patriarchal power relations in a society. In reporting on (sexual) violence against women, media commonly use gender (in)sensitive language, misogynistic and sexist phrases, and rely on hegemonic masculinity as a justifying strategy. This section also problematizes the concept of rape culture; underlying the connection between porn, sex and violence.

4.6.1 Presentation vs. Representation of Mass Media

Despite the traditional understanding that mass-communication is a linear process considering sender/message/receiver, contemporary (cultural) research rather outlines that a message goes through several phases including production, circulation, distribution, consumption, and reproduction. This "complex structure in dominance" implies that the message needs to be shaped according to the language rules that have distinctive, discursive forms in every part of this process.[75] In other words, the message "needs to be told"; it has to "become a 'story' before it can become a communicative event".[76] This means messages are never neutral and objective, rather their form and content depend on the senders' intentions, biases and the media literacy of the receiver. So, when the media claim they present reality impartially, they are actually re-presenting it; re-presenting an object/person to the public which is not a passive receiver of these messages.[77] The inclusion of dominant and positively represented social groups in the media has a strong benefit for them. In contrast, exclusion or misrepresentation of marginalized and subordinate groups further weakens their already fragile social position. Unfortunately, in

[74] Yates (2011).

[75] Hall (2001), p. 508.

[76] Ibid.

[77] Milivojević (2004), p. 12; Valić Nedeljković (2008), p. 447.

the case of powerful, multinational corporate mass media, dominant groups usually take part in the majority of the representing.[78]

4.6.1.1 Representation of Gender Via Media: Ideology, Stereotype and Pornography

Media discourse is a public discourse that has enormous potential for the reproduction of social relations. In terms of gender dichotomies media still resort to new strategies that legitimize these divisions;[79] settings created in gender patriarchal ideologies made a strict boundary between the values of women and men, and their affiliation to public or private, natural or cultural, active or passive. In the informing process, some modern media tend to cultivate desirable notions of gender identities and roles, fixing stereotypes about female inferiority in the popular sphere and representing women differently; from symbolic exclusion to the "ghettoization" of women's interests and experiences.[80] According to the report (2010) of the largest international study of gender in the news media (the Global Media Monitoring Project), women are extremely underrepresented in news coverage as opposed to men.[81] Women make up only 24% of the people in the news (news subjects), usually as a part of the 'ordinary' people categories.[82] Regarding the news content, 46% of stories reinforce gender stereotypes, while only 6% of stories challenge such stereotypes or highlight the problems of gender (in)equality.[83] The consequence of such social action is symbolic gender inequality, defined as "the representation of the principal through an agent to which a certain representative meaning is attributed".[84]

4.6.1.2 Mass Media and Images

Nowadays, contemporary media tend to reinforce stereotypical portraits of gender. This can be via images showing relationships where competent men save incompetent women, women are viewed as devoting and nurturing housewives, whilst men are providers, and women as sexual objects subject to men's desire.[85] By promoting aspects that are not a quality of women's personality, modern media (subtly) continue to reproduce and affirm the patriarchal and traditional roles of women, thereby limiting the professional and socially engaged activities of women.[86] One dimension of the traditional female role, presented as a desirable women's role in a

---

[78] Kellner and Share (2005), p. 370.

[79] Radibratović (2020), p. 14.

[80] Milivojević (2004), pp. 11–12.

[81] Who Makes the News - The Global Media Monitoring Project, http://www.e-alliance.ch/typo3conf/ext/naw_securedl/secure0226.pdf?u=0&file=fileadmin/user_upload/docs/Advocacy_Capacity/2011/3.WACC_Who_Makes_the_News_HIGHLIGHTS.pdf&t=1433999043&hash=a864eea3ea60a0795464f14bf9eb972e, visited 21.04.2021.

[82] Ibid.

[83] Ibid.

[84] Lombardo and Meier (2014), p. 4.

[85] Wood (1994), pp. 33–36.

[86] Filipović and Kuzmanović-Jovanović (2012), p. 19; Lubina and Klimpak (2014), p. 213.

private sphere is taking care of the home, as a devoted mother and loving wife. Through objectification and sexualisation in the public sphere, media promote the other cultural identity of women; a prostitute or concubine.[87] In the current global and local context of tabloidization of media, the real model of prostitution is replaced with different modalities, such as starlets, trendsetters, whose "attractive" physical appearance glorifies the public manifestation of sexuality. Media focus on these female roles is primarily oriented towards commercial purposes, but nothing less in favour of reproducing new modalities of patriarchy—so-called a "new patriarchy".[88]

Despite this pervasive tendency, media should practice a different way of reporting which eliminates, instead of contributing to, these prejudices. Media should report on all genders equally; as for women, they should be represented in all their diversity such as age, social class, ethnicity, level of education, and urban versus rural environment.[89] The media could offer portraits of women from the professional, academic and other spheres that emphasize their professional competence, instead of insisting on their (attractive) physical appearance or only to affirm the image of a happy woman in a traditional family environment.[90] By exploring internal relations of inequality, and structural violence in gender relations, the media should and could contribute to deconstructing stereotypes of the traditional family as the centre of love and harmony. Right-wing defence of the traditional family (as the only real "family" without which nation, state and reproduction/birth rates are put into danger) should be countered by presenting the benefits of alternative forms of families.[91]

4.6.2 Media Reporting on Violence Against Women

Violence against women persists in media through negative, non-ethical and irresponsible discriminatory reporting. This includes the use of stereotypes, relativization of perpetrators' guilt or victim-blaming. This erodes the gravity of the criminal act; by disqualifying the victim by history or quasi-history of his/her private life; allowing explanations or justifications of the circumstances under which an act of violence has occurred, and by subsequent stigmatization of the victim.[92]

▶ **Definition** Violence against women can occur both in the public or private sphere of life. Violence implies an act that results, or would result in, physical, psychological or sexual suffering to women. It can also refers to threats of such acts, coercion or arbitrary deprivation of liberty.[93]

[87] Vujadinović (2016), p. 102.

[88] Vujadinović and Stanimirović (2016), pp. 195, 198, 200.

[89] Filipović and Kuzmanović-Jovanović (2012), pp. 31–32.

[90] Filipović and Kuzmanović-Jovanović (2012), pp. 31–32.

[91] Vujadinović and Stanimirović (2016), p. 198.

[92] Mršević (2017), pp. 5, 8; Babović et al. (2010), p. 30.

[93] UN Declaration on the Elimination of Violence against Women, Article 1, https://undocs.org/en/A/RES/48/104, visited 20.03.2021.

In this sense, we are used to witnessing in the media how women are exposed and publicly objectified, with scarce consequences for the media.

4.6.2.1 Gender (in)Sensitive Language

Gender sensitive language (GSL) is part of a non-discriminatory way of speaking and writing. It reflects the political correctness of the one who uses it, as well as the commitment to eliminate discrimination against sex and desire to achieve gender equality. Advocates of *traditional structural linguistics* outline language as a homogeneous, static and independent system that is completely separate from the social context in which it is used. *Modern sociolinguistics* are of the opinion that language is a product of social interactions; various political, economic and cultural factors can have hidden effects on the system of social relations.[94] One typical language areas where this disparity is most clearly reflected is the asymmetric relationship between members of the society. This refers to the established practice of using the masculine form for titles and professions performed not only by men, but also by women. By using the masculine form to denote the woman's occupation, instead of feminine form, women remain linguistically invisible in the public and political sphere, supporting the patriarchal role model of women in a society.[95] A *critical sociolinguistics* go a step further by claiming these language differences are determined by hegemony and dominance of one group of members of a society over another. Comparatively *theory of dominance* labels men as creators of these discriminatory language practices, which were made with the intention to keep women in a subordinate position.[96]

4.6.2.2 Hegemonic Masculinity

This concept is commonly defined as the prevailing gender norm; the predominant gender construct that can be related to the dominant gender regime and the wider social environment or heteronormative model of gender relations, identities and roles.[97] These gender roles, which were accepted during the process of socialization, are treated as the most culturally desirable within a particular society; "imaginary social standard". These gender regimes lead to the underestimation, and consequently, discrimination of women and any other non-hegemonic identity in public spaces. In Connell's words, hegemonic masculinity "was distinguished from other masculinities, especially subordinated masculinities. Hegemonic masculinity was not assumed to be normal in the statistical sense; only a minority of men might enact it. But it was certainly normative. It embodied the currently most honoured way of being a man, it required all other men to position themselves in relation to it, and it ideologically legitimated the global subordination of women to men".[98] Contrastingly, it is also

---

[94] Filipović (2011), pp. 409–410.

[95] Begović (2015), p. 64; Savić (2004), p. 4; To see more on recommendation for conscientiously, sensitive and non-discriminatory use of language, Savić (2009), pp. 9–27.

[96] Stevanović (2019), pp. 65–69; Filipović (2011), pp. 410–411.

[97] Hughson (2017), pp. 39, 21; Anđelković (2015), pp. 50–51.

[98] Connell and Messerschmidt (2005), p. 32.

defined a "negative standard" in which various subversive patterns of practices primarily reflect male dominance over women, as well as over LGBTQIA+ people. Some of these typical practices are homophobia (seeing homosexuality as counter-hegemony) and male heterosexuality as the only accepted means of expressing sexuality;; seeing women as potential sexual objects to provide sexual validation to heterosexual men.[99] Despite these inner ambivalences, a conventional, heterosexual masculinity is seen as "culturally idealized form of masculine character".[100]

In comparison to the aforementioned rigid conditions of "being a real man", other forms of masculinities are perceived as subordinated, incomplete or marginalized.[101] Being more socially accepted and desirable then homosexual masculinity, heterosexual masculinity "oppresses gayness" in different ways; in terms of gay identity, sexual and mental health.[102] Notwithstanding the fact that the conventional notion of hegemonic masculinity in its essence undoubtedly denies various aspects of gay men lives, paradoxically hegemonic masculinity actually pervades (to a certain extent) different spheres of gay partnerships, such as clothing, public appearance, sexual intercourse, and social engagement.[103] In other words, empirical studies have shown that there is a significant percentage of the gay population that is attracted by strong, dominant, and powerful men, whose appearance could be compared with the dominant male partner in heterosexual relation.[104]

As such, hegemonic masculinity has different forms of legitimation in media reporting. This is particularly evident in gender-based violence cases, where media often tend to somewhat "justify" these acts and excuse the behaviour of perpetrators. In particular, instead of loud and clear qualification of a murder, various headlines romantically refer to the "crime of passion", the "destiny similar to the one of Romeo and Juliet", or stipulate the crime was motivated by some sort of woman's infidelity.[105] In this way, hegemonic masculinity continues to exist and grow; it tacitly overcomes even the gender-based violence cases that are driven by such a concept.[106]

[99] Donaldson (1993), p. 644; Jarić (2006), pp. 175–176; Connell and Messerschmidt (2005), p. 832; More on the critics and suggestions for reformulation of hegemonic masculinity as a very much contested theoretical concept Connell and Messerschmidt (2005).

[100] Donaldson (1993), p. 646.

[101] Connell (1992), p. 736.

[102] Edwards (2018).

[103] Edwards (2018); Lanzieri and Hildebrandt (2011); Ravenhill (2018).

[104] Lanzieri and Hildebrandt (2011), p. 287.

[105] Mršević (2019), p. 105. Headlines are usually shaped like this—"A crime of passion", "Killed a woman because he suspected she was cheating on him", "They ended up as Romeo and Juliet", "After he got fired, he killed his wife and kids" etc.

[106] A good example of consequences of hegemonic masculinity is "honour killing" or "customary killing". This type of violence against women, typical for patriarchal sharia societies (Iran, Pakistan, Jordan, India etc.), where women are murdered by their male family members—fathers, brothers or other relatives, if they have acted in a way that such societies consider as dishonorable, sinful or inappropriate. In addition to strict norms of sharia law, these situations are equally grounded on notion of hegemonic masculinity on which women's fathers and brothers were raised. Hadi (2020); Faqir (2001); Cohan (2010).

4.6.3 Rape Culture and Pornography

Ever since women raised their voices in order not to be seen as a property, the issue of rape became an inseparable part of the public feminist struggle for gender equality and justice. Contemporary feministic studies introduce a different perspective, saying that rape is "a part of a sexist ideology and thus helps to reinforce social and structural injustice".[107] Rape culture refers to an environment in which women's rape is tolerated, trivialised, normalized, eroticised and justified through different social, cultural and structural practices, behaviours and discourses.[108]

4.6.3.1 Theoretical Ideas on Rape Culture and Pornography in Feminist Theory

Although some would say it is less visible than the other forms of violence, sexual violence[109] is more widespread than we think.[110] One form of this sometimes "invisible" violence is rape; "physically forced or otherwise coerced penetration – even if slight – of the vulva or anus, using a penis, other body parts or an object".[111] While rape is still a very contested theoretical concept,[112] 'rape culture' refers to social, cultural and structural discourses and practices that allow, and in different ways support, sexual violence. In rape culture, perpetrators are usually not held accountable for their acts and women victims are systematically disbelieved.[113] Blaming victims for being raped is usually followed by doubts and mistrust in the occurrence of rape, often results in justifying the perpetrator or rationalizing rape as a big misunderstanding.[114] Such an opinion is often grounded in the belief that rapists are a specific type of persons, are not someone known to the victim (although 90% of rapes were committed by someone the victim actually knew),[115] or perceptions that rape could happen only to certain types of women.[116] Such manifestation of rapists

---

[107] Hänel (2018), pp. 9–10, 24.

[108] Powell and Henry (2014), p. 2.

[109] Sexual violence is defined as "any sexual act, attempt to obtain a sexual act, unwanted sexual comments or advances, or acts to traffic, or otherwise directed, against a person's sexuality using coercion, by any person regardless of their relationship to the victim, in any setting, including but not limited to home and work". Kurg et al. (2002), p. 149.

[110] Some public institutions worldwide, such as governments, organizations, health institutions, point out that sexual violence is an epidemic. Powell and Henry (2014), pp. 1–22.

[111] Kurg et al. (2002), p. 149.

[112] Rape has different definitions: legal definition—"a sex without consent", clinical definition—"-any form of forcible sexual assault", or widely accepted definition—"sexual aggression that is not sexually motivated", Savino and Turvey (2005), pp. 2, 7.

[113] Buchwald et al. (1993).

[114] Harding (2015), pp. 9, 23–24.

[115] According to the World Health Organization (2002), overall 35% of women worldwide reported having experienced either physical or sexual violence by a partner, or sexual violence by a friend, family member, acquaintance or stranger, Powell and Henry (2014), p. 1.

[116] Harding (2015), pp. 9, 23–24.

and rape victims do not happen in isolation but rather are part of broader gender inequality regimes. Law and institutions that perpetuate and support rape culture, in an active or passive way, contribute to making rape one form of structural violence.[117]

Regarding the connection between rape and pornography, opinions were polarized and heatly debated between feminists. *Anti-pornography feminism* argue that pornography is one form of a sexual violence against women and a source, and product of, misogyny in a society.[118] According to these academics (some would say radical ones), pornography reflects a patriarchal ideology that treats women as sexual objects, where their depersonalized body parts serve exclusively to please a men's sexual desire. By looking provocative into the camera, the pornographic model expresses a desire and willingness to satisfy the male consumer. In this way, we have an impression that women are helpless and submissive objects of a man's desire. In turn this creates and fosters relations of sexual supremacy and domination, in which increasing younger boys and girls are being socialised.[119] Creating a distorted image of a women's body, sexuality and the sexual act itself, pornography fosters rape myths (especially the one that all women fantasize about being raped), erects sexual violence and tempts rape.[120] Outlining that most female models are in some way forced into pornography, the basic motto of these ideas is; "pornography is the theory, and rape is the practice".[121] However, there is a significant gap between these ideas. *Pro-pornography feminists* (also called "pro-sex" or "sex-positive" feminists) lie on the other side of the debate and emphasize positive effects of the pornography such as: free expression of women's sexuality; a sexual stimulation; a kind of erotic art; a social space for women as producers as well as consumers of pornography, and a way of helping men to become a better lovers.[122] So long as no coercion is used, or degrading, dehumanizing scenes are included, each individual can express his sexual right of self-determination through pornography. These ideas resulted in a minority of feminist pornography, as the industry is male-dominated professionally and so, are the consumer profile and sexual practices offered. Theoretically, it represents an alternative and different kind of pornography where actors

[117] Buchwald et al. (1993).

[118] Valić Nedeljković (2008), p. 449.

[119] Ibid.

[120] Russell (1995), pp. 45–79.

[121] Although this motto, created by Robin Morgan, one of the leaders of international feminist movement in 1960–1970s in USA, was very often quoted and notoriously accepted by other representatives of this movement, Berl Kutchinsky conducted an empirical research with an aim to find a causal link between pornography and rape. He investigated the development of rape and the number of attempted rape during the period 1964–1984 in U.S.A., Denmark, Sweden and West Germany. Seeing that in every country the number of rape didn't increase more than any other nonsexual violent crimes, Kutchinsky dismisses the hypothesis that pornography causes rape. Kutchinsky (1991), pp. 47–64.

[122] Potter (2016) https://www.dissentmagazine.org/article/not-safe-for-work-feminist-pornography-matters-sex-wars, visited 31 October 2021.

give, and are in power to revoke, their consent in every moment. The workplace is safer, cleaner and female performers are allowed to engage more creatively on set. Protecting and respecting actors equally and showing sex in a safe and fun way, feminist pornography promotes "positive sexual role modelling".[123]

4.6.3.2 Strategies and Policies for Overcoming Rape Culture

At first glance, maybe the pervasiveness and frequency of rape looks discouraging, however "safety and security do not just happen: they are the result of collective consensus and public investment".[124] Through united action of different social actors, fertile strategies against rape and sexism in general could be developed.[125] In order to transform a rape-supportive culture, as individuals, we should stop thinking about the victims as strangers, but rather as someone's mother, spouse, sister, daughter or friend .[126] More importantly, as a society, we should focus on the social structures that underpin the various forms of sexual violence.[127] We have to combat the victim-blaming cultural pattern, which holds victims as responsible for the crime itself.[128] In that respect, we need to begin educating our educators and increase participation in, or awareness of, (non)institutionalized organizations devoted to ending violence.[129]

Media (re)present (symbolically constructed) information. As a whistle blower, they may prevent, abolish or condemn gender-based violence in the public domain. Yet, certain media still maintain and reproduce culturally shaped stereotypes, ideologies, (rape) myths and prejudices. Nevertheless, media can be influenced by a public who are awake, critical and responsible, and able to deconstruct, and reconstruct, an offered reality. As selective and critical recipients of media content, we will be capable of: forming our own cultural meanings;, analysing media code; criticizing stereotypes, dominant values and ideologies; recognizing implicit discriminatory or sexist messages, and interpreting the multiple meanings of media messages.[130] In this way, we need to actively change the *status quo*, despite how

---

[123] One of the pioneer of the feminist pornography is Candice Vadala, an ex-pornographic model, who started her own company with the words "these movies are sold based on the women, but our sexuality was completely ignored in them." Potter (2016).

[124] Kurg et al. (2002), p. ix.

[125] Hänel (2018), p. 12.

[126] Savino and Turvey (2005), p. 21; Despite the fact that we, most likely, didn't participate in the very act of rape, nor did we watch or relativize such an act, we should not be turning our head away; instead, we need to take rape accusations seriously, to be supportive to a person that have been raped etc. Harding (2015), p. 47.

[127] Powell and Henry (2014), p. 2.

[128] This attitude towards victims has its roots in gender lessons which have been internalized through growing up and has been maintained through the widely accepted beliefs, opinions and behaviors. As Adichie likes to point out, we "...have been raised to think of women as inherently guilty. And they have been raised to expect so little of men that the idea of men as savage beings with no self-control is somehow acceptable." Adichie (2014).

[129] Harding (2015), p. 37.

[130] Filipović and Kuzmanović-Jovanović (2012), pp. 20–21, 28.

uncomfortable it may be. Widespread attention is required regarding gender-based violence, as one of the basic social mechanisms which maintain and reproduce historically unequal relations of social power between men and women, and other self-identities.

4.7 Gender Inequalities in Public Sphere: Politics, Political Institutions, Parties and Governments, Socio-Legal Perspective[131]

The analysis of the main institutions of contemporary political systems, especially democracies, has traditionally been a subject of study in social sciences in general and particularly political science. The crucial roles of the legislative, executive, and judicial powers in the processes of law-making, implementation, and interpretation have been highlighted. One of the most recent and promising lines of research in the study of these political institutions is related to the implementation of the gender perspective. *Gender perspective* in this sense means that institutions are not gender-neutral; rather, they reproduce prevailing norms and values, including those related to inequalities (roles, stereotypes and legal barriers). An aim of this section is to analyse and illustrate the processes by which the phenomenon of male domination is created, maintained, and reproduced in the spaces of political power. In other words, the goal is to show the formal and informal strategies, procedures, and modes of action through which the asymmetrical power relations between the sexes are perpetuated within the framework of political institutions.

4.7.1 Gender Differential Political Socialization and Political Culture

The concept of *political culture* refers to the set of attitudes, beliefs, values, and evaluations that predominate among citizens in relation to their country's political system, and therefore influence their political behaviour.[132] Through the process of political socialisation, which begins in childhood, attitudes, values, and beliefs about political reality are acquired that allow us to understand the political participation and behaviour of individuals. The political socialization of gender begins mainly within the family, but also in the school.[133] This transmits differentiated political expectations associated with femininity and masculinity. Family is important for

[131] This heading is linked to the Public Law chapter, where some of this matters will be discussed.

[132] Almond and Verba (1963).

[133] As we have stated related to educational systems, traditionally, boys are more stimulated than girls to public acting in schools, expressing themselves and their opinion; they are more trained for decision-making and future accepting public roles. Teaching materials and learning outcomes affiliate public social roles to boys much more than to girls. This is one of the symptoms of the social (inequality) reproduction functions in education that pervades educational systems.

developing the type of personality of the child; either autonomous type of personality (crucial for democratic politics), or the heteronomous one (fitting into all forms of undemocratic political orders). A democratic family tends towards child respect and developing the child's autonomous personality. This is more likely to stimulate less traditional, and more equal, roles for both boys and girls.

This leads to women showing less interest in politics compared to men, less capacity to understand politics and to influence public affairs, as well as seeing themselves as less qualified than men to run for political office.[134]

4.7.2 Gender Gap in Political Participation

Political participation is a key element in democratic systems. It consists of all those actions carried out by citizens; the ultimate aim being to influence the political process, whether in the election of political representatives or in the elaboration and implementation of public policies.

The specialized literature has differentiated between conventional and nonconventional political participation, called "politics in narrow sense" and "politics in wider sense".[135] The former includes actions such as voting, participating in electoral campaigns, joining political parties, and contacting public offices. The latter manifests itself in actions that go beyond the institutionalized channels established in democratic societies, generally expressed in the form of civil society actions of a different nature. This can include mass movements, civic protests, manifestations of civil disobedience, and grass-roots actions by collecting signatures, occupying buildings, boycotting events or blocking traffic. A noteworthy example would be the actions carried out by suffragette movements of the nineteenth century and feminist movements of 20th (and twenty-first century).

Studies analysing the explanatory factors of political participation have classified them into two main types. Internal types refer to individual resources, attitudinal orientations, and values. Factors of an external nature are related to institutional and contextual factors. In relation to internal factors, the position that the individual occupies in the social structure, defined fundamentally by his/her level of education and participation in the labour market, determines the availability of more or less free time to become involved in politics, as well as the greater, or lesser, cognitive ability to assimilate and process political information. Likewise, socialization provides the individual with information, resources and behavioural patterns that can lead to an interest in and participation in politics. In contrast, and in relation to internal resources, individual attitudes and values influence the degree of political involvement, and levels of satisfaction, with the political system.[136] In terms of factors external to the individual that may explain political participation, different

134 Fox, Lawless (2011), pp. 59–73.

135 Keane (2003).

136 Verba et al. (1997), pp. 1051–1072.

characteristics of the political context, related to electoral (in)stability, or the (non)-existence of civic organizations, have been identified as facilitating political participation.[137]

Feminist literature has identified the existence of gender differences in political participation that can be explained by a deficit of resources that women suffer from as a social category. This is based on the unequal distribution of family responsibilities and domestic tasks, the availability of free time, and differentiated role socialization. These differences between men and women in political participation are also based on the prevailing gender culture and organizational practices in the very political and social organizations that are supposed to promote political participation, allocate responsibilities based on sexist stereotypes, or with the establishment of participation activities that are incompatible with care schedules.[138]

4.7.3 Women and Men as Candidates for Political Institutions: The Role of Political Parties

The classical literature on political parties have focused on the study of different aspects related to political parties: the origin and evolution of parties; their main characteristics and functions; the models and sources of party financing; their internal structure and organization and the key role that political parties play in the processes of recruitment and selection of political elites.[139]

Political parties are indispensable instruments in the organization of parliaments and governments. These political institutions are nurtured by leaders who have been selected within the parties and who come to power through elections. Parties not only intervene in the selection of candidates for different electoral contests, but they also intervene in the internal selection processes to define their governing bodies and the leaders of the political party itself.[140]

Feminist literature has focused on the analysis of gender bias in political parties, conveying that women's presence decreases as one moves up the party hierarchy. Moreover, the percentage of women in party membership is significantly higher than the level of women's presence in party executive and central bodies. Several studies draw attention to a certain degree of opacity in the recruitment processes and internal functioning of parties.[141] Feminist literature argues that it is precisely these mechanisms, more or less explicitly, that are behind the lesser presence of women in political parties compared to their male colleagues. This perpetuates a logic of male recruitment and functioning.[142]

---

[137] Kriesi et al. (1992), pp. 219–244.

[138] Lovenduski (2005).

[139] Sartori (1976).

[140] Norris and Lovenduski (1995).

[141] Verge and De la Fuente (2014), pp. 67–79.

[142] Verge and Claveria (2017), pp. 91–114.

4.7.4 Gender and Three Dimensions of Political Representation: Descriptive, Symbolic, and Substantive

Feminist political theory has introduced explanations, ways of understanding and approaches to what political representation entails. Such theory questions and problematises some of the central tenets of the classical literature, showing the importance of power asymmetries between the sexes in the framework of political institutions. This is in relation not only to the differential numerical presence of men and women in parliaments and governments, but also to their symbolic impact and substantive political action. It thus implies the necessity of paying attention to gender and its political implications in the public sphere.[143]

4.7.4.1 Women and Numeric Political Representation: The Relevance of Critical Mass Theory

The descriptive dimension of representation, also known as the demographic, social, or microcosmic approach to representation, focuses on the composition of institutions. This considers that they should be as accurate a reflection as possible of the gender of the population they represent, in order to achieve the best possible articulation of the citizens' interests.[144] *Being* in politics is justified for reasons of equity and fair distribution of social positions and resources. The presence of women is thus an indicator of democratic legitimacy. Within this framework of analysis, '*the theory of critical mass*' becomes particularly relevant. It points out that when traditionally under-represented groups, in this case women, in the political arena reach a critical mass, institutions and public policy will be feminized.[145]

A large body of literature has identified the explanatory factors that determine the level of women's presence in institutions of political representation, especially in parliaments and governments; institutional,[146] socioeconomic,[147] and cultural or ideological factors.[148] Feminist literature has particularly highlighted that quotas are a key institutional mechanism for improving the descriptive dimension of political representation.[149] This, and other related issues, will be discussed in the chapter of Public Law.

Studies linked to women's participation in government show the progressive presence of women in government occupying spaces traditionally considered masculine.[150] However, their differential presence according to ministerial portfolios (greater in areas linked to family, health or education issues) and levels of

[143] Phillips (1995).

[144] Pitkin (1967).

[145] Dahlerup (1988), pp. 275–298.

[146] Caul (1999), pp. 79–98.

[147] Rosenbluth et al. (2006), pp. 165–192.

[148] Norris and Inglehart (2001), pp. 126–140.

[149] Lépinard and Rubio-Marín (2018).

[150] Bauer and Tremblay (2011).

government (higher rates of female presence in local governments than in regional or national governments) highlights the sexist impact of stereotypes and their cultural transfer to the public space.[151] Despite the critical mass, if gender sensitivity among women politicians is absent, insofar as merely following the male political acting model, we would remain at the initial starting point. In this sense, there is a growing body of literature arguing for policy change when women are in power; developing differential skills, concerns and priorities.

4.7.4.2 Women as Political Symbols: Role Model Effect

The symbolic dimension of political representation is analysed on the basis of the feelings, beliefs, and attitudes that the representative awakens, or generates, in the represented. Representation is thus determined by the extent to which citizens recognize, accept, and believe in the symbol of the representative.[152] Analysing the symbolic dimension of political representation from a gender perspective therefore involves showing the process of social construction of men and women as political symbols, and the differential impact that this gender construction can have on representatives and the represented.[153]

It is worth noting here that the literature analysing the interrelations among gender, political representation, and mass media is in terms of the latter's capacity to (re)produce existing social prejudices about women's abilities as political elites.[154] On the other hand, mass media could play the opposite emancipatory role. Nevertheless, women to a greater extent than men, are (re)presented to the electorate on the basis of their physical appearance, age, family model, and lifestyle. This is to the detriment of their reliability as elites, confirming the mass media have the ability to trivialise and render women politicians invisible in symbolic terms. In short, the mass media, in their process of symbolic construction of gender, can reduce or even nullify the possibilities of broadening citizens' views of gender and politics, as well as their perceptions of the role of women in politics.[155]

4.7.4.3 Women Who Are 'Doing' in Politics: A Feminist Agenda and Feminine Political Style

The third dimension of political representation focuses on what, in Pitkin's terms, is known as the 'substantive activity of representation'.[156] Namely, the represented is made present in a legislature by the representative's actions. From this perspective, the focus of attention is on the decisions that are taken in the parliamentary chambers, both in terms of the content of the political process and the form or style in which the representative exercises his or her task. Research has shown that

[151] Claveria (2014), pp. 1156–1176.

[152] Lombardo and Meier (2014).

[153] Childs (2008).

[154] García-Blanco and Wahl-Jorgensen (2013), pp. 422–41.

[155] Verge and Pastor (2018), pp. 26–50.

[156] Pitkin (1967).

women tend to have characteristic priorities and ways of acting, that are manifested in an agenda closer to women's issues and interests. This extends to establishing a different way of doing politics; one more focused on consensus and attention to civil society actors, as opposed to the confrontational and hierarchical style of men.[157] It is also necessary to mention that women in politics sometimes imitate/copy the traditional male role in politics, happening too often, particularly in more traditional societies and authoritarian political orders.

However, when the interrelationships among the three dimensions of political representation was studied in depth, the critical mass theory was progressively replaced by other arguments that showed the importance of *critical actors* who, because of their feminist attitudinal orientations,[158] their seniority as representatives,[159] or their positional power within parliamentary chambers,[160] have the capacity to carry out *critical acts* aimed to improve the female presence in the political life.

4.8 Conclusion

The interplay between social practices and law is studied through sociology of law. This strives to examine law not only as the product of state, but also as a social phenomenon. Moreover, gender as a social construct is regulated by law, itself a social product. Thus, gender and gender relations are very important keys in socio-legal studies.

This chapter gives an in-depth view of how gender stands as an important element of studying law and society, and how the lack of gender perspective in socio-legal research fails to grasp the essence of social relations upon which human lives are built. The chapter's key points are to (1) highlight feminists' critical analysis of gender and gender relations within law, (2) deconstruct power as discursively constructed and dispersed through social institutions, and (3) problematise structural inequalities and violence through feminist socio-legal research and activism.

This chapter elaborates on how gender socialization, and different values, attitudes, norms, behaviours, and expectations in society reinforces traditional gender roles determined by biological sex. Moreover, it reflects on how gender regimes of inequality are affected by intersections including race, class, gender identity, sexual orientation, poverty, disability, and age.

To this end, this chapter examines very important forms of gender structural violence due to gender structural inequalities. Thus, the chapter investigates feminist socio-legal perspectives on matters such as the social family transformation, rape (marital and statutory rape), child marriage, intimate partner violence, economic

[157] Mateo-Díaz (2005).

[158] Tremblay and Pelletier (2000), pp. 381–405.

[159] Beckwith (2007), pp. 27–49.

[160] Kathlene (1994), pp. 560–585.

violence, unequal access to health care and education, unequal labour market, sexual objectification of women, and lack of access to political participation.

Questions

1. **Understanding non-heteronormative and gender variant:** The objective of this activity is to learn what is gender and how gender relations are constituted.
   Choose a few legislations from your home country or a country of choice and investigate how these legislations address, define and approach gender? What type of gender system do they reinforce and how? Write amendments to the legislations by presenting your arguments.
2. **Understanding the effects of structural inequalities:** The objective of this activity is to learn how structural inequalities affect people in public and private sphere.
   Conduct desk research and examine which countries in Europe have legalised or criminalised abortion or forced sterilisation/forced infertility treatment against trans people, ethnical women groups and women with disabilities. Choose two different contexts and find out what have been the driving forces for and against legalising or criminalising such practices. Identify the intersections of power relations between the legal, medical, and social institutions in each context and reflect on how such issues are social problems in need of social solution.
3. **Understanding changes in institutions of family and marriage:** The objective of this activity is to learn about different family models and how policies based on different models of family affect people's experiences in society.
   Share your experiences and discuss how would you problematise and introduce policy changes in the realm of family and marriage.
4. **The welfare state and good practices in attention to equality in the working family and conciliation:** The development of this section will be carried out through a practical exercise by the students. The basis for the analysis and sharing of good practices will be the information provided by, among other organisations, the European Institute for Gender Equality (EIGE), the International Labour Organization (ILO), and other sources of official organisations by country.
   Objectives:
   1. Make visible and highlight successful experiences in certain countries on public policies facilitating the reconciliation of work and family life for men.
   2. Present and analyse employment policies in different countries that have effectively contributed to the reconciliation of work and family life,

(continued)

disaggregated by sex: those aimed at paternity and those aimed at maternity.
3. Determine the frequency with which these practices are used by men and women separately.

5. **Understanding the difference between verbal and non-verbal consent:** This activity is to be performed interactively and in pairs. Each student must clearly show to his/her colleague when he/she feels uncomfortable because of such a colleague's behaviour. Student can express his/her uncomfortableness in three ways: 1. through body language with his/her eyes, 2. through body language with his/her hands and 3. verbally, i.e., by using words. The aim of the exercise is to see that sometimes it is quite difficult to say "no" and that (absence of) consent can be communicated in other ways, which is why we should respect the autonomy of others to understand that sexual acts need to be agreed and accepted by both partners equally.
6. **Understanding the gender-insensitive language:** Students will receive various copies of daily newspapers which reported on gender-based violence. Their task will be to find examples of (in)adequate reporting, i.e., the use of gender-insensitive language, the justification of violence through the practice of hegemonic masculinity, rape myths and forms of rape culture, etc. The goal of this exercise is to learn on the (in)adequate reporting, i.e., how to recognize, define and, finally, recommend more appropriate forms of reporting on gender-based violence.

References

Acker J (2006) Inequality regimes: gender, class, and race in organizations. Gend Soc 20:441–464. https://doi.org/10.1177/0891243206289499

Acker J (2009) From glass ceiling to inequality regimes. Sociologie du Travail 51:199–217. https://doi.org/10.1016/j.soctra.2009.03.004

Adichie CN (2014) We should all be feminists. Vintage

Aguado E (2018) Segregación ocupacional: una mirada crítica a la participación tamizada de las mujeres en el empleo. Occupational segregation: a critical overview of sifting participation of women in employment. Universitat de València, Valencia

Almond G, Verba S (1963) The civic culture. Political attitudes and democracy in five nations. Princeton University Press, Princeton

Anđelković B (2015) Hegemoni maskulinitet u muškim zatvorima u Srbiji. Antropologija 15:49–70

Babović M, Ginić K, Vuković O (2010) Mapiranje porodičnog nasilja prema ženama u Centralnoj Srbiji. SeConS, Beograd

Banakar R (2008) The politics of legal cultures. University of Westminster School of Law Research Paper 10(1)

Bartlett KT (2020) Gender law: after twenty-five years. Duke J Gender Law Policy 27:1–23

Bauer G, Tremblay M (2011) Women in executive power, a global review. Routledge, London

Beckwith K (2007) Numbers and newness: the descriptive and substantive representation of women. Can J Polit Sci 40:27–49
Beghini V, Pozzani U, Cattaneo E (2019) A Quantum Leap for Gender Equality: for a Better Future of Work for All. https://www.ilo.org/global/publications/books/WCMS_674831/lang%2D%2Den/index.htm. Accessed 31 Oct 2021
Begović B (2015) Upotreba rodno osetljivog jezika i prikaz žena u štampanim medijima u Srbiji. CM Komunikacija i mediji 10:59–79
Bermúdez-Figueroa E, Roca B (2019) Silenced narratives of women's participation in labour and political struggle in Spain, 1960–1975. Labor Hist 00:1–14. https://doi.org/10.1080/0023656X.2019.1573976
Bettio F, Verashchagina A (2009) Gender segregation in the labour market: root causes and policy responses in the EU. Luxembourg: European Union. European Commission, Brussels
Billing YD (2011) Are women in management victims of the phantom of the male norm? Gend Work Organ 18:298–317. https://doi.org/10.1111/j.1468-0432.2010.00546.x
Boll C, Lagemann A (2018) Gender pay gap in EU countries based on SES (2014). Luxembourg, Publication Office of the European Union 10. https://doi.org/10.2838/978935
Buchwald E, Fletcher PR, Roth M (1993) Transforming a rape culture. Milkweed Editions, Minneapolis
Butler J (1990) Gender trouble, feminist theory, and psychoanalytic discourse. Routledge, London
Caul M (1999) Women's representation in parliament: the role of political parties. Party Polit 5:79–98
Cebrián López I (2015) Tiempo cotizado, ingresos salariales y sus consecuencias para las pensiones: diferencias por género al final de la vida laboral. Cuadernos de Relaciones Laborales 33:311–328. https://doi.org/10.5209/rev_crla.2015.v33.n2.50318
Chant S (2015) The 'Feminization of Poverty': A Reflection 20 Years After Beijing. https://www.unrisd.org/beijing+20-chant. Accessed 31 Oct 2021
Chatzitheochari S (2012) Class, gender and time poverty: a time-use analysis of British workers' free time. Br J Sociol 63:451–471
Childs S (2008) Women and British party politics: descriptive, symbolic and substantive representation. Routledge, London
Claveria S (2014) Still a 'male business'? Explaining women's presence in executive office. West Eur Polit 37:1156–1176
Cohan JA (2010) Honor killings and the cultural defense. Calif West Int Law J 40:101–175
Conaghan J (2008) Intersectionality and the feminist project in law. In: Intersectionality and beyond. Routledge-Cavendish, pp 37–64
Connell RW (1992) A very straight gay: masculinity, homosexual experience, and the dynamics of gender. Am Sociol Rev 57:735–751
Connell RW (2005) Masculinities. Polity, Cambridge
Connell RW (2006a) Glass ceilings or gendered institutions? Mapping the gender regimes of public sector worksites. Public Adm Rev 66:837–849
Connell RW (2006b) The experience of gender change in public sector organizations. Gend Work Organ 13:435–452
Connell RW (2011) Confronting equality: gender, knowledge and global change. Polity, Cambridge
Connell RW (2016) Masculinities in global perspective: hegemony, contestation, and changing structures of power. Theory Soc 45:303–318. https://doi.org/10.1007/s11186-016-9275-x
Connell RW, Messerschmidt JW (2005) Hegemonic masculinity: rethinking the concept. Gend Soc 19:829–859
Connell RW, Pears R (2015) Gender in world perspective. Polity, Cambridge
Cooper D (1993) An engaged state: sexuality, governance, and the potential for change. J Law Soc 20:257–276
Dahlerup D (1988) From a small to a minority: women in Scandinavian politics. Scandinavian Polit Stud 11:275–298

Donaldson M (1993) What is hegemonic masculinity? Theory Soc 22:643–657
Edwards AM (2018) The role of hegemonic masculinity in gay men's health disparities. University Honors Theses. https://pdxscholar.library.pdx.edu/honorstheses/586/. Accessed 31 Oct 2021
EIGE (2014) Gender inequalities in care and consequences on the labour market. https://doi.org/10.1128/AAC.03728-14. Accessed 31 October 2021
EIGE (2017) Gender issue(s) | European Institute for Gender Equality. https://eige.europa.eu/thesaurus/terms/1196. Accessed 31 October 2021
EPIC (2013) Sweden: Successful reconciliation of work and family life. https://ec.europa.eu/eurostat/statistics-explained/index.php?title=Reconciliation_of_work_and_family_life_-_statistics&oldid=511883. Accessed 31 Oct 2021
Etienne CF (2019) Addressing masculinity and men's health to advance universal health and gender equality. https://iris.paho.org/bitstream/handle/10665.2/49698/v42e1962018.pdf?sequence=1&isAllowed=y. Accessed 31 Oct 2021
European Commission (2014) Tackling the gender pay gap. European Commission, Brussels
European Trade Union Confederation (ETUC) (2014) Bargaining for equality. ETUC, Brussels
EUROSTAT (2019) Education and training in the EU – facts and figures. https://ec.europa.eu/eurostat/statistics-explained/index.php?title=Education_and_training_in_the_EU_-_facts_and_figures
Faqir F (2001) Intrafamily femicide in defence of honour: the case of Jordan. Third World Q 22:65–82
Fawole OI (2008) Economic violence to women and girls: is it receiving the necessary attention? Trauma Violence Abuse 9:167–177
Filipović J (2011) Rod i jezik. In: Milivojević I, Markov S (eds) Uvod u rodne teorije. Mediterran Publishing, Novi Sad, pp 409–419
Filipović J, Kuzmanović-Jovanović A (2012) Vodič za rodno osetljiv pristup medijima u Srbiji – preporuke i dosadašnja praksa. Uprava za rodnu ravnopravnost, Beograd
Fletcher R (2002) Feminist legal theory. An introduction to law and social theory. Hart Publishing, London
Fox RL, Lawless JL (2011) Gendered perceptions and political candidacies: a central barrier to women's equality in electoral politics. Am J Polit Sci 55:59–73
Franzway S, Fonow MM (2011) Making feminist politics: transnational alliances between women and labor. Making feminist politics: transnational alliances between women and labor. University of Illinois Press, Illinois
Fraser N (2000) Rethinking recognition. New Left Rev 3:107–118
Fraser N (2001) Social justice in the knowledge society: redistribution, recognition, and participation. Heinrich Boll Stiftung 5:1–13
Galtung J (1969) Violence, peace, and peace research. J Peace Res 6:167–191
Glasier A, Gülmezoglu M, Schmid GP, Moreno CG, Van Look PFA (2006) Sexual and reproductive health: a matter of life and death. Lancet 368:1595–1607
Hadi A (2020) Honor' killings in misogynistic society: a feminist perspective. AJIS 9:29–37
Hall S (2001) Encoding, decoding. In: During S (ed) The cultural studies reader. Routledge, London, pp 507–517
Hamilton F, La Diega N (2020) Same-sex relationships, law and social change. Routledge, London
Hänel HC (2018) What is rape? Social theory and conceptual analysis. Columbia University Press, New York
Harding K (2015) Asking for it – the alarming rise of rape culture – and what we can do about it. Da Capo Press, Boston
Hartmann H (1981) The family as the locus of gender, class, and political struggle: the example of housework. Signs 6:366–394
Hines S (2010) Recognising diversity? The gender recognition act and transgender citizenship. In: Hines S (ed) Transgender identities. Routledge, London, pp 101–119

Hubbard P, Matthews R, Scoular J (2008) Regulating sex work in the EU: prostitute women and the new spaces of exclusion. Gend Place Cult 15:137–152. https://doi.org/10.1080/09663690701863232
Hughson M (2017) Muškarci u Srbiji – druga strana rodne ne/ravnopravnosti. Institut za kriminološka i sociološka istraživanja, Beograd
International Labour Organization (2020) Facts on women at work. www.ilo.org/gender
Jarić I (2006) Rekonfiguracija hegemonih modela (muških i ženskih) rodnih uloga u procesu transformacije srpskog društva. Filozofija i društvo 30:175–191
Kathlene L (1994) Power and influence in state legislative policymaking: the interaction of gender and position in committee hearing debates. Am Polit Sci Rev 88:560–585
Keane J (2003) Global civil society? Cambridge University Press, Cambridge
Kellner D, Share J (2005) Toward critical media literacy: core concepts, debates, organizations, and policy. Disc Stud Cult Polit Edu 26:369–386
Kirton G (2005) The influences on women joining and participating in unions. Ind Relat J 36:386–401. https://doi.org/10.1111/j.1468-2338.2005.00366.x
Kirton G (2013) Gender and leadership in unions. Florence Taylor and Francis, Florence
Kirton G, Guillaume C (2017) Work, employment and engagement conditions in a female-dominated public service occupation after restructuring/outsourcing. Ind Relat J 48:482–499. https://doi.org/10.1111/irj.12196
Kriesi H, Koopmans R, Duyvendak JW, Giugni M (1992) New social movements and political opportunities in Western Europe. Eur J Polit Res 22:219–244
Krug EG et al (2002) The world report on violence and health. Lancet 360(9339):1083–1088
Kutchinsky B (1991) Pornography and rape: theory and practice? Evidence from crime data in four countries where pornography is easily available. Int J Law Psychiatry 14:47–64
Lanzieri N, Hildebrandt T (2011) Using hegemonic masculinity to explain gay male attraction to muscular and athletic men. J Homosex 58:275–293
Lasio D, Congiargiu N, De Simone S, Serri F (2019) Gender fundamentalism and heteronormativity in the political discussion about lesbian and gay parenthood. Sexual Res Soc Policy 16:501–512
Lépinard E, Rubio-Marín R (2018) Transforming gender citizenship: the irresistible rise of gender quotas in Europe. Cambridge University Press, Cambridge
Lindskog A (2020) The Invisibility of Economic Violence in Swedish Legal and Gender Equality Policy Discourse. http://umu.diva-portal.org/smash/get/diva2:1451156/FULLTEXT01.pdf. Accessed 31 Oct 2021
Lombardo E, Meier P (2014) The symbolic representation of gender. A discursive approach. Ashgate, Surrey and Burlington
Lovenduski J (2005) Feminizing politics. Polity, Cambridge
Lubina T, Klimpak IB (2014) Rodni stereotipi: objektivizacija ženskog lika u medijima. Pravni vjesnik 30:213–231
MacKinnon CA (1983) Feminism, Marxism, method, and the state: toward feminist jurisprudence. Signs J Women Cult Soc 8:635–658
Mateo-Díaz M (2005) Representing women? Female legislators in west European parliaments. ECPR Press, Colchester
Mays JM (2006) Feminist disability theory: domestic violence against women with a disability. Disabil Soc 21:147–158
Mikucka M (2008) Variation in women's employment across European countries: the impact of child care policy solutions. Int J Sociol 38:12–37
Milivojević S (2004) Žene i mediji: Strategije isključivanja. Genero : časopis za feminističku teoriju i studije kulture Special 4–5:11–24
Moodley J, Graham L (2015) The importance of intersectionality in disability and gender studies. Agenda 29:24–33
Mršević Z (2017) Mediji u Srbiji o rodno zasnovanom nasilju u 2015. i 2016. godini: Kako protiv nasilja – uloga medija. https://cpz.rs/Dokumenti/Kako-protiv%20nasilja-uloga%20medija.pdf. Accessed 31 Oct 2021

Mršević Z (2019) Nasilje i mi – mediji o nasilju nad ženama. Institut društvenih nauka, Beograd

Mullins L, Saldivar K (2015) Seven: research associating gender and government privatization: lessons from international literature. Wagadu: a J Transnatl Women's Gender Stud 14:169–186

Namaste V (2000) Invisible lives: the erasure of transsexual and transgendered people. University of Chicago Press, Chicago

Norris P, Inglehart R (2001) Cultural obstacles to equal representation. J Democr 12:126–140

Norris P, Lovenduski J (1995) Political recruitment. Gender, race and class in the British parliament. Cambridge University Press, Cambridge

Nowicka W (2007) The struggle for abortion rights in Poland. Sex Politics–Reports from the Front Lines 167–196

Phillips A (1995) The politics of presence. Oxford University Press, Oxford

Pitkin HF (1967) The concept of representation. University of California Press, Berkeley

Postmus JL, Sara B et al (2011) Understanding economic abuse in the lives of survivors. J Interpers Violence 27:411–430

Potter C (2016) Not Safe for Work: Why Feminist Pornography Matters. https://www.dissentmagazine.org/article/not-safe-for-work-feminist-pornography-matters-sex-wars. Accessed 31 Oct 2021

Powell A, Henry N (2014) Framing sexual violence prevention what does it mean to challenge a rape culture? In: Henry N, Powell A (eds) Preventing sexual violence interdisciplinary approaches to overcoming a rape culture. Palgrave Macmillan, London, pp 1–22

Prieto C, Pérez De Guzmán S (2013) Desigualdades laborales de género, disponibilidad temporal y normatividad social. Revista Espanola de Investigaciones Sociologicas 141:113–132. https://doi.org/10.5477/cis/reis.141.113

Radibratović EM (2020) Rodna dihotomija u diskursu onlajn medija. https://uvidok.rcub.bg.ac.rs/handle/123456789/4011. Accessed 31 Oct 2021

Ravenhill JP (2018) Gay masculinities: a mixed methods study of the implications of hegemonic and alternative masculinities for gay men. University of Sussex, Sussex

Rich A (1980) Compulsory heterosexuality and lesbian existence. Signs J Women Cult Soc 5 (4):631–660

Rich AC (2003) Compulsory heterosexuality and lesbian existence (1980). J Women's Hist 15:11–48

Richardson D (2007) Patterned fluidities:(Re) imagining the relationship between gender and sexuality. Sociology 41:457–474

Rosenbluth F, Salmond R, Thies MF (2006) Welfare works: explaining female legislative representation. Polit Gend 2:165–192

Rottleuthner H (1989) The limits of law: the myth of a regulatory crisis. Int J Sociol Law 17:273–285

Rubery J, Hebson G (2018) Applying a gender lens to employment relations: revitalisation, resistance and risks. J Ind Relat 60:414–436. https://doi.org/10.1177/0022185618766680

Rubery J, Smith M, Fagan C (1998) National working-time regimes and equal opportunities. Fem Econ 4:71–101. https://doi.org/10.1080/135457098338572

Russell DEH (1995) Pornography and rape: a causal model. Prev Hum Serv 12:45–79

Sartori G (1976) Parties and party systems, a framework for analysis. Cambridge University Press, Cambridge

Savić S (2004) Žena skrivena jezikom medija: kodeks neseksističke upotrebe jezika. https://www.zenskestudie.edu.rs/izdavastvo/elektronska-izdanja/casopis-zenske-studije/zenske-studije-br-10/193-zena-sakrivena-jezikom-medija-kodeks-neseksisticke-upotrebe-jezika. Accessed 31 Oct 2021

Savić S, Čanak M, Mitro V, Štasni G (2009) Rod i jezik. Ženske studije i istraživanja i Futura publikacije, Novi Sad

Savino JO, Turvey BE (2005) Defining rape and sexual assault. In: Savino JO, Turvey BE (eds) Rape investigation handbook. Academic, Cambridge, pp 1–22

Snježana M (2001) Javnost i ideološki efekti medija. Reč – časopis za književnost i kulturu, i društvena pitanja 64:151–213
Stevanović MM (2019) Rodno osetljiv jezik u medijskoj praksi u Srbiji. Filologija 19:64–81
Stryker S, Whittle S (2006) The transgender studies reader. Taylor & Francis, Oxfordshire
Tremblay M, Pelletier R (2000) More feminist or more women? Descriptive and substantive representation of women in the 1997 Canadian federal elections. Int Polit Sci Rev 21:381–405
UN Women (2020) Facts and figures: Ending violence against women | What we do. https://www.unwomen.org/en/what-we-do/ending-violence-against-women/facts-and-figures. Accessed 31 Oct 2021
Valić Nedeljković D (2008) Rod i mediji. Uvod u rodne teorije:447–459
Verba S, Burns N, Schlozman KL (1997) Knowing and caring about politics: gender and political engagement. J Polit 59:1051–1072
Verge T, De la Fuente M (2014) Playing with different cards: party politics, gender quotas and women's empowerment. Int Polit Sci Rev 35(1):67–79
Verge T, Claveria S (2017) Party office, homosocial capital and gendered political recruitment. In: Waylen G (ed) Gender and informal institutions. Rowman and Littlefield, London, pp 91–114
Verge T, Pastor R (2018) Women's political firsts and symbolic representation. J Women Polit Policy 39:26–50
Višnjić J, Mirosavljević M (2008) Problem reprezentacije roda u medijima. In: Zaharijević A (ed) Neko je rekao feminizam?- Kako je feminizam uticao na žene XXI veka. Heinrich Böll Stiftung, Beograd, pp 248–262
Vujadinović D (2016) Teorijsko-metodološki okvir za razumevanje rodnih odnosa - slučaj Srbije. In: Lilić S (ed) Pravni kapaciteti Srbije za evropske integracije. Univerzitet u Beogradu, Beograd, pp 99–111
Vujadinović D, Stanimirović V (2016) Rodni odnosi u Srbiji u doba tranzicije - Između repatrijarhalizacije i emancipacije. In: Dajević G, Vranić B (eds) Demokratska tranzicija Srbije - (re)kapitulacija prvih 20 godina. Univerzitet u Beogradu, Beograd, pp 189–215
Walklate S, Fitz-Gibbon K, McCulloch J (2018) Is more law the answer? Seeking justice for victims of intimate partner violence through the reform of legal categories. Criminol Crim Just 18:115–131
Wood JT (1994) Gendered media: the influence of media on views of gender. https://www1.udel.edu/comm245/readings/GenderedMedia.pdf. Accessed 31 Oct 2021
World Health Organization (2002) Report on Violence and Health – 2002. https://www.who.int/violence_injury_prevention/violence/world_report/en/summary_en.pdf. Accessed 31 Oct 2021
Yates CAB (2011) Organizing women in the spaces between home, work and community. Relations industrielles 66:585–604. https://doi.org/10.7202/1007635ar
Young IM (2011) Justice and the politics of difference. Princeton University Press, Princeton

Further Reading

Banakar R, Travers M (2005) Law, sociology and method. Hart Publishing, London
Connell RW, Messerschmidt JW (2005) Hegemonic masculinity: rethinking the concept. Gender Soc 19:829–859
Hunter R (2019) Feminist approaches to socio-legal studies. In: Creutzfeldt N, Mason M, McConnachie K (eds) Routledge handbook of socio-legal theory and methods. Routledge, London, pp 260–272
Masselot A (2007) The state of gender equality law in the European Union. Eur Law J 13:152–168
Munro VE (2016) The Ashgate research companion to feminist legal theory. Routledge, London
Pastor R, Verge T (2021) The symbolic representation of women's political firsts in editorial cartoons. Fem Media Stud:1–16

Feminist Judgments

5

Marco Evola, Ivana Krstić, and Fuensanta Rabadán

Contents

Authors are listed in alphabetical order. Sections 5.4 and 5.6 are authored by Marco Evola, Ivana Krstić authored Sects. 5.2, 5.3.1, 5.3.2.2.1, 5.3.2.2.3, 5.3.2.4 and 5.5. Sections 5.3.2.1, 5.3.2.2.2 and 5.3.2.3 are written by Fuensanta Rabadán Sánchez-Lafuente.

M. Evola (✉)
LUMSA, Department of Law, Palermo, Italy
e-mail: m.evola@lumsa.it

I. Krstić
University of Belgrade Faculty of Law, Belgrade, Serbia
e-mail: ikrstic@ius.bg.ac.rs

F. Rabadán
University of Cadiz, Faculty of Law, Private Law, Cadiz, Spain
e-mail: fuensanta.rabadan@uca.es

D. Vujadinović et al. (eds.), *Gender-Competent Legal Education*, Springer Textbooks in Law, https://doi.org/10.1007/978-3-031-14360-1_5

Abstract

The chapter discusses how the lack of gender knowledge and approach in judicial decision-making can influence the decision and the result of the case. Particular emphasis is given to the role of gender stereotypes and how gender stereotypes bias the working of the bench and the outcome courts achieve. Feminist judgments projects that have been developed worldwide demonstrate that judging is gendered, and women make a difference in the decision-making process. The rising number of women judges makes the bench more representative, although they face many constraints preventing them from asking the woman question. The analysis of the essential features of rewriting judgments in a gender perspective highlights that feminist judgments could contribute to the enhancement and spreading of gender competent legal knowledge.

5.1 Introduction

This section will explain how judges' interpretation of facts relies on their perspective (gender stereotypes), which influences their reasoning and the outcome of cases. Thus leading to discrimination itself. This aspect is usually neglected as there is a perception that judges are very knowledgeable, professional, and objective, while some researches demonstrate that they can be even more biased than the general population.[1] Therefore, it will be explained, having regard to the practice of the Committee on the Elimination of discrimination against women, that gender competent legal knowledge in the judiciary is a necessity to increase the access to justice and more just outcomes of cases with a gender perspective. Gender stereotypes and prejudices will be defined. Finally, the evolution of the gender perspective in the European Court of Human Rights judgments will be studied.

Against the background of stereotypes and prejudices marking the working of the judiciaries, this paper considers the reasons for increasing the representation of women on benches and the limits this solution entrenches. In this perspective, assessing the main features of feminist judgments will substantiate the claim for gender balance in courts and highlight the role it can play in improving and spreading gender competent legal knowledge.

Judges are independent in their assessment of the facts of the case and interpretation of laws, leading to different opinions in the same case. It is particularly evident in cases of international courts when the decision is attached with individual and dissenting opinions. The nature of judicial impartiality, independence, knowledge

[1] For example, Harris and Sen (2018), available at https://scholar.harvard.edu/files/msen/files/bias-judging-arps.pdf; Society for Personality and Social Psychology (2018), available at https://www.sciencedaily.com/releases/2018/04/180403085049.htm.

and experience of judges encourages critical reasoning. However, there is almost no research and perception of how much gender stereotypes can influence the collection of facts and interpretation of existing laws, which are also very often ambiguous.

Gender stereotypes can be defined differently, but one of the possible definitions is:

▶ **Definition** "a generalised view or preconception about attributes or characteristics that are or ought to be possessed by women and men or the roles that are or should be performed by men and women."[2]

Gender stereotypes can be both positive and negative, for example, "women are nurturing" or "women are weak"."[3] However, whether positive or negative, gender stereotypes can have a detrimental effect on both sexes, rightly underlined in the *Konstantin Markin* case before the European Court of Human Rights, which will be mentioned below (Sect. 5.3.2.2).

The usual perception of persons that have gender bias is that women are caretakers at home and in the family, whilst men are meant to be the family's breadwinners.[4] If a person has grown up in that surrounding, it can affect their social identity, anticipated social role, as well as their short-and long-term goals.[5] Nevertheless, if that person is a judge, this perception can lead to a biased decision for example, in divorce cases and especially in regard to custodial rights of children.

In recent years, some feminist scholars have paid particular attention to the issue of judges' bias in delivering judgments and decisions. They raised their voices, by stating that this problem was visible in different jurisdictions and that it can very much influence the reasoning or result of the case.[6] Therefore, several feminist judgments projects around the world very well illustrate that the reasoning or the result of the case can be different if applying a feminist approach.

This chapter contains five sections.

The first one presents different feminist judgment projects that have been developed since 2005. This part covers projects that apply feminist perspectives and rewrite national judgments, and the latest volume rewriting international judgments and decisions.

The second section deals with legal reasoning and underlines the importance of tackling gender stereotyping in decision-making. It was shown that this issue had been neglected, although it can impede access to justice and influence the court reasoning and decision.

---

[2]OHCHR (2014), available at https://www.ohchr.org/Documents/Issues/Women/WRGS/OnePagers/Gender_stereotyping.pdf, last accessed 15 October 2020.

[3]Ibid.

[4]Brewster and Padavic (2000), pp. 477–487.

[5]Eccles et al. (1999), pp. 153–192.

[6]Stanchi et al. (2016), p. 246.

The third section covers the issue of equal representation of men and women in the judiciary and chambers. Although it is essential to achieve greater representation of women on the bench, it is also equally important to train all judges to recognise and combat gender stereotypes and eliminate them during the judicial process. Intersectionality is also more and more important and therefore, this issue needs to cover the representation of women coming from more vulnerable groups in a society.

The fourth section very briefly underlines the importance of rewriting courts' decisions from a gender perspective and its role in the judiciary and society as a whole.

Finally, the last section covers the main features of feminist judgments, dealing with constraints and approaches to feminist judgments.

Learning Goal

The chapter has several learning goals:

- to understand the importance of applying the feminist perspective in legal writing and legal reasoning;
- to identify the main challenges women judges face in applying a gendered law and in working in a legal environment which has been dominated by male judges, highlighting the contribution that feminist judgments can give in order to reshape the legal culture. As well as the main techniques feminist judges can avail themselves of to introduce the feminist view in the everyday working of the bench;
- to be aware how gender perspective and analytical method change the interpretation of facts of the case and/or results of a court decision, which can lead to limited access to justice and/or impunity.

5.2 Feminist Judgements Projects around the World

Feminist judgments projects are a form of 'academic activism,' which appeared worldwide intending to show that prevailing academic and political discourse around the law was limited,[7] especially in terms of failing to make an impact on judicial thinking and judging. The feminist judgment projects emerged from the sense that the judgments did not "do justice" in either process or outcome.[8] Therefore, the primary purpose of feminist judgment projects around the world are to demonstrate that the lack of feminist perspective in key decisions is visible. It leads to unjust results in some cases, while in some other cases it leads to the same result but from different aspects. This perspective is very important as adjudicating is

[7] Hunter et al. (2016), p. 8.

[8] Berger et al. (2020), p. 3.

traditionally seen as a matter for judges themselves and critical assessment in many countries is not a part of legal tradition and culture. In addition, this is a good combination of theory and practice as academics have a possibility to implement the feminist theory in real cases to show different solutions in a concrete case. It is very important as it also shows that "the law is a powerful and productive social discourse which creates and reinforces gender norms".[9]

The feminist projects began in the USA, where two books were published with leading feminist scholars who were invited to rewrite the judgments in the cases *Brown v. Board of Education*[10] and *Roe v. Wade*.[11] Inspired by these publications, in Canada some feminist scholars and litigators, members of the Women's Court, were engaged in writing alternative judgments of some major decisions of the Supreme Court, published in 2007 in the *Canada Journal of Women and the Law*.[12] In Great Britain, *Feminist Judgments: From Theory to Practice* volume was issued in 2010.[13] This book contains twenty-three key decisions of the Court of Appeal and House of Lords, written by feminist legal scholars. In their judgments, the authors dealt with many principles, covering civil law (such as the law of trespass, the test for capacity to marry, the equitable doctrine of undue influence and implied contracts). Other principles dealt with included criminal law (causation, criminal liability for omission and the role of consent in relation to causing actual bodily harm). However, many other areas were also represented including administrative law, migration law, international law, etc. This book was an inspiration for some 25 legal academics and practitioners from across Australia to gather at the workshop in December 2010 and to pursue an Australian project. The Project, which commenced in 2011, is administered by the University of Queensland and in 2014 published its own volume.[14]

The US Feminist Judgments Project gathered a group of leading legal theorists, practitioners, clinicians and law professors who, in a 2016 book *Feminist Judgments: Rewritten Opinions of the United States Supreme Court,* rewrote 25 crucial U.S. Supreme Court cases using feminist reasoning.[15] Also, that following year, the Northern/Irish Feminist Judgments Project published a collection of 26 rewritten judgments.[16] The specific approach of this project was that each judgment also contained an introductory commentary explaining a social background of the case. A wide range of legal areas was represented, such as animal rights, discrimination law, education, employment, evidence, immigration law, medical law, reproductive rights and policing. This book was accompanied by the collection of crucial

[9] Smart (1989).

[10] Balkin (2002).

[11] Balkin (2005).

[12] See Canadian Journal of Women and the Law (2007) 18:1.

[13] Hunter et al. (2010).

[14] Douglas et al. (2014).

[15] Berger et al. (2016).

[16] Enright et al. (2017).

New Zealand judgments. Particular value of this manuscript is the use of complex realities of Maori women's lives.[17]

The Feminist Judgment Project also comprises of some legal academics and practitioners from Africa, India and Scotland, who gathered in July 2019 in Edinburgh to discuss their experience with the Project. The Project from Scotland commenced in 2017, and 2 years later published a volume *Scottish Feminist Judgments: (Re) Creating Law from the Outside.*[18] Academics from India gathered at two workshops and completed a first volume, which consists of 51 judgments.[19] Contributors from Africa launched the project within the Cardiff Law and Global Justice. They had met twice during 2018 intending to discuss the methodology and scope of the future volume, with a focus on decisions from eastern and southern Africa and some cases of the African Commission on Human and People's Rights.[20]

Finally, while all mentioned volumes deal with national judgments, the novelty is the manuscript "Feminist Judgments in International Law", edited by Loveday Hodson and Troy Lavers.[21] This book contains judgments of the Permanent Court of International Justice, the International Court of Justice and the Court of Justice of the EU. Other judgments also include those from the European Court of Human Rights and international courts and hybrid tribunals: International Criminal Court, International Criminal Tribunal for the former Yugoslavia and Special Court of Sierra Leone. Interestingly, it also contains rewritings of a decision of the Committee on the Elimination of all Forms of Discrimination against Women. This book is precious as it also shows that international judges lacked a feminist perspective in some crucial decisions which are a milestone of international law, such as *the Lotus* case. Also, all judgments and decisions were rewritten by several authors working together, compared to other volumes where only one scholar was engaged to rewrite the judgment.

The feminist projects address a range of legal topics and areas such as administrative law, contract law, criminal law, constitutional law, discrimination law, housing, evidence, human rights, etc. However, since 2017, the focus was on specific areas of law, and in this same year, a book on rewriting tax opinions was published,[22] followed by family law, reproductive justice, employment discrimination and tort opinions.[23] However, few case projects mentioned a question of sexual autonomy, sexual equality and identity. For example, the U.S. project deals with

[17] McDonald et al. (2017).

[18] Cowan et al. (2019).

[19] Judgments are available at Righting Together, The Indian Feminist Judgment project, available at: https://www.indianfeministjudgmentsproject.com/cases.

[20] Munro (2020).

[21] Hudson and Lavers (2019).

[22] Crawford and Infanti (2017).

[23] Chamallas and Finley (2020); McGinley and Porter (2020); Rebouchè (2020); Mutcherson (2020).

striking down a state anti-sodomy law on privacy grounds[24] and sexual harassment when the harasser was motivated by the victim's failure to "adhere to masculine (or feminine) stereotypes, including the real or perceived sexual orientation of the victim."[25] The international project included a case of *Goodwin v. the United Kingdom*, decided by the European Court of Human Rights (ECtHR), in which domestic courts refused to recognise the applicant's personal identity.[26] Also, the feminist project, dealing with tax law, contains three opinions which provide new understanding of LGBTQIA+ rights. Issues also include the refusal to grant a medical deduction to a fertile gay man who used reproductive technology in order to have biologically related children. Furthermore, there is the issue of tax deductibility of gender confirmation surgery and lastly the issue of due process and equal protection by treating some state sanctioned same-sex marriages differently from others.[27] With the spread and further development of the feminist judgment projects, it can be expected that more judgments will be rewritten from the gender identity and sexual orientation perspective.

5.3 Gender and Judging

5.3.1 Legal Reasoning

Legal reasoning is the most important logical operation. Depending on different actors in a trial, there are different perspectives on legal reasoning. Clients approach their attorneys with a strong sense of injustice, expecting that they will find legal basis and practice and will integrate this into a persuasive case.[28] Here, legal reasoning is driven by the desired outcome. Legal arguments used by attorneys and evidence provided are essential for the judge's ultimate decision. However, judges will rely on their own background knowledge and experience, thus have their own interpretations of the evidence and understanding of the law. Jurors will stick with instructions on the law and will apply that law to the evidence.[29] Therefore, the most important role in the proceeding is that of a judge who is trained in the law, who applies the law to the facts of the case and relies on different authorities (national case law, international case law and others) to support the main conclusion.

[24] See *Lawrence v. Texas*, 539 U.S. 558 (2003) which was rewritten by Robson (2016), pp. 488–503.

[25] See McGinley (2016), pp. 414–425 at 424.

[26] *Goodwin v. the United Kingdom*, ECtHR, Application No. 28957/95, judgment from 11 July 2002.

[27] See rewritten judgments *Magdalin v. Commissioner*, *O'Donnabhaim v. Commissioner*, and *United States v. Windsor* in Crawford and Infanti (2017), pp. 253–265, 274–297, 306–316.

[28] Ellsworth (2005), p. 685.

[29] Ibid.

There are 2 common methods of reasoning: deductive and analogical. Deductive (rule-based) means that the judge begins with facts of the case, relies on the rule that applies to those facts of the case and delivers a judgement. Rules have at least three parts: (1) a set of elements, called a test; (2) a result that occurs when the test is satisfied; and (3) a casual term which determines whether the result is mandatory, prohibitory, discretionary, or declaratory.[30] However, it is essential to highlight that some rules have exceptions that can change the result if they can be applied in a specific case. On the contrary, analogical legal reasoning means that the judge can examine similarities and differences of the case and previous cases to select an outcome that corresponds to the holding of the case. In contrast to analogical legal reasoning, deductive reasoning is based on distinguishing cases or finding differences among them, the rule does not apply. Reasoning by policy means that a particular rule will be applied to a specific case, if it will create a precedent that would be beneficial for society. Finally, inductive reasoning is the last method, meaning that the lawyer goes from the specific to the general. In other words, the rule is derived from several cases, taking into account their similarities and differences in facts and is synthetised.[31]

All these methods can be used in order to interpret legal norms, which is always indeterminate enough to leave choices of interpretation. If the philosophy behind is gender neutral, the result of the case can be unjust for a party. Therefore, in all legal matters, including interpretation of legal norm, gender perspective should be relevant. But as we will see below, gender stereotypes and prejudices are present in decision making and manifest in the legal rules. This perspective means that it is considered in a process of judgement. Therefore, the writing of legal decisions needs to include legal analyses of social context, including the existence of gender inequalities.

5.3.2 Gender Bias in Court Decisions

5.3.2.1 General Aspects of Gender Bias[32]

The recognition in international and national legal texts of the principle of equality and non-discrimination on the grounds of gender, appears to be an essential first step towards achieving equality between men and women. However, this formal equality has also proved to be insufficient for this purpose. In all areas of society, there are inequalities between women and men based on gender stereotypes or prejudices that cannot be eliminated by simply recognising equality in the rules. It must be borne in mind that, over the centuries, this inequality has been based on the attribution of certain characteristics, functions or roles differentiated by the simple fact of being a

[30]Neumann (2005), p. 16.

[31]See more at Fruehwald (2020), p. 2.

[32]This section has been translated with the translation service of the University Research Institute for Sustainable Social Development (INDESS).

man or a woman in order to keep men in a position of power and women in a position of submission or subjugation.[33]

In order to achieve equality between men and women, the same rights must be recognised for both. Yet but this cannot be done without taking into account the reality of women, the disadvantaged position they have occupied for centuries and which they continue to hold in practice. For example, this happened in the field of work, where labour rights were initially constructed according to a traditionally male parameter in which pregnancy and child-rearing did not exist, because these are traditionally female roles. Thus, placing women at a disadvantage once again, forcing them to choose between either family and work or to face the difficult task of balancing work and family life ("Wollstonecraft dilemma"). The stereotype also persists, to the detriment of men, who want to devote themselves to child-rearing, contrary to what is attributed to them by their gender. All this hinders the creation of a co-responsible parenting model, even though the rules state that fathers and mothers have the same rights and responsibilities over their children. As a result, even though the regulations state that men and women are equal, inequalities based on gender stereotypes persist in different social areas.[34]

Example

The author consulted 30 cases that dealt with custodial rights and the relationship between parents and their children, decided by four appellate courts in Serbia. In most cases, the mother was the sole custodian over the children (around 70%). There is also a growing trend of giving custody to a father. However, it is usually in cases when a mother was characterised as an improper parent due to her unstable personality, had financial difficulties, or a child clearly expressed opinion to stay with a father (sometimes even escaping to live with a father). It was also frequent in cases where a mother was serving a prison sentence, was engaged in jobs that do not correspond to her parenting abilities, such as being characterised of "easy morality" (working as a prostitute).[35] ◄

According to the United Nations Office of the High Commissioner for Human Rights, a gender stereotype is a widely held view or prejudice about attributes or characteristics that men and women possess, or should possess, or about the social roles that both men and women play or should play. A gender stereotype is harmful as it limits men and women's capacity to develop their personal abilities, pursue their professional careers and to make life decisions in general. Harmful stereotypes can be negative (e.g. women are irrational) or seemingly benign (e.g. women are nurturing). For example, based on the latter stereotype, childcare responsibilities

[33] Lousada Arochena (2020), pp. 22–28.

[34] Lousada Arochena (2020), pp. 22–28, 84–85.

[35] Krstic, Gender analysis for the Action "Strengthening the effective legal remedies to human rights violations in Serbia", Council of Europe, 2021. For a more detail study of this issue, see the chapter "Gender competent family law".

often fall mainly on women. Gender stereotyping is the practice of assigning specific attributes, characteristics or roles to an individual person, male or female, only based on their membership in a male or female social group. Gender stereotyping is harmful, as it could lead to violations of fundamental rights and freedoms. An example is the failure to criminalise marital rape, based on the social concept that women are the sexual property of their husbands. A further example is the failure to effectively investigate, prosecute and sentence sexual violence against women, based, for example, on the stereotype that women should protect themselves from sexual violence by dressing and behaving modestly. Wrongful gender stereotypes are a frequent cause of discrimination against women and a contributing factor to the violation of a wide range of rights, including the right to health, adequate standard of living, education, marriage and family relations, work, freedom of expression, freedom of movement, and effective remedy and freedom from gender-based violence.[36]

Therefore, material equality requires removing the gender stereotypes that prevent its achievement through the necessary positive and inclusive measures and actions, but without falling into the trap of paternalism, so that, far from promoting equality, the measures adopted perpetuate these inequalities or stereotypes. Moreover, following a gender perspective is no longer enough to adopt measures focused on a single aspect or sector. Rather, cross-cutting measures are required to remove these gender inequalities or stereotypes, involving different areas (legal, social, educational, etc.) in a connected way (gender mainstreaming).

5.3.2.2 Gender Bias in Court Decisions

The term 'judicial bias' or "judicial stereotyping" can be understood as ascribing particular characteristics, attributes, or roles to individuals, depending on their sex and gender, as well as perpetuating harmful stereotypes by not challenging them.[37] In identifying and combating stereotypes, the judiciary can make a significant contribution to addressing the structural causes of human rights violations and to adopting appropriate, effective and meaningful remedies.[38]

5.3.2.2.1 CEDAW

The main source of obligation to combat gender roles and stereotypes is stipulated in the Convention on the Elimination of All Forms of Discrimination against Women (CEDAW). This Convention underlines in Article 5 (a) that States Parties shall take all appropriate measures to "modify the social and cultural patterns of conduct of men and women, with a view to achieving the elimination of prejudices and customary and all other practices which are based on the idea of the inferiority or the superiority of either of the sexes or on stereotyped roles for men and women." Article 2 (f) reinforces Article 5 (a) by requiring States Parties to take "all

---

[36] https://www.ohchr.org/en/issues/women/wrgs/pages/genderstereotypes.aspx.

[37] OHCHR (2014).

[38] Brems and Timmer (2016), p. 48.

appropriate measures to modify or abolish laws, regulations, customs and practices which constitute discrimination against women." It is clear, from this provision, that the State is responsible to take all appropriate measures to combat gender stereotyping in the judiciary. As it was emphasised in its General Recommendation no. 33 (which will be elaborated in Sect. 5.3.2.2.2), the State needs to provide capacity-building programs for judges, prosecutors, lawyers, law enforcement officials and students on gender equality. As well as to "eliminate gender stereotyping and incorporate a gender perspective into all aspects of the justice system."[39]

These obligations apply to all branches of government, but particularly to the judiciary,[40] and judges themselves need to:

1. refrain from stereotyping (obligation to respect);
2. ensure stereotyping does not infringe human rights (obligation to protect); and
3. ensure women can exercise and enjoy the right to be free from wrongful gender stereotyping (obligation to fulfil).[41]

5.3.2.2.2 General Recommendation No. 33

The Committee on the Elimination of Discrimination against Women[42] has adopted General Recommendation No. 33 on women's access to justice (2015) that, in line with Article 5 a) of CEDAW, there is the obligation of States Parties to adopt the necessary measures to remove gender stereotypes that prevent women from exercising and defending their rights and accessing effective remedies.[43] General Recommendation No. 33 says that "stereotyping and gender bias in the judicial system have far-reaching consequences for women's full enjoyment of their human rights" and that "eliminating stereotyping in the justice systems is a crucial step in ensuring equality and justice for victims and survivors".[44]

It should be borne in mind that the judiciary administers justice in accordance with the law, but that a judges' interpretation of the facts may be conditioned by the existence of gender stereotypes. This may influence their reasoning and the outcome of the case, leading to a discriminatory result.

Thus, even if a law criminalises sexual violence against women, the judge may be contributing to perpetuate a gender stereotype and, ultimately, a situation of inequality. This could be possible if when resolving a specific dispute, the judge considers

---

[39] CEDAW, General Recommendation No. 33 on women's access to justice, CEDAW/C/GC/233 (2015), para. 29.

[40] CEDAW, General Recommendation No. 28 on the Core Obligation of States Parties under Article 2 of the Convention on the Elimination of All Forms of Discrimination against Women, CEDAW/C/GC/28 (2010), para. 39.

[41] Ibid.

[42] On the role of the Committee see the chapter International and European Law.

[43] See, General Recommendation No. 33 of the CEDAW Committee, para. 7.

[44] Idem, paras. 26 and 28.

that the situation was caused by the woman because of the way she was dressed, being alone during the incident, her personal or professional life (promiscuity, prostitution, etc.), character or personality and insufficient resistance even though the male perpetrator was violent. The last reason may be explained with the stereotypical held belief that women enjoy male perpetuated violence during sexual relations.[45] Similarly, when sexual harassment is justified as a supposed demonstration of love or romantic closeness, or denied in the stereotypical belief of male-hunter/female-prey, i.e., domination/submission, on the belief that a man has to behave that way in order to be a man.[46] Another example of gender stereotype is the framing of a murder of the wife (and their children) as family tragedy or act of desperation and not as murder.

Example

The Federal Court of Germany denies murder when "the separation emanates from the victim of the crime and the accused, by committing the crime, deprives himself of what he actually does not want to lose". BGH of 29.10.2008, Az. 2 StR 349/08. ◄

5.3.2.2.3 CEDAW's Jurisprudence

Combating bias among judges is very well perceived in several cases decided by the CEDAW. It was first underlined in *V.K. v. Bulgaria.*

Example

In *V.K. v. Bulgaria,* the applicant alleged to be a victim of domestic violence by her husband. Although she submitted complaints seeking protection from domestic violence, the court refused to issue a permanent order as there was no evidence of domestic violence in the month prior to the hearing, despite the fact that she has been a victim of intimate partner violence for years (first psychological and economic, and then physical violence). The main question before the CEDAW was whether or not the refusal of domestic courts to issue a permanent protection order against the author's husband was arbitrary or otherwise discriminatory. The CEDAW found that domestic courts "focused exclusively on the issue of direct and immediate threat to the life or health of the author and on her physical integrity while neglecting her emotional and psychological suffering", and "unnecessarily deprived themselves of an opportunity to take cognisance of the past history of domestic violence."[47] The CEDAW underlined: "Stereotyping affects women's right to a fair trial and that the judiciary must be careful not to

[45] Lousada Arochena (2020), pp. 120–121.

[46] Lousada Arochena (2020), p. 64.

[47] *V.K. v. Bulgaria*, CEDAW, Communication No. 20/2008, 15 October 2008, para. 9.9.

create inflexible standards based on preconceived notions of what constitutes domestic or gender-based violence."[48] ◄

In another case against the Philippines,[49] the CEDAW was dealing with one employee of the Davao City Chamber of Commerce and Industry in the Philippines. A former President of the Chamber raped her after an evening business meeting. Eight years passed before the court delivered a final judgment, finding that there was insufficient evidence to prove beyond reasonable doubt that he committed the rape. The applicant claimed that the decision was based on several gender-based myths and misconceptions about the rape and victims of rape, which are as follows: (1) women need to physically resist sexual assault; (2) the victim must be timid or easily cowed; (3) women are likely to fabricate allegations of rape; (4) older men lack sexual prowess; and (5) perpetrators of rape are strangers.[50] The CEDAW agreed with the applicant. It found that "the assessment of the credibility of the author's version of events was influenced by a number of stereotypes, the author in this situation not having followed what was expected from a rational and 'ideal victim' or what the judge considered to be the rational and ideal response of a woman in a rape situation.[51] The CEDAW particularly underlined that "stereotyping affects women's right to a fair and just trial and that the judiciary must take caution not to create inflexible standards of what women or girls should be or [. . .] have done when confronted with a situation of rape based merely on preconceived notions of what defines a rape victim."[52]

In another case, the CEDAW found that the court proceedings were based on the "stereotyped perception of the gravity of extramarital affairs by women,"[53] "a stereotyped conception of visiting rights based on formal equality"[54] and concluded that judges often "adopt rigid standards about what they consider to be appropriate behaviour for women and penalise those who do not conform to those stereotypes,"[55] which leads to misinterpretation or misapplication of the law.

The CEDAW also emphasises that gender bias in judiciary can deeply influence the enjoyment of human rights of women.[56] Firstly, it influences the access to justice for women in all legal areas. It also leads to unjust results of the cases, as they are based on preconceived beliefs and myths, rather than relevant facts. It further

[48] *Ibid*, para. 9.11.

[49] *Karen Tayag Vertido v. The Philippines*, CEDAW, Communication No. 18/2008, 22 September 2010.

[50] *Ibid,* para. 3.5.1–3.5.6.

[51] *Ibid,* para. 8.5.

[52] *Ibid,* para. 8.4.

[53] *R.K.B. v. Turkey*, CEDAW, Communication No. 28/2010, 24 February 2012, para. 8.7.

[54] *González Carreño v. Spain*, CEDAW, Communication No. para. 9.4.

[55] *J. I. v. Finland*, CEDAW, Communication No.47/2012, 15 August 2014, para. 8.6.

[56] CEDAW, General Recommendation on women's access to justice, CEDAW/C/CG/33, 23 July 2015, para. 26.

influences the witness credibility. Therefore, stereotyping negatively influences impartiality and integrity of judiciary, "which can, in turn, lead to miscarriages of justice, including the revictimization of complainants."[57] The CEDAW insists that "women should be able to rely on a justice system free from myths and stereotypes, and on a judiciary whose impartiality is not compromised by these biased assumptions."[58]

Example

In *R.K.B. v. Turkey,* the applicant was dismissed for an affair with her male colleague, while at the same time her colleague was not dismissed. Dealing with this case, the CEDAW concluded: "The Committee emphasises that full implementation of the Convention requires States parties not only to take steps to eliminate direct and indirect discrimination and improve the de facto position of women, but also to modify and transform gender stereotypes and eliminate wrongful gender stereotyping, a root cause and consequence of discrimination against women. The Committee is of the view that gender stereotypes are perpetuated through a variety of means and institutions including laws and legal systems and that they can be perpetuated by State actors in all branches and levels of government and by private actors. In this case, the Committee is of the view that the Kocaeli 3d Labour Court has clearly allowed its reasoning based on law and facts to be influenced by stereotypes and the Court of Cassation by failing altogether to address the gender aspect, has perpetuated gender stereotypes about the role of women and men with it being accepted for the latter to have extramarital affairs. The Committee therefore concludes that the State party has violated article 5, paragraph (a), of the Convention."[59] ◄

5.3.2.3 Consequences of Judge's Stereotyping

Stereotypes affect the credibility of women's statements, arguments and testimony, both as parties and as witnesses. They may cause judges to misinterpret or misapply laws or punish women when they consider that the court/the judges have not behaved appropriately according to them. Moreover, not only judges and magistrates, but also prosecutors and all law enforcement officials can allow stereotypes to influence investigations and trials, so that these stereotypes will be present at all stages of the investigation and trial and will ultimately influence the judgement.[60]

---

[57] Ibid.

[58] Ibid, para. 28.

[59] *R.K.B. v. Turkey*, CEDAW, Communication No. 28/2010, 24 February 2012, para. 8.8.

[60] See General Recommendation No. 33 of the CEDAW Committee, paras. 26 and 27.

It should be borne in mind that the adverse effects of judging based on gender stereotypes affect the specific case it resolves around and has a broader projection.[61] Firstly, because the fact that the judge bases his or her judgement on this stereotype contributes to give it legitimacy or institutional backing, as the decision comes from the judiciary, which is ultimately a state power.[62] In the second place, because not holding perpetrators responsible for violations of women's rights creates a culture of impunity. In the third place, because stereotypes compromise the impartiality and integrity of the justice system. Lastly, because stereotyping in the judicial system can lead to a denial of women's right to access justice and the re-victimisation of complainants.[63]

Therefore, the judge in the performance of his or her work must combat gender stereotypes by identifying them in the litigation that he or she resolves. Starting from this point, the judge should avoid the introduction of gender stereotypes in the trial and promote their eradication in the specific case.[64] Gender Prosecution implies the obligation of judges or legal operators to combat these gender stereotypes as part of their commitment to equality. Gender Prosecution must be present when applying the law, interpreting legal norms, assessing the facts or the conduct of the persons involved (victim, aggressor) for the purposes of applying the norm.[65]

In this regard, General Recommendation No. 33 of the CEDAW Committee recommends a series of measures to the Member States, including "awareness-raising and capacity-building for all actors in justice systems and law students to eliminate gender stereotypes."[66]

5.3.2.4 Gender in the Jurisprudence of the ECtHR

The European Convention on Human Rights prohibits discrimination based on sex and gender in Article 14 of the ECHR and in Article 1, Protocol no. 12. It has a very extensive jurisprudence of this matter, although the ECtHR did not focus on gender stereotypes and prejudices in discrimination cases. However, in the *Konstantin Markin* case,[67] the applicant relied on Article 14 (prohibition of discrimination) taken in conjunction with Article 8 (right to respect private and family life). He claimed that he was refused parental leave for his third child on the same level as his female colleagues in an analogous situation. Therefore, he claimed to be a victim of gender discrimination. The ECtHR noted that the improvement of gender equality "is a major goal in the Member States of the Council of Europe", all parties to the

[61] Lousada Arochena (2020), p. 97.

[62] Lousada Arochena (2020), p. 97.

[63] See General Recommendation No. 33 of the CEDAW Committee, par. 26.

[64] Lousada Arochena (2020), p. 97.

[65] Lousada Arochena (2020), pp. 119–121.

[66] See General Recommendation No. 33 of the CEDAW Committee, par. 29.

[67] *Konstantin Markin v. Russia*, ECtHR (GC), Application No. 30078/06, judgment from 22 March 2012.

Convention.[68] Thus, "very weighty reasons had to be put forward for such a difference of treatment to be regarded as compatible with the Convention."[69] The Court further emphasised that "references to traditions, general assumptions or prevailing social attitudes in a given country were insufficient justification for a difference in treatment on the grounds of sex."[70] The Court found that "such difference has the effect of perpetuating gender stereotypes and is disadvantageous both to women's careers and to men's family life."[71] Also, the Court stands that gender stereotypes, "such as the perception of women as primary child-carers and men as primary breadwinners, cannot, by themselves, be considered to amount to sufficient justification for a difference in treatment, any more than similar stereotypes based on race, origin, colour or sexual orientation."[72]

After the Grand Chamber judgment of *Konstantin Markin*, the ECtHR captured even more directly the phenomenon of gender stereotyping in judicial decision-making. In the *Carvalho Pinto* case, the ECtHR found that the higher courts in Portugal diminished the amount of compensation in a case of medical maltreatment, which caused injures that prevented a 50 year old woman to have sexual intercourse with her husband. This was argued to be based on gender stereotypes.[73] The domestic Court found that she was "already fifty years old at the time of the surgery and had two children, that is, an age when sexuality is not as important as in younger years, its significance diminishing with age." Further, they pointed out that she "probably only needed to take care of her husband".[74] However, the ECtHR emphasised that this "assumption reflected a traditional idea of female sexuality as being essentially linked to child-bearing purposes, thus ignored its physical and psychological relevance for the self-fulfillment of women as people."[75] Even more, in two previous similar cases of men aged 55 and 58, domestic courts awarded a very high compensation and concluded that "the fact that the men could no longer have normal sexual relations had affected their self-esteem and resulted in a "tremendous blow" and "strong mental shock".[76] The ECtHR concluded that these considerations show the prejudices prevailing amongst the judiciary in Portugal,[77] which is the first case of this kind. In this case, it was found that stereotypes prevented judges to make an objective assessment of the evidence, which led to denial of justice, even though the applicant had trial by an independent and impartial court. This can have negative

[68] *Ibid,* para. 127.

[69] Ibid.

[70] Ibid.

[71] *Ibid,* para. 141.

[72] *Ibid,* para. 143.

[73] *Carvalho Pinto de Sousa Morais v. Portugal,* ECtHR, Application No. 17484/2015, judgment from 27 July 2017, para. 54.

[74] *Ibid,* paras. 49–50.

[75] *Ibid,* par. 52.

[76] *Ibid,* par. 55.

[77] *Ibid,* par. 54.

consequences both at individual and societal level, as it can lead to impunity for offenders and distrust of the judiciary. This aspect was particularly underlined in *M. C. v Bulgaria*,[78] where it was visible that judiciary can base its assessment on common myths in a rape case.

This aspect was also considered in *J.L. v. Italy*, where the Court dealt with criminal proceedings against seven men who were charged with having committed sexual violence against the applicant and who were acquitted by Italian courts.[79] The Court found that the Florence Court of Appeal failed to protect the applicant from secondary victimisation during the procedure.[80] The Court found that the language and arguments used by the Court of appeal convey prejudices about the role of women in Italian society, which prevents women from effective protection from gender violence -even though the legislative framework is satisfactory. The ECtHR particularly underlined that criminal prosecution and sanctions play a crucial role in the institutional response to gender-based violence.[81] It is therefore essential that the judicial authorities avoid reproducing gender stereotypes in court decisions, especially by demoralising comments in the judgments.[82]

5.4 Gender Imbalance on Benches

Domestic and international adjudicatory bodies have been male arenas for long time. In a male-powered world, the judicial system was not an exception. Poverty, the limited access to legal education and legal profession, stereotypes, gendered-biased mechanisms of appointment or recruitment are the main reasons for women's under-representation in the judiciary.[83] As a consequence, a gendered law has been applied from a gendered bench which is considered as a neutral power because of its own nature.[84]

The wind of gender equality has been blowing in courtrooms and a slow process to grant men and women equal representation on benches has been reshaping the composition of the judicial system.

Example

The 1998 Treaty establishing the International Criminal Court provides that "the States Parties shall, in the selection of judges, take into account the need, within the membership of the Court, for: (...) (iii) A fair representation of female and

[78] *M. C. v. Bulgaria*, ECtHR, Application No. 39272/98, judgment from 4 December 2003.

[79] *J.L. v. Italy*, ECtHR, Application No. 5671/16, judgment from 27 May 2021.

[80] *Ibid*, para. 142.

[81] *Ibid*, para. 141.

[82] Ibid.

[83] Vauchez (2019), para 27.

[84] *Idem*, para. 36.

male judges (Art 36 (8))." The 2004 Protocol to the African Charter on Human and Peoples' Rights creating the African Court establishes: "due consideration shall be given to adequate gender representation in nomination process' (Art 12)". The 1996 Constitution of South Africa refers to the 'need for the judiciary to reflect broadly the racial and gender composition' of the country and mandates that this need 'be considered when judicial officers are appointed' (Art 174 (2)). The requirement that 'the Court shall be composed of judges of both sexes' is established by Article 34 (5) of the organic legislation of 6 January 1989 relative to the Belgian Constitution. ◄

The said process stems from the claim that the representation of women on the bench has to be strengthened since female judges change decision-making in courts.[85] Such a claim has attracted severe criticism, not only among those who oppose gender equality.

This paragraph will make a short review of the comprehensive array of studies on the issue arguing that women judges make a difference. Moreover, attention will be paid to the limits that are entrenched in the simple rising of the number of women judges.

Some authors argue that women judges can empathise with female plaintiffs and witnesses. This ability should support parties and witnesses in their activities before the court, preventing them from experiencing gender oppression in courtrooms (e.g. sexual comments, a male-oriented approach in dealing with the evidence of sexual violence). Furthermore, women on the bench ensure that the court or the parties and their attorneys at law do not act in a sexist or gender-biased manner.[86]

In the same practical vein scholars highlighted that women judges could urge their male colleagues to reason and act without stereotypes and prejudice and to ensure that the working of legal proceedings will not be affected by gender attitudes.[87]

From a different point of view, the outcome women judges can reach has to be connected to the introduction of a gendered sensibility in the decision-making process. This focus on women's sensibility has been developed in two different ways. The first theory points out that women bring their experience of life into legal proceedings which differs from the experience of their male colleagues. In this perspective courts' judgments will express not only men's view of life, but a more comprehensive understanding of human beings. As long as courts are composed of only male judges, their rulings will be the expression of only a male culture and understanding of the law.[88]

The second theory sheds light on the "ethic of care" women make use of arguing that it leads them to judge differently since men judges adopt the "ethic of justice".

[85] Madam Justice Wilson (1990).

[86] Baroness Hale of Reachmond (2008); Schultz (2001); Resnik (1988).

[87] Hale and Hunter (2008); Schroeder (2002); Martin (1993).

[88] Rackley (2013), p. 164.

Men's culture is rooted in an atomistic idea of the human experience and in a hierarchical conception of rights.[89] Women aim at preserving social relationships and combining rights rather than considering them as a source of conflicts. The idea that women's experiences raises the quality of justice is marked by an essentialist approach and does not seem persuasive.[90] The approach fails to take into consideration the variety of women's experience as well as the role that factors such as race, colour and social class play.[91] Furthermore, this essentialist reasoning does not take into consideration the challenges women entering the judiciaries are called on to face and the constraints that could also limit bringing their female life experience into judging or silence their different voice.

Before examining such constraints, it is worth to recall the claims for a gender balance on bench, which are not immediately connected to the practical working of the decision-making process.

A judicial system which is composed of both sexes is perceived by citizens as offering equal opportunities to all individuals irrespective of their sex. The presence of women ensures that the recruitment of judges is based on fair and non-discriminatory procedures which pay attention to individuals' merits.[92] Furthermore, such an arrangement of the bench encourages girls to attend legal education, and to run legal profession or take part in public proceedings for the recruitment of judges.[93]

A different theory refers to the need for the presence of women in courts to ensure representation and legitimacy. Raising the number of women judges enhances the democratic legitimacy of the bench, since a judicial system composed of women and men represents society in all its different components.[94]

The approach at stake seems more persuasive not only because rising the number of women in public bodies enhances democracy, but also for the connection between democracy and the presence of women in courts covers domestic judicial bodies as well as international courts due to the public authority they exercise.[95] Furthermore, anchoring gender balance on bench to democratic representation enables us to take into consideration the constraints women judges are subject to and helps to identify the terms for a substantively different judicial decision-making. Notwithstanding its importance in the light of democratic legitimation, the enrolment of women into the judiciary is insufficient and taken alone, cannot provide a different voice because of structural phenomena which could endanger women's diversity. Constraints that stem from the law courts are to apply, since it is the outcome of gendered political processes where women had no voice in the first place. A further limit originates

[89] West (1988); Du Bois et al. (1985); Gilligan (1982).

[90] Hunter (2008), p. 13; Hunter (1996).

[91] Vauchez (2019), para. 21.

[92] Hale (2001).

[93] Cowan (2013), p. 321; Junqueira (2003), p. 445.

[94] Kenney (2013); Grossman, (2012), p. 661; Malleson (2003).

[95] Vauchez (2019), para. 35.

from the working of the bench. Judges' decision-making has been shaped by a set of norms and traditions which are difficult to dismantle and which were molded by all-male courts. Hunter has pointed out that "these norms include deference to the separation of powers and a limited judicial role, adherence to precedent, incrementalism, and the upholding of 'fundamental principles' of the common law, which may give rise to resistance to legislative reforms that are perceived to contravene those principles."[96]

Moreover, women judges tend to behave in order to be legitimised by their men colleagues. The need for being accepted and recognised as equals urges women judges to conform their work and opinions to those of their male peers.[97] The fear to be disqualified in the eyes of those who have always been sitting on the bench makes no difference in the outcome courts achieve.[98]

Hunter observed that "several studies of women and other non-traditional judges have demonstrated their unwillingness to step out of line, and a feeling that they must distance themselves from any notion of difference in order to establish their judicial authority and to be taken seriously by their peers and the judicial hierarchy."[99]

Female judges' strict acceptance and adherence to the law, a field made by and for men, is strong, due to their need for acceptance in such a male dominated career sector. This, however, prevents them from applying their own judgment and inserting their gender competent knowledge into decision-making. Such a remark does not refer only to those systems in which judges are appointed[100] or are chosen because of political allegiance, such as in international bodies,[101] but also, to the systems which are based on public recruitment through competition, though these latest procedures ensure a wider representation of women on bench.[102]

The phenomena that were briefly described, make it clear that gender balance on the bench is a step towards democratic representation since dismantling a male-biased judicial system entails the involvement of *feminist judges* in the decision-making processes of courts. As Kelley has rightly observed, "we need more feminist judges: judges who understand women's experiences and take seriously harm to women and girls, who ask the gender question, 'How might this law, statute, or holding affect men and women differently?'; who interpret equal protection and discrimination law in light of those provisions' broad social change purposes; who value women's lives and women's work; who do not believe women to be liars, whores, or deserving of violence by nature; who question their own stereotypes and

[96] Hunter (2015), p. 126.

[97] Charlesworth (2019), pp. 485–486; Chappell (2016), p. 91; Aoláin (2015); Graycar (1995), p. 268. On the difficulties women judges face see Tulkens (2014).

[98] Hunter (2015), p. 126; Rackley (2013), pp. 137–138.

[99] Hunter (2015), p. 128.

[100] Vauchez (2019), para. 28.

[101] Charlesworth (2019), p. 484.

[102] Vauchez (2019), para. 29.

predilections and listen to evidence; and who, simply put, believe in equal justice for all."[103]

In other words, the democratic legitimacy of courts can be achieved not only through the presence of women, but rather through feminist judges who contribute to substantial equality by asking the woman question.[104,105] As a consequence, reforms purporting to eradicate gender imbalance on bench are part of a broader process involving the spreading of a gender competent legal knowledge. Feminist judgments do not only demonstrate that women have a different voice but can support the progressive shaping of this legal culture.

5.5 Rewriting Courts' Decisions from a Gender Perspective

The role of the judiciary is to preserve the appearance of neutrality and impartiality. However, it does not mean that the feminist approach should not be applied, especially when it means achieving gender equality and justice. On the contrary, by applying a neutral approach, the judge can come to an unjust, even discriminate result, although some argue that if gender matters, a judgment can be seen as highly divisive.[106] But in many cases, decision making involves a choice between different possible conclusions, which depends on the judge's own approach to the law.[107]

Nevertheless, if a feminist approach is accepted, it does not mean that a judge needs to refer to feminist theories, but rather to have feminist awareness, to bear the understanding on the position of litigants, facts, evidence, and legal rules.[108] In other words, it is enough to be aware of the feminist approach. This would naturally led to practicing and incorporating the realities in which women live, to ask specific type of questions, to raise particular issues, and "to embrace insight and knowledge obtained, by viewing the world through a feminist lens".[109]

It also does not mean that a judge needs to identify himself/herself as a feminist, but the judge should not perpetuate negative characterisation of feminism.[110] Feminism in this sense means a fluid, multidimensional methodology and practice, which aim is to create a world in which women enjoy full personhood.[111] It is important to underline what is meant by feminism, as it has different branches, and represent different strands, such as liberal feminism, radical feminism, Marxist and socialist

[103] Kenney (2013), pp. 15–16.

[104] Hunter (2015), p. 121.

[105] On men judges showing a gender sensitive approach in adjudicating see Yahyaoui Krivenko (2019), p. 201 *et seq.*

[106] Hunter (2012), p. 15.

[107] Hunter (2012), p. 14.

[108] Douglas et al. (2014), p. 7.

[109] Berger et al. (2016), p. 37.

[110] Hunter (2012), p. 8.

[111] Berger et al. (2016), p. 26.

feminism, lesbian feminism, cultural feminism, women-of-colour feminism and postmodern feminism. This approach is very often in a conservative legal profession, where even female judges criticise feminism and refuse to use gender sensitive language.

Some authors provide a checklist of approaches to apply the feminist perspective, such as, among others, to challenge gender bias, and "to contextualise and particularise reasoning from context and making individualised rather than categorical or abstract decisions".[112] It also presupposes, that fact finding and assessment of witness credibility should not be based on stereotypical and gender-based assumptions, as stipulated in the jurisprudence of the ECtHR and the CEDAW.

However, it is important to underline that this approach does not guarantee that the feminist approach will necessarily lead to a different outcome of the case. It can only lead to different facts of the case that will be considered, or the adoption of another understanding of applicable legal principle.[113]

Example

In the Australian Feminist Judgments: Writing and Rewriting Law, it was underlined that in some cases, the result of a rewritten judgment would be the same as the original one. However, even in that case, it is valuable to apply the gender approach: "Most of the feminists included in this collection come to a different conclusion to the original case or to the majority judgment. In seven cases, however, the feminist judgment-writers agree with the outcome of the original decision but take the opportunity to provide a different account of the facts or to adopt another understanding of applicable legal principle, or both. [...] Kylie Burns' judgment in Cattanach v Melchior also concurred with the majority, but her judgment provided an opportunity to address a gap in the majority reasoning in relation to whether pregnancy is a form of economic loss, or some other form of damage or harm."[114] ◄

However, in the majority of cases, a different approach would lead to a different conclusion. Either a legal rule will be interpreted differently or different facts will be considered. Also, it is noticeable that writers who took part in rewriting judgments usually rely on social facts or empirical surveys with the aim to support their view. For example, in one judgment, extra-legal materials were used to demonstrate that women suffer in the workforce, or statistical data was used to find which age group was most vulnerable to sexual assault in Australia.[115] Another approach was to give names to parties, where there are statutory restrictions on identifying the parties.

[112] Hunter (2013), p. 401.

[113] Douglas et alii, p. 21.

[114] Douglas et al. (2014), p. 21.

[115] Douglas et al. p. 26.

Thus, some writers claimed that courts never talk about real children and their names, and that their aim was to humanise the process.[116]

Rewriting judgments has a triple role:

It can show how feminist ideas can be applied in the practice of legal decision-making;

Feminist judgments can provoke critical thinking about judicial decision-making and show how constructing the facts can lead to different case results; and

It can also encourage discussion on particular decisions and to propose a new judicial approach.[117]

5.6 The Main Features of Feminist Judgements

The previous paragraphs made it clear that gender equality entails among other issues the shaping of new techniques of judging through the adoption of the lens of feminism.

The different Feminist Judgments Projects scholars developed focus on several concurring needs: (a) facing the challenges which are embedded in a gendered law; (b) counteracting those stereotypes which affect the working of courts; (c) spurring society to reconsider the relationship between law and gender equality; and (d) displaying that a gender competent legal knowledge can support the achievement of substantial equality. Feminist judgments are based on the idea that law provisions can be applied, taking into consideration the special condition of the women involved in a concrete dispute, notwithstanding law represents the outcome of social and economic processes subjecting women to male domination. Feminist judgments can either give rise to the revision of the gendered approach in the enactment of law and the concepts which are entrenched in the male-dominated assessment of rules, or mold legal concepts.

Example

In rewriting the famous *Lotus Case,*[118] the feminist judges challenged States' sovereignty as a fundamental principle of the international legal system by exposing "the gendered nature of (Western) sovereignty and the gendered personification of States. Strikingly, for their judgment, the feminist chamber decided to adopt the name of the Turkish vessel, 'the Bozkurt', that had collided with the French vessel, 'the SS Lotus', thereby directing us to think about the way in which power structures operate in international decision-making. The re-written judgment also places the case in historical context and opens up

[116] Douglas et al. (eds), p. 30.

[117] Hunter (2012), pp. 219–220.

[118] Permanent Court of International Justice, *The Case of the SS Lotus*, judgment No 9 of 7 September 1927, Publications of the Permanent Court on International Justice, Series A No. 10, p. 4.

questions about the right of women that were not posed by the original tribunal. In finding that Turkey's exercise of jurisdiction did not violate international law, the 'Bozkurt Principle' de-centers State sovereignty and establishes international co-operation as a hallmark of international society."[119] The rewritten judgment sheds light on the masculine nature of the concept of sovereignty, which is grounded on the Western legal culture. Furthermore, the rewritten judgment reshapes the role of international law as an instrument for cooperation between States in making application of a different understanding of sovereignty: "the emergence of the Republic of Turkey is indicative of a new era in international law, one where new States are claiming their sovereignty and thus their entitlement to sit within the international community of nations. This marks the end of an Old European Order [. . .] The Court reflects that Turkey has in effect been 'feminised' by France and other European powers, through capitulations, formal and informal, and through the type of pressure France is asserting via the raising of this case. The Court notes with concern international law's history as one which persistently feminises weaker and primitive peoples, that is non-white non-Europeans. This is just as men, including white men from 'civilised nations', have subordinated women [. . .] The Court relies on an understanding of sovereignty as built on the spirit of co-operation, community and pacific settlement of disputes, one that resists inequalities in power relations between those recognised as States and thereby also challenges nineteenth century and positivist conception of free will, which assume formal equality without considering the substantive inequalities between States."[120] ◀

The consequences of such an effect of feminist judgments will be highlighted after examining the main features marking their writing.

5.6.1 The Constraints on Feminist Judgments

It has been observed that feminist judgments "present what the tribunals *could* or *should* have done rather than what they *would* have done if exposed to feminist thought circulating at the time of the original judgment."[121]

Consequently, writing feminist judgments is subject to the same constraints under which the original judges were called upon to operate.[122] Feminist judgments are decided on at the same time as the original judgments were delivered,[123] and are based on the same facts which were established in the original judgment. The

---

[119] Hodson and Lavers (2019), p. 15. Chinkin et al. (2019), pp. 27–51. On the theory of State see MacKinnon (1989).

[120] Chinkin et al. (2019), pp. 40–41.

[121] Charlesworth (2019), p. 481.

[122] Hunter et al. (2010), p. 13 *et seq.*

[123] On this problem see. Knop (2011), pp. 145–164.

feminist judges are obliged to rely on the same material which was available to the original judges and to take into consideration the proof on which the original judgment was based, comprising expert evidence. The state of the law to which reference can be made is the state existing at the time of the original judgment, which must be applied in accordance with the relevant legislation and precedents. Feminist judges cannot avail themselves of statutory interpretation or the incremental development of the common law. [124] In rewriting appellate judgments, feminist judges limit themselves to the issues and arguments the parties raised in their appeals and the authorities they referred to. In criminal proceedings feminist judgments cannot change the charges the prosecutor made. However, in commenting on the experience of *Feminist Judgments in International Law,* Charlesworth observed that the international feminist judges seem more prepared overall to abandon black letter law and to prefigure an expansive judicial agenda.[125]

Example

"For the Genocide Convention, the feminist ICJ bench establishes a two-pronged mechanism to deal with the impact of reservations that are objected by other States: all Contracting States must specifically accept or reject a reservation, with objecting States clarifying the legal basis of their objection. In the case of an arguably impermissible reservation, a dispute resolution process is engaged. The Court also introduces the notion of placing a time limit on a reservation effectiveness, with review at least every five years."[126] ◀

This difference in the approach towards rewriting judgments could be explained having regards not only to the different features of domestic law and international law, but also to the more evident connection between law and politics marking the latter.

5.6.2 The Feminist Approach to Judgment-Writing

Since the judgments to rewrite are subject to the same procedural rules of the original rulings, feminist judgments can be put into place via the rulings of a single judge or those of a collegiate body. As well as through the use of instruments such as concurring or dissenting opinions, if such instruments are provided for by the statute of the relevant body.

The rewriting judgments projects move from the idea that the original judgment perceived the law wrong or relied on a skewed account of the facts. Instead they

[124] Hunter et al. (2010), p. 15.

[125] Charlesworth (2019), p. 489.

[126] *Idem*, p. 490. For the original advisory opinion see International Court of Justice, Reservations to the Convention on Genocide, Advisory Opinion: I.C. J. Reports 19–51, p. 1.5. For the rewritten advisory opinion see Mc-Call-Smith et al. (2019), p. 55.

involve a series of activities embodying a specific method, making the feminist point of view rise. Hunter has identified several features, marking judgment-rewriting from the practice of feminist judgements.[127] The first of these features is to be found in asking the woman question.[128] Writing a feminist judgment originates from the consciousness that neither the law nor the practices which have been developed in applying it are neutral, thus highlighting the consequences that they produce on women's legal status or socio-economic conditions.

Example

The International Criminal Court convicted Thomas Lubanga Dyilo of the war crimes of the conscription and enlisting of child soldiers under the age of 15 as part of the rebel group he led during the conflict in the Democratic Republic of the Congo.[129] "The re-written judgment clarifies the relationship between the crimes of conscription and enlistment, drawing on feminist insights on the notion of consent. It also highlights the silences of the original judgement in terms of the experiences of the girl child, revisiting what it means to 'actively participate in hostilities'. Finally, it foregrounds the particular gendered experiences of sexual violence that were marginalised in the original judgment. The re-written judgement contextualises the experiences of girl and boy children soldiers and emerges with a more gender-sensitive approach to the questions raised".[130] ◀

The case is also of interest because it embodies some of the difficulties courts may face in assessing criminal cases from a feminist point of view, since adjudicating bodies cannot widen the charges prosecutors made.

Rewriting judgments entails finding out the way in which rules impact women's lives and putting them into fore. This approach is anchored in a shift from the perspective of the subject of law as an atomised individual to human relationality and interdependence. This revision of traditional concepts of law urges feminist judges to set aside intention and to focus on effects of actions.[131]

Example

In the *Mundon*[132] case "the Employment Appeal Tribunal held that an employer would only unfairly dismiss a woman on the basis of her pregnancy if they did so intentionally or if, at the time of the decision to dismiss, they knew that the reason for dismissal was related to her pregnancy. The feminist judgment contends that

---

[127] Hunter (2010), p. 35; Grey and Chappell (2019), pp. 222 *et seq.*

[128] Bartlett (1990), pp. 829–888.

[129] *Prosecutor v Thomas Lubanga Dyilo* (Judgment pursuant to Article 74 of the Statute) ICCC-01/04-01/06 (14 March 2012).

[130] Hodson and Lavers (2019), p. 20; Brunger et al. (2019), pp. 409–443.

[131] Hunter et al. (2010), pp. 21 *et seq.*

[132] Del Monte Foods Ltd v Mundon [1980] ICR 694.

this creates too wide of a 'get out' clause for employers and proposes instead that a dismissal should be considered unfair if it is objectively based on or related to the woman's pregnancy, and that the onus should be on employers to make reasonable inquiries when dismissals are pending to ensure that they will not be unfairly based on pregnancy."[133] ◀

Nowadays, asking the woman question is more and more connected to intersectionality, so that the authors of feminist judgments pay attention to the link between being a woman and other factors such as colour, race, belonging to a minority, social class.

Example

The rewritten decision of the CEDAW Committee in the case *Kell v Canada*[134] widens the perspective of assessment of the law stressing Kell's indigeneity. Ms. Kell, an indigenous woman living in Canada, secured housing pursuant to a legal scheme laying down special rules for indigenous people. Because of the abuse of her partner, Ms. Kell was forced to leave her home. Kell's partner changed the locks and managed to place the lease of the home in his name alone. Ms. Kell's legal battle attempts to regain access to her home was unsuccessful. "In their Views, the feminist chamber argues that her 'intersectional marginality' served to make her invisible to the Canadian legal system; she was a single parent, an indigenous woman and a domestic abuse survivor. Although the original Committee found that Canada had violated certain articles of the Convention, the re-written views foreground the blind spots of legal process, in its analysis and adopts an intersectional approach that highlights in particular the role that Ms. Kelly's indigeneity played in her experience of discrimination and marginalisation."[135] ◀

The second feature of rewriting judgments is including women. In describing this feature, Hunter pointed out that feminist judgments include women "both in terms of writing women's experience into legal discourse (as individual litigants and collectively, drawing on relevant research evidence) and in the construction of legal rules."[136] The method takes shape in telling the story of the case in a manner different from that of the original judgment. This approach enables feminist judges to shed light on the specific circumstances of the persons who are involved in the case, placing instead, the women's conditions at the centre as they emerge from the

[133] Hunter et al. (2010), p. 22; Horton and James (2010), pp. 401–413.

[134] Committee on the Elimination of Discrimination against Women, *Cecilia Kell v Canada*, Communication No. 19/2008, Views adopted by the Committee at its fifty-first session, 13 February to 2 March 2012, CEDAW/C/51/D/19/2008.

[135] Hodson and Lavers (2019), p. 19; Buckner et al. (2019), pp. 333–368.

[136] Hunter (2010), p. 35.

relevant materials. This arrangement is necessary for the achievement of a different outcome in deciding the case.[137]

Example

The case *R v Dhaliwal*[138] offers a good example of this technique. Gurjit Dhaliwal lived with a violent husband and put an end to her life by committing suicide. The extent of Dhaliwal not being involved in the trial is filled up by the writer of the feminist judgment, calling on the Lords to focus on the cruel treatment she was subject to. "The following brief sketch of agreed facts cannot begin to convey the intolerable treatment that the victim, Gurjit Dhaliwal, was subjected to by her husband, Harcharan Dhaliwal, for over a decade. Victims of domestic abuse are too often silenced, metaphorically speaking, by abusers, society and the institutions of the state. The tragic suicide of Gurjit Dhaliwal also renders her voice literally absent from these, and earlier, court proceedings. Posthumous insights from her diaries, witness recollections and official records do, however, provide partial glimpses of her plight."[139] ◄

Moreover, including women could entail walking along paths which have not been explored by the judges and pushing judgments towards new borders, through the widening of the scope of the legal status that are worth to be protected in the case at issue.

Example

The rewritten judgment the ECtHR delivered in *Christine Goodwin v the United Kingdom*[140] clarifies how considering lived experience changes all understanding of the interests involved in a legal dispute and leads to a revisions of traditional legal concepts. The case concerned the construction of gender under international law for Christine Goodwin, a trans woman, who sought legal recognition of her gender before the Court in Strasbourg. The original judgment recognised the breach of art. 8 (right to private life) and art. 12 (right to marry). "The feminist chamber's rewriting of the judgment shows that the original judgment served to reinforce a binary understanding of gender and was silent on a number of important issues. [. . .] a key method adopted by the feminist chamber was to pay greater attention to the lived experiences of Christine Goodwin and the marginalisation, challenges and humiliation she endured because of the incongruence between her lived and legal gender. Significantly, the rewritten judgment frames the obligation on the State as a negative one; that is, the State must refrain

[137] On storytelling see Rackley (2010), pp. 44–56.

[138] R v D [2006] EWCA Crim 1139, [2006] 2 Cr App R 24 (CA).

[139] Burton et al. (2010), pp. 255–272.

[140] Application no. 28957/95, *case of Christine Goodwin v the United Kingdom* (ECtHR 11 July 2002).

from imposing a gender on an individual that she does not identify with. Placing her suffering at the hearth of its reasoning, the feminist judgment also takes Convention jurisprudence into new territory by finding that the State violated Ms. Goodwin right to be free from inhuman and degrading treatment."[141] This is one of the crucial points of the reasoning of the feminist judgment: "the applicant submitted that she has suffered numerous humiliating experiences in her everyday life as a result of her inability to change to her legal sex. Although the applicant did not invoke Article 3 of the Convention in her application, the Court considers that Article to be relevant to her complaint because of the centrality and extent of the claims about humiliation. When taken together, the facts submitted by the applicant—in particular, the alleged discrimination at work; the problem at work arising from the link between her previous sex and her National Insurance number; the difficulties created in dealing with the DSS; the inability to access certain advantages in goods and services because of the requirement to produce a birth certificate; and a fear of reporting crime to the police—suggest that the issue of humiliation is fundamental to every aspect of the applicant's complaint about her inability to reconcile her gender identity with her legal sex. Therefore, the Court considers it appropriate to consider the applicant's complaint under Article 3 of the Convention."[142] ◄

The third feature is the fighting against gender bias which is anchored on those stereotypes marking legal doctrine and judges' reasoning.[143] One of the most relevant expressions of gender bias is the admission of sexual history evidence in rape trials.

Example

The rewritten judgment in *R v A (No 2)*[144] dealt with this problem pointing out that "the treatment of witnesses in court adversely impacts on decisions to report rape to the police. Who would want to put themselves before a voyeuristic court to have their sexual history trawled through and criticised, and often with little direct relevance to the issues at trial? The police and prosecutors often warn witnesses of the harrowing nature of giving evidence at trial, sometimes from the best of intentions, with the result that many withdraw their complaints. Accordingly, while this case is about the admission of evidence at trial, its impact will reverberate throughout the criminal justice system in its dealings with rape."[145] Such a practice stems from the idea that rape trials are "particularly subject to the danger of deliberately false charges, resulting from sexual neurosis, phantasy,

[141] Hodson and Lavers (2019), p. 17.

[142] Bengstone et al. (2019), p. 193, para. 54.

[143] Hunter (2010), p. 35.

[144] R v A (No 2) [2001] UKHL 25, [2002] 1 AC 45.

[145] McGlynn (2010), p. 212, para. 5.

jealousy, spite or simply a girl's refusal to admit that she consented to an act of which she is now ashamed."[146]

The feminist judgment argued for the need to introduce restriction on the use of sexual history evidence in order to protect the women's fundamental rights. "Article 8 of the Convention protects the right to respect for private life [. . .] While it will sometimes be necessary to introduce evidence about a complainant's sexual history, thereby constituting a necessary and justified interference with privacy rights, this is not invariably the case. In particular, it has been demonstrated that many unnecessarily intrusive questions have been asked of complainants, often as a matter of routine; potentially, therefore, in breach of the complainant's article 8 rights. [. . .] Although not argued before us, it seems to me that restrictions on the admission of sexual history evidence may be necessary to ensure compliance with a state's positive obligations, inherent in article 3 of the Convention, to bring perpetrators of rape to justice. [. . .] to the extent that the admission of sexual history evidence impedes proper investigation, prosecution and conviction of perpetrators, restrictions may be justified to ensure compliance with article 3 positive obligations. Indeed, where evidence or questioning is not necessary and reaches the requisite threshold of harm, for example by inducing significant psychological injury, article 3 may be directly engaged. Article 3 is a non-derogable right, meaning that if it is breached, other Convention rights such as the article 6 right to a fair trial do not take precedence."[147] ◄

The fourth feature is contextualisation and particularity. In Hunter's words, it entails "reasoning from context and the reality of women's lived experience; making individualised rather than categorical or abstract decisions; paying particular and careful attention to the individuals before the court; and not judging women for making different choices from those the judge herself would have made."[148]

This technique is strictly connected with the features already examined since it is functional to ask the woman question and to include women in the narrative of the case. However, it possesses its own hallmarks because of the way in which feminist judges make use of in rewriting judgments.

The introduction of social framework material into the judgment is one of the instruments adopted in order to identify the broader context within which the specific facts of the case or the legal items arising from the case have to be placed. This additional material could derive from research evidence on the topics at stake.

[146] Sir. Matthew Hale (1963) quoted at para. 2 of the rewritten judgment.

[147] McGlynn (2010), p. 214, paras. 14–18.

[148] Hunter (2010), p. 35.

Example

In *Baird Textile Holdings v Marks & Spencer PLC*[149] the point of departure of the reasoning of the feminist judgment was the acknowledgment that English contract law does not recognise long-term commercial relationships such as that at stake in the case at issue. The need for aligning English law to commercial practice spurred the feminist judgment to rely on research evidence dealing with the dynamics of commercial relationships: "the umbrella contract is an increasingly popular device which can be used to give recognition to long-term relationships in which a series of orders for goods and services are placed over time. In this context, it should be a matter for concern that a mechanism devised by the marketplace to facilitate efficiency is not fully recognised by our courts. There is now a rich body of academic research detailing what motivates the maintenance of a successful commercial relationship on a day-to-day basis and over time. Counsel for Baird have referred us in particular to the excellent empirical studies of the lived world of contract undertaken by Hugh Beale, Tony Dugdale[150] and Richard Lewis[151] in the United Kingdom, and to Stuart Macaulay[152] and Lisa Bernstein's[153] work in the United States. Reading their research I have been struck by how familiar their findings would sound to lawyers such as myself who spent their formative years at the commercial bar. Professor David Campbell in "Ian Macneil and the Relational Theory of Contract"[154] has aptly observed that we now have so many descriptions of how successful long-term contracts operate in the business world that the real challenge is to determine the extent to which the law of contract is in tune with the standards and expectations of commercial parties. The facts of this case appear to reflect the findings of empirical studies about what binds commercial parties together in successful relationships so well that I would consider it inappropriate not to say something about the enhanced understandings of the commercial sectors which have emerged from academic debate and to reflect on how well the modern law of contract serves the business community."[155] ◀

In other cases, references are made to legal materials which are drawn from international law, the law of other States and domestic sources such as parliamentary debates, policy documents.

[149] Baird Textile Holdings v Marks & Spencer Plc [2001] EWCA Civ 274, [2002] 1 All ER (Comm) 737.

[150] Beale and Dugdale (1975), pp. 2:45–60.

[151] Lewis (1982), pp. 153–175.

[152] Macaulay (1963), pp. 55–67.

[153] Bernstein (1992), pp. 115–157.

[154] Campbell (1991), pp. 3–58.

[155] Mulcahy and Andrews (2010), p. 195, paras. 38 *et seq.*

Example

In rewriting the judgment, the ECtHr delivered in *A, B and C v Ireland*,[156] the feminist Court referred to the domestic laws of European States to argue that abortion is available in virtually all of the states parties on certain fundamental grounds[157] and on statistical data pointing out that "the abortion policies of the Irish government impose a significant burden on women. Official statistics of the United Kingdom demonstrate that 4422 women travelled to that jurisdiction to obtain an abortion in 2009."[158] ◄

But the use of these materials is just one element of feminist judgments since they are marked by the introduction of feminist common knowledge.[159] The knowledge of non-legal items and their evaluation are usually the expression of judges' gendered culture.[160] Feminist judgments dismantle this male appreciation, introducing social experiences into legal discourse counteracting the male mainstream which excludes women from the judicial experience. In so doing, feminist judgments tend to reshape the knowledge of the world in a feminist perspective.[161]

The fifth feature of feminist judgments consists of seeking to remedy injustices and to improve the condition of women's life. Feminist judgments do not stem only from the unsatisfactory solutions of judgments gendered courts delivered. Rewriting judgments is intended to foster the development of gender competent legal knowledge, in order to give new impetus to judicial experience in the wider perspective of contributing to the improvement of women's social and economic conditions. Charlesworth has pointed out that feminist judgments accord prominence to women's and other outsiders lives and voices.[162]

This approach highlights the sixth feature of feminist judgments: promoting substantive equality. Feminist judgments contain a severe criticism of liberalism.[163] The attempt to go beyond the liberal notion of formal equality embodies one of the expressions of this criticism.

[156] App. no.25579/05, *case of A, B and c v Ireland* (ECtHR GC 16 December 2010).

[157] Fenwick et al. (2019), p. 291, para. 38.

[158] *Idem*, p. 297, para. 62.

[159] Hunter (2010), p. 38.

[160] Smart (1989), p. 17; Graycar (1995), p. 269 *et seq.*

[161] Hunter (2013), pp. 399–418.

[162] Charlesworth (2019), p. 488.

[163] Hunter et al. (2010), p. 22.

Example

In *EM (Lebanon) v Secretary of State for the Home Department*[164] the feminist judgment argued that the order of deportation was in breach of the fundamental right to equality: "this House does, however, have a duty to uphold the law, including the law as it derives from regional and international human rights norms. The Convention will preclude the appellant's deportation to Lebanon if it can be shown that she is at real risk of a flagrant breach of her Convention rights such as to have them completely denied or nullified. As I have alluded to above, in my judgment, in this case the appellant's right to gender equality in the enjoyment of her family life, including with her child, and in any legal proceedings that relate to her family life would necessarily be flagrantly breached were she to be returned to Lebanon. This is because, by simple fact of her womanhood, she would be automatically denied custody of her child". As a consequence of this reasoning, the feminist judgment considers the breach of art. 8 ECHR as an unsatisfactory outcome since "to have decided the case on that basis would, in my view, have been to ignore the central feature of this case, namely that the wrong that would be done in Lebanon to this appellant would be most fundamentally to deny her equality because she is a woman."[165] ◀

The last feature of feminist judgments has been identified in drawing on feminist legal scholarship to inform decisions.[166] Feminist judgments are grounded on feminist jurisprudence, though the rewritten judgments make no reference to the theoretical approach grounding it. However, the linkage between gender competent legal knowledge and rewriting judgments comes out from the different techniques that were briefly analysed. The widening of the legal and factual framework, the attention to the specific circumstances of the case, the criticism of liberalism represent the concrete application of the theories which shape the feminist lens feminist judges make use of. The dissenting opinion of the feminist judge in *Prosecutor v Karadžić* helps us to understand the way in which the female theories of law combines the different features of feminist judgments. Thus highlighting the unsatisfactory results of the gendered application of law.

Example

The International Criminal Tribunal for the former Yugoslavia acquitted Karadžić of genocide in the Municipalities of Bosnia Herzegovina for the genocidal intent was not proved. The feminist judgment reached a different

[164] EM (Lebanon) v Secretary of State for the Home Department [2008] UKHL 64, [2009] 1 AC 1198.

[165] Monaghan (2010), p. 458, paras. 23–24.

[166] Hunter (2010), p. 35.

conclusion.[167] "In my judgement, the nature, scale and content of the sexual violence committed in the Municipalities not only amounts to the actus reus of genocide, but also lays bare that the intent in committing crimes of rape, indecent assault, forced gross indecency and assault, sexual slavery, forced prostitution, forced nudity, and forcible impregnation, was to destroy in whole or in part the target group. Through these crimes, domination and absolute control over members of the group was asserted and exercised. These crimes were committed across the length and breadth of the Municipalities, in villages and towns, in public and in private, in streets, in houses, and in detention camps. The number of victims are vast. In the context of patriarchal, patrilineal, religious and conservative communities—and against a backdrop of hundreds of years of ethnic and ethno-religious rivalries and violence, including the perceived genocide of the Serbs in WWII—the only, and compelling, inference to be drawn is that genocidal intent was present."[168] The Author identified the theoretical foundations of this outcome pointing out: "in contrast to the original judgment, this dissenting judgment, written by an individual feminist judge, will use the techniques of asking the woman question, telling women's stories and exploring background context to achieve a richer and more complete picture of the issues before the court. Coupled with a willingness to see and understand both the significance of pattern evidence of sexual violence and its deeply communicative purpose and impact, this judgment clearly finds evidence of genocidal intent."[169] ◀

This latest example makes it clear that the feminist assessment of law could reshape gender relationships. In applying feminist theories to real legal disputes feminist judgments enhance the development of a gender competent legal knowledge and give rise to a virtuous circle between theory and practice. Viewed in this perspective, feminist judgments could remove the limits which are intrinsic to the raising of the number of women in courts.

5.7 Conclusion

Achieving gender equality in access to justice requires the absence of gender stereotypes in the judicial system. This presupposes measures to ensure that the judicial process from its initiation until the delivery of a judgment is free from gender stereotyping. The first step is to achieve a gender balance in court representation. However, the greater proportion will not achieve the greater result in terms of better access to justice and the more just outcome of the case. Therefore, it is essential to monitor judgments and organise training of gender-sensitive judges and jurists, as set out by the CEDAW Committee in its General Recommendation No 33. At the

[167] *Prosecutor v Karadžić* (Judgment) ICTY-95-5/18-T (24 March 2016).

[168] Greenwood (2019), p. 471, para. 70.

[169] *Idem*, p. 453.

international level, for the past decade, the CEDAW Committee has delivered several important decisions which underline the importance of combating gender stereotypes in the judicial making. Also, the ECtHR in several judgments underlines the importance of tackling gender bias in the judiciary. However, there is still a lack of a gender-sensitive approach in some of its decisions.

The rising number of women judges is a step forward towards democratic legitimacy of the judiciary. Still, it cannot dismantle the male-centered mechanisms ruling the proceedings leading to courts' decision-making. The need for a more comprehensive number of feminist judges, highlights the role that rewriting judgments could play in developing gender competent legal knowledge. Nevertheless, the experience of states that face feminisation in the judiciary shows that the more critical issue is to secure that judges take into account the feminist perspective, to understand it, and to apply it when assessing the credibility of a witness, facts of the case and interpretation of the law.

Questions

1. What is considered to be gender stereotyping?
2. Why can gender stereotypes in judicial system hinder women's access to justice?
3. What is the main purpose of feminist judgments projects around the world?
4. What are the gender stereotypes that the CEDAW Committee underlines in case of *Karen Tayag v. Philippines*? What are the rights of Case of *Karen Tayag v. Philippines* that have been violated, according to the CEDAW Committee? What are the recommendations it makes to the Philippine State?
5. What were the gender stereotypes present in case of *Carvalho Pinto v. Portugal*, decided by the ECtHR in 2017?
6. Research and analyse a judgement from the courts in your country that has resolved a case arguing a decision based on gender stereotypes.
7. Research and analyse a judgement from the courts in your country that has resolved a case bearing in mind a gender perspective.
8. What are the main reasons for gender balance on bench?
9. What are the main features of feminist judgments?
10. What are the constraints on rewriting feminist judgments?

References

Aoláin FN (2015) More women – but which women? A reply to Stéphanie Hennette Vauchez. Eur J Int Law 26:229–236

Balkin JM (2002) What Brown v. Board of Education should have said: the nation's top legal expert rewrite America's landmark civil rights decision. New York University Press, New York

Balkin J (ed) (2005) What Roe v. Wade should have said: the nation's top legal experts rewrite American's most controversial decisions. New York University Press
Baroness Hale of Reachmond B (2008) A minority opinion? Proc Br Acad 154:319–336
Bartlett KT (1990) Feminist legal methods. Harv Law Rev 103:829–888
Beale H, Dugdale T (1975) Contracts between businessmen: planning and the use of contractual remedies. Br J Law Soc 2:45–60
Bengstone S, Gonzalez-Salzberg D, Paul J, Hodson L (2019) Christine Goodwin v the United Kingdom. In: Hodson L, Lavers T (eds) Feminist judgments in international law. Hart Publishing, London, pp 175–201
Berger LL, Stanchi KM, Crawford BJ et al (2016) Learning from feminist judgments: lessons in language and advocacy. Tex Law Rev 98:40–70
Berger LL, Stanchi KM, Crawford BJ et al (2020) Teaching with Feminist judgments: a global conversation. Pace Law Faculty Publications, Pace University
Bernstein L (1992) Opting out of the legal system: extralegal contractual relations in the diamond industry. J Leg Stud 21:115–157
Brems E, Timmer A (2016) Stereotypes and human rights law. Intersentia
Brewster KL, Padavic I (2000) Change in gender-ideology. J Marriage Fam 62:477–487
Brunger YM, Irving E, Sankey D (2019) The prosecutor v Thomas Lubanga Dyilo. In: Hodson L, Lavers T (eds) Feminist judgments in international law. Hart Publishing, London, pp 409–443
Buckner IL, Hohmann J, Tramontana E (2019) Cecilia Kell v Canada. In: Hodson L, Lavers T (eds) Feminist judgments in international law. Hart Publishing, London, pp 333–368
Burton M, Munro V, Shah S (2010) R v Dhaliwal. In: Hunter R, MacGlynn C, Rackley E (eds) Feminist judgments. From theory to practice. Hart Publishing, London, pp 255–272
Campbell D (1991) Ian Macneil and the relational theory of contract. In: Campbell D (ed) The relational theory of contract: selected works of Ian Macneil. Sweet & Maxwell, London, pp 3–58
Chamallas M, Finley LM (2020) Feminist judgments: rewritten tort opinions. Cambridge University Press, Cambridge
Chambers L (2007) Unprincipled exclusions: feminist theory, transgender jurisprudence, and Kimberly Nixon. Can J Women Law 18:305–334
Chappell L (2016) The politics of gender justice at the international criminal court. Oxford University Press, Oxford
Charlesworth H (2019) Prefiguring feminist judgments in international law. In: Hodson L, Lavers T (eds) Feminist judgments in international law. Hart Publishing, London, pp 479–493
Chinkin C, Heathcote G, Jones H, Bozkurt C (2019) Bozkurt case, aka the lotus case (France v Turkey): ships that go bump in the night. In: Hodson L, Lavers T (eds) Feminist judgments in international law. Hart Publishing, London, pp 27–51
Cowan RB (2013) Do women in South Africa's courts make a difference? In: Schultz U, Shaw G (eds) Gender and judging. Hart Publishing, London, pp 317–333
Cowan S, Kennedy C, Munro VE (2019) Scottish feminist judgments: (Re) creating law from the outside. Hart Publishing, London
Crawford BJ, Infanti AC (2017) Feminist judgments: rewritten tax opinions. Cambridge University Press, Cambridge
Douglas H, Bartlett F, Luker T, Hunter R (2014) Australian feminist judgments: righting and rewriting law. Hart Publishing, London
Du Bois EC et al (1985) Feminist discourse, moral values and the law: a conversation. Buffalo Law Rev 34:11–87
Eccles JS, Barber B, Jozefowicz D (1999) Linking gender to educational, occupational, and recreational choices: applying the Eccles et al. model of achievement-related choices. In: Swann WB, Langlois JH, Gilbert LA (eds) Sexism and stereotypes in modern society: the gender science of Janet Taylor Spence. American Psychological Association, Washington, pp 153–192

Ellsworth PC (2005) Legal reasoning. In: Holyoak KJ, Morrison Jr RG (eds) The Cambridge handbook of thinking and reasoning. Cambridge University Press, Cambridge, pp 685–704
Enright M, McCandless J, O'Donoghue A (2017) Northern/Irish feminist judgments, Judges' troubles and the gendered politics of identity. Hart Publishing, London
Fenwick E, Guns W, Warwick B (2019) A, B and C v Ireland. In: Hodson L, Lavers T (eds) Feminist judgments in international law. Hart Publishing, London, pp 279–302
Fruehwald ES (2020) Think Like a Lawyer: Legal Reasoning for Law Students and Business Professionals. Independently Published
Gilligan C (1982) In a different voice: psychological theory and women's development. Harvard University Press, Harvard
Graycar R (1995) The gender of judgments: an introduction. In: Thornton M (ed) Public and private: feminist legal debates. Oxford University Press, Oxford, pp 262–282
Greenwood C (2019) Prosecutor v Radovan Karadžić. In: Hodson L, Lavers T (eds) Feminist judgments in international law. Hart Publishing, London, pp 447–476
Grey R, Chappell L (2019) 'Gender just-judging' in international criminal courts: new directions for research. In: Rimmer SH, Ogg K (eds) Research handbook on feminist engagement with international law. Edward Elgar Publishing, Cheltenham/Northampton, pp 213–239
Grossman N (2012) Sex on the bench: do women judges matter to the legitimacy of international courts. Chic J Int Law 12:647–684
Hale B (2001) Equality and the judiciary: why should we want more women judges? Public Law:489–504
Hale B, Hunter R (2008) A conversation with Baroness Hale. Fem Leg Stud 16:237–248
Harris AP, Sen M (2018) Bias and Judging. https://scholar.harvard.edu/files/msen/files/bias-judging-arps.pdf. Accessed 24 Sept 2021
Hodson L, Lavers T (2019) Feminist judgments in international law. An introduction. In: Hodson L, Lavers T (eds) Feminist judgments in international law. Hart Publishing, London, pp 3–21
Horton R, James G (2010) Mundon v Del Monte Foods Ltd. In: Hunter R, McGlynn C, Rackley E (eds) Feminist judgments. From theory to practice. Hart Publishing, London, pp 3–29
Hudson L, Lavers T (2019) Feminist judgments in international law. Hart Publishing
Hunter R (1996) Deconstructing the subjects of feminism: the essentialism debate in feminist theory and practice. Aust Fem Law J 6:135–162
Hunter R (2008) Can feminist judges make a difference? Int J Legal Profess 15:7–36
Hunter R (2010) An account of feminist judging. In: Hunter R, McGlynn C, Rackley E (eds) Feminist judgments. From theory to practice. Hart Publishing, London, pp 30–43
Hunter R (2012) Can feminist judges make a difference. In: Schultz UU, Shaw G (eds) Women in judiciary. Routledge
Hunter R (2013) Justice Marcia Neave: case study of a feminist judge. In: Schultz U, Shaw G (eds) Gender and judging. Hart Publishing, London, pp 399–418
Hunter R (2015) More than just a different face? Judicial diversity and decision-making. Curr Leg Probl 68:119–141
Hunter R, McGlynn C, Rackley E (2010) Feminist judgments: an introduction. In: Hunter R, McGlynn C, Rackley E (eds) Feminist judgments. From theory to practice. Hart Publishing, London, pp 3–29
Hunter R, McGlynn C, Rackley E (2016) Feminist judgments: an introduction in Hunter. In: McGlynn, Rackley (eds) U.S. Feminist judgments: rewritten opinions of the United States Supreme Court. Cambridge University Press
Junqueira EB (2003) Women in the judiciary: a perspective from Brazil. In: Schultz U, Shaw G (eds) Women in the World's legal professions. Hart Publishing, London, pp 437–450
Kenney SJ (2013) Gender and justice: why women in the judiciary really matter. Routledge, London
Knop K (2011) The Tokyo Women's tribunal and the turn to fiction. In: Johns F, Joyce R, Pahuja S (eds) Events: the force of international law. Routledge, London, pp 145–164

Krstic I (2021) Gender analysis for the action "Strengthening the effective legal remedies to human rights violations in Serbia". Council of Europe, Strasbourg
Lewis R (1982) Contracts between businessmen: reform of the law of firm offers and an empirical study of tendering practices in the building industry. J Law Soc 9:153–175
Lousada Arochena JF (2020) El enjuciamiento de género. Dykinson, Madrid
Macaulay S (1963) Non-contractual relations in business—a preliminary study. Am Sociol Rev 28: 55–67
MacKinnon C (1989) Towards a feminist theory for the state. Harvard University Press, Harvard
Malleson K (2003) Justifying gender equality on the bench: why difference won't do'. Fem Leg Stud 11:1–24
Martin E (1993) The representative role of women judges. Judicature 77:166–172
Sir. Matthew Hale (1963) The Proof of Guilt
Mc-Call-Smith K, Smith R, Yahyaoui K (2019) Reservations to the convention on the prevention and punishment of the crime of genocide. In: Hodson L, Lavers T (eds) Feminist judgments in international law. Hart Publishing, London, pp 55–81
McDonald E, Powell R, Stephens M, Hunter R (2017) About feminist judgments of Aotearoa New Zealand, Te Rino: a two-stranded rope. Hart Publishing, London
McGinley AC (2016) Oncale v. Sundowner Offshore Services Inc. In: Berger L, Crawford B, Stanchi K (eds) Feminist judgments: rewritten opinions of the United States Supreme Court, pp 414–425
McGinley AC, Porter NB (2020) Feminist judgments: rewritten employment discrimination opinions. Cambridge University Press, Cambridge
McGlynn C (2010) R v A (No 2). In: Hunter R, McGlynn C, Rackley E (eds) Feminist judgments. From theory to practice. Hart Publishing, London, pp 205–227
Monaghan K (2010) EM (Lebanon) v Secretary of State or the Home Department. In: Hunter R, McGlynn C, Rackley E (eds) From theory to practice. Hart Publishing, London, pp 449–458
Mulcahy L, Andrews C (2010) Baird Textile Holdings v Marks & Spencer Plc. In: Hunter R, McGlynn C, Rackley E (eds) Feminist judgments. From theory to practice. Hart Publishing, London, pp 184–202
Munro VE (2020) Feminist judgments projects at the intersection. Fem Leg Stud 29:251–261
Mutcherson K (2020) Feminist judgements: reproductive justice rewritten. Cambridge University Press, Cambridge
Neumann RK Jr (2005) Legal reasoning and legal writing: structure, strategy, and style. ASPEN Publishers, New York
Rackley E (2010) The art and craft of writing judgments: notes on the feminist judgments project. In: Hunter R, MacGlynn C, Rackley E (eds) Feminist judgments. From theory to practice. Hart Publishing, London, pp 44–56
Rackley E (2013) Women, judging and the judiciary: from difference to diversity. Routledge, London
Rebouchè R (2020) Feminist judgments: family law opinions rewritten. Cambridge University Press, Cambridge
Resnik J (1988) On the bias: reconsideration of the aspirations for our judges. South Calif Law Rev 61:1877–1944
Robson R (2016) Lawrence v. Texas, 539 U.S. 558 (2003). In: Stanchi K, Berger L, Crawford B (eds) Feminist judgments: rewritten opinions of the United States Supreme Court. New York, Cambridge University Press, pp 488–503
Schroeder MM (2002) Judging with a difference. Yale J Law Fem 14:255–261
Schultz J (2001) Can women judges help make civil sexual assault trials more therapeutic? Wisconsin Women's Law J 16:53–66
Smart C (1989) Feminism and the power of law. Routledge, London
Society for Personality and Social Psychology (2018) Gender roles highlight gender bias in judicial decisions. ScienceDaily. https://www.sciencedaily.com/releases/2018/04/180403085049.htm. Accessed 24 Sept 2021

Stanchi KM, Berger L, Crawford BJ (2016) Feminist judgments: rewritten opinions of the United States Supreme Court. Cambridge University Press
Tulkens F (2014) Parity on the bench: why? Why not? Eur Human Rights Law Rev 6:587–595
Vauchez SA (2019) Gender Balance in International Adjudicatory Bodies. https://opil.ouplaw.com/view/10.1093/law-mpeipro/e2699.013.2699/law-mpeipro-e2699. Accessed 24 Sept 2021
West R (1988) Jurisprudence and gender. Univ Chic Law Rev 55:1–72
Wilson B (1990) Will women judges really make a difference? Osgoode Hall Law J 28:507–522
Yahyaoui Krivenko E (2019) Women and the international court of justice. In: Rimmer SH, Ogg K (eds) Research handbook on feminist engagement with international law. Edward Elgar Publishing, Cheltenham/Northampton, pp 190–212

Further Reading

Baetens F (2020) Identity and diversity on the international bench. Who is the judge? Oxford University Press, Oxford
Collado Mateo C (2006) Mujeres, poder y derecho. Feminismo/s 8:15–34
Conaghan J (2018) Gender, law and jurisprudence. In: Auchmuty R (ed) Great debates in gender and law. Palgrave Macmillan, London
Esquembre Valdés MM (2006) Género y ciudadanía, mujeres y Constitución. Feminismo/s 8:35–51
Sanz Hermida AM (2014) Género y sistema procesal. In: Martín López T, Velasco Retamosa JM (eds) La igualdad de género desde la perspectiva social, jurídica y económica. Thomson Reuters-Civitas, Cizur Menor, pp 259–278
Swann WB, Langlois JH, Gilbert LA (1999) Sexism and stereotypes in modern society: the gender science of Janet Taylor Spence. American Psychological Association, Washington
United Nations (2017) Gender equality and Women's empowerment: constitutional jurisprudence. UN Women, New York

Gender Research and Feminist Methodologies

6

Zara Saeidzadeh

Contents

Abstract

This chapter is structured around the issue of gender research and what it means to conduct research with a gender perspective. Thus, it discusses research

Z. Saeidzadeh (✉)
Örebro University, School of Humanities, Education and Social Sciences, Örebro, Sweden
e-mail: zara.saeidzadeh@oru.se

D. Vujadinović et al. (eds.), *Gender-Competent Legal Education*, Springer Textbooks in Law, https://doi.org/10.1007/978-3-031-14360-1_6

methodologies inspired by feminist ontological and epistemological approaches. Drawing on feminist standpoint theory, situated knowledge, feminist poststructuralism and intersectionality, the chapter shows how feminist scholars, especially feminist legal scholars, have adopted feminist epistemologies in challenging gender inequalities in law and society. The chapter draws on legal methods combined with feminist social theories that have assisted feminist scholars to go about legal reforms. Furthermore, focusing on qualitative methods, the chapter explains some of the methods of data collection and data analysis in gender research which have been applied interdisciplinarily across social science and humanities studies. The last part of the chapter concentrates on practical knowledge about conducting gender research that is informed with feminist epistemologies and methodologies. Finally, through some exercises, the students are given the opportunity to design and outline a gender research plan with a socio-legal approach.

6.1 Introduction

Feminist scholars have been conducting research criticizing traditional and male dominated research and knowledge production. Therefore, feminists have proposed alternative methodologies which are informed by a variety of epistemological and ontological approaches across different disciplines including law and sociology. This chapter draws on feminist methodologies including feminist critical legal studies through a gender sensitive lens, in other words, feminist socio-legal approach in gender research (aims, objectives, outcomes).

Learning Goal

- The first learning objective of the chapter is to elaborate on how feminist research methodologies are developed in order to contribute to the production of knowledge about social reality; a production of knowledge that is not based on male dominated perspectives. Thus, it stresses the distinctiveness of feminist methodologies from traditional and patriarchal mainstream methodologies. In the process of knowledge production, feminist researchers have attempted to make connection between the idea of gender, gender equality, experience, and the reality of intersectional gender discrimination. Consequently, feminist research methodologies move from the mainstream scientific methods, from only collecting data for objective purposes, towards gender sensitive data collection and analysis. Feminist methodologies aim to produce knowledge through ethical and political perspectives, which focus on the critique and overcoming of gender blind scientific approach, in addition to the articulation of gender equality

(continued)

contents, concepts, conceptions, aims, objectives and outcomes. Feminist methodologies also aim at producing a so-called situated knowledge, which encompasses active role of the subject of creating the knowledge in the process of knowledge production.

- The second objective of the chapter is to show diversity among feminist epistemologies that opt for challenging power structure in various ways which capture complexities of gender and gender relations. It shows how feminist methodologies have developed from focusing on the category of women to moving beyond emphasizing women's commonality, which risks suppressing important differences existing among women who live life differently. There is a diversity of experiences in different social positions; white, black, heterosexual, lesbian, poor, privileged, colonized.
- The third objective of the chapter is to put an emphasis on qualitative methods in feminist research based on the feminist epistemologies presented in the chapter. Qualitative research method is thought to be the most appropriate to investigate the complex socio-historical, political, relational, structural and material existence of gender. Thus, qualitative methods of data collections such as interviews and documents are described. Qualitative methods of analysis including thematic analysis, document analysis and discourse analysis in conducting socio-legal research are also included.
- Finally, the fourth objective of this chapter is to provide the necessary knowledge and practical skills on academic writing. Writing an academic paper is challenging when it is based on research. Feminist writings are grounded on gender sensitive approach to political and ethical reflections which stand out across disciplines. Such reflections ought to be weighed more in educational purposes.

The key concepts that are covered in this chapter are:

- Gender research
- Epistemology and ontology in feminist research
- Situated knowledge and women's experiences
- Reflexivity and positionality
- Feminist standpoint theory
- Discourse and discursive construction of power
- Feminist legal methods
- Feminist intersectionality research
- Research design and research strategy
- Thematic analysis, critical discourse analysis and document analysis

6.2 Gender Research

This section introduces the notion of gender research, and conducting research from a gender perspective. It explains why it is important to conduct gender research and how methodologies are adopted to carry out research within the field of law and sociology with an emphasis on gender. Applying gender perspective in research refers to the analysis of gender as a social construct that impacts all aspects of people's lives with regards to social interactions and extends to intimate relations. Gender perspective in research questions unequal power relations in social structures. Moreover, gender perspective in social and legal research pays careful attention to the process of knowledge production in relation to power structure and contributes to development of gender equality within law and society.

The kind of research that only documents differences between the sexes offers no understanding of gender relations and gender practices, neither does it elaborate on the gendering process of laws and policies. Therefore, legal scholars have adopted methodologies with gender perspective to show an approach that recognizes multiple dimensions of gendered relations and power structure in the legal system. Gender research in sociological studies problematises hierarchical power relations between genders in everyday life and integrates diversity of social structures such as race, class, ethnicity, sexuality, socioeconomic status, age, and disability into analysis of structural inequalities.[1] What's more, Gender researchers have addressed traditional bias by adopting alternative methods of qualitative and quantitative data collection, that not only pay attention to gender differences, but also captures the complexity of gender relations.[2]

6.2.1 Gender Research in Law and Society

Why is it important to conduct gender research through analysing the interaction between law and society?

The emergence of gender studies as a field of research has contributed to critical study of law as being a rule of the state. Gender studies have explored law as a social process that is discursively constructed. Understanding law as a social phenomenon challenges the mainstream 'black letter' definition of law as fixed and immutable. Gender research that is conducted by sociolegal scholars have attended to the lack of gender sensitivity in law using critical social theories. Examples of such are matters of sexual harassment and domestic violence.

Legal policies are constituted in interaction with social norms and realities that are often gendered. Gendered social relations and practices have taken shape through historicity of sociocultural, political, and economic processes. Therefore, gender research helps to tease out the ways in which legal and social policies and practices

[1] Beetham and Demetriades (2007), pp. 199–216.

[2] Ibid.

shape people's lives. Law is an important and constitutive element of social life and gender is an important and constitutive element of human being. Together, the two are important in such research and more pressing in educational practices of law and gender.

Studying a social phenomenon with an emphasis on gender at interplay between law and society is important in many ways. It analyses law in terms of its power, potential and actual shortcomings in society. It investigates social realities of gender relations and constructions within law. It explores gendered social and legal process, and practices of legislation, judgements, jurisprudence and advocacy among legal professionals and institutions.

6.3 Feminist Research Methodologies

This section covers the ways in which feminist epistemologies as opposed to traditional and objective epistemologies have been developed to adopt methodologies for gender research. Feminist methodologies emerged from feminist politics, being feminist theories and practices. This section reflects on three feminist methodological approaches in studying gender and gender relations, which will be explained in the following subsections.

Feminist research does not stem from a unified set of thought and perspective. However, feminist perspectives do share common ideas. These common ideas imply that feminist research reflects on marginalization of women in social and political life.[3] Moreover, feminist research criticizes dominant norms of science which maintain male superiority by problematising hierarchical gender power relations and by establishing research approaches that are based on equal grounds.[4]

Methodology concerns the use of theories and methods in conducting research, which are informed by different epistemological and ontological approaches. In criticizing traditional and male dominated research, feminists have proposed alternative methodologies which are informed by their epistemology and ontology; the ways in which one understands the world and the knowledge produced about the world.

Feminist methodologies claim that knowledge is produced within a context in which meanings and experience cannot be simply distinguished.[5] In the process of knowledge production, feminist scholars and researchers have tried to make connection between idea, experience, and reality.[6] Moreover, feminist research is based on, and feeds, feminist theoretical perspectives which are a considerable part of feminist politics, challenging male-biased knowledge production and power. Thus, feminist researchers have consciously developed theories based on practice. Therefore, most

[3] May (2002).

[4] Undurraga (2010), pp. 277–281.

[5] Munro and Davies (2016), pp. 261–278.

[6] Ramazanoglu and Holland (2002).

researches that are conducted by feminists draw on experiences, especially women's experiences.[7]

Feminist epistemologies identify how gender influence our conception of knowledge and practices of inquiry.[8] Feminist epistemologies problematize how dominant conceptions and practices of knowledge production exclude and subordinate some groups of people, including women. Thus, feminist epistemologies offer diverse accounts of how to overcome this problem by developing new theories and methods. Central to this endeavour is situated knowledge, a kind of knowledge that reflects a particular position of the knower. Situated knowledge means that the situatedness of the subject in relation to the power structure produces a type of knowledge that problematizes the 'universal' male-dominated knowledge.[9] Donna Haraway reminds researchers how to tell the truth rather than proving how objective is the truth, by introducing the concept of situated knowledge. She encourages feminist researchers to hold on to the notion of partial visions instead of struggling to reduce their research to patriarchal knowledge.[10]

Feminist epistemologies focus on how the social location of an individual affects everyday life experiences, and how social structures are based on factors such as; gender, sexuality, ethnicity, race, age, place and socioeconomic status. These factors are imbued with power which ultimately results in situated knowledge. Thus, feminist epistemologies have opted for various ways to understand social phenomena and the ways in which knowledge is produced. This chapter explains standpoint theory, poststructuralism and intersectionality. However, it should be mentioned that feminist methodologies are developed across disciplines, adopting different approaches including; critical realism, historical materialism, new materialism and social structuralism to name but a few.[11]

Feminist researchers in various disciplines, including feminist legal scholars, have discussed how to incorporate feminist theories, women's experiences and knowledge production through gendered social relations into their analyses. That is to say, the following methodological approaches: standpoint theory, poststructuralism, intersectionality have also been employed by feminist researchers in legal studies. It should be mentioned that the following methodologies are chosen for students to understand how only some feminist methodologies are applied due to the limited scope of this chapter. Therefore, it does not imply rigid classification of these methodologies nor does it suggest they should be prefered in conducting gender research.

[7]Ackerly and True (2010), pp. 464–472.

[8]Anderson (2000).

[9]Haraway (1988), pp. 575–599.

[10]Ramazanoglu, Holland (2002).

[11]For further reading, please see McHugh (2014), pp. 137–164.

6.3.1 Feminist Standpoint Theory

This approach emerged in the 1970s out of discussions among feminists regarding masculinist science defining 'women' based on biology. Sandra Harding and Nancy Hartstock are known to be pioneer of this approach. Feminist standpoint theory finds out how knowledge production is entrenched with power relations. Feminist standpoint varies as different approaches are taken among feminists, which itself informs variety of feminist epistemological positions.

Feminist standpoint's central conception is that women's experiences speak the truth, resulting in the creation of knowledge that is situated in relation to power.[12]

In privileging women's standpoint, this epistemological stand presents strong reasons for how women understand the world differently from men in social division of labour. Feminist standpoint essentially adds gender to the already existing class analysis in scientific research.

Taking a feminist standpoint approach means to emphasize women's lives as they experience life differently from men. This is required to fully understand the relationship between experience, reality and knowledge, meaning it would be possible to remedy the kinds of misrepresentation and exclusion of women from dominant knowledge. According to Patricia Hill Collins, making knowledge claims about women must involve women's concrete experience to make that knowledge claim credible. Women's experiences refer to activities in everyday life including emotions and embodiment.[13]

For feminist standpoint theorists, knowledge is partial and does not implicate universal truth. Instead, it indicates the relations between power and knowledge. Empirical study is needed to investigate the specific forms of power, social relation and social positionality.[14]

Knowledge is constituted through everyday life. The everyday life of people is authoritative knowledge, as Dorothy Smith describes through 'work knowledge'.[15] A woman's standpoint begins to unravel the underpinnings of gender. However, experience must be spoken or written for it to come in to existence, meaning it does not exist before its entry to language as authentic. Therefore, experience is already discursively determined by the discourse in which it is spoken.[16]

Feminist legal scholars have adopted feminist standpoint theory to draw on women's point of view and experiences of matters in life which have been systematically excluded from legislations and supportive legal mechanisms. (Please see all the other chapters of the Textbook especially Sociology of Law chapter).

---

[12] Ramazanoglu and Holland (2002).

[13] Collins (1990), pp. 221–238.

[14] Ramazanoglu and Holland (2002).

[15] Smith (2005).

[16] Smith (2005).

6.3.2 Feminist Poststructuralism

Influenced by literary criticism, poststructuralism emerged in the 1960s in France. Many thinkers of this philosophy such as Jacque Derrida, Michel Foucault and Julia Kristeva were initially structuralist thinkers who became critical to structuralism and abandoned the idea. Therefore, poststructuralism was created. It is fair to say that the work of thinkers who were initially known as structuralists, was developed to a more fluid and complex kind of idea called poststructuralism.

► **Definition** Poststructuralism upholds that language produces meanings which constitutes subjects. Poststructural theories explain how discourse produces subjects. How do discourses function and what are their effects in society.

The lines between postmodernism and poststructuralism are blurry and many have argued that the two cannot be assumed separately. Postmodern theory emerged in response to the limitation of modernism and the metanarratives produced by modernists.[17] Poststructuralism (i.e. Derrida) is usually associated with a theory of knowledge and language, while postmodernism (i.e. Foucault and Lyotard) is often linked to theory of society, culture and history.[18]

Feminists allied with postmodern and post-structural themes on fluidity of identities, and some have opted for deconstruction of identities, such as category of woman. Furthermore, the rejection of epistemology altogether is also said to be taken by postmodern feminists who aim to abandon any attempt to claim knowledge.[19]

Feminist poststructuralism transcends situatedness by stressing on locality, partiality, contingency and ambiguity of any view of the world.[20] Feminists started to revise the standpoint theory. Hartstock, for example, made a revision to her original presentation of standpoint approach, in which she says that emphasizing women's commonality will risk suppressing important differences existing between women and their life experiences in different social positions; white, black, heterosexual, lesbian, poor, privileged, colonized and so on.[21] According to poststructuralism, reality is socially and discursively constructed. Thus, feminist poststructuralists do claim that gender is socially and discursively constructed as a result of the effect of social regulations.

Postmodern feminist researchers criticize feminist standpoint and feminist empiricism for being essentialists in the ways they use identity categories such as women, due to their focus on gender differences that are portrayed as essential and univer-

[17]Leavy (2007), pp. 83–108.

[18]Agger (1991), pp. 105–131.

[19]Ibid.

[20]Anderson (2000).

[21]Benton and Craib (2010).

sal.[22] Poststructuralist scholar Joan Scott criticizes standpoint theory and its focus on women's experience which she argues exists in language and discourse, hence the discourses of women's experiences are constructed beyond the speaker or writer's intention.[23] In poststructuralist epistemology, power is understood as discursive and not the property of one gender. Thus, agency of the subject, according to feminist poststructuralist view is not free from discursive power.

Feminist poststructuralism, usually known as third wave feminism, problematizes the binary category of male and female, and argue that language and discourse create gendered subject through interactive process of everyday life.[24] It shows how relations of power are produced and reproduced. Thus, it subscribes to knowledge being produced discursively through particular social and historical contexts. According to feminist poststructuralism, the subject is basically dead, one's subjectivity and understanding of self is constructed through discourse. Hence, the agency of the subject is limited, as Judith Butler holds that 'the subject is not just a product a constitutive force of her discursive practices, it rather is a disruptor of the process through which she is constituted'.[25]

Feminist legal scholars' approach to law as a social phenomenon, seeing law as being discursively constructed, has led them to decentralize the states' power and push forward for gender equal legal reforms. (please see Sociology of Law chapter).

6.3.3 Feminist Intersectionality

The concept of intersectionality is said to be developed by Black feminism in 1980s, particularly by Kimberlé Crenshaw who focused on the intersection of gender and race. She defined the concept of intersectionality as a different way in which the factor of race, along with gender, affect the ways black women experience employment and social life. The experiences of women of colour were excluded and lost in forms of multiple discrimination and marginalization.[26] It is worth noting that long before the inception of the concept of intersectionality, feminists had already been analysing gender at intersection with other structures of dominations such as class. For example, US feminist anti-slavery movement in the nineteenth century.[27] Therefore, we can say that the early use of the concept of intersectionality in feminist practice was based on the intersection of at least two axes of domination. This included gender and race, or gender and class, yet was not considered in either politics or research. Intersectionality has brought a conceptual shift in feminist philosophy and research through which scholars understand social actors.

---

[22] Leavy (2007), pp. 83–108.

[23] Scott (1991), pp. 773–797.

[24] Davies (2000).

[25] Butler (1993).

[26] Crenshaw (1989), pp. 139–167.

[27] Kaijser and Kronsell (2014), pp. 417–433.

Feminist intersectionality focuses on multidimensional and multi layered understandings of power and knowledge. To understand power relations in production of knowledge, it is important to know how subjects are situated; the situatedness or social location of people in the intersections of power. Situatedness engender knowledge from specific circumstances where power struggle is immediately at work, and when a particular type of knowledge is generated.

The recent work of feminists on intersectionality focuses on multiple forms of systems of dominations and privileges. Thus, in intersectionality research, the perspective of multiple marginalized groups is included in analysis, including the social experiences of privileged groups. The consequence here is to problematise and challenge universalisation.[28] For example, the category of woman as a universal aspect is challenged. Furthermore, intersectionality research illustrates that no one single factor is the reason for marginalisation and dominance; they are part of a broader pattern. According to Kathy Davis, "intersectionality is the interaction between gender, race, and other categories of difference in individual lives, social practices, institutional arrangements and cultural ideologies and the outcomes of these interactions in terms of power".[29]

Power is an important element in intersectional analysis. Feminist studies, together with anti-racist, postcolonial, queer studies, masculinity and disability studies, continue to enhance how norms are constructed and how power relations interact with each other. "Intersections of power can be found in all relations, at all levels of social structure from individual actions to institutional practice".[30]

The aim of employing intersectionality in feminist research is not to simply add as many categories as possible to our analysis, but to broaden the perspective and reflect on what factors may be relevant in a particular context, with specific socio-historical and spatial context. "An intersectional approach goes beyond just identifying power patterns. It is applied to problematizing the underlying social categories and see how these are reinforced or challenged".[31]

Feminist legal scholars have critically analysed the one-dimensional approach of law through intersectional perspective. Intersectional analysis has enabled feminist legal scholars in their legal analysis and judgments to scrutinize the multiplicity of underpinning social structures of both oppression and privilege at macro, meso and micro levels. Thus, relationality of social structures of gender, sexuality, class, race, ethnicity, religion, age, (dis)ability is being analysed with respect to socio-historicity of the context.

The formation of intersectionality has not been without criticism. Scholars often remain critical towards the use of intersectionality as an additional component of research. The critiques extend to debate that in trying to present multiple forms of discrimination and oppression, the grounds of intersectionality are used as additive

[28] Freidenvall and Dahlerup (2019), pp. 230–251.

[29] Davis (2008), pp. 67–85.

[30] Kaijser and Kronsell (2014), pp. 417–433.

[31] Kaijser and Kronsell (2014), p. 422.

and multiplicative approaches. This often reduces oppression to discrete categories of sexism, racism, heterosexism, classism.[32]

6.4 Feminist Legal Methodologies

This section provides an overview of the development of feminist legal methods in doing and making laws. This extends from asking the woman's question, to addressing other genders and multiple forms of gender inequality approach, through methods such as feminist judgments and gender mainstreaming applying intersectional analysis (i.e., gender, race, class, sexuality etc.).

6.4.1 Feminist Legal Methods

What are feminist legal methods? Feminists have long been criticizing law and what the law should entail. Therefore, they have proposed legal reforms which recognize women and other marginalized groups, including provision for, and protection of, their needs and rights in different areas of law.

In order to challenge power structures, feminists have defined their own methods of legal analysis; without having methods, feminists claims about law would have been dismissed.[33] Bartlett explains that "feminists like other lawyers use a range of methods of conventional legal reasoning such as deduction, induction, analogy and general techniques". However, what distinguishes feminist legal methods from the traditional legal methods is that feminist legal methods try to "unveil legal issues which are overlooked and suppressed by traditional methods".[34]

Feminist legal methods are strongly imbued with feminist theoretical and methodological approaches. The following sections explain how feminist legal methods have adopted standpoint theory, by including women's and other 'marginalized' genders into law making and legal reasonings adopting feminist intersectional approach. Furthermore, the section explains how feminist socio-legal scholars have adopted poststructuralist methodologies to problematize gendered power relations. This is achieved through discursive analysis and active engagement with practices of law and society, to rewrite judgments and policies through gender perspective.

6.4.1.1 From women's Question to Multiple Gender Inequality

Feminist legal methods are seen as contributor to the modification of traditional legal methods, dominated by heterosexual male perspective. Legal methods were first initiated and adopted by feminists for practical reasoning and consciousness raising

---

[32] Cor and Chan (2017), pp. 109–132.

[33] Bartlett (2018), pp. 370–403.

[34] Bartlett (1990), p. 830.

on issues experienced by women. Feminist legal methods, according to Bartlett, is about discussions over what kind of methodology feminist legal theory should adopt to identify and problematize the existing legal structure.[35] Feminist legal methods started to develop by problematising those parts of law that are discriminatory towards women. In other words, including women's perspectives into legal methods and ask questions from women's point of views.

Feminist legal methods, three methods as explained by Bartlett, are as follows. The first method is about asking the question of women, which is applied to expose how the substance of law subtly excludes the perspectives of women. So, feminist legal method considers the experience of women and asks the women's question in law.

Example

The case of *Myra Bradwell vs. State of Illinois* in 1873 asked the United States Supreme Court about why women are excluded from practicing law and why women are not included in the privileges and immunities of citizenship according to 14th amendment. This led to Illinois legislation prohibiting gender discrimination in occupation.[36] ◄

The second method regards feminist practical reasoning that is applied to move beyond the traditional notion of legal relevance in legal decision making. Practical reasoning is more sensitive to the cases, instead of simply reflecting already established legal doctrine. In this method, the reasoning is dependent on women's context and experiences, which are unique.

Example

The issue of abortion among teenagers is contingent on specific situations. Actual and specific circumstances might not be in favour of pregnant children who ought to obtain their parents' consent, as it might lead to abusive behaviours of parents forcing pregnancy on the child. ◄

The third method covers consciousness raising, which is applied to examine how legal principles correspond directly with people's personal experience.[37] Consciousness raising is a process through which one reveals experience for collective empowerment. Personal experience becomes a political matter.

[35] Alkan (2013), pp. 83–97.

[36] Bartlett (2018), pp. 370–403.

[37] Ibid.

Example

Women employ consciousness raising method when they share their experiences of rape and sexual assault publicly through MeToo campaign. ◄

Critiques have raised some shortcomings with regards to the practicality of feminist legal methods focusing on women only. They have argued that the focus on the elimination of bias against women is limiting and such methods will be used by legal professionals who are not necessarily feminists, and certainly not all legal decision makers are concerned about the women's question. Moreover, feminist legal method is criticized for its biased focus on women and women's way of thinking, which is discussed to be elevating women over other issues such as disability, racism, poverty and ethnicity to name but a few. It is argued, as a consequence, this would ultimately lead to privilege of women's experiences over other groups of people.[38]

6.4.1.2 Intersectional Perspective in Law

Previously, the dominant kind of civil society activism within the EU had usually focused on one particular identity category when acted against discrimination which resulted in a way that, "the EU equality and anti-discrimination policies addressed specific groups of people as being subject of inequality and discrimination. For example, women, ethnic minorities, sexual minorities were only targeted in relation to one single dimension of inequality and discrimination such as either gender or ethnicity or sexuality".[39] Instead of foregrounding one category over others for addressing discrimination, Hancock has proposed academic researchers should adopt multiple approach to inequality. This approach recognizes that people are not one-dimensional with grounds of inequality being manifold and multiple. In turn, this demands recognition of multiple discriminations in law.[40] However, an intersectionality approach has been argued to replace 'multiple discrimination' approach in research, because the multiple discrimination approach might lead to focusing on inequality grounds at individual level, rather than accounting for discrimination at structural level.

Intersectionality and intersectional perspective in law and policies concerning European institutions has not yet been adequately used to deal with intersectional violence and discrimination. Intersectionality within law reveals and tackles violence against women who are marginalized due to the interplay of different structural and individual reasons.[41] Intersectionality in law is not just about understanding the ways in which discrimination is experienced on grounds of race, ethnicity, gender,

[38] Clougherty (1996), p. 1.

[39] Kantola and Nousiainen (2009), pp. 459–477.

[40] Hancock (2007), pp. 63–79.

[41] Bello (2017), pp. 15–28.

sexuality and so on. Intersectional perspective in law also unveils the structural barriers that produce social inequalities.

Intersectionality in law has been discussed in relation to antidiscrimination laws and gender-based violence in Europe. The problem with law is that it does not acknowledge fluidity and intersecting elements of people's lives. It often focuses on one element of a human being. Most laws tend to adopt a one-dimensional approach. For example, in law on violence against women, the law usually addresses violence as crime that occurred on one ground and that is usually identity.[42] Other grounds of inequality such as sexuality, class, age, ethnicity, disability in protecting violence against women are rarely considered by legal policies.

Although the legal framework of the Council of Europe's Convention for Protection of Human Rights and Fundamental Freedoms (ECtHR) allows lawyers and judges to have an intersectional perspective,[43] it has remained less practiced on the ground among legal professionals and within legal culture. Namely, given the behaviour and attitudes of legal professionals towards law, it is rare to examine, for example, the intersection of heterosexism or patriarchy in relation to sexist or racial behaviour. To demonstrate this, the cases of forced sterilization of Muslim Roma women in the Czech Republic, Slovakia and Hungry at ECtHR which were either settled or declared inadmissible in 2016[44] did not involve intersectional analysis of gender, age, class, ethnicity and religion. Bello discusses how the application of intersectionality within legal reasoning can contribute to protection of Roma women's rights.[45]

An Intersectional approach is also hugely missing within European national and international laws with regards to LGBTQIA+ groups of people who are immigrants, refugees, sex workers, domestic workers, and disabled. The EU policies have not adequately taken an intersectional approach addressing inequalities among and within LGBTQIA+ groups who experience violence and discrimination differently. Moreover, laws and policies often homogenize lesbian, gay, bisexual, transgender, queer, and intersex people as one identity category, lumping them altogether into one cluster of entity. This has often overlooked people's different needs. An inequality ground for a gay person may not be a concern for a trans persons. The intersectional approach within and among each group would allow for specific and common policy objectives.[46]

[42] Bello (2017), pp. 15–28.

[43] Please see https://www.coe.int/en/web/gender-matters/intersectionality-and-multiple-discrimination retrieved 25 June 2021.

[44] Bello (2017), pp. 15–28.

[45] Bello (2009), pp. 11–20.

[46] Cruells and Coll-Planas (2013), pp. 122–137.

6.4.2 Feminist Socio-Legal Methods

The term socio-legal has a broad definition that might differ in different contexts. The main component of socio-legal study is that it acknowledges the law is not just the product of the state. Rather, it is a product of social processes and practices.[47] Feminists have adopted social theories in combination with legal methods to criticize the role of law, not as law in the books, instead law in the context in creating and reinforcing gendered relations and practices. During the past few decades, feminist socio-legal scholars have worked with feminist methodological approaches, including poststructuralism and intersectionality, to highlight the "the implications of gendered power relations in law and society".[48] (see chapter on Sociology of Law).

6.4.2.1 Feminist Judgements

As part of critical legal scholarship and legal reforms, feminist legal scholars, judges, lawyers and activists have engaged in specific cases to provide critical analyses of law in construction of gender. In their attempt to re-write judgments, they tackle power relations and problematise judicial and legal norms embedded in society.[49] Feminist judgements have impacted legal understanding and gender equality policies through socially engaging with matters such as marriage, parenthood, sexual consent, rape, and domestic violence. Moreover, feminist judgements consider the concept of judging as a 'social practice' which does not take place in isolation.[50] (Please see chapter on Feminist Judgement).

6.4.2.2 Gender Mainstreaming

Feminists have defined and debated gender mainstreaming differently, although the transformative potential of gender mainstreaming, that is revealing patriarchal structures and bringing marginalized issues into the centre of policy and law making, has been consistently valued.

Gender mainstreaming became the focus of international attention through adoption of the Beijing platform for action at the UN conference in 1995. The Amsterdam treaty imagined gender equality within all activities in the EU in 1997. The Council of Europe defined gender mainstreaming as a way to call for "incorporation of gender equality perspective into all policies at all levels and stages of policy making".[51] Gender mainstreaming involves discursive analysis of the process and practices, through which laws and policies are created. Dragica Vujadinović emphasizes the necessity of gender mainstreaming to a gender sensitive approach within legal education. Vujadinovic shows how this is mostly non-existent in universities across the globe, including universities in developed 'Western countries'

---

[47] Fletcher (2002), pp. 135–154.

[48] Hunter (2019).

[49] Hunter et al. (2010).

[50] Ibid.

[51] Sainsbury and Bergqvist (2009), pp. 216–234.

and the European Union.[52] Introducing gender mainstreaming projects in different countries depends on their approach to gender equality. For example, a broader approach to gender equality rather than conceiving it in terms of equal opportunities and equal treatment, allows for incorporating gender mainstreaming or a gender sensitive approach in educational practices.

Moreover, gender mainstreaming has provided opportunities for feminists to problematize 'gender blindness' at an institutional level, in public services and private matters.

6.5 Feminist Empirical Methods of Gender Research

This section describes the steps in conducting empirical sociological and qualitative research with a gender perspective. It explains the process of research including research design, research plan, research methods and method analysis. It should be noted that feminist research can be based on empirical as well as theoretical studies.

6.5.1 Feminist Positionality and Reflexivity

Feminist researchers study power relations, and yet unequal power relations are always present between the researcher and the subjects of research. Therefore, it is crucial to reflect upon the existing unequal power relations between the researcher and the research participants throughout the process of knowledge production. One should begin by clarifying one's own positionality in relation to the research, as well as one's position in relation the research participants. Conducting qualitative study based on fieldwork and sharing the findings collected from people, would be best done through destabilising power hierarchies. This is a task that feminist researchers have achieved by applying reflexivity into their theory and methods. Feminist researchers tend to define their positionality within research to avoid claiming objective truth in the process of knowledge production.[53]

Feminist approaches to mainstream methodology vary, because they try to discover reliable accounts of socially constituted 'reality' rather than reproducing the 'objective' truth. Feminists have taken different approaches to challenge mainstream scientific methods of knowledge production, which aim to criticize universal criteria for knowledge claim. The feminist approaches that are elaborated in this chapter are: feminist standpoint theory or epistemology, feminist post-structuralism and feminist intersectionality.

As for research ethics, conducting empirical research based on interviews, for example, require researchers to obtain ethical approval; the practical aspect of research ethics. Ethical considerations in research are not limited to obtaining

[52] Vujadinović (2015), pp. 56–74.

[53] Maxey (1999), pp. 199–208.

permissions. Ethics involve the ways in which the researcher relates to the research participants, and the data and information gathered from the research participants. Feminist research ethics emphasizes on the coproduction of knowledge with the research participants.[54] Researchers need to address ethical issues in qualitative research with regards to informed consent, privacy, and protection of information and lives of research participants, during and after the fieldwork.

6.5.2 Qualitative and Quantitative Research

Due to feminists' criticism of traditional research being reliant on quantitative methods in the social sciences, increased use of qualitative research is suggested to better understand people's social life. The dialogue between quantitative and qualitative researchers has continued for decades, as to which method better captures complexities of social issues. The use of quantitative data in conjunction with qualitative material is encouraged by feminist researchers to develop feminist theories.

► **Definition** Quantitative research has a numeric and statistical approach. It employs strategies and methods of data collection such as surveys and other statistical instruments through which information can be quantified.[55] Quantitative research consists of experiments that either test or confirm the existing theories. Therefore, the research is independent of the researcher in a quantitative method, tending to give an objective account of reality.

Three broad classifications of quantitative research are identified: descriptive, experimental, and causal comparative. The descriptive approach examines the current situation as it exists. The experimental approach investigates an independent variable in a study and then measures the outcome. The causal comparative approach examines how an independent variable is affected by a dependent variable, before analysing the cause-and-effect relationships between the variables.[56] Moreover, different methods of examination are used in quantitative research such as correlational design, observational studies, and survey research.

► **Definition** Qualitative research has a holistic approach. It does not entail a fixed definition, as the nature of qualitative research is deemed 'ever-changing'. This is due to the variety of frameworks and approaches within which researchers conduct qualitative inquiry.[57]

---

[54] Karnieli-Miller et al. (2009), pp. 279–289.

[55] Creswell and David Creswell (2017).

[56] Williams (2007).

[57] Catalano and Creswell (2013), pp. 664–673.

Common characteristics of qualitative research are: (1) it is conducted in a natural setting, (2); directed by the researcher; (3) involving inductive and deductive reasoning; (4) it focuses on participants' views; (5) conducted in a specific context; (6) involves flexibility and creativity during the research process and; (7) is based on the researcher's complex interpretation of the issue, but involves reflexivity.[58] Qualitative research engages with matters in everyday life, discourses, experiences and practices in a variety of dimensions. Poststructuralists have shown particular interests in qualitative research. Feminist research has had a significant impact in developing qualitative research as exists today. Qualitative methods, particularly face-to-face in-depth interviews, have become definitive of feminist qualitative research. Here we focus on interviews and documents as methods of data collection in qualitative research.

6.5.3 Research Plan, Design and Strategy

Before going through the steps of planning research, the following aspects need to be addressed:

In order to conduct the research, there are a few fundamental matters that the researcher needs to address. First, the researcher should know about the nature of the phenomenon, entities or the social reality that are in question. What is the research about? Second, the researcher must have an ontological and epistemological position as to how the researcher thinks the world exists, how knowledge about the world is produced and what social reality is made of. These are the epistemological questions: how social phenomenon can be known and how knowledge can be demonstrated.

Example

If the researcher thinks that social reality is constituted of people, relations, institutions, structures, social process, discourses, practices, and rules, the researcher ought to establish how to investigate the social phenomenon in question, within this framework of understanding of social reality. ◀

The answers to such questions form the strategy of the research. Research strategy is about how the researcher outlines the epistemological and ontological approaches to investigate the subject matter of their research. For instance, a socio-legal approach is a way to strategise research.

The next step is to clarify the aim of the research, that is to find out exactly why the researcher wants to conduct the research. It should be noted that the research objectives are less broad than the research aims and they basically pave the way to achieve the research aims.

---

[58] Ibid.

Example

If the aim of a research is to reduce violence against women in the workplace, the research objectives to achieve this aim would be: (1) understand how violence in workplace is perceived by employers, (2) explore all forms of violence experienced by women during their employment, and (3) investigate employment laws and policy. ◀

The next step is to design the research. Designing research starts after ascertaining the position and approach in conducting the research. Research design is a kind of planning that maps out the ways through which the researcher conducts a study; helping the researcher to conduct an organised and coherent study.[59] In qualitative research, designing starts from the moment the researcher starts to formulate the research questions, problems or hypotheses. A qualitative research design consists of research questions, methods of data collection, methods of analyses and findings. After investigating the topic and reading the literature, the researcher drafts research questions. The questions can be refined later during the research process. After defining the questions, the researcher maps out relevant information for each question. This information concerns the sources of data and material, how to gather data and how to analyse the data.

Example

In studying violence against women in the workplace, one research question could be how violence against women in the workplace is defined by law and policy makers? To answer this question, the researcher needs information or data from specific sources that can answer the question. The sources of data collection to answer the questions would be legal documents and interviews with stake holders. How to collect data from these sources could be gathered through documents and interviews. After gathering the data, the analysis could be done by applying critical discourse analysis and/or policy analysis. This outline is called research design. ◀

6.5.3.1 Socio-Legal Research Strategy

How to design research which investigates the subject matter through a socio-legal approach? One way is to examine how policies and practices of gender at individual, meso and macro levels are influenced by, and influence the subject matter in question, within a specific context that is also contingent on socio-historical background.

Studying 'law in context'[60] as one of the approaches within social-legal research contributes to the production of knowledge that is informed by people's experiences

[59] Creswell and Poth (2016).

[60] Banakar (2015), pp. 41–58.

and existing social issues. In turn, these are tied to the processes of making and implementing law.

The policy research approach to socio-legal research is concerned with issues related to social policy, regulations, implementation, and enforcement. For example, examining how efficient implementation of law can affect access to justice, can be a policy research. The use of survey to evaluate a piece of legislation is another common policy research.[61]

6.5.4 Methods of Data Collection in Qualitative Research

Based on the methodological approaches explained in previous sections, the following methods of data collection have been adopted by feminist researchers cross disciplines, including socio-legal scholars.

6.5.4.1 Interviews

An interview is understood to be a simple conversation that constitutes everyday life. It is a valuable method for gathering knowledge from an individual's experience. An interview constitutes a further way to collect intellectual information in a social process from people.[62] As Kvale and Brinkmann suggest, the act of interviewing is a craft, which means it is based on practical skills and the decisions made by the interviewer during every step of the process.[63] Interview in social research is a guided, informal conversation through which the interviewee and the interviewer contribute to the process of knowledge production. The two sides interact with each other ethically and politically.[64]

Learning how to conduct interviews for social research can be achieved only through engaging in actual interviews. In other words, one learns by doing. However, it is important to consider that interviewing is composed of several general steps. The interviewer logically follows these steps, including; identifying the population, classifying the questions, reaching out to the population, designing the interview guide, determining the location of interviews, recording interviews, transcribing interviews and analysing interviews.[65]

It is up to the researcher to determine what type of interviews are deemed more suitable for answering the research questions; either structured interviews or semi-structured interviews. Semi-structured interviews involve the researchers asking a set of questions from each interviewee. The nature of these interviews, however, allows the interviewee to raise ideas and issues about which the researcher has not

[61] Ibid.

[62] Gubrium and Holstein (2002), pp. 3–32.

[63] Kvale and Brinkmann (2009).

[64] Rubin and Rubin (2011); Brinkmann (2009).

[65] Gubrium and Holstein (2002), pp. 3–32; Kvale and Brinkmann (2009); Rubin and Rubin (2011).

thought. This type of interview is flexible and gives the opportunity for the researcher to receive new questions or change the existing ones.

6.5.4.2 Documents

What are documents? Documents contain texts and sometimes images that have been produced without the researcher's involvement.[66] Documents in social research could include a variety of materials, from personal journals to official organisational records or state datasets. Researchers have also identified other documents for social research, such as maps, photographs, newspaper reports, autobiographies, and even social media or SMS conversations. Electronic and digital documents constitute a significant part of documents in our world today, especially within organizations and institutions.

Documents can also be the sort of data and evidence through which people, groups, institutions, and organizations are accounted for. Documents here are tools to enable understanding of social and organizational practices.[67] Documents exist in many varieties such as legal, medical, financial, personal and so on. In terms of their form, documents can be literary, textual, or visual devices that create information. Therefore, documents are artifacts produced for a particular purpose, representing social conventions, being the analytical component of documents. Amanda Coffey maintains: "documents are social facts which means they are produced, shared and used in socially organized ways".[68] Policy documents, legislations, strategic plans, press release, annual reports, newspaper articles are included as such.

6.5.5 Methods of Analysis in Qualitative Research

Based on the methodological approaches explained in previous sections, the following methods of data collection have been adopted by feminist researchers cross disciplines including socio-legal scholars.

Analysis is a process of generating, developing and verifying concepts.[69] The process of analysis begins even before starting the research project, as researchers choose a topic in which they have prior ideas.[70] Researchers require to have some ideas while collecting information about their studies; these ideas continue to develop during the research process and might modify along the way, by going back and forth between ideas and collected information. Analysis is not the last phase of research, as some might think. It is rather a process that actively involves information gathering.[71] Nevertheless, no consensus is achieved among scholars on

[66] Bowen (2009).

[67] Coffey (2014), p. 368.

[68] Ibid.

[69] Corbin and Strauss (2008).

[70] Bernard et al. (2016).

[71] Coffey and Atkinson (1996).

what analysis means. Despite this lack of consensus, there are common characteristics to all methods of qualitative analysis. These are; reflexivity of the researcher, systematic but not rigid analytical approach, organizing the data, and inductive (that is data led) analysis. In addition, methodological knowledge is required. This does not mean that one should subscribe to one approach only and follow through the entire process. Flexibility and reflexivity should be counted.[72]

Analysis involves interpretation where qualitative researchers translate other people's acts and words. It is not straightforward to convey exact meanings, and therefore, some details may be lost in translation.[73] Interpretation consequently becomes a never-ending process, as researchers must always consider their data; reflect, reinterpret or amend interpretations. This may lead the researcher to new ideas. The process of analysis according to Denzin and Lincoln, is neither terminal nor mechanical. It is an ongoing emergent unfinished, changeable process.[74]

6.5.5.1 Thematic Analysis

As a method of analysing data, thematic analysis searches for themes that emerge from the data or information to describe the phenomenon. "The process of analysis involves identifying themes through reading of the data. These themes become categories of analysis for the researcher".[75]

Thematic analysis can be applied within many ontological and epistemological frameworks. The researcher should make their theoretical approach explicit to the reader, as thematic analysis is a theoretical independent method of analysis.[76] Thematic analysis does not concern counting predetermined words or phrases, rather, it identifies implicit and explicit ideas in the data.

Thematic analysis is 'a method for identifying, analysing and reporting patterns (themes) within data' inductively or deductively.[77] Due to its flexibility, thematic analysis is suitable for analysing a wide range of data types, for instance; interviews, focus group discussion, textual data (i.e., qualitative surveys, diaries), online discussion forums and other textual and visual media sources.[78]

Applying this method in research requires the identification of patterns, paying particular regard to important issues in relation to the research questions and theoretical framework, which must form some level of prevalence across the whole data. Similar to many other qualitative methods, thematic analysis is not a linear process. The researcher moves back and forth between different phases of the process of analysis. A six-phase analytic process is introduced by Terry et al., which are: "1) familiarising with the data, 2) generating codes, 3) constructing

---

[72]Ibid.

[73]Corbin and Strauss (2008).

[74]Denzin and Lincoln (2011).

[75]Fereday and Muir-Cochrane (2006), pp. 80–92.

[76]Terry et al. (2017), pp. 17–37.

[77]Guest et al. (2012), pp. 79–106.

[78]Terry et al. (2017), pp. 17–37.

themes, 4) reviewing potential themes, 5) defining and naming themes, and 6) producing the report".[79]

6.5.5.2 Document Analysis

In qualitative research, document analysis is applied to close examination of documents to understand how they are authored or produced, including how they are used. Much of the organizational knowledge is stored in documents. Social actors are the authors of documents, and the examination of those documents is one way of understanding how social structure operates.[80] Documents also represent reality, albeit in a distorted and selective fashion, and can be used as a medium through which the researcher can find correspondence with the subject of study. However, they cannot be read separately from the social, historical and political contexts.[81]

'Document analysis is a systematic procedure for reviewing and evaluating both printed and electronic materials.[82] Document analysis starts with finding the documents, selecting and synthesizing information in the documents, which then can be organized into themes or categories and interpretation. This process involves content analysis that entails identifying meaningful and relevant passages of the text. Scholars have discussed applying thematic analysis to analyse documents, involving the recognition of patterns within the data and consequently exposing emerging themes.[83]

Document analysis involves data *selection* instead of *collection*. Content information in documents is what the researcher analyses without being involved in gathering it, which is said to be unaffected by the research process. Many documents are publicly available, making it easier for the researcher to access.

Document analysis is used as a single method, in a triangulation, or mixed-methods, where two or more methods are used in research. For example, questionnaires and interviews in research are used in combination with document analysis.[84] As an illustration, gathering and analysing documents such as state laws and institutional regulations, as a stand-alone method provides the researcher in-depth knowledge about the purpose and intentions of the creators of the documents, and how they are used to shape people's lives.

6.5.5.3 Discourse Analysis

Discourse analysis is a method which investigates how meanings are produced within narratives of, for example, conversation, newspapers or interviews. Discourse analysis refers to a set of approaches that can be used to examine the ways in which

---

[79]Terry et al. (2017), pp. 17–37.

[80]Coffey (2014), pp. 367–380.

[81]May (2001).

[82]Bowen (2009).

[83]Fereday and Muir-Cochrane (2006), pp. 80–92.

[84]Bowen (2009).

power relations are reproduced, through the function of language within texts and narratives. Discourse analysis is the result of Foucault's work on discursive construction of power. Hence, it focuses on how power relations are constructed by means of language. Within social science research, discourse analysis takes a political approach by finding out who is constructed as marginalized and who gains hegemony in social relations. Thus, discourse analysis pays attention to the socio-political context of discourse and conveys how people are positioned by dominant discourses.[85]

Discourse analysis method aims to move away from finding truth, instead working towards the functionality of discourse critically. Critical discourse analysis is an interdisciplinary type of discourse studies, examining how 'social practices become contextualized as they are represented in discourse in instances of communication'.[86] Furthermore, critical discourse analysis concentrates on the role of language and communication in discursive construction of social domination, discrimination and social injustice.[87] The analysing process of research, focuses on the use of language to understand how people, practices and processes are represented, and what the underlying forces of such representations are. However, critical discourse analysis does not simply regard texts, rather, establishing what connects the text to a social context where people and events are produced.[88]

Identifying discourses vary among researchers as there is no one way. In common, discourse analysis involves general steps, as any other qualitative methods, such as; formulating research questions, selection of sample, gathering data (i.e., records and documents etc.) and transcribing, coding data before writing up.

Critical discourse analysis of legal documents such as judicial opinions, statutes, constitutions, procedural laws and administrative laws can reveal the subtle and invisible nature discrimination based on gender, sexuality, race, ethnicity, class, religion, nationality etc.

Example

Discourse analysis of a supreme court's judgement on refusing a request of a trans woman to gain the custody of her child or visitation, unravels the discrimination based on discursive practices and policies of creating gendered subjects, gendered roles, womanhood and parenthood. ◀

[85] Hesse-Biber and Leavy (2010).

[86] Breazu (2020).

[87] Van Dijk (1993), pp. 249–283.

[88] Fairclough (2000), pp. 163–195.

6.6 Writing a Research Paper

This section elaborates basic knowledge on how to write a scholarly paper; a paper that is the result of either an empirical or conceptual/theoretical research on gender.

Feminist researchers have published extensively on writings of research, especially research based on fieldwork. Feminist writings have paid special attention to reflexivity or reflection, by emphasizing the complex relationship between the researcher and the research participants in the process of knowledge production in various contexts. Writing on issues related to gender requires critical engagement and more of an explanatory than descriptive writing.

Essential skills for writing rationally and effectively are discussed in many textbooks.[89] These skills include using arguments, building arguments, understanding the cause-and-effect relations, making comparison, using references and describing visual and textual materials.

6.6.1 Structuring a Paper

The structure of the paper is proven to be the most difficult part of writing for writers. The main and few substantial components of a research paper are basically comprised of the introduction, the main text (theory, methods, analysis), the conclusion and references.

The purpose of the introduction in a research paper is firstly, to provide a rationale for the paper and explain why a particular question within the topic of the paper is being investigated. Secondly, it is important to illuminate on why it is interesting for the reader to know about the topic of the paper, particularly the issue in question.

The theory section describes the theoretical tools and concepts that are used to interpret and analyse data. The method section in the main text of the paper elaborates on what kind of data have been gathered for the purpose of this paper and how. It further draws on the methodological approach that has been adopted.

The section on analysis in the paper discusses the interpretation of data within the adopted theoretical framework.

The conclusion is the final section of the paper. The purpose is to summarize the main points of the paper, restates the thesis of the paper and makes final comments of the arguments of the paper.

To write a clear and organized paper, the writer should be especially confident about the ideas contained within. Moreover, it is important that the topic is written with passion.

Some general strategies are suggested for writing which focus on how to manage an academic paper in a timely manner. Planning and revising are the two general strategies that have been found in writing research.

[89] Please see: Bailey (2014); Swales and Feak (1994).

6.6.2 Referencing and Plagiarism

Since writing a scholarly paper depends on the research and studies conducted by others, it is crucial for the writer to indicate the used sources. Providing references and citations are important as it shows that first, the writer has read other people's work on the subject and is aware of the existing literature. As a second function, it allows the reader to find further sources on the topic. Lastly, it prevents plagiarism.[90]

The use of the sources in a research paper can be presented as a citation, summary/paraphrasing or quotation. A list of references including all sources cited in the paper is provided at the end of the paper. There are various referencing systems in academia. Therefore, it is important to know which system to use, and thereafter maintain consistency in referencing throughout the paper.

Plagiarism happens when someone uses an intellectual property that belongs to another without acknowledging or referencing accurately. For example, copying or paraphrasing of texts, images or any other data without correct citation, or acknowledging the source, is plagiarism.

6.7 Exercises

The aim of these exercises is to encourage students to use the knowledge they have acquired in the course and deepen their understanding about feminist methodology and gender research in a practical way.

Questions

1. Understanding feminist Epistemologies in research
   Formulate a research question that investigates a matter in relation to violence and law. Explain the problem and how you understand the problem and why you have chosen to explore it? In your explanation elaborate on your epistemological and ontological approach for carrying out this research.
2. Designing research
   Following previous exercise, in a structured manner, map out how you plan to investigate the research question. Specify the data and material, sources, place and time, methods of data collection as well as methods of analysis for each material or data. You are required to justify your choices.
3. Structuring a scholarly paper
   Following the last two exercises, write a disposition (no longer than 1 page) where you elucidate how you are about to write this paper based on your research. Explain how each section unfolds in the paper including theory, methods, and analysis.

[90] Bailey (2014).

6.8 Conclusion

The learning outcome of this chapter is divided into theoretical and practical outputs. As theoretical outputs, students learn about gender research and what it means to conduct research from a gender perspective. This is achieved through understanding feminist research in the process of knowledge production, in turn informing feminist theory and politics. This is particularly important for applying gender in law and legal education. The chapter focuses on three main feminist methodologies: feminist standpoint; feminist poststructuralism; feminist intersectionality, and how they have been adopted by feminist legal scholars in their analyses of law and legal system. Students also learn about the importance of qualitative methods in conducting gender research with socio-legal approach.

Concerning practical outputs of this chapter, students learn how to conduct qualitative gender research and how to write a research paper. The chapter explains methods of conducting empirical research and how they are applied within feminist studies, with a focus on socio-legal research.

With the aim of mainstreaming gender equality perspective in law and legal education, this chapter has provided a glimpse of what constitutes gender research by reflecting on some feminist methodologies. Thus, it has explained the development of feminist methodologies by describing some ontological and epistemological approaches within feminist theories ad practices. Among feminist methodologies, the chapter has gone through three main feminist methodological approaches to illustrate how each of these approaches see knowledge, and how they understand knowledge is produced. The chapter has focused on feminist legal methodologies, to explain the ways in which legal scholars have adopted different feminist methodological approaches to critically analyse law's perspective on gender. Furthermore, the chapter has shed light on various methods of feminist socio-legal studies, including feminist judgments and gender mainstreaming, to illustrate how feminist legal scholars, lawyers and activists have engaged with such methods that are infused with feminist methodologies, to critically analyse law in construction of gender, and unravel patriarchal and unequal power structures in society.

Critical study of law explores law as a social process that is discursively constructed. Gender research that is conducted by socio-legal scholars points to the lack of gender sensitivity in creating, interpreting and implementing of law. Thus, it deconstructs the 'black letter' definition of law as fixed and immutable, and explores an understanding of law as a social phenomenon which has inherited patriarchal elements of male dominance and power relations. Gender mainstreaming in law has been of the utmost importance for overcoming gender and intersectional power relations, insofar as the critical study of law contributes to overcoming unequal power relations throughout all spheres of peoples` lives, i.e. to problematizing 'gender blindness' at an institutional level, in public services and private matters.

This chapter, and the book as a whole, aims at gender mainstreaming in legal education with a practical intention to contribute to gender mainstreaming in law as being a rule of the state. This is particularly important in legal education, through which future legal professionals and decision-makers are nurtured to become the promoters of gender equality, social justice and the rule of law.

References

Ackerly B, True J (2010) Back to the future: feminist theory, activism, and doing feminist research in an age of globalization. Women's Stud Int Forum 33:464–472

Agger B (1991) Critical theory, poststructuralism, postmodernism: their sociological relevance. Annu Rev Sociol 17:105–131

Alkan Y (2013) Feminist legal methods: theoretical assumptions, advantages, and potential problems. Univ Leicester Sch Law Res Pap 13–12:83–97

Anderson E (2000) Feminist epistemology and philosophy of science. Springer, Heidelberg

Bailey S (2014) Academic writing: a handbook for international students. Routledge, London

Banakar R (2015) Social scientific studies of law. In: Banarkar R (ed) Normativity in legal sociology. Springer, Heidelberg, pp 41–58

Bartlett KT (2018) Feminist legal methods. In: Bartlett K, Kennedy R (eds) Feminist legal theory. Routledge, London, pp 370–403

Beetham G, Demetriades J (2007) Feminist research methodologies and development: overview and practical application. Gend Dev 15:199–216

Bello BG (2017) A look at the socio-legal aspects of intersectionality: an interview with Barbara Giovanna Bello, by Ludivine Royer. Alizés: Revue angliciste de La Réunion 42:15–28

Bello BG (2009) Multiple discrimination between the EU agenda and civic engagement: the long road of intersectional perspective. Roma Rights Q 2:11–20

Benton T, Craib I (2010) Philosophy of social science: the philosophical foundations of social thought. Macmillan International Higher Education, London

Bernard HR, Wutich A, Ryan GW (2016) Analyzing qualitative data: systematic approaches. SAGE Publications, New York

Bowen GA (2009) Document analysis as a qualitative research method. Qual Res J 9:27–40

Breazu P (2020) Representing the Roma in Romanian media: a multimodal critical discourse analysis. Örebro University, Örebro

Brinkmann S (2009) Interviews: learning the craft of qualitative research interviewing. SAGE Publications, New York

Butler J (1993) Bodies that matter: on the discursive limits of sex. Taylor & Francis, London

Catalano T, Creswell JW (2013) Understanding the language of the occupy movement: a cognitive linguistic analysis. Qual Inq 19:664–673

Clougherty LA (1996) Feminist legal methods and the first amendment defense to sexual harassment liability. Neb Law Rev 75:1–27

Coffey A (2014) Analysing documents. In: Flick U (ed) The SAGE handbook of qualitative data analysis. Free University Berlin, Berlin, pp 367–380

Collins PH (1990) Black feminist thought in the matrix of domination. In: Black feminist thought: knowledge, consciousness, and the politics of empowerment, vol 138. Unwin Hyman, pp 221–238

Cor DN, Chan CD (2017) Intersectional feminism and LGBTIQA+ psychology: understanding our present by exploring our past. In: Ruth R, Santacruz E (eds) LGBT psychology and mental health: emerging research and advances. Praeger, Santa Barbara, pp 109–132

Corbin J, Strauss A (2008) Strategies for qualitative data analysis. In: Basics of qualitative research. Techniques and procedures for developing grounded theory. SAGE publications, New York

Crenshaw K (1989) Demarginalizing the intersection of race and sex: A black feminist critique of antidiscrimination doctrine, feminist theory and antiracist politics. Univ Chicago Legal Forum, pp 139–167

Creswell JW, David Creswell J (2017) Research design: qualitative, quantitative, and mixed methods approaches. SAGE Publications, New York
Creswell JW, Poth CN (2016) Qualitative inquiry and research design: choosing among five approaches. SAGE Publications, New York
Cruells M, Coll-Planas G (trans: Pearson, Roland) (2013) Challenging equality policies: the emerging LGBT perspective. Eur J Women's Stud 20:122–137
Davies B (2000) A body of writing, 1990–1999. Rowman & Littlefield, Washington
Davis K (2008) Intersectionality as buzzword: a sociology of science perspective on what makes a feminist theory successful. Fem Theory 9:67–85
Denzin NK, Lincoln YS (2011) The Sage handbook of qualitative research. SAGE Publications, New York
Fairclough N (2000) Discourse, social theory, and social research: the discourse of welfare reform. J Socioling 4:163–195
Fereday J, Muir-Cochrane E (2006) Demonstrating rigor using thematic analysis: a hybrid approach of inductive and deductive coding and theme development. Int J Qual Methods 5:80–92
Fletcher R (2002) Feminist legal theory. In: Banakar R, Travers M (eds) An introduction to law and social theory. Hart Publishing, London, pp 135–154
Freidenvall L, Dahlerup D (2019) Gender, ethnicity, and political inclusion: Intersectionalizing representation. In: Kulawik T, Kravchenko Z (eds) Borderlands in European gender studies. Routledge, London, pp 230–251
Gubrium JF, Holstein JA (2002) From the individual interview to the interview society. In: Gbrium JF, Holstein JA (eds) Handbook of interview research: context and method. SAGE publications, New York, pp 3–32
Guest G, MacQueen KM, Namey EE (2012) Validity and reliability (credibility and dependability) in qualitative research and data analysis. In: Guest G, MacQueen KM, Namey EE (eds) Applied thematic analysis. SAGE Publications, New York, pp 79–106
Hancock A-M (2007) When multiplication doesn't equal quick addition: examining intersectionality as a research paradigm. Perspect Polit 5:63–79
Haraway D (1988) Situated knowledges: the science question in feminism and the privilege of partial perspective. Fem Stud 14:575–599
Hesse-Biber SN, Leavy P (2010) Handbook of emergent methods. Guilford Press, New York
Hunter R (2019) Feminist approaches to socio-legal studies. In: Creutzfeldt N, Mason M, McConnachie K (eds) Routledge handbook of socio-legal theory and methods. Routledge, London, pp 260–272
Hunter R, McGlynn C, Rackley E (2010) Feminist judgments: from theory to practice. Bloomsbury Publishing, London
Kaijser A, Kronsell A (2014) Climate change through the lens of intersectionality. Environ Polit 23: 417–433
Kantola J, Nousiainen K (2009) Institutionalizing intersectionality in Europe: introducing the theme. Int Fem J Polit 11:459–477
Karnieli-Miller O, Strier R, Pessach L (2009) Power relations in qualitative research. Qual Health Res 19:279–289
Kvale S, Brinkmann S (2009) Interviews: learning the craft of qualitative research interviewing. SAGE publications, New York
Leavy PL (2007) Feminist postmodernism and poststructuralism. In: Hesse-Biber SN, Leavy PL (eds) Feminist research practice. SAGE publications, New York, pp 83–108
Maxey I (1999) Beyond boundaries? Activism, academia, reflexivity and research. Area 31:199–208
May T (2001) Social research. McGraw-Hill Education, London
May T (2002) Qualitative research in action. SAGE Publication, New York
McHugh MC (2014) Feminist qualitative research: toward transformation of science and society. In: Leavy P (ed) The Oxford handbook of qualitative research. Oxford University Press, Oxford, pp 137–164

Munro VE, Davies M (2016) The body, bodies, embodiment: feminist legal engagement with health. In: Munro VE, Davis M (eds) The Ashgate research companion to feminist legal theory. Routledge, London, pp 261–278
Ramazanoglu C, Holland J (2002) Feminist methodology: challenges and choices. SAGE Publications, New York
Rubin HJ, Rubin IS (2011) Qualitative interviewing: the art of hearing data. SAGE Publications, New York
Sainsbury D, Bergqvist C (2009) The promise and pitfalls of gender mainstreaming: the Swedish case. Int Fem J Polit 11:216–234
Scott JW (1991) The evidence of experience. Crit Inq 17:773–797
Smith DE (2005) Institutional ethnography: a sociology for people. Rowman Altamira, Lanham
Terry G, Hayfield N, Clarke V, Braun V (2017) Thematic analysis. In: Willig C, Rogers WS (eds) The Sage handbook of qualitative research in psychology. SAGE Publications, New York, pp 17–37
Undurraga R (2010) How quantitative are feminist research methods textbooks? Int J Soc Res Methodol 13:277–281
Van Dijk TA (1993) Principles of critical discourse analysis. Discourse Soc 4:249–283
Vujadinović D (2015) Gender mainstreaming in law and legal education. Анали Правног факултета у Београду 63:56–74
Williams C (2007) Research methods. J Bus Econ Res (JBER) 5:65–72

Further Reading

Callaway H (1992) Ethnography and experience: gender implications in fieldwork and texts. Anthropol Autobiogr 29:29–49
Carastathis A (2014) The concept of intersectionality in feminist theory. Philos Compass 9:304–314
Conaghan J (2008) Intersectionality and the feminist project in law. Routledge-Cavendish, London
DeVault ML (1996) Talking back to sociology: distinctive contributions of feminist methodology. Annu Rev. Sociol 22:29–50
McEwan C (2001) Postcolonialism, feminism and development: intersections and dilemmas. Prog Dev Stud 1:93–111
McLeod J (2020) Beginning postcolonialism. Manchester University Press, Manchester
Mills J, Birks M (2014) Qualitative methodology: a practical guide. SAGE Publications, New York
Nash JC (2008) Re-thinking intersectionality. Fem Rev 89:1–15
Wolf DL (2018) Situating feminist dilemmas in fieldwork. In: Wolf DL (ed) Feminist dilemmas in fieldwork. Routledge, London, pp 1–55
Verloo M (2005) Displacement and empowerment: reflections on the concept and practice of the Council of Europe approach to gender mainstreaming and gender equality. Soc Polit Int Stud Gender State Soc 12:344–365

Part II

Gender in a Public Context

Human Rights Law Through the Lens of the Gender Perspective

7

Marco Evola, Julia Jungfleisch, and Tanasije Marinković

Contents

Authors are listed in alphabetical order. Marco Evola authored Sects. 7.2.4, 7.2.7, 7.3.1–7.3.5; Julia Jungfleisch authored Sects. 7.2.1–7.2.3, 7.2.6 and 7.3.6; Sects. 7.2.5 and 7.2.8 are written by Tanasije Marinković.

M. Evola
LUMSA, Department of Law, Palermo, Italy
e-mail: m.evola@lumsa.it

J. Jungfleisch (✉)
Saarland University, Faculty of Law, Saarbrücken, Germany
e-mail: jungfleisch@europainstitut.de

T. Marinković
University of Belgrade, Faculty of Law, Belgrade, Serbia
e-mail: tanasije.marinkovic@ius.bg.ac.rs

D. Vujadinović et al. (eds.), *Gender-Competent Legal Education*, Springer Textbooks in Law, https://doi.org/10.1007/978-3-031-14360-1_7

Abstract

This chapter will provide an overview on several aspects of the gender perspective in Human Rights Law. The chapter will therefore look at the civil and political rights from a gender perspective, as well as social, economic and cultural rights of women, non-binary and LGBTIQA+ persons. The aim is to increase the students' awareness for the gender perspective in international human rights protection, by providing an overview of currently discussed issues in this area. Such issues include the prohibition of gender-based violence, contemporary forms of slavery and trafficking in persons, the freedom of religion, the right to private life, access to justice for women, women's (political) empowerment, the prohibition of economic and social discrimination, and women's right to education.

7.1 Introduction

Human rights are by their very nature subject to controversy and debate. Gender perspective in human rights renders this debate even more complex, given there is more than one version of gender equality. In addition, some of the well-known attacks on the values of human rights, coming from utilitarianism, communitarianism and cultural relativism, directly target gender equality. The chapter will look at the civil and political rights (Sect. 7.2) as well as social, economic and cultural rights (Sect. 7.3) from a gender perspective.

The covered aspects include: the prohibition of gender-based violence; the prohibition of slavery and trafficking in persons; the freedom of religion; the right to private life; the access to justice for women; women's empowerment; the prohibition of women's economic and social discrimination, and women's right to education.

Learning Goals

The learning goals of this chapter are:

- Increased awareness of the gender perspective in international and comparative law of human rights protection.

(continued)

- Overview of currently discussed problem issues in the area of human rights from a gender perspective.
- Basis for own further engagement of the student with the gender perspective in human rights law.

7.2 Gender Perspective in Civil and Political Rights

7.2.1 The Prohibition of Gender-Based Violence with a Focus on the Istanbul Convention

Gender-based violence (GBV) occurs worldwide; its elimination is therefore part of the UN General Assembly's Agenda for Sustainable Development (Goal 5.2).[1]

The prohibition of GBV can be derived from several guarantees in general human rights treaties, such as the International Covenant on Civil and Political Rights.[2] Pursuant to Art. 2 (1) ICCPR, the right to life (Art. 6), the right to physical and psychological integrity (Art. 17) and the prohibition of torture and inhuman or degrading treatment (Art. 7) have to be respected and ensured by States Parties regardless of gender. As a consequence, these can be read as obliging the latter to protect women from GBV.

GBV against women has furthermore been qualified as discrimination against women. It mirrors a systematic inequality of women and a respective societal structure that supports this inequality, thereby disadvantaging women.[3] Even though the gender-specific Convention on the Elimination of All Forms of Discrimination against Women (CEDAW)[4] does not contain any specific prohibition of GBV, the Committee on the Elimination of Discrimination against Women defines it in its General Comments and requires states to act upon it. GBV *"[...] includes a host of harmful behaviors that are directed at women and girls because of their sex, [...]"*[5] not only in the analogous but also in the digital world.[6]

---

[1] *UN General Assembly (UNGA)*, Resolution A/RES/70/1, Transforming the world: the 2030 Agenda for Sustainable Development, https://www.un.org/ga/search/view_doc.asp?symbol=A/RES/70/1&Lang=E.

[2] ICCPR, 16 December 1966, UNTS vol. 999, p. 171.

[3] See e.g. Committee on the Elimination of Discrimination against Women (CEDAW), General Recommendations No 19 on Violence against Women (1992) and No 35 on Gender-based Violence against Women, Updating General Recommendation No 19 (2017).

[4] CEDAW, General Recommendations supra note 3, stating that the prohibition of gender based violence is a principle of customary international law (para. 2).

[5] Heise et al. (2002), p. 6.

[6] *Human Rights Council,* Report of the Special Rapporteur on violence against women, its causes and consequences on online violence against women and girls from a human rights perspective, A/HRC/38/47, paras. 12ff.

In contrast to CEDAW, the three regional instruments; the Inter-American Convention on the Prevention, Punishment and Eradication of Violence against Women (Convention of Belem do Para),[7] the Protocol to the African Charter on Human and Peoples' Rights on the Rights of Women in Africa (Maputo Protocol)[8] and the Council of Europe Convention on Violence against Women and Domestic Violence (Istanbul Convention)[9] explicitly define GBV. The Istanbul Convention, for example, sets forth in Art. 3 lit. a) that 'violence against women' is

> *"[. . .] a violation of human rights and a form of discrimination against women and shall mean all acts of gender-based violence that result in, or are likely to result in, physical, sexual, psychological or economic harm or suffering to women, including threats of such acts, coercion or arbitrary deprivation of liberty, whether occurring in public or in private life; [. . .]". According to Art. 3 lit. d, 'gender-based violence against women' "shall mean violence that is directed against a woman because she is a woman or that affects women disproportionately".*

A shortcoming of the Istanbul Convention is that it does not acknowledge that gender-based violence can also occur to men, e.g. violence against men because of their homosexual orientation[10] and it leaves non-binary persons outside its protection; "gender" in the sense of the Convention refers exclusively to women and men.[11] Since the Istanbul Convention does not have an individual complaints mechanism, the ECHR remains important for the effective implementation of the prohibition of GBV. The ECtHR uses the Istanbul Convention as a point of reference for interpreting the ECHR[12] and the case law of the Court is of importance for the application of the Istanbul Convention.[13] The prohibition of GBV has been read into the Articles 2, 3, 4, 6, 8, 13, 14 and Art. 1 Protocol 12 to the Convention by the ECtHR.[14]

---

[7]Organization of American States (OAS), Inter-American Convention on the Prevention, Punishment and Eradication of Violence against Women, 9 June 1994.

[8]African Union, Protocol to the African Charter on Human and People's Rights on the Rights of Women in Africa, 11 July 2003.

[9]Council of Europe Convention on preventing and combating violence against women and domestic violence, CETS No. 210.

[10]See the definition of victim in the Explanatory report to the Istanbul Convention, para. 45 (men can merely be victims of domestic violence), see also: Niemi and Sanmartin (2020), p. 81 f.

[11]Art. 3 lit. c Istanbul Convention, Explanatory Report, para. 44.

[12]E.g.: App. No. 41237/14, *Talpis v Italy* (ECtHR, 2 March 2017), para 129; App. No. 49645/09, *Bălşan v Romania* (ECtHR, 23 May 2017), para. 79; App. No. 47666/13, *Ž.B. v Croatia* (ECtHR, 11 July 2017) para 56; App. No. 62903/15, *Kurt v Austria* (ECtHR [GC], 15 June 2021) paras. 167 ff.

[13]Preamble of Istanbul Convention, supra note 10.

[14]A good overview gives the ECtHR Press Unit, Factsheet on Violence against women, available here: https://www.echr.coe.int/Documents/FS_Violence_Woman_ENG.pdf.

7.2.2 The Content and Scope of the Prohibition of GBV

The prohibition of GBV has several dimensions: firstly, the duty to respect, or as described by the ECtHR, negative obligations; secondly, the duty to protect, and thirdly, the duty to ensure, also a part of the aforementioned positive obligations. Said positive obligations entail: *"(1) the obligation to criminalise harmful conduct, (2) the procedural obligation to investigate allegations of criminal conduct, (3) the obligation to take protective operational measures, (4) the obligation to adopt effective regulatory frameworks for general prevention and (5) the obligation to offer remedies."*[15] The Istanbul Convention follows a comparable threefold approach with regard to the positive obligations, the so called "three P approach",[16] ' which can be derived from Art. 1 of the Convention.

7.2.2.1 Negative Obligations

With regard to the negative obligations, the prohibition of GBV requires a state to refrain from gender-based violence (Art. 5 (1) Istanbul Convention). This comes into play e.g. in relation with ill treatment in detention,[17] police violence,[18] and expulsions.[19]

7.2.2.2 Positive Obligations

Positive obligations come into play where, not the state itself (including its organs, agents, etc.) commits an act of GBV, but rather where private individuals trigger the state's duty to protect the victim. The ECtHR, for example, derives positive obligations to protect women from GBV from the right to life (Art. 2 ECHR) and the prohibition of inhuman and degrading treatment (Art. 3 ECHR), as well as the duty to protect the physical and psychological integrity of women from Art. 8 ECHR.[20] Art. 5 (2) of the Istanbul Convention speaks of the concept of "due diligence" instead of positive obligation, but according to the Explanatory report to the Istanbul Convention, the two terms can be used interchangeably.[21] With regard to the implementation of said positive obligations/ due diligence, states are granted a certain discretion.[22] Positive obligations cannot be interpreted in a way where they

---

[15] Stoyanova (2020a), p. 104.

[16] The three P's stand for: Prevention, Protection and Prosecution.

[17] App. No. 52515/99, *Juhnke v Turkey* (ECtHR, 13 May 2008).

[18] App. No. 43347/09, *Ebru Dínçer v Turkey* (ECtHR, 29 April 2019).

[19] See case law on the Factsheet *supra note* 15; (Art. 59ff. Istanbul Convention) and example at 3.1.2.2.

[20] App. No. 87/1997/871/1083, *Osman v UK* (ECtHR, 28 October 1998); App. No. 55354/11, *Civek v Turkey* (ECtHR, 23 February 2016).

[21] See: Explanatory Report to the Istanbul Convention, para 58. For a detailed analysis of the relationship between positive obligations and due diligence and a critique on the interchangeable use of the concepts see Stoyanova (2020a), pp. 95–129.

[22] App. No. 33401/002, *Opuz v Turkey* (ECtHR, 9 June 2009) para. 129.

would impose *"an excessive burden on the authorities"*,[23] but only require the state to do what can reasonably be expected in the respective situation.

Positive obligations/due diligence with regard to the prohibition of GBV require the states, inter alia: to introduce legislation that criminalises GBV (see also Art. 4 Istanbul Convention, Art. 33–42 Istanbul Convention);[24] and to effectively apply and interpret the existing legal framework that criminalises the respective behaviour,[25] in all areas of law, not only criminal law.[26] States are furthermore required to conduct adequate investigations[27] into committed crimes and complaints of GBV[28] and convict perpetrators (Art. 45 (1) Istanbul Convention), as well as to ensure effective proceedings and adequate remedies (Art. 29f. Istanbul Convention; Art. 49–58 Istanbul Convention).

7.2.3 Fields of Application for the Prohibition of GBV

7.2.3.1 Domestic Violence

"Domestic violence as intimate-partner violence includes physical, sexual, psychological or economic violence between current or former spouses as well as current or former partners."[29] In cases of domestic violence, the state has a duty to protect victims and to effectively and adequately investigate and prosecute the perpetrator with a "special diligence":

Example

"160. The Court considers that the circumstances of the attack on the applicant – which has the hallmarks of a form of gender-based violence – should have incited the authorities to react with special diligence in carrying out the investigative measures. Whenever there is a suspicion that an attack might be gender motivated, it is particularly important that the investigation is pursued with vigour."[30] ◀

In principle, more women than men are affected by domestic violence, but not exclusively, as has also been acknowledged by the ECtHR.[31]

[23] App. No. 35810/09, *O'Keefee v Ireland* (ECtHR, [GC], 28 January 2014), para. 144.

[24] With regard to sexual crimes see: App. No. 8978/80, *X and Y v the Netherlands* (ECtHR, 26 March 1985), paras. 23, 26; more general see: *O'Keeffe v Ireland* supra note 25, para. 147.

[25] App. No. 57693/10, *Kalucza v Hungary* (ECtHR, 24 April 2012), paras. 68f.

[26] *Bălşan v Romania,* supra note 13, para 63.

[27] App. No. 12060/12, *M.C. and A.C. v Romania* (ECtHR, 12 April 2016) paras. 107–111.

[28] See e.g.: App. No. 3621/07, *Durmaz v Turkey* (ECtHR, 13 November 2014), paras. 54–68.

[29] Explanatory report to the Istanbul Convention, para. 42.

[30] App. No. 48756/14, *Tërshana v Albania* (ECtHR, 04 August 2020), paras. 153 and 160.

[31] *Opuz v. Turkey*, supra note 24, para. 132.

7.2.3.2 Crimes Committed in the Name of So-called "Honour"

Another aspect of GBV are crimes committed in the name of so-called "honour". What these crimes have in common, is that they are committed mostly by a family member, or a person close to the family. The intent being to punish the victim for the lack of respect for, or in order to ensure her respect for "the sexual and social conduct that is the norm within the community."[32] A typical example is the killing of a woman after the end of a relationship or her breakaway from the family in order to "restitute" the man's, and respectively, the family's so called "honour".

Article 42 of the Istanbul Convention obliges states inter alia to exclude "honour crimes" from the justification grounds. Besides these legislative obligations of states, the well-founded fear of a person to become a victim of a *"crime committed in the name of so-called honour"* can, if substantiated, qualify as a persecution *"within the meaning of Art. 1, A (2) of the 1951 Convention relating to the Status of Refugees and as a form of serious harm giving rise to complementary/subsidiary protection"* (Art. 60 (1) Istanbul Convention) and thus lead to international protection. Equally, *"victims of violence against women who are in need of protection, regardless of their status or residence, shall not be returned under any circumstances to any country where their life would be at risk or where they might be subjected to torture or inhuman or degrading treatment or punishment."* (Art. 61 (2) Istanbul Convention). Even though Art. 59–61 of the Istanbul Convention add to a more gender sensitive (European) Refugee law, the absence of a regulation concerning *"internal flight alternatives"*, lead the ECtHR to refer to the said alternative as a reason for inadmissibility decisions in GBV related asylum cases,[33] creating a gap of (needed) protection.

7.2.3.3 Obstetric Violence

Finally, obstetric violence as an aspect of GBV is not per se new, but has only recently entered public and academic awareness. The Special Rapporteur defines obstetric violence as:

▶ **Definition** *"[. . .] violence experienced by women during facility-based childbirth."*[34] She elaborates further, that *"[s]uch violence is [also] experienced by women and girls when seeking other forms of sexual and reproductive healthcare, including gynaecological examinations, abortion, fertility treatments and contraception and in other sexual and reproductive health contexts."*[35]

---

[32] Grans (2018), p. 137.

[33] Citing ECtHR case law in this regard: Morondo Taramundi (2020), p. 254.

[34] UNGA, Report of the Special Rapporteur on violence against women, its causes and consequences on a human rights-based approach to mistreatment and violence against women in reproductive health services with a focus on childbirth and obstetric violence, A/74/137, para. 12.

[35] *ibid.* para. 9.

Obstetric violence can occur to every person giving birth, however, it is more likely to occur to persons belonging to a minority, migrants, persons with disability or persons who are living with HIV. In other words: *"women [or rather: persons] who experience intersectional discrimination on multiple grounds."*[36] CEDAW and the Istanbul Convention oblige states *"[. . .] to pursue, by all appropriate means and without delay, a policy of eliminating discrimination and gender-based violence against women, including in the field of health"*.[37] This obliges states to effectively combat obstetric violence as a form of GBV, as stated and elaborated in detail by the Committee on the Elimination of Violence against Women in a recent case.[38]

7.2.4 Gender Dimensions of Contemporary Forms of Slavery and Trafficking in Persons

Assessing the laws on slavery and trafficking in persons from a gender perspective, puts into question the effectiveness of the protection the international system affords to women's fundamental rights against the old and new forms of violence.[39] Although the international covenants regulating slavery and trafficking include male victims, the violations of human rights at stake possess special significance with reference to women. Slavery and trafficking stem from the patriarchal culture which commodifies women and subjugate them through the threat or use of violence. Slavery like practices such as enforced prostitution or forced marriages, and the slavery status in which many female household workers are kept, are marked by the conception of women as objects.

Furthermore, a gender-based analysis of the laws on slavery and trafficking highlights the recent phenomena related to the wider processes embedded in globalisation; the international division of labour, migration, and the feminization of poverty.

[36] Zampas et al. (2020), p. 253, (Addition in brackets added by the author).

[37] Report supra note 39, para. 10.

[38] *CEDAW*, Decision concerning communication 138/2018, CEDAW/C/75/D/138/2018.

[39] The Human Rights Council, *Accelerating efforts to eliminate violence against women: preventing and responding to violence against women and girls*, 1 July 2016, A/HRC/RES/32/19 defined violence "any act of gender-based violence that results in, or is likely to result in, physical, sexual or psychological harm or suffering to women and girls of any age, including threats of such acts, coercion of arbitrary deprivation of liberty, whether occurring in public or private life". On violence throughout women's life see Henn (2016), pp. 183–215. See also UN Commission on Human Rights Special Rapporteur Radhika Coomaraswamy, *Report of the Special Rapporteur on Violence against Women, Its Causes and Consequences*, 12 February 1997, UN Doc E/CN.4/1997/47.

7.2.4.1 Slavery and Slave-Related Practices

The elimination of slavery is provided for by the most important international covenants protecting human rights.[40] The legal definition of slavery is contained in the League of Nations Slavery Convention.[41] It establishes that "[s]lavery is the status or condition of a person over whom any or all of the powers attaching to the right of ownership are exercised" (art. 1). The provision enshrines ownership as a main feature of slavery, and slavery-like practices, and covers the complete control a person exercises over their victims. Hence, establishing slavery entails considering the restrictions imposed on the freedom of movement, the control over the personal belongings of the involved individuals, the existence of consent and understanding on the nature of the relationships.[42]

This assessment is anchored in the rationale of the provision. It provides a legal avenue for addressing the new forms of slavery which departed from the "chattel slavery" model, but are marked by elements of control and ownership; the exploitation of domestic workforce and enforced prostitution.

The rules of the Slavery Convention were implemented by the Supplementary Convention on the Abolition of Slavery, the Slave Trade and Institutions and Practices Similar to Slavery of 1956[43] imposing on states parties the further obligation to abolish several practices which were identified as servile status. The Supplementary Convention comprehends among slave-related practices any institution or practice whereby: (i) a woman, without the right to refuse, is promised or given in marriage on payment of a consideration in money or in kind to her parents, guardian, family or any other person or group; or (ii) the husband of a woman, his family, or his clan, has the right to transfer her to another person for value received or otherwise; or (iii) a woman on the death of her husband is liable to be inherited by another person (art. 1). These practices stem from legal arrangements. as well as cultural or religious stereotypes.

This is the legal framework against which to assess enforced prostitution and slavery like conditions of household workers.

Starting from the latter, it has to be observed that tens of thousands of women are domestic workers in private households. This part of the workforce is the most exploited in the world. Housemaids work more than the maximum time per day and

---

[40] See art. 4 Universal declaration of Human Rights; art. 8 of the International Covenant of Civil and Political Rights (Adopted by General Assembly resolution 2200 A (XXI) of 16 December 1966, United Nations Treaty Series, vol. 999, p. 171; entered into force on 23 March 1976); Article 7(2) (c) of the Rome Statute of the International Criminal Court, United Nations Treaty Series, vol. 2187, p. 3, entered into force 1 July 2002, stipulates that "enslavement" is a crime against humanity falling within the jurisdiction of the Court; art 4 of the European Convention of Human Rights.

[41] League of Nations Slavery Convention, United Nations Treaty Series, vol. 60, p. 254; entered into force on 9 March 1927; Rassam, pp. 303–352.

[42] Weissbrot (2002), p. 7.

[43] Supplementary Convention on the Abolition of Slavery, the Slave Trade and Institutions and Practices Similar to Slavery of 1956 (the Supplementary Convention), United Nations Treaty Series, vol. 226, p. 3; entered into force on 30 April 1957.

their salaries are lower than the minimum wage. Furthermore, they are often locked within their workplace and suffer physical and sexual violence.

Example

In the case *Siliadin v France* the plaintiff, a girl who entered France aged 15, worked as housemaid seven days a week from 7.30 a.m. to 10.30 p.m. She received no pay and was obliged to sleep on a mattress on the floor of the baby's room. The Court argued that the girl was held in servitude but not slavery, pointing out that servitude "includes, in addition to the obligation to perform certain services for others [. . .] the obligation for the 'serf' to live on another person's property and the impossibility of altering his condition. [. . .] servitude means an obligation to provide one's services that is imposed by the use of coercion, and is to be linked with the concept of slavery." In applying this assessment the Court focused on the plaintiff's working conditions and her lack of consent and argued that "she [. . .] was vulnerable and isolated, and had no means of living elsewhere than in the home of Mr and Mrs B [. . .] She was entirely at Mr and Mrs B.'s mercy, since her papers had been confiscated and she had been promised that her immigration status would be regularised, which had never occurred. In addition, the applicant, who was afraid of being arrested by the police, was not in any event permitted to leave the house, except to take the children to their classes and various activities. Thus, she had no freedom of movement and no free time As she had not been sent to school [. . .] the applicant could not hope that her situation would improve and was completely dependent on Mr and Mrs B."[44] ◄

Enforced prostitution occurs when a person is obliged, under violence or menace, to supply sexual services in return of money.[45]

Example

In *S.M. v Croatia* the Court dealt with an application lodged by a woman who alleged that a former police man had physically and psychologically forced her into prostitution. The Court stated that "the notion of forced or compulsory labour under Article 4 of the Convention aims to protect against instances of serious exploitation, such as forced prostitution, irrespective of whether, in the particular circumstances of a case, they are related to the specific human-trafficking context. Moreover, any such conduct may have elements qualifying it as "servitude" or "slavery" under Article 4, or may raise an issue under another provision of the Convention."[46] ◄

---

[44] App. Nos. 73316/01, *Case of Siliadin v. France* (ECtHR 26 July 2005), paras. 123–128.
[45] Weissbrot (2002), p. 31; Barry (1995).
[46] App. Nos. 60561/14, *Case of S.M. v. Croatia* (ECtHR GC 25 June 2020), paras. 282–285.

Nowadays the root causes of women slavery are to be found in an extensive array of economic and social factors. Migration gives rise to several kinds of exploitation and female migrants represent the most vulnerable group of women exposed to slavery-like practices.[47] The confiscation of passports or travel documents, the captivity of domestic workers, forced prostitution or the enrolment in the sex industry are some of the practices affecting migrant women and leading to their exploitation combining old stereotypes with new forms of slavery.[48]

7.2.4.2 Trafficking in Persons

The connection between vulnerability and exploitation marks also trafficking in persons which is one of today's most widespread forms of women's exploitation.[49]

In General Recommendation n. 38 the CEDAW Committee observed that a gender analysis of trafficking reveals several root causes, ranging from sex-based discrimination, globally dominant policies, globalised macroeconomic and political factors, the shrinking of the welfare state and discriminatory social and cultural norms engendering the oppression of women.[50]

This analysis relies on the idea that trafficking is a form of violence against women and as such a form of discrimination on grounds of sex so that it occurs not only in cases of sexual exploitation, but also in those activities which have not sexual purposes such as exploitative domestic work and forced marriage.

Trafficking challenges the international system of protection of human rights. Art. 6 CEDAW obliges states to take measures, "including legislation, to suppress all forms of traffic in women and exploitation of prostitution of women". Pursuant to this provision the CEDAW Committee pointed out that a life free from being trafficked must be recognized as a human right and appropriate conditions must be created for that right to be fully enjoyed by women and girls.[51] A definition of trafficking is provided for in the United Nations Protocol to Prevent, Suppress and Punish Trafficking in Persons, Especially Women and Children (hereinafter Trafficking Protocol)[52] which supplements the United Nations Convention against

---

[47] Wijers and Lap-Chew (1997).

[48] On these forms of slavery-like practices see Weissbrot (2002), pp. 11 *et seq;* Bales and Robbins (2001), pp. 18–45.

[49] Obokata (2006).

[50] Committee on the Elimination of Discrimination against Women, *General recommendation No. 38 (2020) on trafficking in women and girls in the context of global migration*, CEDAW/C/GC/38, 20 November 2020, paras. 2–3.

[51] *Idem*, para. 4.

[52] Protocol to Prevent, Suppress and Punish Trafficking in Persons, Especially Women and Children (Trafficking Protocol), supplementing the United Nations Convention against Transnational Organized Crime, Adopted by General Assembly resolution 55/25 of 15 November 2000, Official Records of the General Assembly, Fifty-fifth Session, Supplement No. 49 (A/45/49), vol. I., 60, United Nations, Treaty Series, vol. 2237, p. 319, entered into force 25 December 2003.

Transnational Organized Crime[53] in order to prevent and combat trafficking, to protect the victims of trafficking and to promote cooperation among States Parties (art. 1).[54]

▶ **Definition** Art. 3 (a) of the Trafficking Protocol identifies trafficking through three elements.[55] The first is the action: recruitment, transportation, transfer, harbouring or receipt of persons. The second element is embodied by the means the provision lists: "the threat or use of force or other forms of coercion, of abduction, of fraud, of deception, of the abuse of power or of a position of vulnerability or of the giving or receiving of payments or benefits to achieve the consent of a person having control over another person".[56] The last feature is to be found in the purpose of exploitation.

The Council of Europe Convention on Action against Trafficking in Human Beings (hereinafter the CoE Convention) makes use of the same legal elements to define trafficking (art. 4), but is wider in scope.[57] The Trafficking Protocol covers only transnational trafficking which is connected to organized crime, while the CoE Convention applies to national as well as transnational forms of trafficking in human beings, whether or not connected with organised crime (art. 2).[58] The CoE Convention rules bolster women's protection since the vulnerability stemming from the threat or use or violence rises also in those cases in which individuals act without relying on the intimidating power of a criminal group.

Unlike the Trafficking Protocol and the CoE Convention the CEDAW pushes the focus on the phenomenon from the fight against crime and the management of migration to the protection of rights by imposing positive obligations on states parties with the aim of eradicating the legal, political and economic constraints making women vulnerable to trafficking and sexual exploitation.[59]

The prohibitions contained in the rules on slavery and trafficking aim at protecting human dignity which has been playing a crucial role in their evolutive

[53] United Nations Convention against Transnational Organized Crime Adopted by General Assembly resolution 55/25 of 15 November 2000, Official Records of the General Assembly, Fifty-fifth Session, Supplement No. 49 (A/45/49), vol. I., 60, United Nations, Treaty Series, vol. 2225, p. 209, entered into force 29 September 2003.

[54] Gallagher (2001).

[55] Brewer and Southwell (2018), p. 3; Gallagher (2011), p. 29; Cerone (2007).

[56] For criticism on the clarity of the provision see Noll (2007), pp. 343–361.

[57] Council of Europe Convention on Action against Trafficking in Human Beings, Varsaw 16 May 2005, Council of Europe Treaty Series - No. 197. Sembacher (2006).

[58] App. Nos. 60561/14, *Case of S.M. v. Croatia* (ECtHR 19 July 2018).

[59] Chuang (2012), p. 172. On the root causes and the obligations the CEDAW imposes on States Parties see Committee on the Elimination of Discrimination against Women, *General recommendation No. 38 (2020) on trafficking in women and girls in the context of global migration*, CEDAW/C/GC/38, 20 November 2020, para. 18.

and teleological construing.[60] This is the reason why the practice of the international bodies shows some uncertainties in defining the precise borders between trafficking, slavery, servitude and forced labour.[61]

7.2.5 Religious Freedom for and Against Women

The ECtHR has regularly held that freedom of religion is *"one of the most vital elements that [. . .] make up the identity of believers and their conception of life"* and that it entails freedom to hold religious beliefs and to practice religion. *"While religious freedom is primarily a matter of individual conscience, it also implies, inter alia, [. . .] freedom to manifest one's religion [. . .] in community with others"*.[62] This jurisprudential position has been buttressed by the legal doctrine. Hence, Mahlmann considers that "religion is not an ornamental side issue of human life", but "a central existential concern".[63] And this is true, both for men and women.

Religious freedom, especially in its communitarian dimension, has also become a political argument advanced by the supporters of multiculturalism, committed to strengthening the position of a cultural or religious minority within the larger society. Whilst being perfectly legitimate, this political action has been accompanied by the strengthening of power of cultural and religious leaders over dissidents in their groups; women are often those who bear the brunt of this.[64] Since gender is a social construct, gender identity is created by the norms of behaviour imposed by culture and religion. As a result, in traditionalist cultures and religions there is a "systematic domination of women by men, [. . .] women's exclusion from public power, and [. . .] their subjection to patriarchal power within the family".[65]

For instance, "the authoritarian and hierarchical features of Ibero-Catholic culture appear to be particularly hostile to women's advancement" especially "when seen in light of the traditional sexism of Roman Catholic ethics and secular ideologies like machismo and marianismo".[66] According to some scholars, the endurance of

[60] On the role of human dignity see De Sena (2019).

[61] (ILO, Report of the ILO Committee of Experts on the Application of Conventions and Recommendations, Report III (Part IB), p. 41) paras. 77–78. See also Benjamin Whitaker, Report on Slavery. E/CN.4/Sub.2/1982/20/Rev.1, UN Sales No. E.84.XIV.1, 10 *et seq*. App. Nos. 25965/04, *Case of Rantsev v. Cyprus and Russia* (EctHR 7 January 2010), para. 282. App. Nos. 21884/15, *Case of Chowdury and Others v. Greece* (ECtHR 30 March 2017), para. 93; App. Nos. 58216/2012, *Case of J. And Others v. Austria* (ECtHR 17 April 2017), para. 104; App. Nos. 60561/14, *Case of S.M. v. Croatia* (ECtHR GC 25 June 2020), para. 297, para. 308 *et seq*. On this issue see Stoyanova (2020b); Stoyanova (2017); Stoyanova (2012), pp. 163–194; Gallagher (2009), pp. 789–848; Fitzpatrick (2003), pp. 1143–1167.

[62] App. No. 14307/88, Case of *Kokkinakis v. Greece* (ECtHR, 25 May 1993), para. 31.

[63] Mahlmann (2009), p. 2473.

[64] Phillips (2005), p. 113.

[65] Raday (2003), p. 669.

[66] Htun (2000), pp. 191–192.

Latin-American harsh patriarchal systems, in the field of gender relations, is rivalled only in the Arab world.[67]

Example

If sentencing women to death by stoning for the violation of offense of adultery, in some Islamic countries, may appear as an extreme example of persisting gender inequality, the 2009 Manhattan Declaration, signed by major Christian churches in the USA, bears witness to a fact that there is actually a widespread refusal of religious institutions to abide by the antidiscrimination norms in the western world too.[68] ◀

In response to these phenomena, the 1979 Convention on the Elimination of all Forms of Discrimination Against Women (CEDAW) stipulates that states parties shall take all appropriate measures "to modify social and cultural patterns of conduct of men and women, with a view to achieving the elimination of prejudices and customary and all other practices which are based on the idea of the inferiority or the superiority of either of the sexes or on stereotyped roles for men and women" (Article 5(a)).

Two groups of questions have particularly been in the focus of supranational and national decision makers, as well as the academic community, when it comes to religious freedom for and against women. Those are wearing of headscarves and full-face veils in public places (1), and the performance or assistance in abortion procedures (2).

7.2.5.1 Wearing of Headscarves and Full-Face Veils in Public Places

In a number of cases, the ECtHR examined whether the measures prohibiting women from wearing a headscarves/burkas/niqab[69] infringed upon their freedom to manifest their religion, as guaranteed by Article 9 of the Convention. *Dahlab v. Switzerland* concerned a primary school teacher who was requested by the education authorities to stop wearing the Islamic headscarf in the school where she worked.[70] In *Leyla Sahin v. Turkey*, the applicant, a university student, complained of the Istanbul University regulation restricting the right to wear the Islamic headscarf and the disciplinary measure of suspension taken thereunder against her as a result of her failure to comply with the rules on dress.[71] *S.A.S. v. France* concerned the French law, stating that "no one may, in public places, wear clothing that is designed to conceal the face", which was challenged by women who wished

[67] Chaney (1979), p. 32. Quoted in Htun (2000), p. 192.

[68] Mancini (2014), p. 35.

[69] Burka is "a full-body covering including a mesh over the face", and the niqab "a full-face veil leaving an opening only for the eyes".

[70] App. No. 42393/98, Case of *Dahlab c. Suisse* (ECtHR, 15 February 2001).

[71] App. No. 44774/98, *Case* of *Leyla Sahin v. Turkey* [GC] (ECtHR, 10 November 2005), paras. 16, 21, 24, 70.

to wear burka and niqab in public places.[72] In none of the cases above did the ECtHR find the violation of the right to religious freedom.[73]

Example

In reaching the conclusion that public measures prohibiting women from wearing headscarves and full-face veils did not infringe upon their freedom to manifest their religion, the ECtHR relied on: the consideration that wearing of a headscarf might have some kind of proselytising effect on very young children, "seeing that it appears to be imposed on women by a precept which is laid down in the Koran and which [. . .] is hard to square with the principle of gender equality";[74] the principle of secularism as the paramount value underlying the ban on the wearing of religious symbols in Turkish universities;[75] and, on the argument that the "barrier raised against others by a veil concealing the face breaches the right of others to live in a space of socialisation which makes living together easier".[76] ◄

It is important to note, in this context, that the ECtHR was not convinced by the French Government's submission regarding the legitimate aim pursued by the ban on full-face veils, in so far as it concerned respect for equality between men and women.[77] More concretely, the Court took the view that "a State Party could not invoke gender equality in order to ban a practice that was defended by women – such as the applicant – in the context of the exercise of the rights enshrined" in Article 9 of the Convention, "unless it were to be understood that individuals could be protected on that basis from the exercise of their own fundamental rights and freedoms".[78] The Court also took the view that respect for human dignity could not "legitimately justify a blanket ban on the wearing of the full-face veil in public places", since it was the expression of a cultural identity, which contributed to the pluralism that was inherent in democracy.[79]

No matter how pertinent these arguments are, it is undisputed that the value of cultural identity cannot trump the respect for human dignity. Here, a burka denies human dignity, specifically, the right to individual personality by rendering

[72] App. No. 43835/11, Case of *S. A. S. c. France* [GC] (ECtHR, 1 July 2014), paras. 28 and 76.

[73] For an opposite view of the United Nation Human Rights Committee that the prohibition on wearing in public of clothing designed to conceal the face violated the freedom of religion and the prohibition of discrimination, based on gender and religion, as guaranteed by the International Covenant on Civil and Political Rights, see section 3 of the chapter Gender Equality and Public Law, in this volume.

[74] *Dahlab c. Suisse.*

[75] *Leyla Sahin v. Turkey* [GC], para. 116.

[76] *S. A. S. c. France* [GC], para. 122.

[77] For the inconsistencies in the Convention Case-Law, see Marinkovic (2017), pp. 75–91; see also section 3 of the chapter Gender Equality and Public Law, in this volume.

[78] *S. A. S. c. France* [GC], para. 119.

[79] *Ibid.*, para. 120.

individuality invisible.[80] This is the case with women who do not wear a burka voluntarily, but under the pressure of the patriarchal cultural-religious practices within which they are born and raised. The position of the ECtHR is all the more questionable since under international law, the states are responsible to remove any inconsistency between international human rights of women and religious and customary laws, operating within their territories,[81] including those which are the expression of cultural identity. In this context, it is worthwhile remembering that the CEDAW stipulates that "the term 'discrimination against women' shall mean any distinction, exclusion or restriction made on the basis of sex which has the effect or purpose of impairing or nullifying the recognition, enjoyment or exercise by women, irrespective of their marital status, on a basis of equality of men and women, of human rights and fundamental freedoms in the political, economic, social, cultural, civil or any other field" (Article 1).

7.2.5.2 Performance or Assistance in Abortion Procedures

Dress codes are not the only case where religious norms may come in conflict with the right to dignity and autonomy of women. Other notable cases concern the attempts to read foetus rights, and not women's, rights into mostly silent constitutions;[82] restricting women's right to abortion (see infra 2.4). In Europe, the constitutional disputes surrounding abortion were clearly influenced by the mobilization of Catholic groups resisting women's reproductive autonomy in the name of the sanctity of life. Consequently, "constitutions were called to play a role", through judicial review of constitutionality, against legislative liberalization of access to abortion.[83]

Example

After the collapse of communism and under the influence of the Catholic Church, the Polish Constitutional Court considered that "the very nature of the recognition that human life is a constitutional value implies a necessary limitation on the rights of a pregnant women" and that "one cannot decide about having a child when the child is already evolving in the pre-natal phase". Consequently, it held that the legalization of the acts, which occasioned "the death of the foetus" before it was 12 weeks old, was entirely arbitrary.[84] However, the German Federal Constitutional Court took a more balanced approach. It stated that "there is a

[80] Mahlmann (2009), pp. 2492–2493.

[81] Cf. An-Na'im, pp. 167–168.

[82] The exceptions are: the 1983 reform of the Irish Constitution, under which "the state acknowledges the right to life of the unborn" (Eight Amendment of the Constitution Act); and, the 2011 Fundamental Law of Hungary which provides that "the life of the foetus shall be protected from the moment of conception" (Article II).

[83] Rubio-Marin and Chang (2013), pp. 304–305.

[84] Constitutional Tribunal (Poland), decision dated 28 May 1997 (K. 26/96), in Dorsen et al. (2003), pp. 546–551.

right to life which is inviolable but that foetus is not a 'completed person' and is thus not fully protected". The Court held that "abortion may be permitted in some cases, for which public insurance will not bear the cost".[85] The French Constitutional Council took a position in favour of the right to life, but found no constitutional obstacles to accept the statutory scheme that permitted abortion after mandatory counselling.[86] ◀

The right to women's reproductive autonomy is not secured even when abortion is allowed. Conservative Christian lobbies "advocate a thick conception of religious freedom, one that encompasses an almost unlimited right to conscientious objection".[87] As a result, there has been a multiplication of refusals to deliver services, when the person considers them incompatible with his or her religion. This includes performing abortions or providing assistance and extends to many others actions (selling contraceptives, prescribing prenatal tests, providing reproductive health related information etc.).[88]

Example

In Italy, the Constitutional Court partially decriminalized abortion in 1975, after which a law was enacted, in 1978, to regulate access to abortion services. However, nearly 70 percent of doctors in Italy refuse to perform abortion invoking conscientious objection, thereby denying many women reproductive health care.[89] This has led some authors to conclude that "conscientious objection has turned from an individual right rooted in the freedom of conscience and religion, into a politically motivated collective strategy to undermine the law".[90] ◀

7.2.6 The Right to Respect for Private and Family Life in the Context of (Women's) Reproductive Autonomy and Gender Affirming Surgery

Women's reproductive autonomy, as having the power to decide and control contraceptive use, pregnancy, and childbearing, is explicitly qualified as a human right by the Maputo Protocol (a protocol to the African Charter on Human and People's

85 Dorsen et al. (2003), p. 553.

86 *Ibid.*

87 Mancini (2014), p. 36.

88 *Ibid*; Luciani (2019), pp. 333–334.

89 Mancini (2014), pp. 36–37.

90 *Ibid.*, p. 37; *cf.* Luciani (2019), pp. 332–333.

Rights).[91] On the UN level, as well as the regional European and American level, the protection of said autonomy is guaranteed, not by a specific provision, but by a bundle of provisions, such as *inter alia* the right to life, the right to health, the right to education and the right to respect for private and family life.[92] It is also a Goal of the 2030 Agenda for Sustainable Development to ensure *"universal access to sexual and reproductive health and reproductive rights"* as part of achieving gender equality and women empowerment (Goal 5.6).

The right to respect for private and family life is secured by human rights catalogues on the international[93] as well as the regional level.[94] As a human right, the right to private life generally binds states and protects the individual from state interference, however, it also obliges the state to protect the individual from interference by private individuals.[95]

The right to respect for private and family life *inter alia* protects the development and realisation of a person's personality. This includes a certain freedom from state driven surveillance, as well as the power of disposal over one's own person and the shaping of one's own life. Or as the ECtHR puts it: *"the right to personal autonomy and personal development."*[96]

It goes without saying that the rights connected with reproductive autonomy, and especially the right to respect for private and family life apply also to persons with disabilities,[97] persons who belong to minorities[98] and minors.[99] In other words it

[91] Art. 14 Protocol to the African Charter on Human and People's Rights on the Rights of Women in Africa, 11 July 2003, https://au.int/sites/default/files/treaties/37077-treaty-charter_on_rights_of_women_in_africa.pdf.

[92] See e.g.: Committee on Economic, Social and Cultural Rights (CESCR), General Comment No. 22 and No. 14.

[93] Art. 12 UNGA, Universal Declaration of Human Rights, 10 December 1948, 217 A (III), (UDHR); Art. 17 ICCPR (supra note 2), Art. 16 Convention on the Rights of the Child, 20 November 1989, UNTS 1577, p. 3, (CRC); Art. 14 International Convention on the Protection of the Rights of All Migrant Workers and Members of their Families, 18 December 1990, UNTS 2220, p. 3.

[94] Art. 5 American Declaration of the Rights and Duties of Man; Art. 8 Convention for the Protection of Human Rights and Fundamental Freedoms , ETS No. 005, (ECHR); Art. 7 Charter of Fundamental Rights of the European Union, OJ C 326, 26.10.2012, pp. 391–407 (CFR); Art. 11 (2) OAS, American Convention on Human Rights, "Pact of San Jose", Costa Rica, 22 November 1969; Art. 18 Organization of African Unity (OAU), African Charter on Human and Peoples' Rights ("Banjul Charter"), 27 June 1981, CAB/LEG/67/3 rev. 5, 21 I.L.M. 58 (1982).

[95] App. No. 27617/04, *R.R. v. Poland* (ECtHR, 26. May 2011), para. 184.

[96] App. No. 25579/05, *A, B, C v. Ireland* (ECtHR, 16 December 2010), para. 212.

[97] Articles 23 and 25 UNGA, Convention on the Rights of Persons with Disabilities, UNTS 2515, p. 3; CRPD, General Comment No. 3, paras. 23, 44, 64(b); CRPD Committee, General Comment No. 1, para. 41.

[98] E.g.: App. No 18968/07, *V.C. v. Slovakia* (ECtHR, 08. November 2011).

[99] See e.g.: CRC, General Comment No. 20 (2016), para 39.

applies to especially vulnerable persons and protects their (reproductive) autonomy.[100]

The right to respect for private life protects persons with regard to their gender identification, sexual orientation and their sexual life.[101] Part of the personal autonomy is therefore not only the right to determine one's gender, but also the decision for gender affirming surgery. In this regard, it is important to mention that the right to respect for private and family life furthermore protects the physical and psychological integrity of a person.[102]

7.2.6.1 Several Aspects of (Women's) Reproductive Autonomy

7.2.6.1.1 Medically Assisted Procreation/In Vitro Fertilization

The decision to become parents is part of the private and family life. The ECHR therefore protects the decision to become parents through medically assisted procreation.[103]

The Inter-American Court explicitly decided that the prohibition of in vitro fertilization (IVF) violates inter alia the right to respect for private and family life.[104] Equally the ECtHR decided, that *"moral considerations or [. . .] social acceptability [. . .] are not in themselves sufficient reasons for a complete ban on a specific artificial procreation technique[. . .]."*[105] Even though the court accepts a wide margin of appreciation in this legislative field, at the same time it emphasises the fact that as medically assisted procreation is *"subject to a particularly dynamic development in science and law"*,[106] states need to review their respective laws accordingly to this dynamic and adapt to it.

The decision to refuse fertility treatment that was previously agreed to has to be respected. The person concerned would otherwise have to undergo a forced pregnancy, violating especially their right to health.[107] Equally, the decision to withdraw the consent to the storage and use of embryos by one of the partners has to be respected, even if this ultimately hinders one of them becoming a (genetic) parent.[108]

---

[100] See e.g.: CESCR, General Comment No. 22 (2016), paras. 30, 31.

[101] App. No. 35968/97, *van Kück v Germany* (ECtHR, 12. June 2003), para. 69.

[102] App. No. no. 5410/03, *Tysiąc v. Poland* (ECtHR, 20 March 2007), para. 107.

[103] The ECtHR speaks of "genetic" parents, App. No. 44362/04, *Dickson v. the United Kingdom* (ECtHR, [GC], 04. December 2007), para. 66.

[104] Case No. 257, *Artavia Murillo et. al. v. Costa Rica* (Inter American Court of Human Rights [IACHR], 28 November 2012) para. 294.

[105] App. No. 57813/00, *S. H. and Others v. Austria* (ECtHR, [GC] 03. November 2011), para. 100.

[106] *Ibid.*, para. 118.

[107] CESCR, Views adopted by the Committee under the Optional Protocol to the International Covenant on Economic, Social and Cultural Rights, concerning communication No. 22/2017, para. 11.2.

[108] App. No. 6339/05, *Evans v. the United Kingdom* (ECtHR [GC], 10 April 2007), paras. 90–92.

The question whether national laws that exempt same sex couples from IVF treatment are compatible with the ECHR has not yet been decided.[109] The ECtHR has consistently held that states must guarantee the rights they are obliged to grant under the ECHR in a non-discriminatory manner, in accordance with Article 14. The same applies to such rights which the state guarantees voluntarily, i.e. outside the obligatory rights catalogue enshrined in the ECHR. Thus, insofar as a state has equated same-sex marriage with different-sex marriage, at least the exclusion of married same-sex couples from IVF should be impermissible. If a state allows IVF for unmarried heterosexual couples, Art.14 ECHR arguably requires opening it up to unmarried same-sex couples as well. Besides the access to medically assisted procreation, the ECHR protects also from discriminatory consequences such a treatment might cause and prohibits discrimination on the basis of sex and the manner in which a person gets pregnant:

Example

"1. The applicant entered into an employment contract ten days after she had undergone in vitro fertilisation. When she subsequently went on sick leave on account of pregnancy-related complications, the relevant administrative authority re-examined her health insurance status and rejected her application for insurance as an employed person, concluding that her employment had been fictitious.[. . .] 84. In sum, the Court would reiterate that a refusal to employ or recognise an employment-related benefit to a pregnant woman based on her pregnancy, amounts to direct discrimination on grounds of sex, which cannot be justified by the financial interests of the State [. . .]. On the basis of the foregoing, the Court considers that the difference in treatment to which the applicant, as a woman who had become pregnant by means of in vitro insemination, had been subjected to, had not been objectively justified or necessary in the circumstances."[110] ◀

7.2.6.1.2 Contraception and Abortion

Whereas religious freedom covers the refusal to conduct an abortion as seen above, the right to respect for private and family life not only protects the decision to become a parent, it also protects the decision not to become one. Therefore, courts on the regional level and human rights mechanisms on the international level have found that an absolute ban on abortions[111] and contraception medicine[112] violates the human rights of the concerned (pregnant) persons. Even though a general right to

[109] App. No. 22612/15, *Charron and Merle-Montet v France* (ECtHR, 08. February 2018).

[110] App. No. 54711/15, *Jurčić v Croatia* (ECtHR, 04 February 2021), paras. 1 and 84.

[111] App. No. 57375/08, *P and S v Poland* (ECtHR, 30. October 2012), para. 96; CEDAW, *L. C. v. Peru,* Communication No. 22/2009, CEDAW/C/50/D/22/2009 (25 November 2011), para 9. b) i).

[112] CEDAW, Summary of the inquiry concerning the Philippines, CEDAW/C/OP.8/PHL/1 para. 43.

abortion does not exist,[113] the right to respect for private life necessitates the access to legal abortions, at least for reasons of health and/or well-being.[114] This includes access to information about legal ways for abortions.[115] For the abortion, the consent of the pregnant person is necessary and the views of the person concerned have to be respected when deciding over the termination of the pregnancy.[116]

The right to respect for private and family life therefore necessitates in its procedural aspects that courts investigate whether *"adequate and timely medical treatment"* allowing an informed decision of the pregnant person whether to continue the pregnancy or not, has been granted to the pregnant person.[117] As it is the pregnant person that is primarily affected by the pregnancy, the father of the child does not have to be informed before or about the abortion, the right to private life of the pregnant person prevails.[118]

The legality of sterilization operations as a contraceptive medical treatment depends on the informed consent of the concerned person.[119] Sterilization operations conducted without such consent not only violate the right to respect for private life, but happen especially to persons infected with HIV,[120] persons belonging to minorities (especially Roma women in the European context[121] and indigenous women in South Amerika[122]) or persons who have disabilities[123] and thus are also highly discriminatory.[124] States are required to ensure that no person is subjected to non-consensual sterilisation and that adequate investigations as well as compensation are guaranteed in cases where forced sterilisation was conducted.[125]

---

[113] App. No. 57375/08, *P and S v Poland* (ECtHR, 30. October 2012), para. 96.

[114] Human Rights Committee (HRC), *Mellet v. Ireland*, CCPR/C/116/D/2324/2013, para. 7.7 f.; HRC, Whelan v. Ireland, CCPR/C/119/D/2425/2014, para. 7.8.

[115] HRC, *Whelan v. Ireland,* CCPR/C/119/D/2425/2014, para. 7.6.

[116] *Tysiac v Poland*, supra note 56, para. 117.

[117] E.g.: antenatal screening tests, where genetic disorders, that allow an abortion under the respective national law could have been detected: App. No. 33011/08, *A.K. v. Latvia* (ECtHR, 24. June 2014) paras. 93 f.

[118] App. No. 50490/99, *Boso v Italy* (ECtHR, 5. September 2002).

[119] App. No. 29518/10, *N.B. v Slovakia* (ECtHR, 12 June 2012), para. 73.

[120] E.g.: Case No. SA 49/2012, *Government of the Republic of Namibia v. LM and Others* (Namibia, Supreme Court 3 November 2014).

[121] E.g.: CEDAW, *Ms. A. S. v. Hungary,* CEDAW/C/36/D/4/2004.

[122] E.g.: Inter-American Commission on Human Rights (IACHR), Report No. 71/03. Petition 12.191. Friendly Settlement María Mamérita Mestanza-Chávez, (Peru: IACHR, 2003), accessed August 1, 2019, https://www.cidh.oas.org/annualrep/2003eng/peru.12191.htm.

[123] A case concerning persons with disabilities, but which was held inadmissible: App. No. 61521/08, *Gauer and others v France* (ECtHR, 23 October 2012).

[124] E.g.: Series C No. 336, *I.V. v. Bolivia* (IACHR, 30 November 2016), para. 248 f.

[125] App. No. 15966/04, *I.G. and Others v. Slovakia* (ECtHR, 13 November 2012) paras. 143–146, 169 ff.; App. No. 8759/05, *Csoma v Romania* (ECtHR, 15 January 2013), paras. 65–68; forced sterilisations are also gender-based violence and explicitly prohibited in the Istanbul Convention, Art. 39.

7.2.6.1.3 Giving Birth

Giving birth constitutes an intimate moment in a person's life. Therefore the right to respect for private life requires the consent of the person giving birth to the presence of medical students during birth.[126] Even though "the circumstances of giving birth incontestably form part of one's private life for the purposes of Article 8",[127] the obligation of the state to secure the health and life of the person giving birth and the child, can prevail over the right to respect for private life. This can allow a state to prohibit home births or render it impossible to be assisted by midwives during home births; factually hindering home births.[128] However, the state's duty to protect the life of the child does not automatically outbalance the birthing person's right to respect for private and family life. Precautionary measures to protect a new-born baby's health, such as a court order to return to the hospital, can therefore constitute a violation of Art. 8 ECHR.[129]

7.2.6.2 Legal Aspects of Gender Identification and Gender Affirming Surgery

As mentioned above the right to respect for private and family life protects the gender identification of a person. This right is impaired by national laws that require gender affirming surgery before granting legal gender recognition. On the international level, human rights mechanisms and institutions held that these laws violate various human rights of the persons concerned.[130] On the regional European level, this finding was the end of a development: in 2017 the ECtHR decided in *A.P., Garçon et Nicot v France*[131] that a compulsory sterilisation as a requirement for gender recognition violates the right to respect for private life. The German Federal Constitutional Court rendered a similar decision already in 2011:

Example

> "The permanent nature and irreversibility of transsexual persons' perceived gender cannot be assessed against the degree of the surgical adaptation of their external genitals but rather against the consistency with which they live in their perceived gender. The unconditional prerequisite of a surgical gender reassignment according to [the respective national law] constituted an excessive requirement because it requires of transsexual persons to undergo surgery and to tolerate

---

[126] App. No. 37873/04, *Konovalova v Russia* (ECtHR, 9 October 2014) paras. 47 ff.

[127] App. No. 67545/09, *Ternovszky v. Hungary* (ECtHR, 14 December 2010) para. 22.

[128] App. No. 18568/12, *Pojatina v Croatia*, (ECtHR, 04. February 2019), paras. 89 ff.

[129] App. No. 43643/10, *Hanzelkovi v the Czech Republic* (ECtHR, 11 December 2014), paras. 79 f.

[130] CESCR, General Comment No. 22, para. 58; Méndez (2013), UN Doc. A/HRC/22/53 (2013), para. 78.

[131] App. Nos. 79885/12, 52471/13 and 52596/13, *A.P., Garçon et Nicot v France* (ECtHR, 06. April 2017), paras. 130–135.

health detriments even if this is not indicated in the respective case and if it is not necessary for ascertaining the permanent nature of the transsexuality."[132] ◀

In 2019 there was no need for the ECtHR to decide on whether the requirement of gender affirming surgery violated Art.8 ECHR, because the state concerned did not have *"quick, transparent and accessible procedures for gender recognition procedures"* and thus lacked the necessary regulatory framework which is required by Article 8 in order to ensure the respect for private life.[133] In 2021, the Court explicitly held that *"the refusal of the domestic authorities to legally recognise the applicants' gender reassignment in the absence of gender reassignment surgery amounted to unjustified interference with their right to respect for their private life"*.[134]

7.2.7 Access to Justice for Women

The laws and the socio-economic mechanisms preventing women from having access to justice have been enhancing their subordination. The consciousness that the attainment of the objective of guaranteeing substantial equality entails the enactment of instruments enabling women to bring legal proceedings has been gaining ground in the international system of protection of fundamental rights.

The CEDAW Committee in General Recommendation n. 33 has highlighted that women face challenges entrenched in two situations. On the one side, women are empowered to bring legal actions before courts and tribunals, the challenge here being the law in force is based on traditional gender stereotypes and contains discriminatory rules. On the other side, women have no access to courts and tribunals due to economic, social and cultural factors.[135] In this vein the CEDAW Committee emphasized the existence of "a number of obstacles and restrictions that impede women from realizing their right to access to justice on a basis of equality, including a lack of effective jurisdictional protection offered by States parties in relation to all dimensions of access to justice. These obstacles occur in a structural context of discrimination and inequality owing to factors such as gender stereotyping, discriminatory laws, intersecting or compounded discrimination, procedural and evidentiary requirements and practices, and a failure to systematically

---

[132] English press release to the Judgment of 11 January 2011, 1 BvR3295/07 (German Federal Constitutional Court).

[133] App. No. 29683/16, *X v. the Former Yugoslav Republic of Macedonia* (ECtHR, 17. January 2019), paras. 70 f.

[134] App. Nos. 2145/16 and 20607/16, *X and Y v Romania* (ECtHR, 19. January 2021), para. 168 (translation taken from the press release available at: http://hudoc.echr.coe.int/eng-press?i=003-6910029-9279612).

[135] Committee on the Elimination of Discrimination against Women, *General recommendation No. 33 on women's access to justice*, CEDAW/C/GC/33, 3 August 2015, paras. 22 and 23. Trigoudja (2016), pp. 133–134.

ensure that judicial mechanisms are physically, economically, socially and culturally accessible to all women. All these obstacles constitute persistent violations of women's human rights."[136]

As a consequence, access to justice entails eradicating discrimination through law reforms and providing for legal channels of judicial or quasi-judicial redress. International practice highlights two trajectories in the achievement of the said aims; the enactment of new instruments of protection of women's rights, and a gender sensitive assessment of existing provisions. In describing these trajectories, special attention will be paid to gender-based violence for its role in shaping the relationships between women and men.

7.2.7.1 The Enactment of New Substantial Laws of Protection

Removing the reasons for discrimination marks the provisions of the CEDAW which enshrines the right to access to justice through the obligations art. 2 (b) and art. 2 (c) envisage.[137] The first of the said provision obliges the States Parties to adopt appropriate legislative and other measures to prohibit all discrimination against women. The law aims at reforming existing rules to guarantee equality.

The undertaking art. 2 (b) displays is complemented by the obligation of result art. 2 (c), laying down reference to the judicial dimension of access to justice. The rule provides for the duty "to establish legal protection of the rights of women on an equal basis with men and to ensure through competent national tribunals and other public institutions the effective protection of women against any act of discrimination."

States are therefore called on to establish remedies and to guarantee their availability.

The CEDAW Committee pointed out that the right to justice is multidimensional since it encompasses justiciability, availability, accessibility, good quality, the provision of remedies for victims and the accountability of justice systems.[138] The recommendations the CEDAW Committee adopted in developing the content of the right to access to justice move from the need to give effect to the principle of equality by abolishing "any existing laws, procedures, regulations, jurisprudence, customs and practices that directly or indirectly discriminate against women."[139]

---

[136] Committee on the Elimination of Discrimination against Women, *General recommendation No. 33 on women's access to justice*, CEDAW/C/GC/33, 3 August 2015, para. 3. In para. 8. The Committee added that Discrimination against women, based on gender stereotypes, stigma, harmful and patriarchal cultural norms and gender based violence, which affects women in particular, has an adverse impact on the ability of women to gain access to justice on an equal basis with men. In addition, discrimination against women is compounded by intersecting factors that affect some women to degrees or in ways that differ from those affecting men or other women.

[137] On the overlap between the two rules as regards accesso to justice for women see Byrnes (2012), p. 83.

[138] Committee on the Elimination of Discrimination against Women, *General Recommendation No. 33 on women's access to justice*, CEDAW/C/GC/33, 3 August 2015, para. 1.

[139] *Idem*, para. 25.

In the same perspective of eradicating discrimination, an important step towards women's access to justice is to be found in several international conventions' provisions. Such provisions recognise that violence against women is a discrimination which has to be eradicated to suppress male domination.[140]

7.2.7.2 Gender-Based Assessment of Existing Substantial Laws

The assumption that violence embodies a gender discrimination influences the evolutive interpretation of several provisions of the ECHR.[141] Notwithstanding the low number of female plaintiffs,[142] the ECtHR has divined from art. 14 read in conjunction with 2, 3 and 8 of the Convention, a series of positive obligations intended to protect women against violence, domestic violence and rape. In *Opuz v. Turkey* the Strasbourg Court stated that art. 2 para.1 of the Convention "involves a primary duty on the State to secure the right to life by putting in place effective criminal-law provisions to deter the commission of offences against the person backed up by law-enforcement machinery for the prevention, suppression and punishment of breaches of such provisions."[143] In *M.C. v. Bulgaria* the ECtHR argued that "measures in the sphere of the relations of individuals between themselves" fall within the scope of positive obligations to punish rape arising from art. 3 and art. 8 of the Convention.[144]

7.2.7.3 The Enactment of New Procedural Laws of Protection

The practice on judicial or quasi-judicial redress is marked by the enactment of provision for legal avenues, encompassing an extensive set of measures.

The CEDAW Committee pointed out in General Recommendation n. 28 that pursuant to art. 2 (b) States are obliged to provide reparation to women whose rights under the Convention were violated "such as monetary compensation, restitution, rehabilitation and reinstatement; measures of satisfaction, such as public apologies, public memorials and guarantees of non-repetition; changes in relevant laws and practices; and bringing to justice the perpetrators of violations of human rights of women."[145] Furthermore, the Committee in the already mentioned Recommendation

---

[140] See the Inter-American Convention on the Prevention, Punishment and Eradication of Violence against Women, Protocol to the African Charter on Human and Peoples' Rights on the Rights of Women in Africa (Maputo Protocol), the Council of Europe Convention on Violence against Women and Domestic Violence (Istanbul Convention), the statutes of the ad hoc Tribunals for the former Yugoslavia and Rwanda Choudhry (2018); Koome (2012); Viseur Sellers (2009); Engle (2005).

[141] On the case law of the ECtHR see Radacic (2008).

[142] On the difficulties women face in bringing actions before the ECtHR see Palmer (1996), pp. 223–242; Tulkens (2007), pp. 423–445.

[143] App. Nos. 33401/02, *Case of Opuz v. Turkey* (ECtHR 9 June 2009), para. 128.

[144] App. Nos. 39272/98, *Case of M.C. v. Bulgaria* (ECtHR 4 December 2003), paras. 150–151.

[145] Committee on the Elimination of Discrimination against Women, *General Recommendation No. 28 on the core obligations of States parties under article 2 of the Convention on the Elimination of All Forms of Discrimination against Women*, CEDAW/C/GC/28, 16 December, para 32.

n. 33, stated that the availability of justice systems entails that the States Parties ensure, "in cases of violence against women, access to financial aid, crisis centres, shelters, hotlines and medical, psychosocial and counselling services recommended."[146] Moreover, the Committee divined from the accessibility of justice systems the need for establishing justice access centres providing "legal advice and aid, begin the legal proceedings and coordinate support services for women in several areas including violence against women."[147] The Committee recommended the protection of women's privacy, safety and other human rights during proceedings with reference to the good quality of justice systems.[148] Sexual violence in conflict, or post conflict situations, was also taken into consideration. The Committee argued it is necessary to adopt "institutional reforms, repeal discriminatory legislation and enact legislation providing for adequate sanctions, in accordance with international human rights standards, and determine reparation measures, in close cooperation with women's organizations and civil society, to help to overcome the discrimination that preceded the conflict as regards the provision of remedies."[149]

The Istanbul Convention lays down several provisions purporting the protection of women victims of violence: a) the training of professionals dealing with victims of all acts of violence (art. 15); b) women's right to receive adequate information on available support services and legal measures (art. 19); c) States' duty to provide victims with adequate civil remedies (art. 29) and compensation (art. 30); d) the prohibition of alternative dispute resolution processes, including mediation and conciliation, in relation to all forms of violence covered by the scope of the Convention (art. 48); e) carrying out investigations without undue delay (art. 49); f) the obligation to permit, in any civil or criminal proceedings, evidence relating to the sexual history and conduct of the victim only when it is relevant and necessary (art. 54); g) the protection of the rights and interest of victims at all stages of investigation and legal proceedings (art. 56) and finally; h) victims' right to legal assistance and to free legal aid (art. 57).

7.2.7.4 Gender-Based Assessment of Existing Procedural Rules

The ECtHR has considered art. 2, 3 and 8 of the Convention as the source of positive obligations. Such positive obligations comprise: the enactment of criminal provisions and the adoption of operational measures in order to protect against violence; the setting in place of an efficient and independent judicial system with the aim of protecting vulnerable subjects; preventing vulnerable subjects from being subject to torture, inhuman or degrading treatment, and the guarantee of an effective

[146] Committee on the Elimination of Discrimination against Women, *General recommendation No. 33 on women's access to justice*, CEDAW/C/GC/33, 3 August 2015, para. 16.

[147] *Idem*, para. 17.

[148] *Idem*, para. 18.

[149] *Idem*, para. 19.

system of investigation.[150] This interpretative approach contributes to the protection of women's rights in a limited way; the ECtHR clearly stated that States enjoy a certain margin of discretion in fulfilling the positive obligations at stake. In *M.C. v. Bulgaria*, a case on rape, the ECtHR specified that "the choice of the means to secure compliance with Article 8 in the sphere of protection against acts of individuals is in principle within the State's margin of appreciation".[151] Furthermore, in *Opuz v Turkey* the Court, ruling in a case of domestic violence, stated that " [n]ot every claimed risk to life, therefore, can entail for the authorities a Convention requirement to take operational measures to prevent that risk from materialising. For a positive obligation to arise, it must be established that the authorities knew or ought to have known at the time of the existence of a real and immediate risk to the life of an identified individual from the criminal acts of a third party and that they failed to take measures within the scope of their powers which, judged reasonably, might have been expected to avoid that risk."[152] This discretion could jeopardize the right to access to justice.

Furthermore, access to justice cannot be guaranteed only through the reform of the judicial system. Obstacles which stem from economic, cultural factors and gender stereotypes require to be removed.

7.2.8 Empowering of Women in the Political Sphere

Constitutionalism and citizenship have always been associated with furthering the egalitarian and rights-based vision of political justice. Yet, the birth of constitutionalism did not occur at the same time for men and women. While political equality started to become a reality for men with the late eighteen-century American and French democratic revolutions, for women it was only in the first half of the twentieth-century.[153]

The empowering of women is usually identified with the introduction of female suffrage and gender quotas (1). However, for their empowering to be effective further positive state measures are needed in the public sphere, more specifically prohibition of sexism (2).

[150] App. Nos. 7510/04, *Case of Kontrova v Slovakia* (ECtHR 31 May 2007); App. Nos. 839/02, *Case of Maslova and Nalbandov v. Russia* (ECtHR 24 January 2008); App. Nos. 38478/05, *Case of Sandra Jankovic. v. Croatia* (ECtHR 5 March 2009); App. Nos. 2660/03, *Case of Hajudova v. Slovakia* (ECtHR 30 November 2010); App. Nos. 60561/14, *Case of S.M. v. Croatia* (ECtHR GC 25 June 2020); App. Nos. 41237/14, *Case of Talpis v. Italy* (ECHR 2 March 2017), paras. 99–106. On this case see De Vido (2017).

[151] App. Nos. 39272/98, *Case of M.C. v. Bulgaria* (ECtHR 4 December 2003), para. 150.

[152] App. Nos. 33401/02, *Case of Opuz v. Turkey* (ECtHR 9 June 2009), para. 129.

[153] Rubio-Marin and Chang (2013), p. 301; see also section 4 of the chapter on the Gender Equality and Public Law, in this volume.

7.2.8.1 Female Suffrage and Gender Quotas

The slow recognition of female suffrage was the result of widespread prejudices as to the inherent inequality and division of roles between women and men. Family and household were reserved for women, while the public sphere, especially political life, were the privileges of men. In addition to these stereotypes, various other "concerns" related to the culture and politics of the specific countries, were advanced to maintain the exclusion of women from the political realm.[154]

Example

The religiousness of women was used as an argument against female suffrage in an otherwise progressive Third French Republic. Women were denied political rights as they were considered too prone to clericalism; the cleavage between clericalists and anti-clericalists was a determining one in political life of France at the turn of the twentieth Century.[155] ◄

These factors combined, led to the commencement of the recognition of women's political rights across Europe and North America in the first half of the twentieth century: Norway (1913); United Kingdom (1918); Germany (1918); Canada (1918); Poland (1918); United States (1920); Soviet Union (1924), and Spain (1931). The next milestone for the female suffrage came with the victory of progressive forces in World War Two, in recognition of women's participation in the war, more specifically in France (1944), Yugoslavia (1945), Italy (1945), Romania (1946), Belgium (1948), and Greece (1952). Yet, in Switzerland, it was only in 1971 that men accepted to share the right to vote with women, demonstrating how strongly they cared for their privileges in the political sphere.[156] Furthermore, there were reverse waves in the recognition of female suffrage. In Spain, after the female suffrage was recognized under the Second Republic in 1931, it was suppressed in 1939 with Franco's arrival to power. Female suffrage was restored only in 1978, three years after his death.[157]

Liberal feminist over emphasis on the "sameness" of men and women, and the appropriateness of gender-neutral approaches to overcome the discrimination based on sex or gender proved its limits.[158] Decades after the female suffrage was introduced in law, women were politically underrepresented in reality. The late arrival of women's citizenship to the constitutional project required the introduction of gender quotas in electoral lists. Their function was to enhance equal opportunities for individuals and to ameliorate the position of disempowered groups. It became obvious, as difference feminists argued, that in order to treat men and women

[154] Duverger (1980), p. 115.

[155] *Ibid.*

[156] *Ibid.*

[157] Carrillo (2019), p. 236.

[158] Cf. Jackson (2016), p. 441.

equally, it is (sometimes) necessary to treat them differently (because of history, and/or physiology, and/or culture, and/or political economy).[159]

However, granting women effective political power through gender quotas did not enter the constitutional scene without resistance across the globe.[160] Political and judicial battles ensued, leading to negative reactions of constitutional courts and, at the end, their constitutional entrenchment.[161]

Example

The recognition of the female suffrage in France did not lead to the gradual increase of the female representation. While in 1946 there were 42 women in the National Assembly, in 1962 there were only 8, and there was no more than 36 female deputies when the socialists came to power in 1981. These worrying figures led to the introduction of legislative quotas for women. However, that measure was struck down by the Constitutional Council, in 1982 and once again in 1999, with almost the same reasoning; it contradicted the constitutional principles of the indivisibility of sovereignty and equality before the law. To overcome the resistance of the constitutional judges, the Constitution was amended, first in 1999 and then in 2008. Hence, the new provision of the Fifth French Republic's Constitution stipulates that "statutes shall promote equal access of women and men to elective offices and posts as well as position of professional and social responsibility" (Article 1(2)).[162] In Italy, as in France, women were underrepresented in the political life. In response, measures of affirmative action were undertaken on the national and regional level. Nevertheless, in 1995 the Constitutional Court declared the gender quotas for the representative assemblies unconstitutional, being contrary to the principle of the universal character of political representation. The Court subsequently departed from this position, accepting the measures to promote female representation under the condition it applied only to the extent to which it concerned the opening of chances and not the guaranteeing of seats. It became obvious that a constitutional amendment was required to move from a formal to a substantive understanding of gender equality. After the 2003 reform, the Italian Constitution states that "any citizen of either sex is eligible for public offices and elected positions on equal terms" and that "to this end, the Republic shall adopt specific measures to promote equal opportunities between women and men" (Article 51(1)). Consequently, in another ruling, the Court confirmed that the new constitutional wording implied the principle of substantive gender equality.[163] ◀

[159] *Ibid*; cf. Wacks (2005), pp. 317–318.

[160] For a European perspective, see: Giegerich (2021), 05/21 EN, online via: https://jean-monnet-saar.eu/?page_id=70.

[161] Rubio-Marin and Chang (2013), p. 309.

[162] Roman (2019), pp. 276–277.

[163] Luciani (2019), pp. 344–345.

7.2.8.2 Prohibition of Sexism

Although gender quotas have contributed to the empowering of women, there are still many spheres of public life in which they are not only marginalized, but also degraded and humiliated. The stereotyping of women and the use of misogynistic language have not been eradicated from public discourse, increasing calls for restrictions on the freedom of speech. Pornography, systemic sexual objectification and denigration of women and girls have led some authors to ask themselves rhetorically if women are human.[164] Radical feminists, such as Catharine MacKinnon and Andrea Dworkin, have even pledged for the definition of pornography as a practice of sex discrimination, seeing in it "graphic materials that subordinate women through sexually explicit pictures and words",[165] and have advocated for a ban.

In response to these phenomena, the 2011 Council of Europe Convention on Combating Violence Against Women and Domestic Violence (Istanbul Convention) binds the states to "take the necessary measures to promote changes in the social and cultural patterns of behavior of women and men with a view to eradicating prejudices, customs, traditions and all other practices which are based on the idea of the inferiority of women or on stereotyped roles for women and men" (Article 12(1)). More specifically, Istanbul Convention imposes obligations upon states to "encourage [. . .] media, with due respect for freedom of expression and their independence, to participate in the elaboration and implementation of policies and to set guidelines and self-regulatory standards to prevent violence against women and to enhance respect for their dignity" (Article 17(1)).

Since, the similar provision has been already present in Article 5(a) of 1979 Convention on the Elimination of all Forms of Discrimination Against Women (see section 2c supra), many countries have started regulating freedom of expression with a view to combat sexist remarks.

Example

In 2004 France modified the Law on the Freedom of Press, penalizing speech provoking hatred or violence, as well as discrimination on the ground of sex. In 2017 further legislation was adopted to prohibit discrimination on the grounds of gender identity and sexual identity. Finally, in 2018, the Criminal Code was amended to penalize sexist behaviour, defined as injuring a person's dignity by degrading and humiliating acts, or creating intimidating, hostile or offending situation against another person. Criminal proceedings against French rapper Orelsan point to the complexity of the interpretation and application of the legislative provisions on the prohibition of the sexual discrimination. After he was convicted by the first instance court for his songs, among which one was poetically named *Suce ma bite pour la Saint-Valentin* ("Suck my dick for

[164] MacKinnon (2006), p. 42.

[165] *Ibid.*, p. 118.

Valentine's Day"), Orelsan was acquitted on appeal. In reaching this decision, the appellate court took into account the value of artistic creation and nature of rap music. Here, the court particularly valued freedom of artistic creation; allowing for the expression of minority views, and reflecting a vibrant society. Such minority views hold their own place in a liberal democracy. Rap music was viewed by the court as often brutal, provocative, vulgar and violent in its nature, being the expression of a generation which considered itself as disillusioned and rebelled. The court, then, went on to examine whether Orelsan's music was intended to harm women and to provoke discrimination against them, or to express the discomfort of one part of his generation. An exhaustive and non-truncated listening of his songs led the court to the conclusion that Orelsan did not identify himself with his characters, who are mediocre in their values, and that he did not claim for the legitimacy of their views.[166] ◄

7.3 Gender Perspective in Economic, Social and Cultural Rights

7.3.1 Economic and Social Discrimination of Women

The previous paragraphs clarified that the feminization of poverty[167] and gender-based violence have strengthened women's subordination to men. The connection between the two phenomena has to be evaluated against the framework of the laws protecting women's economic and social rights.

The unequal distribution of wealth between men and women is a final outcome of several processes, ranging from the difficulties women face in accessing education and employment to "the structured relations of production and reproduction that govern the distribution and use of resources, benefits, privileges and authority within the home and society at large".[168] Poverty exposes women to violence, since the lack of economic resources and the difficulties in acceding social protection oblige them to live in violent contexts.[169] Furthermore, the overrepresentation of women in informal, precarious and low-paid sectors[170] of the workforce widens the gap between men and women and exposes the latter to (sexual) harassment in the workplace. It has been rightly observed that the process is circular; violence

[166] Roman (2019), pp. 268, 282–284.

[167] Jänterä-Jareborg (2016), pp. 31–34.

[168] Ertürk (2009), para. 27.

[169] Larking (2019), p. 307.

[170] Committee on Economic, Social and Cultural Rights, *General Comment No. 24 on States obligations under the International Covenant on Economic, Social and Cultural Rights in the context of business activities*, 10 August 2017, Un Doc. E/C.12/GC/24, para. 9.

generates poverty in many cases by preventing women from acceding to education and employment, or obliges them to caring roles.[171]

This brief description illustrating the discrimination of women in economic and social fields makes it clear that equality entails dismantling those power structures which have been shaping economic and social organization.[172] The international system of protection of women's rights has not achieved such an outcome.

7.3.2 The ILO System

The Equal Remuneration Convention (1951) stipulates that States shall promote and ensure the principle of equal remuneration for men and women workers for work of equal value (art. 2).[173] The following Convention n. 111 of 1958 on employment and occupation envisages the adoption of special measures of protection or assistance which are to be deemed non-discriminatory in nature (art. 5).[174] Eventually, the Convention n. 156 of 1981 has fostered the promotion of effective equality of opportunity and treatment between women and men calling States to "make it an aim of national policy to enable individuals to engage in employment and exercise family responsibilities without being subject to discrimination (art. 3).[175]

7.3.3 The ICESCR

The ICESCR affords a limited protection to women's social and economic rights. The Covenant obliges States Parties to take steps with a view to progressively achieving full realization of the rights the Covenant enshrines (art. 2).[176] This obligation is somewhat restrained by further stating that the realizations are to be progressive, referencing "the maximum of [their] available resources." All economic, social and cultural rights the Covenant sets forth are enjoyed by men and women, pursuant to the equal right art. 3 provides for. This provision has to be read in conjunction with art. 2 para. 2 which lists several grounds of prohibited

[171] Goldblatt (2019), p. 360.

[172] On economic and social rights see Chinkin (2014), pp. 134–160; Fredman (2013), pp. 217–241; Otto (2002).

[173] ILO Equal Remuneration Convention, 1951 (No. 100), United Nations Treaty Series, Vol. 165, p. 2181, entered into force on 23 May 1953.

[174] ILO Discrimination in respect of Employment and Occupation Convention, 1958 (No. 111), United Nations Treaty Series, vol. 362, p. 31, entered into force 15 June 1960.

[175] ILO Workers with Family Responsibilities Convention, 1981, (No. 156), United Nations Treaty Series, vol. 1331, p. 295, entered into force on 11 August 1983.

[176] International Covenant on Economic, Social and Cultural Rights, adopted and opened for signature, ratification and accession by General Assembly resolution 2200A (XXI) of 16 December 1966. Entry into force 3 January 1976. 993-1 UNTS 14531.

discrimination, including sex. Pursuant to these provisions the right to equal treatment is not standing alone, but applies to the rights the Covenant establishes.

The equal right of men and women imposes a mandatory and immediate obligation to States Parties[177] to protect, respect and fulfil.[178] This latest obligation contains duties to provide, promote and facilitate. To comply with the obligation at stake, States are empowered to enact temporary measures in the first instance.[179]

7.3.4 The Conventions of the Council of Europe

The European Social Charter[180] and the Revised European Social Charter[181] adopted the same approach of the ICESCR in applying the principle of non-discrimination. The European Social Charter recognises: the right of men and women workers to equal pay for work of equal value (art. 4 (3)); the right of employed women to protection including the protection of maternity; the regulation of night work; the prohibition of employment of women workers in underground mining and in all other unsuitable works (art. 8), and the right of mothers and children to social and economic protection (art. 17).

The Revised European Social Charter widened the scope of the protection of fundamental economic and social rights. It provides for an express right to equal opportunities and equal treatment in matters of employment and occupation without discrimination on the grounds of sex. The obligation lies with States Parties "to recognize the said right and to take appropriate measures to ensure or to promote its application" in the fields of "a) access to employment, protection against dismissal and occupational reintegration; b) vocational guidance, training, retraining and rehabilitation; c) terms of employment and working conditions, including remuneration; d) career development, including promotion" (art. 20) . Moreover, the Revised European Social Charter aims at protecting dignity at work through the promotion of awareness, information and prevention of sexual harassment in the workplace (art. 26). It further imposes on States Parties the duty to take appropriate measures to guarantee the exercise of the right to equality of opportunity and treatment for men and women workers with family responsibilities and between such workers (art. 27). Eventually, art. E of Part V lists sex as a prohibited ground of discrimination in the enjoyment of the rights the Charter sets forth.

[177] Committee on Economic, Social and Cultural Rights, *General Comment No. 16 (2005). The equal right of men and women to the enjoyment of all economic, social and cultural rights (art. 3 of the International Covenant on Economic, Social and Cultural Rights)*, 11 August 2005, E/C.12/2005/4, para. 16.

[178] *Idem*, para. 17.

[179] *Idem*, para. 15.

[180] Council of Europe European Social Charter, Turin 18 October 1961, CETS – No. 35.

[181] Council of Europe Revised European Social Charter, Strasbourg 3 May 1996, CETS No. 163.

7.3.5 The CEDAW

All the international conventions examined above seem to fail to ensure women emancipation. The rules reproduce the divide between public and private sphere since they do not affect the private relationships in which women experience labour segregation, exclusion from social assistance and violence.[182] Moreover, they adopt a male conception of rights, expressed through the use of male language,[183] and aim at extending these rights to women pursuant to the principle of non-discrimination. These do not take into consideration the specific condition of women and the related need for protection. There is no provision affecting the social division of labour, namely the clustering of women in specific labour fields and positions, and no regulation for the unpaid work of caring. No action is envisaged to remove those obstacles to the enjoyment of rights in the field of employment, occupation and social protection stemming from the work in the private sphere of families.

Most of the shortcomings arise from the adoption of a non-discriminatory approach. It is therefore not surprising that such a stance has not been followed in the drafting of the CEDAW, which aims at eliminating discrimination. To achieve the said targets, the Convention puts an end to the distinction between the public and private sphere. Discrimination against women falls within this scope when committed by any person, organization or enterprise. Art. 3 establishes the duty of taking appropriate measures in the economic and social fields to ensure the full development and advancement of women. In this vein the rules art. 11 envisages aim at tackling structural factors of inequality between women and men in employment and occupation. The provision is based "on recognition of the complex realities of women's economic, family and employment situation"[184] and provides for a series of States' obligations to eliminate discrimination. The aims of the rules enacted by art. 11 are to ensure substantial equality through the removal of direct and indirect discrimination affecting women, and preventing them for acceding to occupation. The provision distinguishes two sets of duties which relate to different obstacles to equality. The first set of rules (art. 11 para. 1) aim at granting women the same rights on the basis of equality between women and men. The provisions at stake cover the rights to work, equal employment opportunities, vocational training and retraining, equal remuneration and social security, and finally, free choice of protection and employment.

The second set of rules (art 11 para. 2) targets the prevention of discrimination women face because of marriage and maternity, guaranteeing their effective right to work. This section of the provision relates to structural factors of discrimination. These tend to be entrenched in a model of family relations, the distribution of roles within family, and the cultural stereotypes based on the said organization of society.

[182] On this divide see Charlesworth and Chinkin (2000), p. 238.

[183] E.g. articles 1, 10, 13 and 19 of the European Social Charter and the Revised European Social Charter; Art. 1 para. 1 ICESCR; Chinkin (2014), p. 137.

[184] Raday (2012), p. 281.

The instruments art.11 envisages are connected to the provisions contained in art 1 to 5 of the CEDAW.

Moreover, the system of eradication of discrimination against women set out by art. 11 is strengthened by the provisions contained in art. 13. This imposes on States Parties the duty to "take all appropriate measures to eliminate discrimination against women in other areas of economic and social life". The rule covers the right to self-employed economic activities, food, adequate housing, adequate standard of living, water and sanitation.[185]

Notwithstanding the improvement of the protection of women's economic and social rights the CEDAW has achieved, the root causes of gender discrimination were not erased. Economic and social rights were not conceived for preventing violence against women. Furthermore, the crisis of the conception of labour rights as human rights[186] has undermined the effectiveness of the rights the international conventions lay down.

Moreover, liberalization has pushed several publicly funded social services to the realm of private business, affecting the poorest part of society.[187]

The shrinking of social protection stems also from the policies of loans pursued by the IMF and the World Bank, obliging the recipient States to cut down welfare protection.

The spreading of poverty does not only affect women's rights, exacerbating their discrimination, but contributes to increased violence against women.[188]

7.3.6 Gender Education Gaps and Education as a Pathway Towards Equality

7.3.6.1 The Right to Education

The right to education is enshrined in multiple human rights treaties on the international[189] and on the regional level.[190] It includes the right to primary education,[191]

[185] See Rudolf (2012), pp. 336–355.

[186] Alston (2005).

[187] Larking (2019), p. 307.

[188] Orford (1997), pp. 455–456.

[189] Art. 5 CERD, Art. 13 ICESCR, Art. 10 lit. h) CEDAW, Art. 17 CRC, Art. 4 lit. h) CRPD; Art. 30 UN Convention on the Protection of the Rights of All Migrant Workers and Members of Their Families.

[190] Art. 10 ECHR, Art. 13 ACHR and Art. 9 ACHPR.

[191] This includes grade levels for children between the age of four and twelve according to: International Standard Classification of Education (ISCED) 2011, para. 122, http://uis.unesco.org/sites/default/files/documents/international-standard-classification-of-education-isced-2011-en.pdf.

secondary education, including technical and vocational education, as well as higher education[192] and fundamental education.[193]

According to the Committee on CESCR, States are required to secure the *"availability, accessibility, acceptability and adaptability"*[194] of the respective education or all educational levels. This means that *"functioning educational institutions and programmes have to be available in sufficient quantity within the jurisdiction of the State party. [. . .] educational institutions and programmes have to be accessible to everyone, without discrimination, within the jurisdiction of the State party. [. . .] teaching methods, have to be acceptable (e.g. relevant, culturally appropriate and of good quality) to students and, in appropriate cases, parents.[. . .] education has to be flexible so it can adapt to the needs of changing societies and communities and respond to the needs of students within their diverse social and cultural settings."*[195]

As the right to education is a human right, states have to respect, protect and ensure its enjoyment. The scope of these obligations depend on the level of education; whereas they merely have "to take steps" with regard to the realization of secondary, higher and fundamental education, States have to prioritize the introduction of compulsory, free primary education.[196] Therefore, a national educational strategy including the provision of secondary, higher and fundamental education already suffices, whereas states have a direct obligation to provide primary education.[197]

7.3.6.2 The Prohibition of Discrimination in Education

In 2013, around 60% of the 773 million illiterate people were women.[198] Until today, girls are more likely to drop out of school, or never to go to school at all.[199]

---

[192] Also defined as tertiary education: "[. . .] includes what is commonly understood as academic education but also includes advanced vocational or professional education. [. . .] Bachelor's or equivalent level, Master's or equivalent level, and doctoral or equivalent level, [. . .]" (ISCED 2011, para. 200).

[193] CESCR, General Comment No. 13 (1999), paras. 23, 24: "[. . .] The right to fundamental education extends to all those who have not yet satisfied their "basic learning needs". [. . .] the right to fundamental education is not limited by age or gender; it extends to children, youth and adults, including older persons. Fundamental education, therefore, is an integral component of adult education and life-long learning. Because fundamental education is a right of all age groups, curricula and delivery systems must be devised which are suitable for students of all ages."

[194] *Ibid.* para. 6.

[195] *ibid.*

[196] *ibid.* para. 10.

[197] *ibid.* para. 51 f.

[198] CEDAW, General Recommendation No. 36, para. 2.

[199] Even though the global trend goes towards parity, on the regional level the gap continues to exist: UNESCO Institute for Statistics (UIS) (2019).

The Covid 19-pandemic put over 11 million girls at the risk of dropping out of school.[200]

The right to education is of special importance as it is a prerequisite for the enjoyment of other human rights and (women's) participation in a democratic society, including, but not limited to, the right to work, the right to health (especially concerning reproductive rights)[201] or the freedom of expression.[202] Equal access to education reduces unwanted pregnancies and the mortality of young mothers.[203] Furthermore, women who have received at least a basic education are later able to shape their own lives and are more likely to participate in political life.[204] It is not only gender, but mostly intersectional discrimination that prevents girls from exercising their right to education by attending school. *"Such factors include barriers to access for girls and women from disadvantaged and marginalized groups, exacerbated by poverty and economic crises, gender stereotyping in curricula, textbooks and teaching processes, violence against girls and women in and out of school and structural and ideological restrictions to their engagement in male-dominated academic and vocational fields.*[205] The necessary awareness of potential intersectional discrimination has been emphasized, for example, by the Inter-American Court of Human Rights in a case concerning girls whose parents were migrants.[206]

According to the CEDAW Committee, the right to education is a "tripartite human rights obligation"[207] which means that states firstly have to guarantee the "right of access to education" and ensure equal access. Secondly, they have to guarantee "rights within education", concerning the treatment and opportunity of women in education. Thirdly, they have to ensure, "rights through education", concerning the results of the education for the enjoyment of other human rights.

The gender gap in education is not only a violation of the state's obligations with regard to the right to education, it is also an economically expensive failure. Studies show that the gender gap in employment can cost the economy up to 15 percent of the GDP of the respective country.[208] The better women and girls are educated, the higher the likelihood that they participate in the labour market and contribute to the

[200] For the situation in the context of the Covid 19-pandemic see: UNESCO (2020).

[201] See above Sect. 7.3.4.

[202] ICESCR, General Comment No. 13 para. 1; CEDAW, General recommendation No. 36, para. 1.

[203] Art. 10 h CEDAW requires the states to reduce the lack of education on health issues for women; on the positive outcomes of education and childbirth see: Bhalotra and Clarke (2013), p. 19.

[204] Currently, only 25.5% of the world's parliamentarians are female (https://data.ipu.org/women-averages?month=4&year=2021).

[205] CEDAW, General Recommendation No. 36 (2017), para. 4.

[206] Series C No. 130, *Girls Yean and Bosico v. Dominican Republic* (IACHR, 08. September 2005), paras. 134 and 244.

[207] CEDAW, General Recommendation No. 36 (2017), paras. 13–19.

[208] Cuberes and Teignier (2016), pp. 1–32.

growth of the respective state's economy.[209] It is therefore not only a legal obligation to provide equal education, but also in the economic and financial interest of the state. In order to ensure that the gender education gap is closed, the right to education is complemented by the prohibition to discriminate,[210] obliging states to enable equal access to education regardless of gender or other prohibited grounds of discrimination. This prohibition is reaffirmed in the 2030 Agenda for Sustainable Development (Goal 4) and enshrined in a separate UNESCO treaty; the Convention against discrimination in education of 1960.[211]

7.4 Conclusion

The chapter has shown several aspects of human rights, when interpreted and applied from a gender perspective. States are not only obliged to ensure gender equality by refraining from interventions, but also have positive obligations to adjust their legislation accordingly. This was witnessed in the context of GBV and the right to respect for private life.

Religious freedom "is one of the most vital elements that [...] make up the identity of the believers and their conception of life" *(Kokkinakis v. Greece)*. However, controversies over wearing headscarves and full-face veils in public places, as well as performance and assistance in abortion procedures, bear witness to the fact how religious freedoms play for women, but also against them.

Furthermore, the rules on access to justice contained within international treaties grant states a wide margin of discretion in their implementation. As a consequence, judicial protection cannot dismantle the vicious circle of poverty, violence, and the distribution of labour in which women are kept. Besides judicial rights, political rights are another field where "asking the woman question" furthers and deepens the debate as to the meaning of equality. The late recognition of female citizenship

[209] See on this e.g.: OECD, Gender Equality in Education, Employment and Entrepreneurship: Final Report to the MCM 2012. http://www.oecd.org/employment/50423364.pdf, p. 3.

[210] See for example: Art. 10 CEDAW, Art. 2 (2) CRC read together with Art. 28, 29 CRC; Convention against Discrimination in Education 1960 and on the regional level: Art. 12 of the Protocol to the African Charter on Human and Peoples' Rights on the Rights of Women in Africa; Art. 13 African Youth Charter; Art. 11 of the African Charter on the Rights and Welfare of the Child; Art. 13 African Youth Charter; Art. 11 of the African Charter on the Rights and Welfare of the Child; Art. 14 ECHR read in conjunction with Art. 2 of Protocol 1 (general prohibition of discrimination in Art. 1 Prot. 12); Art. E, 9, 10 and 17 of the European Social Charter; Art. 14 Istanbul Convention; Art.14, 21 and 23 Charta of Fundamental Rights of the European Union; Art. 3, 13 and 16 Additional Protocol to the American Convention on Human Rights in the Area of Economic, Social and Cultural Rights Protocol of San Salvador; Art. 34, 49 and 50 of the Charter of the Organization of American States; Art. 6 Inter-American Convention on the Prevention, Punishment and Eradication of Violence against Women; Art. 9 and 16 Inter-American Democratic Charter; Art. 41 Arab Charta on Human Rights; Art. 31 ASEAN Human Rights Declaration (not legally binding).

[211] UNESCO, Convention against Discrimination in Education, 14 December 1960.

necessitated the introduction of gender quotas and prohibition of sexism for the equality between men and women to be effective.

The feminization of poverty, the privatization of public goods and services, and the distribution of labour have been bolstering men's domination, by creating new forms of women's sexual and labour exploitation. The stress on the management of migration flows has shaped the rules on trafficking marginalising the need for granting victims' rights.

The international standards of protection of women's economic and social rights have not been effective in ensuring equality. This is despite the importance of women's economic, social and cultural rights, not only to reach substantive gender equality, but also for states economies.

Questions

1. Define the legal notion of slavery
2. Identify the elements of trafficking
3. Identify the obstacles women face in having access to justice
4. Why is a religious freedom both an essential component of identity of many women and a challenge to their dignity and autonomy?
5. How do female suffrage and gender quotas empower women and what are the legal controversies surrounding the introduction of gender quotas?
6. Why is the prohibition of sexism important and what are the legal challenges related to the implementation of this measure?
7. Mention the reasons for the failure of economic and social rights to eradicate women discrimination
8. Explain the term "gender-based violence" as used in the Istanbul Convention and explain its strengths and shortcomings.
9. What does the right to respect for private life entail with regard to reproductive rights?
10. How is/can gender equality be ensured when it comes to education?

References

Alston P (2005) Labour rights as human rights. The not so happy state of the art. In: Alston P (ed) Labour rights as human rights. Oxford University Press, Oxford, pp 1–24

Bales K, Robbins PT (2001) No one shall be held in Slavery or Servitude: a critical analysis of international slavery conventions. Hum Rights Rev 2:18–45

Bhalotra S, Clarke D (2013) Educational attainment and maternal mortality. https://unesdoc.unesco.org/ark:/48223/pf0000225945. Accessed 12 Sep 2021

Byrnes A (2012) Art. 2. In: Freeman MA, Chinkin C, Rudolf B (eds) The UN convention on the elimination of all forms of discrimination against women. Oxford University Press, Oxford, pp 71–99

Carrillo M (2019) Espagne. Annuaire international de justice constitutionnelle XXXIV-2018 – Égalité, genre et constitution, pp 223–239

Cerone J (2007) Human trafficking in Max Planck Encyclopedias of International Law

Chaney E (1979) Supermadre: women in politics in Latin America. University of Texas Press, Austin
Charlesworth H, Chinkin C (2000) The boundaries of international law. Manchester University Press, Manchester
Chinkin C (2014) Gender and economic, social and cultural rights. In: Riedel E, Giacca G, Golay C (eds) Economic, social, and cultural rights in international law. Contemporary issues and challenges. Oxford University Press, Oxford, pp 134–160
Choudhry S (2018) Women's access to justice: a guide for legal practitioners. https://rm.coe.int/factsheet-womens-access-to-justice/16808ff44e. Accessed 12 Sep 2021
Coomaraswamy R (1997) Report of the Special Rapporteur on violence against women, its causes and consequences. https://digitallibrary.un.org/record/238264. Accessed 12 Sep 2021
Cuberes D, Teignier M (2016) Aggregate effects of gender gaps in the labor market: a quantitative estimate. J Hum Cap 10:1–32. https://doi.org/10.1086/683847
De Vido S (2017) States' positive obligations to eradicate domestic violence: the politics of relevance in the interpretation of the European Convention on Human Rights. ESIL Reflection 6:1–11
Duverger M (1980) Institutions politiques et droit constitutionnel – I/ Les grands systèmes politiques. Presses universitaires de France, Paris
ECtHR, Factsheet on Violence against women. https://www.echr.coe.int/Documents/FS_Violence_Woman_ENG.pdf. Accessed 12 Sep 2021
Engle K (2005) Feminism and its (dis)contents: criminalizing wartime rape in Bosnia and Herzegovina. Am J Int Law 99:778–816
Ertürk Y (2009) Report of the Special Rapporteur on violence against womens its causes and consequence: political economy of women's human rights. Human Rights Council. https://digitallibrary.un.org/record/656877. Accessed 12 Sep 2021
Fredman S (2013) Engendering socio-economic rights. In: Hellum A, Aasen HS (eds) Women's human rights. CEDAW in international, regional and national law. Cambridge University Press, Cambridge, pp 217–241
Giegerich T (2021) Gender equality and gender quotas for political participation in Europe: comparative, international and supranational perspectives. http://jean-monnet-saar.eu/?page_id=70. Accessed 12 Sep 2021
Goldblatt B (2019) Violence against women and social and economic rights: deepening the connections. In: Rimmer SH, Ogg K (eds) Research handbook on feminist engagement with international law. Edward Elgar Publishing, Cheltenham/Northampton, pp 359–371
Grans L (2018) The Istanbul Convention and the positive obligation to prevent violence. Hum Rights Law Rev 18:133–155. https://doi.org/10.1093/hrlr/ngx041
Heise L, Ellsberg M, Gottmoeller M (2002) A global overview of gender-based violence. Int J Gynecol Obstet 78:5–14. https://doi.org/10.1016/S0020-7292(02)00038-3
Htun M (2000) Culture, institutions and gender inequality in Latin America. In: Harrison LE, Huntington SP (eds) Culture matters. Basic Books, New York, pp 191–192
Jackson VC (2016) Feminisms, pluralisms and transnationalism: on CEDAW and national constitutions. In: Rubenstein K, Young KG (eds) The public law of gender – from the local to the global. Cambridge University Press, Cambridge, pp 437–464
Jänterä-Jareborg M (2016) Women's human rights: international law in the intersection between socioeconomic conditions, culture, tradition and religion. In: Jänterä-Jareborg M, Tigroudja H (eds) Women's human rights and the elimination of discrimination. The Hague Academy of International Law, The Hague, pp 3–98
Koome J (2012) Without these women, the tribunal cannot do anything: the politics of witness testimony on sexual violence at the international criminal tribunal for Rwanda. J Women Cult Soc 38:253–277
Larking E (2019) Challenging gendered economic and social inequalities: an analysis of the role of trade and financial liberalisation in deepening inequalities, and of the capacity of economic and social rights to redress them. In: Harris S, Rimmer KO (eds) Research handbook on feminist

engagement with international law. Edward Elgar Publishing, Cheltenham/Northampton, pp 306–322
Luciani M (2019) Italie. Annuaire international de justice constitutionnelle XXXIV-2018 – Égalité, genre et constitution, pp 327–347
MacKinnon CA (2006) Are women human? – And other international dialogues. The Belknap Press of Harvard University Press, Cambridge/London
Mahlmann M (2009) Freedom and faith: foundations of freedom of religion. Cardozo Law Rev 30: 2473–2493
Mancini S (2014) Strong religions and weak minorities: a cautionary tale from Europe. In: Basta Fleiner LR, Marinkovic T (eds) Key developments in constitutionalism and constitutional law. Eleven International Publishing, Den Haag, pp 33–47
Marinkovic T (2017) Religion in public spaces – controversies in the European Court of Human Right's Case-Law. In: Brunkhorst H, Vujadinović D, Marinkovic T (eds) European democracy in crisis – polities under challenge and social movements. Eleven International Publishing, Den Haag, pp 75–91
Méndez J (2013) Report of the UN Special Rapporteur on torture and other cruel, inhuman and degrading treatment. https://www.ohchr.org/documents/hrbodies/hrcouncil/regularsession/session22/a.hrc.22.53_english.pdf. Accessed 12 Sep 2019
Morondo Taramundi D (2020) Gender-based violence against women and international protection needs - the contribution of the Istanbul Convention. In: Peroni L, Niemi J, Stoyanova V (eds) International law and violence against women: Europe and the Istanbul Convention. Routledge, London, pp 241–265
Niemi J, Sanmartin AV (2020) The concepts of gender and violence in the Istanbul Convention. In: Niemi J, Peroni L, Stoyanova V (eds) International law and violence against women: Europe and the Istanbul Convention. Routledge, London, pp 81–95
Orford A (1997) Locating the international military and monetary interventions after the Cold War. Harv Int Law J 38:443–486
Otto D (2002) Gender comment: why does the UN Committee on economic, social and cultural rights need a general comment on women? Can J Women Law 14:1–52
Palmer S (1996) Critical perspectives on women's rights: the European Convention on Human Rights and fundamental freedoms. In: Bottomley A (ed) Feminist perspectives on the foundational subjects of law. Cavendish, London, pp 223–242
Phillips A (2005) Dilemmas of gender and culture: the judge, the democrat and the political activist. In: Eisenberg A, Spinner-Halev J (eds) Minorities within minorities: equality, rights and diversity. Cambridge University Press, Cambridge, pp 113–134
Radacic I (2008) Gender equality jurisprudence of the European Court of Human Rights. Eur J Int Law 19:841–857
Raday F (2003) Culture, religion and gender. I.CON 1(4):669
Raday F (2012) Art. 11. In: Freeman MA, Chinkin C, Rudolf B (eds) The UN convention on the elimination of all forms of discrimination against women. Oxford University Press, Oxford, pp 281–309
Roman D (2019) France. Annuaire international de justice constitutionnelle XXXIV-2018 – Égalité, genre et constitution, pp 259–287
Rubio-Marin R, Chang W-C (2013) Sites of constitutional struggle for women's equality. In: Tushnet M, Fleiner T, Saunders C (eds) Routledge handbook of constitutional law. Routledge, London, pp 304–305
Rudolf B (2012) Art. 13. In: Freeman MA, Chinkin C, Rudolf B (eds) The UN convention on the elimination of all forms of discrimination against women. Oxford University Press, Oxford, pp 336–355
Sembacher A (2006) The Council of Europe Convention on action against trafficking in human beings. Tulane J Int Comp Law 14:435–454
Stoyanova V (2020a) Due diligence versus positive obligations - critical reflections on the Council of Europe Convention on violence against women. In: Niemi J, Peroni L, Stoyanova V (eds)

International law and violence against women: Europe and the Istanbul Convention. Routledge, London, pp 95–129
Trigoudja H (2016) Droits des femmes et non-discrimination: de l'affirmation des obligations internationales de l'Etat à un droit à l'autoprotection. In: Jänterä-Jareborg M, Tigroudja H (eds) Women's human rights and the elimination of discrimination. The Hague Academy of International Law, The Hague, pp 133–134
Tulkens F (2007) Droits de l'homme, droits des femmes. Les requérantes devant la cour européenne des droits de l'homme. In: Caflisch L, Callewaert J, Liddell R, Mahoney P, Villiger M (eds) Liber Amicorum Luzius Wildhaber. Droits de l'homme—Regards de Strasbourg. Engel, Kehl, pp 423–445
UNESCO (2019) Fact Sheet 56. New methodology shows that 258 million children, adolescents and youth are out of school. http://uis.unesco.org/sites/default/files/documents/new-methodology-shows-258-million-children-adolescents-and-youth-are-out-school.pdf. Accessed 12 Sep 2021
UNESCO (2020) Addressing the gender dimensions of COVID-related school closures. https://unesdoc.unesco.org/ark:/48223/pf0000373379. Accessed 12 Sep 2021
Viseur Sellers P (2009) Gender strategy is not luxury for international courts symposium: prosecuting sexual and gender-based crimes before international/ized criminal courts. Am Univ J Gender Soc Policy Law 17:301–325
Zampas C, Amin A, O'Hanlon L, Bjerregaard A, Mehrtash H, Khosla R, Tunçalp Ö (2020) Operationalizing a human rights-based approach to address mistreatment against women during childbirth. Health Hum Rights J 22:251–264

Further Reading

Allain J (2010) Rantsev v. Cyprus and Russia: The European Court of Human Rights and trafficking as slavery. Hum Rights Law Rev 10:546–557
Allain J (2013) Slavery in international law: of human exploitation and trafficking. Martinus Nijhoff, Leiden
Barry K (1995) The prostitution of sexuality. New York University Press, New York
Bassiouni MC (1991) Enslavement as an international crime. N Y Univ J Int Law Polit 23:445–517
Brewer M, Southwell P (2018) Legal policy and framework on trafficking. In: Southwell P, Brewer M, Ben Douglas-Jones QC (eds) Human trafficking and modern slavery. Law and practice. Bloomsbury Publishing, Haywards Heath, pp 1–12
Chuang J (2012) Art. 6. In: Freeman MA, Chinkin C, Rudolf B (eds) The UN convention on the elimination of all forms of discrimination against women. Oxford University Press, Oxford, pp 169–196
De Sena P (2019) Slaveries and new slaveries: which role for human dignity?. http://www.qil-qdi.org/wp-content/uploads/2019/12/02_New-Slaveries_DE-SENA_FIN.pdf. Accessed 12 Sep 2021
Dorsen N, Rosenfeld M, Sajó A, Baer S (2003) Comparative constitutionalism – cases and materials. Thomson West, St. Paul
Eskitaşçıoğlu İ (2019) Access to menstrual products is a constitutional right. Period.: On period poverty and the (un)constitutionality of Tampon tax. https://verfassungsblog.de/access-to-menstrual-products-is-a-constitutional-right-period/. Accessed 12 Sep 2021
Fitzpatrick J (2003) Trafficking as a human rights violation: the complex intersection of legal frameworks for conceptualizing and combating trafficking. Mich J Int Law 24:1143–1167
Fortas AC (2016) Droit international et genre. In: Jänterä-Jareborg M, Tigroudja H (eds) Women's human rights and the elimination of discrimination. The Hague Academy of International Law, The Hague, pp 3–98
Gallagher A (2001) Human rights and the new UN protocols on trafficking and migrant smuggling: preliminary analysis. Hum Rights Q 23:975–1004

Gallagher A (2009) Human rights and human trafficking: quagmire or firm ground? A response to James Hathaway. Va J Int Law 49:789–848

Gallagher A (2011) The international law of human trafficking. Cambridge University Press, Cambridge

Grossman N (2019) Feminist approaches to international adjudication. https://opil.ouplaw.com/view/10.1093/law-mpeipro/e3350.013.3350/law-mpeipro-e3350. Accessed 12 Sep 2019

Haverkamp R, Herlin-Karnell E, Lernestedt C (2019) What is wrong with human trafficking? Critical perspectives on the law. Hart Publishing, London

Hellum A, Aasen HS (2013) Women's human rights. CEDAW in international, regional and national law. Cambridge University Press, Cambridge

Henn EV (2016) Gender injustice, discrimination and the CEDAW: a women's life course perspective. In: Jänterä-Jareborg M, Tigroudja H (eds) Women's human rights and the elimination of discrimination. Brill/Nijhoff, Leiden/Boston, pp 183–215

Lamont R (2013) Beating domestic violence? Assessing the EU's contribution to tackling violence against women. Common Market Law Rev 6:1787–1807

Meix-Cereceda P (2020) Educational values in human rights treaties: UN, European, and African international law. Hum Rights Rev 21:437–461. https://doi.org/10.1007/s12142-020-00599-6

Nanda P, Cherif Bassiouni M (1971) Slavery and the slave trade: steps toward eradication. Santa Clara Law Rev 12:424–442

Noll G (2007) The insecurity of trafficking in international law. In: Chetail V (ed) Globalization, migration and human rights: international law under review. Bruylant, Bruxelles, pp 343–361

Obokata T (2006) Trafficking of human beings from a human rights perspective. Martinus Nijhoff Publisher, Leiden

Paulk LB (2014) Embryonic personhood: implications for assisted reproductive technology in international human rights law. Am Univ J Gender Soc Policy Law 22:781–823

Peroni L (2018) The protection of women asylum seekers under the European Convention on Human Rights: unearthing the gendered roots of harm. Hum Rights Law Rev 18:347–370. https://doi.org/10.1093/hrlr/ngy004

Pizzarossa LB (2018) Here to stay: the evolution of sexual and reproductive health and rights in international human rights law. Laws 3:1–17

Scarpa S (2018) Contemporary forms of slavery. https://www.europarl.europa.eu/RegData/etudes/STUD/2018/603470/EXPO_STU(2018)603470_EN.pdf. Accessed 12 Sep 2021

Stoyanova V (2012) Dancing on the borders of article 4: human trafficking and the European Court of Human Rights in the Rantsev Case. Neth Q Hum Rights 30:163–194

Stoyanova V (2017) Human trafficking and slavery reconsidered: conceptual limits and states' positive obligations in European law. Cambridge University Press, Cambridge

Stoyanova V (2020b) The Grand Chamber Judgment in S.M. v Croatia: human trafficking, prostitution and the definitional scope of Article 4 ECHR. https://strasbourgobservers.com/2020/07/03/the-grand-chamber-judgment-in-s-m-v-croatia-human-trafficking-prostitution-and-the-definitional-scope-of-article-4-echr/. Accessed 12 Sep 2021

Suzor N, Dragiewicz M, Harris B, Gillett R, Burgess J, van Geelen T (2019) Human rights by design: the responsibilities of social media platforms to address gender-based violence online. Policy Internet 1:84–103

Wacks R (2005) Understanding jurisprudence – an introduction to legal theory. Oxford University Press, Oxford

Weissbrot D (2002) Abolishing slavery and its contemporary forms. United Nations, New York/Geneva

Westendorp I (2012) The Women's Convention Turned 30. Intersentia, Cambridge

Whitaker B (1982) Report on slavery. https://digitallibrary.un.org/record/33645?ln=fr. Accessed 12 Sep 2021

Wijers M, Lap-Chew L (1997) Trafficking in women, forced labour and slavery-like practices in marriage, domestic labour and prostitution. Foundation Against Trafficking in Women, Utrecht

The Evolving Recognition of Gender in International and European Law

8

Rigmor Argren, Marco Evola, Thomas Giegerich, and Ivana Krstić

Contents

Authors are listed in alphabetical order. Rigmor Argren authored Sects. 8.2.2–8.2.4 and Sect. 8.3; Marco Evola authored Sect. 8.6. Sections 8.1.3 and 8.5 are written by Thomas Giegerich and Ivana Krstić authored Sects. 8.1.2, 8.2.1 and 8.4.

R. Argren (✉)
Örebro University, School of Law, Psychology and Social work, Örebro, Sweden
e-mail: Rigmor.Argren@oru.se

M. Evola
LUMSA Department of Law, Palermo, Italy
e-mail: m.evola@lumsa.it

T. Giegerich
Europa-Institut, Saarland University, Saarbrücken, Germany
e-mail: giegerich@europainstitut.de

I. Krstić
University of Belgrade, Faculty of Law, Belgrade, Serbia
e-mail: ikrstic@ius.bg.ac.rs

D. Vujadinović et al. (eds.), *Gender-Competent Legal Education*, Springer Textbooks in Law, https://doi.org/10.1007/978-3-031-14360-1_8

Abstract

This chapter explains the development of international and European law from a gender perspective and describes how the process from a gender-neutral to a gender-sensitive approach was developed.

Since 1945 and the adoption of the UN Charter, the idea of achieving greater gender equality was merged into many international documents, including the first catalog of women's rights—Convention on the Elimination of all Forms of Discrimination against Women. Many principal and subsidiary bodies were established, contributing to the elimination of gender discrimination and to awareness-raising on some critical issues which were an impediment to achieving gender equality. Twenty years ago, UN Security Council Resolution 1325 was adopted, due to a global effort to establish a platform as a foundation to national and international policies to ensure greater protection of women and girls, during and after, armed conflicts. International Humanitarian Law, enshrined in the Geneva Conventions, also has rules that specifically seek to protect women during armed conflicts. Also, International Criminal Law has been developed to recognize extreme forms of sexual violence as international crimes.

On the European level, under the auspices of the Council of Europe, several international conventions were adopted to achieve gender equality. One of the main instruments, the European Convention on Human Rights, provides broad protection from discrimination based on gender, established in a comprehensive jurisprudence of the European Court of Human Rights. The EU has a set of primary and secondary sources on anti-discrimination, which provides comprehensive protection from gender discrimination and serves as an inspiring model to States candidates and other European countries.

8.1 International Law and Gender Equality

8.1.1 Introduction

This chapter deals with international and European law from the perspective of gender equality. It is divided into two major parts. The first part (Sects. 8.1–8.4) covers universal sources and bodies established with the aim to promote and protect gender equality, while the second (Sects. 8.5–8.6) deals with sources developed under the auspices of the Council of Europe and EU law.

The first part is divided into four sections.

The first section briefly explains how international law developed from gender-neutral to a branch of law that considers gender equality and sketches the Convention on the Elimination of Discrimination against Women and Optional Protocol as the main UN treaties for the advancement of women's rights.

The second section covers other gender-related sources and activities at the UN level. This part covers UN main and subsidiary bodies which serve as a catalyst to the advancement of gender equality.

The third section outlines particular aspects of International Humanitarian Law. This part covers the legal provisions that protect women during armed conflict as well as the provisions in place for the prevention of sexual violence during armed conflict.

The fourth section presents the development of gender perspective into International Criminal Law and recognition of gender-based persecution in the statutes and practice of international, hybrid and national courts and tribunals.

The second part deals with the European law and consists of two sections. Thus, section five gives an overview of the gender aspects of the European Convention on Human Rights and case-law of the European Court of Human Rights as well as of other gender-relevant treaties and policies of the Council of Europe.

Finally, the sixth section focuses on primary and secondary law of the European Union, arguing that the existing rules on gender equality are functional to fair competition of the internal market and fail to promote substantial equality.

8.1.2 Traditional Gender-Neutral Approach of Public International Law and the Development of Gender Perspective (Ivana Krstić)

Three foundational approaches to the international legal order were framed in early to mid-seventeenth-century Europe by Hugo Grotius, the founder of the science of international law, with his capital work, *De jure belli ac pacis* (1625),[1] together with

[1] Hershey (1912), p. 30.

Thomas Hobbes and Samuel Pufendorf.[2] The Peace of Westphalia (1648) is considered to be the beginning of modern international law. After the end of the Thirty Years War, two main ideas emerged: the rise of modern states and sovereignty. The notion of sovereignty was developed in writings of political theorists, such as Jean Bodin, Thomas Hobbes, John Locke and Jean-Jacques Rousseau.[3] Therefore, international law was a result of certain theories and principles and international practice, which did not include women and their perspective in its development and were gender-free.

In the second half of the nineteenth century, various women's organizations were first established, with the creation of the International Council of Women in April 1888.[4] Representatives of 53 women's organizations from 9 countries gathered together in Washington D.C. advocating for human rights of women. After World War I, the first universal organization was established as a League of Nations. Women's organizations participated at the 12th meeting of the League of Nations Committee at the Peace Conference in Paris, but their participation was limited to matters which the committee thought were directly relevant for women.[5] However, they presented "The Women's Charter," which underlined the importance of separating the nationality of women from their spouses, prohibiting human trafficking of women and girls, and achieving equality of men and women in the area of labour.[6] The League of Nations Covenant prescribed in Article 7 that all positions in this organizations were equally open to men and women.[7] This opened the possibility to some of these women to continue their efforts through the work of the League of Nations, and through the work of the International Labour Organization, also established in 1919. However, foundations and human rights development originated only with the establishment of the United Nations.

In 1945, the UN Charter was adopted, reaffirming in its Preamble faith in equal rights of men and women. The UN further committed itself to promote universal respect for human rights without distinction as to, among others, sex.[8] As the UN

[2]Besson and Tasioulas (2010), pp. 33, 34.

[3]Bederman (2002), p. 4.

[4]International Council for Women, History, available at: http://www.icw-cif.com/01/03.php, accessed 10 April 2021.

[5]Those issues were women's employment rights, prostitution, prison reform, child marriage and trafficking of women and children. The Inter-Allied Women's Conference as a response to Paris Peace Conference, EuroClic, 4 December 2019, available at: https://www.euroclio.eu/2019/12/04/the-inter-allied-womens-conference-as-a-response-to-paris-peace-conference/, accessed 9 July 2021; See also Women and Global Diplomacy: from Peace Movements to the United Nations, UN Research Guides, available at: https://libraryresources.unog.ch/womendiplomacy/leagueofnations, accessed 9 July 2021.

[6]More on the work of the women's organizations in the League of Nations see Miller (1994), pp. 219–245.

[7]The Covenant of the League of Nations, including amendments adopted to December 1924, available at: https://avalon.law.yale.edu/20th_century/leagcov.asp, accessed 10 April 2021.

[8]Article 55 of the UN Charter.

Charter did not contain any human rights catalogue, it was agreed to prepare a draft human rights declaration. At the end of 1945, US President Harry Truman appointed Eleanor Roosevelt, First Lady during Franklin D. Roosevelt's administration from 1933 to 1945, as a member of the US delegation, expecting her to assist in the purpose to create conditions of mutual trust and economic and social well-being of all people around the world.[9] Eleanor Roosevelt was an active humanitarian, working on civil rights protections. In April 1946, she became chair of the UN Commission on Human Rights (HRC) and, together with Hansa Mehta, delegate from India and the only other female delegate at that time, was advocating for the adoption of the human rights declaration. They were also advocating for changing the wording of Article 1: "All men are born free and equal" to "All human beings are born free and equal."[10] As Howard Zinn has written, the use of the word 'men' indicated that women were "beyond consideration as worthy of inclusion", and were politically invisible.[11] Therefore, with the more justifiable use of the word 'human beings', any doubt that rights equally belong to both, men and women, were dispelled.

The Universal Declaration of Human Rights (UDHR) was adopted in 1948.[12] It contains several provisions which are relevant from the perspective of gender equality, but with particular attention to Article 2 which prescribes that everyone is entitled to all rights without distinction, among others, of sex. Article 16 further proclaims equality of spouses, while Article 25(2) protects motherhood. Many other provisions are also relevant from the perspective of gender equality. Bearing in mind that the UDHR was a non-binding instrument, the work on two main human rights treaties commenced in 1951, and in 1966 they were adopted. The International Covenant on Civil and Political Rights (ICCPR) and the International Covenant on Economic, Social and Cultural Rights (ICSCR) contain many important provisions, as well as the provision that States Parties will respect and guarantee everyone within their jurisdiction all rights without distinction of any kind, including, sex.[13] In 1967, the General Assembly adopted a Declaration on the Elimination of Discrimination against Women, acknowledging in its Preamble that women were greatly contributing to social, political, economic and family life and that full and complete development of a country, the welfare and peace in the world required their maximum participation.[14] In 1979, this declaration was transformed into the first gender-specific convention—the Convention on the Elimination of All Forms of Discrimination against Women (CEDAW), which prohibits gender discrimination in

[9] Letter, Harry Truman to Eleanor Roosevelt, 21 December 1945, available at: https://artsandculture.google.com/exhibit/eleanor-roosevelt-and-the-united-nations/ARaxRSs-, accessed 15 April 2021.

[10] Scroll Staff (2019), available at: https://scroll.in/announcements/946351/human-rights-day-2019-history-the-women-who-shaped-the-udhr-and-theme, accessed 15 April 2021.

[11] Zinn (2015), p. 73.

[12] General Assembly, Resolution A/RES/217 (III), 10 December 1948.

[13] Article 2(1) ICCPR; Article 2(2) ICSCR.

[14] General Assembly, Resolution 2263 (XXII), 7 November 1967.

all areas of life. CEDAW lists women's human rights to equality and non-discrimination and identifies the range of actions that States must take to achieve this equality. Article 7 stipulates that women's equality must be implemented in public and political life, enabling their participation in non-governmental organizations and associations and securing a more active role in international organizations and State delegations. After the adoption of CEDAW, many other international instruments relevant for gender equality were adopted. The practice of international judicial and quasi-judicial bodies was advanced, recognizing the position of women to a much greater extent.

8.1.3 The First Catalogue of Women's Rights on UN Level: General Aspects and Overview of CEDAW

8.1.3.1 CEDAW's *Raison d'être* Undermined by Reservations

The preamble of CEDAW explains the Convention's *raison d'être* by underlining that "despite [the previous] instruments extensive discrimination against women continues to exist" and points out that "a change in the traditional role of men as well as the role of women in society and in the family is needed to achieve full equality between men and women".

Among the nine core human rights treaties on UN level, CEDAW is one of the most widely accepted with currently 189 States Parties, important outsiders being Iran, Somalia, Sudan and the USA (the latter has at least been a signatory since 1980). Yet CEDAW is also subject to a great number of general and indeterminate reservations, such as reservations attempting to subordinate treaty obligations to domestic or religious laws and traditions. Many of these are incompatible with the Convention's object and purpose and thus impermissible under Art. 28 (2) CEDAW.[15] States apparently felt politically compelled to join CEDAW, even though they do not share its main goal. Other States have objected to those far-reaching reservations.

Example

Reservation by Saudi Arabia:

"... In case of contradiction between any term of the Convention and the norms of Islamic law, the Kingdom is not under obligation to observe the contradictory terms of the Convention ..."

Objection by Germany:

"The Government of the Federal Republic of Germany is of the view that the reservation, with regard to compatibility of CEDAW rules with Islamic law, raises doubts as to the commitment of the Kingdom of Saudi Arabia to

[15] Chinkin (2010), paras 16–17. In General Recommendation no. 4 (1987), the CEDAW Committee expressed concern in this regard and suggested withdrawal of such reservations.

CEDAW. The Government of the Federal Republic of Germany considers this reservation to be incompatible with the object and purpose of the Convention. . . . This objection does not preclude the entry into force of the Convention between the Federal Republic of Germany and the Kingdom of Saudi Arabia."[16] ◀

According to the International Law Commission's "Guide to Practice on Reservations to Treaties" of 2011, an impermissible reservation is devoid of any legal effect so that the reserving State is bound by the treaty without the benefit of the reservation, unless it expresses a contrary intention.[17] The ILC's solution may go beyond the customary international law rules on reservations.

8.1.3.2 Obligations of States Parties

Art. 1 CEDAW defines "discrimination against women" as, "any distinction, exclusion or restriction made on the basis of sex which has the effect or purpose of impairing or nullifying the recognition, enjoyment or exercise by women, irrespective of their marital status, on a basis of equality of men and women, of human rights and fundamental freedoms in the political, economic, social, cultural, civil or any other field". In Arts. 2–6, CEDAW sets forth the fundamental obligations of States Parties. Most importantly, they have to eradicate discrimination by public authorities and institutions, ensure effective protection of women against discrimination and "take all appropriate measures to eliminate discrimination against women by any [private] person, organization or enterprise" (Art. 2).[18] Art. 4 (1) CEDAW permits "temporary special measures aimed at accelerating de facto equality between men and women . . ."

Art. 5 CEDAW obliges States Parties to modify social and cultural patterns of conduct in order to eliminate prejudices and stereotypes and redirect family education toward common responsibility of men and women in the upbringing and development of their children. Arts. 7–9 CEDAW clarifies obligations concerning equal rights and non-discrimination in political and public life. Arts. 10–16 CEDAW prescribe action to be taken against discrimination in various sectors such education, health care and family relations.

According to Art. 23 CEDAW, the Convention enshrines only minimum standards of equality, leaving the States Parties free to enact provisions "more conducive to the achievement of equality between men and women". Art. 24 CEDAW obliges the States Parties to undertake all necessary measures at the national level aimed at achieving the full realization of CEDAW rights.[19]

---

[16] United Nations Treaty Collection, Status of Treaties – CEDAW, https://treaties.un.org/Pages/ViewDetails.aspx?src=IND&mtdsg_no=IV-8&chapter=4&clang=_en.

[17] Paras. 4.5.1.–4.5.3. (https://legal.un.org/ilc/texts/1_8.shtml).

[18] Chinkin (2010), para. 8.

[19] For more detailed information on CEDAW, see Chapter on Human Rights.

8.1.3.3 Implementation

A Committee on the Elimination of Discrimination against Women consisting of independent experts is established to monitor compliance (Art. 17–22 CEDAW).[20] States Parties have to submit regular reports to that Committee which can make individual or general recommendations.[21] The Optional Protocol (OP) to CEDAW,[22] with currently 114 States Parties, has introduced an individual communication procedure which can be initiated by victims of violations of CEDAW rights against a State Party (Art. 2–7 OP). The Committee can also conduct a confidential inquiry *ex officio* if it receives "reliable information indicating grave or systematic violations by a State Party" of CEDAW rights (Art. 8–10 OP). States Parties can opt out from that inquiry procedure.[23]

8.2 Other Gender-Related Sources and Activities at Universal Level

8.2.1 The Role of UN Bodies in Achieving Gender Equality

Different bodies were established within the UN system to pay particular attention to women's rights.

The Economic and Social Council (ECOSOC) is a main body of the UN with a mandate to promote social and economic progress, health issues, human rights without discrimination based on race, sex, language, or religion. One of its subsidiary bodies is the Commission on the Status of Women (CSW), established in 1946 as the principal global intergovernmental body with the aim to promote gender equality.[24] Each year, during a two-week long annual session, it discusses the most comprehensive global policy agenda for the empowerment of women—the 1995 Beijing Declaration and Platform for Action.[25] The Beijing Declaration affirms that women's rights are inalienable, integral and an indivisible part of human rights. This platform covers 12 areas of concern: poverty, education and training, health, violence, armed conflict, economy, power and decision-making, institutional mechanisms, human rights, media, environment, and the girl child. ECOSOC also established another subsidiary body, the UN Commission on Human Rights, which

[20] Hellum and Ikdahl (2019).

[21] Chinkin (2010), paras. 13–14.

[22] 6 October 1999 (UNTS, vol. 2131, p. 83). For more detailed information, see Chapter 7 on Human Rights.

[23] Chinkin (2010), paras. 11, 15.

[24] ECOSOC Resolution 11(II), 21 June 1946.

[25] Beijing Declaration, Platform for Action, 4th World Conference on Women, 4–15 September 1995.

ceased to exist with the creation of the Human Rights Council (HRC), a subsidiary body of the General Assembly.

The HRC was established in 2006 with the aim to further advance human rights among UN Member States. There are different mechanisms that this body can use in order to focus on the protection of women around the globe. The HRC can act under the complaint procedure alleging widespread and systemic human rights violations in a certain country, as was the case with Eritrea, where it examined different human rights violations, including violence against women.[26] It can call special sessions to address violations of women's rights. Rape and sexual violence were at the attention of the special session on situation in Darfur,[27] and gender inequality and sexual violence in relation to the Democratic Republic of Congo.[28]

Example

The Human Rights Council stated the following: "Sexual violence has been a defining feature of the armed conflicts in the DRC and conflict parties have not assumed their responsibilities reaffirmed also by Security Council resolutions 1325 (2000) and 1820 (2008) on women, peace and security. During her visit in July 2007, the Special Rapporteur on violence against women found that sexual violence against women was particularly dramatic in the Kivus, where non-state armed groups, including foreign militia, committed sexual atrocities that were of an unimaginable brutality and aimed at the complete physical and psychological destruction of women with implications for the entire society."[29] ◄

The role of special procedures is to examine particular thematic issues or the human rights situation in a certain country. For instance, a Special Rapporteur on violence against women, including its causes and consequences was appointed by the Human Rights Commission in 1994,[30] but since March 2006, the Special Rapporteur reports to the Human Rights Council.[31] The Rapporteur has issued several thematic reports; a report on violence against women journalists addressing challenges faced by women journalists,[32] and Covid-19 and the increase of domestic

[26] HRC, Resolution 21/1, Situation in Eritrea, 9 October 2012.

[27] Report of the High-Level Mission on the situation of human rights in Darfur pursuant to Human Rights Council decision S-4/101, A/HRC/4/80, 9 March 2007, para. 39.

[28] A/HRC/10/59, paras. 35–42, and A/HRC/13/63, paras. 26–34.

[29] Human Rights Council, Combined report of seven thematic special procedures on technical assistance to the Government of the DRC and urgent examination of the situation in the east of the country, A/HRC/10/59, 5 March 2009, para. 35.

[30] Human Rights Commission, Resolution 1994/45, 4 March 1994.

[31] Human Rights Council decision 1/102, 30 June 2006. Its mandate was renewed in 2019 by Resolution 411/17, 11 July 2019.

[32] Combating Violence against Women Journalists, Report of the Special Rapporteur on Violence against Women, its causes and consequences, A/HRC/44/52, 6 May 2020.

violence against women.[33] The role of special procedures mandates holders to improve knowledge on human rights, taking women into account'[34] The HRC can also address gender issues through its universal periodic review (UPR), which is an opportunity to regularly assess the compliance by all UN Member States with international obligations in relation to women's rights.

Example

Honduras, within the universal periodic review for Serbia welcomed the acceptance of the recommendations "related to reinforcing measures to eradicate all forms of social stigmatization, discrimination and violence on grounds of sexual orientation, gender identity and HIV status, adopting specific measures to prevent and combat discrimination against women and girls with disabilities, redoubling efforts destined to promote tolerance towards minorities, reinforcing measures to prevent and combat trafficking in persons and approving a policy addressing internal displacement in Serbia."[35] ◄

In 2010, the General Assembly also created UN Women, the United Nations Entity for Gender Equality and the Empowerment of Women, as a result of years of negotiations between UN Member States, to address serious challenges in its effort to promote gender equality.[36] UNWOMEN supports Member States in designing laws, policies, programmes and services which are necessary to ensure that the Sustainable Development Goals[37] are implemented and that women participate equally in all aspects of life.

8.2.2 Women, Peace and Security: Resolution 1325, and Onwards

2020 was the 20th anniversary of the adoption of United Nations (UN) Security Council (SC) Resolution 1325 on Women, Peace and Security (WPS).[38] The passing of Resolution 1325 was seen as a global effort to establish a platform on which to base national and international policies with the aim of ensuring greater protection of women and girls, during and after conflict, equal participation in all efforts of women and girls in the maintenance of peace and security, mainstreaming of gender

---

[33] Violence against Women, its causes and consequences, Report of the Special Rapporteur on Violence against Women, its causes and consequences, A/75/144, 24 July 2020.

[34] Women's Rights are Human Rights, United Nations Human Rights Office of the High Commissioner, New York and Geneva, 2014, p. 21.

[35] Report of the Human Rights Council on its thirty-eighth session, 38/114, Outcome of the universal periodic review: Serbia, 29 June 2018, para. 816.

[36] General Assembly, Resolution 64/289.

[37] The 2030 Agenda for Sustainable Development.

[38] SC Resolution 1325, 31 October 2000.

perspectives in peace operations and the implementation of specialized training for all personnel deployed in affected areas. In other words, the WPS agenda is now seen to be constructed around the following five pillars: prevention, protection, participation, relief and recovery.[39]

Example

"Noting the need to consolidate data on the impact of armed conflict on women and girls [the Security Council],

1. Urges Member States to ensure increased representation of women at all decision-making levels in national, regional and international institutions and mechanisms for the prevention, management, and resolution of conflict;
2. Encourages the Secretary-General to implement his strategic plan of action (A/49/587) calling for an increase in the participation of women at decision-making levels in conflict resolution and peace processes;
3. Urges the Secretary-General to appoint more women as special representatives and envoys to pursue good offices on his behalf, and in this regard calls on Member States to provide candidates to the Secretary-General, for inclusion in a regularly updated centralized roster;
4. Further urges the Secretary-General to seek to expand the role and contribution of women in United Nations field-based operations, and especially among military observers, civilian police, human rights and humanitarian personnel;
5. Expresses its willingness to incorporate a gender perspective into peacekeeping operations, and urges the Secretary-General to ensure that, where appropriate, field operations include a gender component."[40] ◀

8.2.3 After a Journey of Twenty Years

Since the adoption of SC Resolution 1325, almost half of the UN member States have launched National Action Plans[41] to increase women's participation in security processes. The seminal work of the Security Council in passing SC Resolution 1325 has since 2000 been followed by further resolutions; (a) Prevention of and response

[39] Coomaraswamy et al. (2015), p. 329. Available from: https://reliefweb.int/sites/reliefweb.int/files/resources/UNW-GLOBAL-STUDY-1325-2015.pdf.

[40] SC Resolution 1325, 31 October 2000.

[41] As of 16 March 2021, 90 States have established National Actions Plans. http://1325naps.peacewomen.org/, accessed 16 March 2021. For visualised content analysis see: Hamilton and Shepherd (2020). Available at https://www.wpsnaps.org/.

to conflict-related sexual violence[42] and (b) Women's participation and leadership in peace making and conflict prevention.[43] Furthermore, States started to take national initiatives that related to their own armed forces,[44] and of enacting national legislation that aims to ensure that women are fully included in discussions concerning peace and security.[45] These are some examples of the progress that has been made, although the proliferation of actors engaged in the WPS work and the broadening and deepening of the WPS agenda cause scholars to describe its reach as "extensive, contested and uncertain."[46]

Women undisputedly deserve a place at the table in peace negotiations, as well as access to political power, post-conflict, when peace has been established. However, it has been suggested that seeing 'womenhood in itself' as an antidote to armed conflict, may be to regard conflict dynamics too simplistically.[47] Although not statistically verified, there are some indications in research of a correlation between gender equality in a State and avoidance of interstate conflict escalation.[48] Other research has indicated that women are inclined to promote negotiations in intrastate conflicts.[49] Furthermore, when it comes to budgetary decisions, women tend to give priority to investment in welfare[50] areas rather than military. As well as noting the strategic role women may play in peace negotiations, there are particular challenges faced by women who have taken direct part in hostilities when seeking to re-integrate into their societies after a conflict has ended.[51] Research has found that these women and girls are often perceived to have broken deep rooted gender norms in their societies by engaging in what is traditionally seen as masculine behaviour. This is repeatedly found to make their re-integration even more difficult.[52]

---

[42] See SC Resolution 1820, 19 June 2008; SC Resolution 1888, 30 September 2009; SC Resolution 1960, 16 December 2010; SC Resolution 2106, 24 June 2013 and SC Resolution 2467, 23 April 2019.

[43] SC Resolution 1889, 5 October 2009; SC Resolution 2122, 18 October 2012; SC Resolution 2242, 13 October 2015 and SC Resolution 2493, 29 October 2019.

[44] See for instance the Swedish Ordinance with instructions for the Swedish Armed Forces (Swedish Code of Statutes 2007:1266) which stated that the Armed Forces are required to operate in accordance with UN Security Council Resolutions 1325 and 1820. Tengroth, in Tengroth, Lindvall (2015), p. 74. Available at: ihl-and-gender-151110.pdf (rodakorset.se), accessed 17 March 2021.

[45] See in this regard The US Women, Peace, and Security Act of 2017 signed into law on 6 October 2017.

[46] Basu et al. (2020), p. 2.

[47] Sassòli (2019), p. 557.

[48] Caprioli and Boyer (2001), p. 516.

[49] Nagel (2020), p. 2.

[50] Bolzendahl and Brooks (2007), pp. 1509–1534.

[51] Barth (2002).

[52] Ibid.

8.2.4 WPS Areas Under Debate

While the importance of States' engagement with the WPS agenda cannot be overestimated, the nature of their engagement can give rise to questions. States from the global North tend to refer to WPS in their role as donors or contributors of troops. The result of this is that they display WPS in a manner Basu refers to as 'outward-oriented', that is deflecting attention away from the State in the Northern hemisphere. Correspondingly, States in the global South seemingly have to a lesser extent internalized the WPS policies in their national frameworks, with WPS references being promoted through donor policies and the aid channelled by inter-governmental organisations.[53] Also from the perspective of individuals, there are areas within the WPS discourse that are increasingly debated.

It has been pointed out that the explicit focus on women in the WPS discourse has rendered the vulnerabilities of men and boys invisible,[54] not least in relation to sexual violence, when the victim is male. Furthermore, in the context of armed conflict, there have been examples when widespread perception that a civilian population[55] is mainly made up of women and children has in effect, rendered civilian men and boys extremely vulnerable.[56] More recently, attention has been drawn to new themes in connection with the WPS agenda. This includes intersections between countering violent extremism and WPS, the invisibility of race and sexuality in WPS discourse and practice, and the engagement of men within and alongside the WPS agenda.[57]

8.3 Protecting Women Under International Humanitarian Law

International Humanitarian Law (IHL) seeks to regulate situations where any normal and peaceful human relations have failed. The use of armed force is a pre-requisite for this legal regime to come fully into play. Despite the challenging circumstances for IHL, there are numerous historic examples dating back thousands of years, of societies that developed rules on what was, and was not, seen as permissive behaviour during armed conflict,[58] not only in general terms, but also to a certain extent with specific regard to women. It is the aim of this section to outline these provisions.

[53] Basu et al. (2020), p. 8.

[54] Myrttinen, in Davies, True (2018), p. 88.

[55] Under international humanitarian law, the distinction between civilians and members of the armed forces is the lynch pin for the legal protection of this regime. See below, footnote 63, with accompanying text.

[56] See generally Carpenter (2003), pp. 661–694.

[57] Basu et al. (2020), p. 2.

[58] Crawford and Pert (2020), p. 4.

It is fundamental to note that victims on both sides of the conflict; women, men, girls and boys, need to be protected from war crimes. To achieve any respect for IHL, it is necessary for it to apply equally to all the parties involved, regardless of, and separate from issues relating to the resort to force.[59] For IHL to be applicable, the conduct must have a connection (the nexus) with either an international armed conflict (IAC), or a non-international armed conflict (NIAC).[60] Thus, in the case of IAC, applicable treaty law consists of the Geneva Conventions I-IV[61] and Additional Protocol I. If the conflict falls into the category of NIAC, then Common Article 3 of the Geneva Conventions applies together with Additional Protocol II. Lastly, there are also customary law provisions that apply in IAC as well as NIAC.[62] Separately, irrespective of the nature of the conflict, international human rights law will of course remain in force, but the State may derogate from certain human rights provisions "in time of public emergency which threatens the life of the nation".[63]

8.3.1 General Protection of the Civilian Population

IHL rests on distinguishing two groups of people, namely civilians and members of the armed forces. This principle of distinction is a cardinal principle, and it is paramount to the whole construction of IHL. Furthermore, the principle of distinction extends beyond human beings, and also applies to civilian objects and military objectives.[64] It is worth noting that IHL, by design, deals with the protection of *groups* of people rather than with individuals. This is clearly visible in the four Geneva Conventions as each apply to 'categories of war victims'[65] as defined by the

[59] Sassòli (2019), p. 19.

[60] An IAC involves at least two State parties, whereas the parties to NIAC must involve a State and a sufficiently organized armed group (or groups) on the other hand. Sassòli (2019), p. 6.

[61] 1949 Geneva Convention for the Amelioration of the Condition of Wounded and Sick in Armed Forces in the Field of August 12, 1949, (1950) 75 UNTS 31–83 [Geneva Convention I]; 1949 Geneva Convention for the Amelioration of the Condition of Wounded, Sick and Shipwrecked Members of Armed Forces at Sea of August 12, 1949, (1950) 75 UNTS 85–133 [Geneva Convention II]; 1949 Geneva Convention Relative to the Treatment of Prisoners of War of August 12, 1949 (1950) 75 UNTS 135–285 [Geneva Convention III]; 1949 Geneva Convention Relative to the Protection of Civilian Persons in Time of War of August 12, 1949 (1950) 75 UNTS 287–417 [Geneva Convention IV].

[62] For a good overview of applicable customary law rules, please visit the Customary IHL Database, available here: https://ihl-databases.icrc.org/customary-ihl/eng/docs/home.

[63] Article 4, 1966 International Covenant on Civil and Political Rights, *entered into force* 23 March 1976; 999 UNTS 171; the corresponding provision in the ECHR, Article 15, explicitly includes 'war' as a circumstance which permits derogation. 1950 Convention for the Protection of Human Rights and Fundamental Freedoms, adopted 3 September 1953, 213 UNTS 222.

[64] Dinstein (2016), p. 72.

[65] Sassòli (2019), p. 8.

treaties.[66] Historically, it is held that women predominantly were seen as civilians, which is not, nor has ever been, a matter of a single truth. Women can be, and increasingly are, members of the armed forces, joining fighting rebel groups[67] and are deployed in United Nations peace-keeping missions.[68] When it comes to the protection of women, IHL is predominantly concerned with issues of motherhood, such as pregnancy, childbirth and new-born babies.[69] Considering the general protection outlined so far, Gardam and Jarvis have noted that of the 42 provisions in IHL treaty law that mention women, almost half concern matters such as pregnant or nursing mothers.[70] It has been noted by scholars, that concerning women, IHL has not only an old-fashioned language,[71] but also gives special protection to women based on assumptions of women as a vulnerable group, rather than based on concepts of equality.

It is a customary rule of IHL that "[a]dverse distinction in the application of international humanitarian law based on race, colour, sex, language, religion or belief, political or other opinion, national or social origin, wealth, birth or other status, or on any other similar criteria is prohibited."[72] This is the case in IAC[73] as well as NIAC.[74] The notion of adverse distinction is used to signify that although discrimination is prohibited, there are circumstances when the law recognises the need for certain priorities in terms of urgent needs.[75]

Many of the IHL provisions about women are concerned with particular vulnerabilities. For example, Geneva Convention IV holds that "[...] Women shall be especially protected against any attack on their honour, in particular against rape, enforced prostitution, or any form of indecent assault.[...]"[76] This provision is also echoed in Additional Protocol I, stating that "Women shall be the object of special respect and shall be protected in particular against rape, forced prostitution,

---

[66]Geneva Convention I protects wounded and sick members of the armed forces in the field; Geneva Convention II protects wounded, sick and shipwrecked members of armed forces at sea; Geneva Convention III regulates the treatment of prisoners of war and Geneva Convention IV protects civilian persons in the hands of a party to the conflict of which they are not nationals.

[67]Durham and O'Byrne (2010), p. 37.

[68]The increase of female UN troops remains painstakingly slow, having moved from 1% of the troops in 1993, to 4,8% some thirty years later. For updated figures see: https://peacekeeping.un.org/en/women-peacekeeping, accessed 11 March 2021.

[69]Additional Protocol I, Article 8(a) incorporates these women as protected persons who are 'wounded and sick'.

[70]Gardam and Jarvis (2001), p. 93.

[71]Sassòli (2019), p. 282.

[72]Henckaerts and Doswald-Beck (2005), p. 308.

[73]Article 16 of Geneva Convention III, and Article 13 of Geneva Convention IV and Article 75(1) of Additional Protocol I.

[74]The relevant treaty provisions are Common Article 3 of the Geneva Conventions, and Article 4(1) of Additional Protocol II.

[75]Henckaerts and Doswald-Beck (2005), p. 309.

[76]Geneva Convention IV, Article 27(2).

and any other form of indecent assault."[77] The disparity in these two provisions is the scope of application: the former applies in essence to civilian women who are 'protected persons' in the sense of Geneva Convention IV, which means that the occupying States own national's are not covered. The provisions of Additional Protocol I cover all civilian women in IAC.[78]

8.3.2 Protection of Women as Members of the Armed Forces

IHL prohibits girls and boys below the age of 15 from taking direct part in hostilities.[79] As international law holds that childhood ends at the age of 18,[80] many States have opted to extend the protection of minors from taking direct part in hostilities to the age of 18. State parties[81] to the Optional Protocol to the Convention on the Rights of the Child[82] are also committed to take any feasible measures to prevent the recruitment of girls and boys under 18 into rebel forces.[83]

With regards to prisoners of war (POW), IHL provisions demand "respect for their person and their honour".[84] It is commonly accepted that the notion of *honour* encapsulates protecting prisoners of war from rape.[85] Explicitly, women who become prisoners of war are to "be treated with all the regard due to their sex and shall in all cases benefit by treatment as favourable as that granted to men."[86] The provisions allow for beneficial treatment, based on rank and sex.[87] This is necessary in order to make substantial equality possible, rather than remain fixated on formal equality.[88]

[77] Additional Protocol I, Article 76(1).

[78] Dinstein (2016), p. 187.

[79] Additional Protocol I, Article 77(2) and Additional Protocol II Article 4(3)(c).

[80] See Convention on the Rights of the Child, 1577 UNTS 3, *entered into force* 2 September, 1990, Article 1.

[81] As of February 2021, 170 countries are State Parties to the Optional protocol to the CRC, with an additional 10 countries being signatories. See https://indicators.ohchr.org/, accessed 11 March 2021.

[82] Optional Protocol to the Convention on the Rights of the Child on the Involvement of Children in Armed Conflicts, 2173 UNTS 222 *entered into force* 12 February, 2002.

[83] *Ibid.*, Article 4.

[84] Geneva Convention III, Article 14.

[85] Pictet (1960), p. 147.

[86] *Ibid.* See also Anna Crows analysis of the meaning of 'regard', in Crowe (2016), available at http://hrp.law.harvard.edu/wp-content/uploads/2016/12/Anna-Crowe_HRP-16_001.pdf, accessed 13 March 2021.

[87] Geneva Convention III, Article 16.

[88] Dörmann et al. (2020), para 1749.

Although IHL provides some particular protection to women who become POWs,[89] they are not by law granted the privilege to be searched by a woman, as is the case with civilian female internees in the hands of the adverse powers, as stipulated by Geneva Convention IV, Article 97. Prescott has also pointed out that in terms of participatory influence among prisoners of war, IHL may well be indirectly discriminating women in camps where no officers are held, because detained prisoners of war are allowed to elect their representative by secret majority ballot.[90] This may result in men voting for male representation; the law does not ensure gender representation. If officers are present, they are to be the representatives without election irrespective of their sex.[91]

8.3.3 Prohibition of Sexual Violence During Armed Conflict

From a gender perspective, mention needs to be made of situations when gender stereotypical behaviours or features are being encapsulated in the commission of war crimes. An example would be when detainees (prisoners of war as well as civilians) become victims of rape[92] and other forms of sexual violence, or when women (civilian as well as members of the armed forces) become perpetrators of sexual violence as war crimes.[93] The issue of bringing perpetrators of sexual violence and rape, as a war crime, to justice has made significant progress through the work of international criminal tribunals, such as the tribunals for the former Yugoslavia (ICTY)[94] and Rwanda (ICTR).[95] Against an historic backdrop that lacked examples of prosecuting such conduct as war crimes,[96] these acts are now firmly incorporated and criminalized in the ICC statute, regardless of whether the victim is male or female, or the act took place in an IAC or a NIAC.[97]

---

[89] IHL proscribes separate dormitories for women and men (Geneva Convention III Article 25); separate hygiene facilities (Geneva Convention III Article 29); repatriation or relocation to neutral countries if possible, for pregnant female prisoners of war (Geneva Convention III, Annex I A (3) (f)). Similarly, female prisoners of war with infants and small children may also be relocated to neutral countries (Geneva Convention III, Annex I B (7)).

[90] Prescott (2019), p. 184.

[91] Geneva Convention III, Article 79.

[92] This is discussed by Bradley (2020), pp. 381–422.

[93] IHL foresees that war crimes can be committed by women and men, be it civilians or members of the armed forces, in that it obliges States to "search for *persons*" that are alleged to have committed or ordered the commission of war crimes. See Geneva Convention I, Article 49; Geneva Convention II, Article 50; Geneva Convention III, Article 129; and Geneva Convention IV, Article 146.

[94] 1993 Statute of the International Tribunal for Former Yugoslavia, UN Doc. S/25704 at 36, Annex.

[95] 1994 Statute of the International Tribunal for Rwanda, UN Doc. S/Res/955 Annex.

[96] Durham and O'Byrne (2010), p. 35.

[97] 1998 Rome Statute of the International Criminal Court, *entered into force* 1 July 2002; 2187 UNTS 3, Article 8(2)(b)(xxi).

As noted in the opening of this section, IHL has origins that reach back thousands of years and that can be traced back in treaty law more than 200 years.[98] It is of no surprise that the treaties bear linguistic marks of explicit, as well as implicit attitudes and perceptions towards women and gender from past times. Furthermore, it is a longstanding truth that gender-based stereotype views tend to be exacerbated during armed conflict when the social fabrics of communities dissolve.[99] Nevertheless, the drafters of the IHL treaties set out to create rules of humanity and respect for the human being in physical as well as moral terms to be applicable in the most extreme circumstances imaginable. Whereas the protective obligations of IHL should not be undermined, a gender analysis study of IHL can be an enlightening undertaking that puts the spotlight on stereotypes and provides additional avenues of legal interpretation to strengthen the implementation of and respect for the laws of war.

8.4 International Criminal Law and Gender Perspective

International Criminal Law is a branch of International Public Law designed to prohibit heinous crimes, such as genocide, war crimes, crimes against humanity and the crime of aggression, and to hold perpetrators of those crimes accountable. While the Nuremberg and Tokyo tribunals did not pay attention to sexual crimes, the evolution of international law brought a gender dimension.[100] The International Criminal Court (ICC), as well as the ICTY and the ICTR have special provisions on sexual violence in their statutes. The crime of rape became a constituent element of crimes against humanity in the statute of the ICTY, while forced prostitution is recognized as a war crime by the statute of the ICTR. The ICC statute also addresses conflict-related sexual and gender-based violence and includes rape, sexual slavery, enforced prostitution, forced pregnancy, enforced sterilization, or any other form of sexual violence of comparable gravity as a part of crimes against humanity.[101] In addition, the Statute defines 'forced pregnancy'.[102] Conflict related sexual and gender-based violence can also constitute grave breaches of Geneva conventions and war crimes.[103]

[98]Most notably the 1864 Convention for the Amelioration of the Condition of the Wounded in Armies in the Field, which is the forerunner to modern days Geneva Conventions I-IV, and the 1868 Declaration Renouncing the Use, in Time of War, of Explosive Projectiles Under 400 Grammes Weight.

[99]Gardam and Jarvis (2000), pp. 6–7.

[100]Delpia (2014), pp. 39, 179.

[101]Article 7 (1) g) of the Rome Statute. See also Art. 7 (3) of the Rome Statute.

[102]Article 7 (2) f) of the Rome Statute.

[103]Article 8 (2) b) xxii.

Example

António Guterres, the UN Secretary General, underlined the following: "Conflict-related sexual and gender-based violence (SGBV) is a widespread weapon of war—seen in conflicts in the Central African Republic, the Democratic Republic of Congo, Mali, Darfur and Syria, to name but a few. It is used to terrorize, to degrade, to punish communities and to ethnically "cleanse." Women and girls are predominantly the victims; but men and boys are also targeted and suffer. Survivors are often marginalized and stigmatized, with little hope of seeing their attackers brought to justice."[104] ◀

Despite this legal recognition, there has been only one conviction for sexual violence crimes at the ICC in a case of Bosco Ntaganda so far.[105] When Fatou Bensouda, the former Prosecutor of the ICC, took office in 2012, she published a policy paper on Sexual and Gender-Based Crimes, and the prosecution assumed a more proactive role.[106]

Example

Fatou Bensouda, the former ICC Prosecutor, emphasised the role of all actors in combating sexual and gender-based crimes: "Each of us has a role to play. It is hoped that the Policy will also serve as a guide to national authorities in the exercise of their primary jurisdiction to hold perpetrators accountable for these crimes. United in our efforts, we can end the silence that has surrounded sexual and gender-based crimes for far too long and give victims the ultimate tool in combatting such crimes: a voice backed by the force of the law."[107] ◀

The role of hybrid courts is also relevant in this area of law. Sexual violence was a key characteristic of the Sierra Leone conflict and Jalloh documented the battle faced by prosecutors in the Special Court for Sierra Leone in their intention to indict gender-based crimes.[108] It is worth mentioning the role of national transitional

[104] UN Secretary-General, António Guterres, Eliminating Sexual Violence in conflict through the ICC, Coalition for the ICC, 20 June 2017, available at: https://www.coalitionfortheicc.org/news/20170620/eliminating-sexual-violence-conflict-through-icc, accessed 9 July 2021.

[105] Ntaganda case: ICC Appeals Chamber confirms conviction and sentencing decisions, International Criminal Court, 30 March 2021, available at: https://www.icc-cpi.int/Pages/item.aspx?name=pr1582, accessed 9 July 2021. See also Forlani, available at: https://www.mukwegefoundation.org/guest-blog-prosecution-sexual-violence-icc-problems/, accessed 4 May 2021.

[106] ICC, Policy on Sexual and Gender-Based Crimes, June 2014, available at: https://www.icc-cpi.int/iccdocs/otp/Policy_Paper_on_Sexual_and_Gender-Based_Crimes-20_June_2014-ENG.pdf, accessed 4 May 2021.

[107] ICC Prosecutor Fatou Bensouda, Policy Paper on Sexual and Gender-Based Crimes, 5 June 2014, available at: https://www.icc-cpi.int/pages/item.aspx?name=pr1011, accessed 9 July 2021.

[108] Jalloh (2020).

justice mechanisms in this respect. On 14 April 2021, the Colombian Special Jurisdiction for Peace (JEP), established by the final peace agreement between the Colombian Government and the Revolutionary Armed Forces of Colombia - People's Army, recognized new ground for persecution as a crime against humanity. The JEP's Chamber for the Acknowledgment of Truth held that gender-based violence also covers sexual orientation and gender identity.[109] It was acknowledged that the violent acts committed against the five LGBTQIA+ persons demonstrated "the indelible traces of the barbarity against diverse sexual orientations and gender identities in an armed conflict."[110] The next step would be to assess if the alleged crimes constitute persecution of LGBTQIA+ persons as a crime against humanity.

8.5 Gender Perspective of Council of Europe Agreements and Activities

While "the maintenance and further realisation of human rights and fundamental freedoms" is among the aims of the Council of Europe (CoE), the CoE Statute[111] nowhere expressly refers to equal rights of men and women, in contrast to the UN Charter. Neither has the CoE produced any general agreement specifically protecting the human rights of women, in parallel with CEDAW or the Protocol to the African Charter on Human and Peoples' Rights on the Rights of Women in Africa.[112] Yet, the European Convention for the Protection of Human Rights and Fundamental Freedoms (ECHR)[113] covers the human rights of women, non-binary and transgender persons. Moreover, there are several gender-relevant CoE agreements and gender-specific provisions in other CoE agreements, as well as gender-related policies by the CoE.

8.5.1 European Convention on Human Rights and Gender: General Aspects and Overview

The ECHR does not enshrine any gender-specific rights. It mentions women (beside men) only in Art. 12 ECHR on the right to marry. The general anti-discrimination provision in Art. 14 ECHR guarantees the enjoyment of the Convention rights and freedoms without discrimination on suspect grounds and includes "sex" in the non-exhaustive list of such grounds.

---

[109] Abouelddahab, *Ejiltalk*, 4 May 2021.

[110] Ibid.

[111] 5 May 1949 (ETS No. 1).

[112] 11 July 2003 (https://au.int/sites/default/files/treaties/37077-treaty-charter_on_rights_of_women_in_africa.pdf).

[113] 4 November 1950, as amended (ETS No. 5).

Among the rights which the Protocols have added to the Convention catalogue, only Art. 5 of Protocol No. 7[114] is gender-related. It sets forth that "[s]pouses shall enjoy equality of rights and responsibilities of a private law character between them, and in their relations with their children, as to marriage, during marriage and in the event of its dissolution." States are permitted to take such measures as are necessary in the interests of the children. Art. 1 of Protocol No. 12 extends the general prohibition of discrimination in Art. 14 ECHR to any right set forth by law and prohibits discrimination by any public authority, leaving the list of suspect grounds in Art. 14 ECHR ("sex") unchanged. The preamble of Protocol No. 12 reaffirms that "the principle of non-discrimination does not prevent States Parties from taking measures in order to promote full and effective equality, provided that there is an objective and reasonable justification for those measures", thus permitting affirmative action in favour of disadvantaged persons, including women.

The European Court of Human Rights (ECtHR) that is charged with ensuring the observance of the engagements undertaken by the States Parties (Art. 19 ECHR) has progressively developed the Convention rights and the prohibition of discrimination in order to effectively guarantee gender equality and protect gender identity as well as sexual orientation.[115]

Example

ECtHR, Grand Chamber judgment of 22 March 2012, Konstantin Markin v. Russia, Appl. No. 30078/06, para. 127:

"The Court further reiterates that the advancement of gender equality is today a major goal in the member States of the Council of Europe and very weighty reasons would have to be put forward before such a difference of treatment could be regarded as compatible with the Convention ... In particular, references to traditions, general assumptions or prevailing social attitudes in a particular country are insufficient justification for a difference in treatment on grounds of sex. For example, States are prevented from imposing traditions that derive from the man's primordial role and the woman's secondary role in the family ..." ◀

The ECtHR has extended the prohibition of discrimination in Art. 14 ECHR to discrimination based on sexual orientation as well as transsexualism, recognized a right under Art. 8 ECHR for homosexual couples in a stable relationship to have access to a civil union or registered partnership (although not yet to marriage) and the duty of States to protect homosexuals from homophobic violence (Art. 3 in conjunction with Art. 14 ECHR).[116] While the right to marry pursuant to Art. 8 and/or Art. 12 ECHR was extended to transsexuals, their position in this regard has not yet been

[114] 22 November 1984 (ETS No. 117).

[115] See the regularly updated Factsheets on Gender Equality, Gender Identity and Sexual Orientation Issues by the Court's Press Unit, available at https://www.echr.coe.int/Pages/home.aspx?p=press/factsheets&c=.

[116] See sources cited in the preceding footnote.

fully aligned with that of cisgender persons.[117] ECtHR has also used Art. 4 ECHR to protect women from becoming victims of human trafficking, and sexual, or other, forms of exploitation.[118] In the context of gender identity and equality, two approaches by the ECtHR can come into conflict—the progressive interpretation extending the protective scope of Convention rights and the granting of a wide margin of appreciation to States in the absence of a European consensus.

Example

ECtHR, judgment of 26 July 2005, Siliadin v. France, Appl. No. 73316/01, para. 121:

"[. . .] Sight should not be lost of the Convention's special features or of the fact that it is a living instrument which must be interpreted in the light of present-day conditions, and that the increasingly high standard being required in the area of the protection of human rights and fundamental liberties correspondingly and inevitably requires greater firmness in assessing breaches of the fundamental values of democratic societies [. . .]"

ECtHR, judgment of 16 July 2014, Hämäläinen v. Finland, Appl. No. 37359/09, paras. 74–75:

"[. . .] [I]t cannot be said that there exists any European consensus on allowing same-sex marriages. Nor is there any consensus in those States which do not allow same-sex marriages as to how to deal with gender recognition in the case of a pre-existing marriage. [. . .] In the absence of a European consensus and taking into account that the case at stake undoubtedly raises sensitive moral or ethical issues, the Court considers that the margin of appreciation to be afforded to the respondent State must still be a wide one [. . .] This margin must in principle extend both to the State's decision whether or not to enact legislation concerning legal recognition of the new gender of post-operative transsexuals and, having intervened, to the rules it lays down in order to achieve a balance between the competing public and private interests." ◀

With the evolution of the legal and moral standards across Europe regarding gender equality and identity, the Court's interpretation of the ECHR will become more progressive and the States' margin of appreciation narrower.[119]

In 2007, a gender issue under Art. 22 ECHR was referred to the ECtHR by the Committee of Ministers (CM) for an advisory opinion pursuant to Art. 47 ECHR: the question whether the list of candidates for the post of judge at the ECtHR nominated

[117] ECtHR, Grand Chamber judgment of 11 July 2002, Christine Goodwin v. UK, Appl. No. 28957/95; Grand Chamber judgment of 16 July 2014, Hämäläinen v. Finland, Appl. No. 37359/09.

[118] ECtHR, judgment of 26 July 2005, Siliadin v. France, Appl. No. 73316/01; judgment of 7 January 2010, Rantsev v. Cyprus and Russia, Appl. No. 25965/04; Grand Chamber judgment of 25 June 2020, S.M. v. Croatia, Appl. No. 60561/14.

[119] See, e.g., ECtHR, judgment of 19 January 2021, X and Y v. Romania, Appl. Nos. 2145/16 and 20607/16, para. 166.

by a State Party, which satisfied the criteria enshrined in Art. 21 ECHR, could be refused by the Parliamentary Assembly (PACE) solely because it did not include at least one woman (women being under represented in the Court). The Court answered that "although the aim of ensuring a certain mix [including gender mix] in the composition of the lists of candidates is legitimate and generally accepted, it may not be pursued without provision being made for some exceptions designed to enable each Contracting Party to choose national candidates who satisfy all the requirements of Article 21 § 1." It was therefore not compatible with the ECHR that PACE did not allow any such exception.[120] PACE has adapted its practice on single-sex lists accordingly.[121]

8.5.2 Other Gender-Relevant CoE Treaties

The European Social Charter (revised),[122] the companion to the ECHR, includes several gender-specific provisions in Part II: Art. 4 (3) on the right of men and women workers to equal pay for work of equal value; Art. 8 on the right of employed women to protection of maternity; Art. 20 on the right to equal opportunities and equal treatment in matters of employment and occupation without discrimination on grounds of sex; Art. 26 (1) on the right to be protected from sexual harassment. Moreover, in Part V, Art. E guarantees the enjoyment of the Charter rights without discrimination on suspect grounds and includes "sex" in the non-exhaustive list of such grounds (in parallel to Art. 14 ECHR). There is a gender-specific provision in Art. 14 of the Convention on Human Rights and Biomedicine[123] prohibiting the use of techniques of medically-assisted procreation for the purpose of choosing a future child's sex.

The Council of Europe Convention on Action against Trafficking in Human Beings[124] is formulated in gender-neutral terms, but since most victims are women (and children), it is in substance a treaty for the protection of women.[125] When defining the purposes of the Convention, Art. 1 (1) twice refers to the need to guarantee gender equality. Art. 3 enshrines the non-discrimination principle according to which the implementation of the Convention provisions shall be secured without discrimination on suspect grounds such as sex.[126] Pursuant to Art.

---

[120] ECtHR, Grand Chamber Advisory Opinion No. 1 of 12 February 2008, paras. 53–54.

[121] Parliamentary Assembly, Procedure for the election of judges to the European Court of Human Rights (SG-AS (2020) 03rev4), 4 December 2020, paras. 10, 18–20 (https://assembly.coe.int/LifeRay/CDH/Pdf/ProcedureElectionJudges-EN.pdf).

[122] 3 May 1996 (ETS No. 163).

[123] 4 April 1997 (ETS No. 164).

[124] 16 May 2005 (CETS No. 197).

[125] Explanatory Report to the Convention, paras. 1, 3 (https://rm.coe.int/CoERMPublicCommonSearchServices/DisplayDCTMContent?documentId=09000016800d3812).

[126] Such a provision has become a general standard in recent CoE agreements.

17 of the Convention, in applying measures to protect and promote the rights of victims each Party shall "aim to promote gender equality and use gender mainstreaming in the development, implementation and assessment of the measures."

The gender-specific primary objective of the Council of Europe Convention on Preventing and Combating Violence against Women and Domestic Violence[127] becomes apparent from its title and is confirmed by the preamble. Art. 4 (3) requires the Parties to implement the Convention without discrimination on the usual list of suspect grounds, but adding "gender" to "sex". Art. 6 of the Convention deserves to be quoted in full: "Gender-sensitive policies: Parties shall undertake to include a gender perspective in the implementation and evaluation of the impact of the provisions of this Convention and to promote and effectively implement policies of equality between women and men and the empowerment of women."

8.5.3 Gender-Related Policies of the CoE

Since the Second (Strasbourg) Summit of 1997 and the Third (Warsaw) Summit of 2005, real equality between men and women in all spheres of society, including equal participation in democracy and gender mainstreaming, has been high on the agenda of the CoE.[128] Both the CM[129] and PACE[130] have been involved with various gender-related declarations,[131] recommendations[132] and resolutions[133] on a broad range of topics. The ECtHR takes these documents into consideration when interpreting the provisions of the ECHR and Protocols.[134]

Three subsidiary bodies are worth mentioning in this context:

---

[127] 11 May 2011 (CETS No. 210).

[128] Giegerich and Jötten (2017), paras 26.44 ff.

[129] The CM has a Rapporteur Group GR-H – Human Rights whose main fields of activity include anti-discrimination, diversity and inclusion (Steering Committee on Anti-Discrimination, Diversity and Inclusion [CDADI]) as well as gender equality (Gender Equality Commission [GEC]).

[130] PACE has a Committee on Equality and Non-Discrimination with a Sub-Committee on Gender Equality.

[131] See, e.g., Declaration of the Committee of Ministers on the need to intensify the efforts to prevent and combat female genital mutilation and forced marriage in Europe of 13 September 2017.

[132] See, e.g., Recommendation CM/Rec(2010)5 of the CM to member states on measures to combat discrimination on grounds of sexual orientation or gender identity of 31 March 2010; Recommendation CM/Rec(2010)10 of the CM to member states on the role of women and men in conflict prevention and resolution and in peace building of 30 June 2010; Recommendation CM/Rec(2019) 1 of the CM to member states on preventing and combating sexism of 27 March 2019.

[133] See, e.g., PACE Resolution 2191 (2017) 'Promoting the human rights of and eliminating discrimination against intersex people of 12 October 2017; PACE Resolution 2306 (2019) 'obstetrical and gynaecological violence' of 3 October 2019. For earlier examples, see Giegerich and Jötten (2017), para 26.52.

[134] Giegerich and Jötten (2017), para 26.63.

The Gender Equality Commission (GEC) was established by the CM in order to "steer the CoE's intergovernmental work in the field of gender equality and advise the CM on appropriate action to be taken in its field of competence, taking due account of relevant transversal perspectives."[135] The GEC is charged with promoting "gender equality as a visible priority for the Organisation (internally and externally)".[136] It supports the implementation of the newest CoE Gender Equality Strategy 2018–2023.[137] That Strategy is based on the following definition: "*Gender equality entails equal rights for women and men, girls and boys, as well as the same visibility, empowerment, responsibility and participation, in all spheres of public and private life. It also implies equal access to and distribution of resources between women and men.*"[138]

Example

The Gender Equality Strategy 2018–2023 pursues six strategic objectives, addressing intersectionality as a transversal issue:[139]

"1) Prevent and combat gender stereotypes and sexism.

2) Prevent and combat violence against women and domestic violence.

3) Ensure the equal access of women to justice.

4) Achieve a balanced participation of women and men in political and public decision-making.

5) Protect the rights of migrant, refugee and asylum-seeking women and girls.

6) Achieve gender mainstreaming in all policies and measures."[140] ◀

The second subsidiary body is the European Commission against Racism and Intolerance (ECRI).[141] It was set up by the First (Vienna) Summit of 1993 as an independent human rights monitoring body. While mainly focussing on racism, it has also addressed homo- and transphobic intolerance and discrimination since 2013.[142]

The third subsidiary body is the Commissioner for Human Rights that was instituted by the CM as "a non-judicial institution to promote education in, awareness of and respect for human rights, as embodied in the human rights instruments of the CoE."[143] Part of the thematic work of the Commissioner is devoted to women's

---

[135] GEC current terms of reference (https://rm.coe.int/tor-gec-2020-2021/1680997efd). For GEC's predecessors, see Giegerich and Jötten (2017), para 26.49 ff.

[136] Id.

[137] Adopted by the CM on 7 March 2018 (https://rm.coe.int/strategy-en-2018-2023/16807b58eb).

[138] Para. 2 (italics in the original).

[139] Id., para. 21.

[140] Id., para. 35.

[141] https://rm.coe.int/leaflet-ecri-2019/168094b101.

[142] See ECRI Factsheet on LGBTI issues of 1 March 2021 (https://rm.coe.int/ecri-factsheet-lgbti-issues/1680a1960a).

[143] Art. 1 (1) of Resolution (99) 50 of 7 May 1999.

rights and gender equality,[144] including women's sexual and reproductive health rights,[145] and the human rights of LGBTQIA+ people.[146]

8.6 EU Law and Gender Equality (Marco Evola)

8.6.1 Gender Equality in the EU Legal System

The principle of equality is one of the general principles of the EU legal system.[147] In applying this principle the Court of Justice (hereinafter CJEU) has stated that it possesses the nature of a fundamental right.[148] Gender equality embodies one of the expressions of the principle of equality and shares the same legal features. The CJEU made this point clear in *Defrenne III* ruling that "There can be no doubt that the elimination of discrimination based on sex forms part of those fundamental rights."[149]

The Court's assessment of gender equality sheds light on the legal framework the founding Treaties and the Charter of Fundamental Rights of the European Union (hereinafter CFREU) shape. The Lisbon Treaty stipulates that equality between men and women is one the founding values of the Union (art. 2 TEU). Pursuant to this provision, EU law has to tackle gender issues in order to promote substantial equality[150] beyond the mere formal approach embedded in the principle of non-discrimination. From this perspective, outlawing gender discrimination contributes to the development of the EU social policy, a result stemming from art. 3 TFEU, which combines the promotion of social protection with that of equality between women and men. In the same vein art. 23 CFREU provides that equality between women and men must be ensured in all areas, including employment, work and pay. This set of rules recognises the existence of stereotypes shaping the division of labour and requiring women and men to perform different roles in society. In

[144] See, e.g., the human rights comment "Remove obstacles to the work of women's rights defenders", 2015 (https://www.coe.int/en/web/commissioner/-/remove-obstacles-to-the-work-of-women-s-rights-defenders).

[145] See the issue paper "Women's sexual and reproductive health and rights in Europe", 2017 (https://rm.coe.int/women-s-sexual-and-reproductive-health-and-rights-in-europe-issue-pape/168076dead).

[146] See, e.g., the issue paper "Human rights and intersex people", 2017 (https://rm.coe.int/human-rights-and-intersex-people-issue-paper-published-by-the-council-/16806da5d4).

[147] Joined cases 117-76 and 16-77, Albert Ruckdeschel & Co. and Hansa-Lagerhaus Ströh & Co. v Hauptzollamt Hamburg-St. Annen; Diamalt AG v Hauptzollamt Itzehoe (ECJ 19 October 1977), para. 7; Case C-115/08, Land Oberösterreich v ČEZ (ECJ 27 October 2009), para. 91. On EU non-discrimination law see Fredman (2011); Bell (2011), pp. 611–639.

[148] Case C-144/04, *Werner Mangold v Rüdiger Helm* (ECJ 22 November 2005), paras. 94–96; Koukoulis-Spiliotpoulos (2005), p. 330; Muir (2013), pp. 1231–1254.

[149] Case 149/77, Gabrielle Defrenne v Société anonyme belge de navigation aérienne Sabena (ECJ 15 June 1978), paras. 26–27.

[150] Scholars also proposed the notion of transformative equality. See Fredman (2003), pp. 111–118.

order to dismantle this structuring of gender relationships the TFEU lays down gender mainstreaming committing the EU institutions to eliminate inequalities and promote equality between men and women in its actions (art. 8 TFEU) and to combat discrimination based, among other grounds, on sex and sexual orientation in defining and implementing its policies and actions (art. 10 TFEU). This duty is general in nature since it does not cover only the traditional field of employment, thus making it clear that gender equality is not a special issue.[151]

Furthermore, pursuant to art. 21 TEU, gender equality is one of the principles and objectives of the EU external action.[152]

Three legal items rise from EU law as well as the rulings of the CJEU. The first issue concerns the scope of equality. The express reference to women and men in art. 2, art. 3 TEU and art. 23 CFREU might entail a binary conception of gender. However, it could be argued that EU law on gender has to be applied to any discrimination based on sexual orientation guaranteeing LGBTQIA+ individuals' rights.

The second issue relates to the objective of EU gender law. In this perspective it is doubtful whether EU law is shaped to attain substantial equality through the guarantee of diversity or to remove differential treatment through the eradication of discriminatory rules and practices.

The third item refers to the role of gender equality law in the wider framework of the EU policies since the rules on gender might be functional to the working of the common market rather than contribute to the setting up of a social policy at the EU level.[153]

The EU has limited or no power on issues which are of utmost importance in the perspective of women's emancipation: gender-based violence, reproductive rights, family law, women's participation to political life and their representation in public institutions, contract law, and children's custody. In the same vein it is to be added that the EU has no competence on those thorny legal items which are a crucial pivot point in outlawing discrimination on the ground of sexual orientation: marriage of homosexual couples, recognition of civil union, adoption and legal status of same-sex partnerships.

Notwithstanding the Treaty's boundaries on its action, the EU has been playing a crucial role in equality. A first reason for that role is to be found in the influence of EU anti-discrimination law on the domestic legal system of Member States on sex equality[154] . This is due not only to the direct effect and supremacy of EU law,[155] but

---

[151] Beveridge et al. (2000); Pollack and Hafner-Burton (2000) pp. 432–456.

[152] Thies (2019), pp. 429–454-, pp. 433 *et seq.*

[153] Case 439/75, Gabrielle Defrenne v Société anonyme belge de navigation aérienne Sabena (ECJ 8 April 1976), paras. 9–10.

[154] Tridimas (2006), p. 102.

[155] Cichowski (2004), pp. 147–196.

also to the continuous dialogue between the CJEU and national judges.[156] A second reason is entrenched in the case law of the CJEU. The arrangement of the EU competences has not prevented the Court from exercising its control over Member States laws regulating fields not falling within the competences of the Union, for they could affect the effectiveness of EU gender equality law.[157] From this point of view, gender equality is part of wider trends in EU law.[158]

The problematic legal items stemming from the laws on non-discrimination are the eventual result of a long process which is the necessary starting point in the assessment of EU gender equality.

8.6.2 The Development of EU Law on Gender Equality

EU anti-discrimination law on the ground of gender has been shaped neither to pursue a consistent and systematic design of gender relationships, nor to give an answer to the demand for equality with a view to mould a defined arrangement of equality in the gender perspective. As a consequence, the rules outlawing gender discriminations are piece-meal.

The Treaty of Rome laid down the duty of Member States to ensure that men and women receive the same pay for work of equal value (art. 119) in order to establish fair competition in the internal market by putting an end to wage disparities between the Member States. The CJEU highlighted that the principle of equal pay is an expression of a principle of non-discrimination which was wider in scope since it extended to employment.[159]

Furthermore, the Community adopted laws aiming at outlawing discrimination in the following fields: (a) employment:[160] (b) social security;[161] (c) self-employed

[156] On the relationship between EU Law and the German and Dutch law see Mulder (2017), pp. 66 *et seq.*

[157] Case C-117/01, K.B. v National Health Service Pensions Agency and Secretary of State for Health (ECJ 7 January 2004).

[158] Lefevre (2004), pp. 501–516; Mickliz and De Witte (2012).

[159] Barnard (1999), pp. 215–279; Rönmar (2020), pp. 612–642.

[160] Council Directive 75/117/EEC of 10 February 1975 on the approximation of the laws of the Member States relating to the application of the principle of equal pay for men and women OJ L 45, 19.2.1975, pp. 19–20. The Directive is no longer in force. Council Directive 76/207/EEC of 9 February 1976 on the implementation of the principle of equal treatment for men and women as regards access to employment, vocational training and promotion, and working conditions, OJ L 39, 14.2.1976, pp. 40–42. The Directive is no longer in force.

[161] Council Directive 79/7 of 19 December 1978 on the progressive implementation of the principle of equal treatment for men and women in matters of social security, OJ L 6, 10.1.1979, pp. 24–25. Council Directive 86/378/EEC of 24 July 1986 *on the implementation of the principle of equal treatment for men and women in occupational social security schemes*, OJ L 225, (1986), pp. 40–42. The Directive is no longer in force.

capacity;[162] (d) pregnancy and motherhood;[163] (e) parental leave;[164]and (f) judicial protection of women's rights.[165] The reforms of the Treaties have bolstered the action of the EU.

The EU citizenship endowed also non-economic migrants with the right not to be discriminated against on grounds of nationality in the access to the social assistance of the hosting country (see *infra* Sect. 8.6.6).

The Amsterdam Treaty made the principle of equal pay part of the social policy of the EU (art. 155 TFEU para. 1 (i)), laid down the principles of equal opportunities and equal treatment of men and women in matters of employment and occupation, including the principle of equal pay for equal work or work of equal value. (art. 157 para. 3 TFEU), enabled Member States to maintain or adopt positive measures, established gender mainstreaming (art. 8 and 10 TFEU)[166] and conferred on the EU the competence to combat discrimination based on various grounds, such as sex or sexual orientation.[167]

The CFREU devotes two provisions to gender discrimination, a choice highlighting its importance in EU law and its extensive policy development.[168] The first limb of art. 21 prohibits any discrimination on various grounds such as sex and sexual orientation, enabling the EU to face multiple discrimination cases because of the extensive and non-exhaustive array of forbidden status.[169]

Art. 23 CFREU recognizes the existence of inequalities to the detriment of women and provides two different rules. The first paragraph of art. 23 obliges the EU and the Member States to ensure equality in all areas, including employment, work and pay. Art. 23 para. 2 regulates positive actions laying down a provision that is a step back compared to art. 157 par. 4 TFEU since the former considers positive

---

[162] Council Directive 86/613/EEC of 11 December 1986 on the application of the principle of equal treatment between men and women engaged in an activity, including agriculture, in a self-employed capacity, and on the protection of self-employed women during pregnancy and motherhood, OJ L 359, (1986), pp. 56–58. The Directive is no longer in force.

[163] Council Directive 92/85/EEC of 19 October 1992 on the introduction of measures to encourage improvements in the safety and health at work of pregnant workers and workers who have recently given birth or are breastfeeding (tenth individual Directive within the meaning of Article 16 (1) of Directive 89/391/EEC), OJ L 348, (1992), pp. 1–8.

[164] Council Directive 96/34/EC of 3 June 1996 *on the framework agreement on parental leave concluded by UNICE, CEEP and the ETUC*, OJ L 145, (1996), pp. 4–9. The Directive is no longer in force.

[165] Council Directive 97/80/EC of 15 December 1997 *on the burden of proof in cases of discrimination based on sex*, OJ L 14, (1998), pp. 6–8. The Directive is no longer in force.

[166] Lewis (2006), p. 427. Shaw (2002), pp. 213–226, p. 221, highlights that mainstreaming could be reduced to the ticking of boxes.

[167] On the different grounds of discrimination EU law forbids see Ellis and Watson (2012), pp. 22–42.

[168] Kilpatrick (2014), p. 582.

[169] Idem, p. 591. On multiple discrimination see Schiek and Lawson (2011).

actions as permissible derogations while the latter acknowledges that positive measures are a means to promote substantial gender equality.[170]

The EU has adopted a series of directives to rationalize the existing laws and to widen the scope of the action in gender sensitive issues (see Sect. 8.6.4).

8.6.3 EU Primary Law and Gender Equality

EU primary laws have different functions within the multi-layered legal framework on gender equality.[171]

A first group of primary laws is composed of rules the CJEU utilises as a benchmark against which the action of the EU institutions or the rules of the Member States can be checked.

This group of rules comprises the general principle of non-discrimination on the ground of sex the CJEU considers a fundamental right of the EU.[172] However, the reasoning of the rulings in *Mangold*[173] and *Kücükdeveci*[174] on the relationships between a general principle of non-discrimination and directives intended to apply that principle, could open new avenues of protection in the field of equality law, since the principle of sex discrimination could become a source of rights which are to be protected in horizontal disputes.[175]

Art. 21 CFREU is the second primary law belonging to this first group.[176] However, as regards art. 21 of the Charter the most recent developments of the Court's case law might entail a broader application of the provision at stake.

In *Egenberger* the CJEU dealt with the application of the principle of non-discrimination on grounds of religion in horizontal litigations and stated that art. 21 para. 1 CFREU has direct effect so that "the national court would be required to ensure within its jurisdiction the judicial protection for individuals flowing from Articles 21 and 47 of the Charter, and to guarantee the full effectiveness of those articles by disapplying if need be any contrary provision of national law."[177] The reasoning could lead the Court to apply art. 21 CFREU in disputes between individuals arising from discrimination on grounds of sex or sexual orientation. Such an outcome would contribute to enhance the system since the CJEU has always

---

[170] Millns (2017), p. 258.

[171] On this distinction see Muir (2018), pp. 61 *et seq.*

[172] Case 149/77, Gabrielle Defrenne v Société anonyme belge de navigation aérienne Sabena, (ECJ 15 June 1978), paras. 26–27.

[173] Case C-144/04, Werner Mangold v Rüdiger Helm (2005).

[174] Case C-555/07, Seda Kücükdeveci v Swedex GmbH & Co. KG (2010).

[175] Ellis and Watson (2012), p. 138.

[176] The CJEU, case C-236/09, *Association Belge des Consommateurs Test-Achats ASBL and Others v Conseil des ministres* (2011), paras. 30–34 referred to art 21 and art. 23 of the Charter in assessing the validity of art. 5 para. 2 of Directive 2004/113.

[177] Case C-414/16, Vera Egenberger v Evangelisches Werk für Diakonie und Entwicklung e.V (2018), para. 79.

pointed out that directives have not direct effect in horizontal disputes. Hence, in *Cresco Investigation,* a case on discrimination based on religion, the CJEU stated that "where discrimination contrary to EU law has been established, as long as measures reinstating equal treatment have not been adopted, observance of the principle of equality can be ensured only by granting to persons within the disadvantaged category the same advantages as those enjoyed by persons within the favoured category."[178]

A second group of primary laws is composed of those provisions playing a dual role. Firstly, primary law is a benchmark. Secondly, the provisions "define the scope and content of EU regulatory intervention in domestic policies".[179] Art. 157 TFEU is one of the provisions of this group.

Example

Ms. Defrenne was hired by SABENA as an air hostess. Pursuant to the provision of a collective agreement Ms. Defrenne's contract ended when she reached the age of 40. Ms. Defrenne brough a legal action arguing that she was victim of sex discrimination compared to her male colleagues. The CJEU in *Defrenne II* ruled that art. 157 TFEU is sufficiently clear and precise and unconditional to produce direct effect in the legal order of Member States.[180] ◄

A third group of primary laws cover those rules which confer upon the EU the power to adopt laws aiming at giving effect to the prohibition of discrimination. Two provisions on sex discrimination are at stake: art. 19 and art. 157 para. 3 TFEU.

The fourth group of primary rules is composed of Art. 2 and 3 TEU which are not binding but play a role in construing EU laws.

The last set of primary laws group Art. 8 and art. 10 TFEU and art. 23 CFREU and impose upon EU institutions and Member States the obligation to integrate gender equality in all polices.

8.6.4 Gender Equality and EU Secondary Law

The directives on gender equality set up identical tools to combat gender discrimination: direct discrimination, indirect discrimination, harassment and sexual harassment, positive actions, the burden of proof.[181] It is necessary to highlight that the principle of non-discrimination on the ground of sex is supplemented by a series of

---

[178] Case C-193/17, Cresco Investigation GmbH v Markus Achatzi (2019), para. 79.

[179] Muir (2018), p. 68.

[180] Case 43/75, Gabrielle Defrenne v Société anonyme belge de navigation aérienne Sabena (ECJ 8 April 1976), para 39.

[181] Prechal (2004) p. 533; Muir and De Witte (2017) p. 137.

directives regulating part-time work, fixed-term employees and temporary agency work which are examined in the chapter on labour law.

8.6.4.1 Equal Treatment of Men and Women in Employment and Occupation

Directive 2006/54[182] on equal treatment in employment and occupation is framed in four titles. The Directive's purpose is the implementation of the principle of equal opportunities and equal treatment (art. 1) in the following areas: (a) access to employment, including promotion, and to vocational training; (b) working conditions, including pay; and (c) occupational social security schemes.

The laws aim at making implementation more effective through a series of instruments; remedies and penalties, the softening of the burden of proof, victimisation, equality bodies, social dialogue and dialogue with NGOs. Moreover, the title devotes rules to the prevention of discrimination, gender mainstreaming and the dissemination of information.

8.6.4.2 Equal Treatment of Men and Women in Social Security Schemes

Equal treatment in the field of statutory social security is provided for by Directive 79/7 prohibiting direct and indirect sex discrimination (art. 4 para. 1) as regards the following risks: sickness, invalidity, old age, accidents at work and occupational diseases, and unemployment. The Directive also covers social assistance, as it is intended to supplement or replace the schemes on the risks already mentioned. The Directive applies to the working population including: self-employed persons; workers and self-employed persons whose activity is interrupted by illness, accident or involuntary unemployment; persons seeking employment, and retired or invalided workers and self-employed persons (art. 2).

Directive 2006/54 repealed Directive 86/378 that extended the principle of equal treatment to occupational social security schemes. The two directives supported the process of market integration for social policy is subordinated to economic policy and purports the promotion of economic targets, mainly as regards the labour market.[183] EU law does not cover social assistance benefits resulting in no protection against the risk of poverty which affects women more than man.[184]

8.6.4.3 The Directive on Pregnant Workers

Directive 92/85 was adopted to improve the safety and health at work of pregnant workers and workers who have recently given birth or are breastfeeding (art. 1).

The Directive prohibits the dismissal of workers during the period from the beginning of their pregnancy to the end of the maternity leave (art. 10 par. 1), but

---

[182] Directive 2006/54/EC of the European Parliament and the Council of 5 July 2006 on the implementation of the principle of equal opportunities and equal treatment of men and women in matters of employment and occupation (recast), OJ L 204, (2006), pp. 23–36.

[183] Hodson and Maer (2001), pp. 719–746; Carmel (2003).

[184] Hervey (2005), p. 310.

Member States are not obliged to guarantee the reinstatement in post. Consequently, the system provides a weak protection in this instance.

8.6.4.4 The Directive on Parental Leave

Parental leave should foster the emancipation of women from a model of family life in which they are charged with the task of providing care, an arrangement which is one of the reasons why women face difficulties in accessing the labour market. Directive 2010/18 on parental leave[185] sets minimum standards to reconcile work with family and confers upon men and women workers the right to a parental leave, which in principle, should be provided on a non-transferable basis.

Member States enjoy a wide margin of discretion in determining the conditions of access, whether the leave should be compensated, whether it should cover full or part-time work, and on the remedies in case of less favourable treatment or dismissal on the grounds of an application for, or the taking of, parental leave. However, it is unlikely that men would accept the leave because of the leeway on the mandatory nature of compensation, therefore the law failed to enhance a redistribution of roles within family and to set aside the stereotype of men as breadwinners,[186] legitimating women's social role of childbearers and childrearers.[187]

Most of the highlighted limits mark Directive 2019/1158, which is to repeal Directive 2010/18[188] from 2 August 2022, notwithstanding various important reforms it introduces. Directive 2019/1158 establishes the paternity right (art. 4) and obliges Member States to take appropriate measures to prohibit the dismissal of those who benefitted from paternity or parental leave (art. 12). However, the new directive ensures Member States the leeway they enjoyed pursuant to the rules of Directive 2010/18.

8.6.4.5 Equal Treatment Between Men and Women in an Activity in a Self-Employed Capacity

Directive 2010/41[189] refined the existing rules in order to put into effect the principle of equal treatment between men and women engaged in an activity in a self-employed capacity, or contributing to the pursuit of such an activity, as regards those aspects not covered by Directives 2006/54/EC and 79/7/EEC (art. 1). The Directive stipulates that there shall be no discrimination whatsoever on grounds of

[185] Council Directive 2010/18/EU of 8 March 2010 implementing the revised Framework Agreement on parental leave concluded by BUSINESSEUROPE, UEAPME, CEEP and ETUC and repealing Directive 96/34/EC (Text with EEA relevance), OJ L 68, (2010), pp. 13–20.

[186] Lewis (2006), p. 429 raises this criticism on the rules of Directive 96/34.

[187] Fourbet (2002), pp. 219–246.

[188] Directive (EU) 2019/1158 of the European Parliament and of the Council of 20 June 2019 *on work-life balance for parents and carers and repealing Council Directive 2010/18/EU,* OJ L188, (2019), pp. 79–93. See Waddington and Bell (2021); Weldon-Johns (2021).

[189] Directive 2010/41/EU of the European Parliament and the Council of 7 July 2010 *on the application of the principle of equal treatment between men and women engaged in an activity in a self-employed capacity* and repealing Council Directive 86/613/EEC, OJ L 180, (2010), pp. 1–6.

sex in the public or private sectors, either directly or indirectly, for instance in relation to the establishment, equipment or extension of a business or the launching or extension of any other form of self-employed activity (art. 3 para. 1). The focus on the principle of non-discrimination prevents the directive from fostering women's self-employed capacity which stems, among other factors, from the distribution of roles within family and the difficulties in accessing education.

8.6.4.6 Equality Between Men and Women in the Access to and Supply of Goods and Services

Sexual discrimination affects women's ability to be fully and successfully integrated into economic and social life. Moving from this assumption Directive 2004/113 purports to guarantee the principle of equal treatment between men and women in the access to and supply of goods and services.[190]

Pursuant to art. 3, the Directive "shall apply to all persons who provide goods and services available to the public irrespective of the person concerned as regards to both the public and private sectors, including public bodies and which are offered outside the area of private and family life and the transactions carried out in this context."

The Directive envisages wide-ranging exceptions (art. 4 para. 5) and lays down specific provisions on actuarial factors in insurance contracts which legitimize different offers to men and women (art. 5). This arrangement severely curtails the potential for reshaping private contractual relationships[191] since in the fields of goods and services, mainly insurance services, the treatment of women is handled differently to the treatment men are granted.[192]

8.6.4.7 Sexual Orientation and Equal Treatment in Employment and Occupation

Directive 2000/78 encompasses various prohibited types of discrimination including sexual orientation.[193] Art. 3 stipulates that the Directive shall apply to all persons, as regards both the public and private sectors, including public bodies, in relation to: (a) conditions for access to employment, to self-employment or to occupation; (b) access to all types and to all levels of vocational guidance, and vocational training; (c) employment and working conditions, including dismissals and pay;

[190] Council Directive 2004/113/EC of 13 December 2004 implementing the principle of equal treatment between men and women in the access to and supply of goods and services, OJ L 373, (2004), pp. 37–43.

[191] Schiek (2005), p. 434.

[192] Hervey (2005), p. 310. The Court Case C-236-09, *Association Belge des Consommateurs Test-Achats ASBL and Others v Conseil des ministres* (1 March 2011), paras. 30–32 struck down art. 5 para. 2 of the Directive because it enabled the Member States to maintain without temporal limitation an exemption from the rule of unisex premiums and benefits working against the objective of the Directive itself and breaching art. 21 and 23 CFREU.

[193] Council Directive 2000/78/EC of 27 November 2000 establishing a general framework for equal treatment in employment and occupation, OJ L 303, (2000), pp. 16–22.

and (d) membership of, and involvement in, an organisation of workers or employers, or any organisation whose members carry on a particular profession, including the benefits provided for by such organisations.

A difference in treatment does not constitute discrimination where it is based on a characteristic which constitutes a genuine and determining occupational requirement, by reason of the nature of the particular occupational activities concerned or of the context in which they are carried out, provided that the objective is legitimate and the requirement is proportionate (art. 4 para. 1).

8.6.5 Citizenship of the Union and Gender Equality

The setting up of the EU citizenship did not purport to the tackling of gender discrimination. However, the right of residence and the right not to be discriminated against on grounds of nationality have been construed by the Luxembourg Judge in a manner which contributed to the protection and enforcement of women's rights; the Court has linked stay and access to social assistance in the hosting country to caretaking.

In *Martinez Sala*[194] the Court stated that an EU citizen lawfully residing in another country has the right to equal treatment as regards to access to a child-raising allowance in the host Member State.

Furthermore, in *Baumbast*[195] the CJEU ruled that the parent who is the primary carer of children, having the right to reside in a Member State, is entitled to reside with them in order to enable them to exercise the right of residence. In the same vein the exercise of the rights EU citizenship guarantees led the Court to endow the third-country nationals who are carers with the right of residence in *Chen*[196] and *Ruiz Zambrano*.[197]

Example

The preliminary ruling the CJEU delivered in the *Ruiz Zambrano* case concerned the refusal of the Belgian authorities to regularize the stay of Mr. and Ms. Ruiz-Zambrano, a couple of third-country nationals whose children held Belgian nationality. The Court stated that "article 20 TFEU precludes national measures which have the effect of depriving citizens of the Union of the genuine enjoyment of the substance of the rights conferred by virtue of their status as citizens of the Union (. . .). A refusal to grant a right of residence to a third country national with dependent minor children in the Member State where those children are nationals

[194] Case C-85/96, *María Martínez Sala v Freistaat Bayern* (ECJ 1998), paras. 61–65.

[195] Case C-413/99, Baumbast and R v Secretary of State for the Home Department (ECJ 2002), para. 75.

[196] Case C-200/02, Kunqian Catherine Zhu and Man Lavette Chen v Secretary of State for the Home Department (ECJ 2004), paras. 44–47.

[197] Case C-34/09, Gerardo Ruiz Zambrano v Office national de l'emploi (ONEm) (ECJ 2011).

and reside, and also a refusal to grant such a person a work permit, has such an effect."[198] ◀

The connection between caring and the right of residence limits States' power to expel unlawful stayers. In *Carpenter* the CJEU pointed out that the order of deportation of Ms. Carpenter would prevent Mr. Carpenter from providing services since the former took care of the latter's children when he was abroad to run his business.[199]

Scholars argued that these rulings give EU citizenship a social content going beyond the economic dimension of the rights embedded in EU laws, since the CJEU valued the care work women and mothers do, highlighting that this work is not usually considered as a source of rights.[200]

However, in the more recent *Dano* case the CJEU adopted a narrower interpretation of the rules on citizenship and stated that the claim of a Romanian woman to have access to social assistance benefits for herself and her son was unfounded.[201]

Furthermore, it could be argued that the case law of the CJEU stereotypes women as caregivers rather than promoting gender equality.

8.6.6 Gender Equality Beyond Equality Between Women and Men

The reference to equality between women and men that art. 2 TEU and art. 23 CFREU establish relates to "socio-economic role expectations around division of labour".[202] In this perspective the rationale behind the two rules is to dismantle those factors which distribute roles in family, employment, and society, giving rise to inequality.

A cautious approach marks the way in which the CJEU has managed the thorny issues related to the legal status of transsexuals and homosexuals.[203]

As regards transsexuals, the Court ruled that the principle of non-discrimination on grounds of sex "cannot be confined simply to discrimination based on the fact that a person is of one or other sex" but its scope is also "such as to apply to discrimination arising, as in this case, from the gender reassignment of the person concerned."[204]

[198] *Ibidem*, paras. 42–43.

[199] Case C-60/00, Mary Carpenter v Secretary of State for the Home Department (ECJ 2002), paras. 45–46.

[200] Millns (2017), p. 258. Cheltenham, p. 263. See Baer (2004), p. 112 who considers citizenship in the light of the CFREU and argues that the latter reacts to social exclusion by establishing rights of solidarity.

[201] Case C-333/13, Elisabeta Dano and Florin Dano v Jobcenter Leipzig (ECJ 2014), paras. 82–84.

[202] Schiek (2014), p. 645.

[203] Gallo et al. (2015).

[204] Case C-13/94, *P v S and Cornwall County Council* (ECJ 1996), paras. 17–20.

The Court has adopted a different stance towards homosexuality. In the first stage of its case law the CJEU excluded that same-sex partnerships and married couples are comparable.[205]

In *Maruko*[206] and *Römer*[207] the Court illustrated that a comparison can be made between same-sex partnerships and married couples.

Example

Römer, who was in a stable same-sex partnership, claimed the same treatment of married couples as regards his pension scale. The Court held that "first, it is required not that the situations be identical, but only that they be comparable and, second, the assessment of that comparability must be carried out not in a global and abstract manner, but in a specific and concrete manner in the light of the benefit concerned. (. . .) the Court (. . .) on the basis of the analysis of German law carried out by the court which made the reference for a preliminary ruling, according to which there was a gradual harmonisation in German law of the regime put in place for registered life partnerships with that applicable to marriage, (. . .) made it clear that registered life partnership is to be treated as equivalent to marriage as regards the widow's or widower's pension."[208] ◄

In the following *Hay* case the comparability was affirmed in a horizontal dispute. The Court stated that "as regards the very existence of discrimination, it is apparent from the Court's case-law that a Member State's rules which restrict benefits in terms of conditions of pay or working conditions to married employees, whereas marriage is legally possible in that Member State only between persons of different sexes, give rise to direct discrimination based on sexual orientation against homosexual permanent employees in a PACS arrangement who are in a comparable situation."[209]

In these rulings the Court based its reasoning on a broader interpretation of Directive 2000/78.[210] In so doing the Court showed its reluctance to extend the *Mangold* jurisprudence to discrimination based on sexual orientation.[211] The protection of homosexuals within the EU legal system falls short of the protection which is guaranteed within the ECHR (see Sect. 8.5.1 in this chapter).

---

[205] Case C-294/96, Lisa Jacqueline Grant v South-West Trains Ltd (ECJ 1998), para. 35.

[206] C-267/06, Tadao Maruko v Versorgungsanstalt der deutschen Bühnen (ECJ 1 April 2008), paras. 67–73.

[207] C-147/08, Jürgen Römer v Freie und Hansestadt Hamburg (ECJ 10 May 2011).

[208] *Ibidem* para. 42.

[209] Case C-267/12, Frédéric Hay v Crédit agricole mutuel de Charente-Maritime et des Deux-Sèvres (ECJ 2013), para 41.

[210] Zaccaroni (2017), p. 183 argues that the broad interpretation of Directive 2000/78 may be justified only in light of the particular importance of the principle of non-discrimination.

[211] Amalfitano (2018), p. 133.

8.7 Conclusion

International law is a result of particular theories and international practice that were gender-free and did not include women and their perspectives in its development. In the second half of the nineteenth century, various women's organizations were first established. They participated at the Peace Conference in Paris, advocating for separating the nationality of women from their spouses, prohibiting human trafficking of women and girls, and achieving equality of men and women in the area of labour. Some of the members of those organizations were very active and took part in the League of Nations and the International Labour Organization. In 1945, the UN Charter was adopted, reaffirming in its Preamble a faith in equal rights of men and women. Since then, many international documents were adopted, and bodies were established to achieve greater gender equality. In 1979, the first gender-specific convention,the Convention on the Elimination of All Forms of Discrimination against Women was adopted, prohibiting gender discrimination in all areas of life.

Resolution 1325 was passed in the Security Council more than twenty years ago. It has since been followed by several more resolutions, covering the two areas of (a) Prevention of and response to conflict-related sexual violence and (b) Women's participation and leadership in peace making and conflict prevention. Global work on the WPS agenda remains challenging, as it engages a vast number of actors and stretches over several agendas. Nevertheless, some progress is also noted; almost half of the UN member States have developed their National Action Plans, as envisaged by the resolution. These States regularly engage in the revision process with regards to their plans. Work continues to engage the remaining States in this process.

International humanitarian law is an inherently male-normative branch under international law, since armed conflict is a context traditionally associated with masculinity. This is evident in the language of the Geneva Conventions and their Additional Protocols, whose history goes back to a time when women did not take part in public life, even less so in deliberations of international public law. The treaties bear their mark of time: they speak about women as objects whose honour needs protection. Even if we today may perceive the language as outdated, this does not render the provisions void of legal protection. Interpreting the norms in light of their object and purpose remains the most constructive approach today.

While the ECHR does not contain gender-specific rights, its prohibition on gender-based discrimination is strictly enforced by the ECtHR. The primary objective of the Council of Europe Convention on Preventing and Combating Violence against Women and Domestic Violence is gender-specific. That Convention is the crowning achievement of the CoE's longstanding gender-related policies.

The EU has shaped gender law focusing mainly on labour law. The laws the EU enacted ensure fair competition in the common market and do not dismantle the social and economic structures and cultural stereotypes segregating women in the labour market. A similar reasoning applies to the laws on self-employed activities and the rules on access to and supply of goods and services. The limits on women's access to social assistance and the restrictions on the enactment of positive actions clearly convey that EU gender law is anchored in the principle of non-discrimination, failing to promote substantial equality.[212]

In the same vein, it is to be observed that the fragmentation of the rules outlawing discrimination contained in a set of directives regulating specific prohibited statuses, jeopardizes the efficacy of the system in tackling multiple discriminations, a phenomenon which is of growing importance.[213]

Eventually, the Court's care in handling transsexual and homosexual persons rights lowers the standard of protection EU law envisages in comparison with the jurisprudence of the ECtHR.

Questions

1. What are the principal and subsidiary organs within the UN system which deal with gender equality?
2. What is the main UN body for gender equality?
3. Explain the main features of CEDAW.
4. Which provisions of the ECHR and Protocols are particularly important from a gender perspective?
5. Describe the ECtHR's approach to gender-related discrimination.
6. Describe the role EU primary law plays in the case law of the Court of Justice on gender equality.
7. Define direct and indirect discrimination.
8. Describe the case law of the Court of Justice on sexual orientation discrimination.
9. More than twenty years have now passed since the Security Council passed resolution 1325. Many actors have engaged with the agenda over the years. What are the key gains of the resolution? What are the contemporary challenges with its implementation? Discuss.
10. Does it matter under IHL whether the rape victim is a civilian, a combatant, a fighter, a militant sympathizer, or a terrorist? Why?

References

Amalfitano C (2018) General principles of EU law and the protection of fundamental rights. Edward Elgar Publishing, Cheltenham/Northampton

Baer S (2004) Citizanship in Europe and the construction of gender by law in the construction of gender by law in the european charter of fundamental rights. In: Knop K (ed) Gender and human rights. Oxford University Press-Oxford, Collected courses of the academy of European law, pp 83–112

Barnard C (1999) Gender equality in the EU: a balance sheet. In: Alston P, Bustelo M, Heenan J (eds) The EU and human rights. Oxford University Press, Oxford, pp 215–279

---

[212] Fenwick and Hervey (1995).

[213] Solanke (2021), p. 93.

Barth EF (2002) Peace as disappointment: the reintegration of female soldiers in post-conflict societies: a comparative study from Africa. https://www.prio.org/utility/DownloadFile.ashx?id=470&type=publicationfile. Accessed 4 Oct 2021
Basu S, Kirby PC, Shepherd LC (2020) Women, peace and security: a critical cartography. In: Basu S, Kirby PC, Shepherd LC (eds) New directions in women, peace and security. Bristol University Press, Bristol, pp 1–28
Bederman DJ (2002) The spirit of international law. The University of Georgia Press, Athens/London
Bell M (2011) The principle of equal treatment: widening and deepening. In: Craing P, De Burca G (eds) The evolution of EU law. Oxford University Press, Oxford, pp 611–639
Besson S, Tasioulas J (2010) The philosophy of international law. Oxford University Press, Oxford
Beveridge F, Stephen K, Nott S (2000) Making women count: integrating gender into law and policy-making. Routledge, London/New York
Bolzendahl C, Brooks C (2007) Women's political representation and welfare state spending in 12 capitalist democracies. Soc Forces 85:1509–1534
Bradley SF (2020) Protection of detainees from sexual violence under international humanitarian law. J Confl Secur Law 25:381–422
Caprioli M, Boyer MA (2001) Gender, violence, and international crisis. J Confl Resolut 45:503–518
Carmel E (2003) What is European and social about European social policy? Some remarks on the open of co-ordination. Paper for ESP Anet Conference Copenhagen 14–17 November
Carpenter CR (2003) 'Women and Children First': gender, norms, and humanitarian evacuation in the Balkans 1991–95. Int Organ 57:661–694
Chinkin C (2010) Women, rights of, international protection. Max Planck Encyclopedia of Public International Law (OUP online)
Cichowski RA (2004) Sex equality. In: Sweet AS (ed) The judicial construction of Europe. Oxford University Press, Oxford, pp 147–196
Coomaraswamy R et al (2015) Preventing conflict, transforming justice, securing the peace: a global study on the implementation of United Nations Security Council Resolution 1325. UN Women, New York
Crawford E, Pert A (2020) International humanitarian law. Cambridge University Press, Cambridge
Crowe A (2016) "All the regard due to their sex": women in the Geneva Conventions of 1949. Harvard Research Working Paper Series, HRP
Delpia I (2014) Women in international criminal law. Gend Laws War 39:183–204
Dinstein Y (2016) The conduct of hostilities under the law of international armed conflict. Cambridge University Press, Cambridge
Dörmann K, Lijnzaad L, Sassòli M, Spoerri P (2020) Commentary on the Third Geneva Convention: Convention (III) relative to the treatment of prisoners of war. Cambridge University Press, Cambridge
Durham H, O'Byrne K (2010) The dialogue of difference: gender perspectives on international humanitarian law. IRRC 92:31–52
Ellis E, Watson P (2012) EU anti-discrimination law. Oxford University Press, Oxford
Fenwick H, Hervey TK (1995) Sex equality in the single market: new directions for the European Court of Justice. Common Mark Law Rev 32:443–470
Fourbet P (2002) Does EC pregnancy and maternity legislation create equal opportunities for women in the EC labor market? The European Court of Justice's Interpretation of the EC pregnancy directive in *Boyle* and *Lewen*. Mich J Gend Law 8:219–246
Fredman S (2011) Discrimination law. Oxford University Press, Oxford
Gallo D, Paladine D, Pustorino P (2015) Same-sex couples before national, supranational and international jurisdictions. Springer, Heidelberg
Gardam J, Jarvis MJ (2000) Women and armed conflict: the international response to the Beijing platform for action. Colum Hum Rights Law Rev 32:1–66
Gardam J, Jarvis MJ (2001) Women, armed conflict, and international law. Springer, New York

Giegerich T, Jötten S (2017) Anti-discrimination policy. In: Schmahl S, Breuer M (eds) The Council of Europe. Oxford University Press, Oxford, pp 589–616
Hamilton C, Shepherd LJ (2020) WPS National Action Plans: content analysis and data visualisation, v2. Online, at https://www.wpsnaps.org/, last visited 5 September 2022
Hellum A, Ikdahl I (2019) Committee on the Elimination of Discrimination Against Women (CEDAW), Max Planck Encyclopedia of International Procedural Law (OUP online)
Henckaerts J-M, Doswald-Beck L (2005) Customary international humanitarian law, vol I. Cambridge University Press, Cambridge
Hershey AS (1912) History of international law since the peace of Westphalia. Am J Int Law 6:30–69
Hervey TK (2005) Thirty years of EU sex equality law: looking backwards, looking forwards. Maastricht J Eur Comp Law 12:307–325
Hodson D, Maer I (2001) The open method as a new mode of governance: the case of soft economic policy co-ordination. J Common Mark Stud 39:719–746
Jalloh CC (2020) The legal legacy of the Special Court for Sierra Leone. Cambridge University Press, Cambridge
Kilpatrick C (2014) Article 21 – non-discrimination. In: Peers S, Hervey T, Kenner J, Ward A (eds) The EU Charter of Fundamental Rights. A commentary. Hart Publishing, Oxford/Portland, pp 579–604
Koukoulis-Spiliotopoulos S (2005) The amended equal treatment directive (2002/73): an expression of constituional principles/fundamental rights. Maastricht J Eur Comp Law 12:327–368
Lefevre S (2004) The interpretation of community law by the Court of Justice in areas of national competence. Eur Law Rev 29:501–516
Lewis J (2006) Work/family reconciliation, equal opportunities and social policies. The interpretation of policy trajectories at the EU level and the meaning of gender equality. J Eur Public Policy 13:420–437
Mickliz HW, De Witte B (2012) The European Court of Justice and the Autonomy of Member States. Intersentia, Antwerp
Miller C (1994) "Geneva - the key to equality": inter-war feminists and the League of Nations. Women's Hist Rev 27:219–245
Muir E (2013) The transformative function of the EU equality law. Eur Rev Priv Law 21:1231–1254
Millns S (2017) Gender and constitutionalism in the European Union. In: Irving H (ed) Constitutions and gender. Edward Elgar Publishing, Cheltenham/Northampton, pp 252–267
Muir E (2018) EU equality law. The first fundamental rights policy of the EU. Oxford University Press, Oxford
Muir E, De Witte B (2017) The procedural and institutional dimension of EU anti-discrimination law. In: Rossi LS, Casolari F (eds) The principle of equality in EU law. Springer, Heidelberg, pp 133–149
Mulder J (2017) EU non-discrimination law in the courts. Hart Publishing, Oxford/Portland
Myrttinen H (2018) Locating masculinities in WPS. In: Davies SE, True J (eds) The Oxford handbook of women, peace, and security. Oxford University Press, Oxford
Nagel RU (2020) Gendered preferences: how women's inclusion in society shapes negotiation occurrence in intrastate conflicts. J Peace Res:1–16
Pictet JS (1960) The Geneva Conventions of 12 August 1949: Commentary, vol III. International Committee of the Red Cross, Geneva
Pollack MA, Hafner-Burton E (2000) Mainstreaming gender in the European Union. J Eur Public Policy 3:432–465
Prechal S (2004) Equality of treatment, non-discrimination and social policy: achievements in three themes. Common Mark Law Rev 41:533–551
Prescott JM (2019) Armed conflict, women and climate change. Routledge, London/New York

Rönmar M (2020) Labour and equality law. In: Peers C, Peers S (eds) European Union law. Oxford University Press, Oxford, pp 598–627
Sassòli M (2019) International humanitarian law: rules, controversies, and solutions to problems arising in warfare. Edward Elgar Publishing, Cheltenham/Northampton
Schiek D (2005) Broadening the scope and the norms of EU gender equality law: towards a multidimensional conceptions of equality law. Maastricht J Eur Comp Law 14:427–466
Schiek D (2014) Art. 23. Equality between women and men. In: Peers S, Hervey T, Kenner J, Ward A (eds) The EU Charter of Fundamental Rights. A commentary. Hart Publishing, Oxford/ Portland, pp 633–660
Schiek D, Lawson A (2011) European Union non-discrimination law and intersectionality. Investigating the triangle of racial, gender and disability discrimination. Routledge, London/ New York
Shaw J (2002) The European Union and gender mainstreaming: constitutionally embedded or comprehensively marginalised? Fem Leg Stud 10:213–226
Solanke L (2021) The EU approach to intersectional discrimination in law. In: Abels G, Krizsan A, MacRae H, van der Vleuten A (eds) The Routledge handbook of gender and EU politics. Routledge, London/New York, pp 93–104
Staff S (2019) Human Rights Day 2019: history, the women who shaped the UDHR and theme. https://scroll.in/announcements/946351/human-rights-day-2019-history-the-women-who-shaped-the-udhr-and-theme. Accessed 15 Apr 2021
Tengroth C (2015) The Swedish armed forces and gender in military operations. In: Tengroth C, Lindvall K (eds) IHL and gender: Swedish experiences. Swedish Red Cross, Stockholm, pp 73–77
Thies A (2019) The EU's law and policy framework for the promotion of gender equality in the world. In: Giegerich T (ed) The European Union as protector and promoter of equality. Springer, Heidelberg, pp 429–454
Tridimas T (2006) The general principles of EU law. Oxford University Press, Oxford
Waddington L, Bell M (2021) Similar, yet different: the work-life balance directive and the expanding frontiers of EU non-discrimination law. Common Mark Law Rev 58(5):1401–1432
Weldon-Johns M (2021) EU work-family policies revisited: finally challenging caring roles. Eur Labour Law J 12(3):301–321
Zaccaroni G (2017) Differentiating equality? the different advancements in the protected grounds in the case of the European court of justice. In: Rossi S, Casolari F (eds) The principle of equality in EU law. Springer, Heidelberg, pp 167–195
Zinn H (2015) A people's history of the United States. Harper Collins Publ., New York

Further Reading

Aboueldahab S (2021) Gender-based persecutions a crime against humanity: a milestone for LGBTI rights before the Colombian Special Jurisdiction for Peace. https://www.ejiltalk.org/gender-based-persecution-as-a-crime-against-humanity-a-milestone-for-lgbti-rights-before-the-colombian-special-jurisdiction-for-peace/. Accessed 4 Oct 2021
Bradley SF (2020) Protection of detainees from sexual violence under international humanitarian law. J Confl Secur Law 25:381–422
Charlesworth H, Chinkin C, Wright S (1991) Feminist approaches to international law. Am J Int Law 85:613–645
Chimni BS (2017) Feminist approaches to international law. The work of Hilary Charlesworth and Christine Chinkin. Oxford University Press, Oxford
Chinkin C (1995) Feminist critiques of international law and their critics. Third World Leg Stud 13: 1–16
Chinkin C (2010) Feminism, approach to international law, Max Planck Encyclopedias of International Law

Cichowski RA (2004) Women's rights, the European Court, and supranational constitutionalism. Law Soc Rev 39:489–512

Fellmeth AX (2013) Feminism and international law: theory, methodology and substantive reform. Hum Rights Q 22:658–733

Fredman S (2003) Beyond the dichotomy of formal and substantive equality. Towards a new definition of equal rights. In: Boerefijn I, Coomans P, Goldschmidt J, Holtmaat R, Wolleswinkel R (eds) Temporary special measures. Accelerating de facto equality of women under Article 4(1) UN Convention on the elimination of all forms of discrimination against women. Intersentia, Antwerp, pp 111–118

Freeman MA, Rudolf B, Chinkin C (eds) (2012) The UN convention on the elimination of all forms of discrimination against women: a commentary. Oxford University Press

Mulder J (2020) Indirect sex discrimination in employment. Theoretical analysis and reflections on the CJEU case law and national application of the concept of indirect sex discrimination. https://op.europa.eu/de/publication-detail/-/publication/c7a7c5be-86d1-11eb-ac4c-01aa75ed71al. Accessed 4 Oct 2021

Gender Equality Aspects of Public Law

9

Marko Davinić, Eleonor Kristoffersson, and Tanasije Marinković

Contents

Authors are listed in alphabetical order. The chapter is the result of the collective work of all three authors but that the Sects. 9.2 and 9.3 were written by Tanasije Marinković, Sect. 9.4 by Marko Davinić and Sects. 9.5 and 9.6 by Eleonor Kristoffersson.

M. Davinić (✉) · T. Marinković
University of Belgrade, Faculty of Law, Belgrade, Serbia
e-mail: markod@ius.bg.ac.rs; tanasije.marinkovic@ius.bg.ac.rs

E. Kristoffersson
Örebro University, School of Law, Psychology and Social Work, Örebro, Sweden
e-mail: eleonor.kristoffersson@oru.se

D. Vujadinović et al. (eds.), *Gender-Competent Legal Education*, Springer Textbooks in Law, https://doi.org/10.1007/978-3-031-14360-1_9

Abstract

This chapter portrays the initial appearance of modern public law in late eighteen-century Europe as homocentric, and its gradual profiling, in the centuries to follow, across the globe, as gender-balanced. It also addresses the reforming force of the international instruments in achieving gender-balanced public law on a national level, as well as the inherent limits of those instruments due to the inevitable pluralism of public law approaches to gender equality in areas of reasonable disagreement. Furthermore, authors will analyse structural, institutional, and cultural factors that play a part in the underrepresentation of women at all worldwide governmental levels. However, they emphasise that electing more women in state institutions is only the first step. What is necessary is to ensure that women have a tangible impact on public policies. Thus, they conclude that empowering women is a multi-layered process that is much more complex than choosing an equal number of women in state institutions. Public law aspects on gender-based violence as well as anti-discrimination measures are also included in this chapter.

9.1 Introduction

This chapter deals with fundamental constitutional law and administrative law institutions and their re-evaluation based on the gender equality principle. Readers will be stimulated to better conceive the meaning and importance of the gender equality principle in the area of public law, but also the challenges to its effective implementation.

The second section portrays the development of the modern public law from the homocentric, through the gender-neutral to the gender-competent public law. It points out that the birth of modern public law is very much related to the rise of the secular and liberal state and its upshot: the clear delineation between public and private spheres. This divide contributed in its own way to the exclusion of women from the public realm and their subjection to male domination within the family for over one and a half centuries.

The third section addresses the structural processes on the international and national level bolstering the profiling of gender-competent public law. It emphasises the importance of universalism in public law approaches to gender equality, as embodied in the international instruments which provide focal points for local reforms. However, it also draws attention to the inevitability of pluralism in those approaches in areas of reasonable disagreement, as exemplified by the inherent tensions between freedom of religion and gender equality.

The fourth section deals with representation of women in all levels of government and political life. Subtopics, which will be addressed in this section, are obstacles and of importance to women's political representation, international norms and standards in this area, the role and impact of the Inter-Parliamentary Union (IPU) in the political representation of woman, and the "Women's Power Index," as a new interactive tool.

The fifth section deals with public law and gender-based violence. Not only criminal law, but also public law may play an important role against gender-based violence. In this section, the role of, for example, education law and health care law is discussed.

In the sixth section public law aspects of anti-discrimination law are discussed. Whereas most countries in the world recognise the principle of non-discrimination, its enforcement and the effectiveness of the respective laws vary widely. Measures that are discussed in this section are discrimination ombudsmen, access to justice and information on the legal concept of discrimination.

Learning Goals

- Readers should be able to grasp that gender-balanced public law is the result of a long historical process and that even nowadays there are parts of the world where it is not achieved. As well as this, there is a pluralism of understanding as to what the gender-balanced public law implies.
- Readers should be able to understand the obstacles and importance of women's political representation as well as international norms and standards in this area.
- Readers should be able to understand the relation between gender discrimination and gender-based violence.

9.2 From Homocentric to Gender-Competent Public Law

The struggle for a more gender-balanced public law is historically grounded in the rejection of the public privileges based on gender, and in the understanding that gender equality in the public realm needs to be not only formal but also substantive. This struggle unfolded in a dialectical process, comprising three different stages. In stage one, differences—whether real or constructed, between men and women provided grounds for treating women as inferiors.[1] It is within this homocentric context that the modern public law was born (Sect. 9.2.1). In stage two, women made claims to equality, by stressing similarities between themselves and men and downplaying differences.[2] As a result, public law became more gender-balanced, in fact gender-neutral (Sect. 9.2.2). In stage three, women pursued equality in a way that accounted for differences between genders, without disadvantaging

[1] Rosenfeld (2003), p. 620.

[2] *Ibid.*

themselves.[3] Consequently, gender-competent public law has been gaining momentum (Sect. 9.2.3).

9.2.1 The Birth of Modern (Homocentric) Public Law

Modern public law appeared as a consequence of the switch from both a religious to secular state and from an absolutist to liberal state, at the time of the Enlightenment in eighteen-century Europe.[4] The replacement of the religious paradigm by secularism, relegated the religion (and education which was attached to it) to the private sphere; whereas the triumph of the liberal state reserved economic and social matters to the realm of free market and civil society. The end result was a clear delineation between public and private spheres, which proved to not only be important for the profiling of modern public law, but also for *homocentric* public law.

In ancient and medieval Europe, political power, law and religion were united.[5] Although the two authorities—religion and state—were distinct and occasionally in conflict, they generally cooperated and supported each other.[6] Nevertheless, the attempts of various popes to seize the worldly sword (political authority) in addition to their spiritual sword (religious authority) led to the resistance of princes, kings and emperors and their gradual independence from them. Hence, the emergence of absolutist monarchies, in which the king was the sovereign by the grace of God, but was separated from the church. This paved the way for political authority to become somewhat secularised.[7] With the bourgeois eighteen-century revolutions, such as the American (1776) and French (1789), the process of gradual secularisation of the state was completed. Backed up ideologically by the liberally oriented social contract theories, the concept of a "popular sovereignty, was finally able to replace the concept of sovereignty of the king by the grace of God".[8] Religion was relegated to the private sphere and public law became secular.

Limited government "by consent," implied a fundamental transformation of the understanding of public law. Constitutional and administrative law regulated the public sphere of a liberal state, leaving the economy, religion and family matters to the private realm. Yet, that consent did not encompass women, who were considered to be inferior to men. In this first stage of the dialectical process, unfolding towards a more gender-balanced public law, the difference was correlated to inequality—those who were considered different were legitimately treated better or worse.[9]

[3] *Ibid.*

[4] *Cf.* Raday (2003), p. 663.

[5] Fleiner and Fleiner (2009), p. 309.

[6] *Ibid.*

[7] *Ibid.*, p. 315.

[8] *Ibid.*, p. 316.

[9] Rosenfeld (2003), p. 620.

Example

The fundamental constitutional document of that period, the French Declaration of the Rights of Man and of the Citizen, proclaimed "freedom and equality in rights of *man* at birth" (1789). This prompted Olympe de Gouges to draft the Declaration of the Rights of Woman and of the Female Citizen affirming that "*woman* is born free and remains equal to man in rights" (1791). ◀

Despite these efforts of early feminists, Napoleon's legislation (1804) characterised women as "lifelong, irresponsible minors".[10] Even a century later, public lawyers preached that constitutional equality not only allowed for differences of treatment, including between men and women, but that it ordained them when they derived from the nature of life and social reality.[11]

Democratic revolutionary struggles brought society to the realms of the Enlightenment , leaving nonetheless women in the obscurity of the medieval times. A negative conception of freedom, typical for the public law of the liberal state, cherished "the right to be left to do or be what [he] is able to do or be without interference from other persons, reinforces the status quo of women's social subordination", while concealing it simultaneously.[12] Furthermore, it allowed for domestic violence, which was neither gender-neutral nor random, to be viewed as something "personal", "private" or a "family matter". Hence it was not considered as a human rights violation, *per se*, or was even treated as justified.[13] The systematic exclusion of women from the public realm and their subjection to patriarchal authority within the private sphere of family continuously persisted (see Sects. 9.5 and 9.6 *infra*).

Therefore, the public/private dichotomy came under the attack of the feminist critique very early on (see Feminist Political Theories chapter). "Such a division of spheres, by ignoring the political character of power unequally distributed in family life, does not recognise the political nature of the so-called private life".[14] However, "once we admit the idea that significant differences between men and women are created by the existing division of labo[u]r, within the family, it becomes increasingly obvious just how political of an institution the family is".[15] Furthermore, feminist critique rightly contributed to the understanding of violence against women as a public crime in the sense that beatings "kept women from leaving, [and] kept them providing sexual, housework and child care services as male entitlements".[16]

---

[10] Romany (1994), p. 95.

[11] Orban (1911), p. 117. Quoted in Renauld and Verdussen (2019), p. 150.

[12] Romany (1994), p. 93.

[13] Copelon (1994), pp. 116–117.

[14] Romany (1994), p. 94.

[15] Okin (1989), p. 115. Quoted in: Romany (1994), p. 94.

[16] Romany (1994), p. 95.

9.2.2 Gender-Neutral Public Law

It took more than a hundred years for Olympe de Gouges' fight to start bearing fruits. The gradual change of the *homocentric* paradigm towards more gender-balanced public law took place only in the twentieth century, as a result of various political movements. These movements claimed for the rights of women to be treated like men.[17] In this second stage of the dialectical process, feminist movements argued for political and civil equality by stressing similarities between the sexes and downplaying differences. Since these claims were made in a setting dominated by men, the identity that women had to embrace in their quest for equality was a male-oriented identity.[18]

The first steps to political equality for women were made at the turn of the twentieth century, with the consecration of female suffrage. But even then, women's political equality was understood to be compatible with their civil inequality.[19] "In western liberal democracies, it was not until 1945 and, as a rule, not before the 1960s and 1970s that marriage and family law, regarded as the paradigmatic realms of tradition, were systematically reformed to ensure women's full equality with men [. . .], a task undertaken by constitutional litigation and legal reform in Asia only in the late 1980s and 1990s".[20]

Example

In Germany, female suffrage was recognised in 1918. In the next step, the 1919 Weimar Constitution set forth that "men and women shall as a rule have the same civil rights and duties" (Article 109 (2)). The comprehensive formal equality of men and women was entrenched only in 1949, in the Basic Law (Article 3 (2)). Yet, it was not until the 1970s that gender equality was fully implemented in German family law.[21] ◄

9.2.3 Gender-Competent Public Law

Today, of the 194 constitutions in the world, almost two-thirds guarantee equality on the basis of sex. However, the question remains of how much actual change was made by the worldwide sweep of gender equality provisions.[22]

---

[17] Vujadinović (2019), pp. 99–107.

[18] Rosenfeld (2003), p. 620.

[19] Rubio-Marin and Chang (2013), p. 301.

[20] *Ibid.*

[21] Arnold (2019), pp. 98 and 100–101.

[22] Young (2016), pp. 1 and 3.

For this reason, the "second birth" of modern public law implies not only the embracement of equality for all: men, women, and since recently, non-binary gender (see example *infra*); but also, of substantial equality as opposed to formal equality. The increasing recognition of positive state duties to ensure that gender equality is effectively achieved also calls for the expansion of the reach of public law into what was once free market relations and private domains of marital and family relations.

Example

The Constitution of Argentina empowers the Congress "to legislate and promote positive measures, guaranteeing true equal opportunities and treatment, the full benefit and exercise of the rights recognised by this Constitution and by the international treaties on human rights in force, particularly referring to children, *women*, the aged and disabled persons" (Section 75 (23) emphasis added). ◀

To achieve second stage "equality as identity," (gender-neutral public law) women had to downplay their feminine specificities, which would be perceived as obstacles to access the world of men.[23] For example, the women's right to political equality could only be conceived in the same terms as the free suffrage for men. However, in stage three, women pursued equality in a way that accounted for differences between the genders without disadvantaging themselves. For instance, they demanded gender quotas for electoral lists so that they could be effectively empowered, whilst not renouncing their marital, family and other life roles (see Sect. 9.4 *infra*).

The need to confront the social reality and fight effectively against gender inequalities has led to the internationalisation of fundamental rights (see Sect. 9.3 *infra*). This trend has imposed international obligations upon states, extending the domain of public law and of their responsibility. For example, the 2011 Council of Europe Convention on Combating Violence Against Women and Domestic Violence (Istanbul Convention) binds the states to "take the necessary legislative and other measures to promote and protect the right for everyone, particularly women, to live free from violence in both the public and private sphere" (Article 4).

Furthermore, gender-sensitive public law goes beyond binary female-male understanding of gender equality.

Example

Correlating difference to equality, the German Federal Constitutional Court found in 2017 that the German Civil Status Act violated the fundamental right to free development of personality by not allowing for the positive entry in the birth register of a non-binary legal gender option. The proceedings were brought by a complainant who had been assigned the female sex and who had been

[23] Rosenfeld (2003), p. 620.

registered as a girl in the birth register; but who had an atypical set of chromosomes (so-called Turner syndrome), and permanently identified neither as female nor as male. The complainant filed an application for a positive entry as "inter/diverse" in the birth register. However, the registry office rejected the application, claiming that the Civil Status Act did not permit such an entry.[24] The Federal Constitutional Court held that the general right of free development of personality, protected under Article 2 (1) of the German Basic Law, included the protection of the gender identity "which is usually a constitutive aspect of an individual's personality".[25] More specifically, the Court reasoned that "the official assignment of sex is of paramount importance for one's individual identity [. . .]: sex determines entitlements and obligations provided for by law; it also often forms the basis for identifying a person, and, beyond legal provisions, gender identity is also significant in everyday life"; and that "the gender identity of persons who can be assigned neither the male nor the female sex is protected as well".[26] As a result, the Court considered that the Civil Status Act interfered "with the general right of personality in its manifestation as protection of one's gender identity".[27] For that purpose, the Court recalled that under civil status law, a person's sex had to be documented in the birth register; that the only positive categories available for this were "female" and "male"; and, that there was no further category. Thus the Court concluded that if a child could not be assigned either the female or the male sex, no positive entry could be made in the birth register; and that the complainant had to tolerate an entry that did not correspond to their constitutionally protected gender identity.[28] ◀

9.3 Universalism and Pluralism in the Public Law Approaches to Gender Equality

Whereas the previous chapter exposes the unfolding dialectical processes leading to the gender-competent public law, this chapter attempts to elucidate the structural developments on the international and national level buttressing these trends. In that respect, legal norms embodied in the international instruments such as the 1950 European Convention on Human Rights, the 1966 International Covenant on Civil and Political Rights, the 1979 Convention on the Elimination of all Forms of Discrimination Against Women (CEDAW), or the Istanbul Convention, and in the practice of their (quasi-)judicial institutions, provide focal points for local reforms

[24] 1 BvR 2019/16 (10 October 2017) [English translation of the ruling provided by the Federal Constitutional Court], para. 1.

[25] *Ibid.*, paras. 38–39.

[26] *Ibid.*, paras. 39–40.

[27] *Ibid.*, para. 42.

[28] *Ibid.*

and fight against discriminatory cultural patterns. They symbolise the universalism in public law approaches to gender equality (Sect. 9.3.1).

Although gender-balanced public law is gaining momentum across the world, there are still numerous sub-groups and whole societies where patriarchy prevails. Stereotyping women exclusively as mothers and housewives, in a way that limits their opportunity to participate in public life, is widespread even nowadays: in Kuwait women were until recently (2005) ineligible for public posts.[29] Similarly, while Germany introduced the non-binary gender option for official records, in Benin, Senegal or the Ivory Coast, intersex is a social taboo.[30] It follows that public law responses to gender inequalities are very much culturally predetermined.

Hence, there is not merely one universal version of gender equality, just as there is more than one school of feminism. Accordingly, there will often be a wide range of public law issues that constitutional and administrative law aiming for gender equality should consider. A pluralism of legitimate approaches should address them, especially in areas of reasonable disagreement. These areas normally appear when the wide margin of appreciation is accorded to the Member States or when the (quasi-)judicial institutions, established by the international instruments, take divergent positions to the same set of legal issues (Sect. 9.3.2).

9.3.1 Universalism in Public Law Approaches to Gender Equality

Contemporary development of public law, in particular of constitutional law, is marked by the interplay between the international and national legal systems, leading to the internationalisation of constitutionally entrenched fundamental rights. The internationalisation of constitutional law took place through the vertical convergence of international law norms and constitutional texts, as well as of the case-law of the (quasi-)judicial bodies entrusted with their enforcement. Good domestic practices, which have been previously "upgraded" to international standards, serve both as principles governing the functioning of international institutions and as points of reference for the evaluation of national public law norms. The vertical convergence is manifested in the international law's impact on the national constitution-making, public law reforms and judge-made law.[31]

Example

The Canadian Charter of Rights and Freedoms incorporates two international covenants—one on Civil and Political Rights and one on Economic, Social and Cultural Rights. Both covenants guarantee gender equality, while no fewer than

[29] Al Fili (2019), p. 371.

[30] Niasse (2019), p. 432.

[31] Peters and Preuss (2013), p. 34.

15 international human rights documents are annexed to the Constitution of Bosnia and Herzegovina, including the CEDAW. ◄

Rubio-Marin and Morgan categorised domestic public law incorporations of gender rights flowing from international legal instruments. Accordingly, there are three major forms of incorporation of international human rights law: assimilation, supplementation and adaptation. Assimilation takes place in the moments of constitution-making and constitution-amending, when international human rights law directly influences the drafting of fundamental domestic rights. Supplementation is manifested in the constitutionally mandated hierarchical ordering of international and national law in such a way that they become an integrated system of internally applicable law. Adaptation involves processes, be they constitutionally required or judicially constructed, through which the interpretation and application of the fundamental domestic rights is influenced by international law. These types of incorporations of international gender norms and jurisprudence have helped shape domestic public law, in a number of countries, either by expanding, complementing or concretising relevant constitutional provisions.[32]

CEDAW has been particularly praised for its accomplishment on behalf of gender equality. It has been argued that even when national governments have hypocritical commitment to women's equality, the activists are given a basis for action and for demanding more equality. Much of the CEDAW Committee's work, in reviewing country reports and identifying the next steps for countries seeking to achieve CEDAW's goals, has received the approval of professionals defending different strands of feminism.[33] Yet, the CEDAW Committee process has also raised concerns for being insufficiently sensitive to the pluralism of its state parties. Jackson draws attention to the impulse to standardise from the top down, under the CEDAW regime in areas of reasonable disagreement.[34] Relying on the arguments of feminist pluralism, constitutional diversity and epistemological humility, she claims that there may be benefits of a certain degree of "space" between international human rights treaties, as interpreted by their expert committees, and the regimes of national law.[35]

9.3.2 Pluralism in Public Law Approaches to Gender Equality

The dialectical march towards gender-competent public law did not end the dilemma as to the best way of achieving gender equality. As it was previously shown, universalism did provide for some guidance in that respect, but has also been criticised for its tendencies to impose too singular a vision. Also, there are areas in

[32] Rubio-Marin and Morgan (2006), pp. 115 and 118–119.

[33] Jackson (2016), p. 449.

[34] *Ibid.*, p. 450.

[35] *Ibid.*, p. 462.

which international instruments purposefully accord a wide margin of appreciation to the Member States; or in which the (quasi-)judicial institutions, established by those instruments, take different or even opposing positions to the same set of legal issues.

Public law performs multiple functions. Other than also setting gender equality, it provides the frameworks for the protection of rights and liberties. In that sense, gender equality commitments may come into conflict with other rights-based commitments.[36] One of those rights, standing very high on the list of public law commitments, is the right to freedom of religion.

In the words of the ECtHR, freedom of religion is "one of the most vital elements that go to make up the identity of believers and their conception of life" and it entails "freedom to hold [...] religious beliefs and to practice [...] religion".[37] The relegation of religion to the private sphere did make public law secular and free from religion (see Sect. 9.2 *supra*), but it did not free the state from the duty to secure the exercise of religious freedom through public law mechanisms. The ECtHR "has frequently emphasised the State's role as the neutral and impartial organiser of the exercise of various religions," as well as that the "State's duty of neutrality and impartiality is incompatible with any power on the State's part to assess [...] the ways in which those beliefs are exercised".[38]

While religion is so highly valued, due to its importance for the identity of believers, many of the religious practices support patriarchal gender relations, specifically the subjection of women to male domination within the family.[39] One of those religious practices, with respect to which there is a reasonable disagreement across the globe, is the dress code for Muslim women in public spaces. Four types of female coverings have been the object of intensive legal debates for the past three decades: the hijab (a headscarf tied under the chin), the burka (a full-body covering including a mesh over the face), the niqab (a full-face veil leaving an opening only for the eyes) and the burkini (a full body swimsuit). The clash between cultural-religious and gender equality arguments "has risen as a constitutional issue in secular countries, where religious Muslim communities demand that their women and girls observe the dress code".[40] In theocratic Islamic states, a woman's dress code is mandatory and severely punishable for any breach.[41]

There has been a series of administrative and judicial cases on the wearing of the hijab in educational institutions and workplaces in France,[42] Switzerland,[43] and Turkey.

---

[36] *Cf. Ibid.*, pp. 460–461.

[37] App. No. 44774/98, *Case of Leyla Sahin v. Turkey* [GC] (ECtHR, 10 November 2005), para. 104.

[38] *Ibid.*, para. 107.

[39] Raday (2003), p. 672.

[40] *Ibid.*, p. 690.

[41] *Ibid.*

[42] Roman (2019), pp. 285–286.

[43] Hottelier and Carron (2019), pp. 473–474.

Example

The ECtHR considered that the ban on wearing the Islamic headscarf in institutions of higher education, in Turkey, did not constitute an unjustified interference with the right to freedom of religion as guaranteed by the European Convention on Human Rights. In reaching this ruling, the ECtHR pointed out the Member States' margin of appreciation and took into account, *inter alia*, the emphasis placed in the Turkish constitutional system on the protection of the rights of women and gender equality; as well as that the ban applied to universities in which the equality before the law of men and women was being taught and practiced.[44] ◄

The conflicts over wearing burkas and niqabs in public places have arisen as major political and even constitutional issues in France,[45] Belgium,[46] Italy,[47] Norway,[48] and Switzerland.[49]

Example

When the question of prohibition, regarding the wearing of clothing, designed to conceal the face in public, came before the ECtHR, it held again that this measure was not an unjustified interference with the right to freedom of religion, as guaranteed by the Convention "having regard in particular to the breadth of the margin of appreciation afforded to the respondent State in the present case".[50] However, the ECtHR considered that such a measure could not have been justified "in the name of gender equality", but for the purpose of the constitutional concept of "living together".[51] In contrast, the United Nation's Human Rights Committee took the view that that same prohibition violated the freedom of religion and the prohibition of discrimination based on gender and religion, as guaranteed by articles 18 and 26 of the International Covenant on Civil and Political Rights.[52] The Committee observed, inter alia, that the concept of "living together" was very vague and abstract, and that the "State party has not identified any specific fundamental rights or freedoms of others that are affected by the fact

[44] App. No. 44774/98, *Case* of *Leyla Sahin v. Turkey* [GC], paras. 115–116.

[45] Roman (2019), pp. 286–287.

[46] Renauld and Verdussen (2019), pp. 172–173.

[47] Luciani (2019), pp. 346–347.

[48] Smith (2019), p. 378.

[49] Hottelier and Carron (2019), pp. 474–475.

[50] App. No. 43835/11, Case of *S. A. S. c. France* [GC] (ECtHR, 1 July 2014), paras. 129, 155 and 157.

[51] *Ibid.*, paras. 119 and 121–122.

[52] CCPR, C/123/D/2807/2016, Case of *Miriana Hebbadj v. France*, paras. 7.17 and 8; CCPR, C/123/D/2747/2016, Case of *Sonia Yaker v. France*, paras. 8.17 and 9.

that some people present in the public space have their face covered, including fully veiled women".[53] ◀

Finally, even "Islam on the beach" had its administrative and judicial repercussions. In the summer of 2016, certain municipal authorities on the French Riviera banned the use of the full body swim-suits on their beaches, under the pretext that this type of clothing was contrary to the principle of secularism and/or that the ban was protecting the public order. On the one hand, the administrative judges did not accept the argument of secularism considering that it was a principle which imposed obligations upon the public authorities and not the individuals. On the other hand, the protection of public order was a legitimate aim for the limitation of an individual, since there were cases of violence between the Maghrebinian families, whose female members were wearing hijabs or burkas, and the locals.[54] However, it remained unclear how the wearing of these garments on the beach, such as the hijab or burka, could in itself disturb public order. The idea to ban the wearing of the burkini on the beach was also present at the time in Belgium.[55]

9.4 Representation of Women in All Levels of Government and Political Life

9.4.1 Obstacles and Importance of Women's Political Representation

Although women constitute approximately one half of the world population, they are underrepresented at all governmental levels around the world. Multiple structural, institutional and cultural factors play a part in the current situation, where women are politically underrepresented. Many studies show a direct correlation between the social and economic position of women in society and their participation in political life.[56] Thus, "socio-economic obstacles include poverty and unemployment, lack of adequate financial resources, illiteracy and limited access to education, choice of professions and the 'dual burden' of family and a full-time job. Women take on a disproportionate share of household tasks which makes a political career almost impossible."[57] In addition, institutional barriers are usually an important reason for systematic differences in women's representation between comparable societies. For

[53] *Miriana Hebbadj v. France*, para. 7.10; *Sonia Yaker v. France*, para. 8.10.

[54] Hochmann, https://verfassungsblog.de/islam-on-the-beach-the-burkini-ban-in-france/, accessed October 17, 2021; Roman (2019), p. 286.

[55] Renauld and Verdussen (2019), p. 173.

[56] Delys (2014), p. 8.

[57] Bari, https://www.un.org/womenwatch/daw/egm/enabling-environment2005/docs/EGM-WPD-EE-2005-EP.12%20%20draft%20F.pdf, last accessed October 17, 2021; Quoted in: Delys (2014), p. 8.

example, difficulties in obtaining support from political parties and securing campaign funding. Moreover, "many studies showed that much more women are being elected under proportional party lists, in contrast to majoritarian single-member constituencies".[58] In that sense, the proportional representation system "provides an incentive for parties to broaden their appeal by adding women to their party lists. The majoritarian single-member system, in contrast, usually only allows for one candidate per district to be chosen".[59] Finally, the political culture is often based on traditional attitudes regarding women, emphasising women's primary roles as mothers and housewives, not as decision-makers.[60]

Example

The President of the European Commission Ursula von der Leyen expressed her feelings regarding a diplomatic protocol incident ("Sofagate") that happened during her visit to Turkey in April 2021. Only two chairs were prepared for the three presidents in the room: "I am the first woman to be President of the European Commission. I am the President of the European Commission. And this is how I expected to be treated when visiting Turkey two weeks ago, like a Commission President, but I was not. I cannot find any justification for the way I was treated in the European Treaties. So, I have to conclude, it happened because I am a woman. Would this have happened if I had worn a suit and a tie? In the pictures of previous meetings, I did not see any shortage of chairs. But then again, I did not see any women in these pictures, either."[61] ◄

There are different arguments which are brought forward when discussing the importance of women's representation. "The justice argument claims that women have a right to half of the seats since they make up half of the population; the experience argument holds that women have different experiences, either biologically or socially constructed, that should be represented as well; the interest argument grants that women and men have conflicting interests and that these interests cannot be represented by men; the symbolic argument says that every female politician acts a role model for all women, regardless of political views or party membership and will attract other women to the political arena; the critical mass argument states that women are able to achieve solidarity of purpose to represent women's interests when they achieve certain levels of representation; and the democracy argument asserts that the equal representation of women and men

[58] Norris (2000), pp. 348–351; Quoted in: Delys (2014), p. 9.

[59] *Ibid*, p. 9.

[60] *Ibid*, pp. 9–10.

[61] *Speech by President von der Leyen at the European Parliament Plenary on the conclusions of the European Council meeting of 25-26 March 2021 and the outcome of the high-level meeting between the EU and Turkey*, 26 April 2021: https://ec.europa.eu/commission/presscorner/detail/en/speech_21_1965.

enhances the democratization of governance in both transitional and consolidated democracies."[62]

Many authors emphasise the importance of 'critical mass' for women's political representation, which means that only a considerable minority of women will be able to impose topics which are important for them and to encourage other females to enter the political arena.[63] Furthermore, Atkeson suggests that "viable women candidates lead women to feel more connected to and a part of the political system in a way that they do not when they look around and see only men".[64]

Example

Upon reflecting on her historic run for the US vice-presidency in 1984, as the first female vice-presidential nominee, representing a major American political party, Geraldine Ferraro stated that, "women across the country have told me what a huge personal impact my nomination had on their lives. Many took risks and tried new challenges, saying, 'If you could do it, so could I.' Others have thanked me for opening doors."[65] ◄

Of course, it is not just about the sheer number of women in politics that is at stake, but also the quality of their activities and their sensitivity for gender equality approaches. This cultural (mindset) approach should not be overlooked when discussing women's political representation.

9.4.2 International Norms and Standards in the Area of Political Participation of Women

A number of international norms and standards relate to women's leadership and political participation. Among them the most prominent are:

- The 2011 UN General Assembly resolution on women's political participation (A/RES/66/130)
- The 2003 UN General Assembly resolution on women's political participation (A/RES/58/142)
- Council of Europe, Recommendation Rec (2003) 3 of the Committee of Ministers on balanced participation of women and men in political and public decision making
- The 1995 Beijing Declaration and Platform for Action
- The UN Economic and Social Council resolution 1990/15

[62] Dahlerup (1978), pp. 139–162; Quoted in: Delys (2014), pp. 7–8.

[63] Similar in: Delys (2014), p. 11.

[64] Atkeson (2003), p. 1043.

[65] *Ibid*, pp. 1043–1044.

- The 1979 Convention on the Elimination of All Forms of Discrimination against Women (CEDAW)[66]

It is important to emphasise that some of the listed documents regulate solely on the area of political participation of women, while others have a broader scope, regulating political and other types of participation.

The 2011 UN General Assembly resolution on women's political participation (A/RES/66/130) highlighted that "the active participation of women, on equal terms with men, at all levels of decision-making is essential to the achievement of equality, sustainable development, peace and democracy", and that "women in every part of the world continue to be largely marginalised from the political sphere, often as a result of discriminatory laws, practices, attitudes and gender stereotypes, low levels of education, lack of access to health care and the disproportionate effect of poverty on women". The General Assembly "reaffirms its resolution 58/142 of 22 December 2003 on women and political participation, and calls upon all States to implement it fully". Furthermore, it "calls upon all States to eliminate laws, regulations and practices that, in a discriminatory manner, prevent or restrict women's participation in the political process". The General Assembly urged all States to take numerous actions to that end.[67]

The 2003 UN General Assembly resolution on women's political participation (A/RES/58/142) affirmed that "the empowerment and autonomy of women and the improvement of their political, social and economic status are essential to the achievement of representative, transparent and accountable government, democratic institutions and sustainable development in all areas of life". Furthermore, it recognised "that the active participation of women, on equal terms with men, at all levels of decision-making is essential to the achievement of equality, sustainable development, peace and democracy". However, this document expressed concerns that, "despite general acceptance of the need for gender balance in decision-making bodies at all levels, women are still largely underrepresented at most levels of government, especially in ministerial and other executive bodies, and in legislative bodies". Taking all that into account, the General Assembly urged states and invited the private sector, non-governmental organisations and other actors of civil society, to take appropriate measures to strengthen the process of political participation of women.[68]

Council of Europe, Recommendation Rec (2003) 3 of the Committee of Ministers on balanced participation of women and men in political and public decision-making, recommended that the governments of Member States, among

[66] UN Women, *Global norms and standards: Leadership and political participation*: https://www.unwomen.org/en/what-we-do/leadership-and-political-participation/global-norms-and-standards.

[67] The 2011 UN General Assembly resolution on women's political participation (A/RES/66/130): https://www.un.org/ga/search/view_doc.asp?symbol=A/RES/66/130.

[68] The 2003 UN General Assembly resolution on women's political participation (A/RES/58/142): https://www.un.org/ga/search/view_doc.asp?symbol=A/RES/58/142.

other things, "commit themselves to promote balanced representation of women and men by recognising publicly that the equal sharing of decision-making power between women and men of different background and ages strengthens and enriches democracy".[69]

Example

"For the purpose of this recommendation, balanced participation of women and men is taken to mean that the representation of either women or men in any decision-making body in political or public life should not fall below 40%".[70] ◀

The 1995 Beijing Declaration and Platform for Action was adopted by 189 UN Member States and is still considered to be the most ambitious and progressive document ever made for advancing women's rights. It made comprehensive commitments under 12 critical areas of concern and has remained a powerful source of guidance and inspiration.[71] One of those areas is called "Women in power and decision-making" and it is acknowledged in the Declaration that "without the active participation of women and the incorporation of women's perspective at all levels of decision-making, the goals of equality, development and peace cannot be achieved" (para. 181). It is also recognised that "despite the widespread movement towards democratisation in most countries, women are largely underrepresented at most levels of government, especially in ministerial and other executive bodies and have made little progress in attaining political power in legislative bodies" (para. 182). The Platform for Action envisages measures which should provide women's equal access to and full participation in power structures and decision-making (Strategic objective G.1) and increase women's capacity to participate in decision-making and leadership (Strategic objective G.2). Those actions are expected to be taken from different actors: the UN, governments, international organisations, national bodies, the private sector, political parties, trade unions, employers' organisations, research and academic institutions, subregional and regional bodies, non-governmental and women's organizations, and industrial and professional entities.[72]

The UN Economic and Social Council resolution 1990/15, among other actions, called on governments, political parties, trade unions, professional and other representative groups "to increase the proportion of women in leadership positions to at

[69] Council of Europe, Recommendation Rec (2003) 3 of the Committee of Ministers to member states on balanced participation of women and men in political and public decision making, paragraph 1: https://rm.coe.int/1680519084.

[70] Appendix to Recommendation Rec (2003) 3.

[71] UN Women, *The Beijing Platform for Action: inspiration then and now*: https://beijing20.unwomen.org/en/about.

[72] Beijing Declaration and Platform for Action, Beijing+5 Political Declaration and Outcome, UN Women, United Nations 1995, reprinted by UN Women in 2014, pp. 119–126: https://beijing20.unwomen.org/~/media/headquarters/attachments/sections/csw/pfa_e_final_web.pdf#page=125.

least 30 percent by 1995. This was suggested in order to achieve equal representation between women and men by the year 2000". Further, to "institute recruitment and training programmes to prepare women for those positions".[73]

The Convention on the Elimination of All Forms of Discrimination against Women (CEDAW) was adopted by the United Nations General Assembly in December 1979 and entered into force as an international treaty in September 1981.[74] Political participation is regulated in two articles in this document. In Article 7, it stipulates that states "shall take all appropriate measures to eliminate discrimination against women in the political and public life of the country and, in particular, shall ensure to women, on equal terms with men, the right: (a) to vote in all elections and public referenda and to be eligible for election to all publicly elected bodies; (b) to participate in the formulation of government policy and the implementation thereof and to hold public office and perform all public functions at all levels of government; (c) to participate in non-governmental organisations and associations concerned with the public and political life of the country". Furthermore, Article 8 of the Convention regulates, that states "shall take all appropriate measures to ensure to women, on equal terms with men and without any discrimination, the opportunity to represent their Governments at the international level and to participate in the work of international organisations".[75]

9.4.3 The Role of the Inter-Parliamentary Union (IPU) in the Political Representation of Women

The Inter-Parliamentary Union (IPU) is one of the leading international organisations for the empowerment of women. Its work is directed towards three main objectives: "increasing the number of women in parliament through well-designed quotas and parliamentary caucuses, supporting women in parliament, and transforming parliaments into gender-sensitive institutions that deliver on women's rights".[76] Furthermore, the IPU has recognised gender equality as a key component of democracy in its documents. For example, in the 1997 Universal Declaration on Democracy, the IPU highlighted "the direct link between democracy and the balanced participation of men and women in politics, and in particular in parliament".[77]

[73]The UN Economic and Social Council resolution 1990/15: https://www.un.org/ga/search/view_doc.asp?symbol=E/1990/90.

[74]Convention on the Elimination of All Forms of Discrimination against Women New York, 18 December 1979: https://www.ohchr.org/EN/ProfessionalInterest/Pages/CEDAW.aspx.

[75]Convention on the Elimination of All Forms of Discrimination against Women New York, 18 December 1979: https://www.ohchr.org/EN/ProfessionalInterest/Pages/CEDAW.aspx.

[76]See: IPU, *Gender Equality*: https://www.ipu.org/our-impact/gender-equality.

[77]*Implementation of the IPU Strategy for 2012-2017, Gender Mainstreaming at IPU*, IPU Governing Council, Geneva, 9 October 2013, p. 1: https://www.ipu.org/about-ipu/gender-equal-ipu.

According to data from the Inter-Parliamentary Union (IPU), "with a global average of 25 per cent women, most parliaments remain male-dominated, and women MPs are often under-represented on decision-making bodies."[78]

Regarding women's participation in parliament, one can conclude from relevant data that constant progress has been evident in the previous years. However it is still insufficient and slow. It means that at the current rate, it would take "another 50 years before gender parity is achieved in parliaments worldwide".[79]

Example

"The United States made history in 2020 with the election for the first time of a woman as Vice President. Vice President Kamala Harris also constitutionally becomes President of the Senate. With Nancy Pelosi as Speaker of the House of Representatives, both chambers of the US Congress are now presided over by women".[80] ◄

As far as women ministers are concerned, they mainly cover areas of social and women's affairs, gender equality, environment and energy. However, as of 1 January 2021, there are just 13 countries with women holding 50 per cent or more ministerial positions.[81]

Example

Countries with women holding one half or more ministerial positions are as follows: Nicaragua—58.82%, Austria—57.14%, Belgium—57.14%, Sweden—57.14%, Albania—56.25%, Rwanda—54.84%, Costa Rica—52.00%, Canada—51.43%, Andorra, Finland, France, Guinea-Bissau, Spain—50.00%.[82] ◄

Despite overall improvement across the globe, the number of countries with no women ministers as of 1 January 2021 increased to 12, compared to nine in the year before.[83]

Example

As of 1 January 2021, there are no women in the governments of Azerbaijan, Armenia, Brunei Darussalam, D.P.R. Korea, Papua New Guinea, Saint Vincent

[78] IPU, *Gender Equality*: https://www.ipu.org/our-impact/gender-equality.

[79] *Proportion of women MPs inches up but gender parity still far off* (published on: 5. 3. 2021): https://www.ipu.org/news/women-in-parliament-2020.

[80] *Ibid.*

[81] Women in politics: new data shows growth but also setbacks, (published on 10. 3. 2021): https://www.ipu.org/news/women-in-politics-2021.

[82] *Ibid.*

[83] *Ibid.*

and the Grenadines, Saudi Arabia, Thailand, Tuvalu, Vanuatu, Vietnam and Yemen.[84] ◀

The IPU and the CEDAW Committee have urged parliaments and governments worldwide to adopt National Action Plans in order to reach the goal of gender parity in politics by 2030. The main measures to be taken to achieve this goal are as follows:

1. Reforming legal frameworks, which implies:
   - Adoption of electoral gender quotas (as reserved seats, legal candidate quotes or political party quotes);
   - Reformation and enactment of comprehensive legislation that guarantees gender equality in all areas of life;
   - Limitation on spending on electoral campaigns;
2. Making institutions gender-sensitive and gender-responsive, which implies:
   - Adopting the target of parity in all spheres of public life, at both the national and subnational levels;
   - Ensuring that internal rules and codes of ethics help prevent all forms of discrimination and gender-based violence against women
   - Establishing mechanisms for gender mainstreaming in state institutions.
3. Ensuring a conducive environment for gender equality, which implies:
   - Fighting against negative gender stereotypes;
   - Mobilising all media formats in order to implement information campaigns and raise awareness on the importance of this issue;
   - Reorganisation of political parties to be more favourable for women's participation;
   - Protecting and supporting women's human rights defenders and NGO representatives;
   - Promoting gender equality in educational curriculum.[85]

Example

"The Liberal Democrats in the UK wondered what it was that kept women out of politics and set up a campaign with the name "Cash, Confidence and Culture" which addresses the three main obstacles newcomers in politics face."[86] ◀

[84] *Ibid.*

[85] *Joint Call by IPU and CEDAW Committee on International Women's Day 2021*, (published on: 8. 3. 2021): https://www.ipu.org/iwd-2021-statement; About importance of gender quotas, see also: Giegerich (2021), https://jean-monnet-saar.eu/wp-content/uploads/2021/05/Symposium-Gender-Parity_updated-version_II.pdf.

[86] See: Delys (2014), p. 19.

Electoral gender quotas have appeared as one of the main instruments for tackling the underrepresentation of women around the world and have been introduced in more than 130 countries in the last few decades.[87] In general, there are three main types of electoral gender quotas:

1. Political party quotas (voluntary party quotas)
2. Candidate quotas
3. Reserved seats

Political party quotas are not regulated by law. Instead, they are introduced by the internal acts of the parties (they are voluntary, not mandatory for parties), and they usually determine the minimum number of seats that must belong to women on electoral lists (for example, 40%). On the other hand, candidate quotas and reserved seats are introduced by national legal acts (Constitution or election laws). The differences between them is that candidate quotas require the percentage of women on electoral lists of political parties (in this case, it is not voluntary), while reserved seats determine the percentage of women who must be elected (share of women in institutions after the elections).

Reserved seats provide more guarantees for the election of a woman than any other option. Thus, introducing candidate quotas requiring a certain minimum of each gender on an electoral list (for example, 40%) does not automatically result in women winning that percent of seats. Political parties may meet that requirement, but they can place women at the bottom of the lists, making their election much more difficult.[88]

Some may argue that "quotas imply that politicians are elected because of their gender, not because of their qualifications." On the other hand, there is a counterargument that "women are just as qualified as men, but women's qualifications are downgraded and minimised in a male-dominated political system".[89]

However, setting quotas for women isn't a silver bullet for achieving gender equity and well-being. Thus, it is emphasised that "one cannot deal with the problem of female representation by a quota system alone. Political parties, the educational system, NGOs, trade unions, churches—all must take responsibility within their own organisations to systematically promote women's participation, from the bottom up [...]".[90]

---

[87] Krook and Zetterberg (2017), p. 1; See also the Global Database of Gender Quotas in parliaments worldwide, as a joint project of International IDEA, Inter-Parliamentary Union and Stockholm University: https://www.idea.int/data-tools/data/gender-quotas/country-overview.

[88] Dahlerup (2005), p. 150.

[89] *Ibid*, pp. 143–144.

[90] Dahl, former Speaker of Swedish Parliament, quoted in Dahlerup (2005), p. 143.

9.4.4 The Women's Power Index

In 2020, the Women and Foreign Policy program launched the "Women's Power Index" as a new interactive tool. It ranks 193 UN Member States according to their progress toward gender parity in political participation and analyses the proportion of women who serve as heads of state or government, in cabinets, national legislatures, as candidates for national legislatures, local government bodies, and visualises the gender gap in political representation.[91] The index points out that the number of female heads of states has increased over the last three decades. Nevertheless, women remain underrepresented at all levels of government.[92]

Example

As of March 29, 2021, out of 193 countries only 22 have a female head of state or government. Only 13 have at least 50 percent women in the national cabinet and only three have at least 50 percent women in the national legislature.[93] ◄

Vogelstein and Bro argue that political representation of women is important for a multitude of reasons. They summed up that , "increasing women's political representation is not simply a matter of fairness -- it is also a strategic imperative".[94] Firstly, women are more likely to cross party lines to find common ground. In that way, they manage to overcome the differences much easier than their male counterparts.[95] Furthermore, experience shows that female lawmakers are more likely to advocate for policies that support social welfare, health, education and gender equality, especially laws on parental leave and childcare, domestic violence, rape and sexual harassment.[96]

Example

"Research on *panchayats* (local councils) in India discovered that the number of drinking water projects in areas with women-led councils was 62 per cent higher than in those with men-led councils. In Norway, a direct causal relationship

[91] See: Vogelstein and Bro (2020), *Women's Power Index*: https://www.cfr.org/article/womens-power-index; See also: https://www.unwomen.org/-/media/headquarters/attachments/sections/library/publications/2020/women-in-politics-map-2020-en.pdf?la=en&vs=827.

[92] Vogelstein and Bro (2020): https://www.cfr.org/blog/womens-power-index-tracks-womens-political-representation.

[93] Vogelstein and Bro (2020), *Women's Power Index*: https://www.cfr.org/article/womens-power-index.

[94] Vogelstein and Bro (2018), https://edition.cnn.com/2018/11/09/opinions/year-of-woman-goes-global-bro-vogelstein/index.html.

[95] *Ibid.*

[96] *Ibid.*

between the presence of women in municipal councils and childcare coverage was found".[97] ◀

Finally, women in politics promote stability of the country and reduce the possibility for state-perpetrated human rights abuses, such as political imprisonment, torture, disappearances, killings and even decrease the risk of international conflict.[98]

Example

One study found that, "as the percentage of women in the legislature increases by 5%, a state is nearly 5 times (4.86) less likely to use violence. At a normative level, this also suggests that the pursuit of gender equality in societies throughout the world may have positive effects for the lessening of violence at national, transnational, and international levels".[99] ◀

Vogelstein and Bro point out that "electing women does not guarantee those outcomes. Holding political office is just the first step to wielding political power; in many countries, institutional structures and political systems still limit women's ability to influence policy. Women are not a homogenous group, and not all female leaders will be cooperative, peaceful, or advocate for laws that strengthen gender equality [. . .]. Regardless of outcome, as the number of women leaders increases, more women will likely be inspired to become politically engaged."[100]

9.5 Public Law and Gender-Based Violence

Gender-based violence may be defined as "violence that reflects the existing asymmetry in the power relations between men and women and that perpetuates the subordination and devaluation of the female as opposed to the male".[101] Gender-based violence is a health issue that threatens girls' and women's wellbeing, health, and overall life quality all over the world. Gender-based violence occurs both in peacetime and in war. Rape, sexual slavery, enforced prostitution, forced pregnancy, enforced sterilisation and any other form of sexual violence of comparable gravity are, under the Statute of Rome, considered as a crime against humanity when committed as a part of a widespread or systematic attack directed against any civilian

[97] UN women: *Facts and figures: Leadership and political participation*: https://www.unwomen.org/en/what-we-do/leadership-and-political-participation/facts-and-figures.

[98] Vogelstein and Bro (2018), https://edition.cnn.com/2018/11/09/opinions/year-of-woman-goes-global-bro-vogelstein/index.html.

[99] Caprioli and Boyer (2001), p. 514.

[100] Vogelstein and Bro (2021), *Women's Power Index*: https://www.cfr.org/article/womens-power-index#chapter-title-0-2LC/.

[101] Reed et al. (2010), p. 348.

population with knowledge of the attack.[102] According to the World Health Organisation (WHO), one third of the women in the world have experienced sexual and/or physically intimate partner violence.[103] Equally, almost one third (27%) of the women aged 15–49 years who have been in a relationship, report that they have been subjected to a form of physical and/or sexual violence from their partner.[104] Globally, 38% of all murders of women are committed by intimate partners.[105]

The WHO defines intimate partner violence as "a behaviour by an intimate partner or ex-partner that causes physical, sexual or psychological harm, including physical aggression, sexual coercion, psychological abuse and controlling behaviours. Sexual violence is any sexual act, attempt to obtain a sexual act, or other act directed against a person's sexuality using coercion, by any person regardless of their relationship to the victim, in any setting".[106] Sexual violence includes, according to the WHO, "rape, defined as the physically forced or otherwise coerced penetration of the vulva or anus with a penis, other body part or object, attempted rape, unwanted sexual touching and other non-contact forms".[107]

The WHO reports demonstrate that gender-based violence is a huge world-wide health issue . Adding other aspects, such as race, social class and sexual orientation, is important to understand the issue in more detail.[108] Research shows that partner violence is not limited to men's violence against women but that it may happen in all forms of partner constellations.[109] The complexity of the issue is not limited to gender, but the gender aspect is important to understand violence.

The public-private divide allows states to clean their hands of any responsibility for what happens in the private sphere and only take responsibility for the public sphere. What belongs to the private and to the public sphere differs over time and between regions and states. The definition of the public-private divide is thus of relevance of which responsibility the state has for gender-based violence, which happens between private individuals.

The WHO provides different explanations for gender-based violence. There are individual factors such as a history of exposure of child maltreatment, harmful use of alcohol, marital discord and dissatisfaction and difficulties to communicate between partners.[110] Applying the public-private divide, society has a role in protecting children from maltreatment and to offer treatment for alcoholism. Forcing

[102] Article 7 of the Rome Statute of the International Criminal Court, https://www.icc-cpi.int/resource-library/documents/rs-eng.pdf, accessed 26.04.2021.

[103] World Health Organisation (WHO), Violence against women, 21 March 2021, https://www.who.int/news-room/fact-sheets/detail/violence-against-women, accessed 27.04.2021.

[104] *Ibid.*

[105] *Ibid.*

[106] *Ibid.*

[107] *Ibid.*

[108] See Kaladelfos and Featherstone (2014), p. 236.

[109] See Reed et al. (2010), p. 349 with references.

[110] Barr (2018).

grown-ups to treat their own alcoholism, would in most societies be considered a violation of the right to personal integrity. At the same time, having a system for voluntary treatment of alcoholism is an obvious part of public society.

Other explanations are lower levels of education, low levels of women's access to the labour market, weak legal sanctions for sexual violence and a low level of equality in forms of discrimination roles.[111] Here, the role of society is clearer for example, in giving access to education to everybody. The latter however, requires a well-functioning state apparatus, where the public sector has the financial resources to provide equal opportunities. In education, the state may be proactive in counteracting gender-based violence. In higher education in Sweden for example, knowledge about men's violence against women is a compulsory integral part of the education to become a lawyer, medical doctor, nurse, psychologist, social worker, physiotherapist and dentist.[112] Knowledge about such violence is considered crucial to save lives.[113] The aim is that students shall gain knowledge about how to both discover and prevent men's violence against women, may it be physical or other forms of violence.[114]

Example

In the Syllabus for the first semester of the Swedish law programme at Örebro University, there is the following course aim:

"Be able to describe the basic features of the problem concerning men's violence against women and violence in close relationships and in this context describe in what way this is relevant to the legal profession."

This is how it is reflected in the course content part of the syllabus:

"During the course, the issue of men's violence against women and violence in close relationships is introduced and discussed at an overall societal level but also from a gender perspective and what significance this has for the legal profession."

Men's violence against women is also an examination:

"Introduction of men's violence against women and violence in close relationships - Seminar, 1.5 higher education credits (Exam code: A023)

Active participation in seminars and group assignments."

The seminar is graded with "pass" or "fail". Just to have pass or fail for this subject at the first semester is motivated by the fact that most students are complete beginners on discussing men's violence against women. ◀

---

[111] *Ibid.*

[112] Appendices to *Högskoleförordningen* (1993:100), the Higher Education Ordinance.

[113] Socialdepartementet, Kunskap om mäns våld mot kvinnor obligatoriskt i jurist- och läkarutbildningarna, 17 March 2017, https://www.regeringen.se/pressmeddelanden/2017/03/kunskap-om-mans-vald-mot-kvinnor-obligatoriskt-i-jurist%2D%2Doch-lakarutbildningarna/, accessed 27.04.2021.

[114] *Ibid.*

One field within public law that plays an important role is health care legislation. In article 20 of the 2011 Council of Europe Convention on preventing and combatting violence against women and domestic violence (the Istanbul Convention),[115] the contracting parties are obliged to "take the necessary legislative or other measures to ensure that victims have access to health care and social services. These services must be adequately resourced and professionals are trained to assist victims and refer them to the appropriate services". Sweden has a long tradition of gender equality and this has a central position in Swedish policy.[116] Still, Swedish health care law has just recently started to expressively address men's violence against women.[117] The first binding regulations on violence in close relations, which were applicable to both health care and social work, were enacted in 2014.[118] These regulations are however gender neutral. Men's violence against women, which is addressed in public policy and regulations on higher education is not reflected in any binding norms in relation to health care. Furthermore, the legal obligations in the regulations are vaguely defined.[119] This vagueness in practice, leaves it to the discretion of the health care actors to decide on how to deal with victims of gender-based violence.

Public law measures against gender-based violence may also be found in police law. In Germany for instance, police law empowers the police to expel violent partners from the flat for up to ten days: "Expulsion from the flat: In order to avert a danger to the life, limb or freedom of a female or male fellow resident, the police may expel the person from whom the danger emanates from the flat and the immediately adjacent area and prohibit him or her from returning."

Example

Another example is the obligation of State Parties to the Istanbul Convention to prevent violence against women and domestic violence by ordering a perpetrator to leave the victim's residence, or prohibiting the perpetrator from entering the victim's residence in situations of immediate danger (Art. 52). By allowing the victim to stay at the residence "it shifts th[e] burden to the perpetrator,"[120] who is required to leave the residence for a "sufficient time" instead of the victim. This emergency tool gives the victim the necessary time to seek long-term restraining or protection orders (as required under Art. 52 Istanbul Convention).

[115] https://rm.coe.int/168008482e, accessed 27.4.2021.

[116] See Öhman et al. (2020), p. 3.

[117] Öhman et al. (2020), p. 2.

[118] SOSFS 2014:4 Socialstyrelsens föreskrifter och allmänna råd om våld i nära relationer, https://www.socialstyrelsen.se/regler-och-riktlinjer/foreskrifter-och-allmanna-rad/konsoliderade-foreskrifter/20144-om-vald-i-nara-relationer/, accessed 27.4.2021.

[119] Öhman et al. (2020), p. 9.

[120] Council of Europe, 'Emergency Barring Orders in Situations of Domestic Violence: Article 52 of the Istanbul Convention, A Collection of Papers on the Council of Europe Convention on Preventing and Combating Violence against Women and Domestic Violence', June 2017.

In Germany, for example, such an emergency barring order (EBO) can be issued by the police for up to 14 days.[121] ◄

Since gender-based violence is just starting to become recognised in law, more sophisticated issues such as gender-based violence for transgender women, in relation to public law, is even more rare. There are however, studies on gender-based violence in health care, education and police encounters for transgender women in Latin America and the Caribbean.[122] In this research it was found that transgender women experienced gender-based violence when they obtained state-issued identity documents or when they used identity documents that conflicted with their gender identity.[123] Legislation that potentially could improve this situation are modernised gender identity laws and to give the right to self-determine the name and gender that appears on official documents.[124] Another conclusion that was drawn in regard to legislation, is that to achieve equality for trans people there is a need to design and implement public policies that reach beyond the elimination of discrimination and violence. Thus enabling conditions for all trans persons to live their lives to full potential.[125]

9.6 Public Law Aspects of Antidiscrimination Law: Enforcement of Antidiscrimination Law by Public Law Mechanisms

Studies show that states that have ratified the Convention on the Elimination of All Forms of Discrimination against Women (CEDAW)[126] thus, have anti-discrimination rules in their constitutions or elsewhere in their legislation, are more likely to adopt full legal protection against domestic violence. Anti-discrimination laws therefore, play an important role in changing prejudices, customs and traditions and other practices based on the idea of the inferiority of women. This section puts focus on public law mechanisms against discrimination and how those mechanisms may function as awareness raising in education and training of professionals.

Discrimination against women is defined in CEDAW as "any distinction, exclusion or restriction made on the basis of sex which has the effect or purpose of impairing or nullifying the recognition, enjoyment or exercise by women, irrespective of their marital status, on a basis of equality of men and women, of human rights and fundamental freedoms in the political, economic, social, cultural,

[121] See e.g. § 29a General Law for the Protection of Public Safety and Order in Berlin, Germany.

[122] Lanham et al. (2019), p. 37.

[123] *Ibid*, p. 43.

[124] *Ibid.*

[125] *Ibid.*

[126] https://www.ohchr.org/EN/ProfessionalInterest/Pages/CEDAW.aspx, accessed 28.4.2021.

civil or any other field."[127] The states that have ratified CEDAW have obliged themselves to condemn discrimination against women in any form. They have agreed to embody the principle of equality between men and women in their constitutions or other legislation and ensure the practical realisation of the principle (Article 2(a)). They should "prohibit discrimination by law and impose sanctions against discrimination, give access to justice in discrimination cases and refrain from engaging in any act of discrimination against women". Furthermore, the contracting states should take measures to eliminate discrimination against women by any person, organisation or enterprise and abolish all laws, regulations, customs and practices that constitute discrimination against women, including penal provisions.[128]

Most countries in the world embrace the principle of equality and non-discriminatio but in practice, the protection is broader in some and narrower in other countries.[129] Only Iran, Sudan and Somalia have taken no action to ratify CEDAW.[130] In Asian, European and South American laws, antidiscrimination is a constitutional principle. In Argentina, Brazil, the Czech Republic, Germany, India, Israel, Japan and Spain, it is a fundamental right. Antidiscrimination laws cover a wide range of activities, such as housing, employment, education, health, or access to public and private areas.[131]

To make discrimination laws more effective all over the world, the access to justice is crucial. If a court procedure is necessary and it is expensive and slow, the discrimination laws will not be effectively in practice.[132] A public law measure that may be a best practice, is a discrimination ombudsman, who may assist people who have been subject to discrimination. A discrimination ombudsman may work actively against discrimination, in relation to employers and other actors.[133] Furthermore, a discrimination ombudsman may supervise employers and other actors and make binding decisions on how the actor must act in the future to avoid discrimination.[134] Finally, a discrimination ombudsman may assist and represent persons in court proceedings. A practical issue in any court proceeding is the issue of proof. Where gender equality is weak in practice, it may be difficult for the victim to be believed.

[127] Article 1 CEDAW.

[128] Article 2 CEDAW.

[129] Mercat-Bruns et al. (2018), p. 3.

[130] United Nations Human Rights. Office of The High Commissioner, Convention on the Elimination of All Forms of Discrimination Against Women, Last updated 20 June 2016, https://www.ohchr.org/Documents/HRBodies/CEDAW/OHCHR_Map_CEDAW.pdf, accessed 28.4.2021.

[131] Mercat-Bruns et al. (2018), p. 5.

[132] *Ibid*, p. 7.

[133] See Diskrimineringsombudsmannen, Vad gör DO, https://www.do.se/om-do/vad-gor-do/, accessed 27.4.2021.

[134] *Ibid.*

To pursue legal proceedings against somebody for discrimination may have a high price, especially if the proceedings are not successful. It is thus important, that discrimination laws contain a prohibition of reprisals for persons who reports or complain of discrimination or participates in an investigation into discrimination. Otherwise, it is likely that many cases are never reported. The limited amount of damages that victims of discrimination get, in the case that court proceedings are successful, may further discourage the victim from initiating a legal action.[135]

Effectiveness of anti-discrimination laws may be measured by the degree of compliance.[136] Anti-discrimination laws have a symbolic value and demonstrate that gender equality is an important issue, which in turn reduces gender-based and domestic violence. This is maybe the most important function of those laws. There are many ways to achieve compliance. One is awareness in public policy and to openly communicate that gender equality is an important issue. Another is to create gender awareness early in the education of children and young people . To respect and promote equality in education is a cornerstone in many educational systems.[137] To actively educate in gender equality and non-discrimination of women may be more controversial. Public law governing schools may have an important role to play in this respect. Also, the proactive role of a discrimination ombudsman, who works proactively in relation to employers and other stakeholders may increase the degree of compliance.

To make anti-discrimination laws effective in practice, it is important to efficiently communicate to the stakeholders what discrimination is. This is a matter for public law and a public authority such as a discrimination ombudsman. In Sweden for instance the discrimination ombudsman communicates with film material and in text form and explains what discrimination is. Besides Swedish, the communication is in Arabic, Bosnian, Croatian, Dari, English, Finnish (also the version spoken in Tornedalen), French, German, Persian, Polish, Romani (Aril, Gurbet, Kaldaresh, Lovari and the Swedish version), Sami (North, South and from the Luleå region), Serbian, Somalian, Spanish, Tigrinya and Yiddish. It is also communicated in sign language and easy-to-read language and there is also the option to listen to the text.[138] Here is an example of how the Swedish discrimination ombudsman communicates discrimination:[139]

---

[135] Mercat-Bruns et al. (2018), pp. 7–8.

[136] *Ibid*, p. 11.

[137] See e.g. Benjamin (2013), p. 197.

[138] Diskrimineringsombudsmannen, https://www.do.se, accessed 28.4.2021.

[139] Diskrimineringsombudsmannen, Disadvantaging a person on parental leave is prohibited, https://www.do.se/other-languages/english/disadvantaging-a-person-on-parental-leave-is-prohibited/, accessed 28.4.2021.

Example

Pregnancy and parental leave

"The prohibition against disadvantaging a person taking parental leave covers in principle all situations that may arise between an employer and an employee or job-seeker. It makes no difference whether there is an intention to disadvantage or not. It is the effect or the result that determines whether it is a case of disadvantage. Examples of disadvantage include:

- Not being given a job or promotion
- Being transferred or relocated to less favourable duties or working conditions
- Lagging behind in salary
- A trial period of employment is terminated or does not result in permanent employment
- Being subjected to victimisation or other harassment by the employer that causes discomfort and suffering."[140] ◀

As important as knowing what discrimination is, is to know what discrimination is not. Initiating a discrimination issue against an employer based on a misunderstanding on the concept of discrimination is not wise. Thus, the Swedish discrimination ombudsman gives examples on what discrimination is not, in the case of pregnancy and parental leave:[141]

Example

"There are some situations where the prohibition of disadvantage to a person on parental leave does not apply. These are situations where certain conditions or treatment are a necessary consequence of the parental leave, such as:

- not paying salary to the person on parental leave (does not apply to agreed top-up salary during parental leave)
- not employing a jobseeker who intends to be on leave during a large part or the entire period of employment (applies to temporary employment)
- changing a person's duties when he/she returns from parental leave if the previous duties no longer exist"[142] ◀

[140] Diskrimineringsombudsmannen, Disadvantaging a person on parental leave is prohibited, https://www.do.se/other-languages/english/disadvantaging-a-person-on-parental-leave-is-prohibited/, accessed 28.4.2021.

[141] *Ibid.*

[142] Diskrimineringsombudsmannen, Disadvantaging a person on parental leave is prohibited, https://www.do.se/other-languages/english/disadvantaging-a-person-on-parental-leave-is-prohibited/ accessed 28.4.2021.

9.7 Conclusion

Modern public law appeared with the rise of the secular and liberal state at the time of the Enlightenment in eighteen-century Europe. "Government by consent," implied a fundamental change of the nature of constitutional and administrative law. Yet, women were not included in that consent. The systematic legal and factual domination of women by men, in the public and private spheres, continuously persisted. The gradual shift from a homocentric to a more gender-balanced public law took place only in the second half of the twentieth century, under the pressure of various political movements. The "second birth" of the modern public law signified not only the embracement of equality for both men and women, but also for the non-binary gender, as well as of substantial equality as opposed to formal equality. The increasing recognition of positive state duties to ensure gender equality in practice also meant the expansion of the reach of the public law. Public law used to be reserved for the free market relations and private domains of marital and family relations.

Although gender-balanced public law is gaining momentum across the world, there are still many sub-groups and whole societies in which patriarchy prevails. National public law responses to gender inequalities are very much culturally predetermined. In that respect, international legal norms embodied in the CEDAW, the International Covenant on Civil and Political Rights, the European Convention on Human Rights or the Istanbul Convention and in the practice of their (quasi-)judicial institutions provide focal points for local reforms and fight against discriminatory cultural patterns. However, there is not always one, universal version of gender equality, just as there is more than one school of feminism. Accordingly, there is a wide range of public law issues that constitutional and administrative law aiming for gender equality should consider and a pluralism of legitimate approaches addressing them. The pluralism of approaches particularly appears in areas in which international instruments accord a wide margin of appreciation to the Member States or in which the (quasi-)judicial institutions established by those instruments take divergent positions to the same set of legal issues.

Although women constitute approximately one-half of the world population, they are underrepresented at all governmental levels worldwide. Multiple structural, institutional and cultural factors play a part in this phenomenon. The situation is improving from year to year. However, this process is not fast and efficient enough, especially in developing countries. All international documents in this field emphasise the direct link between the equal representation of women in public life and the process of democracy. Sure, there is no doubt that democratic values cannot be achieved as long as women are underrepresented in public affairs. However, electing more women in state institutions is only the first step. What is necessary is to ensure that they have a tangible impact on public policies. They should not serve only as décor and reason for praise before foreign diplomats and international institutions. Thus, empowering women is a multi-layered process that is much more complex than choosing an equal number of women in state institutions. Consequently, this process requires the active involvement of all segments of the state and society.

Even though most countries in the world recognise principles of non-discrimination of women, every third woman in the world has been subject to a form of gender-based violence. Still, the existence of anti-discrimination laws in a country, plays a role in reducing gender-based violence. Anti-discrimination laws are however not alone the solution on either gender-based violence or discrimination of women.

People who meet persons who are subject to gender-based violence in their profession, such as lawyers, psychologists, medical staff and social workers, need education and knowledge about gender-based violence to see the signs, encounter the victims in the right way and to help them. Bringing gender-based violence as a subject into education laws is a public law measure that may be efficient. Binding regulations in relation to gender-based violence for health care is another important public law measure.

Anti-discrimination laws have an important signal value in recognising that women shall not be discriminated. Anti-discrimination laws as such, do not however abolish discrimination of women. Creating an anti-discrimination law that is effective in practice contains many challenges. For example, a female employee takes a risk when reporting her employer for discrimination in working life. A public law measure that may make this easier is a discrimination ombudsman, who can make binding decisions, but also inform employers, employees and other stakeholders on what discrimination is and what is not.

In discussions on equal representation, gender equality and discrimination of women, ethnicity, sexual orientation, societal class, and age need to be taken into consideration. There are cumulative disadvantages if many of these and other similar aspects are present. Furthermore, a wealthy, heterosexual, white women may be better-off regarding discrimination and other disadvantages than a poor, trans-sexual immigrant. Thus, when designing public law measures, they need to include more aspects than only gender, without missing out the gender issue.

Questions

1. What were the historical and ideological preconditions for the profiling of modern public law and why it is considered as homocentric in its initial stage?
2. What is the rationale behind gender-neutral and gender-sensitive stages of development of modern public law?
3. Why is there pluralism in the public law approaches to gender equality and how do the tensions between some aspects of freedom of religion and gender equality exemplify it?
4. What are the main obstacles for political representation of women worldwide?
5. Explain the main arguments which are brought forward when discussing the importance of women's representation.

(continued)

6. Does only a larger number of women in state institutions guarantee their greater political influence?
7. What is the relevance for private-public divide in relation to gender-based violence?
8. Which public law measures may have an effect against gender-based violence? Mention some examples from the text and some examples from any other jurisdiction that you know.
9. Why is there still discrimination, even though most countries have discrimination laws in place?
10. If you compare discrimination of women with other discrimination grounds (race, sexual orientation, disability, age. . .), which public law measures should, according to your view, be the same for all kinds of discrimination, and in which regard are specific measures needed?

References

Al Fili M (2019) Koweït. Annuaire international de justice constitutionnelle XXXIV-2018 – Égalité, genre et constitution. https://www.persee.fr/doc/aijc_0995-3817_2019_num_34_2018_2701. Accessed 9 Oct 2021

Arnold R (2019) Allemagne. Annuaire international de justice constitutionnelle XXXIV-2018 – Égalité, genre et constitution. https://www.persee.fr/doc/aijc_0995-3817_2019_num_34_2018_2688. Accessed 9 Oct 2021

Atkeson LR (2003) Not all cues are created equal: the conditional impact of female candidates on political engagement. J Polit 65:1040–1061

Bari F (2005) Women's political participation: issues and challenges. https://www.un.org/womenwatch/daw/egm/enabling-environment2005/docs/EGM-WPD-EE-2005-EP.12%20%20draft%20F.pdf. Accessed 9 Oct 2021

Barr N (2018) Shifting Tides. Dramatic social changes mean the welfare state is more necessary than ever, finance and development.. https://www.imf.org/external/pubs/ft/fandd/2018/12/pdf/redesigning-the-welfare-statebarr.pdf. Accessed 12 Apr 2020

Benjamin M (2013) Equality in education law and policy. Cambridge University Press, Cambridge

Caprioli M, Boyer MA (2001) Gender, violence, and international crisis. J Conflict Resolut 45:503–518

Copelon R (1994) Intimate terror: understanding domestic violence as torture. In: Cook RJ (ed) Human rights of women - national and international perspectives. University of Pennsylvania Press, Philadelphia, pp 116–153

Dahlerup D (1978) Women's entry into politics: the experience of the Danish local and general elections 1908–20. Scand Polit Stud 1:139–162

Dahlerup D (2005) Increasing women's political representation: new trends in gender quotas. In: Ballington J, Karam A (eds) Women in parliament: beyond numbers. International Institute for Democracy and Electoral Assistance, Stockholm, pp 141–153

Delys S (2014) Women & political representation, handbook on increasing women's political participation in Georgia, Human Rights Education and Monitoring Center. https://rm.coe.int/1680599092. Accessed 9 Oct 2021

Fleiner T, Fleiner LRB (2009) Constitutional democracy in a multicultural and globalised world. Springer, Heidelberg

Gender Quotas Database. IDEA. https://www.idea.int/data-tools/data/gender-quotas/country-overview. Accessed 9 Oct 2021
Hochmann T (2021) Islam on the Beach – The Burkini Ban in France. https://verfassungsblog.de/islam-on-the-beach-the-burkini-ban-in-france/. Accessed 9 Oct 2021
Hottelier M, Carron D (2019) Suisse. Annuaire international de justice constitutionnelle XXXIV-2018 – Égalité, genre et constitution. https://www.persee.fr/doc/aijc_0995-3817_2019_num_34_2018_2707. Accessed 9 Oct 2021
Inter-Parliamentary Union (2013) Gender equal IPU. https://www.ipu.org/about-ipu/gender-equal-ipu. Accessed 9 Oct 2021
Inter-Parliamentary Union (2020) The IPU women in parliament report. https://www.ipu.org/women-in-parliament-2020. Accessed 9 Oct 2021
Inter-Parliamentary Union (2021a) Joint call by IPU and CEDAW Committee on International Women's Day 2021. https://www.ipu.org/iwd-2021-statement. Accessed 9 Oct 2021
Inter-Parliamentary Union (2021b) Proportion of women MPs inches up but gender parity still far off. https://www.ipu.org/news/women-in-parliament-2020. Accessed 9 Oct 2021
Inter-Parliamentary Union (2021c) Women in politics: new data shows growth but also setbacks. https://www.ipu.org/news/women-in-politics-2021. Accessed 9 Oct 2021
Jackson VC (2016) Feminisms, pluralisms and transnationalism: on CEDAW and national constitutions. In: Rubenstein K, Young KG (eds) The public law of gender – from the local to the global. Cambridge University Press, Cambridge, pp 437–464
Kaladelfos A, Featherstone L (2014) Sexual and gender-based violence: definitions, contexts, meanings. Aust Fem Stud 29:233–237
Krook ML, Zetterberg P (2017) Introduction, gender quotas and women's representation – new directions in research. In: Krook ML, Zetterberg P (eds) Gender quotas and women's representation, new directions in research. Routledge, London
Lanham M, Ridgeway K et al (2019) We're going to leave you for last, because of how you are: transgender women's experiences of gender-based violence in healthcare, education and police encounters in Latin America and Caribbean. Violence Gend 6:37–46
Luciani M (2019) Italie. Annuaire international de justice constitutionnelle XXXIV-2018 – Égalité, genre et constitution. https://www.persee.fr/doc/aijc_0995-3817_2019_num_34_2018_2699. Accessed 9 Oct 2021
Mercat-Bruns M, Oppenheimer DB, Sartorius C (2018) Comparative perspectives on the enforcement and effectiveness of antidiscrimination law: challenges and innovative tools. Springer, Heidelberg
Niasse CB (2019) Sénégal, Bénin, Côte d'Ivoire. Annuaire international de justice constitutionnelle XXXIV-2018 – Égalité, genre et constitution. https://www.persee.fr/doc/aijc_0995-3817_2019_num_34_2018_2706. Accessed 9 Oct 2021
Norris P (2000) Women's representation and electoral systems. In: Rose R (ed) International encyclopedia of elections. CQ Press, Washington, pp 348–351
Öhman A, Burman M, Carbin M, Edin K (2020) The public health turn on violence against women: analysing Swedish healthcare law. Public Health Gend Equal Policies 20:753
Okin SM (1989) Justice, gender, and the family. Basic Books, New York
Orban O (1911) Droit constitutionnel de la Belgique, t. III. Dessain & Giard & Brière, Liège/Paris
Peters A, Preuss UK (2013) International relations and international law. In: Tushnet M, Fleiner T, Saunders C (eds) Routledge handbook of constitutional law. Routledge, London, pp 142–146
Raday F (2003) Culture, religion and gender. ICON 1:663–715
Reed E, Raj A, Miller E, Silverman JG (2010) Losing the "gender" in gender-based violence: this missteps of research on dating and intimate partner violence, violence against women 16(3):348
Renauld B, Verdussen M (2019) Belgique. Annuaire international de justice constitutionnelle XXXIV-2018 – Égalité, genre et constitution. https://www.persee.fr/doc/aijc_0995-3817_2019_num_34_2018_2690. Accessed 9 Oct 2021
Roman D (2019) France. Annuaire international de justice constitutionnelle XXXIV-2018 – Égalité, genre et constitution. https://www.persee.fr/doc/aijc_0995-3817_2019_num_34_2018_2696. Accessed 9 Oct 2021

Romany C (1994) State responsibility goes private: a feminist critique of the public/private distinction in international human rights law. In: Cook RJ (ed) Human rights of women- national and international perspectives. University of Pennsylvania Press, Philadelphia, pp 85–116
Rosenfeld M (2003) Towards a reconstruction of constitutional equality. In: Dorsen N, Rosenfeld M, Sajó A, Baer S (eds) Comparative constitutionalism – cases and materials. Thomson West, St. Paul
Rubio-Marin R, Chang W-C (2013) Sites of constitutional struggle for women's equality. In: Tushnet M, Fleiner T, Saunders C (eds) Routledge handbook of constitutional law. Routledge, London, pp 301–312
Rubio-Marin R, Morgan MI (2006) Constitutional domestication of international gender norms: categorizations, illustrations and reflections from the nearside of the bridge. In: Knop K (ed) Gender and human rights. Oxford University Press, Oxford, pp 113–152
Smith E (2019) Norvège. Annuaire international de justice constitutionnelle XXXIV-2018 – Égalité, genre et constitution. https://www.persee.fr/doc/aijc_0995-3817_2019_num_34_2018_2702. Accessed 9 Oct 2021
Speech by President von der Leyen at the European Parliament Plenary on the conclusions of the European Council meeting of 25-26 March 2021 and the outcome of the high-level meeting between the EU and Turkey. https://ec.europa.eu/commission/presscorner/detail/en/speech_21_1965. Accessed 9 Oct 2021
UN Women (1995) (Reprinted 2014). Beijing Declaration and Platform for Action, Beijing+5 Political Declaration and Outcome. https://www.unwomen.org/en/digital-library/publications/2015/01/beijing-declaration. Accessed 9 Oct 2021
UN Women (2021) Facts and figures: leadership and political participation. https://www.unwomen.org/en/what-we-do/leadership-and-political-participation/facts-and-figures. Accessed 9 Oct 2021
Vogelstein RB, Bro A (2018) The 'Year of the Woman' goes global. https://edition.cnn.com/2018/11/09/opinions/year-of-woman-goes-global-bro-vogelstein/index.html. Accessed 9 Oct 2021
Vogelstein RB, Bro A (2020) Women's power index tracks women's political representation. https://www.cfr.org/blog/womens-power-index-tracks-womens-political-representation. Accessed 9 Oct 2021
Vogelstein RB, Bro A (2021) Women's Power Index. https://www.cfr.org/article/womens-power-index#chapter-title-0-2. Accessed 9 Oct 2021
Vujadinović D (2019) Rod i pravna regulativa. In: Vujadinović D, Stanimirović V (eds) Studije roda. Univerzitet u Beogradu – Pravni fakultet, Beograd, pp 99–107
Young KG (2016) Introduction: a public law of gender? In: Rubenstein K, Young CG (eds) The public law of gender: from the local to the global. Cambridge University Press, Cambridge, pp 1–47

Further Reading

Adams K, Byrnes A (2000) Gender equality and the judiciary: using international human rights standards to promote the human rights of women and the girl-child at the national level. Commonwealth Secretariat, London
Ahrens P, Chmilewski K, Lang S, Sauer B (2020) Gender equality in politics: implementing party quotas in Germany and Austria. Springer, Heidelberg
Ahrens P (2018) Actors, institutions, and the making of EU gender equality programs. Palgrave Macmillan, London
Celis K, Childs S (2014) Gender, conservatism and political representation. ECPR Press, Colchester
Coles A, Gray L, Momsen J (2015) The Routledge handbook of gender and development. Routledge, London
Cox Han L, Heldman C (2017) Women, power, and politics: the fight for gender equality in the United States. Oxford University Press, Oxford

Elman AR (2008) Sexual equality in an integrated Europe: virtual equality. Palgrave Macmillan, London

Hattery AJ, Smith E (2019) Gender, power, and violence: responding to sexual and intimate partner violence in society today. Rowman & Littlefield Publishers, Lanham

Hoard S (2015) Gender expertise in public policy: towards a theory of policy success. Palgrave Macmillan, London

Jacquot S (2015) Transformations in EU gender equality: from emergence to dismantling. Palgrave Macmillan, London

Jamil I, Aminuzzaman SM et al (2020) Gender mainstreaming in politics, administration and development in South Asia. Palgrave Macmillan, London

Kantola J (2010) Gender and the European Union. Red Globe Press, Gordonsville

Krook ML, Zetterberg P (2015) Gender quotas and women's representation: new directions in research. Routledge, London

Lomazzi V, Crespi I (2019) Gender mainstreaming and gender equality in Europe: policies, culture and public opinion. Policy Press, Bristol

Lombardo E, Forest M (2012) The Europeanization of gender equality policies: a discursive-sociological approach. Palgrave Macmillan, London

Lovenduski J (2006) State feminism and political representation. Cambridge University Press, Cambridge

Matland R, Montgomery K (2003) Women's access to political power in post-communist Europe. Oxford University Press, Oxford

Muriaas RL, Wang V, Murray R (2019) Gendered electoral financing: money, power and representation in comparative perspective. Routledge, London

Osborn TL (2012) How women represent women: political parties, gender, and representation in the state legislatures. Oxford University Press, Oxford

Pini B, McDonald P (2011) Women and representation in local government: international case studies. Routledge, London

Rai SM (2003) Mainstreaming gender, democratizing the state, institutional mechanisms for the advancement of women? Manchester University Press, Manchester

Rubenstein K, Young KG (2018) The public law of gender: from the local to the global. Cambridge University Press, Cambridge

Squires J (2007) The new politics of gender equality. Red Globe Press, Gordonsville

Thames FC, Williams MS (2015) Contagious representation: women's political representation in democracies around the world. NYU Press, New York

Williams SH (2009) Constituting equality: gender equality and comparative constitutional law. Cambridge University Press, Cambridge

Gender Perspective of Social Security Law 10

María Angustias Benito Benítez and Carmen Jover Ramírez

Contents

Authors are listed in alphabetical order. Maria Angustias Benito Benítez authored Sect. 10.1–10.3 and Carmen Jover Ramírez wrote Sect. 10.4–10.7. Sect. 10.8 was written by both authors.

M. A. Benito Benítez (✉) · C. Jover Ramírez
Labour and Social Security Law, University of Cadiz, Faculty of Law, Cadiz, Spain
e-mail: angustias.benito@gm.uca.es; maricarmen.jover@uca.es

D. Vujadinović et al. (eds.), *Gender-Competent Legal Education*, Springer Textbooks in Law, https://doi.org/10.1007/978-3-031-14360-1_10

Abstract

The main purpose of Social Security Law is to regulate the social protection provided to those who, while carrying out a professional activity, find themselves in situations of need that are protected by the different Social Security systems of states. The purpose of these systems is to guarantee the welfare state and, therefore, they are increasingly inclined to extend their subjective scope of protection beyond those who carry out a professional activity. The gender perspective is not alien to Social Security law. It is essential to analyse Social Security from a gender perspective, not only because it includes protected situations arising from the very nature of women, but also due to the consequences the traditional distribution of roles between men and women has had in the field of Social Security. Both these issues will be studied in this chapter.

10.1 Introduction

The close connection between Social Security Law and Labour Law requires the study of both areas to be undertaken 'hand-in-hand', as covered in the chapter "Gender perspective of Labour Law". The impact of the gender perspective on Social Security law requires analysis to account for labour law issues in the strict sense of the term, such as, the suspension of the employment relationship. It can also extend to tangential issues intrinsic to labour law, such as the prevention of occupational hazards.[1] However, our analysis will focus on the impact of this gender perspective on Social Security.[2] In light of the above, it must be said that Social Security includes, among its protected situations, situations directly related to women, such as pregnancy, maternity or breastfeeding. Contemporaneously, other situations are included which, being common to all human beings, have not been hermetically sealed from the gender perspective. Despite it being thought at first that the objective nature of such situations would not allow any subjective interference, they are in fact determined by the gender of the person affected. A conclusion can consequently be discarded in the face of the evidence shown by reality.

This chapter will therefore analyse these and other issues, both in which the impact of the gender perspective is obvious and required by the very idiosyncrasy that shapes gender, as well as those in which this idiosyncrasy appears in an

[1] Vid. Chapter Gender Perspective of Labor Law.

[2] According to William Beveridge (British Minister who is considered the father of Social Security by his 1942 Report Social "Insurance and Allied Services", known as the Beveridge Report), Social Security is understood as the set of measures adopted by the State to protect citizens against those individual risks that will never cease to occur, no matter how optimal the overall situation in which society lives.

overlapping but no less incisive way. It cannot be forgotten that, although the protection provided by the Social Security system is based on occupational benefits as an employee or self-employed worker, the system has extended its range of protection beyond this sphere. This (protection) has even come under the umbrella of a broader concept of social protection; closely linked to the welfare state and includes complementary measures of protection outside the Social Security system, such as social assistance, third level benefits or complementary level benefits.

10.2 The Scope of the Statutory Social Security Schemes

The origins of Social Security as we know it today can be traced back to the industrial revolution of the nineteenth century. The appalling working conditions to which workers were exposed (long working hours, lack of health and safety protection measures, low pay, child labour, etc.), were aggravated in the case of women and led to the materialisation of a series of risks which had to be dealt with. The notion of social risk appears as opposed to individual risk. Social risk is characterised by the concurrence of two elements; an objective element, and a subjective element. The first entails the generality of the incidence of risk, since it threatens any person. In other words, it is inherent to the very life of human beings in society. The second is the general conviction that the individual alone cannot protect her or himself against the risk, but that it is necessary to organise a collective response to it. This is necessary as the individual does not have the technical and economic means necessary to protect her or himself against such risk, given the generality of the risk, and that its origin is not attributable to the specific individual, It should be pointed out that the emergence of both elements is not simultaneous in time. While the objective element, the generality of the risk, was known from the first stages of the provision of work, even in the primitive forms of slavery and servitude, the emergence of the second element, the concern to arbitrate mechanisms of protection against these risks, arises with the establishment of capitalism; the industrial and bourgeois revolution. It was at this historical moment that awareness of the inadequacy of the protection techniques that had hitherto been used to protect against these risks, came to light. These non-specific techniques, such as individual savings, insurance contracts or mutual-based solidarity systems, were not able to respond to the so-called "social question" arising from the industrial and bourgeois revolution. Thus, during the second half of the nineteenth century, specific protection techniques emerged, including social insurance.

10.2.1 The Right to Social Security: A Gendered Consideration

10.2.1.1 The Backgrounds of the Present-Day Social Security Systems: Bismarck System and Beveridge System

The origin of social insurance, as a response to the inadequacy of non-specific protection techniques, dates back to 1881 and was introduced by German Chancellor von Bismarck. The first social insurances were thus created; to provide due protection against the materialisation of the contingencies they protected. These included health insurance, industrial accident insurance, and invalidity and old-age insurance, emerging in Germany as protection mechanisms. The Bismarckian system took the private insurance model as a reference, adapted to the protection of what we have called social risks. Its characteristics include: its compulsory nature; its constitution and financing, involving not only the employee, but also the employer and the State, and the public or quasi-public assumption of its management. However, its closed sphere in terms of its markedly professional subjective scope and the plurality of insurances, combined with the consequent dispersion of protected risks, management and financing, highlighted the need to give way to a new system of protection. Thus, in 1942, the publication of the first Beveridge Report in the United Kingdom marked the first step towards the Social Security system. This system has certain peculiarities and differences with respect to the social insurance system. The Social Security system advocated by Beveridge was characterised by an extension of the personal scope of coverage with a tendency towards universality: protection for all citizens and even residents in the country; the tendency towards protection against any risk that might cause a situation of destitution or economic need; seeking to guarantee a minimum income and solve the lack of income as quickly as possible; financing of a fundamentally fiscal origin, either directly (taxes) or indirectly (contributions), and the public nature of Social Security through the direct intervention of the State in its management by means of a single entity that integrates the various social insurances, thus recognising its public service character.

Notwithstanding the above, it should be pointed out that, at present, neither of the two models exists in a pure state, but rather the features and characteristics of one and the other are converging in a single model in which the inspiring principles of both are included. It is true that, depending on the system adopted by each country and even depending on the benefits of the model itself, the welfare or contributory nature prevails.

Therefore, the characteristics of each model are:

Welfare model:
- financing almost exclusively through taxation
- protection only for real situations of economic need
- protection guarantees a vital minimum
- benefits, that are essentially uniform, regardless of the financial contributions of the protected person to the financing of the system.

Contributory model:
- financing basically by contributions
- guaranteeing benefits whose amount depends on the time and value of previous contributions
- benefits tending to guarantee the levels of income received prior to the materialisation of the protected situation that constitutes the situation of need.

What unites the two systems is that "both models in their application and practical evolution in the national systems have a more or less universalist vocation: they maintain a tendency towards a joint treatment of risks (although the differentiated consideration of risks continues to exist); the financing tends more and more to become mixed, with more or less predominance, of financing through contributions; charged to quotas and general State budgets, and finally, both models have attempted to rationalise public management in an increasingly unified manner, although there are also various forms of private collaboration".[3]

They are both part of the so-called welfare state, promoted by all Member States of the European Union in the second half of the twentieth century with the aim of improving the quality of life of citizens. The models of social protection are determined by the social objectives of each State; the responses given by each State to social problems give rise to different models of social protection. However, the authors highlight these models have a common element in presenting a structure in which non-contributory social benefits are combined with contributory pensions and supplementary schemes.[4]

In view of the differences between the various national legislations, the EU decided to coordinate the Social Security systems of the Member States with Regulations rather than harmonizing them with Directives.[5] This coordination will ensure equal treatment for workers who are nationals of Member States, their dependants and heirs. This ensures that when workers exercise their free movement within the Union, they retain rights and benefits acquired, or those in the process of being acquired.

10.2.1.2 The Gender Perspective in the Bismarck System and Beveridge System: Current Implications

The characteristics of each social security model, and the inclination in the configuration of existing models towards one or the other, has an important impact on gender related situations. The situation of women in the labour market, in all its phases and aspects, access to employment, promotion and professional development as well as voluntary exit or not, have important implications in the field of Social Security. The characteristics of the model adopted and the gender aspects in the context of the social protection provided by the system will depend on the characteristics of the model adopted. The characteristics of the contributory model indicated above and the situation of women in the labour market (shorter periods of contribution to social security systems than men, late entry to the labour market or interruptions due to assuming the role of caregiver) assume that said model is not the

[3] Monereo Pérez (2015); Conde-Ruiz and González (2016), pp. 461–490.

[4] Millán García (2005), p. 197.

[5] "Regulation (EC) No 883/2004 of the European Parliament and of the council of 29 April 2004 on the coordination of Social Security systems" and "Regulation (EC) No 987/2009 of the European Parliament and of the Council of 16 September 2009 laying down the procedure for implementing Regulation (EC) No 883/2004 on the coordination of Social Security systems".

most beneficial for the social protection of women. In addition, lower contributions for lower-ranking jobs, part-time contracts or the incidence of pay discrimination, mean that an eminently contributory model has negative repercussions on the social protection that women can receive from it. In contrast, the welfare model can be characterised by its almost exclusively tax-based financing, and the protection only for real situations of economic need. In turn, this guarantees a vital minimum, with benefits that are tendentially uniform regardless of the economic contributions of the protected subject to the financing of the system. Consequently, it is possible to avoid the negative consequences that other models, as described above, can have on the social protection provided to women by ensuring that in similar situations of need, men and women will be able to obtain the same social protection provided by the Social Security system.

The pillars on which the Beveridge model was based,[6] some of which are still in place today, must be analysed from a gender perspective. This will make it possible to respond to current situations in which the binomial of women and social security continues to require special attention. The main issue continues to be the need to protect women from unpaid work, childcare and care of the elderly, which keeps them away from the labour market and in a situation of lack of protection. A social security system is advocated in which paid and unpaid work is respected; men and women have to be protected from situations of need, both in the exercise of their professional activities and in the assumption of care functions.[7] This is not at odds with the economic development of the countries For example, Nordic countries, (Finland, Denmark and Sweden) are some of the most competitive economies in the world, despite their strong social protection.[8]

10.2.2 Conditions of Access to the Statutory Social Security Schemes

In the context of the 1970s when the first gender equality Directives entered into force, one of the areas of concern was Social Security, giving rise to the Social Security Directive. This Directive is the first and only binding instrument in the field of social security. Its existence has made it possible to purge national legislation of direct discrimination, and its transcendental importance now lies especially in the detection of indirect discrimination.

The material scope of the Social Security Directive covers statutory schemes providing protection against the risks of sickness, invalidity, old age, industrial accident and occupational disease, and unemployment.[9] Unlike the risks traditionally included in national social security systems, it does not apply to survivors' benefits, nor to family benefits, except in the case of increases in benefits intended to

[6]Dale and Foster (1986), pp. 16–17.

[7]Pascal (1997), p. 233.

[8]Pampillón Olmedo (2008), pp. 155–165.

[9]Art. 3.

cover the aforementioned risks. It also includes social assistance, only if it is intended to supplement or complement the protection against some of the foreseen risks. With the exclusion of survivors' benefits and family benefits, one of the shortcomings of this Directive in the fight against the structural discrimination suffered by women becomes evident. These benefits are the ones most often reproducing gender stereotypes, particularly the importance of the family policy adopted by each State to achieve the full integration of women in the labour market and in the strengthening of co-responsibility.

> The Social Security Directive excludes certain matters from its scope of application, granting full powers to national legislators in this respect: the determination of pensionable age for the purpose of granting old-age and retirement pensions, and the possible consequences thereof for other benefits; advantages in respect of old-age pension schemes granted to persons who have brought up children; the acquisition of benefit entitlements following periods of interruption of employment due to the bringing up of children; the granting of old-age or invalidity benefit entitlements by virtue of the derived entitlements of a wife; the granting of increases for long-term invalidity, old-age, accidents at work and occupational disease benefits for a dependent wife. These are exceptions in the progressive application of the principle of equal treatment, the maintenance of which is also subject to periodic reviews to be carried out by the Member States "*in order to ascertain, in the light of social developments in the matter concerned, whether there is justification for maintaining the exclusions concerned*".[10]

There are three starting points to bear in mind. First, the instrument through which the protection of the Social Security system is provided; the benefit (either in kind or in cash). Secondly, access to this protection and, therefore, the conditions that a person has to comply with to obtain this protection. Thirdly, the impact of the principle of equal treatment and non-discrimination.

Regarding the first starting point, the ECJ has reiterated in its case law that a benefit will be considered a Social Security benefit, for the purposes of the European coordination rules on Social Security, when "*it is granted to its beneficiaries, regardless of any individual and discretionary assessment of personal needs, on the basis of their legally defined situation and insofar as the benefit refers to one of the risks expressly listed in those rules*",[11] as referred to in Article 3 of *Regulation (EC) 883/2004*[12] This Article mentions, as regards its material scope, all legislation concerning the branches of Social Security relating to "sickness, maternity and equivalent paternity benefits, invalidity, old age, survivors' benefits, benefits in respect of accidents at work and occupational diseases, unemployment benefits, early retirement, family benefits and death grants". The application of that

[10] Art. 7 (2).

[11] For all of them, Cases C-216/12 y C-217/12 In Joined (ECJ, 19 September 2013).

[12] Regulation (EC) 883/2004 of the European Parliament and of the Council of 29 April 2004.

Regulation is excluded when "a Member State assumes responsibility for the damage caused to persons and provides for compensation, such as those granted to victims of war and military action or their consequences; victims of crime, murder or terrorist acts; victims of damage caused by agents of the Member State in the performance of their duties, or victims who have suffered damage for political or religious reasons or because of their origin, are outside the scope of Social Security".

With regard to the second question, the requirements, it should be pointed out that, despite their differences in each of the possible models existing within the European Union, they can be reduced to three types: inclusion in the corresponding Social Security system; prior deficiency or prior contribution period required for access to these benefits, and specific requirements according to the nature of the protected situation itself.

With regard to the third question, mention should be made of the Council Directive *"on the progressive implementation of the principle of equal treatment for men and women in matters of Social Security"*.[13] However, the time which has elapsed since its entry into force means that, while maintaining in essence the objective set out in Article 1 of the Directive, *"namely the progressive implementation, in the field of Social Security and other elements of social protection provided for in Article 3 thereof, of the principle of equal treatment for men and women in matters of Social Security!"*, the changing social reality and social developments have called for new responses to ensure the applicability of this principle in the reality which now prevails. This is a function in which the role assumed by the ECJ through its case law has been of relevance.[14]

The importance of gender equality in the Social Security systems is also emphasized by Article 1 of Directive 2006/54/EC (the Equal Treatment Directive)[15] which states that its purpose is to ensure the application of the principle of equal opportunities and equal treatment of men and women in matters of employment and occupation, in particular occupational Social Security schemes.

Both Directives explicitly mention the conditions for access to Social Security benefits.

[13] Council Directive of 19 December 1978 "on the progressive implementation of the principle of equal treatment for men and women in matters of Social Security" (79/7/EEC).

[14] As an example, Case C-450/18, WA v Instituto Nacional de la Seguridad Social (INSS) (ECJ, 12 December 2019) where it is indicated that Directive 79/7 must be interpreted as meaning that it precludes national legislation, which makes provision for the right to a pension supplement for women who have had at least two biological or adopted children and who are in receipt of contributory pensions under a scheme within the national Social Security system, while men in an identical situation do not have a right to such a pension supplement.

[15] Of the European Parliament and of the Council of 5 July 2006 "on the implementation of the principle of equal opportunities and equal treatment of men and women in matters of employment and occupation".

Article 4.1 of the Social Security Directive[16] for example states that: "the principle of equal treatment shall mean that there shall be no discrimination whatsoever on grounds of sex, either directly or indirectly, in particular as regards marital or family status, in particular as regards the scope of schemes and the conditions of access to them, the obligation to contribute and the calculation of contributions, as well as the calculation of benefits". Article 2(f) of the Equal Treatment Directive[17] provides that "schemes not covered by Council Directive 79/7/EEC, the purpose of which is to provide benefits intended to supplement or replace the benefits provided by statutory Social Security schemes, whether membership of such schemes is compulsory or optional, to employed or self-employed workers in an undertaking or group of undertakings, or in a branch of the economy or occupational or cross-industry sector". Article 5 of Equal Treatment Directive prohibits any direct or indirect discrimination on grounds of sex, in particular as regards the scope of these schemes and the conditions of access to them, the obligation to pay contributions and the calculation of contributions and benefits, including increases due for spouses and dependents, and the conditions for the duration and maintenance of entitlement to benefits.

The following sections will analyse the generic requirements for access to the benefits provided by the Social Security systems. The characterisation of this access is often directly related to the gender issue and requires action on the part of the public authorities, some of which is already underway.

10.2.2.1 The Inclusion in the Social Security System

The first requirement governing eligibility for the protection granted by social security systems is to be included in their personal scope of application. This requirement is met not only, and exclusively, by the performance of an occupational activity but also by family ties with the principal subject for certain benefits. By way of example, the protection afforded in the event of death and survival.

The Equal Treatment Directive expressly prohibits direct and indirect discrimination on grounds of sex in the application of occupational social security schemes.[18] It also sets out some examples of matters which, in relation to inclusion in social security schemes, are to be regarded as contrary to the principle of equal treatment if they are based directly or indirectly on sex.[19] These include: provisions defining the persons eligible to "participate in an occupational social security scheme"; provisions establishing "the compulsory or optional nature of participation in a scheme", or "laying down different rules as regards the age of entry into a scheme".

---

[16] Directive 79/7/ EEC.

[17] Directive 2006/54/EC.

[18] Article 5(a) that: "occupational social security schemes shall not discriminate directly or indirectly on grounds of sex with regard to the scope of application of such schemes".

[19] Article 9(1)(a), (b) and (c).

10.2.2.2 The Obligation to Contribute and the Calculation of Contributions

The second of the requirements for entitlement to certain benefits, without prejudice to some exceptions, is the demand for a prior period of contribution to the system. This requirement is increased in the case of contributory benefits par excellence, such as old age or retirement pensions, where longer contribution periods are required.

From a gender perspective this requirement can be criticized. Women's contribution careers tend to be shorter than men's; they may enter the labour market later, suffer frequent interruptions due to dedication to family care, or are only able to accept part-time work.

In this respect, the Equal Treatment Directive recognises the prohibition of any direct or indirect discrimination on grounds of sex in occupational social security schemes. This extends to: the obligation to contribute; the calculation of contributions, the calculation of benefits, including increases due for spouses and dependants, and the conditions for the duration and maintenance of entitlement to benefits.[20] The directive furthermore indicates those provisions which are based directly or indirectly on sex in order to establish different conditions for the granting of benefits, or to reserve benefits for workers of one sex. Establishing different levels of benefits, or different levels of contributions for workers or employers, without prejudice to the exceptions provided for, would infringe the principle of equal treatment.[21] Exceptions, in the latter case, provide for the possibility of setting different levels in the case of defined-contribution schemes, if the aim is to equalise or approximate the amounts of pension benefits for both sexes or, in the case of funded defined-benefit schemes, where the employers' contributions are intended to supplement the financial allocation needed to cover the costs of such defined.

It should be noted that the difficulty lies in identifying those measures which will lead to indirect sex discrimination. While there are fewer provisions which explicitly differentiate on the grounds of sex in terms of the obligation to contribute to the social security system, or in the calculation of benefits, there are often measures which are apparently neutral but factually have a negative effect on women's eligibility for benefits, and on the determination of the amount of benefits.

Example

The calculation of a part-time worker's contributory retirement pension by multiplying the regulatory base by a percentage depends on the length of the contribution period (a period to which a part-time coefficient is applied) gives rise to indirect discrimination. This measure particularly disadvantages women

[20] Article 5 b) and c).

[21] Article 9(1)(h)(i) and (j).

workers in relation to men workers;[22] it is mostly women who hold part-time contracts.[23] ◀

10.2.2.3 Other Conditions of Access

In addition to inclusion in the corresponding social security system and the prior contribution requirement, age is a prerequisite for access to certain benefits. For example, the old-age or retirement pension is understood as the typical age pension.

The Equal Treatment Directive states, in similar terms, that provisions based on sex, directly or indirectly, to establish different rules as regards the age of entry into a scheme or to impose different retirement ages, must be considered to be contrary to the principle of equal treatment. This is without prejudice as, stated by Article 13 of the Directive, due to the fact that men and women may require a flexible retirement age under the same conditions, and therefore not considered incompatible with the Directive.

The principle of equal treatment between men and women, and the prohibition of direct or indirect discrimination on grounds of sex, extends to any other condition which may be required for access to the protection of the social security system concerned. This is clear from Article 9(1)(e) of the Directive, by holding that any provision which lays down different conditions for the granting of benefits, or reserves such benefits to workers of one of the sexes, infringes that principle of equality.

Example

In a preliminary ruling the ECJ held that national legislation which, in the event of voluntary early retirement of a worker enrolled in the general social security scheme, makes that worker's right to an early retirement pension subject to the condition that the amount of that pension is at least as much as the minimum pension amount that worker would be entitled at the age of 65, is not discriminatory. The consequence is justified by legitimate social policy objectives (on the condition it is unrelated to sex-based discrimination) even if that law supposes an unfavourable consequence to women compared to men.[24] This discretion lies with the court in question to determine. ◀

---

[22] Case C-161/18, Violeta Villar Láiz v Instituto Nacional de la Seguridad Social (INSS), Tesorería General de la Seguridad Social (TGSS) (ECJ, 8 May 2019).

[23] Vid. Gender Statistics Database, Full-time and part-time employment by sex, age and occupation in eige.europa.eu.

[24] Case C-843/19, INSS v BT (ECJ, 21 January 2021).

10.3 Gender Perspective in Health Insurance

The protection provided by social security systems in situations of need, in which women may find themselves as a result of biological maternity, comes from the legislation protecting the health and safety of working women in such circumstances. We refer to Council Directive 92/85/EEC (Pregnant Workers Directive).[25] The protection afforded during these situations will be examined in this subchapter, with the exception of the protection afforded during maternity leave, which is analysed thereafter.

10.3.1 The Protection in the Event of Sickness (Health Care and Sickness Benefits)

Article 5 of the Pregnant Workers Directive provides that, in cases where there is a risk to the safety or health of the worker or an effect on pregnancy or breastfeeding, the employer must take the necessary measures to prevent the worker from being exposed to that risk. To this end: the working conditions and/or working time of the worker concerned may be temporarily adapted; the job may be changed if such adaptation is not possible, and if such a change is not technically and/or objectively possible or cannot reasonably be required for duly justified reasons, the worker concerned shall be excused from work for the whole period necessary for the protection of her safety or health. In the latter case, in accordance with Article 11 of the Directive, either the maintenance of remuneration and/or the provision of an adequate allowance must be ensured.

In response to this requirement, the different social security systems have included in their protective action benefits that respond to this aim, which will be analysed below.

10.3.1.1 The Protection During the Pregnancy

Without prejudice to the provision of health care to which the worker may be entitled for illnesses arising from pregnancy, as well as her right to attend prenatal examinations with guaranteed remuneration,[26] the Union legislator provides for financial protection in those situations in which the working woman has to give up her job as a result of the incompatibility of her job with her pregnancy. The financial benefit provided by the social security system, identified as risk during pregnancy benefit, may, in accordance with the provisions of Article 11(4) of the Directive, be subject by the Member States to the condition that the worker in question fulfils certain requirements. This does not include requiring periods of previous work of

[25] Council Directive 92/85/EEC of 19 October 1992 "on the introduction of measures to encourage improvements in the safety and health at work of pregnant workers and workers who have recently given birth or are breastfeeding".

[26] As provided for in Article 9 of Directive 92/85 EEC.

more than 12 months immediately prior to the expected date of childbirth. Thus, for example, in the Spanish social security system, entitlement to the benefit for risk during pregnancy only requires compliance with the condition of being registered in the social security system, and in a situation of registration, no prior contribution period is required.[27]

10.3.1.2 The Protection During the Breastfeeding

Similarly in relation to risks during breastfeeding, the Pregnant Workers Directive recognises the right for the worker to maintain her remuneration, or the right to an allowance, during the time she is unable to carry out her professional activity. The conditions for access to this financial protection are also left to the legislation of the Member States.

Example

In the case of the Spanish social security system, for example, the economic benefit for risk during breastfeeding shall be granted to the working woman under the same terms and conditions as those laid down for the economic benefit for risk during pregnancy.[28] ◄

10.3.2 The Perspective of Gender in the Protection of Accidents at Work and Occupational Diseases

A comparative study of accidents at work suffered by men and women shows that in all the countries of the European Union, the percentage of accidents at work suffered by men is higher than that suffered by women.[29] Denmark, Ireland and Luxembourg, are the countries where the difference is smallest.[30] The characteristics of the profession also have an influence on these percentages. In occupations related to management or administration, technical profiles or liberal professions,[31] the percentage of accidents at work suffered by women exceeds that of men in countries

[27] Article 187 of the Ley General de la Seguridad Social (General Law on Social Security), the consolidated version of which was approved by Real Decreto Legislativo 8/2015 (Royal Legislative Decree 8/2015) of 30 October 2015 (BOE No 261, 31 October 2015).

[28] Article 189 of the Ley General de la Seguridad Social (General Law on Social Security), the consolidated version of which was approved by Real Decreto Legislativo 8/2015 (Royal Legislative Decree 8/2015) of 30 October 2015 (BOE No 261, 31 October 2015).

[29] Information Resource: EIGE, Persons reporting an accident at work by sex, age and size of Enterprise, https://eige.europa.eu/gender-statistics/dgs/indicator/ta_wrklab_wrk_cond_wrkhealthsaf_acc_gen__hsw_ac9.

[30] Ibid.

[31] About liberal professions, vid. In extenso: European economic and social Committee, The State of Liberal Professions Concerning Their Functions and Relevance to European Civil Society, EESC/COMM/05/2013.

including Denmark, Luxembourg, Austria, Finland and Sweden.[32] Notwithstanding the above, the data show that more women than men report a work-related health problem.[33]

Statistics further convey that women suffer more frequently from bullying, harassment, or humiliating behaviours in the workplace.[34]

The protection provided by social security schemes for accidents at work and occupational diseases must also respect the principle of equal treatment and non-discrimination. This follows from a joint interpretation of Articles 6 and 7 of the Equal Treatment Directive, stating that there shall be no direct or indirect discrimination on grounds of sex within the scope of application of occupational social security schemes, including those providing protection against the risk of accidents at work and occupational diseases.

Thus, in principle, the requirements for access to benefits deriving from occupational contingencies, and the amount corresponding to them, should not include any differentiation on the grounds of gender. This is without prejudice to the possible indirect effects of any wage discrimination that may exist in the development of certain benefits, due to the chain relationship between the remuneration received, the contribution bases and the regulatory bases determining each benefit.

Example

Finish law[35] provides that the lump sum benefit paid to a man is lower than that paid to a woman, both being the same age and under the same circumstances, because life expectancy—different for men and women—is applied as actuarial calculation criterion for determining its amount. The Finnish Government specifies that "the differentiation on account of sex is necessary to avoid placing women at a disadvantage compared to men. Since women have a statistically longer life expectancy than men, the lump-sum compensation to remedy the harm suffered for the remainder of the injured person's life must be higher for women than for men". Thus, in its view, the provisions do not discriminate between men and women. However, the ECJ established that Article 4(1) of the Social Security Directive must be interpreted as precluding Finnish legislation because "it must be noted that the taking into account of a factor based on remaining life

[32] Information Resource: EIGE, Persons reporting an accident at work by sex, age and occupation, https://eige.europa.eu/gender-statistics/dgs/browse/ta/ta_wrklab/ta_wrklab_wrk/ta_wrklab_wrk_cond/ta_wrklab_wrk_cond_wrkhealthsaf/ta_wrklab_wrk_cond_wrkhealthsaf_acc/ta_wrklab_wrk_cond_wrkhealthsaf_acc_inter/ta_wrklab_wrk_cond_wrkhealthsaf_acc_inter_occ.

[33] Information Resource: EIGE, Persons reporting a work-related health problem by sex, age and NACE Rev. 2 activity, https://eige.europa.eu/gender-statistics/dgs/indicator/ta_wrklab_wrk_cond_wrkhealthsaf_incid__hsw_pb6b.

[34] Information Resource: EIGE, Psychological violence, https://eige.europa.eu/gender-statistics/dgs.

[35] Finnish Law on accident insurance (tapaturmavakuutuslaki) of 1982, as amended in 1992 ('the Law on accident insurance') and "Decision No 1662/453/82 of the Finnish Ministry of 30 December 1982 on the criteria for capital values of statutory accident insurance".

expectancy is not provided for either in Article 4(2) of that Directive, which concerns the provisions on the protection of women on the grounds of maternity or in Article 7(1) of that Directive, which enables the Member States to exclude from its scope a certain number of rules, advantages and benefits as regards social security".[36] ◄

10.4 Gender Perspective in the Protection of Maternity, Paternity and Family

This section will analyse the protection offered by social security, to the exercise of maternity rights and those aimed at reconciling work and family life. This protection is marked in European legislation by the competence retained by Member States over social protection,[37] creating complexity in the adoption of commitments.

The importance of such rights having economic protection stems from the fact that this circumstance functions as a factor that enhances their enjoyment. When sufficient and adequate economic protection is guaranteed, parents will have fewer problems in exercising their rights. Eliminating the inconveniences involved in the exercise of reconciliation rights is essential from a gender perspective, because it enhances the exercise of these rights by men, guaranteeing the presence of men in family responsibilities and the reversal of roles.

In addition, such subsidies must be sufficient and adequate so the protected situations do not generate an economic loss during their enjoyment (especially when their enjoyment is mandatory).

10.4.1 Maternity Benefits

The Pregnant Workers Directive,[38] requires Member States to take the necessary measures to ensure that workers are granted maternity leave of at least 14 uninterrupted weeks, allocated before and/or after confinement, in accordance with national legislation and/or practice. This must include compulsory maternity leave of at least two weeks, allocated before and/or after confinement,[39] and leave for prenatal examinations without loss of pay if such examinations take place during working hours.[40] The Directive guarantees that during this period an adequate remuneration and/or benefit is recognized. This stipulates an income at least equivalent to the one

[36] Case C-318/13 X (ECJ, 3 September 2014).

[37] Article 151 of Consolidated version of the Treaty on the Functioning of the European Union (OJ C 202).

[38] OJ L 348, (1992).

[39] Article 8.

[40] Article 9.

the worker would receive in the event of a break in her activities for health reasons, subject to any ceiling laid down under national legislation.[41] With regard to the amount of the remuneration or benefit and, specifically, with regard to the requirement that it be adequate, the ECJ has had occasion to rule as follows:

Example

In a case against the German federal minister for Education and Research[42] the court analysed whether the financial coverage during a leave from work and during maternity leave requires the payment of an availability allowance when, during these periods, the right to remuneration equivalent to the average salary received during a previous reference period is recognized. The ECJ came to the conclusion that the financial coverage must be adequate, but not necessarily full.

This precedent was confirmed two years later.[43] There the ECJ analysed the remuneration consequences of a change of job for a flight attendant who, during her pregnancy, was posted on the ground. In that case, the court came to the conclusion that she is not entitled to the remuneration that she received on average before the transfer, but she was entitled to the basic salary and to the components of the remuneration, or to the complements inherent to her professional condition. This included those complements related to her hierarchical superior status, seniority or professional qualifications. It excluded those that depend on the exercise of specific functions under singular conditions and that tend to compensate the inconveniences inherent to such exercise. ◀

The last attempt to reform the text of the Pregnant Workers Directive took place with a proposal in 2008.[44] Despite approval from the European Parliament in 2010, it was withdrawn in 2015 (by the Commission?). Among the proposed amendments, the European Parliament emphasized that not only should an adequate remuneration be guaranteed, but one similar to that received and also sufficient. Further amendments included provisions to prevent such enjoyment from having repercussions on future benefit rights, indicating that “the Member States should prevent this possibility and compensate for the possible loss of pension rights”. To this end, the amendment indicated that “*a period of maternity leave must not be prejudicial to the worker's pension rights and must be counted as a period of*

[41] Article 11.

[42] Case C-194/08, Gassmayr v Bundesminister für Wissenschaft und Forschung (ECJ, 1 July 2010).

[43] Case C-471/08, Parviainen v Finnair Oyj (ECJ, 1 July 2010).

[44] Proposal for a Directive of the European Parliament and of the Council amending Council Directive 92/85/EEC on the introduction of measures to encourage improvements in the safety and health at work of pregnant workers and workers who have recently given birth or are breastfeeding, COM(2008) 637 final.

employment for pension purposes, and workers must not suffer any reduction of pension rights through taking maternity leave".[45]

10.4.2 Paternity Benefits

Reconciliation rights formulated in a gender perspective must be formulated in an individualized manner and be non-transferable. Reconciliation measures require to be individualized in order to promote male exercise of these rights. Accordingly, they must attribute an individual right to each parent without the possibility of transfer, either by creating male entitlements or reserving a period of indistinct parental leave for the father. The most representative measure for the purposes of co-responsibility or reconciliation in terms of gender is paternity leave.

To this effect, the first action of the European Union towards the creation of rights involving the presence of the other parent, arrived with the Directive 96/34/EC (Parental Leave Directive).[46] Its character was limited by omission of some type of economic compensation; it did not establishing incentives for paternal enjoyment, or contain provisions on the needs of care for dependent elderly people. Such omissions motivated the approval of the new Council Directive. The Directive 2010/18/EU (Revised Parental Leave Directive)[47] recognised that its precedent had been insufficient to allow both parents to exercise their rights on equal terms. This failure required to be rectified, and a financial benefit during paternal leave to be guaranteed, as "many families may not afford to do so".[48] Further, the leaks in the non-transferability in which the conciliatory rights must be configured, prevented "a greater involvement of fathers in caring responsibilities".[49]

The Revised Parental Leave Directive recognized an individual right to parental leave for workers, men and women, on the birth or adoption of a child. This is in order to care for the child up to a certain age, set at eight years old. A minimum duration of 4 months is guaranteed, of which one month would be non-transferable. At the end of the leave the worker would be entitled to occupy the same or equivalent

[45]European Parliament legislative resolution of 20 October 2010 on the proposal for a directive of the European Parliament and of the Council amending Council Directive 92/85/EEC on the introduction of measures to encourage improvements in the safety and health at work of pregnant workers and workers who have recently given birth or are breastfeeding (COM(2008)0637 – C6-0340/2008 – 2008/0193(COD)).

[46]Council Directive 96/34/EC of 3 June 1996 "on the framework agreement on parental leave concluded by UNICE, CEEP and the ETUC", OJ L 145 (1996).

[47]Council Directive 2010/18/EU of 8 March 2010 "implementing the revised Framework Agreement on parental leave concluded by BUSINESSEUROPE, UEAPME, CEEP and ETUC", OJ L 68 (2010) and repealing Directive 96/34/EC.

[48]Proposal for a Directive of the European Parliament and of the Council on work-life balance for parents and carers and repealing Council Directive 2010/18/EU, COM/2017/0253 final - 2017/085.

[49]Proposal for a Directive of the European Parliament and of the Council on work-life balance for parents and carers and repealing Council Directive 2010/18/EU, COM/2017/0253 final - 2017/085.

job and to maintain the rights acquired, and in the process of acquisition, on the date of commencement of the leave.

However, despite the fact that in its fifth clause, the Directive warns of "the importance of the continuity of the entitlements to social security cover under the different schemes", it still reiterates that "all matters regarding social security in relation to this agreement are for consideration and determination by Member States and/or social partners according to national law and/or collective agreements".[50] In short, the Revised Parental Leave Directive was not the breakthrough that was expected.

In this vain, in 2017 the Commission submitted its proposal for a directive on work-life balance for parents and carers.[51] The objectives set out in this Proposal focus on combating the under-representation of women in employment and supporting women's careers; improving the conditions for reconciling their professional and private tasks. The aim being to combat the triple gender gap: employment; pay, and pensions.

Directive (EU) 2019/1158 (Work-Life-Balance Directive),[52] highlights that "[t] he imbalance in the design of work-life balance policies between women and men reinforces gender stereotypes and differences between work and care". In order to encourage men to assume family responsibilities in the moments after the birth of a child, the Directive creates paternity leave as a "leave from work for fathers or, where and insofar as recognised by national law, for equivalent second parents, on the occasion of the birth of a child for the purposes of providing care".[53] Previous attempts to amend the Pregnant Workers Directive that aimed, among other measures, to incorporate paternity leave failed. With regard to the proposal to amend the Pregnant Workers Directive in 2008, the European Parliament proposed changing its name to include paternity leave and adoption leave.[54]

In this regard Article 4 of Directive (EU) 2019/1158 (Revised Work-Life-Balance Directive) requires Member States to ensure

> "that fathers or, where and insofar as recognised by national law, equivalent second parents, have the right to paternity leave of 10 working days that is to be taken on the occasion of the birth of the worker's child. Member States may

---

[50] Clause 5.5.

[51] https://www.consilium.europa.eu/en/policies/work-life-balance/; The Proposal for a Directive of the European Parliament and of the Council on the reconciliation of the working and family life of parents and carers, which would repeal Directive 2010/18/EU.

[52] Directive (EU) 2019/1158 of 20 June 2019 "on work-life balance for parents and carers and repealing Council Directive 2010/18/EU", OJ L 188 (2019), published on July 12, 2019.

[53] Art. 3.1.a.

[54] European Parliament legislative resolution of 20 October 2010 on the proposal for a directive of the European Parliament and of the Council amending Council Directive 92/85/EEC on the introduction of measures to encourage improvements in the safety and health at work of pregnant workers and workers who have recently given birth or are breastfeeding (COM(2008)0637 – C6-0340/2008 – 2008/0193(COD)).

> determine whether to allow paternity leave to be taken partly before or only after the birth of the child and whether to allow such leave to be taken in flexible ways. The right to paternity leave shall not be made subject to a period of work qualification or to a length of service qualification. The right to paternity leave shall be granted irrespective of the worker's marital or family status, as defined by national law".

The remuneration or benefit to be received is regulated in article 8, which provides that

> "such payment or allowance shall guarantee an income at least equivalent to that which the worker concerned would receive in the event of a break in the worker's activities on grounds connected with the worker's state of health, subject to any ceiling laid down in national law. Member States may make the right to a payment or an allowance subject to periods of previous employment, which shall not exceed six months immediately prior to the expected date of the birth of the child".

The Revised Work-Life-Balance Directive underlines the relevance of economic coverage to guarantee its exercise, encouraging Member States to "provide for a payment or an allowance for paternity leave that is equal to the payment or allowance provided for maternity leave at national level", since the objectives of both permits are similar.

10.4.3 Family Benefits

Together with paternity leave, the most relevant rights created by Directive (EU) 2019/1158 are the new content parental leave, and a new caregiver's leave and absence from work due to force majeure. As this chapter has pointed out, the failure of the previous Directives was the lack of a financial benefit during parental leave, and the non-transferability in its formulation; reflecting the data that "most fathers did not take advantage of their right to parental leave, transferring a considerable proportion of it to mothers".[55]

▶ **Definition** Parental leave is an individual right "of four months that is to be taken before the child reaches a specified age, up to the age of eight, to be specified by each Member State or by collective agreement.";[56]

Carers' leave is an individual right "*of five working days per year.*";[57]

---

[55] Proposal for a Directive of the European Parliament and of the Council on work-life balance for parents and carers and repealing Council Directive 2010/18/EU, COM/2017/0253 final - 2017/085.

[56] Art. 5.

[57] Art. 6.

Time off from work is "the right to time off from work on grounds of force majeure for urgent family reasons in the case of illness or accident making the immediate attendance of the worker indispensable.[58]

Regarding the economic protection of these rights, only parental leave is attributed a remuneration; determined by the Member States or the social partners. The renumeration requires to be established to facilitate parental leave for both parents equally.[59] The Revised Work-Life Balance Directive underlines the importance of an adequate level of the respective payments and allowances that are guaranteed by it.[60]

With regard to caregiver's leave, the Directive stresses that although the Member States are free to decide whether to grant remuneration or a financial benefit, "*they are encouraged to introduce such a payment or an allowance in order to guarantee the effective take-up of the right by carers, in particular by men*".[61] Therefore, the importance of economic protection for the rights aimed at reconciliation as a stimulus for its exercise, especially for men, must be emphasized; this financial incentive promotes the reversal of roles in the assumption of family responsibilities. Childcare should not cause a financial loss, nor affect the future acquisition of benefit entitlements (for example, when a minimum contribution period is required prior to the event that causes the protection). Social security systems should provide this dual protection for all genders equally.

The ECJ has had occasion to rule on the amount to be received during parental leave, although there was no such coverage at the time, the rulings highlighted the full competence of the Member States:

Example

In 2009[62] the Court held that it was not discriminatory treatment on grounds of sex contrary to the Social Security Directive, for a national regulation to calculate the social benefit for permanent disability of a female worker according to the salary, reduced due to a reduction in her working hours for childcare and not according to what she would have received if she had maintained her full-time working hours. This case is of great relevance, since the distorting element, the reduction of working hours, was connected to the exercise of a right to conciliation. The Directive does not make it compulsory to grant social security benefits to persons who take care of their child. The financial implications that a decision declaring discriminatory treatment may have on the system are a condition for the rulings of the Court of Justice. Therefore, when such repercussions are not at

[58] Art. 7.

[59] Art. 8.

[60] Directive (EU) 2019/1158, L 188/82 (31).

[61] Directive (EU) 2019/1158, L 188/83 (32).

[62] Case C-537/07, Gómez-Limón v Instituto Nacional de la Seguridad Social (ECJ, 16 July 2009).

stake, the commitment to gender equality is strengthened, "transferring to the scope of parental leave the doctrine of indemnity derived from the exercise of maternity rights".[63] This decision has to be seen in light of the ECJ's decision adopted in a further case[64] where the Court analysed the salary that should be taken into account in the calculation of compensation for dismissal, when the worker had enjoyed a reduced working day for care. The Court concluded it should be calculated by taking into account the salary corresponding to the full working day, and not the salary received during the reduced working day. As we can see, this protection was not applied in a case involving the Spanish National Institute of Social Security.[65] Article 7(1)(b) of the Social Security Directive safeguards the competence of the Member States to grant advantages to people who have taken on the care of children and who have therefore suffered a chain of disadvantages; a reduction in their professional career; and consequently in their contribution to Social Security, both of which affects future access to benefits. Advantages which, depending on the Directive, may be directed at the retirement age (for example, in reducing the age required for access) or at granting specific benefits (for example, in Spain, suspension of employment to care for a child does not interrupt the contribution to Social Security). ◀

10.5 Gender Gaps in the Pension System

10.5.1 Pension System: Old-Age, Invalidity and Survivors Pensions

The Social Security Directive has not been updated or amended to date. Although it has led to the elimination of direct and indirect discrimination, it has not been sufficient to promote gender equality; women are still generally under-protected in the Social Security systems. Rectification of this would require a radical change in said systems. The Social Security Directive certainly proclaims equal treatment between men and women in Social Security matters. However, reducing it to benefits related to the employment relationship, the Directive does not extend beyond the strict labour sphere, in which there are undoubtedly differences between women and men. There is no recognition of acting in other spheres that reflect the role that has traditionally been attributed to women in the family structure. Remedying this would promote the individualization of the rights of access to Social Security benefits; recognising work performed in the home, and especially in the care of dependent persons (elderly, sick, etc.).

The Social Security Directive excludes certain matters from its scope of application. Of all the matters excluded from the scope of application of the Directive, the

[63] Lousada Arochena (2014).

[64] Case C-116/08, Meerts contra Proost NV (ECJ, 22 October 2009).

[65] Case C-537/07, Gómez-Limón v Instituto Nacional de la Seguridad Social (ECJ, 16 July 2009).

setting of different ages for access to retirement on the basis of sex should be highlighted. Its importance derives from the fact it conditions their access and configuration to such an important contributory benefit as retirement, directly connected with the profile that generally characterizes their insurance careers. Bearing in mind that the Directive does not establish a maximum period of time for the duration of such an exception, the survival of such exceptions in domestic regulations has been extended to the present day. However, it generalized the forecast of a gradual regime to achieve equalization, [66] in compliance with the indications contained in the *White Paper of 2012* promoting the equalization of retirement ages; "this persistence of gender inequalities on the labour market leads to lower pension entitlements for women".[67] This legal incentive to the retirement of women, prior to those of men, only increases their risk of poverty.

Example

In a case which arose as a result of a reform in the United Kingdom, according to which the retirement age for women would gradually increase from 60 to 65 years. A woman considered that such a change would harm her in the future and filed a complaint before the ECtHR. In its judgement the ECtHR was adamant in stressing that the difference between men and women in terms of retirement ages is currently not justified.[68] *"[A]s the Court found in Stec and Others, [. . .], providing for women to receive the State Pension five years earlier than men was originally justified as a means of mitigating financial inequality arising out of women's traditional unpaid role of caring for the family in the home rather than earning money in the workplace. However, as social conditions changed and increasing numbers of women were no longer substantially prejudiced because of a shorter working life, the difference in the pensionable age for men and women ceased to be justified".*[69] ◄

However, the ECJ through case law, has gradually established a restrictive interpretation of the exception, making the following clarifications: the possibility of establishing different retirement ages is exceptional; the consequences that may arise for other benefits are limited to existing discrimination in other systems that are necessarily and objectively linked to the difference in age; and, if national legislation does not provide for such a difference or has eliminated it, it is not possible to establish ex novo or reinstate such an exception.[70]

---

[66] The countries that maintain a different retirement age for men and women, with an indication of those that have adopted reforms to achieve homogenization, can be observed in: https://www.missoc.org/missoc-database/comparative-tables/results/.

[67] European Commission, White Paper, An Agenda for Adequate, Safe and Sustainable Pensions, Brussels, 16.2.2012, COM(2012) 55 final, p. 12.

[68] App. Nos. 26252/08, Case S.V. Richardson v. UK (ECtHR, 10 April 2012).

[69] Paragraph 23.

[70] Case De Vriendt, C-377/96 (30 April 1998), Case Van Cant, C-154/92 (25 May 1993).

First, direct discrimination was eliminated from the national social security rules. The Court of Justice detected overt discrimination that referred to the concept of "married woman" or "head of household" which reflected the subordinate position attributed to women with respect to the home and work. Thus, we can cite cases of direct discrimination against women: when married women who cohabited with their husbands or were dependent on them were denied access to disability benefits, while married men were granted such benefits under the same conditions; when married women were granted a reduced unemployment benefit in terms of amount and duration, as opposed to those enjoyed by single women and men, married or single, and when, for a certain period of time, the calculation of retirement and old-age pensions for working women was based on lower wages than those of male workers.[71]

The ECJ has also found discrimination against men. For example, in a case that analysed a Belgian law on self-employed workers that provided for the possibility for married women, widows and students to be assimilated to persons who do not have to pay any social security contributions when their income did not reach a minimum level.[72] The ECJ considered the national legislation to be contrary to the Directive, since it did not grant the same possibility to married men or widowers who fulfilled all the conditions required.

Of greater interest have been the pronouncements of the ECJ regarding the possible existence of indirect discrimination, being most common at present. The reasons alleged to objectively justify the existing difference acquire great relevance when it is aimed at achieving a legitimate aim of the social policy of the Member State.

Other examples of indirectly discriminatory regulations are: when an increase in the amount of a disability benefit is provided, taking into account the marital status and income of the spouse to guarantee a minimum subsistence; or, when the granting of, or amount of a pension increase depends on the income of the beneficiary's spouse.[73]

Example

In a case an Austrian law regulating a complex system of pension revaluation was discussed, with the increase foreseen for the year 2008 being less advantageous for one group (affecting a greater number of female pensioners) and more beneficial for another group (being mostly male pensioners). The ECJ concluded that: *"a national arrangement which leads to the exclusion, from an exceptional pension increase, of a significantly higher percentage of female pensioners than male pensioners"* cannot be justified *"by the fact that women*

[71] Case Drake, C-150/85 (24 June 1986), Case NV, sentencia de 4 de diciembre de 1986), Case McDermott y Cotter, C-286/85 (24 March 1987), Case Brouwer, C-577/08 (29 July 2010).

[72] Case C-373/89, "Integrity" v Rouvroy (ECJ, 21 November 1990).

[73] Case Teuling, C-30/85 (11 July 1987), Case Molenbrok, C-226/91 (19 November 1992).

who have worked become entitled to a pension at an earlier age or that they receive their pension over a longer period, or because the compensatory supplement standard amount was also subject to an exceptional increase in respect of the same year 2008".[74]

In conclusion, and as the specialized doctrine has stated, the Court of Justice usually justifies Public Social Security measures causing an adverse impact when their purposes fall within the social policy competences of the Member States, showing "enormous caution in the face of the possible economic consequences derived from its decisions and the fear of interfering in the social policies of the national legislator".[75] ◄

10.5.2 Access to Pension System Benefits (Public and Supplementary—Occupational and Personal—Pension Schemes)

For decades we have been witnessing a strengthening of supplementary, occupational and personal, pension schemes by the European Commission. However, concern has been expressed about the lesser possibilities for women to access and benefit from these systems due to their unequal situation in the labour market. In the following paragraph we will highlight the main aspects of European regulation that have had the greatest gender impact.

With regard to the public system, we have had the opportunity in the second section of this chapter to examine in depth the requirements for enjoying protection and its gender impact. In the previous section, we also examined the issue of the different ages for access to retirement according to sex.

Of these requirements, we can now underline the importance of the requirement of a minimum contribution period, since it has a significant impact on women. In the first place, when the contribution to the system is suspended due to childcare. Therefore, we must reiterate the importance of granting economic benefits that are accompanied by the corresponding contribution to the system. Secondly, because it affects a group of workers with a predominantly female presence, part-time work.

Example

Indirect discrimination continues to be detected in the regulation of the rights of part-time workers in the Social Security system. In a case involving the Spanish General Treasury of the Social Security[76] the Court declared the Spanish

---

[74] Case C-123/10, Brachner contra Pensionsversicherungsanstalt, (ECJ, 20 October 2011).

[75] Lousada Arochena (2014).

[76] C-385/11, Elbal Moreno v Instituto Nacional de la Seguridad Social (INSS) y Tesorería General de la Seguridad Social (TGSS) (ECJ, 22 November 2012).

legislation regulating the social protection of part-time workers was contrary to the prohibition of indirect discrimination on grounds of sex. In sharp contrast, no adverse impact was detected in another case against the (same?) Spanish institution,[77] handed down on the formulation of the mechanism for the integration of gaps applicable to part-time workers. Finally, in the most recent case,[78] the court referred to unemployment protection in which the ECJ detected the discriminatory treatment existing in the computation of contributions to determine access to the benefit. Are these three separate cases involving the same Spanish institution? ◄

Occupational regimes were adopted in the Council Directive 86/378/EEC (Equal Treatment in Social Security Schemes Directive).[79] This Directive was affected by the expansive case law developed by the Court of Justice. Consequently, the Directive was subject to modification a decade later, due to its content being exhausted by case law. The profound recasting process is contained in the Equal Treatment Directive whose Chapter II of Title I under the heading "Equal treatment in occupational social security schemes" devotes articles 5 to 13 to this end. The Directive is applicable to 'occupational social security schemes', including those schemes that are not governed by the Social Security Directive, whose purpose is to provide workers "*benefits intended to supplement the benefits provided by statutory social security schemes or to replace them, whether membership of such schemes is compulsory or optional*".[80]

As for employer's contributions to defined benefit plans, financed by capitalization, differences are accepted by the regulations when such contributions are intended to complete the financial allocation necessary to cover the costs of such defined benefits. These considerations mean that actuarial factors can be used on the basis of sex to produce legitimate differentiations, which the ECJ has ruled on in several cases.[81] In these cases, factors linked to demographic hypotheses were analysed, based on the higher life expectancy of women. This implies that their future pension will be more onerous than that of men, requiring higher contributions from the employer. Indeed, based on forecasts, the Plan's financing mechanism made adjustments to the pensions to be paid, using a series of objective elements including: the profitability of the Plan's investments; the rate of salary increase, and certain demographic hypotheses, such as those relating to the life expectancy of the workers. The ECJ held in both cases, that: "*the use of actuarial factors varying*

[77] Case C-527/13, Cachaldora Fernández v Instituto Nacional de la Seguridad Social (INSS) y Tesorería General de la Seguridad Social (TGSS) (ECJ, 14 April 2015).

[78] Case C-98/15, Espadas Recio v Servicio Público de Empleo Estatal (ECJ, 9 November 2017).

[79] Council Directive 86/378/EEC of 24 July 1986 "on the implementation of the principle of equal treatment for men and women in occupational social security schemes", OJ L 225 (1986).

[80] Art. 2 f).

[81] Case C-200/91, Coloroll Pension Trustees v Russell and Others, (ECJ 28 September 1994), and the Case C-152/91, Neath v Steeper (ECJ, 22 December 1993).

according to sex in funded defined benefit occupational pension schemes does not fall within the scope of Article 119 of the Treaty. Consequently, inequalities in the amounts of capital benefits or substitute benefits whose value can be determined only on the basis of the arrangements chosen for funding the scheme are likewise not struck at by Article 119".[82] The court further ruled in other cases that the cause of discrimination was not the sex itself but the change of sex.[83] Specifically, the right of a worker's transsexual partner to access a survivor's pension was denied; the pension was limited to married couples and compliance with this requirement was impossible for same-sex couples. In the case in question, despite having physically changed sex, the claimant could not legally do so, hence the impossibility of getting married. The Court of Justice declared that it is an internal decision of each country to reserve certain benefits to married couples, excluding those who have not married, without any discrimination being invoked. However "*inequality of treatment which, although it does not directly undermine enjoyment of a right protected by Community law, affects one of the conditions for the grant of that right*"[84] by preventing the enjoyment of a benefit which constitutes an element of remuneration, must be considered contrary to article 141 TFEU.

Finally, the importance of ensuring that pensions are adequate, and the role of supplementary pensions, needs to be emphasized; "from an adequacy perspective, the main function of supplementary pensions is to enhance the income maintenance capacity of pension systems".[85] However, the Commission noted in the aforementioned White Paper that "*addressing gender equality aspects will also be crucial in order to avoid widening the existing gender gaps, as women currently have fewer opportunities to build up supplementary retirement savings than men*".[86]

10.5.3 Differences in Pension Income Between Women and Men

The cumulative negative effects of the labour and wage gap over the course of a person's working life subsequently spread to access, and value of, pensions, thus, creating or compounding the existing gender gap. As established earlier "the gender pension gap mostly reflects gender pay inequalities (which lead to lifetime earnings inequality and result from differences in past employment, including work intensity

[82] Paragraph 10.

[83] Case C-117/01, K.B. v National Health Service Pensions Agency and Secretary of State for Health (ECJ, 7 January 2001).

[84] Paragraph 20.

[85] European Commission, The 2018 Pension Adequacy Report: current and future income adequacy in old age in the EU, p. 79: "Supplementary pensions are pension schemes that can be accessed on the basis of professional activity (occupational pensions) or individual pension savings contracts (personal pensions), and that provide additional retirement savings, complementing statutory pensions".

[86] European Commission, White Paper, An Agenda for Adequate, Safe and Sustainable Pensions, Brussels, 16.2.2012, COM(2012) 55 final.

and career breaks) and the extent to which pension design features mitigate these differences".[87]

The gender gap in pensions has become the most recent expression of gender discrimination arising from the social and labour situation of women that requires to be addressed. The European Parliament pointed out "*the imperative need to reduce gender gaps in pay and pension*", underlining the increased number of women "*living in poverty and exclusion, especially older women, whose average pension level is 39% lower than that of men*".[88]

As the Council recognizes, "the gender gap in pensions has received less attention to date than the gender gap in salaries".[89] The phenomenon only recently acquired its own individualization, which must be addressed and eliminated. The gender pension gap in the European Union reaches an average differential of 30.1%,[90] constituting one of the obstacles "for the economic independence of women in old age, a time when women also face a higher risk of poverty than men".[91]

The need to carry out actions from both a curative and preventive perspective, for both current and future pensioners, has been reinforced. The *Strategic engagement for gender equality 2016-2019*[92] contains as priority areas, among others, the reduction of existing gender disparities in pay, income and pensions, in order to combat poverty among women. In relation to achieving such objectives, it underlines the relevance of addressing "the causes and consequences of the gender pension gap need to be addressed, as this is an obstacle to the economic independence of women in old age, when they face a higher risk of poverty than men".[93] As key actions, it stipulates the further development of a comprehensive set of measures to address all causes of the gender gap in pensions, in cooperation with the Member States. This includes the requirement to measure and monitor the gender gap in pensions, and to introduce measures to mitigate gender-related factors,[94] for example in relation to caregiving.

The *A Union of Equality: Gender Equality Strategy 2020-2025* emphasizes that, "accumulated lifetime gender employment and pay gaps result in an even wider

[87]European Commission, Social Protection Committee, The 2018 Pension Adequacy Report: current and future income adequacy in old age in the EU Volume I, 2018.

[88]European Parliament resolution of 10 March 2015 on progress on equality between women and men in the European Union in 2013 (2014/2217(INI)).

[89]Council Of The European Union, Equal income opportunities for men and women: closing the pension gender gap, Brussels, 19 June 2015.

[90]European Commission, A Union of Equality: Gender Equality Strategy 2020-2025, Brussels, 5.3.2020 COM(2020) 152 final.

[91]Council Of The European Union, Equal income opportunities for men and women: closing the pension gender gap, Brussels, 19 June 2015.

[92]Commission's 2016-2019 strategic engagement for gender equality.

[93]Commission's 2016-2019 strategic engagement for gender equality, p. 12.

[94]Communication from the Commission to the European Parliament, the Council, the European Economic and Social Committee and the Committee of the Regions, A Union of Equality: Gender Equality Strategy 2020-2025, Brussels, 5.3.2020, COM(2020) 152 final.

pension gap and consequently older women are more at risk of poverty than men. Eliminating the gender pay gap requires addressing all of its root causes, including women's lower participation in the labour market, invisible and unpaid work, their higher use of part-time work and career breaks, as well as vertical and horizontal segregation based on gender stereotypes and discrimination".[95]

10.5.4 Measures to Reduce the Gender Pension Gap

The European institutions have continued to work intensively to promote gender equality and are currently committed to combating the persistent triple gender gap; labour, wages and pensions. Various policies are therefore being implemented with this focus.

To combat the triple gender gap, efforts have focused on promoting a greater incorporation of women into the labour market; previously undermined by the attribution of gender roles that link women to conciliatory needs. The objective is to guarantee women's economic independence, increasingly linked to generic benefits for the economy and society. To this end, the *Gender Equality Strategy 2020-2025* prioritises the reduction of existing gender disparities in pay, income and pensions in order to combat poverty among women.[96]

The focus is on the promotion and protection of employment in key areas of gender inequalities: maternity; reconciliation, and part-time work. We will now focus on part-time work, given the previous sections have covered maternity and reconciliation. In this respect, we can observe a change of direction in the European guidelines. Although part-time work continues to be a mechanism by which people manage to remain in the labour market, the consequences of forging a working career built solely or preferably on part-time work are recognized. Consequently, it is emphasized that the percentage of women working part-time is an indicator of gender equality in the labour market. Part-time work is an important factor in keeping women in the labour market, especially after becoming mothers, particular attention must be drawn to the corresponding serious disadvantages; it is one of the key elements contributing to the gender wage gap. In turn, this hinders present and future economic independence, insofar as its impact on access to social protection, especially in terms of unemployment benefits and pensions.

In relation to the gender gap in pensions,[97] the European Union has suggested that possible gender biases in pension systems should be addressed. It stresses the

[95] Communication from the Commission to the European Parliament, the Council, the European Economic and Social Committee and the Committee of the Regions, A Union of Equality: Gender Equality Strategy 2020-2025, Brussels, 5.3.2020, COM(2020) 152 final.

[96] Communication from the Commission to the European Parliament, the Council, the European Economic and Social Committee and the Committee of the Regions, A Union of Equality: Gender Equality Strategy 2020-2025, Brussels, 5.3.2020, COM(2020) 152 final.

[97] "Pension systems can either attenuate or widen the gap. There are two direct mechanisms in the pension system that mitigate the gender gaps in pensions at the lower and the upper tails of the

importance of carrying out gender impact assessments prior to the adoption of reforms (also in the adoption of public policies), as well as the adoption of measures that "*mitigate the negative impacts of work interruptions due to family responsibilities, part-time work and slow wage progression on pension rights*".[98] In short, it is stated that "*the reconciliation model proposed by the European Union closes the way to the use of part-time work as an instrument to solve the tensions between work and family life*".[99]

Example

The promotion by European institutions of measures to mitigate the gender gap in pensions led Spain to create a specific measure for this purpose; the "*maternity supplement in the contributory pensions of the Social Security system*".[100] This instrument is granted as compensation for the "*demographic contribution to Social Security*", which was declared discriminatory by the ECJ,[101] given that its application was intended only for women. The court declared that the measure does not bring "*a remedy for the problems which they may encounter in the course of their professional career, and that supplement does not appear to compensate for the disadvantages to which women are exposed by helping them in that career and, thus, to ensure full equality in practice between men and women in working life* without "*men who find themselves in an identical situation not [being] entitled to such a pension supplement*" declaring it as direct discriminatory treatment on grounds of sex. The supplement was subject to a modification that would lead to its reformulation of its name and content, generating the "contributory pension supplement for the reduction of the gender gap". The controversial reference to maternity and demographic contribution is eliminated, now the expressly stated objective of the measure is the elimination of the gender gap in pensions. ◀

In order to combat the gender gap in pensions, multiple actions must be taken as a whole; "pension systems cannot compensate for all the consequences of adverse events and developments that build up over people's working lives".[102]

---

distribution. First, basic and minimum pensions provide a lower bound for pensions. At the other end of the distribution, the ceiling for coverage or a direct cap on pensions provides an upper bound for pensions paid". European Commission, The 2018 Pension Adequacy Report: current and future income adequacy in old age in the EU, p. 78.

[98]Council Of The European Union, Equal income opportunities for men and women: closing the pension gender gap, Brussels, 19 June 2015.

[99]Martínez Yáñez (2015).

[100]Article 60 of the Spanish General Law on Social Security.

[101]Case C-450/18, WA v Instituto Nacional de la Seguridad Social (ECJ, 12 December 2019, C-450/18).

[102]European Commission, The 2018 Pension Adequacy Report: current and future income adequacy in old age in the EU, p. 78.

10.6 Gender Perspective in the Protection in the Event of Unemployment

In accordance with the provisions of Article 3.1 a) of the Social Security Directive, this Directive includes within its scope of application, the protection of the risk of unemployment to be provided by national regimes. As indicated in the preceding paragraphs, the principle of equal treatment must be respected with regard to: the requirements demanded; calculation of the amount of the benefit; the conditions governing its duration, and the requirements to be met to maintain this benefit. Such requirements and conditions need to be established by each of the Member States, without prejudice to the provisions in the "Regulation (EC) no 883/2004 (Social Security Systems Regulation).[103]

10.7 Gender Perspective in Social Assistance and Pension Plans and Complementary Welfare Schemes

The Social Security Directive, as stated in Article 3(1)(b), includes in its scope of application provisions relating to social assistance, insofar as they are intended to supplement or replace the schemes referred to in point (a). These provisions must therefore be covered by the principle of equal treatment, as provided for therein.

What is social assistance and how does it differ from Social Security benefits? Social assistance benefits are usually universal and complementary to Social Security benefits; beneficiaries are required to meet certain conditions, mainly related to an income ceiling. They are financed by the State, generally through the General State Budget. On the other hand, Social Security benefits require that the beneficiary has normally contributed to the system as a result of an occupational activity, and therefore are financed from these contributions.

Example

Examples of social assistance benefits, are:

a) family financial assistance in cash or in kind, which is granted to families to meet the basic needs of dependent minors when they lack sufficient financial resources to do so. This is aimed at preventing, reducing or eliminating factors that generate situations of difficulty or social risk for minors. This favours their permanence and integration in the family and social environment, thus avoiding situations of lack of protection that could arise if the same circumstances continue
b) assistance aid for illness or old age

[103] Regulation (EC) no 883/2004 of the European Parliament and of the council of 29 April 2004 on the coordination of Social Security systems.

c) minimum income guarantee subsidy in favour of persons whose own or family income is insufficient to cover basic needs. ◀

The study of social protection cannot be concluded without mentioning the complementary level of protection, or third level. This level includes those benefits that are complementary to those provided by the public system and granted by the employer; through collective bargaining agreements, and pension plans(for the purposes of this study, those in which the employer is responsible for recognising the benefits granted by these plans).[104] There are several pronouncements of the ECJ in this respect, where the gender perspective has been taken into account in a broader vision, by considering "sexual orientation" as a possible cause of discrimination. This requires reliance not on the Social Security Directive, but on Council Directive 2000/78/EC (Equal Treatment in Employment Directive);[105] Article 3 of the Directive itself provides that it does not apply to payments of any kind made by public or similar schemes, including public Social Security or social protection schemes. This does not preclude its applicability to the so-called "supplementary level of protection". Thus, the ECJ has held that Article 1, in conjunction with Article 2, of the Equal Treatment in Employment Directive precludes legislation under which the surviving partner of a registered partnership, after the death of the other partner, is not entitled to a survivor's pension equivalent to that granted to a surviving spouse simply because it is not expressly recognised for the latter. This despite the fact that, with regard to survival benefit, national law treats registered same-sex partners the same as spouses.[106]

10.8 Conclusion

Social Security, as analysed above, includes among its protected situations, situations directly related to the status of women, such as pregnancy, maternity or breastfeeding. However, the gender perspective has not been immune to the protection provided by Social Security systems in situations of need, generated by the materialisation of a risk. Situations of need, in principle, should be neutral regarding to the necessary requirements for its protection. Nevertheless, inclusion in the Social Security systems and access requirements, mainly in terms of prior qualifying periods or the determination of their amount, have required the interpretation of the ECJ when determining the applicability of the principle of equal treatment in this area. Notwithstanding the above, the European Union legislation currently applicable in this area, the Social Security Directive, is proving to be insufficient as a result

[104] In extenso, Natali, Pavolini, Vanhercke (2020).

[105] Council Directive 2000/78/EC (Equal Treatment in Employment Directive) of 27 November 2000, establishing a general framework for equal treatment in employment and occupation, OJ L 303, 2.12.2000, pp. 16–22.

[106] Judgment of the Court (Grand Chamber) 1 April 2008, Case C-267/06, Maruko.

of the new emerging social reality. It is the ECJ which, through its rulings, is managing to adapt the Directive to this reality. Perhaps it is time to call for the adaptation of European Union regulations on Social Security to the gender perspective, understanding this in its broadest sense, in order to take into account any emerging personal situation.

Questions

1. Nowadays, is there only one Social Security Model?
2. Which is the model whose characteristics benefit more women than men, taking into account the labour market?
3. Explain the reasons that justify your answer in the previous question.
4. Which are the European Law rules to ensure respect for the basic principle of equal treatment in the Social Security?
5. Why is the role of the Court of Justice relevant to implement the principle of equal treatment between women and men in social protection?
6. What are the factors that generate the gender pension gap?
7. Indicate possible measures to reduce the pension gap.
8. Why is the provision of a financial allowance relevant to reconciliation rights?
9. What is the purpose and scope of the Directive 79/7/EEC?
10. Does the Directive allow Member States to set different ages for access to retirement based on gender?

References

Conde-Ruiz JI, González C (2016) From Bismarck to Beveridge: the other pension reform in Spain. SERIEs 7:461–490

Dale J, Foster P (1986) Feminists and state welfare. Routledge, London

EIGE. Persons reporting an accident at work by sex, age and size of enterprise. https://eige.europa.eu/gender-statistics/dgs/indicator/ta_wrklab_wrk_cond_wrkhealthsaf_acc_gen__hsw_ac9. Accessed 9 Nov 2021

ETUI (2018) Occupational welfare in Europe: risks, opportunities and social partner involvement. https://www.etui.org/publications/books/occupational-welfare-in-europe-risks-opportunities-and-social-partner-involvement. Accessed 9 Nov 2021

European Commission (2012) White Paper, an agenda for adequate, safe and sustainable pensions. European Commission, Brussels

European Commission (2018) Social Protection Committee, The 2018 Pension Adequacy Report: current and future income adequacy in old age in the EU, vol I. European Commission, Brussels

European Commission (2020) A Union of Equality: Gender Equality Strategy 2020-2025. European Commission, Brussels

García AM (2005) La protección social en la Unión Europea, ¿un modelo homogéneo?. http://repositori.uji.es/xmlui/bitstream/handle/10234/85450/Millan_Garcia_La_proteccion_social_en_la_UE_2005.pdf?sequence=1&isAllowed=y. Accessed 9 Nov 2021

Lousada Arochena JF (2014) El derecho fundamental a la igualdad efectiva de mujeres y hombres. Tirant lo Blanch, Valencia

Martínez Yáñez N (2015) Flexibilidad del trabajo a tiempo parcial y conciliación de la vida laboral y familiar. In: Méndez LM (ed) Conciliación de la vida laboral y familiar y crisis económica: Estudios desde el derecho internacional y comparado. Delta, McHenry, pp 165–182
Monereo Pérez JL (2015) William Henry Beveridge (1879 1963): the construction of modern Social Security systems. Revista de Derecho de la Seguridad Social 4:279–305
Pampillón Olmedo R (2008) The nordic economic model. Revista de Economía Mundial 18:155–165
Pascal G (1997) Social policy: a new feminist analysis. Routledge, London

Further Reading

de la Corte Rodríguez M (2019) EU law on maternity and other child related leaves – impact on gender equality, bulletin of comparative labour relations. Wolters Kluwer, Barcelona
De la Corte Rodríguez M (2021) Recent cases and the future of Directive 79/7/CEE on equal treatment for men and women in Social Security: how to realise its full potential. Eur J Soc Secur 23
Goldblatt B (2016) Developing the right to social security – a gender perspective. Routledge, London
Steinbiller S (2009) Gender aspect of social security and pensions. In: United Nations Economic Commission for Europe, gender gap and economic policy – trends from the UNECE region, pp 69–86
Tobler C (2011) Test-Achats or: the limits of lobbying. Eur Gender Equal Law Rev 2:1–3

Gender Equitable Taxation 11

Marco Cedro, Eleonor Kristoffersson, Teresa Pontón Aricha, and Lidija Živković

Contents

Authors are listed in alphabetical order. Marco Cedro authored Sect. 11.4, Sect. 11.2 is written by Eleonor Kristoffersson. Teresa Pontón Aricha wrote Sect. 11.1, Lidija Živković Sect. 11.3 and the conclusion is authored by Teresa Pontón Aricha and Lidija Živković.

M. Cedro
LUMSA, Palermo, Italy
e-mail: m.cedro@lumsa.it

E. Kristoffersson
Örebro University, School of Law, Psychology and Social Work, Örebro, Sweden
e-mail: eleonor.kristoffersson@oru.se

T. Pontón Aricha
University of Cadiz, Faculty of Law, Jerez de la Frontera, Spain
e-mail: teresa.ponton@uca.es

L. Živković (✉)
University of Belgrade, Faculty of Law, Belgrade, Serbia
e-mail: lidija.zivkovic@ius.bg.ac.rs

D. Vujadinović et al. (eds.), *Gender-Competent Legal Education*, Springer Textbooks in Law, https://doi.org/10.1007/978-3-031-14360-1_11

Abstract

From Adam Smith's 1776 classic "The Wealth of Nations" until modern times, the principle of fairness has remained one of the crucial principles on which tax systems are to be based. However, even modern tax and budgetary systems are far from being gender equitable. This chapter provides an analysis of the ways in which taxation, as well as the subsequent spending of resources collected therewith, influence gender equality within a household, at the workplace and within the broader economy. This analysis should enable the reader to utilise the gender equality principle as a framework for re-evaluating the applicable national and international sources of tax law, as well as public expenditure management on various levels of the government. This chapter will show why gender equality should become a priority for governments when creating their fiscal policy and executing their budgets.

11.1 Introduction

One of the main legal concepts that will accompany us throughout our lives is tax. Taxation is essential for our decision-making, whether business or personal, and it must be fair. All of us have heard the quote: "In this world nothing can be said to be certain, except death and taxes." This quote has been attributed to Benjamin Franklin, written in 1789 in his letter to Jean-Baptiste Le Roy, but it was not Franklin who wrote this. Its author is Christopher Bullock who, in The Cobbler of Preston in 1716, said "It is impossible to be sure of anything but Death and Taxes".[1] This fallacy serves us with a dual purpose: firstly, to demonstrate the importance of a matter sometimes forgotten in the legal world due to its economic consequences, and secondly, to invite the reader of these pages to challenge traditional conventions. We accept certain issues that are not such. Although we thought that the quote was associated with Franklin, it actually is not. In most cases we are going to face a taxation in which the language is formally egalitarian but are going to discover that its effects are not. The concept of a taxpayer seems neutral and alien to gender issues,

[1] Bullock (1716).

but the configuration and evolution of the tax system that we are studying shows us that this is not the case.

The first point to be addressed is that fair taxation is essential for sustaining public expenditures and the welfare state in which we live in both developed and developing countries. In 1776 Adam Smith said: "The subjects of every state ought to contribute towards the support of the government, as nearly as possible, in proportion to their respective abilities".[2] This principle is still in force, equality and equity in taxation make taxes good. It is important both how we tax and how we collect tax. So, if the system is harmful from the point of view of gender equality, it will not be a fair system. It should be noted that no principle or guideline is introduced that is not already recognised in the field of both international and domestic taxation where equality, equity and tax justice are established as essential principles and values.

On the other hand, taxation has two indivisible dimensions. Taxation is closely linked to state sovereignty. Taxes serve as the basis for meeting the needs of citizens and provide economic incentives that affect different areas such as the labour market, consumption, investments, etc. And one essential need is gender equality. In modern times, tax systems seem to have evolved to a theoretical equality since they are based on concepts such as economic capacity, income and consumption. This contains in itself an important fallacy since the tax system really becomes a discriminating element, depending on the gender of the taxpayer whether man, woman or third gender, but is hidden by neutral legislative language. Throughout this chapter we will address the aforementioned evolution of tax systems. Most of the systems in European countries have been created taking into consideration the concept of a traditional family with a father who obtains the income and a mother who takes care of the household and children. However, this approach is no longer valid. Our tax laws must advance and adapt to a different reality for which they are not yet prepared. In fact, it privileges or penalises people's family choices and circumstances, which means that it excludes and discriminates.

Section 11.2 will provide an overview and an explanation of the basic tax law concepts necessary for proper understanding of the following sections. Furthermore, it will analyse the evolution of modern tax systems from a gender perspective. An overview and analysis of crucial sources of public international law relevant for analysing tax systems from a gender perspective will be provided. Finally, the concept of the welfare state and its importance for the improvement of the position of women and minorities in society will be explained.

The manner in which tax systems around the world discriminates against certain groups of the population on the basis of gender will be analysed in Sect. 11.3, within the framework of various taxes: personal income taxes, corporate income taxes, property and wealth taxes, as well as consumption taxes. Whereas gender biases are more evident in the field of personal income taxation, this section will show that other types of taxes also contain gender biases that, although less evident, deserve to be addressed.

[2] Smith (1776), Bk 5 Chpt 02 (II).

At the end of this chapter, the other side of state budgets will be addressed from a gender perspective—the side of public spending. The question of public expenditures is closely related to the preceding sections which deal with the configuration of the tax system itself and the tax policies implemented to achieve equality. Therefore, Sect. 11.4 will show why it is so important that the budgeting is conducted in such a way that it takes into account the gender effects of public spending and what tool is utilised to achieve that.

Learning Goals

- Students should understand that taxes have a transversal character and affect all legal activities and businesses, rendering not only their economic but also legal analysis necessary.
- Students should understand that it is necessary to address the question of gender from the point of view of both the drafting as well as imposition of tax laws and understand the meaning and importance of the concept of gender responsive budgeting.
- Students should be able to identify and distinguish between implicit and explicit discrimination within a certain tax system.

11.2 The Relevance of Taxation for Gender Equality

The first section of the main part provides a framework for understanding the gender perspective of key tax law concepts and sets the basis for the re-evaluation thereof on the basis of gender equality principle.

11.2.1 Basic Tax Law Concepts and Gender Equality Related Issues

As long as men and women face different socio-economic realities, equal tax laws will affect them differently.[3] From the previous chapters in this book we have learnt that women spend more time at home with their children than men and that they earn less than men. Women in general own less capital than men. From a tax law perspective, this has implications for taxation of capital gains and dividends from the holding of corporate shares.[4] Women own less businesses than men and are underrepresented in corporate boards and among senior managers.[5] Furthermore, the

[3] Harding et al. (2020). https://oecdecoscope.blog/2020/06/01/in-tax-gender-blind-is-not-gender-neutral-why-tax-policy-responses-to-covid-19-must-considerwomen/. Accessed 11 April 2021.

[4] See Perez-Navarro and Harding (2021). https://www.oecd.org/tax/tax-policy/presentation-march-on-gender-2021-in-tax-gender-blind-is-not-gender-neutral.pdf. Accessed 11 April 2021.

[5] Ibid.

consumption patterns differ between men and women, which may have implications for indirect taxes.[6]

To be able to dig into the gender related issues in taxation, basic knowledge of crucial tax law concepts is needed. Taxation is not only fundamental to all states to secure state revenue, but is also an important political tool. "No taxation without representation" is originally a slogan from the American Revolution, which has become a basic principle in many democratic states. The people have the right to impose taxes on themselves through representation in the parliament, and taxes shall not be imposed by a foreign state or by a king or queen. Thus, taxes differ between jurisdictions around the world.

There are many initiatives on coordinating tax laws and taxing rights. Within the EU, value added tax (VAT),[7] some excise duties, such as excise duties on alcohol and tobacco,[8] and parts of the corporate tax are harmonised.[9] The Organisation for Economic Cooperation and Development (OECD) is active in coordinating taxation in the field of transfer pricing, VAT and electronic commerce and services.[10] There is also an extensive web of bilateral and multinational tax treaties allocating taxing rights on income and property between the states.

Even though all states have designed their tax systems differently and their tax structure and tax rates differ, there are similarities. For example, personal and corporate income is normally taxed, there is normally both general and specific taxes on consumption, as well as property and/or wealth taxation.

Personal income tax is levied on salaries, pensions, personal business activities, and other categories of personal income. The taxable amount on which personal income tax is charged is normally income minus deductible costs. This applies to persons who are subject to unlimited taxability in the specific state, most often residents of that state. Persons who are subject to limited taxability, normally non-residents, may be taxed only with respect to income the source of which is within the territory of the state in question. In such cases, the tax rate is normally lower and the right to deduct costs is limited.

Corporate income tax is paid by legal persons, such as limited companies. Not all legal persons are, however, taxable persons for corporate income tax purposes. In

---

[6] Ibid.

[7] Council Directive 2006/112/EC of 28 November 2006 *on the common system of value added tax.*

[8] See e.g. Council Directive 92/83/EEC of 19 October 1992 on the harmonization of the structures of excise duties on alcohol and alcoholic beverages and Council Directive 2011/64/EU of 21 June 2011 on the structure and rates of excise duty applied to manufactured tobacco.

[9] Council Directive (EU) 2016/1164 of 12 July 2016 laying down rules against tax avoidance practices that directly affect the functioning of the internal market.

[10] OECD Transfer Pricing Guidelines for Multinational Enterprises and Tax Administrations 2017, https://www.oecd.org/tax/transfer-pricing/oecd-transfer-pricing-guidelines-for-multinational-enterprises-and-tax-administrations-20769717.htm, OECD International VAT/GST Guidelines, https://www.oecd.org/ctp/international-vat-gst-guidelines-9789264271401-en.htm. Accessed 12 April 2021.

some jurisdictions, such as Sweden and Finland,[11] partnerships and limited partnerships are not subject to corporate income tax, even when they are legal persons. Instead, their partners are taxed. If the partner is a limited company, the income from the partnership will be subject to corporate income tax, whereas if the partner is an individual, the income will be subject to personal income tax as a personal business income. Also, income of a controlled foreign corporation (CFC) will be taxed as income of its shareholders, in jurisdictions in which a particular CFC tax regime applies. Corporate income tax is basically calculated in the same manner as personal income tax, namely revenues minus deductible costs. The corporate income tax regulations are more extensive and complex than the tax rules for personal income taxation, since transactions within groups of companies, dividends and restructurings of companies need to be specifically regulated. Legal persons that operate for the public good, such as non-profit organisations, religious communities and foundations may be tax exempt. The corporate tax rates differ widely around the world, from 0% up to 50%.[12]

Consumption taxes are indirect taxes. That means that they can be passed on to another entity or individual. The taxable person and the person who ultimately bears the burden of taxation are different persons. Indirect taxes are generally levied by the manufacturer or the supplier and passed on to the consumer. Consumption taxes are either general or specific. A general consumption tax is levied on all consumption of goods and normally also services, as a main rule, whereas specific consumption taxes are called excise duties and are only levied on certain goods and services. Excise duties are normally levied at products that are considered harmful, it may be for people's health or the environment. Excise duties are applied to steer the consumption. The most common general consumption tax is VAT, also called the goods and services tax (GST). VAT is applied in more than 165 countries all over the world. The only main economy that does not apply VAT is the United States. In the United States, however, other consumption taxes, such as the so called use tax and sales tax, are levied at state and municipal level. VAT is levied each time at a taxable person, typically a businessperson, supplies goods and services for consideration. The supplier adds the tax to the price of the goods or services. That is how the VAT is passed on to the supplier. This tax is called output VAT. From the output VAT, input VAT is deducted. Input VAT is the VAT that taxable persons pay when they acquire goods and services. The difference between input VAT is paid to the tax administration. If the input VAT exceeds the output VAT, the taxable person will get a refund from the tax administration.

[11] Chap. 5 Sec. 1 of the Swedish income tax act (1999:1229) and Sec. 4 of the Finnish Income Tax Act 30.12.1992/1535).

[12] See OECD, Corporate Tax Statistics Database, https://www.oecd.org/tax/tax-policy/corporate-tax-statistics-database.htm. Accessed 12 April 2021.

Property tax may refer to recurrent and non-recurrent taxes on the use, ownership, or transfer of property.[13] Property taxes include taxes on immovable property and net wealth, taxes on the change of ownership of property through inheritance or gift and taxes on financial and capital transactions.[14] Net wealth taxes are applied in a minor number of countries. Austria, Denmark, Germany, Finland, Luxemburg, and Sweden are examples of countries that have abolished their wealth taxes.

11.2.2 Evolution of Modern Tax Systems from a Gender Perspective

In modern tax systems, tax provisions explicitly discriminating against women are not common.[15] There are however examples of such provisions from modern times. The Netherlands granted married men a higher tax-free allowance than women until 1984.[16] Until 2021, married women needed the permission of their husbands to talk to the tax administration and to file taxes under their own name on the Island of Jersey.[17] But most modern tax systems do not differentiate between men and women.

Many modern tax systems are still family-based and not individual-based.[18] The idea behind family-based taxation is that they ensure families with the same total income pay the same total income tax, irrespective of who has earned the income.[19] This may seem fair from the family's perspective, but looking at it from an individual perspective, the second earner pays higher taxes on the margin than a single earner would.[20] A family-based tax system also builds upon the nuclear family as the norm. Single parent families do not receive the same advantages as the nuclear family with two parents. This also applies to same sex couples who do not have equal rights in family law, and for example do not have the right to marriage. In individual-based tax systems, the family circumstances are not taken into consideration for tax purposes. Instead, there may be subsidies such as child benefits that may compensate families.

Women are also more often second earners in the household than men. Out of the OECD countries, only Israel has a tax system that makes a second earner pay less tax than a single earner.[21] In Hungary, Lithuania, Austria, Latvia, Norway, Finland,

---

[13] OECD Data, Tax on Property, https://data.oecd.org/tax/tax-on-property.htm. Accessed 12 April 2021.

[14] Ibid.

[15] Harding et al. (2020).

[16] Ibid.

[17] Ibid.

[18] OECD (2016), "Special feature: Measuring the tax wedge on second earners", in *Taxing Wages 2016*, OECD Publishing, Paris, 32.

[19] Ibid.

[20] Ibid.

[21] Perez-Navarro and Harding (2021).

Sweden, Australia, New Zealand, Chile and Mexico a single earner and second earner are taxed equally. But in Germany, Denmark, Belgium, Slovenia, Iceland, Turkey, Poland, France, Italy, Czech Republic, Portugal, Netherlands, United States, Slovak Republic, Greece, Luxembourg, Japan, United Kingdom, Canada, Spain, Ireland, Switzerland, Korea, and Estonia, a second earner pays higher tax than a single earner.[22] This may create an incentive for the second earner not to enter working life.[23]

Even though the family-based systems reasonably may be questioned from a gender neutrality perspective, there is no clear trend that more and more countries are moving toward individual-based systems.

A current development is to apply a reduced VAT on feminine hygiene products. Since exclusively women use these products, it is a tax reduction specifically directed at women. Reduced tax rates and exemptions in the field of VAT seldomly reach the consumers on a long-term basis but tend to increase the profit of the supplier. This is because prices are set primarily by supply and demand, and not by the level of VAT. Thus, the apparently women-directed VAT cut may as well end up increasing the profit of the sellers and manufacturers of these products, which are probably more often men than women.

Example

An example for this is the reduction of the taxation of feminine hygiene products in Germany in 2020. Until then tampons, pads etc. were taxed with 19% VAT instead of the usual 7% VAT for everyday items. According to Article 99 of the Council Directive 2006/112/EC of 28 November 2006 on the common system of value added tax, the minimum taxation rate is 5%.

Along with other measures, such as free sanitary products in public buildings, the UK abolished the taxation of feminine hygiene products completely in order to end period poverty. Although it is not guaranteed that women financially benefit in the end due to rising prices, it has at least a symbolic value for promoting women. ◄

11.2.3 Sources of Public International Law Relevant for Taxation from a Gender Perspective

As mentioned above, each state has its own taxing rights. In international law however, there is a growing focus on the states' obligations to distribute tax burdens equally, to take the taxpayers' ability to pay taxes into account and to use the tax

[22] Ibid.

[23] Ibid.

revenue equally.[24] There are no specific international conventions regulating taxation from a gender perspective. However, human rights treaties, as well as the UN Universal Declaration of Human Rights, the International Covenant on Economic, Social and Cultural Rights, regional human rights covenants, and the Declaration of the Rights of Indigenous Peoples also apply to taxes.[25] The same goes for the Convention on the Elimination of All Forms of Discrimination against Women.[26]

The fifth of the UN's goals on Sustainable Development is gender equality.[27] Target 5.4 provides for the recognition and valuation of unpaid care and domestic work through the provision of public services, infrastructure and social protection policies and the promotion of shared responsibility within the household and the family as nationally appropriate. This is highly relevant, when women worldwide spend more than 250% more time in unpaid work than men every day.[28] Despite the complexity caused by reduced VAT rates and VAT exemptions, Lahey proposes that food, childcare, transportation, and equipment for paid work, should be exempt from VAT.[29] This should be done in order to safeguard women from pressure to increase their work time in unpaid and thus untaxed household or business work.[30]

Target 5 a of the fifth of the UN's goals on Sustainable Development (gender equality) is to "[u]ndertake reforms to give women equal rights to economic resources, as well as access to ownership and control over land and other forms of property, financial services, inheritance and natural resources, in accordance with national laws." As long as men own more than women in general, and own more business shares than women, then tax cuts for capital gains, dividends and immovable property as well as lower corporate tax rates and corporate tax incentives will mainly benefit men.[31] Target 5.c. sends a positive signal to the legislator, including the tax legislator: "Adopt and strengthen sound policies and enforceable legislation for the promotion of gender equality and the empowerment of all women and girls at all levels".

Taxpayers' rights are the human rights of taxpayers.[32] The International Bureau of Fiscal Documentation's Observatory on the protection of taxpayer rights (IBFD OPTR) states that "the current growth of the investigative powers of the tax administrations, which aims at tackling tax avoidance, tax evasion and aggressive tax planning, necessitates a balancing with the provision of timely and effective

---

[24] Lahey (2018), p. 8.

[25] Ibid.

[26] Ibid.

[27] United Nations, Department of Economic and Social Affairs, Sustainable Development, The 17 Goals, https://sdgs.un.org/goals. Accessed 12 April 2021.

[28] Lahey (2018), p. 9.

[29] Ibid, p. 58.

[30] Ibid.

[31] Perez-Navarro and Harding (2021).

[32] Observatory on the protection of taxpayer rights, https://www.ibfd.org/Academic/Observatory-Protection-Taxpayers-Rights. Accessed 12 April 2021.

protection to taxpayer rights".[33] It is, according to the IBFD OPTR, "possible to establish principles, minimum standards and best practices that ensure the enjoyment of those taxpayer rights within the scope of human rights".[34] The US Centre for Taxpayers' Rights has also recently widened its scope to include gender issues in the concept of taxpayers' rights. Even though taxpayers' rights do not yet have any status as human rights for taxpayers, they constitute an important feature in the tax discourse.

11.2.4 Fiscal Policy, Welfare State and Gender Perspective as a Precondition for a Fairer Tax System

A welfare state may be defined as "a system whereby the state undertakes to protect the health and well-being of its citizens, especially those in financial or social need, by means of grants, pensions and other benefits". When the welfare state concept was introduced in the mid-twentieth century, most people used to get married and stayed married.[35] The wife was the caregiver, and the husband was the family provider.[36] The man stayed in the same job, with the same basic training for many years, maybe a lifetime.[37] This is not how it works today. Lifetime work is rare, there is a continuous need for updating one's skills, marriages often end in divorce and parenthood is not tied to marriage or heterosexuality.[38] These are however not the only changes. Technology continues to replace humans in the workforce, even when it comes to intelligence. Further, the population is ageing, which creates demographic changes. In total, this means that the concept of the welfare state, as well as the methods to create welfare, need to be updated.

Tax systems play an important role in creating a welfare state. Taking on the gender perspective, tax systems should be designed in a gender-neutral way regarding both how to spend tax revenue and how to collect the taxes. The main function of all tax systems is to collect revenue. A fundamental issue is whether the tax system should do more than that, and to what extent. Should the tax system take family circumstances into consideration or not to compensate for a maintenance burden? If the tax system does this, for example by applying a family-based calculation of personal income tax, the concept of the welfare state should not be based on how family life was in the mid-twentieth century but how it is now. All kinds of family constellations must be taken into account when designing the tax system. In addition, achieving a fair taxation for the second earner in relation to an individual earner

[33] Ibid.

[34] Ibid.

[35] Barr (2018), p. 17, https://www.imf.org/external/pubs/ft/fandd/2018/12/pdf/redesigning-the-welfare-state-barr.pdf. Accessed 12.04.2020.

[36] Ibid.

[37] Ibid.

[38] See ibid.

risks making the tax system complex and can create loopholes. Thus, an easier way to go may be to do less through the tax system but let the tax system collect revenue in an as neutral and effective way as possible and make more targeted efforts to redistribute the resources when building the welfare state.

Experiences from the dual income tax system, which is common in the Nordic countries such as Norway and Sweden, with a lower flat tax on capital and corporate income and a progressive tax for labour income shows that a broad tax base creates an efficient tax system regarding collecting state revenue and building a welfare state.[39] A broad tax base means that many persons pay tax, not only the richest persons. In countries where many women do not work outside the home, there is a huge unutilised tax base. Thus, tax systems that make it profitable for the family if women remain at home may lock-in potential tax revenue.

11.3 The Effects of Tax Structure on Gender Equity: Recognising Gender Biases

This chapter will focus on the revenue side of the government fiscal policy, by analysing gender biases permeating today's tax systems. Tax systems of modern (both developed and developing) countries are based on the principle of plurality of tax forms. Consequently, gender biases generally differ among various taxes within the same tax system. The analysis in the following sections will present the ways in which the design of various taxes (personal income tax, property and wealth tax, corporate income tax, as well as various consumption taxes) negatively affects gender equality, through gender biases.

Gender bias may take explicit or implicit forms.[40] Explicit gender bias depends on the language used in the tax legislation and presupposes that tax legislation explicitly treats men and women differently. As such, explicit gender bias is relatively easy to identify. Usually, textual interpretation of the legislative provision in question should suffice in identifying an explicit bias. On the other hand, implicit gender bias means that provisions contained in tax legislation tend to have different implications for men and women, although the text of the provisions does not differentiate explicitly between them.[41] Implicit gender bias is far more difficult to identify, as it presupposes that the effect of a certain tax provision on wellbeing of men, on the one hand, and wellbeing of women, on the other, is assessed. This will generally require an evaluation that is highly dependent on what social and economic behavior is regarded as desirable in a specific society. [42] Such evaluation essentially

[39] See Sørensen (2005), p. 27.

[40] Stotsky (1996). https://www.elibrary.imf.org/doc/IMF001/02720-9781451852226/02720-9781451852226/Other_formats/Source_PDF/02720-9781455230235.pdf. Accessed 12 April 2021.

[41] Ibid.

[42] Ibid.

boils down to the respective roles men and women are thought to have within a society in question.

While explicit discrimination is always intentional, implicit discrimination may often not be. Explicit gender bias is to a large extent eliminated from the modern tax systems of democratic countries. However, the same is far from true when it comes to implicit gender bias.

11.3.1 Gender Issues in Personal Income Taxation

In personal income taxation, both explicit and implicit gender biases are present. Moreover, personal income tax is generally regarded as a form of taxation in which explicit gender bias is most commonly found.[43] There are two basic models of personal income tax systems: global and schedular.[44] Since the schedular model presupposes that the tax liability is determined taking into account only the income in question (and not the taxpayer receiving the income), explicit gender bias will not generally occur in its context. On the other hand, within the global model, tax liability is determined by considering the comprehensive economic and personal situation of the specific taxpayer. This is why gender biases are far more common within the global model.

Depending on the manner in which taxpayers file their tax returns, the global model of personal income taxation may be based on (a) individual (also referred to as separate) filing and (b) joint filing. [45] Individual filing means that each individual within the household is required to file its own tax return, provided that they have taxable income for the relevant taxable period. On the other hand, joint filing presupposes that the filing unit is the married couple, i.e. married couples are required or given the option to file a joint tax return, on the basis of which their income is treated as one. [46] Being treated as one, their income will be taxed under a consolidated rate schedule. Based on the above described differences, individual and joint filing systems encompass different gender biases.

Within the system of individual filing, one of the more prevalent gender biases results from the manner in which income derived from sources other than employment is distributed between spouses. While employment income is as a rule allocated to the spouse who earned it, other income may be allocated between spouses in various ways. One way which represents an explicit bias is the attribution of all income, or income other than the wife's employment income to the husband. Such

---

[43] Stotsky (1997), p. 31. https://www.imf.org/external/pubs/ft/fandd/1997/03/pdf/stotsky.pdf. Accessed 14 April 2021.

[44] It should however be borne in mind that pure global and pure schedular systems are not too common in modern tax systems. Presently, the majority of countries employ a mixture of the two models (e.g. global model with schedular elements, dual income tax, or flat tax).

[45] McCaffery (1999), p. 16.

[46] Caparo (2014), p. 9.

an approach used to be applicable in Britain with respect to property and other unearned income.[47] A more extreme example was present in Singapore, where all income of a married woman was allocated to her husband.[48] Similar explicit gender bias is present in some countries in which income from family business is attributed in its entirety to the husband, regardless of the spouse's contribution to the joint family business. There were also examples of global models of personal income taxation which prescribed different tax rates for income derived by men and women, with a higher tax rate being applicable to married women (South African Republic, until 1995). [49] Explicit bias may also be found in the manner tax deductions and exemptions are allocated between spouses. Numerous jurisdictions provide for tax allowances for a financially dependent member of the household. Such allowances typically favour households based on a male breadwinner and female carer model as opposed to households in which both spouses are both breadwinners and carers. [50] One form of discrimination is that the tax system provides a higher amount of a certain category of allowance to a husband than to a wife or stipulates that the allowance is only available to the husband. The effect of such allowances is that the husband is 'paid' for the unpaid labour provided within the household by the wife. Namely, the allowance leads to an increase in disposable income of the household, which is often not allocated to the wife, but to the husband who maintains the control over it.[51]

Within the system of joint filing, explicit bias is less prevalent. A common way of discriminating against women is the requirement that the tax return is submitted in the name of the husband exclusively (Britain until 1990, France until 1986, Switzerland).[52] Due to the fact that the tax unit is the couple, the system of joint filing cannot implement explicit bias within the tax rate structure. [53] On the other hand, implicit gender bias is fairly common. One of the most prevalent implicit biases is present in income tax systems with progressive tax rates and joint filing. Such a framework discriminates against secondary earners, since their income is taxed at a higher marginal rate (because the rate is determined taking into account the aggregated income of both spouses) than it would have been without the joint filing. This is so because the income of a secondary earner is added on top of the primary earner's income and as such it 'draws' the total income into the higher tax bracket. This phenomenon is referred to as secondary-earner bias.[54] It provides an incentive

[47]McMahon (2010), p. 182.

[48]Bun (1995), p. 422.

[49]Valodia et al. (2001), p. 86.

[50]Caparo (2014), p. 10.

[51]Ibid.

[52]McMahon (2010), p. 173; Stotsky (1996), p. 6. https://www.elibrary.imf.org/doc/IMF001/02720-9781451852226/02720-9781451852226/Other_formats/Source_PDF/02720-9781455230235.pdf. Accessed 09 June 2021.

[53]Grown (2005), p. 15.

[54]McCaffery (1999), p. 19.

for the secondary earner to not enter the working force or withdraw from it. As it is women who are more often secondary earners in the family, they are more often adversely affected.

Example

In Morocco, if the husband is the one filing a tax return, the wife will be automatically regarded as his 'dependent'. However, if it is the wife who is filing a tax return, she needs to prove that she is the breadwinner in the household and that her husband and children are financially dependent on her. If she fails to provide sufficient documentary evidence, she will effectively pay more tax compared to the man in the same situation.[55] ◀

Another prevalent occurrence in developing countries is that the majority of women fall outside the income tax net. [56,57] What this means is that, even when they are formally employed, women tend to earn incomes which are so low that they do not even trigger income tax. While this results in not paying income tax, at the same time it means that these women will not be able to benefit from various allowances (e.g. for dependent children) provided for under the income tax legislation. This shows that the tax system should be very carefully utilised as a means of achieving goals relevant for gender equality.

Example

Until 2011, India was the only country to have applied a personal income tax system explicitly discriminating against men. It presupposed that women were subject to a higher tax threshold which meant that they could generate higher income before they became liable to tax. However, due to the exceptionally low number of women earning enough income to be subject to tax in India, this measure was abandoned. It was evident that its effect on gender equality was actually negligible.[58] ◀

[55]El Bouazzaoui et al. (2010), pp. 187–188.

[56]The reason is not only that a large proportion of women is unemployed, but also that even women who are in employment tend to be employed in low paid jobs. For example, in South African Republic 73% of employed women earn income below the income tax threshold. See: Budlender et al. (2010), p. 210. In India, only 0.27% of all working-age women generate income above the income tax threshold. See: Chakraborty et al. (2010), p. 103.

[57]When it comes to developed countries, informal sector of the economy accounts for only 18% of employment, whereas in developing countries 80% of all employment takes place in the informal economy.

[58]For more details see: Capraro (2014), p. 13.

11.3.2 Gender Issues in Corporate Income Taxation

Corporate income tax is often assumed to be gender neutral, because it concerns the taxation of the body corporate which is a non-gender specific entity in law. [59] Evidently, since corporate income taxes apply to legal persons instead of individuals, they cannot contain explicit gender bias. However, it is not the legal entity which effectively bears the economic burden of this tax. [60] This is why implicit gender bias may indeed result from the application of corporate income tax. Just like in the case of indirect taxes, the burden of corporate income tax is passed on. Nevertheless, there still is no consensus among the economists on the question of who exactly bears the burden of corporate income tax: shareholders, capital providers, [61] legal entity's employees, [62] or consumers. [63] Consequently, the identification of possible implicit gender biases in corporate income taxation will depend on the position taken vis-à-vis the alleged incidence thereof. [64]

Since women are well under-represented within the category of corporate shareholders, a potential decrease in corporate income tax burden, leading in turn to an increase in after-tax profits, will benefit women disproportionately less than it will benefit men. [65] In the same vein, the increase in additional bonuses caused by this policy choice will benefit women less than men, as women are far less often members of corporate boards. [66] This is a rather important implication for gender equality since during the last several decades, countries around the world have witnessed considerable corporate income tax cuts in the so-called 'race to the bottom' as a part of international tax competition.

Modern corporate income tax legislation is laden with a variety of incentives. They may be introduced to provide support to certain industries (e.g. incentives granted to the film industry), activities (e.g. incentives for investment in research and development), or taxpayers of a specific size (e.g. incentives for micro, small and medium enterprises). However, studies evaluating the effects of such incentives

[59] European Parliament (2017), Gender equality and taxation in the European Union, DG for Internal Policies, p. 35. HMRC & HM Treasury (2011), Overview of Tax Legislation and Rates, A-50, available at: https://wbg.org.uk/wp-content/uploads/2016/12/RRB_Reports_7_282363355-1.pdf. Last accessed: 16 April 2021.

[60] The term usually used to refer to the manner in which the economic burden of a tax is distributed within the economy is tax incidence or, more specifically, economic tax incidence. See: Gruber (2016), p. 587.

[61] See: Fox (2020), p. 92.

[62] Fuest et al. (2015), pp. 393–418, 415.

[63] Avi-Yonah (2020), p. 653.

[64] Stotsky (1996), p. 16.

[65] European Parliament (2017), Gender equality and taxation in the European Union, DG for Internal Policies, 36.

[66] UK Women's Budget Group (2011), The Impact on Women of the Budget 2011, 9, available at: https://wbg.org.uk/wp-content/uploads/2016/12/RRB_Reports_7_282363355-1.pdf. Last accessed: 16 April 2021.

usually do not take into consideration their impact on gender equality.[67] Tax incentives may easily reinforce the existing implicit gender biases of corporate income tax by providing support to businesses in industries with predominantly male workforce or male shareholders. A very popular category of tax incentives that disproportionately benefits men are tax incentives for start-ups, because women are under-represented among early stage entrepreneurs.[68]

11.3.3 Gender Issues in Property and Wealth Taxation

In the present day still, numerous jurisdictions around the globe deny women the right to own and inherit property.[69] And even in countries in which women are allowed to hold formal title to property, they tend to utilise this right considerably less frequently than men.[70] This is particularly true in the case of land.[71] Unfortunately, there are no comprehensive empirical studies focused on the impact of property and wealth taxation on gender equality.

In general terms, an increase of taxes on wealth, such as recurrent property taxes or net-wealth taxes, could benefit women by allowing for a reduction of other taxes—a burden which falls predominantly on women. Alternatively, it could increase resources needed by the governments to deliver social services (daycare, care for the elderly) whose indirect beneficiaries are principally women.[72] On the other hand, lowering rates for property taxes in cases of women-owned or

[67] European Parliament (2017), Gender equality and taxation in the European Union, DG for Internal Policies, 36.

[68] Ibid.

[69] Jurisdictions implementing the most restrictive laws with respect to women's right to own and inherit property are located in Middle East, North Africa and South Asia. See: Almodóvar-Reteguis (2019), available at: https://blogs.worldbank.org/opendata/where-world-do-women-still-face-legal-barriers-own-and-administer-assets. Last accessed: 9 June 2021. Moreover, a study conducted by the World Bank shows that the dynamic of reforms geared towards gender equality in property and inheritance law is the slowest, compared to reforms in other social-economic spheres, e.g. access to employment, pension rights or business financing opportunities. See: World Bank (2019b), available at: https://thedocs.worldbank.org/en/doc/702301554216687135-0050022019/original/WBLDECADEOFREFORM2019WEB0401.pdf. Last accessed: 9 June 2021.

[70] World Bank (2019a), available at: https://www.worldbank.org/en/news/press-release/2019/03/25/women-in-half-the-world-still-denied-land-property-rights-despite-laws. Last accessed: 9 June 2021.

[71] Only 20% of land across the world is owned by women. In more than 90 countries, women do not have equal rights as men when it comes to land ownership. Villa (2017), available at: https://www.weforum.org/agenda/2017/01/women-own-less-than-20-of-the-worlds-land-its-time-to-give-them-equal-property-rights/#:~:text=rights%20to%20land.-,Women%20own%20less%20than%2020%25%20of%20the%20world's%20land.,percentage%20as%20low%20as%2010.&text=Yet%20female%20farmers%20lack%20equal,in%20more%20than%2090%20countries. Last accessed: 15 April 2021.

[72] Hodgson and Sadiq (2017), p. 119.

jointly-owned real estate, especially land, could incentivise registration of such property in women's names.[73]

Inheritance tax and net wealth tax[74] are generally considered to contribute to the reduction of wide spread wealth inequality. In this respect, their introduction or increase may be seen as promoting gender equality.

11.3.4 Gender Issues in the Taxation of Consumption

To reiterate, the two main consumption taxes present in the majority of today's tax systems are the VAT and excise duties. Whereas VAT is a broad-based consumption tax intended to apply to the comprehensive definition of consumption, excise duties are selective taxes on consumption of only a few items such as alcoholic beverages, tobacco products, and fuels. While explicit gender bias is generally not present within the legislation on VAT and excise duties, these forms of taxation do cause implicit gender bias.

At first glance, VAT may look somewhat like a business tax, because it is collected by businesses. On the contrary, it is a tax on private individual and household consumption.[75] VAT is generally regarded as a regressive tax because it is more burdensome to the poor. This is because the poor spend a larger proportion of their income on consumption than the rich do. Actually, the share of consumption expenditures falls with the increase of disposable income.[76] This alone could lead us to identify an implicit gender bias, as around the world there are more women than men in the lowest income deciles and far more men in the highest.[77]

Regressive impact of VAT is to a certain extent mitigated by allowing for the supply of certain goods and services to be either zero-rated, exempt, or taxed at a reduced rate. Consequently, each country that applies VAT has its own rate structure. It is exactly these preferential treatments that may induce implicit gender

[73] Joshi (2016), p. 2, available at: https://opendocs.ids.ac.uk/opendocs/bitstream/handle/20.500.12413/13066/ICTD_SumBrief%236_OnlineNew2.pdf?sequence=1&isAllowed=y. Last accessed: 15 April 2021.

[74] Net wealth tax is a comprehensive tax on net worth of an individual, i.e. the value of individual's total property reduced by debt. See: Thuronyi (2003), p. 329. Only a handful of jurisdictions across the globe apply the net wealth tax. In the European Union, only France and Spain have net wealth taxes in their respective tax systems.

[75] Lahey (2018), p. 46.

[76] Of course, in absolute terms, the rich will always spend more than the poor. What we are interested in here is the proportion of disposable income that may be saved, as opposed to disposable income that may be spent on consumption. Whereas the poor can hardly save anything, i.e. they spend most of their income, the rich are able to save a larger proportion of their income.

[77] Lahey (2018), p. 45. UN Women (2017), UN Women and the World Bank unveil new data analysis on women and poverty, available at: https://www.unwomen.org/en/news/stories/2017/11/news-un-women-and-the-world-bank-unveil-new-data-analysis-on-women-and-poverty. Last accessed 15 April 2021.

biases.[78] Preferential regimes are usually applied to goods and services that are commonly regarded as (a) necessities, such as food, children's clothes, medicines, as well as (b) merit goods, such as education, health services, etc. Implicit gender bias results from the fact that men and women have different consumption patterns when it comes to some of these products.[79] Empirical studies have shown that women tend to spend relatively higher proportions of their income than men on buying necessities and merit goods. Women are primarily responsible for household purchases of basic goods and services related to nutrition, health care, education and care of children and the elderly.[80] In this respect, tax policy designers should bear in mind that increasing VAT for example on textbooks and stationery material could reduce women's disposable income more than it does in the case of men. This could, in turn, damage their bargaining power within the household and at the same time, strengthen the existing inequalities therein.[81]

Excise duties target specific goods which are considered to be detrimental to consumer's health or the environment: the so-called demerit goods.[82] Therefore, excise duties are intended to function as a corrective mechanism, i.e. to prevent the overconsumption thereof. Like VAT, excise duties also disproportionately encumber lower income groups. It is lower income groups who generally consume more demerit goods. However, at the same time, goods targeted by excise duties are disproportionately consumed by men, for which reason these taxes are implicitly biased against men. Nevertheless, within the context of a household this could actually lead to other members of the said household reducing their consumption of other (non-excise) goods, so that the male breadwinner can maintain the consumption of taxed goods.[83] This is just one way in which bargaining power imbalance within the household could lessen the implicit bias against men.[84]

11.4 Gender Responsive Budgeting

Probably the most important result of the twentieth century was the entry of women and gender-sensitive persons into the political, social and economic life of our nations. But the goal for the future years is to erase gender inequality, especially eliminating gender disparities in health care, paid employment, participation in

[78] Stotsky (1996), p. 13.

[79] Ibid, p. 9. It is, however, rather difficult to ascertain the exact patterns since the consumptions of such goods and services occurs within a household that comprises both men and women.

[80] Joshi (2016), p. 2.

[81] Valodia (2009), pp. 141–142.

[82] Musgrave and Musgrave (1989), p. 404.

[83] Stotsky (1997), p. 32, available at: https://www.imf.org/external/pubs/ft/fandd/1997/03/pdf/stotsky.pdf. Last accessed: 14 April 2021.

[84] Ibid., p. 32.

society and political bodies.[85] Since 1979, the UN underlines the importance of gender equality in the UN Convention on the Elimination of All forms of discriminations against women (CEDAW). To reach these ambitious aims, governments need to improve public policies to avoid gender discrimination.

11.4.1 Basic Budgeting Concepts and Gender Equality Related Issues

As we know, money collected by taxation is used by governments to fund public services and satisfy public needs, for contributing to general well-being. It is clear that taxation must consider inequalities, and these inequalities can be compensated for by the redistribution of money, services and goods through public expenditure.

Economic policies (both macroeconomic and microeconomic policies) are often thought of as gender neutral. Budgeting is generally considered a gender-neutral policy instrument. But that is a mistake: the budget is not gender neutral, but rather gender blind. Some examples of gender biases in taxation, both explicit and implicit, have been analysed in the previous section. Moreover, budgeting policies can hide gender biases too. Public accounting policies are not gender sensitive and have a negative impact on women compared to men. It must be understood that by maintaining gender inequality, these policies also have a negative impact from an economic point of view, making it difficult for all categories to access work or business.

It is clear that governmental budgets reflect political priorities. If we neglect this distinct impact on people, we perpetuate economic disparities and disable the improvement of social roles various groups individuals hold. National or local budgets do not affect individuals directly, but the choices contained in the national or local budget, impacting the market demand or public services, influence employment, family life, healthcare, price level and so on. Individuals in general have different economic roles and, consequently, different economic and social power. In most cases, women and minorities are at a disadvantage. The apparent neutrality of the public budget hides the fact that, often, women and third-gender persons do not have the same variety of choices (political, social, economic) in relation to others.

If we consider gender inequality as inefficient, both from the point of view of access to work and business, and as a lack of participation in political life, it becomes clear that the government (and parliament) can use the money raised through taxes to reduce inequality. By orienting public finances, it is possible to redistribute wealth and fight against women's poverty and gender inequality. Public spending encompasses gender bias and produces gender-disparate effects on distribution of public services and wealth. Usually, government budget is considered as a monetary quantification of political objectives,[86] but we must understand that the public

[85] Stotsky (2016), see also the chapter on Public Policies in this book.

[86] Hyndman et al. (2014), pp. 388–408.

budget is the result of political negotiations and it is influenced by political and social contests and values. Public budget is the reflection of the government's interpretation of these values through the use of public expenditures. Very often public policies do not consider the unpaid work of women enough, especially during economic crises.[87] Women become the last resort of families, compensating for insufficient public healthcare or social services. Public budgets do not recognise the role of women (nor individuals of third-gender and non-binary individuals) in the economy and society. To achieve equity and redistribution of wealth, considering the limited public resources, it is necessary to set the objectives of public finance taking into account these needs.[88] Recently, UN statements (Millennium Development Goals and Sustainable Development Goals, especially action n. 5) reiterated the need to adopt and strengthen sound policies and enforceable legislation for the promotion of gender equality.

Fiscal policies determine the composition of expenditure, and expenditures can consent investments and benefits to influence private behaviours in a gender responsive way. A high level of taxation and a similar level of public expenditures can contribute to an inclusive growth,[89]sustaining investments that reduce gender gap. Moreover, austerity measures after the financial crisis were executed without regard to gender bias. By cutting public expenditures or reducing taxation, governments cannot drive budget priorities towards improving the opportunities for minorities, boosting welcoming culture towards gender equality and avoiding the lack of integration into social life.

11.4.2 Gender Responsive Budgeting Is an Evolution from a Gender Perspective

Gender equality has been at the centre of the debate in recent years. At first the issue of women's empowerment was the subject of attention and it was evaluated how public policies can affect women, men and people in general in different ways.[90]

Through the initiatives of gender responsive budgeting (GRB) it is possible to try to reduce inequalities by operating through the public budget. The term "GRB" considers all efforts aimed at reducing inequalities between women and men, introducing greater attention to gender issues in the drafting of public budgets.[91]

[87] United Nations. 2015. Transforming our world: The 2030 agenda for sustainable development. A/RES/70/1.

[88] Budlender (2005), https://www.ndi.org/sites/default/files/Gender%20Responsive%20Budgeting%20Trainers%20Manual.pdf. Last accessed 18 September 2021.

[89] Birchall and Fontana (2015).

[90] Lavena and Riccucci (2012), pp. 122–136.

[91] Bureau for Gender Equality. 2006. Overview of Gender-responsive Budget Initiatives. ILO Staff on the Relevance of Gender-responsive Budget Initiatives in Promoting Gender Equality in Decent Work Country Programmes. https://www.ilo.org/wcmsp5/groups/public/%2D%2D-dgreports/%2D%2D-gender/documents/publication/wcms_111403.pdf. Accessed 29 April 2021.

First, it is important to understand that a GRB is not a "woman-oriented budget", or a "gender-oriented budget". The GRB concept is different from a budget in which wealth is divided exactly between men and women (or others). GRB introduces a new concept of public budgeting: governments must consider gender-oriented policies as an objective of public budget, and measure the effects of budget implementation on reducing the gender gap.[92] The GRB can be defined as the set of public economic policies that contribute to the achievement of gender equality and respect for human rights.[93] After all, the GRB is a tool that uses budgeting to reduce gender inequality.[94] In this way, taxes and expenses are also considered in order to promote gender equality and the personal development of people, modifying the process of preparing the public budget, modifying society and supporting gender equality. The best definition of GRB is given by the Council of Europe: "Gender budgeting is an application of gender mainstreaming in the budgetary process. It means a gender-based assessment of budgets, incorporating a gender perspective at all levels of the budgetary process and restructuring revenues and expenditures in order to promote gender equality."[95]

Through this new vision of budgetary policies, the government uses public resources in such a way as to increase equality. Also, to increase the efficiency of economic policies, helping an inclusive and sustainable growth.[96]

To achieve these goals, it is necessary to examine the public budget to assess how public spending affects men and women differently.[97] The GRB requires that governments think about gender impact at all stages of the budget cycle.[98] According to the GRB idea, the law must require the government to consider gender-based objectives while writing the budget. It is also important that the law enforces government evaluation of the potential impact of each measure or legal draft considering its gender effects.

The concept was introduced in Australia in the 1980s but it was the World Conference on Women in Beijing in 1995 that the idea was developed.[99] Some countries or local governments adopted GRB policies: Belgium (2007), Australia (1983), Spanish region of Andalusia (2003), Austria (2004), France (2000 and

[92] Stephenson (2018). DOI: 10.21201/2017.1848.

[93] United Nations. 2015. Transforming our world: The 2030 agenda for sustainable development. A/RES/70/1.

[94] Council of Europe. 2005. Final report of the Group of Specialists on Gender Budgeting (EG-S-GB), EG-S-GB (2004) RAP FIN; Equality Division, Directorate-General of Human Rights, Council of Europe, Strasbourg, p. 10, available at http://www.mpsv.cz/files/clanky/12462/GenderBudgeting-report2005_En.pdf.

[95] Council of Europe. 2005. Final report of the Group of Specialists on Gender Budgeting.

[96] European Institute for Gender Equality – EIGE. 2017. Gender Budgeting, ISBN 978-92-9493-897-8, DOI: 10.2839/07916.

[97] Directorate General of Human Rights. 2005. Gender budgeting. Final report of the Group of specialists on gender budgeting (EG-S-GB). Strasbourg: Council of Europe.

[98] Stephenson (2018).

[99] Stotsky (2016).

2010), Sweden (2002), UK (1997), and several countries in the Americas (e.g., Brazil, Chile, Mexico, and Peru). Also, the Finance Ministers of Jamaica, Romania, Mauritania, Morocco, Nigeria and Rwanda, as well as the World Bank proposed the creation of a group to promote gender equality through public budgeting.[100] More than 80 countries have introduced some kind of GRB efforts in the public budget's cycle and the vast majority of OECD countries (90%) report using tools to promote gender equality.[101] However, few nations reached substantive changes in fiscal policy or purpose of expenditures.

Example

Many efforts can be made and they may take many forms.

In Austria, aspects of gender equality have been considered in the federal budget since 2005. Similarly, in Italy and France, a gender budgeting activity is attached to the state budget.[102]

Furthermore, the EU considers the gender-based view in all its budgetary activities. This activity is important for cooperation programs with developing countries. think of the European Consensus on development or the EC Regulation no. 806/2004 on the promotion of gender equality in development cooperation. For the EU is essential to promote gender equality in all EU development cooperation policies, strategies and interventions in developing countries, such as India, the Philippines, Morocco and Uganda.

Moreover, gender budgeting has a firm basis in the Treaty on the Functioning of the European Union, especially its Article 8. The European Parliament and the Council of the EU have repeatedly called on the Member States to develop and implement gender budgeting. Some developed countries, e.g. the US have no rules about GRB, and the US also have not (yet) ratified the CEDAW[103] although some sub-state governments have implemented CEDAW ordinances.[104] ◀

In light of the foregoing, a new gender-sensitive budgeting methodology provides a better understanding of the use of revenue and expenditure. This is particularly useful from a political point of view, as it identifies when gender bias occurs. Analysing the public budget with a gender-oriented view can help identify where corrective actions need to be implemented.

This working method can be applied to any type of budget system at all levels of government. To function properly, this approach requires the widest participation of citizens in national or local budget planning. In fact, some local authorities have

[100] Ibid.

[101] Downes et al. (2017), pp. 1–39. https://doi.org/10.1787/budget-16-5jfq80dq1zbn.

[102] https://www.oecd-ilibrary.org/sites/fb46acfc-en/index.html?itemId=/content/component/fb46acfc-en.

[103] Fragoso and Enríquez (2016).

[104] Moser and Korac (2020).

understood that through their budget sensitivity to this issue, they can meet the needs of women and men (e.g. Andalusia, and some cities in Italy).

State intervention through public economic policies reduces inequality. The interest of the state is to eliminate discrimination, which damages growth and is socially and politically unsustainable. Obviously, we are still a long way from the effective implementation of public policies that can fully achieve these objectives and the GRB is a useful tool. The GRB can use public spending to help achieve three goals: (1) redistribute wealth to unpaid workers; (2) reduce gender asymmetries; (3) change the allocation of public resources to vulnerable people.

It can be assumed that a gender-oriented budget includes public spending on public work programs for women or non-binary individuals, on childcare, on training courses for women in non-traditionally female fields, funding a share of places reserved for women or gender-oriented (especially for public administration).

Gender-specific spending is aimed at the different needs of men and women, to encourage their participation in politics, in a more incisive way than traditional taxation and spending. At the same time, a GRB can develop the access to education, healthcare, social and political bodies for everybody, avoiding gender bias and limiting gender burden. For example, governments can establish specific expenditure on female healthcare programs in schools, both for students and teachers. Further examples of gender-specific expenditures might concern funding of programmes intended to increase women's participation in technical jobs, or men's participation in householding or childcare activities. This kind of strategy can have beneficial spill-over effects in other fields of public life, reducing unemployment or illness, for example.

A good GRB plan needs a focus on available synergies. We have some examples of how the GRB works. Successful promotion of gender equality is related to the level of spending devoted to basic services, according to inclusiveness criteria.[105] But evidence suggests that few programmes exist for childcare, for example, and direct provisions work better than parent subsidies.[106]

Greater public investments are important but are not sufficient. A GRB must contain some specific gender-based expenditures, as well expenditures to change the gender profile of certain areas (work access, recruiting opportunities). A GRB can provide expenditure specifically targeted toward vulnerable people (women, elderly, not binary), and expenditure targeted toward equality (especially for recruitment, education, childcare). Expenditure may be earmarked to finance equal opportunities in government employment. This would also improve the gender focus of the entire public administration. But also, the general expenditures directed to all individuals can be used to obtain a new "gender breakdown" (healthcare, agricultural supports).

[105] Birchall and Fontana (2015).

[106] Fontana and Elson (2014), p. 459.

11.4.3 Transparency and Participatory Budgeting Are the First Stage of the Creation of GRB

To ensure these results, it is important that the impact of the measures on different social groups is made known to the public. Using disaggregated data it is possible to understand if the expenses are adequate and to evaluate the short and long term results.

It is necessary to introduce constant monitoring during the implementation of the public budget, evaluating the results achieved in reducing the gender gap.

A gender disaggregated tax analysis is also important: the impact of direct and indirect taxation can be different.

First, it is useful to analyse, in a disaggregated way for men and women, the benefits of all budgetary measures, considering female and male users differently (and, probably, it is preferable to also disaggregate by income, class, position, age, work, educational qualification).

Only in this way will decision-making processes be more transparent. Therefore, knowing the disaggregated data, it is possible to intervene by modifying the financial allocations in order to promote gender equality or add specific policy measures to make the policy more "gender sensitive".

In this way, the influence of national or local policies on the allocation of resources is more transparent, making it clear that apparently gender neutral social and political institutions sometimes transmit gender bias.

A gender-oriented fiscal statement, which assesses the gender impact of the public budget, can be an information tool on the impact of public economic policies and the corrective measures the government intends to take.

Example

One of the most important hypotheses of GRB is created in France and is called "Le Jaune Budgétaire".[107] This is an annex to the budget in which, annually, each ministry reports the analysis of its gender budget. It is an enormous knowledge tool for public stakeholders and citizens in general. In Italy, since 2016 the "Gender Report" is attached to the state balance.[108] The publication of these tools makes the data transparent and allows the effects of inclusive fiscal policies to be assessed. ◀

[107] https://www.budget.gouv.fr/documentation/documents-budgetaires/exercice-2021/le-projet-de-loi-de-finances-et-les-documents-annexes-pour-2021.

[108] https://www.rgs.mef.gov.it/VERSIONE-I/attivita_istituzionali/formazione_e_gestione_del_bilancio/rendiconto/bilancio_di_genere/index.html.

11.4.4 GRB Is a Tool to Realize Fairer Budgeting System

Although a variety of GRB practices have been introduced in many Western countries and also in some developing nations, too much political, economic and social inequalities continue to remain in society because GRB is not fully embedded in the budget cycle. Public budgets usually do not respect all GRB matters, and cannot resolve the unequal distribution of resources and possibilities.

However, GRB can potentially play a new role to fight against gender inequality. Following GRB rules, governments can obtain fair externalities and social outcomes, like improving healthcare or education, reducing expenses in these fields. Gender budgeting is good budgeting because GRB is not only the budget for women or various minorities, but a budget that considers all the people obtaining fair externalities and reaching equity. Indeed, GRB helps fiscal policies to reach redistributive goals of taxation.

Finally, GRB is an instrument for stimulating economic growth, enabling more persons to express their personality in economy and society thereby creating new wealth for the whole nation. GRB initiatives can lead to a more efficient use of resources, especially resources which are mostly related to poverty reduction and human development.

Gender equality is a fundamental human right. But it can also bring socioeconomic benefits.[109] Reducing gender inequality has positive effects on the economy, public health, job quality and administrative transparency.[110] The European Institute for Gender Equality – EIGE reports that "between 6.3 million and 10.5 million additional jobs in 2050 due to improvements in gender equality by addressing gender segregation in educational choices and increasing the participation of women in science, technology, engineering and mathematics (STEM), with about 70% of these jobs taken by women".[111] With less gender inequality, economic growth could be achieved at a time of difficulty!

In conclusion, fairer taxation must take into account gender differences and not reinforce inequalities. At the same time, better management of public spending can reduce gender-based disparities (explicit or implicit). Gender budgeting tools contribute to the transparency of public administration. The GRB can also be a tool for verifying the promises relating to "gender equality" and the gender sensitivity of its policy.

Gender budgeting represents a crucial tool with which to promote equal opportunities. If the choice of how to collect taxes and spend public money reflects the priorities of the nation, the GRB is the tool to stimulate a perspective of gender equality and reorganization of resources.

---

[109] European Institute for Gender Equality – EIGE (2017), Gender Budgeting.

[110] Elborgh-Woytek et al. (2013). http://www.imf.org/external/pubs/ft/sdn/2013/sdn1310.pdf.

[111] European Institute for Gender Equality – EIGE (2017), Gender Budgeting.

11.5 Conclusion

Tax systems, which at first glance appear to be gender neutral, may actually generate and perpetuate gender inequalities due to their anachronistic design. The manner in which tax systems around the globe are designed, often fails to take into consideration circumstances in which modern societies function, be it distribution of gender roles within the household, at workplace, or within the economy in general. Indeed, progress is being made in this respect. However, public finance has only recently acknowledged the importance of the effects of public policies on gender equality. Numerous jurisdictions have eliminated explicit gender biases from their tax systems, but many examples of implicit gender biases still persist. It is thus crucial to analyse and highlight the negative gender equality effects of tax legislation in order to be able to provide a viable remedy. Moreover, not only tax policy, but also budgetary policy needs to integrate a gender perspective. The way in which countries allocate and spend resources collected through taxation and other channels, is crucial for reducing gender disparities. GRB is therefore an extraordinarily valuable tool in achieving this goal. Having said that, it should be borne in mind that cultural differences will inevitably continue to exert influence on what is to be regarded as gender bias, and how it should be eliminated.

Questions

1. Is taxation gender neutral?
2. Is gender equality recognised within the framework of taxpayer rights?
3. Does the design of tax systems based on traditional family schemes produce gender discrimination?
4. Can a tax system be fair without taking into account a gender perspective?
5. Should the different tax administrations carry out their fiscal policy considering the gender perspective?
6. What is the difference between explicit and implicit gender bias within a specific tax system?
7. Try to identify an explicit or an implicit gender bias within the framework of (a) personal income tax, (b) corporate income tax, (c) property or wealth tax and (d) consumption taxes within the framework of your national tax legislation?
8. Why is it important to include gender-oriented perspectives in budget analysis?
9. Does the GRB include only gender-based expenditure?
10. Is it important that the GRB consider gender disaggregated data for evaluating budget outcomes?

References

Almodóvar-Reteguis NL (2019) Where in the world do women still face legal barriers to own and administer assets? https://blogs.worldbank.org/opendata/where-world-do-women-still-face-legal-barriers-own-and-administer-assets. Accessed 12 Sep 2021

Avi-Yonah RS (2020) A new corporate tax. Tax Notes Fed:653–660

Barr N (2018) Shifting tides. Dramatic social changes mean the welfare state is more necessary than ever. https://www.imf.org/external/pubs/ft/fandd/2018/12/pdf/redesigning-the-welfare-state-barr.pdf. Accessed 12 Sep 2021

Birchall J, Fontana M (2015) The gender dimensions of expenditure and revenue policy and systems. https://www.shareweb.ch/site/DDLGN/Documents/Gender%20dimensions%20of%20expenditure%20and%20revenue%20policy%20and%20systems.pdf. Accessed 12 Sep 2021

Budlender D (2005) Gender responsive budgeting: manual for trainers. https://www.ndi.org/sites/default/files/Gender%20Responsive%20Budgeting%20Trainers%20Manual.pdf. Accessed 12 Sep 2021

Budlender D, Casale D, Valodia I (2010) Gender and taxation in South Africa. In: Caren Grown C, Valodia I (eds) Taxation and gender equity. Routledge, London, pp 206–232

Bullock C (1716) The cobbler of Preston: as it is acted at the Theatre-Royal in Drury-Lane. By his majesty's servants. W. Wilkins, London

Bun SK (1995) Income taxation of the husband and wife. Singap J Leg Stud 2:422–457

Bureau for Gender Equality (2006) Overview of gender-responsive budget initiatives. ILO Staff on the Relevance of Gender-responsive Budget Initiatives in Promoting Gender Equality in Decent Work Country Programmes. https://www.ilo.org/wcmsp5/groups/public/%2D%2D-dgreports/%2D%2D-gender/documents/publication/wcms_111403.pdf. Accessed 12 Sep 2021

Caparo C (2014) Taxing men and women: why gender is crucial for a fair tax system. Christian Aid, London. https://www.christianaid.ie/sites/default/files/2016-03/taxing-men-and-women-gender-analysis-report-jul-2014.pdf. Accessed 12 April 2021

Capraro C (2014) Taxing men and women: why gender is crucial for a fair tax system. Christian Aid, London. https://www.christianaid.ie/sites/default/files/2016-03/taxing-men-and-women-gender-analysis-report-jul-2014.pdf. Accessed 12 Sep 2021

Chakraborty P, Chakraborty L, Karmakar K, Kapila SM (2010) Gender equality and taxation in India. In: Caren Grown C, Valodia I (eds) Taxation and gender equity. Routledge, London, pp 94–118

Council of Europe (2005) Final report of the group of specialists on gender budgeting. https://rm.coe.int/1680596143. Accessed 12 Sep 2021

Directorate General of Human Rights (2005) Gender budgeting. Final report of the group of specialists on gender budgeting (EG-S-GB). Council of Europe, Strasbourg

Downes R, von Trapp L, Nicol S (2017) Gender budgeting in OECD countries. OECD J Budg 3:1–39. https://doi.org/10.1787/budget-16-5jfq80dq1zbn

El Bouazzaoui A, Fazouane A, Jalal H, Saidi S (2010) Gender equality and taxation in Morocco. In: Caren Grown C, Valodia I (eds) Taxation and gender equity. Routledge, London, pp 179–205

Elborgh-Woytek K et al (2013) Women, work and the economy: macroeconomic gains from gender equity, International Monetary Fund staff discussion note. http://www.imf.org/external/pubs/ft/sdn/2013/sdn1310.pdf. Accessed 12 Sep 2021

European Institute for Gender Equality – EIGE (2017) Gender budgeting. https://eige.europa.eu/publications/gender-mainstreaming-gender-budgeting. Accessed 12 Sep 2021

Fontana M, Elson D (2014) Public policies on water provision and early childhood education and care: do they reduce and redistribute unpaid work? Gend Dev 22:459–474

Fox EG (2020) Does capital bear the U.S. corporate tax after all? New evidence from corporate tax returns. J Empir Leg Stud 17:71–115

Fragoso LP, Enríquez CR (2016) Western hemisphere: a survey of gender budgeting efforts. https://www.imf.org/en/Publications/WP/Issues/2016/12/31/Western-Hemisphere-A-Survey-of-Gender-Budgeting-Efforts-44146. Accessed 12 Sep 2021

Fuest C, Peichl A, Siegloch S (2015) Do higher corporate taxes reduce wages? Micro evidence from Germany. Am Econ Rev 108:393–418

Grown C (2005) What gender equality advocates should know about taxation. https://www2.unwomen.org/-/media/files/un%20women/grb/resources/what%20gender%20equality%20advocates%20should%20know%20about%20taxation.pdf?vs=5712. Accessed 12 Sep 2021

Gruber J (2016) Public finance and public policy. Worth Publishers, New York

Harding M, Perez-Navarro G, Simon H (2020) In tax, gender blind is not gender neutral: why tax policy responses to COVID-19 must consider women. https://oecdecoscope.blog/2020/06/01/in-tax-gender-blind-is-not-gender-neutral-why-tax-policy-responses-to-covid-19-must-consider-women/. Accessed 12 Sep 2021

HMRC, and HM Treasury (2011) Overview of tax legislation and rates. https://assets.publishing.service.gov.uk/government/uploads/system/uploads/attachment_data/file/207419/022_fb20013_ootlar.pdf. Accessed 12 Sep 2021

Hodgson H, Sadiq K (2017) Gender equality and a rights-based approach to tax reform. In: Stewart M (ed) Tax, social policy and gender: rethinking equality and efficiency. ANU Press, Canberra, pp 99–129

Hyndman N, Liguori M, Meyer RE, Polzer T, Rota S, Seiwald J (2014) The translation and sedimentation of accounting reforms: a comparison of the UK, Austrian and Italian experiences. Crit Perspect Account 25:388–408

Joshi A (2016) Tax and gender in developing countries: what are the issues? ICTD Summary Brief 6. https://opendocs.ids.ac.uk/opendocs/bitstream/handle/20.500.12413/13066/ICTD_SumBrief%236_OnlineNew2.pdf?sequence=1&isAllowed=y. Accessed 15 April 2021

Lahey KA (2018) Gender taxation and equality in developing countries: issues and policy recommendations. Discussion Paper. UN Women, New York

Lavena C, Riccucci NM (2012) Exploring gender mainstreaming in the European Union. Int J Public Adm 35:122–136. https://doi.org/10.1080/01900692.2011.616991

McCaffery EJ (1999) Taxing women. The University of Chicago Press, Chicago

McMahon S (2010) London calling: does the U.K.'s experience with individual taxation clash with the U.S.'s expectations. Saint Lewis Univ Law J 55:159–220

Moser B, Korac S (2020) Introducing gender perspectives in the budgetary process at the central government level. https://www.tandfonline.com/doi/pdf/10.1080/01900692.2020.1755683. Accessed 12 Sep 2021

Musgrave R, Musgrave P (1989) Public finance in theory and practice. McGraw-Hill Book Company, New York

Perez-Navarro G, Harding M (2021) In tax, gender blind is not gender neutral; how tax policy in times of COVID-19 must consider women, 26 March 2021, OECD. https://www.oecd.org/tax/tax-policy/presentation-march-on-gender-2021-in-tax-gender-blind-is-not-gender-neutral.pdf. Accessed 11 Apr 2011

Smith A (1776) An inquiry into the nature and causes of the wealth of nations

Sørensen PB (2005) Dual income taxation: why and how? https://www.cesifo.org/DocDL/cesifo1_wp1551.pdf. Accessed 12 Sep 2021

Stephenson M-A (2018) A guide to gender-responsive budgeting. https://policy-practice.oxfam.org/resources/rough-guide-to-gender-responsive-budgeting-620429/. Accessed 12 Sep 2021

Stotsky J (1996) Gender bias in tax systems. https://www.elibrary.imf.org/doc/IMF001/02720-9781451852226/02720-9781451852226/Other_formats/Source_PDF/02720-9781455230235.pdf. Accessed 12 Sep 2021

Stotsky J (1997) How tax systems treat men and women differently. Finance & Development. https://www.imf.org/external/pubs/ft/fandd/1997/03/pdf/stotsky.pdf. Accessed 12 Sep 2021

Stotsky J (2016) Gender budgeting: fiscal context and current outcomes. https://www.imf.org/en/Publications/WP/Issues/2016/12/31/Gender-Budgeting-Fiscal-Context-and-Current-Outcomes-44132. Accessed 12 Sep 2021

Thuronyi V (2003) Comparative tax law. Kluwer Law International, The Hague

UK Women's Budget Group (2011) The impact on Women of the Budget 2011. https://wbg.org.uk/wp-content/uploads/2016/12/RRB_Reports_7_282363355-1.pdf. Accessed 12 Sep 2021
UN Women (2017) UN Women and the World Bank unveil new data analysis on women and poverty. https://www.unwomen.org/en/news/stories/2017/11/news-un-women-and-the-world-bank-unveil-new-data-analysis-on-women-and-poverty. Accessed 12 Sep 2021
United Nations (2015) Transforming our world: the 2030 agenda for sustainable development. https://sdgs.un.org/2030agenda. Accessed 12 Sep 2021
Valodia I (2009) Gender, poverty and taxation: an overview of a multi-country study of gender and taxation. Gender Poverty Reduct 23:137–147
Valodia I, Smith T, Budlender D (2001) Has gender-based tax reform been good for all South African women? Agenda: Empowering Women Gender Equity 47:83–88
Villa M (2017) Women own less than 20% of the world's land. It's time to give them equal property rights. https://www.weforum.org/agenda/2017/01/women-own-less-than-20-of-the-worlds-land-its-time-to-give-them-equal-property-rights/#:~:text=rights%20to%20land.-,Women%20own%20less%20than%2020%25%20of%20the%20world's%20land.,percentage%20as%20low%20as%2010.&text=Yet%20female%20farmers%20lack%20equal,in%20more%20than%2090%20countries. Accessed 12 Sep 2021
World Bank (2019a) Women in half the world still denied land, property rights despite laws. https://www.worldbank.org/en/news/press-release/2019/03/25/women-in-half-the-world-still-denied-land-property-rights-despite-laws. Accessed 12 Sep 2021
World Bank (2019b) Women, business and the law: a decade of reform. https://thedocs.worldbank.org/en/doc/702301554216687135-0050022019/original/WBLDECADEOFREFORM2019WEB0401.pdf. Accessed 12 Sep 2021

Further Reading

Anuradha J (2016) Tax and gender in developing countries: what are the issues? https://opendocs.ids.ac.uk/opendocs/bitstream/handle/20.500.12413/13066/ICTD_SumBrief%236_OnlineNew2.pdf?sequence=1&isAllowed=y. Accessed 12 Sep 2021
Bettio F, Rosselli A, Vingelli G (2002) Gender Auditing dei Bilanci Pubblici, Mimeo. Fondazione A. J. Zaninoni, Bergamo
Budlender D, Elson D, Hewitt G, Mukhopadhyay T (2002) Gender budgets make cents: understanding gender responsive budgets. The Commonwealth Secretariat, London
Budlender D (2007) Gender-responsive call circulars and gender budget statements. Guidance Sheet Series 1 January
Cottarelli CC (2011) Revenue mobilization in developing countries. International Monetary Fund. https://www.imf.org/external/np/pp/eng/2011/030811.pdf. Accessed 12 Sep 2021
Elson D (1999) Gender budget initiatives. Commonwealth Secretariat, London
European Union, Support for local-level gender-responsive budget (GRB) initiatives. http://ec.europa.eu/comm/europeaid/projects/gender/projects_unifem_en.htm. Accessed 12 Sep 2021
Khalifa R, Scarparo S (2020) Gender responsive budgeting: a tool for gender equality. Crit Perspect Account. https://doi.org/10.1016/j.cpa.2020.102183
Sharp R (2003) Budgeting for equity. Gender budgeting initiatives within a framework of performance-oriented budgeting. United Nations Development Fund for Women (UNIFEM), New York

Public Policies on Gender Equality 12

Vanesa Hervías Parejo and Branko Radulović

Contents

Authors are listed in alphabetical order. Sect. 12.2 was written by Branko Radulović and Sect. 12.3 was authored by Vanesa Hervías Parejo. Sect. 12.1 and 12.4 were written jointly.

The University Institute of Research for Sustainable Social Development INDESS of the University of Cadiz has collaborated in this work by providing support for specialised translations.

V. Hervías Parejo (✉)
Area of Social Work and Social Services, Department of Labour and Social Security Law, University of Cadiz, Faculty of Labour Sciences, Cádiz, Spain
e-mail: vanesa.hervias@uca.es

B. Radulović
Economics and Economics Analysis of Law, University of Belgrade, Faculty of Law, Belgrade, Serbia
e-mail: bradulovic@ius.bg.ac.rs

D. Vujadinović et al. (eds.), *Gender-Competent Legal Education*, Springer Textbooks in Law, https://doi.org/10.1007/978-3-031-14360-1_12

Abstract

Gender inequality represents a substantial and persistent public problem. Public policies may have a major impact on gender equality and attaining equal access to opportunities, resources, and rights for women, men, and other gender identities. This chapter provides key insights, directions, good practices, and methodologies from existing literature on gender implications of public policies. It also briefly reviews key gender-sensitive policy initiatives and frameworks, gender mainstreaming and tools such as gender impact assessment, gender sensitive budgeting or policy evaluation. This chapter further considers key gender sensitive policies including family and work-life balance policies, equality policies in the labour and political sphere, diversity, anti-discrimination and anti-violence policies, and education and science policies for gender equality.

12.1 Introduction

Public policy is often defined as a course of government action (or inaction) in response to specific public (societal) problems.[1] Public policy as a result of a political process may take the form of a law, regulation, government decision, strategy, programme, or other policy documents that aim to achieve specific societal goals or resolve public problems.[2] Today, gender inequality is perceived as a substantial and persistent public problem, especially evident in economic, educational and political representation, health gaps, as well as discrimination against women or LGBTQIA+ population. However, the identification of gender inequality as a major societal problem is a relatively recent phenomenon. Despite some advances, the placement of gender equality on the top of policymakers agendas did not materialize until the second half of the twentieth century. It was from this point onwards that countries, albeit to varying degrees, began to systemically devise policy interventions to address gender inequality. This eventually led to gender sensitive policy making. In each stage of policy process policymakers take into account gender equality issues and objectives: problem definition and agenda setting; policy measures formulation and adoption; policy implementation, and policy evaluation that may lead to termination or modification.

Research has shown that greater gender equality, particularly in education and employment, positively influences long-term economic growth and development.[3] This is particularly relevant for the less developed and developing countries, where

[1] Kraft and Furlong (2018).

[2] Knill and Tosun (2012).

[3] Kabeer and Natali (2013) and Klasen (2002).

women still face substantial barriers to the formal labour market, do not have equal opportunities to get higher education, and are less likely to occupy managerial or administrative positions. Hence, countries with more room to reduce gender inequality have much to gain, as gender inequality hinders economic development.[4] However, there is no solid empirical support for the opposite effect. Namely, economic growth and changes associated with economic development are not sufficient to eradicate gender inequality. Formal and informal institutions will often prevent gender equality even in the face of economic advancement.[5] By constraining women's empowerment and participation in the labour force and/or access to resources, gender inequality is cemented and will not easily be changed in the course of development.[6] Hence, the decrease of gender inequality is neither inevitable nor precipitous and public policies are needed to promote gender equality.

Example

Despite socio-economic developments, women in the EU still face pay inequality and persistent gender discrimination.[7] In 2019 the gender employment gap (the difference between the employment rates of men and women aged 20 to 64) was 11.5%. Similarly, the gender pay gap for 2019 in the EU stands at 14.1%, only narrowing slightly over the last decade. The pay gap is the result of various factors: the presence of women in relatively low-paying sectors; difference in work-balance choices; the existence of the 'glass ceiling', and discrimination in professions and organizations. ◄

The impact of public policies on gender equality across policy areas has been well documented in literature.[8] Various public policies such as labour market measures, childcare and maternity leave policies reduced employment and pay gaps. However, public policy process and decisions are affected by various socio-economic conditions, cultural norms and values, political context and ideology.[9] The resulting gender related policy measures are the consequence of complex interactions between these factors.

The need to incorporate public policies and respective policy measures that promote gender equality raises several questions. First, how to integrate gender perspectives in public policymaking? Gender perspective represents a framework that enables questioning of existing relationships and concepts, facilitating the identification and examination of existing gender related biases. This requires a systematic approach that takes into account the gender related experience,

---

[4] Galor and Weil (1996).

[5] Marchand and Parpart (1995) and Parpart (1993).

[6] Morrisson and Jütting (2008).

[7] Rubery et al. (2005), Azmat and Petrongolo (2014), Ahmed et al. (2013) and Miller (2009).

[8] Profeta (2020).

[9] Inglehart and Norris (2003) and Ignjatović and Bošković (2013).

perceptions, and concerns throughout the public policy cycle. Second, how to make those involved in the process know how to make policy? This requires gender equality training and skills to use methodological approaches that enable the integration of gender perspective into policy making. These approaches are based on various tools that will be presented in Sect. 12.2. The next section reviews key policy initiatives and frameworks, gender mainstreaming as a leading approach to integrate gender issues into public policy making, and several tools including gender impact assessment, measurements of gender inequality, gender equality plans, gender budgeting and evaluation of policies. Section 12.3 discusses specific gender sensitive public policies: family and work-life balance policies, equality policies in the labour and political sphere, diversity, anti-discrimination and anti-violence policies, and education and science policies for gender equality. Section 12.4 draws a conclusion. This chapter will also provide several case studies.

Learning Goals

The learning objectives of this chapter are as follows:

- To learn about the responses that public authorities are implementing to combat gender inequality and the main instruments to measure such inequalities.
- To learn what equality policies and plans are, what they consist of, as well as what gender impact assessment is and how it is carried out.
- To study specific gender-sensitive policies such as gender-sensitive social policies, policies to reconcile work and family life, policies promoting equality in the labour and political sphere, policies in favour of diversity and against discrimination and violence, and educational and scientific policies for gender equality.
- To understand the importance of teaching and learning about gender competent public policies

12.2 Gender Equality in Public Policies

12.2.1 Gender-Equality Policy Initiatives

Equality between women and men without distinction as to race, colour, language, religion, political opinion, national or social origin, property, birth or other status is a universal legal principle recognised in Articles 1 and 2 of the 1948 Universal Declaration of Human Rights. This equality was reaffirmed twenty years later with the 1968 Teheran Proclamation, which assessed the progress achieved since the adoption of the Universal Declaration of Human Rights and set out an agenda for the future. Other developments at the international level have included: the 1952 Convention on the Political Rights of Women; the 1967 Declaration on the

Elimination of Discrimination against Women; the 1979 Convention on the Elimination of All Forms of Discrimination against Women; the Fourth World Conference on Women, and the adoption of the 1995 Beijing Declaration and Platform for Action. More recently, other actions in favour of equal opportunities for women and men have been developed: (1) the Beijing+5 Conference in 2000, "Women 2000: Gender Equality, Development and Peace for the 21st Century"; (2) the Beijing+10 Conference in 2005, following the Fourth World Conference on Women and implementing the Beijing Declaration and Platform for Action 2005; (3) the World Summit in 2005, which strengthened the United Nations system for the protection of human rights; (4) the World Summit on Women in 2005, which strengthened the United Nations (UN) system for the protection of human rights; (5) the creation of UN Women 2010 as the UN entity for gender equality and women's empowerment, and (6) Beijing+15 in 2010, the follow-up to the Fourth World Conference on Women and the implementation of the Beijing Declaration and Platform for Action.

Example

The United Nations has repeatedly invited governments and other social agents to integrate a gender perspective in their legislation, policies, plans, programmes and projects. For example, in all of the recently-developed Sustainable Development Goals (SDGs), women have a critical role to play, with many specific objectives being dedicated to the women's equality and empowerment. ◀

At the level of the European Union, equality has also been exalted as a supreme value by promoting equality between women and men (Article 2 and Article 3(3) of the Treaty on European Union (TEU) and Article 21 of the Charter of Fundamental Rights of the European Union). The Union has been given the task of eliminating inequalities and promoting equality between women and men by "mainstreaming the gender dimension" in its actions (Article 8 TFEU). For example, the Union and the Member States have undertaken to combat domestic violence in all its forms, to prevent and punish such criminal acts and to provide support and protection for victims (Declaration N° 19 annexed to the Final Act of the Intergovernmental Conference, which adopted the Treaty of Lisbon). Contemporaneously, the TFEU addresses the principle of equal pay for equal work for men and women and authorises positive action to empower women (Article 157). The Union is empowered to act in the broader field of equal opportunities and equal treatment in employment and occupation (Article 153). This provides for the possibility of adopting legislative measures to combat all forms of discrimination, including on the grounds of sex (Article 19) and states the need to combat violence against women (Article 168).

Example

In the European Union various directives and regulations are worth mentioning, such as: (1) Directive 2002/73/EC, reforming Directive 76/207/EEC, on the implementation of the principle of equal treatment for women and men as regards access to employment, training, career advancement and working conditions; (2) Directive 2004/113/EC, on implementing equal treatment as regards the principle of equal treatment between women and men in the access to, and supply of, goods and services, and (3) Directive 2006/54/EC of the European Parliament and of the Council of 5 July 2006 on the implementation of the principle of equal opportunities and equal treatment of men and women in matters of employment and occupation. This last Directive defines direct discrimination, indirect discrimination, harassment and sexual harassment and calls on employers to take preventive measures to combat sexual harassment. It toughens sanctions when discriminations occur and establishes bodies responsible for promoting equal treatment between women and men in the Member States. Regulation 1922/2006 establishes the European Institute for Gender Equality, which works to implement equality measures throughout Europe. Finally, without wishing to be exhaustive, the following should be noted: (1) Council Directive 79/7/EEC of 19 December 1978 on the progressive implementation of the principle of equal treatment for men and women in matters of social security; (2) Council Directive 92/85/EEC of 19 October 1992 on the introduction of measures to encourage improvements in the safety and health at work of pregnant workers and workers who have recently given birth or are breastfeeding; (3) Council Directive 2004/113/EC of 13 December 2004 implementing the principle of equal treatment between men and women in the access to and supply of goods and services; (4) Council Directive 2010/18/EU, and (5) Council Directive 2010/18/EU of 8 March 2010 implementing the revised Framework Agreement on parental leave. ◄

12.2.2 Gender Mainstreaming

The most widely used approach to realize gender equality and deal with gender implications of public policies is gender mainstreaming. Gender mainstreaming represents an approach that should ensure policy development assesses and integrates gender-related issues.[10] The concept has been promoted by international organizations including the United Nations, Council of Europe, European Union, Organization for Economic Cooperation and Development,[11] and is embraced as a central component to policymaking process internationally. Gender mainstreaming also refers to the inclusion of gender expertise into the policy process.

[10]The concept of mainstreaming has been translated as gender mainstreaming, but it was initially unrelated to the concept of gender. The concept dates back to the 1980s when environmental policymakers in the UK realised the need to raise awareness of environmental issues at institutional and societal levels. Thus, they initiated the incorporation of "environmental sensitivity" into all interventions, which led to mainstreaming as a strategy.

[11]Daly (2005).

The OECD provides the most useful definition; “Gender mainstreaming refers to the integration of a gender perspective throughout the policy cycle, including the preparation, design, implementation, monitoring, and evaluation of public policies, with an aim to promote equality and combat gender discrimination”.[12] Similarly, the Council of Europe defines gender mainstreaming as the “reorganisation, improvement, development and evaluation of policy processes”;[13] and proposes that a gender equality perspective should be incorporated into all policies, at all levels and stages, by the actors usually involved in adopting policy measures. In this respect, gender mainstreaming is generally based on the idea that there is no gender-neutral policy. This means that the implemented actions have a positive or negative impact on people’s lives, that is, women, men and the LGTBQIA+ community.

The origin of gender mainstreaming lies in the conviction that inequalities are present in all areas of life, rooted in social structures and dynamics. These inequalities derive from social and cultural structures, modelled on standards that are presumed to be neutral but are, in reality, masculine. For this reason, this strategy aims to deconstruct the dominant patriarchal model, integrating the gender perspective and the effective equality of women and men in a transversal manner in all political initiatives.[14] This same strategy understands that in order to achieve gender equality, it is not enough to implement gender equality policies and measure their effectiveness.

Example

The gender impact assessment that will be reviewed in the next subsection represents a recent approach to promote effective equality between women and men. This approach is based on the idea that inequalities are recurrent and, therefore, it is necessary to consider the principle of equality as an objective that, in an integrated manner, permeates decision-making, design, management, implementation, monitoring and evaluation of all public policies and not just equality policies.[15] Based on the above, gender impact assessment proposes to rely on three types of strategies to achieve effective equality between women and men from the perspective of gender mainstreaming. These strategies are reparation, adaptation and transformation[16] and can be applied in a complementary manner to formulate and reformulate policies, plans and programmes. The reparation strategy aims at formal equality between men and women. An example of a reparation strategy is equal treatment legislation and mechanisms to ensure compliance with such laws. The adaptation strategy of actions and measures

[12] OECD (2018).

[13] Council of Europe (1998), p. 12.

[14] Souto Galván (2012).

[15] Rees (1998).

[16] Lombardo (2003).

understands that equal treatment does not automatically lead to equal outcomes. On this basis, it establishes the need to create specific measures and services for women and men. An example of an adaptation strategy would be positive action programmes in favour of women. The transformation strategy considers the necessary transformation of institutions and their policies to overcome the androcentric perspective. Gender mainstreaming represents an example of the transformation strategy. It consists of assessing the different implications of any policy action on different genders to break the dominant model.[17] ◄

12.2.3 Gender-Sensitive Public Policies and Gender (Equality) Impact Assessment

Gender equality assessment should start as early as possible, preferably from the initial stage of the policy planning process. Several EU Member States are forerunners in gender-based public policy analysis. For example, in the Netherlands, a framework for gender (emancipation) impact assessment was introduced in 1992.[18] In the EU, to ensure gender equality in policy impact assessment, various methods were developed, including gender indicators, gender analysis, gender impact assessment, gender budgeting, and policy monitoring and evaluation.

Example

The European Institute for Gender Equality (EIGE) created a gender mainstreaming toolkit.[19] The toolkit focuses on three assessment stages: gender relevance assessment; gender impact assessment, and gender equality assessment. In the first stage, once the public policy and its purpose have been defined, it is necessary to determine its gender relevance. The scope of public policies that have a substantial gender component is rather broad. They are most often, but not exclusively, related to social policies. Hence, all policies which influence our daily life need to be assessed from the gender perspective. Whether a concrete policy is gender-relevant depends on whether it affects women and men and other gender identities regarding their access to and control of resources.[20] Once it is determined that public policy is gender-sensitive, the next step is to assess the gender impact. The impact on socio-economic or another status for women, men, and other gender identities may be direct or indirect. Some policy measures may have a direct and immediate effect. In contrast, others have an indirect effect (for example, affecting target companies in which women are employees). Finally, in

[17] Barrère Unzueta (2010).

[18] Verloo and Roggeband (1996) and Roggeband and Verloo (2006).

[19] EIGE (2017).

[20] EIGE (2017).

the third stage it is necessary to examine whether the proposed policy measure will contribute to gender equality. ◀

Gender impact assessment in public policies offers the opportunity to systematically examine the repercussions of policies and programmes on women and men, making it a powerful tool for influencing public authorities and private organisations' main social and economic decisions.[21] For instance, the European Commission defines gender impact assessment as follows: "Gender impact assessment is the process of comparing and assessing, according to gender-relevant criteria, the current situation and trend with the expected development resulting from the introduction of the proposed policy".[22] Alternatively, we may define Gender (equality) impact assessment (GIA) as a systematic and orderly process whereby key effects on gender inequality are assessed. Gender inequalities may have different forms: inequality in the household or individual income; access to public services; behavioural inequalities (such as labour force participation), and unpaid work as examples. Besides gender inequalities, other inequalities matter for policy assessment (disability, immigration status, race). These inequalities intersect; policy impacts on gender may be experienced differently depending on whether they are affected by other imbalances.[23] Hence, gender-sensitive public policies should be subject to intersectional analysis whenever feasible. Neglecting intersectional issues may lead to wrong policy prescriptions and missed opportunities.

Assessment should determine and, if possible, quantify inequalities and causal relationships between inequalities and policy options. Additionally, it should assess how this situation would evolve without policy intervention. Finally, there are several options (policy measures) that may achieve the same general policy goal, but that might have a different impact on gender inequalities. If the same goal can be achieved by policies that reduce rather than increase those inequalities, then such policies should be preferred. For example, if a specific policy option is preferable, but it leads to increased gender inequalities, then additional measures should be adopted to mitigate and reduce these impacts.[24] Gender policy impact assessment should be distinguished from a narrower concept of gender analysis. A gender analysis examines how the allocation of resources, authority, representation, and decision-making vary among diverse genders. Hence it provides contextual analysis and identifies existing gender inequalities and considers drivers that led to the current conditions and possibilities to affect the proclaimed goals regarding gender equality.[25]

[21] Goizueta Vértiz (2020).

[22] European Commission (1999), p. 8.

[23] Himmelweit (2018).

[24] Gensana Riera (2015).

[25] Stufflebem (2001).

In general, any public policy analysis must generate information on three types of issues:[26] (1) values, whose achievement is the main test of whether a social problem has been solved; (2) facts, whose presence may limit or enhance the achievement of values; and (3) actions, whose adoption may result in the achievement of values and the resolution of problems. With regard to the analysis and evaluation of gender equality policies, it is possible to distinguish three perspectives. The first is the empirical perspective which describes the causes and effects of a given public policy. This perspective focuses on facts and the type of information generated is denominational or designative: "An example of this perspective would be describing, explaining or predicting the public spending on public policies against social exclusion or gender violence".[27] The second is the evaluative perspective, which determines the value of a public policy: "An example of this perspective would be evaluating the different ways of distributing public spending based on the public policies implemented".[28] The third and final perspective is the normative perspective, which recommends future actions to solve public problems. This perspective focuses on action, and the type of information generated is that of recommendation or advice (*advocative*): "Thus, for example, a guaranteed minimum income policy can be recommended to alleviate social inequality problems".[29] From this perspective, the impact assessment of gender equality policies can contemporaneously include the empirical, evaluative, and normative perspective in all phases of the process.

12.2.4 Measuring Gender Inequality

Policies, as well as academic literature on cross-national and individual country gender inequalities, usually draw on data from several international organizations.[30] These indicators measure inequalities and discrimination regarding access to education, health care, political representation, earnings or income. The aggregate indices that have received particular attention recently are the Gender Development Index (GDI) and Gender Empowerment Measure (GEM): "The GDI is the unweighted average of three indices that measure gender differences in life expectancy at birth, gross enrolment, literacy rates, and earned income. The GEM is also an unweighted average of three variables reflecting the importance of women in society. They include the percentage of women in parliament, the male/female ratio among administrators and managers and professional and technical workers, and the

[26] Dunn (1981), p. 36.

[27] González Orta (2020).

[28] Gensana Riera (2015).

[29] Cruz-Rubio (2017).

[30] The UNDP Human Development Report, the UN World's Women surveys, the OECD Gender, Institutions and Development Data Base (GID-DB), the World Bank's gender statistics database—GenderStats.

female/male GDP per capita ratio calculated from female and male shares of earned income".[31] The validity of these aggregate indices has been often criticized.[32] More recently, other data sets are becoming popular. For example, the OECD Gender Data Portal includes selected indicators shedding light on gender inequalities in education, employment, entrepreneurship, governance, health, and development.[33]

Example

The Gender-Equality Index (GEI) developed by the European Institute for Gender Equality (EIGE) measures the progress of gender equality in the EU.[34] GEI shows the areas that need improvement and aims to support policymakers to design more effective gender equality measures. GEI examines how disability, age, education, country of origin, and family type intersect with gender to result in different outcomes. In the EU, GEI has increased rather slowly from 63.8 in 2010 to 67.9 in 2020. ◀

12.2.5 Gender Budgeting[35]

Conducting "ex-ante" gender impact assessments represents an opportunity to analyse potential impacts of adopted gender sensitive policies, from the perspective of elimination of gender inequalities based on: indicators on the current situation; results foreseen, and their impact. Next step towards full institutional integration of gender mainstreaming would be to integrate the gender perspective in all phases of the budget cycle.[36] Gender budgeting integrates a gender perspective into the budgetary process, aiming to achieve gender equality. Introduction of gender sensitive budgeting informs allocation decisions and ensures that women and men have equal access to resources, are able to decide on them equally, and receive equal benefits from the use of those resources. Hence, gender budgeting aims to improve resource allocations by achieving more gender equal outcomes.[37]

The implementation of gender budgeting requires the assessment, restructuring, monitoring and evaluation of achievements from a gender perspective. Hence, gender budgeting relies on the use of various analytical tools within the budget process. The approach is not yet widely implemented; in 2017, only a half of OECD

[31] Kardam (2005), p. 2.

[32] Dijkstra (2006) and Dijkstra and Hanmer (2000).

[33] Jütting et al. (2008).

[34] EIGE (2020).

[35] For a detailed review, see Chapter on Gender equitable taxation of this Textbook.

[36] OECD (2018).

[37] O'Hagan (2018).

members stated that they have incorporated or plan to incorporate gender budgeting into budget process.

12.2.6 Equality Plans

Various institutional frameworks and methods for gender-related analysis and evaluation have been developed. Governments often adopt a medium- to- long term vision statement that conveys a country's objectives for a gender-equal society.[38] These visions set expectations and are used as a benchmark for measuring reduction in gender inequality. To be successfully implemented, they should reflect the needs of stakeholders (governmental institutions, social partners, and civil society), have clearly defined roles, responsibilities, and accountability, and strong commitment from policymakers. These goals, often termed equality plans, are the primary tool that articulates gender equality policies. Thus, implemented actions by public authorities gender equality are normally contemplated in equality plans. Equality plans are a set of objectives and measures, taken and approved by a government. Generally, the must be carried out at different administrative and governmental levels and within a specific period, ranging from two to five years. The objective of equality plans usually includes all aspects or areas that affect women: education, work, culture, health, legislation, politics, leisure, environment, and rural environment. Therefore, equality plans are designed to be a common umbrella under which all public actions concerning gender equality of a given government are explicit. The plans often involve, at least formally, other administrative or governmental levels and non-governmental organisations. This renders equality plans the primary tool that articulates gender equality policies.

12.2.7 Impact Evaluation in Gender Policies: Functions and Purpose

Evaluation in the framework of public policies and gender equality policies has undoubtedly been the least studied phase.[39] In this sense, the policy cycle theory proposes the possibility of studying a specific public policy by breaking down its policy cycle into different phases. Although the organisation and number of phases depend, in many cases, on the author, following the work of Hogwood and Gunn, we can distinguish the following phases: (1) the definition of the problem and its entry into the agenda of the public authorities, (2) the formulation of proposals and the adoption of decisions, (3) its implementation, (4) the evaluation of the results and (5) the eventual termination of the initiated policy (1984, p. 4). However, a common element in all the classifications reviewed is that impact evaluation is usually considered one of the final public policy stages. Alongside this, most authors state

[38] OECD (2018).

[39] Ballart (1996).

that the process of agenda entry, formulation, implementation and evaluation is, in fact, a circular process that constantly feeds back on itself.[40]

Impact evaluation is not done in the abstract but is intended to improve the programmes and policies evaluated; to provide accountability and/or exemplify and illustrate future actions. Various works point to three functions, depending on the intended use of impact evaluation of gender equality policies: (1) *improvement*; (2) recapitulation, *accountability*; and (3) *enlightenment*.[41] Regarding the first function, that of improving the evaluated programme or policy, evaluation is conceived as a methodological artefact that allows for feedback and learning about one's practice. In this sense, evaluation is an essential instrument for the improvement, enhancement and guarantor of the quality of a service or programme. Logically, this function reinforces the focus on the specific and determined context of what is being evaluated, the differentiated needs of the people receiving these services and of all the agents involved in the service, especially the staff who provide it and the organisation that promotes it.[42]

Accountability would be the second function of impact evaluation. In this respect, the evaluation of equality policies must serve as an instrument to hold accountable different levels of responsibility for the management, results and impact of each of the plans and programmes implemented.[43] Thus, citizens have the right to know where public funds are being spent and how effectively and efficiently those funds are being allocated, managed and used. In addition to these two functions, evaluation can fulfil a third function to shed light on possible future actions. The ultimate meaning of impact evaluation is the evaluation of a particular programme in a given context, situation, and time to its improvement. However, impact evaluations provide systematic information that allows for a general approach to specific public problems; the impact may go beyond what was expected a priori.[44]

The purpose of impact evaluation of gender policies should also be to assess their usefulness in achieving social welfare. In this respect, social utility becomes another critical element of impact evaluation, achieved by recognising and involving different stakeholders in the evaluation process.[45] Above all, impact evaluation should be helpful through its practical orientation; an evaluation intended to play a role in future actions favouring gender equality.[46] Impact assessment has traditionally been conceived to measure the results and effects of a policy or programme. In this sense, some authors have also pointed out the retrospective character of impact evaluation. From this perspective, impact evaluation seems to claim only to provide information

[40]Birckmayer and Weiss (2000). For a detailed review of gender responsive budgeting see Chapter on Gender equitable taxation of the Textbook.

[41]Stufflebem (2001).

[42]Weiss (1998).

[43]Bickman (1994).

[44]Berk and Rossi (1990).

[45]Nelson (1996).

[46]Patton (1997).

on what has happened or is happening[47] As the analysis of what impact assessment entails in gender equality policies has broadened, however, this exclusively retrospective character has become less clear. Recently, in some international bodies and some countries, such as Sweden, "ex-ante" evaluation modalities are being developed, making it difficult to classify it as a purely retrospective activity. The above, and similar examples, have led to the abandonment of the idea that impact assessment focuses exclusively on the outcome of processes. Therefore, no one disputes today that impact evaluation can cover the different phases of policies or programmes favouring. gender equality, from their design or conception to the measurement of their final impact.[48] It is precisely this breadth that allows the evaluation of gender equality policies to be an integral part of the life of equality policies and to serve as a useful methodological tool for the entire process.

12.3 Gender Sensitive Policies

This section will discuss key gender sensitive policies that are used in different sectors and take various forms.[49] Social policies for gender equality deal with problems related to family, reconciliation, work and parental leave, time use, time for caring for the elderly and other dependents, and equal access to society's goods and services. Likewise, social policies aimed at gender equality impact the search for equity in the labour market, in access to employment and labour contexts in general. In addition to the above, university spaces are no stranger to social policies for gender equality, nor are the public contexts where political representation and participation occur. Finally, social policies favouring equality are concerned with devising actions to protect the environment against gender violence and eradicating multiple discrimination based on gender, ethnicity, religious beliefs, origin and other diversities such as functional and sexual diversity.

Social policies for gender equality are the set of principles, norms and objectives explicitly formulated and sanctioned by public authorities, aimed at achieving de jure and de facto equality between women and men.[50] Gender equality policies aim to achieve greater equality of opportunities between women and men by influencing the socio-economic and cultural conditions that prevent and hinder such equality.[51] The following are some of the social policies that promote gender equality and their main limitations.

[47] Rist (1990).

[48] Bachi (1996).

[49] Jacquot (2015).

[50] García Prince (2008).

[51] Bustelo (2004).

12.3.1 Family and Work-Life Balance Policies[52]

The establishment in 1960s of the dominant welfare model is patriarchal and legitimises an unequal allocation of responsibilities and an overburdening of women in the family sphere. Thus, women are primarily responsible for household chores, care roles, the transmission of values, morality and conduct, and families' general welfare.[53] For their part, family policies that promote equality focus mainly on external family support services. Some of the most common resources are childcare facilities, day-care centres and home care. In addition are leaves of absence and reductions in working hours.[54] The benefits and deductions proposed and/or implemented also include: maternity leave, paternity leave, breastfeeding, other paid leave, economic benefits for dependent children, care allowances and deductions in the personal income tax return.

Family policies that promote gender equality are based on two main ideas. The first is that it is not only family members who are capable of providing the best care. The second is that family care is a source of enrichment and satisfaction for the people involved. Thus, depending on the country, other strategies are related to childcare services, actions to provide care for dependents, care throughout the life cycle and the intensification of care at certain points in life.[55] As for the limitations of the family policies in place, they can be grouped into five categories: (1) the insufficient supply of public services and resources made available; (2) the weakening of the social network of support and favours; (3) insufficient attention to the needs of increasingly diverse families; (4) the belief that, for balance, actions must be aimed primarily at women, and (5) the presumption that it is women who will have to make more concessions and bear the most significant burden in those areas not covered by the policies.[56]

12.3.2 Equality Policies in the Labour and Political Sphere[57]

Concerning labour policies, in industrially advanced societies employment occupies a pre-eminent place in the shaping of identity. In this context women suffer from disadvantages; they do not have equal access, opportunities nor equal pay in all sectors and professions.[58] Equality employment policies have been concerned with promoting women's access to paid work and female employment promotion. Other measures implemented have consisted of making employment more flexible,

[52]For a detailed review of the legislative framework see Chapter on Family law of this Textbook.

[53]Meil (2011).

[54]Otero Hermida (2016).

[55]Cohen and Samzelius (2020).

[56]Gallardo (2021).

[57]For a detailed review see chapters on the Labour law and Human rights of this Textbook.

[58]Puleo (2014).

including overtime as actual working hours, reducing productive working time without undermining pay, telecommuting and teleworking. Similarly, measures such as the regulation of working hours, school, business and public administration hours are proposed.[59] The limitations of these policies include the following: (1) they are limited to particular areas and sectors of the labour market; (2) they are not concerned with informing, incentivising and encouraging potential employers to implement them; (3) they are mainly targeted at women, leading to situations of discrimination (for example, if only women consider part-time work) and, finally, (4) they are not always aimed at promoting gender equality. The challenges for equality policies in the field of employment continue to be the following: (1) to guarantee equal opportunities and non-discrimination; (2) to maintain an effective system of protection against unemployment that includes active policies, unemployment protection policies and employment integration policies for groups with particular difficulties in finding employment, and (3) to promote an entrepreneurial and business culture.

Policies for women's equal political participation are concerned with combating horizontal and vertical discrimination, establishing lines of action to establish quotas, and favouring equal representation.[60] At present, other challenges remain: (1) achieving substantive representation of women, which can be achieved to the extent that an increase of women in decision-making bodies leads to an improvement in the representation of their interests;[61] (2) adapting the agenda for gender equality, and (3) promoting increases in budgets to achieve the above challenges[62]

12.3.3 Diversity, Anti-discrimination and Anti-violence Policies[63]

This section focuses specifically on the problems faced by LGBTQIA+ people, women victims of gender-based violence and the policies implemented in favour of diversity and against discrimination and anti-violence. LGBTQIA+ people suffer discrimination on the grounds of sexual orientation and gender identity. This increases when other variables such as gender, ethnicity, age, religious beliefs, functional diversity, health, social class, economic status and political orientation come together. LGBTQIA+ people also suffer denial of rights, murder, non-lethal violence (such as threats, coercion, beatings, kidnappings), harassment, rape, sexual abuse, torture and other ill-treatment.[64] Social and institutional discrimination against LGBTQIA+ people take place in personal development, family, education, employment, health and equal access to goods and resources. The policies to be

[59] Beveridge (2021) and Pastor et al. (2017).

[60] Aldeguer Cerdá (2020).

[61] Freeman (2010).

[62] Bjørna (2012).

[63] For a detailed review see chapters on the Criminal law and Human rights of this Textbook.

[64] Montenegro et al. (2020).

implemented should focus on reviewing, holistically and with a rights-based approach, the serious situation of discrimination and violence experienced by these people and formulating lines of action to promote their rights and freedoms in equality.[65]

Gender violence suffered by women is a social problem of international scope, where it is possible to distinguish particularly vulnerable groups such as older women[66] and women with disabilities.[67] Violence against women persists over time without the formulation of social policies capable of preventing and stopping it. The main limitation of policies against gender violence is that they try to fight it with mainly punitive actions, forgetting that various factors involved are intertwined in the socio-patriarchal system. In this sense, policies against gender-based violence should aim to change the social system itself: the structural, cultural and subjective factors of the gender model. Thus, policies should focus not only on the victims, but also on the rehabilitation of aggressors and raising awareness of the law, institutions and (within?—unsure of meaning) society.[68] Consequently, measures should aim to change hierarchical and sexist gender relations based on stereotypes. Gender roles that foster inequalities are crucial to generating violence and abuse against those considered inferior. In addition to the above, the strategies implemented should be comprehensive and aimed at the education system, the labour market, the media and families to influence and transform the values of children and young people.[69]

12.3.4 Education and Science Policies for Gender Equality

A feminist analysis of the university (what university- or if no university it would be university system or structure) primarily leads us to question the percentage of women rectors worldwide, which is much lower than that of men.[70] An even more pronounced look leads us to analyse the (not always) gender-balanced composition of the governing teams and the structures that guarantee equality in the university. Women working at universities continue to carry the most significant burden of care tasks without economic compensation and, in some cases, without social recognition.[71] This translates into difficulties for access and promotion in university and management careers, and a decrease in women's quality of life compared to men. The organisation of some curricula in morning and afternoon sessions, the working day of administrative, service, teaching and research staff means that many women have to carry out what is known as the second and third working day: work at home,

[65] Jiménez Rodrigo (2020).

[66] Bermúdez Figueroa and Hervías Parejo (2021).

[67] Hervías Parejo and Minguela Recover (2021).

[68] Vélez Bautista and Serrano Barquín (2018).

[69] Vera (2020).

[70] OECD (2021).

[71] Hervías Parejo (2019).

teaching or management, and positions of political responsibility.[72] Finally, universities are no strangers to situations of gender-based violence, sexual and workplace harassment and LGTBQIA+ phobia. In this context, policies for gender equality in the university (as above, system or structure) consider the implementation of leaves of absence, measures to favour reconciliation, co-responsibility and breastfeeding spaces, toy libraries and summer schools. Furthermore, they are concerned with promoting equality and combating discrimination, gender-based violence and sexual and sexist harassment.[73] Among the challenges of equality policies in the university sphere, the following stand out: (1) responding to the diversity of needs and the motivations and interests of university communities; (2) making gender and equality an issue of interest to the entire university community; (3) making the working day and teleworking more flexible; (4) promoting transversality in undergraduate, postgraduate and master's degree training; (5) promoting the transfer of equality to society as a whole; (6) stimulating the institutionalisation of networking, and (7) promoting gender mainstreaming in higher education, for example, by integrating a gender perspective into curricula, textbooks and pedagogical approaches.

12.4 Conclusion

Public policies have often been viewed as gender-neutral interventions. However, even public policies that appear to be gender-neutral may substantially impact gender equality. Nowadays, gender mainstreaming has been embraced across countries as an approach to reduce gender inequality. Several elements are important for an effective and sustainable integration of gender perspective into public policies. First, a comprehensive strategic framework is required. Most countries adopt strategic documents that outline general gender equality goals and set priorities, timelines, general and specific objectives and expected outcomes. This provides a basis for effective gender sensitive policy planning across various sectors and organizations. Second, effective tools of implementation, such as gender impact assessment, gender sensitive budgeting and policy evaluation are needed to ensure the integration of gender mainstreaming at all levels of the policy process to promote gender equality. Third, political commitment to provide clear roles, responsibilities and a supportive environment is required to facilitate capacity development, stakeholder's participation, and effective oversight. The last two elements are necessary to implement, monitor and evaluate gender sensitive policies.

The changing role of women and LGBTQIA+ in the population influences the use of gender sensitive public policies. Namely, the relationship between public policies and gender equality is bidirectional.[74] On the one side, public policy may support

[72]Puleo (2014).

[73]Ruiz Bravo López and Sánchez Barrenechea (2019) and Vujadinović et al. (2020).

[74]Duflo (2012).

gender equality. On the other side, the role and status of women's empowerment and leadership can only be conducive to the promotion of gender equality.[75]

Social policies have the most prominent role in promoting gender equality. These policies deal with problems related to families and their diversity, the reconciliation of family and professional life, work and parental leave, the use of time, time for caring for the elderly and other dependents, and equal access to the goods and services offered by society. Likewise, gender equality policies impact the search for equity in the labour market, access to employment and the protection of groups and special vulnerability situations. In addition to the above, the spaces of representation and political participation are not alien to gender sensitive issues either. In this case, strategies focus on combating inequality and promoting the representation of women's interests on an equal footing. Such policies are also concerned with alleviating discrimination and gender-based violence by focusing on protecting diversity in all areas of human development and aiming to change the social system itself:. the structural, cultural and subjective factors of the gender model. Finally, gender equality policies are formulated and implemented in university settings. In this context, actions aim to make the working day and telework more flexible, promote transversality, foster transfer and stimulate networking.

Questions

- **Case study 1.** Gender mainstreaming is based on the idea that there are no gender-neutral policies. This means that the implemented actions have a positive or negative impact on people's lives, that is, women, men and the LGTBQIA+ community. In recognition of this reality, the United Nations has repeatedly invited governments and other social agents to integrate a gender perspective in their legislation, policies, plans, programmes and projects. Students are asked to select two countries and compare how their governments have or have not integrated the gender perspective in their public policies. In this sense, they will also have to assess whether the public strategies implemented have applied gender mainstreaming.
- **Case study 2.** The Gender-Equality Index (GEI) developed by the European Institute for Gender Equality (EIGE) measures the progress of gender equality in the EU.[76] GEI shows the areas that need improvement and aims to support policymakers to design more effective gender equality measures. GEI examines how disability, age, education, country of origin, and family type intersect with gender to result in different outcomes. Students are asked to select the gender equality indices of two countries and to draw out similarities and disparities from a study of their gender equality legislation.

(continued)

[75] Profeta (2020).

[76] EIGE (2020).

- **Case study 3.** Using Gender, Institutions and Development Database OECD available at https://stats.oecd.org/Index.aspx?DataSetCode=GIDDB2019, students are asked to visit the Data Portal, select the main indicators of gender inequality and draw at least five conclusions about them.
- **Case study 4.** The OECD Gender Data Portal includes selected indicators shedding light on gender inequalities in education, employment, entrepreneurship, governance, health, and development. Students are asked to select a country and establish benchmark indicators in the area of discrimination in the family. Using additional sources, students should provide context and set the public policy goals for a five-year period.
- **Case study 5.** Inequalities are recurrent and, therefore, it is necessary to consider the principle of equality as an objective that, in an integrated manner, permeates decision-making, design, management, implementation, monitoring and evaluation of all public policies and not just equality policies. Students are asked to discuss the concept of gender inequality and reach consensus on a common definition. Also, using additional sources, students should provide context and state the objectives of public policies to combat gender inequality.
- **Case study 6.** Equality plans are a set of objectives and measures taken and approved by a government and must be carried out at different administrative and governmental levels and within a specific period ranging from two to five years. The objective of equality plans usually includes all aspects or areas that affect women, i.e. education, work, culture, health, legislation, politics, leisure, environment, and rural environment. Students are asked to carry out a comprehensive search for international public legislative and technical instruments in favour of equality of women and men in the world.
- **Case study 7.** In the EU, to ensure gender equality in policy impact assessment, various methods were developed, including gender indicators, gender analysis, gender impact assessment, gender budgeting, and evaluation. Students are asked to assess the implementation of such strategies in chosen Member States and in third countries and give some examples and whether they are proving successful.
- **Case study 8.** Gender impact assessment proposes to rely on three types of strategies to achieve effective equality between women and men from the perspective of gender mainstreaming. These strategies are reparation, adaptation and transformation and can be applied in a complementary manner to formulate and reformulate policies, plans and programmes. In this exercise, students are asked to review what these actions consists of and to find applied examples of such strategies in policies implemented at the international level.

(continued)

- **Case study 9.** The invisibility of care: "Care policies" are those whose programmes, plans and regulations seek to promote equality between women and men in their provision. Spanish state laws include Law 39/1999, of 5 November, to promote the reconciliation of work and family life for workers; Law 39/2006, of 14 December, on the Promotion of Personal Autonomy and Care for Dependent Persons; and Organic Law 3/2007, of 22 March, for the effective equality of women and men. These laws are analysed in detail, and no precise definition of the concept of care is found. The conclusion is that the laws mentioned above silence the explicit visibility of care, although it is an essential part of citizens' needs. Based on the previous case study, students are asked to select a country other than Spain and analyse the legislation related to care in that country to deduce whether care is explicitly included and regulated in these laws or whether, on the contrary, it is made invisible.
- **Case study 10.** The difficult reconciliation of work and family life and the ethnicity of care in rich countries: in rich countries, older people are increasingly cared for by immigrants from developing countries, which monetises and makes visible the previously invisible care and assigned to women in the family. Based on the above case study, students are asked to find international or national legal foundations to help them position themselves for or against the following construct: Care is a derivation of gender because its provision has been assigned to women.

References

Ahmed AM, Andersson L, Hammarstedt M (2013) Are Gay men and Lesbians discriminated against in the hiring process? South Econ J 79:565–585

Aldeguer Cerdá B (2020) The impact of quotas on the political representation of women in Les Corts (1995-2019). Corts: Parliam Law Yearb 33:239–279

Azmat G, Petrongolo B (2014) Gender and the labor market: what have we learned from field and lab experiments? Labour Econ 30:32–40

Bachi CL (1996) The politics of affirmative action. SAGE Publications, London

Ballart X (1996) Theoretical models for the practice of programme evaluation. In: Brugé J, Subirats J (eds) Readings in public management. Ministerio para las Administraciones Públicas, Madrid, pp 321–351

Barrère Unzueta MÁ (2010) Intersectionality as a challenge to gender mainstreaming in public policies. Basque J Public Adm 87–88:225–252

Berk RA, Rossi PH (1990) Thinking about program evaluation. SAGE Publications, Newbury Park

Bermúdez Figueroa E, Hervías Parejo V (2021) Gender violence against elderly women. In: Caramés CF (ed) Women particularly vulnerable to gender-based violence: women with disabilities and older women. Tirant Lo Blanch, Madrid, pp 47–82

Beveridge F (2021) 'Going soft'? Analysing the contribution of soft and hard measures in EU gender law and policy. In: The Europeanization of gender equality policies. Palgrave Macmillan, London

Bickman L (1994) An optimistic view of evaluation. Eval Pract 15:255–259
Birckmayer JD, Weiss CH (2000) Theory-based evaluation in practice. What do we learn? Eval Rev 24:407–431
Bustelo M (2004) The evaluation of gender policies in Spain. Los libros de la Catarata, Madrid
Council of Europe, DAC (1998) DAC (OECD) guidelines and concept guide on equality between women and men. Ministry of Foreign Affairs, Madrid
Cruz-Rubio CN (2017) Revisiting the politics of public policy evaluation. More local power 31:8–11
Daly M (2005) Gender mainstreaming in theory and practice. Soc Polit: Int Stud Gend State Soc 12: 433–450
Dijkstra AG (2006) Towards a fresh start in measuring gender equality: a contribution to the debate. J Hum Dev 7:275–283
European Commission (1999) Annual Economic Report. Part 1. https://ec.europa.eu/economy_finance/publications/pages/publication8067_en.pdf
Freeman J (2010) Building a base: women in local party politics. In: Crooks ML, Childs S (eds) Women, gender and politics. Oxford University Press, Oxford, pp 89–96
Gallardo M (2021) Does maternity affect women's careers?: Perceptions of working mothers in academia. Educación XX1: Revista de la Facultad de Educación 24:405–428
Galor O, Weil DN (1996) The gender gap, fertility, and growth. Am Econ Rev 86:374–387
García Prince E (2008) Equality, equity and gender mainstreaming policies: what are we talking about? Conceptual framework. Spain-UNDP, Catalonia
Gensana Riera MÁ (2015) Gender impact assessment and gender social responsibility, instruments for achieving effective equality between women and men. Autonomous University of Barcelona, Barcelona
Hervías Parejo V (2019) The future of gender equality policies in Andalusian universities. An approach from comparative politics. Quorum Libros SL y Instituto de la Mujer, Cádiz
Himmelweit S (2018) Gender equality impact assessment: a core element of gender budgeting. In: O'Hagan A, Klatzer E (eds) Gender budgeting in Europe. Palgrave Macmillan, London, pp 89–108
Ignjatović S, Bošković A (2013) 'Are we there yet?' Citizens of Serbia and public policy on gender equality within the EU accession context. Eur J Women's Stud 0:425–440
Inglehart R, Norris P (2003) Rising tide: gender equality and cultural change around the world. Cambridge University Press, Cambridge
Jacquot S (2015) Transformations in EU gender equality: from emergence to dismantling. Palgrave Macmillan, London
Jiménez Rodrigo ML (2020) Possibilities of documentary research for the intersectional analysis of equality policies. Fem Res 2:319–331
Jütting JP, Morrisson C, Dayton-Johnson J, Drechsler D (2008) Measuring gender (in)equality: the OECD gender, institutions and development data base. J Hum Dev 9:65–86
Kabeer N, Natali L (2013) Gender equality and economic growth: is there a win-win? IDS Working Papers:1–58
Klasen S (2002) Low schooling for girls, slower growth for all? Cross-country evidence on the effect of gender inequality in education on economic development. World Bank Econ Rev 16: 315–373
Knill C, Tosun J (2012) Public policy: a new introduction. Palgrave Macmillan, Basingstoke
Lombardo E (2003) Gender mainstreaming in the European Union. Aequalitas Equal Oppor Women Men Law Rev 10–15:6–11
Marchand MH, Parpart JL (1995) Feminism/postmodernism/development. Routledge, London
Meil G (2011) Individualisation and family solidarity. Soc Stud Collect 32
Miller K (2009) Public policy dilemma—gender equality mainstreaming in UK policy formulation. Public Money Manag 29:43–50
Nelson BJ (1996) Public policy and administration: an overview. In: Goodin RE, Klingemann H-D (eds) A new handbook of political science. Oxford University Press, Oxford, pp 551–592

O'Hagan A (2018) Conceptual and institutional origins of gender budgeting. In: O'Hagan A, Klatzer E (eds) Gender budgeting in Europe. Palgrave Macmillan, London, pp 19–42
Organisation for Economic Co-operation and Development, OECD (2018) Development Co-operation Report. https://www.oecd.org/social/development-co-operation-report-20747721.htm
Organisation for Economic Co-operation and Development, OECD (2021). https://www.oecd.org/
Otero Hermida P (2016) The impact of gender and equality policies on employment at the local level. Doctoral thesis. University of Santiago de Compostela, Santiago
Parpart JL (1993) Who is the 'Other'?: A postmodern feminist critique of women and development theory and practice. Dev Change Int Inst Soc Stud 24(3):439–464. https://doi.org/10.1111/j.1467-7660.1993.tb00492.x
Patton MQ (1997) Utilisation-focused evaluation. The new century text. SAGE Publications, Thousand Oaks
Profeta P (2020) Gender equality and public policy: measuring progress in Europe. Cambridge University Press, Cambridge
Puleo AH (2014) Ecofeminism for another world. Cátedra, Madrid
Rees T (1998) Mainstreaming equality in the European Union. Routledge, London
Rist RC (1990) Program evaluation and the management of government. Patterns and prospects across eight nations. Transaction Publishers, New Brunswick
Ruiz Bravo López PM, Sánchez Barrenechea J (2019) Gender equality policies in higher education institutions. In: Pastor I (ed) Gender equality in Europe and Latin America: higher education, violence and regional integration policies. Publicacions de la Universitat Rovira i Virgili, Tarragona, pp 35–50
Souto Galván C (2012) Principle of equality and gender mainstreaming. Dykinson SL, Spain
Stufflebem DL (2001) Evaluation models. Jossey-Bass, San Francisco
Vélez Bautista G, Serrano Barquín H (2018) Gender violence, masculinities and public policies. Sociol Issues 22:151–176
Vera L (2020) Gender approach, gender violence and public policies: an approach from the social sciences to the Ecuadorian legal framework. ReHuSo: J Humanistic Soc Sci 1:19–32
Verloo M, Roggeband C (1996) Gender impact assessment: the development of a new instrument in the Netherlands. Impact Assess 14:3–20
Weiss CH (1998) Have we learned anything new about the use of evaluation? Am J Eval 19:21–33

Further Reading

Badgett MVL, Waaldijk K, van der Meulen Rodgers Y (2019) The relationship between LGBT inclusion and economic development: macro-level evidence. World Dev 120:1–14
Bjørna H (2012) Women in charge: politics in a women majority local council in Australia. Commonwealth J Local Gov 10:51–69
Chelimsky E (1998) The role of experience in formulating theories of evaluation practice. Am J Eval 19:35–55
Cohen S, Samzelius T (2020) Through the lens of single parenthood: a comparative snapshot of the impact of neoliberal welfare, housing and employment policies on single mothers in the UK and Sweden. Feminismo/s 35:127–153
Dijkstra AG, Hanmer LC (2000) Measuring socio-economic GENDER inequality: toward an alternative to the UNDP Gender-Related Development Index. Fem Econ 6:41–75
Duflo E (2012) Women empowerment and economic development. J Econ Lit 50:1051–1079
Dunn WN (1981) Public policy analysis: an introduction. Prentice-Hall, Englewood Cliffs
European Institute for Gender Equality (EIGE) (2017) Gender impact assessment: gender mainstreaming toolkit. Publications Office of the European Union, Luxembourg
European Institute for Gender Equality (EIGE) (2020) Gender Equality Index 2020: key findings for the EU. European Institute for Gender Equality, Vilnius

Fuentes Rodríguez F (2018) Gender violence in the workplace: sexual harassment and gender-based harassment in the Spanish legal system. In: de Reboleño Lastortres EG (ed) The university as a subject that transforms social reality in terms of gender equality. Agencia Andaluza de Cooperación Internacional para el Desarrollo, Cádiz, pp 51–65
Goizueta Vértiz J (2020) Parity democracy and gender impact in public policies: analysis of the case of the Basque Autonomous Community. Polit Law J 109:153–190
González Orta LC (2020) The impact of global policies on national legislation - the case of the Convention on the Elimination of All Forms of Discrimination against Women (CEDAW) in Spain. Public Policy Manag Anal 24:106–119
Hervías Parejo V (1984) The future of gender equality policies in Andalusian universities. An approach from comparative politics. Quorum Libros SL y Instituto de la Mujer, Cádiz
Hervías Parejo V, Minguela Recover MÁ (2021) Women with disabilities victims of gender violence. In: Caramés CF (ed) Women particularly vulnerable to gender-based violence: women with disabilities and older women. Tirant Lo Blanch, Madrid, pp 87–110
Hogwood BW, Gunn LA (1984) Policy analysis for the real world. Oxford University Press, Oxford
Jacquot S (2010) The paradox of gender mainstreaming: unanticipated effects of new modes of governance in the gender equality domain. West Eur Polit 33:118–135
Kardam N (2005) Turkey's engagement with global women's human rights norms. Ashgate Publishers, London
Kraft ME, Furlong SR (2018) Public policy: politics, analysis, and alternatives. CQ Press, Washington
Montenegro M, Montenegro LCH, Carlos L, Torres-Lista V (2020) LGBTIQ+ people's rights, gender agenda and equality policies. Encuentros. J Hum Sci Soc Theory Crit Think 11:9–23
Morrisson C, Jütting Johannes JP (2005) Women's discrimination in developing countries: a new data set for better policies. World Dev 33:1065–1081
Pastor I, Merino PP, Coronas TT (2017) Equality policies in employment. In: Pastor I, Martín LR, Galindo MZ (eds) Gender equality policies and integration in Europe and Latin America. Aranzadi, Cizur Menor, pp 191–207
Roggeband C, Verloo M (2006) Evaluating gender impact assessment in the Netherlands (1994-2004): a political process approach. Policy Polit 34:615–632
Rubery J, Grimshaw D, Figueiredo H (2005) How to close the gender pay gap in Europe: towards the gender mainstreaming of pay policy. Ind Relat J 36:184–213
Vujadinović D, Kovačević L, Marinković T et al (2020) Achieving gender equality at the University of Belgrade Faculty of Law – research and policy study. Faculty of Law, University of Belgrade, Belgrade
World Bank (2012) World development report. Gender equality and development. World Bank, Washington

Gender Competent Criminal Law 13

María Acale Sánchez, Ivana Marković, and Susanne Strand

Contents

Authors are listed in alphabetical order. Sections 13.1, 13.2.2, 13.3.3, 13.3.5, 13.4 and the questions are written by Ivana Marković. Sections 13.2.1 and 13.2.3–13.2.5 are written by María Acale Sánchez, translated by María del Mar Martín Aragón. Susanne Strand authored Sects. 13.3.1, 13.3.2 and 13.3.4.

M. Acale Sánchez
University of Cadiz, Faculty of Law, International Public, Criminal and Procedural Law, Jerez de la Frontera, Spain
e-mail: maria.acale@gm.uca.es

I. Marković (✉)
University of Belgrade, Faculty of Law, Criminal Law, Belgrade, Serbia
e-mail: ivana.markovic@ius.bg.ac.rs

S. Strand
Örebro University, School of Law, Psychology and Social Work, Örebro, Sweden
e-mail: Susanne.strand@oru.se

D. Vujadinović et al. (eds.), *Gender-Competent Legal Education*, Springer Textbooks in Law, https://doi.org/10.1007/978-3-031-14360-1_13

Abstract

The following chapter deals with the general and special part of criminal law from a gender perspective. It analyses, in particular, the provisions from the Council of Europe Convention on preventing and combating violence against women and domestic violence, the Istanbul Convention, from 2011. The Istanbul Convention is the most comprehensive international legal instrument that outlines binding obligations to states to prevent and combat violence against women and girls. Furthermore, the Istanbul Convention contains several institutes and behaviours that have to be criminalised in the respective national jurisdictions, covering and combining dogmatics and criminal policy issues with a foundation substantially based on gender. The chapter also explores gender issues in a more general way, interpreting criminal law and its challenges towards gender equality. The special part raises questions regarding criminal law and its compatibility with the Istanbul Convention and national laws.

13.1 Introduction

The first part of the chapter on gender competent criminal law will analyse relevant aspects and institutes of the general part of criminal law, while the second part will deal with particular criminal offences that are important and highly topical from a gender perspective—physical and psychological domestic violence, stalking, sexual violence, and violations of women's integrity by forcing them to abortion, sterilisation, marriages, etc. This twofold structure reflects, on the one hand, the traditional and recognisable systematisation of criminal law dogmatics into a general part and a special part. On the other hand, it enables the deduction of certain punishable behaviour.

The bigger picture namely shows: even though the law in general enforces and justifies dominant relationships of power, criminal law mandates socially acceptable behaviour in the most direct manner.[1] One may add—not only mandates but also necessarily sanctions it. While this is common ground for the Theory of Criminal Law, it is a new momentum to include the gender perspective in dogmatic terms. It is also something that has been mainly overlooked by gender studies so far, as they focus on the context of crime. The focus has primarily been on either the results (i.e., as shown in statistics) or the social basis for this development (i.e., inequality, violence), but not specifically on the legal text, its wording, interpretation, examples from jurisdiction, etc. By adding the dogmatic component, it would complete the holistic approach to criminal law questions and gender. Of course, this will not be

[1] Roberts (1994), p. 1.

possible extensively (meaning ubiquitously, finding flaws in each and every legal regulation), nor should it be. In fact, the precise identification and analysis of relevant gender-related and problematic aspects of a particular legislation would lead to well-founded, reasoned, solution-oriented proposals. And last but not least, it would do justice to the *ultima ratio* nature of Criminal Law.

Learning Goals

The learning goals for this chapter are

- Understanding the relationship and the interaction between criminal law and gender.
- Knowing the importance and content of the particular gender-related criminal provisions of the Istanbul Convention.
- Being able to understand current common problems of Gender and Criminal Law, as well as to become able to recognise and anticipate further developments; both positive and negative.

The Istanbul Convention

The Istanbul Convention (CETS No. 210) titled "Council of Europe Convention on preventing and combating violence against women and domestic violence" was enacted 7 May 2011. The first ten ratifications, including eight Member States, were done by 1 August 2014.[2] By 20 July 2021, 35 countries have signed the Treaty, of which eleven have not yet ratified it.[3]

"This new landmark treaty of the Council of Europe opens the path for creating a legal framework at a pan-European level to protect women against all forms of violence, and prevent, prosecute and eliminate violence against women and domestic violence."[4]

It covers eight specific areas: psychological violence, stalking, physical violence, sexual violence, rape, forced marriage, female genital mutilation, forced abortion, forced sterilisation, and sexual harassment.

As part of the Istanbul Convention, a specific monitoring system (Group of Experts on Action against Violence against Women and Domestic Violence - GREVIO) was put in place to evaluate if the Treaty's implementation has been done by those who have signed it. For the Istanbul Convention to be effective, it

[2] The Treaty is open for signature by the Member States of the Council of Europe, the Non-Member States which have participated in its elaboration and by the European Union, and for accession by other Non-Member States. https://www.coe.int/en/web/conventions/full-list/-/conventions/treaty/210/signatures?module=signatures-by-treaty&treatynum=210, last accessed 20 July 2021.

[3] Full list (coe.int).

[4] Full list (coe.int).

must be followed up, and feedback of shortcomings needs to be presented to countries so they can be remedied.

Being the first internationally legally binding instrument that is establishing a comprehensive legal framework for the protection from all forms of violence[5] that is basically gender-related, the Istanbul Convention will be of the most outstanding importance and will be the centre of the analysis. It contains introductory provisions on criminal law and gender, penalties and the perpetrator. The Istanbul Convention has been recognised as essential for gender competent criminal law, providing a new basis and enhancing the development regarding respective offences. This is because it entails provisions that go beyond the usual regulation of international documents, providing an entry into dogmatics of criminal law, yet from a gender point of view. In the Preamble of the Convention, this link is underlined by the acknowledgments of the structural nature of violence against women as gender-based violence; that women and girls are exposed to a higher risk of gender-based violence than men, but also that men may be victims of domestic violence as well.

13.2 General Part

13.2.1 Typicity

Typicity in criminal violations is a direct consequence of implementing the legality principle in criminal law within *civil law* systems. Further, this needs to be complemented with the case law interpretation limited by the prohibition of analogy *in malam partem*.[6] Nevertheless, the enforcement of the legality principle in criminal law does not downplay the work developed by the case law, intended to interpret the facts and include them in the appropriate norm. Nevertheless, case law is the main vehicle for law creation in the *common law*[7] systems. The differences in the source system are not an obstacle for countries to sign international conventions, by which they assume legal compromises regulating issues in a specific direction. Still, different countries have different challenges and would thereby come up with different solutions. This way, as time goes by, international conventions would

[5] https://www.coe.int/de/web/conventions/full-list/-/conventions/treaty/210/signatures?module=treaty-detail&treatynum=210, last accessed 20 July 2021.

[6] Donini (2017), p. 24.

[7] From this point of view it is essential for our democratic societies to have legal operators trained to apprehend the presence of gender based violence in each case.

facilitate the standardisation of criminal laws from different countries and make both comparative legal research and education easier to conduct.[8,9]

The ratification of the Istanbul Convention[10] has opened up a reform process of different legal systems within the States parties.[11] Among these processes, the reform of the criminal code to contextualise the provisions made in the Istanbul Convention in the various national areas will be incorporated. Further, the specific indications made in the Istanbul Convention around the crimes that should be punished in the national legal systems will supposedly guarantee a standard orientation of the European criminal policy. However, if the States include elements that are vague, undefined, or difficult to determine when transposing the Istanbul Convention, the guarantee inherent to the legality principle could be violated.

Thus, the provisions made by the Istanbul Convention within the range of criminal typicity have a dual nature. On the one hand, Articles 33 et seq. set standards around the need for criminal punishment for specific behaviours in each State Party, such as psychological violence, stalking, physical violence, sexual violence, including rape, forced marriage, female genital mutilation, forced abortion and forced sterilisation and sexual harassment.[12] On the other hand, each of these behaviours has its peculiarities, but they also share some common features, which the theory of crime has traditionally solved.

Typicity is the dogmatic category of the crime, including the legal goods that are to be protected. It means a kind of conversation between the lawmaker and society, i.e., general prevention, where one can assume that man does not commit these forbidden behaviours. Further, typicity can be considered a public performance of

---

[8] Wilson describes the reasons that justified the approval in the United Kingdom of *Sexual Offences Act* in 1976, which recognizes types of sexual aggression that differs from vaginal intercourse, Wilson (2011), pp. 19–20. Armenta Deu makes a reference of the knead within the *civil law* system that the court judges and doesn't have to have "direct or indirect legislative facultations". Armenta Deu (2012), p. 25.

[9] So court preparation to deal with this task turns out as essential specifically when talking about crimes that in many cases go unnoticed, camouflage under non-violent daily life, invisivilized to reality if they are not interpreted from a gender-based legal point of view. See Chap. 3 in this textbook.

[10] That was assumed as its own by the European Union 11 May 2017. Recently the European Union in its "Gender equality strategy factsheet" given by the European Parliament 21 March 2021 "calls for preparatory actions to be started now in order to launch additional legally binding measures and an EU framework directive to prevent and combat all forms of gender based violence, addressing among other issues, female genital mutilation (CGM), forced abortion, sterilization and marriages, and for it to include sexual exploitation, trafficking, cyber violence, the publication of revenge porn and online hate speech against women with a strong intersectional approach what comes initially to stand in the areas of crime to encompass specific forms of gender based violence in accordance with Article 83(1) of the TFEU; recalls that these new legislative measures should be complementary to the ratification of the Istanbul Convention."

[11] In this case, State parties are those states who have signed the Istanbul Convention.

[12] It is to be highlighted that there is no reference to human trafficking overall if we take under consideration that women are the priority victims as in the case of forced marriages, sexual exploitation or pornography). These provisions might be complemented with Council of Europe Convention 197 made in Varsovia, 16 May 2005.

the current criminal policy. Taking these under consideration, we can consider typicity as an educational preventive and democratic task because it protects the legal goods.

Indeed, the first task to be addressed within typicity should be identifying the legal goods that sustain the criminal behaviour. According to this, the Preamble of the Istanbul Convention establishes that those behaviours are

> "a serious violation of the human rights of women and girls and a major obstacle to the achievement of equality between women and men", at that the time that it recognises that "women and girls are exposed to a higher risk of gender-based violence than men"

However, this is just a listing of political-criminal interests protected by the Istanbul Convention, not identifying common legal goods.[13] Therefore, the importance of the Istanbul Convention is on the protection of life, health freedom, sexual freedom, and sexual and reproductive rights, which identify all the independent legal goods for each corresponding crime.

While identifying the protected interest for each crime, a study related to the holder's consent should be done. There will not be a violation of sexual freedom or forced marriage, or sexual harassment if the victim agrees to these activities, making them available legal goods. Nevertheless, how the availability for such legal goods is defined is not a common consensus, such as life (homicide/euthanasia) or abortion. The consent needs to be given lawfully to be considered adequate. Regarding these essential elements, Art. 36 (2) of the Istanbul Convention establishes the requirement of consent for sexual crimes, pointing that

> "consent must be given voluntarily as the result of the person's free will assessed in the context of the surrounding circumstances"[14]

[13] In the opposite direction the Inter-American convention on the prevention, punishment and eradication of violence against women convention, Convention of Belem do Para (July, 9, 1994) given by the Organization of American States identifies in its Article 6 the right of every woman "to be free from violence", including rights to life, integrity, freedom, dignity, protection within the law and the courts, association, religious freedom and equality in the access to public function and participation in public issues. The different crimes regulated in the Criminal Codes should be read according to these superior right in order to understand that these crimes attack several legal interest for the purposes of Istanbul Convention is not possible to make visible.

[14] This provision is in the base of the reform that different criminal codes are suffering regarding sexual crimes, as for instance, *Fünfzigstes Gesetz zur Änderung des Strafgesetzbuches zur Verbesserung des Schutzes der Sexuellen Selbstbestimmung,* November 4, 2016; Law n° 2018-703 du 3 août 2018 renforçant la lutte contre les violences sexuelles et sexistes; Article 375 in Belgium criminal code, from the reform made in February 2016; Sweden criminal code, after the reform in 2018. It has also meant that the Spanish parliament made a reform these crimes with the Organic Law draft on Integral Guarantee of Sexual Freedom, 3 May 2020.

In sum, only voluntary and free consent, "in the context of the surrounding circumstances", which gives an absolute relativism to the main act of consenting, is legitimate to decriminalise a behaviour.

Moreover, the typical behaviour is an essential element since it's the image within the criminal regulation of a code of values that allows punishing the most severe behaviours against the most essential legal goods. The decision made by the Istanbul Convention is related to a double judgement of proportionality, whereby it is stated that due to the importance of these legal goods, i.e., psychological violence, harassment, physical violence, sexual violence (including rape), forced marriages, female genital mutilations, abortion, forced sterilisation and sexual-harassment, the offences against them should be criminalised. These offences are the most severe ways of attacking women and girls for the protected legal goods.

Typicity also includes the characteristics of the perpetrator and the victim that are not included in the specific crimes definition given by the Istanbul Convention. Regardless, from a criminological point of view, these behaviours are mostly committed by male perpetrators towards female victims. Nevertheless, personal/relational(?) circumstances that amend the criminal liability are expressly stipulated so that the penalty would increase in such cases.

> "the offence was committed against a former or current spouse or partner as recognised by internal law, by a member of the family, a person cohabiting with the victim or a person having abused her or his authority" (Art. 36 (a))

Further, within typicity, there is no provision determining the sex of the individuals, neither the perpetrator nor the victim, not even for the aggravation of the penalty. In such a manner that the decision to increase the penalty when the perpetrator and the victim are masculine or feminine, respectively, is related to criminal policy reasons that exceed what is established in the Istanbul Convention.[15]

Theory of crime points out that the objective elements[16] should be covered by the wilful misconduct of the perpetrator, which is the case for offences included in the Istanbul Convention. On the other hand, there is no provision related to these behaviours committed due to negligence. This does not mean that these behaviours have to be punished according to international law but that they can be punished or not according to internal criminal law.

The subjective part of the offence description is not as simple as it seems. It has to be taken into consideration that it is the definition of "violence against women" (Art. 3 (a)), which characterises all of these behaviours as "ways of discrimination," which in turn are used to name gender-based violence acts. This might suggest that

---

[15] This decision has been accepted by many Latin American countries which have signed the Convention of Belem do Pará so they have decided to punish the crime of *feminicidio*. Spain also took the decision with the organic law LO 1/2004. *See* Acale Sánchez (2006).

[16] Despite all the specific ones that the lawmaker could include in each crime regulation.

applying the term "violence against women" to all gender-based crimes would not be possible unless the definition was fulfilled.

Example

For example, harming several people against their physical integrity—men and women—with a car bomb couldn't be considered "violence against women" because there might not be any factors to infer that this attack was gender-based. In the same meaning, a bomb that crashes into a population is not directed to kill both "men and women". ◀

On these bases, it needs to be determined if these behaviours are suitable for an aggravation based on discrimination. This will depend on whether the national lawmaker establishes a specific reference to violence against women during the offence regulation or not. In case they do, it would be suitable to apply the criminal offense and the aggravation at the same time.

13.2.2 Unlawfulness (Defenses, Justification)

Unlawfulness, in the continental European legal system usually the third element of crime,[17] can be found at two points when considering gender. On the one hand, it can be seen at general justification grounds. Those classic or common justification grounds are known in basically all legal orders. They are usually regulated by law and/or developed and complemented by doctrine and jurisprudence. Analysing the gender component can be done from both the perpetrator's and the victim's perspectives.

On the other hand, specific defences appear in this context as well. They are basically applicable to a particular gender as they derive from its specific state or situation. Furthermore, the provision from Art. 42 on unacceptable justifications for crimes from the Istanbul Convention is to be highlighted. It excludes certain traditions, cultural and religious patterns as justifications in the internationally most important document on protecting women from violence.

It should be noted that the notion of defences includes grounds for eliminating not only unlawfulness but also guilt as a (fourth) element of crime. This joint approach is the consequence of the impact of the Anglo-American doctrine and jurisprudence. This is important to annotate, as gender theory originates from the USA and is dominated by it.

Legal history and precedents have formulated many of the common criminal defences to account solely for male crimes.[18] At the same time, certain defences can be described as exclusively female, like neonaticide/infanticide (often also

[17] See Marković (2015), pp. 285–300.

[18] See Yeo (1993), pp. 104–116.

formulated as specific crime),[19] marital coercion, premenstrual syndrome and battered woman syndrome.[20]

Also, when it comes to elements that concern guilt, some of the novel defences that are brought into the courtroom include Amnesia, Post-Traumatic Stress Disorder (PTSD), Battered Women Syndrome (BWS), Multiple Personality Disorder (MPD), and Postpartum Depression (PPD). Many of them are more relevant to women than men, especially BWS and PPD.[21] There is a tendency to regard women as psychiatrically disordered.[22] Women are more likely than men to be found not guilty by reason of insanity (although it concerns a small number as such), to succeed in a plea of diminished responsibility (as in the case of BWS, which is medically accepted as a mental disease) and, if found guilty, to receive psychiatric disposal.[23] Problems in this regard are the stigma that goes with mental health issues and the potentially longer incarcerations. This "medicalisation" of women was (is) viewed as patronising and offensive but can be of significant benefit to women homicide defendants.[24] Different sentencing patterns based on gender, above all in cases of domestic homicide, were determined in a study which put 29 male and 29 female perpetrators in comparison before the Supreme Court of Victoria (Australia) in the period from 1985 until 1991.[25] The behaviour of female offenders was more often explained by psychiatric grounds. On the one hand, the acts of women, their mental state, ability to reason and criminal intent have been evaluated through the lens of femininity and domesticity. On the other hand, the treatment of women as "passive recipients of crime", that are submissive and in need for protection,[26] has resulted in milder sentences. Women have been treated with more sympathy and were sentenced to less strict or even non-custodial sentences compared to male offenders, it has been argued.[27] It seems unlikely that a woman can commit a crime out of less excusable motives, like gain or simply pleasure. The medicalisation of female offenders is thus based on the perception of female criminality as being the result of victimisation (which is often, but not always the case); of them being physically weaker, more emotional and in more need to be protected.[28] The outcome of this stereotype is that women are patronised, but also that they are, due to the assumption of their inferior situation, treated milder than men. Finally, and in general terms, it has to be noted that female offenders make up only a very small percentage of

---

[19]See Marković (2012a), pp. 77–95. See also Chap. 2.

[20]Nicolson (2000), p. 160.

[21]Forsythe and Miller (2014), p. 66.

[22]McColgan (2000), p. 138.

[23]On the issue of different assumptions on male and female criminal behaviour, with regard to *mens rea*, see Allen (1987).

[24]McColgan (2000), p. 140.

[25]Armstrong (1999), pp. 67–77.

[26]Ibid., pp. 68, 74.

[27]For a list of literature see Armstrong (1999), p. 67.

[28]Ibid., p. 76.

perpetrators.[29] This means that the medicalisation of female defendants does exist and that it is premised on gender stereotypes; while at the same time, it has a limited impact in the overall context of crime and sentencing.

Speaking about general terms, the classic justification grounds from a gender perspective can roughly be divided into (1) gender-specific, (2) gender-dominant, (3) gender-variant, and (4) gender-cultural.[30]

When it comes to defending before the Court, two defences that women in substantial numbers employ are provocation and diminished responsibility. What should be more often used, as doctrine suggests, is justifiable force.[31] By this, the division of "sudden and temporary loss of control" as premised on masculinity and "slow burn anger" as a specific characteristic for women[32] would diminish and hence put the issue of proportionality into a new perspective.[33]

As mentioned before, a particularity is that Art. 42 of the Istanbul Convention regulates unacceptable justifications for crimes, including crimes committed in the name of so-called "honour".[34]

Chapter V of the Istanbul Convention is dedicated to substantive law; in Articles 33–48 explicitly to criminal matters. The scientific and practical focus was on the eight specifically regulated intentional conducts that are to be criminalized in the respective jurisdictions. Yet, institutions from the general part are also present, albeit only three of them. Besides aiding or abetting and attempt (Art. 41), justifications are the subject of Art. 42—"unacceptable justifications for crimes, including crimes committed in the name of so-called "honour".

In the first paragraph of Art. 42, it is regulated that

> "parties shall take the necessary legislative or other measures to ensure that, in criminal proceedings initiated following the commission of any of the acts of violence covered by the scope of this Convention, culture, custom, religion, tradition or so-called "honour" shall not be regarded as justification for such acts. This covers, in particular, claims that the victim has transgressed cultural, religious, social or traditional norms or customs of appropriate behaviour"

The second paragraph states that

> "parties shall take the necessary legislative or other measures to ensure that incitement by any person of a child to commit any of the acts referred to in paragraph 1 shall not diminish the criminal liability of that person for the acts committed"

[29] McColgan (2000), p. 138.

[30] Denno (1994), p. 84.

[31] McColgan (2000), p. 137.

[32] Ibid., p. 145.

[33] Ibid., p. 146.

[34] See Nicolson and Bibbings (2000). See also Chap. 7.

The Article is completing and specifying the provisions of Article 12, namely that

> "parties shall take the necessary measures to promote changes in the social and cultural patterns of behaviour of women and men with a view to eradicating prejudices, customs, traditions and all other practices which are based on the idea of the inferiority of women or on stereotyped roles for women and men (1) and that they shall ensure that culture, custom, religion, tradition or so-called "honour" shall not be considered as justification for any acts of violence covered by the scope of this Convention (5)"

In other words, Art. 42 rules out, expresses what cannot constitute a justification ground. Bearing in mind the sheer number of possible justifications, their normative regulations, and understandings in different jurisdictions, the legislative formulation chosen in the Istanbul Convention is a good compromise to satisfy the primary goals envisaged by the Convention.

Furthermore, focusing on justifications to the conducts prohibited in the Istanbul Convention, the Explanatory Report to the Council of Europe Convention on preventing and combating violence against women and domestic violence (CoE Report), a valuable instrument for the authentic interpretation of the Convention, confirms that".[35]

As a conclusion to the question of unlawfulness, it can be said that women are more often treated as "medicalised" (4th element: guilt), which can be viewed as patronising behaviour. On the other hand, this could also mean less strict convictions or acquittals and could be regarded as a positive aspect. Other justification grounds, such as provocation, are rarely confirmed in cases involving women. What is undisputed is that so-called honour killings[36] primarily affect women and girls and must be seen as an unacceptable "justification ground", originating in culture and religion.

13.2.3 Guilt

Committing an act—knowingly or by negligence—considered by the law as a crime without any existing complete justification grounds is not enough to impose a penalty because the guilt must be both established and analysed. Guilt individualises the legal system reaction for the individual who has committed the unlawful act that brings to light that they cannot (cases of inculpability) or do not want to assume the

[35] CoE Report, 2011, ch. 216.

[36] In the Oxford Handbook of Gender, Sex, and Crime, honour killings are described as "an extreme type of gendered domestic violence, with peculiar characteristics related to the social and cultural traditions of tribal, patriarchal societies. The killings are motivated by the goal to restore a family's collective reputation that has been damaged by the victim's violation of very strict norms regulating female sexuality, and are viewed by the assailants as a legitimate punishment, often condoned by local communities and tolerated by state agencies." Oberwittler and Kasselt (2014), p. 652.

valuing content of the criminal rule. This means that an alleged perpetrator who does not plead guilty to the crime committed does not participate externally in the importance of legal goods protected by the criminal system. Further, violence against women is a crime category that examines issues that differ in scope from those examined in typicity and unlawfulness.

The Istanbul Convention does not make any specific provision in this sense, so this decision has to be made by national criminal law. Thus, special attention should be made to the intervention of the Group of Experts on Action against Violence against Women and Domestic Violence (GREVIO), which must ensure the proper enforcement of the Istanbul Convention and detect violations, direct or indirect, made, executive or judgmental, by the States enforcement politics.[37]

So, the FRA Report *Violence against women:*[38] *an EU-wide survey* made in 2014 concludes that there is a "relationship between a woman's partner's heavy alcohol use and increased violence."

In view of this evidence, this report states that "heavy alcohol use needs to be highlighted and addressed as a factor contributing to men's violence against women in intimate relationships. National violence prevention measures should consider addressing heavy alcohol use." Despite this criminological data, it is not enough to verify alcohol abuse as the cause for criminal purposes such as intimate partner violence. It is necessary to pinpoint that alcohol abuse affects the capacity to understand the reality of the acts committed under the influence and that the perpetrator acts accordingly to this understanding in order for the alcohol abuse to reflect the judgement of guilt adequately.

Individual issues related to how the perpetrator could have determined the commission of the crime by not knowing, understanding, the prohibition of the behaviour, or wrongly thinking that there was a justification ground are also analysed within guilt. The treatment of mistake on prohibition has similar regulations within European Criminal codes, which are exempt from criminal liability if the mistake was invincible and to attenuate the penalty if beatable. There is no specific provision in the Istanbul Convention about the mistake of the (elements of the crime or prohibition) as it only establishes that the justification of these actions in the name of honour is unacceptable. Erasing these justifications, in general, does not prevent that for specific cases, prohibition could be invoked based on nonconforming beliefs from ethnic minorities or cultural groups that do not share the egalitarian respect of human rights for men and women in European culture.[39] Problems arising from the criminal law are important to examine further since it affects all internal legal systems that develop the positive general prevention task

[37] As an example see GREVIO's (Baseline) Evaluation Report on legislative an other measures giving effect to the provisions of the Council of Europa Convention on Preventing and Combating Violence against Women and Domestic Violence (Istanbul Convention): Spain, 25 November 2020 (www.coe.int/conventionviolence).

[38] European Union Agency of Fundamental Rights. The survey can be found at https://fra.europa.eu/sites/default/files/fra-2014-vaw-survey-at-a-glance-oct14_en.pdf.

[39] Sumalla and María (2005), p. 805.

with respect to human rights for every person. This would be the solution to erase the possibility of invoking nonconforming beliefs to exempt or attenuate the penalty in these cases. It is not enough that criminal codes punish genital mutilation: the important thing is that all the legal systems ensure that women have a healthy sex life.

13.2.4 Sentencing

The theory of crime offers important elements to specify the criminal liability that even though not belonging to typicity, unlawfulness, or guilt, still determines the penalty: the Istanbul Convention refers to them.

13.2.4.1 Aggravating Circumstances

Article 46 of the Istanbul Convention establishes a list of aggravating circumstances. Still, it does not provide a list of attenuating ones, so this would be a task for the Member States' criminal codes. However, the Istanbul Convention states risk factors for intimate partner violence. In the theory of crime, these circumstances modify the perpetrator's criminal liability as an extra to the committed crime that justifies the aggravation of the penalty. This extra could be related to the same legal goods protected by the crime in particular or related to other crimes of a different nature.

Circumstances in Art. 46 could be organised into three groups.

The first group can be explicitly related to the victim. The offence was committed

> (a) "against a former or current spouse or partner as recognised by internal law, by a member of the family, a person cohabiting with the victim or a person having abused her or his authority;" (c) "against a person made vulnerable by particular circumstances" (d) "against or in the presence of a child"

However, only under point (c) specifically mentions the victim's vulnerability, even though according to point (a) it considers that these family ties facilitate the commission of these kinds of crimes. This makes the victims particularly vulnerable when they are being subdued to a victimisation process by those who share or have to share with them. If there is an increased knowledge of these victim vulnerability factors in the criminal justice system, the penalties can be harsher since these are aggravating factors for the crime committed.

The second group is related to perpetrator characteristics. The commission of the crime, or crimes, were committed:

> (b) "repeatedly", (e) "by two or more people acting together", (i) "the perpetrator had previously been convicted of offences of a similar nature"

As it can be seen, these risk factors are focused on recidivism, having more than one perpetrator. Although one perpetrator commits most intimate partner violent crimes, the Istanbul Convention also intends to prevent crimes committed in a collective perspective, such as so-called honour-based violence. As for the commission in the group, the Istanbul Convention highlights the greater ease for the commission of the crime, placing the victim in a transitory situation of extraordinary abandonment.

The third group would be those circumstances that take into consideration the way the crime has been committed, where the offence

> (f) "was preceded or accompanied by extreme levels of violence", (g) "was committed with the use or threat of a weapon", (h) "resulted in severe physical or psychological harm for the victim"

As it can be seen, the fact that the violent act has been preceded or accompanied by "extreme levels of violence"[40] or has resulted in severe physical or psychological harm is taking into consideration the extension of the harm committed to the protected legal goods. For its part, the use of weapons in the commission of the crime entails a greater endangerment of the legal assets involved than when they are not present at the crime scene.

13.2.4.2 Aiding or Abetting and Attempt

The prescriptions of the Istanbul Convention are not limited to the punishment but also to what is established in Art. 41 related to aiding or abetting

> "parties shall take the necessary legislative or other measures to establish as an offence, when committed intentionally, aiding or abetting the commission of the offences established in accordance with Articles 33, 34, 35, 36, 37, 38.a and 39 of this Convention"

All crimes included in the eight areas of the Istanbul Convention are regulated within these articles, except genital mutilation in letters b) and c) from Art. 38 and sexual harassment from Art. 40. There are no established reasons explaining what has led the Istanbul Convention creators to make this decision.

Further, usually, there is one individual perpetrator in crimes of domestic violence. However, it is possible to ask for liability of other family members in specific situations due to their omissive behaviour. This will be the case for the mother who, although unable to do so, does not hinder the father from exercising violence (physical, psychological or sexual) against their child. The discussion is nevertheless open to the possibility to regulate that in every criminal code, the perpetrator can also be the person who uses omissive behaviours. For the given example, if the act omitted by the mother is determining the violent situation to continue, she could be

[40] This element is completely undetermined, so the courts would have to give it substance.

considered as co-perpetrator in commission by omission for the crimes of bodily injury, threat, or sexual aggression that has been committed actively by the other perpetrator. Another issue that is open for debate is how national courts can enforce this if regulations change.

This article also establishes specific provisions about the punishment of attempt:

> "parties shall take the necessary legislative or other measures to establish as offences, when committed intentionally, attempts to commit the offences established in accordance with Articles 35, 36, 37, 38.a and 39 of this Convention"

This provision does not affect all perpetrators; those who use psychological violence (Art. 33), harassment (Art. 34), and sexual harassment (Art. 40) are not included, again without any hint on the reasons for doing so. It would be necessary to pay attention to the punishment of the attempt in the Member States' criminal codes and check if it is required to carry out some legal foresight or if it is related to the appreciation by the courts. However, problems that could arise that should be considered are if an attempted homicide also could be considered a crime of completed actual bodily harm. In this sense, the highest penalty for each crime would have to be taken into account when choosing what crime to charge the perpetrator for in court, considering that this would be the preferential rule.

13.2.4.3 Reporting

The Istanbul Convention leaves an open door to the possibility that a third person could report these incidents because of the understanding that the victims are not capable of it in many cases. This is a way of counteracting the regulation that had been ruling in many countries during many times. The victims should initiate the criminal process in cases that violate sexual freedom or involve mistreatment. At the same time, the forgiveness of the offended would be admitted as an exemption of penalty (as it has been for years in the area of sexual crimes). Both requirements mean a procedural corralling for the victim. If the victim did not report the crimes or once reported and the perpetrator was condemned, they forgave the perpetrator. At the end of the whole process, the victim and the perpetrator would then return to their family environment. This would create a situation for the perpetrator, not just to repeat violent abuse but also to increase its intensity. The official statistics show that victims reporting the incident are one of the reasons that amplify the mistreatment not just in absolute numbers but also in weight.[41]

[41] Nevertheless, crimes against sexual freedom need and a specific mention as they are fairy likely to include a re-victimization process, preventing the victim to start a de-victimization process because of the public opinion or the justice administration proceedings. This is why until it can be assured that this re-victimization process is not going to exist, the general requirement is that the victim is the one to report the crime so she could evaluate the pros and cons of this reporting. See Acale Sánchez (2019), p. 9.

Many countries have erased these procedural disadvantages, which has enabled other people to intervene just to stop these violent situations. In many cases, family members are aware of the reality that victims are living with. Together with people in the neighbourhood, they can be essential witnesses of these criminal acts that usually take place within the family environment. Friends are a stronghold for victims until the perpetrator gets to break the links between them and are the ones that can help victims by reporting these violent acts. These violent acts have then moved from the private to the public scene.

All these provisions have been considered by the Istanbul Convention. Art. 27 encourages the Member States to take measures to make "any person witness" report to organisations and competent authorities the violent acts that could be considered violence against women or domestic violence. This way, the victim's report is not the only way to initiate the criminal process, leaving a possibility for third persons or the public ministry to do it. Moreover, this could be considered a positive change, not a negative change that includes violating the privacy of victims who do not want to report. Nevertheless, this is an existing risk in every kind of crime. For example, see crimes against life for crimes against freedom of movement. Therefore, it should not be considered more important for gender-based violence.[42]

Likewise, Art. 28 makes specific provisions on reports made by professional staff submitted to confidentiality rights "under appropriate conditions, of their reporting to the competent organisations or authorities if they have reasonable grounds to believe that a serious act of violence covered by the scope of this Convention, has been committed and further serious acts of violence are to be expected." Although this pursues a good goal, the practice could raise questions concerning victims who choose not to go to official control institutions, increasing their risk for further violent victimisation. For instance, a new violent action generated as a consequence of a new accusation.

13.2.5 Penalties

The Istanbul Convention goes beyond defining behaviours that should be punished as crimes in national criminal codes. It also makes specific provisions on penalties. These penalty regulations highlight the Istanbul Convention's interest in punishing the perpetrator, preventing the victim from suffering collateral damages from the imposition or implementation of the penalty itself.[43]

[42] Acale Sánchez (2013), p. 218.

[43] It should also be avoided the secondary victimization process where the victims suffer collateral harms that are different from the ones generated by the crime itself. But the Directive 2012/29/EU of the European Parliament and of the Council of 25 October 2012 establishing minimum standards on the rights, support and protection of victims of crime, and replacing Council Framework Decision 2001/220 JHA, does it. It raises the struggle against this phenomenon because from a pragmatic point of view, the reporting process may be seen as discouraging.

These punishments do not only have to be out from a criminal law perspective since civil consequences also follow from a crime. There are two provisions in this sense within the Istanbul Convention. On the one hand, Art. 30 refers to the victim's right to receive compensation by the perpetrator, enshrining the State's subsidiary civil liability in case of insolvency with the right to subsequently ask the perpetrator for the refund of the amount[44] On the other hand, in the case of forced marriages, Art. 32 establishes that they are considered void or dissolved, without meaning excessive economic or administrative burdens for the victim. void or dissolved, without meaning excessive economic or administrative burdens for the victim.

In terms of criminal consequences from committing a crime within the Convention, Art. 45 establishes that the Member States would implement legal or other measures that may be necessary to punish the described behaviours with "effective, proportionate and dissuasive sanctions, taking into account their seriousness".

This specific framework for punishment expressly mentions imprisonment that allowed extradition and other measures like "monitoring or supervision of convicted persons" or "withdrawal of parental rights, if the best interests of the child, which may include the safety of the victim, cannot be guaranteed in any other way" (Art. 45).

This does not prevent the Istanbul Convention from including another kind of penalty. Art. 45 (2) establishes the possibility of "monitoring or supervision of convicted persons". This penalty has demonstrated a potential control capability over the convicted person, warranting, at the same time, the integrity without using the pricey and stigmatising imprisonment. And indeed, penalties that involve limitations in the convicted person's movement have to consider that its implementation affects at least two persons, the perpetrator and the victim. Further, due to the commission of the crime, "both are condemned not to get close to each other". But if the victim consents to what the law is forbidding, the approaching, the critical distancing turns into a penalty for both. In a sense, if the victim decides that after the violence, they want to carry on with the relationship, this critical distancing will mean a penalty for both of them due to a crime one of them committed.[45]

The Istanbul Convention does not ignore the economic dependency that could exist between victims and others. Hence, paragraph two in Art. 48 establishes that "to ensure that if the payment of a fine is ordered, due account shall be taken of the ability of the perpetrator to assume his or her financial obligations towards the victim".

The Istanbul Convention also refers to preventive intervention and treatment programs that are not just geared towards preventing domestic violence perpetrators so they can adopt a non-violent behaviour in their interpersonal relationships to

[44]Number three of Article 30 makes a provision of the utmost importance course concerning the need to ensure the right to compensation within a "reasonable term", so the big team could receive it at times as close as possible to when the crime was committed. Because this is the moment when the victim is going to need every kind of support: including the economic one.

[45]Acale Sánchez (2006), p. 330.

prevent new violence and change the violent behaviour patterns, but also prevent recidivism making particular reference to sexual violence (Art. 16). Then plantation of these programs is related to the need to ensure

> "the safety of, support for and the human rights of victims are of primary concern and that, where appropriate, these programmes are set up and implemented in close coordination with specialist support services for victims"

The integration of victims in the implementation of treatment programs for abusers will be only if victims agree and where assessed appropriately, according to Art. 48 Member States should take legal measures

> "to prohibit mandatory alternative dispute resolution processes, including mediation and conciliation, in relation to all forms of violence covered by the scope of this Convention" (Art. 48).

The efficacy of some programs has been proved effective, although not all. In a sense, perpetrators who followed these kinds of programs "were more likely to leave violence during a one-year follow-up period and to refuse their controlling and intimidating acts". But also their partners' statements have proved that "the range of these acts had been reduced and happened less frequently".[46] As Echeburúa states, mistreatment acts and recidivism have been reduced at least in one-third of the cases. Also victims and abusers have improved their wellness.[47]

Even though these programs' efficacy relies on their design, from a material point of view, its content, dosage, and implementation should be conducted by human behaviour experts, who can consider the specific needs of the case and design the implementation plan according to this. It would be useless to apply standard programs that don't consider the different features of these convicted perpetrators.

13.3 Special Part

The Istanbul Convention constitutes eight specific areas; psychological violence, stalking, physical violence, sexual violence, rape, forced marriage, female genital mutilation, forced abortion, forced sterilisation, and sexual harassment. Countries in Europe already have laws against violent crimes such as murder and assault. Some countries also have specific laws targeting violent men abusing women. In this special part of the chapter, laws explicitly targeting men's violence towards women will be highlighted.

[46]Dobash and Dobash (2005), p. 147.

[47]Echeburúa et al. (2001), pp. 25 ff.

13.3.1 Psychological and Physical Violence

Intimate partner violence towards women is defined as

▶ **Definition** "any acts of physical (including sexual), psychological, or economic violence committed by a current or former male partner",[48]

where every third woman in the world is estimated to be victimised.[49] It is a global public health problem found in all countries and occurs across all socioeconomic, religious, and cultural groups. Violence can be conducted in various ways, although it shares several core characteristics. Further, legislation to combat such violence differs worldwide, to some degree driven by patriarchal structures where women are traditionally subordinate to family structures, and gender equality is low. Subsequently, violence towards women is more accepted within such structures since it is more accepted for men to control women, and thereby such acts are not seen as crimes.[50]

Psychological violence is a severe form of domestic violence and can be as damaging to the victim as physical violence. It is defined according to Art. 33 as

▶ **Definition** "the intentional conduct of seriously impairing a person's psychological integrity through coercion or threats".

This includes the perpetrator insulting, belittling, humiliating, harassing, intimidating or threatening the victim with any type of violence. Further, controlling behaviours such as isolating the victim from friends and family, denying them the right to work, or seeking medical help are examples of psychological violence. As part of the isolation, the victim becomes dependent on the perpetrator, and thereby it will be much harder to leave the abusive relationship.

Further Art. 33 states the importance of criminalising these behaviours. However, it can be somewhat difficult to gather evidence for psychological violence, since the intent to harm a person's integrity is not explicitly defined. For example, it will be specifically hard to gather evidence to strengthen the case if the victim has agreed to live with the perpetrator. One could argue that the holder of the legal goods thereby gives consent, and there would then not be a violation of the law. However, such consent cannot be seen as voluntary according to the intent of the Istanbul Convention. Legislators thereby have to be very explicit in creating the law to ensure the implementation of Art. 33 in their jurisdiction. The national legislations have primarily focused on either harassment or threats to combat psychological violence. However, that doesn't capture the psychological violence as described within the Istanbul Convention. As an attempt to combat psychological violence, The UK

[48] European Institute for Gender Equality [EIGE], 2021.

[49] Devries et al. (2013).

[50] Tran et al. (2016).

enacted the law on controlling and coercive control as an attempt to identify and combat psychological violence.

Example

"The Law on Controlling and Coercive Control in the U.K, Section 76 of the Serious Crime Act 2015 - Controlling or Coercive Behaviour in an Intimate or Family Relationship". The law defines the criminalised behaviours as "repeatedly or continuously engages in behaviour towards another person (B) that is controlling or coercive" ◀

Physical violence is defined in Art. 35 as

▶ **Definition** "the intentional conduct of committing acts of physical violence against another person".

This includes all types of physical violence regardless of its severity. It ranges from pushes, kicks, grabbing the victim's hair to aggravated assault and lethal violence.

Women subjected to repeated and systematic intimate partner violence redefine their understanding of violence as it progresses and becomes normalised.[51] This means that victims of intimate partner violence gradually accept the less severe actions as the violence escalates into more severe physical violence. To some extent, the perpetrator controls the victim in every aspect; how she should behave, what she may say, think, feel, and whom she meets. Further, victims believe that they are the cause of the violence due to the perpetrator imposes that they are misbehaving, not pleasing them, or conforming to their desires. Therefore, he has to punish them for that. The victims' self-confidence and self-appraisal fade away and the abuser has total control over the victim. Moreover, due to this normalisation, neither the victim nor the perpetrator identifies themselves as abused or an abuser. They have both been normalised to the situation, and therefore only the most severe forms of violence might be defined as violent. When the violence turns into more severe forms, victims start reporting the violence to the police. Therefore, when examining what type of crimes are being reported, charged, and convicted, most are severe, and thereby the less severe violence such as psychological violence are seen as parts of the physical violence, although they are violent acts in themselves. The purpose of the Istanbul convention is that this type of intimate partner violence will be recognised regardless of severity and as stipulated in Art. 1 (a), the purpose is to

> "protect women against all forms of violence, and prevent, prosecute and eliminate violence against women and domestic violence"

[51] Lundgren (2012) and Pornari et al. (2013).

National legislations have gender-neutral laws targeting violent acts committed towards both men and women by both men and women. However, this is not enough to combat men's violence against women, since the laws are too general and don't pick up on the different forms of violence in intimate partner relationships. Therefore, new legislation specifically targeting these issues is necessary. One good example of legislation combating both psychological violence and physical violence is the Swedish law explicitly targeting men's violence against women, which is in line with the definition of Art. 33 and Art. 35.

Example

Sweden has enacted unique legislation explicitly aimed at combating men's repeated (defined as occurring on more than one occasion) violence towards women with the offense of Gross Violation of a Woman's Integrity (in Swedish Grov kvinnofridskränkning), which was enacted in the Swedish Penal Code in 1998 [52]. ◀

The offense is overarching and is applied when a woman's self-confidence is severely damaged by her current or former partner's repeated and systematic abuse. The purpose of the law was to recognise the repeated and systematic nature of violence against women in intimate relationships and the impact of such abuse according to the normalisation. In doing so, it is necessary to appropriately punish the perpetrator.[53] One of the advantages of this law is that it combines crimes standing by themselves and is considered less severe in line with the legislation. Still, when adding them into one, the law stipulates that committing several less severe crimes, such as threatening, harassing, damaging property, etc., becomes a severe crime. This is aggravating, and in line with the Istanbul Convention, these crimes should therefore be punished harder. The Swedish law was enacted in 1998, which was almost a decade before the Istanbul Convention was enacted. It should be seen as an example of how legislators can stipulate laws to target men's violence towards women, including all forms of violence.

13.3.2 Stalking

Stalking is addressed as a specific area of the Istanbul Convention. The lifetime prevalence of stalking, as defined by Art. 34

▶ **Definition** "the intentional conduct of repeatedly engaging in threatening conduct directed at another person, causing her or him to fear for her or his safety",

[52] Further, perpetrators of IPV can be of either gender and a separate offense, Gross Violation of a Person's Integrity, exists which includes male victims of IPV and children as victims of family violence.

[53] Burman (2010).

have been found to be about 9.0–19.3% including both men and women in Europe, although most victims are women.[54] Although criminalised in the USA, U.K, and Australia since the mid-1990s, most European nations implemented anti-stalking laws later. Notably, due to the absence of stalking laws over the years, relatively little is known about the prevalence of stalking in Europe, the nature and impact of victimisation, police knowledge, and practice in European jurisdictions.

Stalking includes unwanted communication such as phone calls, SMS, and text messages in different forms of social media, but also leaving notes and sending letters is part of the communication. Furthermore, attempts to contact victims, such as approaching victims outside their workplace, home, favourite gym, etc., are also common. The stalking escalates from attempts to communicate to more approaching behaviours, which can result in violent acts.[55]

Stalking laws in Europe have mainly been enacted from 2000 to 2011. The national laws are primarily described as overarching offences, as stipulated in many laws. It includes repeated acts that individually can be defined and charged as an offence. Assault, threats, harassment, breaching restraining orders and similar offences are crimes that constitute the stalking offence for which the prosecutor may lay charges.

Moreover, this makes the definition of stalking behaviour somewhat different from the laws of stalking, depending on how the law in each nation is defined. The laws include fewer behaviours than the broader definition of stalking as established by the Istanbul Convention. To a large part, it is the psychological violence that is difficult to prove as a crime. The harassment can continue since it is not illegal to park outside the store where victims are shopping, or showing up outside their work to do an errand in a place nearby, although it is not a coincidence that they appear at the same site. The stalker has planned it this way. Yet, it cannot be proven as harassment in a court of law. However, the victim will be subjected to psychological violence, knowing that they have nowhere to go to escape the stalker.

Stalking is a highly gendered crime where most stalkers are men (82%) stalking women.[56] In community samples, about one-third of stalkers are ex-partners, acquaintances and strangers, respectively. However, in police samples, most of the stalkers reported are ex-partners. This could, to some extent, be explained by ex-partners having been violent towards their partner during the relationship as well, of which some have been reported. This may have lowered the threshold for reporting stalking when that occurred. The criminal justice system has more experience and knowledge on how to handle intimate partner violence than stalking, which might indicate that there is a routine in place for how to handle victims of intimate

[54] BRÅ (2006), Dressing et al. (2007), Finney (2006) and Stieger et al. (2008).

[55] McEwan et al. (2009) and Strand and McEwan (2012).

[56] ABS (2006), Baum et al. (2009), Belfrage and Strand (2009), BRÅ (2006), Dressing et al. (2005), Finney (2006), Logan (2020), Maran and Varetto (2017), McEwan and Strand (2013), Mullen et al. (1999), Stieger et al. (2008) and Strand and McEwan (2011); Tjaden and Thoennes (1998).

partner violence, regardless if it includes stalking or not. Victims of non-ex-intimate stalking are more challenging to handle due to less knowledge on that form of stalking.

Moreover, a relatively large body of research has accumulated over the years examining what people recognise as stalking and what factors influence judgments about the severity of stalking situations.[57] Stalking by strangers is judged to be more severe and more fearful than stalking by former intimate partners; male stalkers are perceived to be more harmful than females; stalking is unlikely to be recognised if it does not involve overt aggression. These misperceptions have been identified and exist even though there is empirical evidence showing that ex-intimate partners are more likely to be violent; that male and female stalkers are equally violent, and that stalking causes psychological and social harm to victims regardless of the victim's gender and whether or not the stalking involves violence.[58] Fear of the stalker is closely linked to these misperceptions, leading to the victim misjudging the seriousness of the stalking situation and consequently not reporting to the police. However, few victims of stalking report crimes to the police, of which only a few perpetrators will be charged, prosecuted, convicted and sentenced for their crime, specifically in rural areas.[59] The legislation needs to keep up with such crimes where psychological violence stands for most crimes and is a risk factor for escalation and more severe physical violence.

To conclude, for the criminal justice system to work, crimes need to be reported. Since stalking is defined as a behaviour including criminal offences, there must be effective stalking laws enacted to combat stalking. The Istanbul Convention specifically addresses stalking as an area to combat men's violence against women, but there is still more work to be done in order for legislation to be effective.

13.3.3 Sexual Violence, Including Rape and Sexual Harassment

Sexual violence is one of the main subject matters of criminal law in general and marks critical areas of society and behaviour that are to be put under special scrutiny of the legislator. It is, of course, of particular interest for the gender perspective.

The broad field of sexual violence, including rape is brought together in Article 36:

Article 36 Istanbul Convention

[57] Mullen et al. (2009).

[58] Strand and McEwan (2011), Purcell et al. (2005) and Weller et al. (2013).

[59] Logan and Walker (2017) and Maran and Varetto (2017).

(1) Parties shall take the necessary legislative or other measures to ensure that the following intentional conducts are criminalised:
  a. engaging in non-consensual vaginal, anal or oral penetration of a sexual nature of the body of another person with any bodily part or object;
  b. engaging in other non-consensual acts of a sexual nature with a person;
  c. causing another person to engage in non-consensual acts of a sexual nature with a third person.

(2) Consent must be given voluntarily as the result of the person's free will assessed in the context of the surrounding circumstances.

(3) Parties shall take the necessary legislative or other measures to ensure that the provisions of paragraph 1 also apply to acts committed against former or current spouses or partners as recognised by internal law.

Paragraph 1 of the Article covers all forms of sexual acts (penetration/other non-consensual sexual acts) that are performed on another person without her or his consent and which are committed intentionally. What "intentional" means in this context is to be interpreted by domestic law.[60] Penetration can be vaginal, anal or oral with any bodily part or object (lit. a). It has to be of a "sexual nature". This means that acts that lack sexual connotation or undertones are not included,[61] which can be seen as a restricting or redundant element of the offense when penetration is included. What does not fall under the first case group is covered by other acts of sexual nature (lit. b). Beside the direct perpetrator ship, other forms of participation (lit. c) are included as well if it

> "causes another person to engage in non-consensual acts of a sexual nature with a third person."

All of the above-mentioned acts have to be non-consensual. Paragraph 2 specifies that consent must be the result of free will (voluntarily) and assessed in the context of the surrounding circumstances. This context-sensitive assessment of the evidence is highly significant, as sexual violence usually takes place in environments without witnesses and often between persons that know each other, that are personally engaged or even married or divorced. The personal connection is recognised as (ir)relevant and regulated by Paragraph 3 (the provisions apply also when acts are committed against former or current spouses or partners). The sexual act has to be evaluated with regard to the absence of consent; regardless of the respective relationship between the perpetrator and the victim. Acknowledging that sexual violence is a common form of the exercise and abuse of power,[62] it is pivotal to exclude any possible exceptions to criminalisation and prosecution of those perpetrators of sexual offences against current or former spouses. Not everything is covered by this

[60]Explanatory Report, para. 189.

[61]Ibid., para. 190.

[62]Ibid., para. 194.

regulation, as the connected issue of the existence of "marry your rapist" laws shows.[63]

Furthermore, the assessment of evidence and by this, the evaluation of all circumstances, has to be done case-by-case, taking into consideration that the behavioural responses to rape and other forms of sexual violence differ and cannot be formed into a set of typical reactions.[64] The Explanatory Report of the Convention is very explicit about that, stating that "it is equally important to ensure that interpretations of rape legislation and the prosecution of rape cases are not influenced by gender stereotypes and myths about male and female sexuality."[65]

This approach is expected to widen the understanding of non-consensual acts, to change the notion of consent by the State Parties. One particular case of the European Court of Human Rights (ECtHR) is often recalled.

Example

In M.C. v Bulgaria, the applicant alleged that she had been raped by two men on 31 July and 1 August 1995, when she was 14 years and 10 months old. The ensuing investigation came to the conclusion that there was insufficient proof of the applicant having been compelled to have sex. ◀

The investigation was closed. The summary of the rule of law in this case was that the termination of an investigation in a rape case that is based on the premise that insufficient proof of physical force, but without taking into account if the victim was subjected to forceful circumstances, means that the Member State "in the case fell short of the requirements inherent in the States' positive obligations – viewed in the light of the relevant modern standards in comparative and international law – to establish and apply effectively a criminal-law system punishing all forms of rape and sexual abuse."[66]

The following statement from the Courts' assessment is to be highlighted with regard to the gender context, without mentioning the term gender:

> "the Court is persuaded that any rigid approach to the prosecution of sexual offences, such as requiring proof of physical resistance in all circumstances, risks leaving certain types of rape unpunished and thus jeopardising the effective protection of the individual's sexual autonomy. In accordance with contemporary standards and trends in that area, the Member States' positive obligations under Articles 3 and 8 of the Convention must be seen as requiring the penalisation and

[63] "Marry your rapist" laws shield from prosecution or exempt rapists and similar perpetrators (of sexual assault, abduction, etc.) from punishment if they marry their victims.

[64] In this regard also: ibid., para. 192.

[65] Ibid.

[66] Case of *M.C. v. Bulgaria*, Application no. 39272/98, Judgment from 4 December 2003, para. 185.

effective prosecution of any non-consensual sexual act, including in the absence of physical resistance by the victim."[67]

What is explicitly mentioned is the context-sensitive assessment:

"Regardless of the specific wording chosen by the legislature, in a number of countries the prosecution of non-consensual sexual acts in all circumstances is sought in practice by means of interpretation of the relevant statutory terms ("coercion", "violence", "duress", "threat", "ruse", "surprise" or others) and through a context-sensitive assessment of the evidence."[68]

The ECtHR has taken the gender of the victim and her non-physical defence to rape into account. However, the Istanbul Convention gives the state parties room for specific wording of their domestic laws and the factors they will consider when excluding voluntarily given consent.[69]

The criminalisation of sexual violence, including rape, is completed by the obligation to establish aiding or abetting, as well as attempt as offences (Art. 41).

The range and normative intensity of regulation changes when it comes to sexual harassment, provided in Article 40:

"Parties shall take the necessary legislative or other measures to ensure that any form of unwanted verbal, non-verbal or physical conduct of a sexual nature with the purpose or effect of violating the dignity of a person, in particular when creating an intimidating, hostile, degrading, humiliating or offensive environment, is subject to criminal or other legal sanction."

First of all, the consequence of the offence of sexual harassment could be a criminal or "other legal sanction". The drafters of the Convention have left it to the State Parties to decide where to become active in order to tackle and sanction this behaviour, as long as the measures that are undertaken are effective. Background to this is that some members have expressed concern about the criminalisation of this offence,[70] as it is often committed at work and regulated by labour law. The Explanatory Report refers to that: "While generally considering it preferable to place the conduct dealt with by this article under criminal law, the drafters acknowledged that many national legal systems consider sexual harassment under civil or

[67] Ibid., para. 166.

[68] Ibid., para. 161.

[69] Explanatory note, para. 192.

[70] Sosa (2020), p. 38.

labour law. Consequently, Parties may choose to deal with sexual harassment either by their criminal law or by administrative or other legal sanctions, while ensuring that the law deals with sexual harassment."[71]

However, the CoE acknowledged in a Resolution from 2017 the need to hinder sexual harassment in the public sphere.[72] Of course, with the intensified digitalisation, sexual harassment online (on social media, digital platforms, etc.), becomes more and more an issue to solve. Contrary to the "usual" sexual harassment at the workplace, where the victim and perpetrator know each other, stand in hierarchy to one other (harassment committed in the context of abuse of power, promise of reward or threat of reprisal)[73] and have a discriminatory context that goes beyond sexual connotation, the relationship in digital sexual harassment is often simply non-existent. The perpetrator and victim do not know each other personally ("live") and the perpetrator has fewer obstacles to overcome, due to anonymity provided by the world wide web is harder to be identified, etc.

Furthermore, the obligation to introduce measures against sexual harassment is not limited to the work and education context, as done so in the Gender Equality Directive of the EU.[74]

The types of conduct that are covered by Article 40 are summed up in three principal forms of behaviour: verbal, non-verbal and physical conduct. They have to be of sexual nature and unwanted by the victim. "Unwanted" and "non-consensual" (like in Article 36) are albeit very similar, from a dogmatic point of view not necessarily identical. While "non-consensual" has at least been specified in the rest of the provision, "unwanted" is a less sharp term. If it means "imposed by perpetrator", as suggested in the Explanatory Report (para. 208), then it should be re-formulated or even erased, as logically speaking, some kind of "wanted" sexual harassment contradicts itself and the rest of the provision. The second part of the provision, namely, specifies the effects of this behaviour as

> "violating the dignity of a person, in particular when creating an intimidating, hostile, degrading, humiliating or offensive environment".

As the Explanatory Report admits, the context is of high importance, as it reflects "a pattern of behaviour whose individual elements, if taken on their own, may not necessarily result in a sanction."[75]

---

[71] Explanatory Report, para. 207.

[72] See Parliamentary Assembly, Resolution 2177 (2017), Putting an end to sexual violence and harassment of women in public sphere, available at https://pace.coe.int/en/files/23771.

[73] Explanatory Report, para. 209.

[74] Gender Equality Directive (Dir 2006/54/EU), available at: https://eur-lex.europa.eu/legal-content/EN/TXT/?uri=celex%3A32006L0054. See also Niemi and Sanmartin (2020), p. 88.

[75] Explanatory Report, para. 208.

13.3.4 Forced Marriage and Female Genital Mutilation

Honour-based violence and oppression are considered a global public health problem and are highlighted by several international health organisations.[76] The United Nations Population Fund (UNFPA) estimated that around 5000 girls and women are murdered each year due to honour-based killings. Further, the UN states that globally there are 765 million child marriages, which annually affects about 12 million girls. About 200 million, annually 3.9 million girls and women are genitally mutilated.

In the Preamble of the Istanbul Convention, it states that the Member States should:

> "Recognising, with grave concern, that women and girls are often exposed to serious forms of violence such as domestic violence, sexual harassment, rape, forced marriage, crimes committed in the name of so-called "honour" and genital mutilation, which constitute a serious violation of the human rights of women and girls and a major obstacle to the achievement of equality between women and men"

However, there is no further definition of honour-based violence. Sweden uses the following definition

▶ **Definition** "Honour-based violence is based on strong patriarchal and heteronormative notions, where specific expressions regarding the control of girls and women's sexuality are central and strongly linked to the collective norms. The family's reputation and respect are seen as dependent on girls', and women's actual or alleged innocence and chastity"[77]

Young victims of such violence describe that life is characterised by control and limitations, where sexuality and love before marriage can have severe consequences.[78] Growing up and being fostered in a culture of honour is a major influencing factor on an individual's opportunities to create their own life independently and on equal terms. Areas that are often controlled and surrounded by restrictions or prohibitions are access to; finances, friends, leisure, mobile phone, internet, clothes, and make-up.[79] The restrictions affect the opportunities to make one's own life choices, such as choosing a partner, not being allowed education, or being denied work.[80] In the event of breaching norms of honour, the collective's

---

[76] UNFPA (2000).

[77] SOU (2020), p. 57.

[78] Björktomta (2019), Eldén (2003) and Sedem et al. (2014).

[79] Björktomta (2019).

[80] Eldén (2003).

honour and reputation must be restored by punishing the norm-breaker, which can result in severe or even deadly violence.

Areas of a patriarchal structure that support a collectivist clan society have been found to be characterised by high mortality and fertility, poverty, low social mobility, and a lack of democracy and human rights. However, clan structures do not necessarily include honour-based violence.[81] Instead, it is the clan's norm formation around chastity and innocence that is a determining factor as to whether there is an honour culture or not. In societies where there is a culture of honour, equality and women's equal value are rejected, ultimately with a lack of human rights (UNFPA 2020).

Children exposed to honour-based violence are at risk of being taken abroad with the intention of fostering them, since the family considers them to have breached the honour of the family and disgraced them. The only way to restore the honour is to agree to what the patriarch of the family decides. Art. 37 explicitly state that this has to be criminalised

> "(1) Parties shall take the necessary legislative or other measures to ensure that the intentional conduct of forcing an adult or a child to enter into a marriage is criminalised. (2) Parties shall take the necessary legislative or other measures to ensure that the intentional conduct of luring an adult or a child to the territory of a Party or State other than the one she or he resides in with the purpose of forcing this adult or child to enter into a marriage is criminalised"

When abducting children and young adults, which often occurs in a war-torn country, the young person is placed with relatives or in various types of institutions. The abduction occurs because the young person is being accused of following and living according to Western society's values or being involved in crime.

Further, in certain cultures, genital mutilation is part of their rites. For families within this culture, it might be essential to follow this to retain their honour. Art. 38 states that all types of genital mutilation should be criminalised

> "(a) excising, infibulation or performing any other mutilation to the whole or any part of a woman's labia majora, labia minora or clitoris; (b) coercing or procuring a woman to undergo any of the acts listed in point a; (c) inciting, coercing or procuring a girl to undergo any of the acts listed in point a."

During fictional holiday trips or other made-up travels to relatives in their country of origin, which often occur in the summer, the abducted person is lured into the trip and follows on false premises. They are at risk of being subjected to forced or child marriage or genital mutilation, threats, coercion, or violence by their family. Here, the issue of jurisdiction becomes important. It is important to note that the Istanbul Convention states in Art. 44 that

[81] Makram (2019).

"States shall endeavour to take the necessary legislative or other measures to establish jurisdiction over any offence established in accordance with this convention, where the offence is committed against one of their nationals or a person who has her or his habitual residence in their territory".

This means that States have the possibility to establish their jurisdiction in cases where female genital mutilation is committed abroad to a woman/girl who has her habitual residence on their territory. As a consequence of this provision, this could prevent families of these women/girls to briefly return to their country of origin (as said, mostly disguised as vacation) only to force them to undergo the mutilation.[82]

Article 42 states that legislators should be aware that committing crimes in the name of honour is no justification of crimes

"The commission of any of the acts of violence covered by the scope of this Convention, culture, custom, religion, tradition or so-called "honour" shall not be regarded as justification for such acts. This covers, in particular, claims that the victim has transgressed cultural, religious, social or traditional norms or customs of appropriate behaviour"

13.3.5 Forced Abortion and Forced Sterilisation

Forced abortion and forced sterilisation are regulated by Article 39. There, it is stipulated that

"Parties shall take the necessary legislative or other measures to ensure that the following intentional conducts are criminalised:

a) performing an abortion on a woman without her prior and informed consent;

b) performing surgery which has the purpose or effect of terminating a woman's capacity to naturally reproduce without her prior and informed consent or understanding of the procedure".

A common element for both offences, that aim at terminating reproduction one-time or permanently is the prior and informed consent of the woman. Here, the general theory of consent can be narrowed to consent in medical interventions,

[82] This aspect was outlined, as far as EU Countries are concerned, by the European Commission in its 2013 Communication, p. 5. De Vido (2015), p. 101.

and this further into consent of the two specific interventions of abortion and sterilisation. A consent can be regarded as valid when the following requirements are cumulatively fulfilled: entitlement to dispose of the legal good; statement of consent; the ability to consent, without defect of consent and informing the patient prior to the procedure ("informed consent").[83] With regard to the respective legal good—it will most probably, but not exclusively, fall under the integrity of life and limb; with regard to the statement of consent—its form, scope, time and revocability will be of concern; and with regard to an informed consent—it will depend on the respective legal acts in the respective countries that define this in more detail (i.e. on moment of information, its scope, information about side effects, etc.).[84]

These two offences add up and complete the description of Chapter V as entailing "unacceptable and punishable acts (. . .) that injure women physically, sexually, psychologically and reproductively."[85] The explicit mention of the reproductive aspect is a direct acknowledgement of the gender-related aspect of this form of violence. Bearing in mind that forced abortion and forced sterilisation, beside FGM and forced marriage, and contrary to sexual assault, rape and domestic violence are not universally criminalised, its inclusion in the catalogue of criminal behaviour fosters a uniform approach across the states that have ratified the Istanbul Convention.[86]

At the same time, the reverse situation—forcing a woman to carry a child she has not wanted to conceive, is not regarded as violence by the Convention.[87] By contrast, the CEDAW General Recommendation No. 35 sees forced pregnancy, forced continuation of pregnancy and criminalisation of abortion as forms of gender-based violence,[88] in terms of violations of women's sexual and reproductive health and rights, that "depending on the circumstances, may amount to torture or cruel, inhuman or degrading treatment."[89]

According to Article 41 of the Convention, aiding and abetting, as well as the attempt to commit forced abortion and forced sterilisation are to be established as offences. In line with the criminal law doctrine, the Article specifies that those punishable behaviours are all performed intentionally.

For this crime, states can formulate reservations, meaning that the statute of limitation may not impede the victim to initiate the process after she has come of age, in line with Article 58:

[83] Marković (2012b), p. 315.

[84] Ibid.

[85] Peroni (2020), p. 47.

[86] In this regard also: Jurasz (2015), p. 5.

[87] Niemi and Sanmartin (2020), p. 89.

[88] Ibid.

[89] Convention on the Elimination of All Forms of Discrimination against Women, General recommendation No. 35 on gender-based violence against women, updating general recommendation No. 19, para. 18.

> "Parties shall take the necessary legislative and other measures to ensure that the statute of limitation for initiating any legal proceedings with regard to the offences established in accordance with Articles 36, 37, 38 and 39 of this Convention, shall continue for a period of time that is sufficient and commensurate with the gravity of the offence in question, to allow for the efficient initiation of proceedings after the victim has reached the age of majority."

Last but not least, the issue of double criminality is mentioned in Article 44 (3), concerning certain offences. According to the principles of international law on jurisdiction in criminal matters, double criminality is required when the country where the crime was committed is different from the country where the perpetrator was prosecuted. Yet this requirement of the crime to be stipulated as such in both countries is excluded for rape, forced marriage, FGM, forced abortion and forced sterilisation:

> "For the prosecution of the offences established in accordance with Articles 36, 37, 38 and 39 of this Convention, Parties shall take the necessary legislative or other measures to ensure that their jurisdiction is not subordinated to the condition that the acts are criminalised in the territory where they were committed"

Cyprus, Greece, Romania, Serbia, Slovenia, and Sweden made use of this option and expressed reservations without clarification, whereas France, Denmark, Switzerland and North Macedonia added clarifications to their reservations.[90] It should also be noted that other offences from Chapter V are not included.

13.4 Conclusion

The Istanbul Convention, through the analysis of particular provisions on criminal law, has been confirmed as the anchor point of the intersection between gender and (substantial) criminal law, which so far has not had as many contact points as other fields of academic interest.

Speaking in terms of the general concept of crime, the Convention offers provisions on all of its elements. Typicity, especially the identification of legal goods that have to be protected, is manifested through specifications of behaviours that are to be criminalised—psychological violence; stalking; physical violence; sexual violence, including rape; forced marriage; female genital mutilation; forced abortion and forced sterilisation and sexual harassment; almost all of them being gender-related. Unlawfulness (or justification) offers various examples where its connection to gender becomes clear in general terms. At the same time, the Istanbul Convention contains a regulation on the exclusion of unacceptable justifications for crimes, including crimes committed in the name of so-called "honour". Guilt as the

[90] Burek (2020), p. 284.

last element of crime, though not specifically regulated by the Convention, appears in various contexts of gender equality (insanity based on substance abuse, diminished responsibility, mistake of law, etc.).

Mirroring the content of the principle of legality, elements that specify criminal liability have also been regulated—aggravating circumstances, as well as the traditional institutes of aiding or abetting and attempt. There are also provisions on reporting; created to encourage and facilitate access to justice for the victims.

Requirements will remain ineffective if their breach is not sanctioned. Hence, penalties are another important issue that the Istanbul Convention covers.

When talking about the special part, particular focus is put on the most gender-relevant offences: psychological and physical violence; stalking; sexual violence, including rape, and sexual harassment; forced marriage and female genital mutilation; forced abortion and forced sterilisation. Even among them, the depth and scope of the connection to gender varies. Looking, for example, at stalking: this overarching offense differs from its definition in various national laws, includes (but is not always recognised as such) psychological violence, and is hence difficult to prove. It is a highly gendered crime, where the majority of perpetrators are men stalking women. On the other hand, there is some kind of equality when it comes to the gender of the offender: male and female stalkers are equally violent. Lastly, the consequences of crime are similar: the harm is (also) manifested in psychological and social terms, regardless of the gender of the victim. Ironically, when it comes to stalking, we can observe a kind of reversed gender equality, both as perpetrators, as well as victims.

On the other side, female genital mutilation, forced marriage, forced abortion and forced sterilisation are crimes that derive from the very basis of gender, sexual reproduction (directly or indirectly) and physical integrity of the victim.[91]

The aspiration of the creators of the Istanbul Convention to

> "create a Europe free from violence against women, and domestic violence"

as stated in its Preamble is, of course, solemnly far-fetched. A realistic view at the respective provisions and the statistical outcomes in the respective countries with regard to violence against women and girls speaks a different language. And yet, it is the best unifying international legal instrument we have so far.

Ironically enough, Turkey, the first country to sign the Istanbul Convention and its name giver, is now the first country to withdraw from it.[92] This negative precedent shows that besides consensus in creating the legal basis and implementation of it, continuity is the third essential factor. Another current example is the rise of

---

[91] This is valid even in cases of forced marriage, where (mostly women and girls) are forced to marry early and consequently to give birth to children earlier than it would happen outside a forced marriage.

[92] https://www.europarl.europa.eu/doceo/document/E-9-2021-001699_EN.html, last accessed on 5 May 2021.

domestic violence and cases of violence against women during the COVID 19 pandemic. It indicates that social rethinking and mutual respect are still lacking when it comes to the basic aspects of gender equality, such as the right to physical and mental integrity.

Questions

1. When does the gender perspective occur as necessary in criminal law?
2. How was the relationship between the dogmatic of criminal law and gender shaped so far?
3. Does gender perspective change the mainstream criminal law creation, interpretation, and implementation, and if so, how?
4. What is the importance of the Istanbul Convention, particularly from the gender point of view?
5. What institutes of criminal law does the Istanbul Convention entail? How are they regulated?
6. What are the particularities of unlawfulness as element of crime and gender? What does the so-called medicalisation of female offenders mean?
7. What are the issues of sentencing and gender?
8. How are forced marriage, female genital mutilation, forced abortion, forced sterilisation, and stalking, as highly gender-sensitive crimes regulated?
9. What forms of violence does the Istanbul Convention criminalise? How do they differ among each other and how is the gender aspect incorporated in every one of them?
10. What conclusions can be drawn in general on criminal law and gender?

References

Acale Sánchez M (2006) La discriminación hacia la mujer por razón de género en el Código penal. Reus, Madrid

Acale Sánchez M (2013) Justicia penal y género. Revista Eletrônica de Direito Penal, AIDP---GB Ano 1 1(1), Junho

Acale Sánchez M (2019) Violencia sexual de género contra las mujeres adultas. Especial referencia a los delitos de agresión y abusos sexuales. Tirant lo Blanch, Valencia

Allen H (1987) Justice unbalanced: gender psychiatry and judicial decisions. OU Press, Milton Keynes

Armenta Deu T (2012) Sistemas procesales penales. La justicia penal en Europa y América. Marcial Pons, Barcelona

Armstrong I (1999) Women and their 'uncontrollable impulses': the medicalisation of women's crime and differential gender sentencing. Psychiatry Psychol Law 6(1):67–77

Australian Bureau of Statistics ABS (2006) 2005. Personal Safety Survey. Australia

Baum K, Catalano S, Rand M, Rose K (2009) Stalking victimization in the United States. National Crime Victimization Survey. Special Report. NCJ 224527. U.S. Department of Justice, Washington D.C.

Belfrage H, Strand S (2009) Validation of the guide for stalking assessment and management in Swedish law enforcement. Int J Police Sci Manag 11:67–76

Björktomta S-B (2019) Honor-based violence in Sweden – norms of honor and chastity. J Fam Violence 34:449–460

BRÅ, National Council of Crime Prevention (2006) Stalking in Sweden. Prevalence and measures (Report 2006:3). www.bra.se

Burek W (2020) Reservations and declarations under the Istanbul Convention. In: Niemi J, Peroni L, Stoyanova V (eds) International law and violence against women. Europe and the Istanbul Convention. Routledge, London, pp 277–295

De Vido S (2015) Culturally motivated crimes against women in a multicultural Europe. The case of criminalization of FGM in the 2011 CoE Istanbul Convention. https://edizionicafoscari.unive.it/media/pdf/books/978-88-6969-054-9/978-88-6969-054-9-ch-05.pdf. Accessed 27 Oct 2021

Denno D (1994) Gender, crime, and the criminal law defenses. J Crim Law Criminol 85:80–180

Devries K et al (2013) The global prevalence of intimate partner violence against women. Science 340:1527–1528. https://doi.org/10.1126/science.1240937

Dobash RP, Dobash RE (2005) Efectividad de los programas penales de tratamiento de maltratadores. In: Moliné JC, Pijoan EL (eds) La delincuencia violenta ¿prevenir, castigar o rehabilitar? Tirant lo Blanch, Valencia, pp 147–190

Donini M (2017) An imposible Exchange? Prove di dialogo tra civil e common lawyers su legalitá, morale e teoria del reato. Rivista Italiana di Diritto e Procedura 1:14–47

Dressing H, Kuehner C, Gass P (2005) Lifetime prevalence and impact of stalking in a European population epidemiological data from a middle-sized German city. Br J Psychiatry 187:168–172

Dressing H, Gass P, Kuehner C (2007) What can we learn from the first community-based epidemiological study on stalking in Germany? Int J Law Psychiatry 30:10–17. https://doi.org/10.1016/j.ijlp.2006.03.006

Echeburúa E, Fernández-Montalvo J, de la Cuesta Arzamendi JL (2001) Psicopatología clínica. legal y Forense 1:19–31

Eldén Å (2003) Heder pÅ liv och död. VÅldsamma berättelser om rykten, oskuld och heder. Avhandling Socialt arbete. Uppsala Universitet, Uppsala

Finney A (2006) Domestic violence, sexual assault and stalking: findings from the 2004/05 British Crime Survey. British Home Office

Forsythe S, Miller MK (2014) Novel defenses in the courtroom. Jury Expert 26:66–78

Jurasz O (2015) The Istanbul Convention: a new chapter in preventing and combating violence against women. Aust Law J 89:619–627

Logan TK (2020) Beyond a dichotomy: threat context factors associated with fear and stalker capability of harm among women stalked by (ex)partners, close acquaintances, and distant acquaintances/strangers. J Threat Assess Manag 7:13–28

Logan TK, Walker R (2017) Stalking: a multidimensional framework for assessment and safety planning. Trauma Violence Abuse 18(2):200–222

Lundgren E (2012) Våldets normaliseringsprocess och andra våldsföreståelser. kartläggning [The normalisation process of violence and other understanings of violence]. Riksorganisationen för kvinnojourer och tjejjourer i Sverige (ROKS), Växjö

Makram O (2019) Det är moralen – inte klanen. Nättidskriften Kvartal / riksorganisationen GAPF. https://kvartal.se/medverkande/omar-makram/. Accessed 27 Oct 2021

Maran DA, Varetto A (2017) Motives to report stalking cases to the police: a comparison between a large city and a small town in Italy. J Aggress Maltreat Trauma 26(5):507–524

Marković I (2012a) Krivično delo ubistva deteta pri porođaju. In: Taboroši S (ed) Razvoj pravnog sistema Srbije I harmonizacija sa pravom EU. Pravni fakultet Univerziteta u Beogradu, Beograd, pp 77–94

Marković I (2012b) Preduzimanje medicinskog zahvata kao osnov isključenja protivpravnosti – sa posebnim osvrtom na nepostojanje pristanka pacijenta. In: Ignjatović D (ed) Kaznena reakcija u Srbiji, II deo. Pravni fakultet Univerziteta u Beogradu, Beograd, pp 306–324

Marković I (2015) Neka osnovna pitanja u vezi sa objektivnom stranom protivpravnosti. In: Ignjatović D (ed) Kaznena reakcija u Srbiji, V deo. Pravni fakultet Univerziteta u Beogradu, Beograd, pp 285–300

McColgan A (2000) General defences. In: Nicolson D, Bibbings L (eds) Feminist perspectives on criminal law. Cavendish, London, pp 137–158

McEwan TE, Strand S (2013) The role of psychopathology in stalking by adult strangers and acquaintances. Aust N Z J Psychiatry 47:546–555

Mullen PE, Pathé M, Purcell R, Stuart G (1999) Study of stalkers. Am J Psychiatry 156:1244–1249

Nicolson D (2000) What the law giveth, it also taketh away: female-specific defences to criminal liability. In: Nicolson D, Bibbings L (eds) Feminist perspectives on criminal law. Cavendish, London, pp 159–182

Nicolson D, Bibbings L (2000) Feminist perspectives on criminal law. Cavendish, London

Niemi J, Sanmartin AV (2020) The concepts of gender and violence in the Istanbul Convention. In: Niemi J, Peroni L, Stoyanova V (eds) International law and violence against women. Europe and the Istanbul Convention. Routledge, London, pp 77–94

Oberwittler D, Kasselt J (2014) Honor killings. In: Gartner R, McCarthly B (eds) The Oxford handbook of gender, sex, and crime. Oxford University Press, Oxford, pp 652–670

Peroni L (2020) Unleashing the gender equality potential of the Istanbul Convention. In: Niemi J, Peroni L, Stoyanova V (eds) International law and violence against women. Europe and the Istanbul Convention. Routledge, London, pp 43–56

Pornari CD, Dixon L, Humphreys GW (2013) Systematically identifying implicit theories in male and female intimate partner violence perpetrators. Aggress Violent Behav 18:496–505. https://doi.org/10.1016/j.avb.2013.07.005

Purcell R et al (2005) Association between stalking victimisation and psychiatric morbidity in a random community sample. Br J of Psychiatry 187:416–420

Roberts D (1994) The meaning of gender equality in criminal law. J Crim Law Criminol 85:1–14

Sedem M et al (2014) Fear of the loss of honor: implications of honor-based violence for the development of youth and their families. Child Youth Care Forum 44:225–237

Sosa L (2020) The Istanbul Convention in the context of feminist claims. In: Niemi J, Peroni L, Stoyanova V (eds) International law and violence against women. Europe and the Istanbul Convention. Routledge, London, pp 25–42

SOU (2020) Ett särskilt hedersbrott. Betänkande av hedersbrottsutredningen. Statens Offentliga Utredningar, Stockholm

Stieger S et al (2008) Lifetime prevalence and impact of stalking: epidemiological data from Eastern Austria. Eur J Psychiatry 22(4):235–241

Sumalla T, María J (2005) Artículo 149. In: Olivares GQ, Prats FM (eds) Comentarios al Nuevo Código penal. Aranzadi, Pamplona, pp 93–100

Tjaden P, Thoennes N (1998) Prevalence, incidence, and consequences of violence against women: findings from the National Violence Against Women Survey. National Institute of Justice. Research in Brief. Centers for Disease Control and Prevention U.S. Department of Justice, Washington D.C.

Tran TD, Nguyen H, Fisher J (2016) Attitudes towards intimate partner violence against women among women and men in 39 low- and middle-income countries. PLoS ONE 11(11). https://doi.org/10.1371/journal.pone.0167438

UNFPA (2000) The state of world population 2000. Lives together, worlds apart. United Nations: UNFPA

UNFPA (2020) State of World Population 2020: against my will - defying the practices that harm women and girls and undermine equality. United Nations: UNFPA
Weller M et al (2013) Police and public perceptions of stalking: the role of prior victim-offender relationship. J Interpersonal Violence 28:320–339
Wilson W (2011) Criminal law. Pearson, Wales
Yeo S (1993) Resolving gender bias in criminal defenses. Monash Univ Law Rev 19:104–116

Further Reading

Burman M (2010) The ability of criminal law to produce gender equality: judicial discourses in the Swedish criminal legal system. Violence Against Women 16:173–188
Dressing H et al (2014) Cyberstalking in a large sample of social network users: prevalence, characteristics, and impact upon victims. Cyberpsychol Behav Soc Netw 17:61–67
Finney A (2006) Domestic violence, sexual assault and stalking: findings from the 2004/05 British Crime Survey. British Home Office, London
McEwan TE et al (2009) Violence in stalking situations. Psychol Med 39:1469–1478
Mullen PE et al (2009) Stalkers and their victims. Cambridge University Press, Cambridge
Sheridan L, Grant T (2007) Is cyberstalking different? Psychol Crime Law 13:627–640
Strand S, McEwan TE (2011) Same-gender stalking in Sweden and Australia. Behav Sci Law 29: 202–219
Strand S, McEwan TE (2012) Violence among female stalkers. Psych Med 42:545–556

Gender Perspective of Victimization, Crime and Penal Policy

14

Beatriz Cruz, Natalija Lukić, and Susanne Strand

Contents

Authors are listed in alphabetical order. Beatriz Cruz wrote Sect. 14.4, Natalija Lukić authored Sect. 14.2 and Susanne Strand wrote Sect. 14.3. The authors jointly worked on Sect. 14.1 and 14.5.

B. Cruz
University of Cadiz, Faculty of Law, International Public, Criminal and Procedural Law, Jerez de la Frontera, Spain
e-mail: beatriz.cruz@gm.uca.es

N. Lukić (✉)
University of Belgrade, Faculty of Law, Criminal Law, Belgrade, Serbia
e-mail: natalija.lukic@ius.bg.ac.rs

S. Strand
Örebro University, School of Law, Psychology and Social Work, Örebro, Sweden
e-mail: Susanne.Strand@oru.se

D. Vujadinović et al. (eds.), *Gender-Competent Legal Education*, Springer Textbooks in Law, https://doi.org/10.1007/978-3-031-14360-1_14

Abstract

This chapter examines three criminological perspectives through a gender lens. The first part is dedicated to crime and gender. This chapter presents official data of reported and convicted persons in European countries, discussing crime trends and the different involvement of sexes in certain criminal offences. Further, this chapter points to possible differences in the ethology of crime from a gender perspective at three levels: individual; family, and social. The second section deals with gender and criminal victimization, with special attention dedicated to issues of domestic violence and sexual crimes. The third section of this chapter analyses the penal policy of the courts. Data is presented on sentencing practices in European countries, with an emphasis on certain criminal offences. Besides data on imprisonment, attention is paid to other penal sanctions. This section of the text further explains possible factors related to the different sentencing of women and men. They are divided into two categories: the first is those mainly related to socio-economic characteristics and crime committed; the second is those that reflect courts as gender institutions. Finally, this chapter gives explanations of different treatments of trans offenders in the criminal justice system.

14.1 Introduction

Women commit significantly fewer crimes compared to men. This applies to practically all crimes, while differences can be observed in terms of higher, or lower, frequency in participation of women in the commission of certain criminal offences. Additionally, the number of female crimes is relatively small, and therefore, a slight increase in absolute numbers may lead to the conclusion of an inexplicably high increase. According to Heidensohn, between 10% and 20% of all individuals dealt with criminal proceedings in several European countries were women.[1] At the same time, historical studies show that this share, with occasional deviations, does not significantly differ from today.[2] Although crime rates rose during the twentieth century, women's crime remained stable or even declined slightly.[3] However, self-reported studies on delinquency have shown that more girls than boys are unwilling to admit committing an offence. This led to a conclusion that the gender gap, especially with respect to youth crime, is narrower.

[1] Heidensohn (1991), p. 57.

[2] Burman (2004), p. 43.

[3] Heidensohn (1991), p. 57.

Furthermore, the increase of arrested, convicted, and imprisoned females, especially for assault and drug-related crimes, suggested that they are becoming more violent.[4] As for the characteristics of women's crime, unlike men, females commit less serious criminal offences, such as theft, handling stolen goods, drug offences, prostitution, fraud, forgery, and minor motoring offences.[5] In addition, women who commit crimes, in most cases, do so for the first time. Only a small number of women could fall into the category of professional perpetrators.[6]

The most common victims of violent crimes are men, as men are the most common perpetrators of violent crimes. However, this varies across types of violent crimes. Male victims of homicide are more common than female victims. The relationship between perpetrators and victims differs; while an acquaintance or stranger more often kills men, women are more often killed by a current or former intimate partner. "Women are much more likely than men to be targets of certain kinds of victimization, such as rape and domestic violence".[7] Despite these differences, explanations of victimization cannot be based only on gender perspective without considering other victimological factors that influence the probability of victimization, including class, and race. Furthermore, considering different rates of victimization across countries, wider social, economic, and political circumstances as well as social norms should also be taken into consideration.

Many researchers pay attention to the penal policy of courts from a gender perspective. Although some scholars assert that women have been treated more leniently than men, others point out that women commit less serious crimes, especially less violent crimes. Together with the notion that they are less often recidivist, helps to explain this possible difference. Although the percentage of women in prisons is generally stable, the past few decades have been characterized by a greater increase in female's share in penal institutions in some countries. There are different explanations for this increase. While some assert that women have become more violent and have become more involved in crime generally, other points to changes in reactions of formal social control. Regarding gender differences in sentencing, the distinction between legal and extra-legal factors can be observed, which is discussed in detail in the final section of this chapter.

All of these issues are of great importance for policymakers. Analysis of criminal offending, as well as victimization, shows that in many cases these experiences represent an expression of gender that must be understood in intersection with class and race. The criminological aspect is valuable because it can reveal: the real extent of crime and victimization; the role gender plays; the forms of victimization that are not regulated by criminal law, and the impact and consequences on victims. Policymakers should use this knowledge with respect to crime prevention, the

[4] Cauffman (2008), p. 122.

[5] Burman (2004), p. 42.

[6] Heidensohn (1985), p. 61.

[7] Britton (2011), p. 82.

creation of gender-sensitive criminal law legislation and the application of legal norms in practice.

14.2 Gender and Crime

14.2.1 Crime Trends in Europe from Gender Perspective

There are nine possible data sources regarding gender, crime, and criminal justice in Europe,[8] but none of these offer complete information. Despite some gaps, the European Sourcebook on Crime and Justice Statistics (hereinafter European Sourcebook)[9] could be considered the most reliable source according to some views.[10] Therefore, the section briefly presents data from it.

As for the crimes committed by women in European countries, it is noticeable that there are large differences.

According to the latest available data from the European Sourcebook for 2015 (police statistics), the percentage of women in relation to total offenders per 100,000 population varies and ranges from at least 4.5% (Georgia) to 26.2% (Greece). Among the countries with higher percentages of women are Germany, Luxembourg, Poland, Austria. In contrast a share of less than 8% was recorded in Albania, Croatia, Montenegro, Azerbaijan, and Moldova (Table 14.1). For the period 2006–2015, data is available for 15 European countries, of which eight show a percentage increase in women's share. At the same time, the increase in the total number of perpetrators per 100,000 population increased in only two of these eight countries. Other countries showed a decline in the rate of perpetrators, either with or without significant variations.[11]

[8]The United Nations Survey on Crime Trends and the Operation of Criminal Justice Systems, The World Prison Brief, the European Sourcebook of Crime and Criminal Justice Statistics, the Eurostat Data Collection, the International Crime Victimization Survey, the European Commission for the Efficiency of Justice, Statistiques Pénales Annueles due Conseil de l'Europe (SPACE), the International Self-Delinquency Study and the International Violence against Women Survey. According to: Gelsthorpe and Larrauri (2014), pp. 391–392.

[9]This source is regularly developed by experts in the framework of the Council of Europe, including not just statistical but also information on rules and definitions behind the data. The last edition is the sixth, updated to April 9th 2021.

[10]Gelsthorpe and Larrauri (2014), p. 374.

[11]Aebi et al. (2021). Retrieved from: https://wp.unil.ch/europeansourcebook/printed-editions-2/.

Table 14.1 Percentage of women from European countries among offenders in 2015—criminal offences: total

State	Total offenders per 100,000 pop.	of which % women	State	Total offenders per 100,000 pop.	of which % women
Albania	1178.6	7.9	Italy	1586.3	18.5
Armenia	364.4	12.2	Latvia	1169.9	12.5
Austria	2918.8	20.8	Lithuania	919.5	10.5
Azerbaijan	170.1	6.9	Luxembourg	5051.2	23.7
Bulgaria	566.8	13.4	Moldova	482.7	7.7
Croatia	1425.7	7.9	Montenegro	579.7	7.1
Cyprus	698.3	8.7	Netherlands	1784.3	16.3
Czech Republic	966.1	15.6	Poland	840.4	11.3
Finland	4788.1	18.6	Portugal	1803.1	20.2
France	1748.4	17.9	Serbia	694.5	10.9
Georgia	567.8	4.5	Slovenia	2191.9	18.6
Germany	2917.6	24.8	Spain	684.9	13.9
Greece	1022.5	26.2	Sweden	1796.5	20.9
Hungary	1004.4	16.3	Switzerland	1670.5	20.2
Iceland	1176.8	23.0	Ukraine	313.1	11.7
Mean	1335	15.0	Minimum	0	4.5
Median	1013	14.8	Maximum	5051	26

Source: European Sourcebook of Crime and Criminal Justice Statistics 2021, sixth edition

Example

In the period 2006–2015, an obvious decrease in the homicide rate of reported female offenders has been recorded. Whereas in 2006, the mean value for the percentage of women reported for homicide was 9%, and 13.1% in 2010, in 2015 this share was less than 1% in all countries that submitted data. On the other hand, an increased percentage of women's share for bodily injury can be noticed (data was observed for minor and aggravated forms of bodily injury since this data is the most complete). Of the 18 countries that submitted data, for at least 2 years in the observed period from 2006–2015, an increase was recorded in almost 14 countries (close to 80%).[12] ◄

According to the latest available data for 2015 for conviction statistics (Table 14.2), the mean value of the share of women was 13.8%. The lowest percentage share of convicted women was 5.4% (Turkey), whilst the highest value in the same year was recorded in England and Wales (29.5%). A high percentage of convicted women (more than 20%) was also registered in Luxembourg, Cyprus and Finland.[13]

[12] *Ibid.*

[13] *Ibid.*

Table 14.2 Percentage of women from European countries among convicted persons in 2015—criminal offences: total

State	Total offenders per 100,000 pop.	of which % women	State	Total offenders per 100,000 pop.	of which % women
Albania	559	5.5	Latvia	481	11.8
Armenia	94	7.7	Lithuania	636	9.6
Austria	374	14.2	Luxembourg	1498	20.8
Belgium	1614	18.3	Netherlands	546	12.6
Bulgaria	386	8.4	Poland	684	10.3
Croatia	308	11.4	Portugal	597	12.2
Cyprus	6387	20.0	Serbia	494	9.2
Czech Republic	622	15.1	Spain	673	13.6
Finland	3321	20.8	Sweden	1095	17.3
France	864	10.1	Switzerland	1505	16.8
Georgia	406	6.3	Turkey	1971	5.4
Germany	911	19.8	Ukraine	222	11.6
Hungary	728	11.8	UK: England and Wales	2158	29.5
Italy	363	16.6	UK: Northern Ireland	1317	16.8
Latvia	481	11.8	UK: Scotland	1860	16.9
Mean	1014	13.8	Minimum	94	5.4
Median	622	12.6	Maximum	6387	29.5

Source: European Sourcebook of Crime and Criminal Justice Statistics 2021, sixth edition

Example

The mean value of women convicted of homicide ranged from 7% in 2006 to 9.5% in 2015. Austria and Finland are leading countries in terms of women being convicted for homicide in 2015, accounting for 16%. The lowest percentage of convicted women for this crime was in Turkey (2.6%) and Albania (2.9%). Another example is the crime of fraud. The smallest percentage in 2015 was recorded in Georgia (0.4%), while the highest percentage was in Scotland (48.6%). A high percentage was also recorded in the Czech Republic (34.1), Germany (33.9%), Finland (33.8%), England and Wales (32.7%), and Switzerland (31.9%).[14] ◄

The comparison with police records for many countries is not possible due to a lack of data. For the countries that submitted data, it can be concluded that many countries do not follow the trend; changes in conviction records do not follow changes in police statistics. Albania is an example of opposite trends, with an increase in the share of women in police records, while there is a decrease in the

[14] *Ibid.*

judicial statistics. The situation is similar in Sweden, displaying an increase in the number of women in police statistics, whilst a decline in judicial statistics. In Finland, on the other hand, in the period of 2006–2015, there is a decline of women in police records and an increase in judicial records. An example of similar trends can be found in Poland, where there is a continuous increase in the percentage of women in both data sources.[15] Therefore, even without detailed analysis, there are no similarities between European countries. The claims in literature on the increase in the gender gap should be interpreted with caution since they may refer only to countries where these studies were conducted.

A study conducted by Jennifer Schwartz, for example, included data on reported and convicted women in the USA, Canada, United Kingdom, Finland, Norway, Sweden. The study started from the assumption that the real increase in female crime should be reflected across each stage of the criminal justice system.[16] The author analysed the assault to homicide ratio and the case flow from arrest to imprisonment. One of the conclusions of this study is that the United Kingdom represents an outlier in terms of growth in the female percentage of prosecutions. In Sweden, Norway, and Finland, the female share was fairly stable. Thus, the United Kingdom, but not the Scandinavian countries, witnessed a sustained and sizeable increase (10%) in the period 1997–2006. The author concluded this gives support to policy change explanation, rather than an actual change in female criminal behaviour.[17]

Judicial statistics data often do not indicate a match between the trend of the percentage of share of women, and the trend of convicted persons in relation to 100,000 of the population. This must be taken into consideration before making any conclusions. It is possible that other external factors could explain both the increase or decrease in crime of females and males.

Example

In Germany during the period from 2011–2015, there was an increase in the share of convicted women, while at the same time, a decrease in the rate of all convicted persons was recorded. A similar situation was found in England and Wales, Poland, Finland, Armenia, Croatia. In comparison the situation is quite the opposite in Albania, with an increase in the rate of convicts, accompanied by a lower percentage of convicted women.[18] ◄

In literature, the increase in women's crime is usually explained in two ways. According to the first view, the liberalization of women in terms of their status and changing gender roles, leads to an increase in committed criminal acts. These changes create more opportunities, enabling women to become perpetrators more often.[19] In addition, it is argued that the „changing gender-role expectations have

---

[15] *Ibid.*

[16] Schwartz (2013), pp. 809–810.

[17] *Ibid.*

[18] Aebi et al. (2021).

[19] Chu et al. (2021), p. 2.

allowed for greater freedom and assertiveness, that these changes have "masculinized" female behaviour and engendered in women an "imitative male machismo competitiveness".[20] While Adler advocated the thesis of masculinization and predicted an increase in violent offences committed by women, Simon highlighted the importance of higher involvement in the labour market to increase the number of opportunities for crimes, primarily property and occupational.[21] The opposite thesis concerns economic marginalization, claiming changes in women's lives are reflected in a deteriorated economic status, higher divorce rates, and, consequently, a larger number of single mothers have led to an increase in women's participation in crime. This could be explained by the fact that women's personal and economic position is more dependent on the private sphere than men. Family relations, especially when it comes to traditional gender roles, act preventively in terms of women's participation in crimes.[22] The weakening of traditional family ties and social control, a characteristic of social development, together with possible stress and frustration of women due to a marginalized economic position, can lead to greater involvement in crime.[23] Certainly, women who belong to marginalized groups, such as minorities, low income women, and those who live in disorganized urban areas, are the most affected.[24] The thesis of economic marginalization starts from the fact that most convicted women are far from being liberated, and instead, they disproportionally come from the "underclass".[25] As an example, for Russia, it is stated that "the increased number of Russian women involved in criminal cases is linked to increasingly worse socio-economic conditions, an increase in psychological disorders and problems of dependency on psychoactive substances, and also increasingly stronger discrimination".[26]

The results of the conducted studies indicate different conclusions. It is pointed out that the improvement of the status of women acts in the direction of reducing violent crimes, primarily homicide, while at the same time leading to an increase in other forms of crime such as property crimes, drug offenses, fraud. A study conducted by Simon for the period of 1963–1970, included analysis of the crime rate of women in 25 countries, concluding that the greatest increase was recorded in countries with advanced industrial and technological development. In a study covering 30 years (1962–1995), the results still indicated a similar conclusion.[27] The results of this cross-national study indicated that "in those nations where women have more years of schooling, higher representation in the labour force and lower fertility rates they are more likely to be involved in the property offences of as theft and especially fraud".[28] The study, which analysed data on women's crime for 2006

[20] Steffensmeier et al. (2006), p. 74.

[21] According to: Britton (2000), p. 61.

[22] Steffensmeier et al. (2006), p. 74.

[23] Agha (2009), p. 578.

[24] Steffensmeier et al. (2006), p. 74.

[25] Wang (2021), p. 3.

[26] Lysova (2014), p. 5.

[27] Chernoff and Simon (2000), p. 9.

[28] Chernoff and Simon (2000), pp. 16–17.

for 27 European countries, reiterates the importance of the thesis on liberalization and its impact on the growth of property crimes such as larceny, fraud, embezzlement and theft.[29] Contrarily, Reckdenwald and Parker point to the importance of economic marginalization on female crime and confirm that this factor is relevant in explaining property crimes (specifically robbery), drug-related crimes, homicide in partner relations, and domestic violence. Still, the authors concluded that economic marginalization has a different impact on robbery and drug-related crimes than domestic violence. Pressure and frustration due to limited resources, social support, and power have a decisive role here.[30] Hunnicut and Broidy indicate that liberation and economic marginalization interact. They found statistical support for the influence of economic marginality on female conviction rates. Still, the positive relationship was confirmed between two emancipation variables (women in industry and age-dependency ratio) and female conviction rates.[31]

However, it can be argued the increase in female crime is not the result of changes in their behaviour, but a change in penal policy.[32] Steffensmeier et al. state that "policy change actually consists of the following three elements: a) elasticity of violence definitions, b) the broadness of offence categories, c) the variability in the gender/violence relationship depending on behavioural or item content."[33] The first element means that citizens, police, and other officials have considerable discretion in defining violence. The second element implies that definitions of crimes, such as simple and aggravated assault, are broad and encompass various behaviours. Finally, the third element implies that the gender gap is smaller in the case of less severe acts of violence, which have a lower degree of guilt, take place in a private setting and against the inmate.[34]

It should be noted that media portrayal has considerable impact with regards to these changing patterns in the criminal justice system regarding women and, especially, juvenile girls..[35] As Chesney-Lind says: "When male juvenile violence increases, the media response is "So, what else is new?", whereas violence of juvenile girls represents a threat for a social order".[36] Although official statistics and victimization reports do not support assertions of the increase of female crime, juvenile girls are in many media covers, books, and commentaries portrayed as "mean", "sneaky", "lying" and "cruel".[37]

[29] Chu et al. (2021), p. 18.

[30] Reckdenwald and Parker (2008), p. 220.

[31] Hunnicut and Broidy (2004), pp. 150–151.

[32] Steffensmeier et al. (2006), p. 77.

[33] Steffensmeier et al. (2006), p. 77.

[34] Steffensmeier et al. (2006), p. 77.

[35] Heidensohn and Silvestri (2012), p. 340.

[36] Chesney-Lind and Shelden (2014), p. 16.

[37] Males (2010), p. 14.

14.2.2 Factors of Criminal Offending from Gender Perspective

Male dominance in crime influenced theoretical explanations in criminology, which in principle did not take into account the gender-difference. The low participation of females in crime is one of the reasons for the neglect of women criminals in criminology. However, as Smart notes, female criminality has not been perceived as great a threat to society as male's criminality, not only because of the rarity of women's criminal offences, but because of the nature of these offences. Unlike men, women mostly commit less serious crimes.[38] Daly and Chesney-Lind assert that "criminology is androcentric, shaped by male experiences and understanding of the social world. These realties shape theories of crime which neglect female's experiences as perpetrators or victims".[39] Therefore, the question arises whether and how pathways to crime for men and women differ?

According to the Pathway theory, men and women enter the criminal justice system differently. Some of the factors of more importance for female criminality are a history of personal abuse, mental illness, substance abuse, economic and social marginality, homelessness, and relationships.[40]

Qualitative studies in feminist criminology pointed to different pathways of female crime. One of the most cited is Daly's classification that includes five pathways: (1) *harmed and harming women* are those who were abused or neglected as children. These women are identified as a "problem child", who "acts out" and becomes violent when drinking alcohol. Drug problems and psychological problems are also common in this group; (2) *battered women* are those in a relationship with violent men or they have recently ended such a relationship; (3) *street women* are pushed out, or they run away from abusive households to the streets. They usually commit drug-related offences, theft, and prostitution; (4) *drug-connected women* are addicted to drugs via a relationship with a boyfriend or they sell drugs; (5) *other women* commit crimes due to immediate economic circumstances or greed. Their crimes are not related to drug addiction nor street life.[41]

According to Daly, "pathways of harming and harmed men, street men, drug-connected men were also identified, but 35% males in the sample took male-only pathway". Men were classified into the following categories: (1) 'explosively violent men', used violence to control/dominate others; (2) 'bad luck men', either in the wrong place at the wrong time, used by other men, or reacting to harassing men; and (3) 'masculine gaming men', engaged in crime as a form of recreation/means to demonstrate masculinity. This classification did not fit male's pathways to crime.[42]

Russell et al., in their research, also made comparisons between female's and male's pathways to prison, identifying the following common trajectories: (1) peer

[38] Smart (1995), p. 16.

[39] According to: Simpson (1989), p. 605.

[40] Gehring (2018), p. 116.

[41] Daly (1992), p. 28.

[42] Cited from: Russell et al. (2020), p. 539.

group association/deviant lifestyle; (2) harmed and harming, and (3) economically motivated. In contrast, two pathways were marked as women only: (1) adulthood victimisation and dysfunctional intimate relationships, and (2) naivety and deception. Further, an economically motivated pathway consisted of two types: (1) economic, familial provisioning (in most cases, women commit property offences, half of them lived in poverty. Usually, they had dependent children and other family members financially dependent on them), and (2) greed (exclusively to males).[43]

With respect to gender perspective in the following text this chapter presents some of these crime factors on three different levels: individual, family, and social/societal.

14.2.2.1 Individual-Level

One of the first considerations of the factors to explain women's crime is stated by Lombroso, who, *inter alia,* asserts that women's crime is a consequence of their biological inferiority. He claimed that female offenders are doubly deviant. Firstly, because they represent an anomaly concerning male criminals, and secondly, women act against their biological nature by committing criminal acts.[44] Although such ideas are outdated,[45] the issue of biological factors is still relevant. As men commit violent crimes incomparably more often, there are opinions that biological predispositions can explain this.[46] However, detailed analysis of research conducted in the domain of genetics, structural brain imaging, neuropsychology, psychophysiology, and hormones related to antisocial behaviour indicated that many of these risk factors are associated not only with the antisocial and criminal behaviour of men, but also women.[47] Dunedin Multidisciplinary Health and Development Study testing neurological abnormalities and heart rate was unable to establish a significant difference between genders.[48] As for possible differences, some authors point to brain asymmetry. Greater frontal activation is found on the right, than on the left, in the brains of antisocial females. This was not found in antisocial boys.[49] Further, female crime could be affected by menstruation and premenstrual syndrome. Dalton is one of the proponents of this connection. Using a sample of female prisoners, she examined how the menstrual cycle phases are related to committing crimes. She concluded that almost half of the respondents in the sample committed a crime

[43] Ibid, pp. 559–559.

[44] Gelsthorpe (2004), p. 16.

[45] These opinions have been criticized because they have not taken into account factors such as class, race, economic status which are of great importance in crime etiology. See: Smart (1995), p. 18. On the other hand, Naffin states that Lombrosian thoughts are abandoned in respect to explanations of male crime, but that "our concept of female offender still rests firmly in biological mould"—Naffin (2016), p. 70.

[46] Gelsthorpe (2004), p. 16.

[47] Portnoy et al. (2014), p. 275.

[48] Moffit et al. (2004), p. 105.

[49] Goldweber et al. (2009), p. 219.

during or immediately before menstruation.[50] In respect to males, it has been tested whether testosterone is related to aggressiveness in boys, however conclusions point to the importance of mediating social factors.[51]

In addition to the aforementioned biological explanations, other potential explanations for female crime can be found in psychological theories. Freud, for example, believed that women were inferior to men. Thomas develops the myth of the manipulative women, while Pollak states that women are inherently inconsistent, cunning, vindictive, more capable of manipulating, and are without passion.[52] As for some peculiarities of personality characteristics, Dunedin‘s study shows that there are no significant differences between male and female offenders in relation to intelligence, reading achievement, difficult temperament, hyperactivity or internalizing problems.[53] There are opinions that the crime rate of women is lower because they adopt social cognitive abilities earlier in life and have better pro-social skills.[54] Further, Gilligan's theory of moral development could be used as an explanation for the lower involvement of women in crime. According to this theory, men often make moral decisions based on an ethic of justice (sets of rules and principles), whereas women's decisions are based on "ethic of care".[55] Women will consider how the commission of crime would affect their family members dependent upon them. If their needs (for example, for food) outweigh the "immorality of crime", then it is possible for a woman to commit the crime.[56]

When it comes to the relation between mental illness and crime, scientific conclusions are inconsistent. A study conducted in Finland on homicide offenders found no gender differences in psychiatric disorders.[57] A meta-analysis that included 62 conducted studies indicated that mental illness was not more common among female prisoners than men. The study shows that personality disorders are more prevalent in the male population in prisons, however women with this type of disorder are not negligible.[58] For perpetrators of domestic violence, and also for victims, it is stated that there are no significant differences from the gender aspect when it comes to antisocial personality traits and borderline personality traits.[59] However, there are also conclusions that a larger proportion of female offenders encounter mental health problems, as a consequence of higher levels of violence.[60] The higher share of women prisoners with mental health problems than men does not

---

[50] Dalton (1961), pp. 1753–1754.
[51] Sylvers et al. (2009), p. 154.
[52] Klein (2009), pp. 376–379, 383–384.
[53] Moffit et al. (2004), pp. 98–99.
[54] Gelsthorpe (2004), pp. 19–20.
[55] Simpson (1989), p. 620.
[56] *Ibid.*
[57] Putkonen et al. (2011), p. 57.
[58] Jones (2008), pp. 173–174, according to: Lukić (2019a), p. 338.
[59] Hilinski-Rosick (2016), p. 52.
[60] According to Gartner and Jung (2014), p. 430.

necessarily mean that it is a risk factor, but rather the higher proportions reflect the prevalence of mental illness in the general population. Alternatively, this could simply be a reaction to incarceration.[61]

Addiction to alcohol and narcotics should also be mentioned at the individual level, bearing in mind this is a factor associated with many crimes. For example, no significant gender difference was found in respect to homicide offenders.[62]

14.2.2.2 Family Level

The family environment is primarily important for the understanding of juvenile delinquency. Several factors stand out in this context: inadequate parenting styles; family disorganization; low socio-economic status of the family; domestic violence; alcohol and psychoactive substance abuse of parents, and parental crime. The question is whether these factors act differently, taking into account the gender of juveniles. The educational style differs depending on the gender of the child. Daughters are generally treated more leniently, and unlike sons, they are under greater control and restrictions, so that "bad things" do not happen to them while growing up.[63] Heimer and De Coster emphasize that differences between female and male juvenile violence, depends not only upon levels of parental control, but also upon types of control. According to these authors, "girls" learning of violent definitions will be shaped primarily by the indirect control achieved through emotional bonding to families. In contrast, boy's learning of violent definitions will be shaped primarily by more direct parental control, including supervision and coercive discipline.[64] In the theory of power control, Hagan pointed out differences in the control over girls in patriarchal, matriarchal, and egalitarian families. It is concluded that with the transition to egalitarian family forms, there will be a decrease in the delinquent behaviour of young men and an increase in female delinquency, caused by the greater level of power that women gain at work and home.[65]

Studies show that witnessing criminal offences, as well as personal experience of victimization, within the family are associated with juvenile delinquency. Unlike men, who suffer such events for a short time before they react, the situation is different for girls. They tend to internalize these problems through withdrawal, depression and suicide. After several negative experiences, they react aggressively.[66] In order to escape from victimization within the family, many girls run away from home, steal and leave school.[67] Russel et al. emphasize that abuse and neglect in childhood of females are more related to substance abuse, school failure, and victimization in adulthood in comparison to men. While men with troubled

[61]Hedderman (2004), p. 239.

[62]Putkonen et al. (2011), p. 97.

[63]Siegel and Welsh (2011), p. 155.

[64]Heimer and De Coster (2011), p. 352.

[65]Messerschmidt (2009), p. 435.

[66]Hawkins Anderson (2012), p. 44.

[67]Gehring (2018), p. 118.

childhood more often harmed others, internalization of trauma was more common for women (via substance abuse).[68] Previously, family conflicts were thought to have more impact on males than on female juveniles, and only for the status offences was it the opposite.[69] However, recent research shows that the frequency of domestic abuse was the highest in aggressive girls,[70] with studies generally illustrating that girls are more often abused within families than boys.[71] Childhood victimization is related to later violent behaviour, nonetheless, results of empirical studies are different.[72] Asscher et al. find that sexual victimization was a stronger predictor for sex offences of males, any form of violent victimization was a predictor of violent offences for males, whilst only physical abuse was a predictor for female violence.[73] Studies further convey childhood exposure to intimate partner violence is of great importance in the later manifestation of violence for both men and women.[74]

Victimization by a partner is one of the factors that could lead a woman to commit a crime, as already mentioned in the pathways of female's crime. This type of domestic violence is known as "violence resistance." Usually, offenders are women who previously suffered "intimate terrorism", a severe, one-sided violence and typically male to female.[75] Although female partners also victimize men in cases other than self-defense, empirical research emphasizes that domestic violence has more severe consequences (especially physical injuries) for women.[76] Often, violence by women occurs in the context of ongoing aggression and violence.[77] Extending beyond men victimized by female partners, the literature should pay more attention to gay and lesbian couples. Estimates of the prevalence of domestic violence among same-sex partners are different; possibly due to the, even higher, reluctance of gay and lesbian victims to report that a partner has victimized them.[78]

Example

According to some estimates, "the majority of women prisoners have been victims of one or more types of violence, both as children and adults, and many were in violent relationships before their arrests".[79] Contemporaneously, research over the past three decades shows that three-quarters of all-male victimizations in

[68] Russell et al. (2020), p. 559.

[69] Chesney-Lind (1987), p. 219, according to: Lukić (2019b), p. 264.

[70] Chesney-Lind and Shelden (2014), pp. 55–58.

[71] Belknap and Holsinger (2006), p. 56.

[72] Belknap and Holsinger (2006), p. 51; Robertson and Burton (2010), p. 323.

[73] Asscher et al. (2015), p. 220.

[74] Williams et al. (2014), p. 366.

[75] Williams et al. (2014), p. 367.

[76] Dobash and Dobash (2004), p. 328.

[77] *Ibid.*

[78] Hilinski-Rosick (2016), p. 53.

[79] Marcus-Mendoza (2016), p. 214.

the context of partner homicide were preceded by partner violence against a female perpetrator.[80] ◄

14.2.2.3 Social and Societal Level

Socialization of both women and men into sex roles takes place not only within the family but also within other social circumstances. These include occupational structures, peer groups, and culture.[81] Some authors characterize social networks as social level, whereas cultural and societal norms and beliefs (such as gendered power relations, gendered behavioural expectations, gendered (in)equality) would be a societal level.[82] According to Bertrand, "our culture condones and even expects a certain amount of acting out and aggressive behaviour in young boys, but it is less tolerant of the foibles of young girls."[83] Sutherland and Cressey highlighted that the gender gap in crime would be the lowest in countries in which females have the greatest freedom and equality with men, such as Western Europe, Australia, Canada, and the United States, and highest in countries in which females are closely supervised, such as Algeria. This difference between female and male crime varies with the social positions of the sexes in different groups within a nation, age, size of a community and the crime rate in an area.[84]

Consequently, the liberalization of women should have an impact on behaviour change and gender mainstreaming. In white-collar and corporate crime, women are mostly involved in simpler crimes such as fraud or embezzlement. In contrast, crimes such as securities trading or restrictive agreements are mostly committed by men; fewer women are in higher positions in companies and consequently, they have fewer opportunities to commit these crimes. The motives may also differ; while women commit crimes to satisfy some of their own or the family's needs, men do so because of status.[85]

Example

The results of one conducted research at the European level show that, at least when it comes to the average level of white-collar crime (e.g., occupational fraud), there is no gender difference. Females are twice as likely to commit crimes of asset misappropriation as their male counterparts.[86] ◄

---

[80] Doerner and Lab (2012), p. 213.

[81] Naffin (2016), p. 81.

[82] Korkmaz (2021), pp. 159–160.

[83] Naffin (2016), p. 74.

[84] Sutherland and Cressey (1978), pp. 132–133.

[85] Hilliard and Neidermeyer (2018), p. 815; Holtfreter (2014), p. 497.

[86] Hilliard and Neidermeyer (2018), p. 832.

However, the conducted research does not show that female criminals are emancipated.[87] On the contrary, most female offenders come from disorganized social backgrounds and have low socio-economic status. Although many women are employed, a large proportion is still economically marginalized, doing occasional or low-paid jobs. Turning to criminal activities may prove to be a logical outcome for some of these women.[88] Smart points out that "while middle-class women have benefited from changes in labour market, the position of black and working-class women may actually have deteriorated."[89] More frequent divorces also contribute to the worsening economic situation of an increasing number of women who are single mothers.[90]

The contribution of the feminist studies is also reflected in the question of what the characteristic of men is, not as members of the working class, subordinate individuals or migrants, rather the male gender itself in causing them to commit crimes. Researchers who studied rape, domestic and relationship violence concluded that men see these crimes as the ultimate masculine accomplishment.[91] However, this position has been criticized by arguing that masculinity depends upon class, race, and age. If there is no possibility to demonstrate masculinity by using legitimate means, it is likely that a crime will be committed.[92] Proving masculinity is not just about street crimes but also corporate crimes. Just as masculinity can be a reason for men to commit crimes, the question is whether the committing of crimes by women is the manifestation of their femininity? Although some authors explain women's crime in terms of a means of doing femininity, others point to the necessity to question the explanations in terms of doing masculinity or femininity. Firstly, the tendency to view women's actions only as an expression of "femininity" and men's of "masculinity" is a tautology and restricted to gender dualism. Secondly, gender inequalities should be coupled with those of race, class, and age.[93] Barak et al. examine several research results and conclude that there is no standardized "class" experience, "race" experience, or "gender" experience, rather there is a repertoire of interacting class, race, and gender identities.[94] This intersectional approach advocates multiracial (multicultural) feminism as well.[95] This perspective emphasizes that differences in respect to class, race, sexuality, age, physical ability and nationality are as important as gender. Gender should not have primacy over other forms of inequality that have multiple and cross-cutting effects on the micro and macro level. These claims are based on the critiques of the dominance approach,

[87] Chesney-Lind and Shelden (2014), pp. 135–138.

[88] Marsh et al. (2006), pp. 158–159.

[89] Heidensohn (1985), p. 157.

[90] Blanchette and Brown (2006), pp. 31–32.

[91] Britton (2000), p. 37.

[92] Messerschmidt (2011), p. 359.

[93] Miller (2014), pp. 26–29.

[94] Barak et al. (2010), p. 25.

[95] Burgess-Proctor (2006), p. 35.

according to which all women universally suffer the effects of patriarchy. On the contrary, the existence of diversity among women should be acknowledged.[96] This perspective offers an explanation for the fact that not all marginalized women opt for criminal offending, while some affluent middle-class women do commit crimes. The decision whether to conform to legal order or not, and to achieve goals or desires, is determined by the way a concrete person navigates through different forms of oppressions.[97] Class, race and gender have the possibility to enhance a position in a society, or to constrain choices. For example, men have more choices than women, whites have more choices than minorities and the rich have more chances than the poor.[98]

14.3 Criminal Victimization from a Gender Perspective

14.3.1 Domestic Violence

The Istanbul Convention, the Council of Europe Convention on preventing and combating violence against women and domestic violence (CETS No. 210), was opened for signature on 11 May 2011. Ten years later, it has been signed by 45 countries, of which 33 have ratified the convention. In this treaty, violence against women is.

▶ **Definition** "Defined as any act that causes 'physical, sexual, psychological or economic harm or suffering to women, including threats of such acts, coercion or arbitrary deprivation of liberty, whether occurring in public or in private life'.

Domestic violence is a recognized global public health problem, where one out of three women have been subjected to such violence during their lifetime, and combatting men's violence towards women is on the agenda for the World Health Organization.[99]

In Europe, one in three women have experienced physical and/or sexual violence since the age of 15, 1 in 20 have been raped, one in two have been sexually harassed, and one in five have been stalked.[100] However, this differs across countries; those with a larger population with low economic status have higher rates of domestic violence. The opposite also holds true; countries with a larger population with high economic status has lower rates of domestic violence. Additionally, the highest rates of domestic violence are found in Sub-Saharan Africa and the lowest rates in East

[96] Burgess-Proctor (2006), p. 34.
[97] Bernard (2013), p. 8.
[98] Lynch (2016), p. 7.
[99] EIGE (2021); WHO (2021).
[100] EIGE (2021).

Asia.[101] Furthermore, repeated victimization in terms of recidivism is high, ranging from 15% to over 40%.[102]

Most studies in Western societies show a heterogeneous group of abusers, regardless of ethnicity, culture, or gender.[103] Although the type of violence and behaviours might differ across countries due to national legislation, abusers are more similar than different and can be found in all societies. One typology consists of two subtypes, the general violent and the family only perpetrators, can be used to describe the most common perpetrators of domestic violence.[104] The first subtype is the general violent abuser. This is the man who might have a criminal lifestyle, including being violent towards others. The second subtype is the family-only abuser who is only violent towards the victim and, in some cases, family members. They are otherwise rather well-adjusted in society. The major difference is that the general violent abuser is more difficult to handle; he does not follow regulations set by the state and thereby has a higher risk for recidivism. In contrast, the family only abuser follows the rules to a greater extent, decreasing the risk for relapse. However, both types are at risk for recidivism if no risk management is set in.[105]

The cost of gender-based violence has been estimated to be 109 billion Euros per year in the EU. The costs are split into provision and services: health, social welfare, and justice (38.9%); physical and emotional impact (48.2%), and lost economic output (11.6%). Additionally, 1.3% has been spent on specialized services to prevent violence, such as shelters, helplines, support centres and counselling.[106] Although the costs are huge, little money is spent on preventing and supporting victims. Most victims are women; there is an undefined and unwritten law that women should voluntarily help their sisters in need. However, it is unreasonable that states depend on sisterhood to be the foundation of the risk management needed to help and support women victimized by severe violence. Non-governmental organizations (NGOs) are the foundation of the supportive work done to protect women. First, they need to be funded properly, and second, they cannot be the sole and primary services to support victims of domestic violence.[107] It is a state obligation under the Istanbul Convention and CEDAW. This varies across countries, depending on how welfare systems are managed. Even in countries with a well-organized large welfare system like Sweden, NGOs are not well funded by the government; they rely upon voluntary work by women to protect and support victims of domestic violence.

The victim support services provided, build to some extent on the ideal victim of domestic violence. This has resulted in domestic violence being synonymous with

[101] WHO (2021).

[102] Belfrage and Strand (2012), Goldstein et al. (2016) and Loinaz (2014).

[103] Dixon and Browne (2003), Petersson and Strand (2020), Thijssen and de Ruiter (2011) and Tran et al. (2016).

[104] Petersson (2020).

[105] *Ibid.*

[106] EIGE (2021).

[107] See Chap. 13 in this book.

men's violence against women. Nils Christie's theory of the "ideal victims" from the mid-1980s is a theory consisting of six characteristics. To be an ideal victim, the victim should be: (1) weak; (2) involved in a respectful project; (3) be in a legitimate place; while the perpetrators should be (4) "big and evil"; (5) unknown to the victim, and (6) the victim should also be powerful enough to claim victim status. Therefore, according to Christies theory the ideal victim of domestic violence would be a woman (weak), a mother (respectful project), who is non-violent, no history of substance abuse and engaged in a respectable work, or a stay-at-home-mom (be in a legitim place). At the same time, her abuser is a man who commits severe violent crimes (big and evil). She also has to be strong enough to seek and claim help (powerful to claim victim status). The support system is predominantly set up to fit this profile. If the victim is not an "ideal victim", it will be much more difficult to get support. For instance, some shelters are only available for female victims and their young children. A consequence of this is that women who with a teenage son might not be welcome to stay at the shelter.

Moreover, the support services are not equipped to handle either male victims of partner violence or LGBTQIA+ victims of such violence. Not being an "ideal victim" makes it even more difficult to report the crime since they don't feel that society could offer them help or support. They also have more difficulties reporting the violence since they might not be well received, nor taken seriously.[108]

Male victims of domestic violence do not receive the same attention as female victims due to a misperception that it is rare. In reality, including less severe violence which does not demand hospital care, it is almost as common as for women. A U.S. study estimated prevalence rates of women being violent towards their male partners to range between 23% and 29%.[109] However, when it comes to the severe violence that needs medical attention, men's violence towards women is by far the most common type of domestic violence.

Domestic violence includes sexual minorities as defined by the Gender Equity Resource Centre (2019) as "members of sexual orientations that are marginalized, such as LGBTQIA+ identities". However, the scarce research on domestic violence in couples consisting of sexual minorities mainly focuses on same-sex couples, where studies show that domestic violence is as common, or even more common, in same-sex relationships. In a Nationwide survey in the U. S, results show that lesbian women are even more victimized than heterosexual women, ranging from 43% to 48%, while 26% of gay men were victimized.[110]

---

[108] Oskarsson and Strand (2021).

[109] Black et al. (2011).

[110] Kuehnle and Sullivan (2003), Peterman and Dixon (2003), Oskarsson and Strand (2021) and Pattavina et al. (2007).

14.3.2 Sexual Crimes

According to crime statistics in Europe,[111] the rate of sexual violence per hundred thousand inhabitants varied between 1.98 and 162.03 in 2009, increasing to 3.36 and 274.81 in 2018. Liechtenstein had the median value at 23.61. The countries with the highest sexual violence rates in 2018 were England and Wales, Scotland, Northern Ireland, Sweden, and Iceland, all above 158.13. The lowest rates were seen in Greece, Albania, Montenegro, and Cyprus, below 3.94. In 2018, the median rate for being a victim of rape was 0.75, varying from 0.00 to 15.18 for men. For women, the median was 8.07, varying from 1.91 to 147.63. Furthermore, the median rate for being a victim of sexual assault was 4.79 and varied from 0.19 to 25.89 for men. The median rate for women was 25.65, varying from 1.39 to 201.09.[112]

Example: The Nordic Paradox

The highest rates for rape can be found in Norway (15.18 for men and 75.78 for women), and Sweden, (10.25 for men and 147.63 for women). For sexual assault, the highest rate can be found in Sweden, for both men (25.89) and women (201.09). The gender equality index for the EU-28 is 67.9, where the highest value can be found in Sweden 83.8.[113] The Nordic paradox is somewhat contradictory; at Nordic countries, particularly Sweden, have both the highest gender equality index and the highest rates of gender-based violence, according to the crime statistics.[114] One explanation for this could be that reaching gender equality means that gender norms are put out of balance, leading to more violence by men. Another explanation could be that it reflects victims being freer to talk about gender-based violence, thereby increasing reporting. However, many of the explanations further confirm the existence of the paradox. More research is needed to find the answers to this knowledge gap.[115] ◀

[111] Official statistics from police data of 41 European countries are part of the official crime statistics Eurostat. Overall, over a 10-year period (2008–2018) crime rates of assaults, car thefts, and robbery are decreasing in society. Furthermore, intentional homicides have decreased with 30% in the EU-27 from 2008 to 2018.

[112] Crime Statistics (2021). Eurostat Database—Crime and criminal justice—Eurostat (europa.eu).

[113] EIGE (2021).

[114] Gracia and Merlo (2016).

[115] *Ibid.*

14.4 Gender Perspective in Relation to Penal Policy

It is a widespread opinion that women are treated more leniently than men by the criminal justice system. This "chivalry" approach[116] is noticeable in respect to the imposition of penal sanctions. It can also be found in criminal law, in police reaction and in the different treatments of men and women in prisons.[117] The focus in this chapter is primarily on the penal policy of the courts due to the text limit. Apart from presenting imposed penal sanctions from a European perspective, this part of the chapter analyses whether courts actually have different approaches in imposing penal sanctions on men and women.

14.4.1 Penalties and Sanctions on Women in Europe: Official Data

Relating to the first issue, it is not possible to determine a difference in the imposition of sanctions in Europe between men and women, and to its effective implementation.[118] The data available does not allow a comparative analysis, due to the differences between the regulations within the European area and the availability of information. In any event, the main sources of information on these topics are:[119] (1) The Council of Europe Annual Penal Statistics, with two reports, SPACE I, on imprisonment,[120] and SPACE II, on non-custodial sanctions and measures,[121] and (2) The European Sourcebook.[122]

According to SPACE I and II, the progression of imprisonment and non-custodial sanctions imposed on women in the European context is as follows:

(a) Concerning imprisonment, SPACE I shows that the percentages have remained stable for the last years, where 95% of the population consists of men and 5% of women. Although there are differences between countries, in 2020, Latvia had the highest rate (8.6%) within the countries with at least one million inhabitants whereas Albania had the lowest (1.8%), the under-representation of women in correctional institutions remains consistent in Europe. This stabilization of the

[116] This theory, made by Pollak in 1950, stablishes that women receive better treatment than men as an expression of the general attitude of protection from men towards women. Goethals et al. developed this idea in the 90s, proposing two specific assumptions: (1) Women receive a gentler treatment than men committing the same crime (2) Chivalry is an exclusively male feature, so this gentler treatment wouldn't take place when judges are females (Goethals et al. 1997, p. 222).

[117] Acale Sánchez (2019), pp. 1–15.

[118] Heidensohn (2012), p. 128.

[119] For a comparative with imprisoned women worldwide, see World Female Imprisonment List, made by the Institute for Criminal Policy Research (last available data from 201): https://www.prisonstudies.org/research-publications?shs_term_node_tid_depth=27.

[120] https://wp.unil.ch/space/space-i/.

[121] https://wp.unil.ch/space/space-ii/.

[122] https://wp.unil.ch/europeansourcebook/.

imprisonment rate for women in the last years has been preceded, nevertheless, by an increase in the convictions rates of women in Europe as of the year 2000. This is similar to that produced in the rest of the world, according to the last edition of the "World Female Imprisonment List" (2017).[123] In particular, from 2000 onwards, the numbers for imprisoned women worldwide increased by 53%, whereas it was just 20% during the same period for men.[124] These figures are despite the little evidence to show that female criminality has increased, in their number or seriousness.[125] This is better known as a "criminal paradox". This is a trend explained through the verification of two reasons: an increase of the judicial punitiveness against crimes committed by women; and regulatory changes to increase the minimum penalty of several crimes. Examples of the latter include changes to public health. This mainly affects female offenders,[126] and especially migrant ones.

(b) In connection with non-custodial sanctions and measures, considered by the SPACE II as sanctions under the probation agencies' responsibility, a lower level of difference it is noted between men and women, nonetheless extreme. In 2019, the average percentage of men serving a non-custodial sanction was 89%, whereas for women the figure stood at 11%. In fact, the percentage of women serving such kinds of sanctions is consistently higher, except for Greece and Serbia, than the percentage for imprisoned women (around 6% of the total imprisoned population).[127] The explanation for these differences may be related to the lesser seriousness of the offences, coupled with an estimate of a lower rate of recidivism for women. Non-custodial measures may be considered more appropriate in those conditions.

This data is consistent with the findings published in the European Sourcebook of Crime and Criminal Justice Statistics. The results include the confirmation that the percentage of imprisoned women is still low, with an average of 5%. This reflects the general trend from the first edition of this Sourcebook in 1996. In fact, the slight change in the percentage moving from 4.9% in 2011 to 5.2% in 2016 is evidence, together with a similar trend in foreign population, of the relative stability of the European prison population.

In terms of specific crimes percentages, the results show: total convictions (imprisonment and non-custodial) imposed on women was 13.8% in 2015; they were sentenced to imprisonment for intentional homicides (9.5%), 9.8% assault (9.8%); causing serious injuries (7.4%), sexual assaults in general (1.6%); rape (1%); child sexual abuse (1.5%); robbery (6.15), theft (15.8%); fraud (23.4%); cyber fraud (27.4%), document forgery (16.9%); money laundering (24.5%);

[123] Phoenix (2018), p. 185.

[124] Rope and Sheahan (2018), p. 16; Prison Reform Trust (2017).

[125] Malloch and McIvor (2012).

[126] Rope and Sheahan (2018), p. 16.

[127] Aebi et al. (2020), p. 9.

corruption offenses (12%), and drug trafficking (8.5%). The low data relating to sexual offences is expected, as is the higher concentration for crimes against property, both being similar to previous years. The representation of drug trafficking as lower than for violent crimes (both for homicides and injuries), conveys a change in those traditionally considered as women crimes. This may be due to legislative reforms in a de-criminalizing way. Therefore, the analysis shows concurrent progress for both groups of crimes, based on data from the European Institute for Crime Prevention and Control for the period 2010–2015.

Finally, the data from the European Sourcebook 2021 allows us to confirm that, at least as a general trend beyond the differences among countries, the recidivism rate is higher for men. This reflects the differences between the sexes in their criminal career; violence is more frequently associated with men and significantly less so for women.

14.4.2 Gender Differences in Sentencing

The first issue to address is related to the question around the differences made by the courts when judging crimes committed by men and women. The answer is not affirmative or negative; the research shows there are more factors to be considered, beyond gender, to explain the differences in the conviction rate for men and women in Europe, the USA, and worldwide.

The role of gender in court decisions finds a paradigmatic exponent in Grühl, Welch, and Spohn. This study concluded that adult women were treated more leniently than men; they were less likely to receive tougher penalties and imprisonment, or provisional detention as a precautionary measure. To explain this situation, they exposed several reasons:[128] (1) Judges thinking of women as individuals to be protected; (2) differences in female criminality (less violence and a lack of criminal records are among mitigating circumstances). Aggravating circumstances may include taking advantage of a victim's lack of defence and committing crimes against life in the intimate environment, and (3) the presence of other factors like race-based discrimination that would have an indirect impact on the sentence. These assumptions alone are unable to explain the complexity of these differences. Nevertheless, it provides a working basis for a research area that still produces g relevant knowledge, to ensure equal legal treatment by the criminal system.

In view of this complexity, the section presents the main conclusions to this respect by presenting differences based on the initial focus of each research, the comparative variables, and the explanation to interpret the results. Regarding the approaches, it is possible to make the main distinction, between whether a perspective is based on generalized court chivalry or on a critical perspective. It is therefore

[128] Gruhl et al. (1984), pp. 464–467.

possible to show the criminal decision as a reflection of gender stereotypes in the society, especially those ones that directly affects family relationships.[129]

Various researches attempt to explain benevolent treatment received by female offenders, in the understanding that this is a common situation. Reference can be made to studies analysing the influence of gender and race in homicide sentencing in the USA. It has been found that men, youth, and repeat offenders are imprisoned for longer periods in cases of homicides.[130] More recently, Leiber and Peck proved that women are 25% less likely proceed to the next stage of criminal procedure (court) than men.[131] However, the possibility of receiving an advantage in terms of dismissal is related mainly to misdemeanours. Otherwise, some researchers conclude that women are more likely to receive a non-custodial sentence. Although, when women are sentenced to imprisonment, they have the same length probability as men.[132] The results of these researchers, whose main thrust is to prove the influence of gender in the criminal response and the presumption of a general "gentlemanly and paternalistic treatment" to female offenders, could be systematized according to the knowledge they bring regarding other gender adjuvants factors. These are promoters of differences in sentencing:

Gender and race: there are a wide variety of studies on race and gender as determinants of the criminal response. These have produced different results, although the majority conclude that Black women are more likely to receive a longer penalty than Caucasian and Hispanic ones,[133] and more likely than Caucasians to be sentenced to imprisonment.[134] Regarding the effective completion of the imprisonment, Black women serve a lower percentage of the penalty imposed than Black men, however still higher than white and Hispanic women.[135]

Age: several studies confirm that women in higher age groups are more likely to receive an imprisonment penalty.[136] Nevertheless, other researchers claim just the opposite; better conditions for younger women are related to the most common use of parole, whereas the probability of being punished with this penalty, rather than none, is higher than for older women.[137]

Level of education and employment: some researchers have found that women with a higher level of education are more likely to receive an imprisonment sen-

---

[129] In this last sense see Daly (1987), pp. 154–155.

[130] Franklin and Fearn (2008), p. 285.

[131] Leiber and Peck (2015), p. 784.

[132] Freiburger and Hilinski (2013), pp. 75–79.

[133] Albonetti (2002), pp. 39–60. In the opposite direction, Demuth and Doerner (2014), p. 261.

[134] Spohn and Beichner (2000), pp. 167–169; Goulette et al. (2015), p. 412.

[135] Bradley and Engen (2016), p. 269.

[136] Spohn and Beichner (2000), p. 173.

[137] Freiburger and Hilinski (2013), pp. 69–71.

tence,[138] whereas others have shown just the opposite.[139] The same applies to employment.

Criminal Records: some studies show that women with criminal records are more likely to be condemned. This factor is also crucial to decide the severity and length of the penalty.[140]

Type of crime committed: several researchers have focused their attention on proving the relation between criminal response against women and type of crime, not on a gender roles basis, but in the gentle treatment female offenders receive generally. Among these studies, it can be found that those focused on proving the reaction against drug-related crimes committed by women. In this area, some researchers expose that although women are not judged more severely than men, they are more likely to receive an imprisonment penalty in those cases.[141] This result partly contradicts the results in other studies that showed more beneficial treatment for women involved in crimes against property or drug-related crimes, whilst they are more likely to receive severe treatment than men when they were involved in violent crimes.[142] Regarding serious offences, the latest research seems to confirm the initial scenario of better treatment to female offenders. For instance, these are the results of a study where penalties for men and women who were perpetrators of multiple homicides and were compared. This research would reject: (a) better treatment for women was based on the relationship dynamics between perpetrators, giving women a passive role in the shadow of man; and (b) gender and criminal records as the most influential factor for most severe penalties.[143] This is the conclusion reached by other studies focused on the treatment of sexual female offenders, however this infringes social stereotypes related to women in the sexual area and in the caring function, especially when regarding child victims. In particular, sexual male offenders receive tougher penalties than women. This creates assumptions that women receive special court protection, regardless of the social and gender rules violated when committing those crimes.[144] These results are confirmed by similar studies questioning the myth of the "evil woman", even though sexual crimes are perceived as typically male crimes and far removed from female sexuality stereotypes.[145]

In addition to these results, the intersectional approach suggests taking into consideration the influence of all these factors in terms of vulnerability and inequality. This requires to include legal variables to explain most of the changes in the enforcement of judgments and the valuation of concurrent circumstances during the

[138] Freiburger (2011), pp. 143–167.

[139] Brennan (2006), p. 86.

[140] Demuth and Doerner (2014), p. 257.

[141] Freiburger (2010), p. 388.

[142] Rodriguez et al. (2006), p. 335.

[143] Fridel (2019), p. 333.

[144] Embry and Lyons (2012), pp. 157–158.

[145] Deering and Mellor (2009), pp. 409 ff.; Hassett-Walker et al. (2014), pp. 80–81.

resocialization process.[146] This approach means a questioning of gender perspective in the explanation of violence against women[147]; this explanation analysed a single axis of inequality that, at best, added some individual variables (such as age, race, or education level) and behavioural aspects (criminal records, type of crime) out of context. Intersectional perspective highlights two main risks of this gender-based analytic structure: invisibility of differences between individual and structural features of people expressing conditions different from heteronormativity and (dis)-ability; and the failure to question the idea that these differences could have different analytic values in different moments (mainly due to law changes and to personal and affective circumstances in each rehabilitation process).

Studies consider criminal court systems as a gender institution whose actions reproduce and perpetuate gender inequalities, reflecting traditional thoughts on how to treat men and women. In this understanding, some authors stated that women could receive tougher treatment, regardless of the crime they committed, simply because they were violating gender rules. Nowadays, this theory, better known as "evil woman theory" or "selective chivalry",[148] poses that gentle treatment would only act upon behaviours linked to female social roles. In contrast, the penalty would increase in those crimes that violate female gender roles, double deviance,[149] perceived as "male crimes".[150] Nevertheless, it is important to qualify this statement by focusing, not just on the nature of crime, more or less linked to gender roles, but on the existence of a specific context of group, or family framework, to reproduce the disparities of the patriarchal order. This is the idea highlighted by: studies addressing the influence on children or dependent people; studies on crimes meaning a double deviation based on gender stereotypes; references to a gender-based assessment of culpability capacity, and the latest developments on the influence of gender equality in the enforcement of sentences.

Dependent children: results on this differ. Various studies[151] proved that mothers are more likely to receive longer penalties or imprisonment. Whereas the majority of studies noted just the opposite.[152] A common explanation is that better treatment underlies that idea of family protection and the traditional role of women in the family; the caretaker, protector, and facilitator of the children's education. The seriousness of the penalty seems to be linked to a failure in their caregiver role[153] and to the prediction of negative consequences for children and dependent people

---

[146] Gaub and Holtfreter (2015), pp. 306 ff.

[147] Sokoloff and Dupont (2005), pp. 38–41; Nixon and Humphreys (2010), p. 139.

[148] The evil woman hypothesis would assume women are sentenced more harshly than men for offenses which reflects a severe departure from gender roles, Embry and Lyons (2012), pp. 148–149.

[149] Heidensohn (1985).

[150] Rodriguez et al. (2006), p. 332.

[151] Brennan (2006), p. 86; Griffin and Wooldredge (2006), pp. 914–915.

[152] Spohn and Beichner (2000), p. 173; Koons-Witt (2002), pp. 313, 317; Daly (1987), pp. 167–168.

[153] Freiburger (2010), pp. 387–388.

derived from custodial sentences.[154] However, taking into consideration family responsibilities is a protective factor for both men and women. This hypothesis is apparently confirmed by a further study, where paternity and maternity had no effect on the length of the sentence compared to people with no children. It did reveal, nonetheless, different effects in the penalty depending on gender-based parental models. In particular, mothers living with their children prior to arrest were more likely to receive a more lenient sentence, whereas this feature, or the involvement in family duties, does not correlate in the same way for men.[155] Higher penalties imposed on mothers seem to depend on the type of crime committed, in terms of violating or not the social gender roles; courts perceive these kinds of behaviours as a risk for their children and dependents.[156]

Crime is considered as double-gender deviance: although some studies have revealed better treatment for female offenders in serious crimes, not relating to female criminality, it is also true that in specific crimes, a tougher treatment for female offenders has been witnessed, for example domestic crimes with a woman as victim,[157] partner violence with a man as the victim[158] and violent sexual crimes. Regarding the last, an emotional perspective has been found in the facts narrative when compared to the same crimes committed by men, promoting the idea of the women as a villain and unfeminine.[159]

Assessment of guilt in female offenders: studies related to the interpretation of female crime highlight female offenders are seen as victims of their own past, context, and destiny.[160] Consequently, they are likely to be diagnosed as mentally disturbed.[161] It is therefore common to find mitigating circumstances: passive and assistance involvement during when more than one person commits the crime[162]; greater willingness to collaborate with the clarification of the facts, and more possibilities of regret.

Influence of structural gender equality: although researchers in this area have highlighted that this influence is minimal in explaining the individual sentences, some structural variables revealed significant effects, both for men and women. This is the case for countries with higher female participation in the work area; this is related to a reduction in punitiveness. Correspondingly, those countries with a higher proportion of women with university degrees are more likely to impose a custodial sentence.[163]

[154] Koons-Witt (2002), p. 306.
[155] Tasca et al. (2019), p. 1911.
[156] Hagan and Nagel (1983), pp. 116–117.
[157] Romain and Freiburger (2016), p. 207.
[158] Franklin and Fearn (2008), p. 282.
[159] Damiris et al. (2020), pp. 9–10, 12.
[160] O'Hara (1998), pp. 91–92.
[161] Allen (1987).
[162] Crew (1991), p. 72.
[163] Nowacki (2019), p. 15.

This overview of different approaches and research aimed to verify gender-based differences in sentencing, allowing us to confirm the need to contextualize different variables under family or group criteria in playing a role in the understanding of women's crimes, as well as the tendency to read this context from patriarchal stereotypes and asymmetries.

In addition, it is necessary to highlight that the tools implemented to reach more judicial impartiality, Sentencing Guidelines,[164] do not seem to have eliminated those differences. This verifies the existence of an unavoidable scope of discretion in every interpretative process, that could be influenced not just by stereotypes and personal views, but also by judges' feelings, thoughts, and reasoning.

14.4.3 Features in Criminal Treatment of Trans Offenders

Transgender people are overrepresented in the criminal system; in the USA, ex-convict transgender women represent 21%, trans people, genderqueer people or transgender men represent 10%. Their proportion in the rest of the adult population is only 5%.[165] The explanation of this is mainly based on: (1) increased social vulnerability, as a consequence of family rejection, bullying, and discrimination in different life areas such as employment, housing, identity documents, and social welfare; and (2) direct or indirect criminalization of this community.[166] An obvious example of this last aspect could be found in the sexual work field, which is usually performed by racialized trans women.

Usually, the treatment during trial is not appropriate: they are often denied to be named as they would like; their guilt is attempted to be linked to "ambiguity" based on their identity, and they find special challenges to have a specialized legal defence. This increases the possibilities of pre-trial detention and a tougher punishment (Lambda Legal's Survey). The highest probability of getting a tougher penalty as sex offenders is also documented.[167] Unfortunately, the research on this is extremely low. It is therefore necessary to frame specific studies to assess their extension, and depth in the criminal justice system, to enforce additional protective tools.[168]

During imprisonment,[169] trans people are subjected to high-risk conditions: being victims of harassment; sexual assault; health challenges, and lack of respect in their daily life. This results in an important hardening of physical and psychological

[164] A detailed explanation of the implementation of neutral guidelines in the judicial area in order to avoid preferential or discriminatory treatment of offenders based on race, social status and specially gender, could be found in Nagel and Johnson (1994), pp. 190–197.

[165] Center of American Progress and Movement Advancement Project (2016).

[166] Grant et al. (2011), pp. 158 ff.

[167] Mogul et al. (2011).

[168] Ryan (2016): www.lag.org.uk.

[169] Bassichis (2007), p. 35.

effects; in many instances, the custodial sentence is served in isolation to ensure safety.[170]

14.5 Conclusion

Traditional explanations of crime have not taken into account the role of gender. Feminist approaches in criminology have made great contributions in respect to gender issues. Firstly, they tried and succeeded in moving from the "androcentric" positions within criminological thought, in order to include women as victims, offenders and employees in the criminal justice system. Before feminists works, crimes such as domestic violence and sexual harassment have been neglected and treated as a private matter. Feminists have also contributed in the development of research methodology that focused on qualitative approach, as more appropriate in respect to female victims. After the inclusion of women as another sex in criminology, feminists continued their efforts by paying more attention to different categories of women and acknowledging that not all women suffer the same experiences. This means that women of colour, indigenous and migrant women should also be included in research. Further developments went beyond simplistic division between sexes and instead focused on theorizing of gender (Chesney-Lind)[171] and promoting an intersectional approach, in which gender represents just one level of oppression. The twenty-first century is characterized by backlash politics which posits women as violent as men and that juvenile girls are becoming increasingly violent. This is supported by a more punitive approach of formal social control toward women, as well as by moral panics in societies. Feminists criticize this situation and assert that women are not becoming more violent; the increase of reported and convicted women is the consequence of changed policies. However, analysis of data for European countries for reported and convicted persons shows great differences between countries in respect to the share of women offenders. It is further observable that the higher percentage of women offenders is related to certain criminal offences such as fraud. In contrast, women are far less reported or convicted of homicide. In order to explain these differences, beside classical criminological theories, gender oriented theoretical approach is necessary and useful. It is this perspective that emphasized the importance of intersection of criminalization and victimization in many cases, of which domestic violence is an example. This does not mean that all female offenders have experienced victimization. Many of them opt for criminal behaviour for other reasons, profit is just one among many motives. In contrast, males are also victims of domestic violence, however they have been neglected as victims in literature. Gay couples also report domestic violence, and so it is obvious that we must go beyond traditional views of male offenders and female victims.

[170] Lydon et al. (2015): https://www.blackandpink.org/wp-content/uploads/2020/03/Coming-Out-of-Concrete-Closets-incorcporated-Executive-summary102115.pdf.

[171] Chesney-Lind (2006), p. 8.

Contrary to other regions, Europe shows general stability in respect to the percentage of females sentenced to imprisonment. Of course, there are differences between countries and between criminal offences. This illustrates the need to interpret crime, victimization, and penal policy in every country in correlation to the general picture. Relating to sanction policy, the text has pointed to the existence of the main controversy over the general treatment (favourable or unfavourable) female offenders receive on a gender basis. This issue is not to be solved under just one perspective, with the data available at present. It requires a different approach based on the type of crime and other variables; race, ethnic minority group, criminal records, and children or dependents. These variables, jointly with gender, seem to significantly influence the punishment the offender is going to receive. In addition, overrepresentation of trans-inmates in the criminal execution system has been revealed, together with a discriminatory and biased treatment during the sentencing process. At this point, it is important to highlight the lack of research on this specific topic; providing no possibility for detailed and concluding knowledge.

Questions

1. How would you explain different crime rates of sexes between European countries?
2. In what ways can formal social control affect fluctuations in women's crime?
3. How would you explain the larger involvement of women in the commission of certain criminal offences such as fraud, theft, and bodily injury?
4. What are possible explanations of lower participation of women in crime?
5. To what extent could theories of masculinity explain the overrepresentation of men in criminal behaviour?
6. How can the suppression of domestic violence influence the crime of women and men?
7. In which ways criminalization and victimization of women intersect?
8. Has any relevant change referred to gender occurred over the last few years in applying penalties? If the answer is yes, please point out which one.
9. Which are the main approaches to explain the gender-based difference of treatment for offenders by criminal institutions?
10. Is there any special feature on the criminal treatment trans-people receive by criminal justice?

References

Acale Sánchez M (2019) Penal and custodial control of female criminality in Spain from a gender perspective. Soc Sci 52:1–15

Aebi M, Hashimoto YZ, Tiago MM (2020) Probation and prisons in Europe, 2019: key findings of the SPACE reports. Council of Europe, Strasbourg

Aebi M et al (2021) European Sourcebook of Crime and Criminal Justice Statistics 2021, 6th edn. https://wp.unil.ch/europeansourcebook/printed-editions-2/6th-edition/. Accessed 12 Nov 2021

Agha S (2009) Structural correlates of female homicide: a cross-national analysis. J Crim Just 37: 576–585

Albonetti C (2002) Gender and ethnicity on length of imprisonment under the federal sentencing guidelines for drug trafficking/manufacturing offenders. J Gend Race Just 39:39–60

Allen H (1987) Justice unbalanced: gender, psychiatry and judicial decisions. Open University Press, Milton Keynes

Asscher JJ, Van der Put CE, Stams GJJM (2015) Gender differences in the impact of abuse and neglect victimization on adolescent offending behavior. J Fam Violence 30:215–225

Barak G, Leighton P, Flavin J (2010) Class, race, gender and crime, the social realities of justice in America. Rowman & Littlefield Publishers, Inc, Lanham

Bassichis MD (2007) 'It's War in Here': a report on the treatment of transgender and intersex people in New York State men's prisons. Sylvia Rivera Law Project, New York

Belfrage H, Strand S (2012) Measuring the outcome of structured spousal violence risk assessments using the B-SAFER: risk in relation to recidivism and intervention. Behav Sci Law 30(4): 420–430. https://doi.org/10.1002/bsl.2019

Belknap J, Holsinger K (2006) The gendered nature of risk factors for delinquency. Fem Criminol 1:48–71

Bernard A (2013) The intersectional alternative: explaining female criminality. Fem Criminol 8:3–19

Black MC, Basile KC, Breiding MJ, Smith SG, Walters ML, Merrick MT et al (2011) The national intimate partner and sexual violence survey (NISVS): 2010 Summary report. Atlanta

Blanchette K, Brown SL (2006) The assessment and treatment of women offenders. Wiley, Chichester

Bradley MS, Engen RL (2016) Leaving prison: a multilevel investigation of racial, ethnic, and gender disproportionality in correctional release. Crime Delinq 62:253–279

Brennan P (2006) Sentencing female misdemeanants: an examination of the direct and indirect effects of race/ethnicity. Justice Q 23:60–95

Britton DM (2000) Feminism in criminology: engendering the outlaw. Ann Am Acad Pol Soc Sci 571:57–76

Britton DM (2011) The gender of crime. Rowman & Littlefield Publishers, Inc, Lanham

Burgess-Proctor A (2006) Intersections of race, class, gender and crime, future directions for feminist criminology. Fem Criminol 1:27–47

Burman M (2004) Breaking the mould. Patterns of female offending. In: McIvor G (ed) Women who offend. Jessica Kingsley Publishers, London, pp 38–65

Cauffman E (2008) Understanding the female offender. Futur Child 18:11–42

Center of American Progress and Movement Advancement Project (2016) UNJUST: how the broken criminal justice system fails transgender people. https://www.lgbtmap.org/policy-and-issue-analysis/criminal-justice-trans. Accessed 12 Nov 2021

Chernoff N, Simon RJ (2000) Women and crime the world over. Gend Issues:5–20

Chesney-Lind M (1987) Girls and violence, an exploration of the gender gap in serious delinquent behavior. In: Crowell DH, Evans IM, O'Donell CR (eds) Childhood aggression and violence, sources of influence, prevention and control. Plenum Press, New York, pp 207–230

Chesney-Lind M (2006) Patriarchy, crime and justice, feminist criminology in an era of backlash. Fem Criminol 1:6–26

Chesney-Lind M, Shelden RG (2014) Delinquency and juvenile justice. Wiley Blackwell, Chichester

Chu DC, Hebenton B, Toh A (2021) Gender equality and female offending: evidence from international data sources. Int J Offender Ther Comp Criminol 65:1–24

Crew KB (1991) Sex differences in criminal sentencing: chivalry or patriarchy? Justice Q 8:59–83

Dalton K (1961) Menstruation and crime. Br Med J 30:1752–1753
Daly K (1987) Discrimination in the criminal courts: family, gender, and the problem of equal treatment. Soc Forces 66:152–175
Daly K (1992) Women's pathways to felony court: Feminist theories of lawbreaking and problems of representation. S Calif Rev Law Women's Stud 2:11–52
Damiris IK, McKillop N, Christensen LS, Rayment-McHugh S, Burton K, Patterson T (2020) Gendered judicial discourse in the sentencing of sexual offenders: a new explanatory model. Curr Issues Crim Just:1–20
Deering R, Mellor D (2009) Sentencing of male and female child sex offenders: Australian study. Psychiatry Psychol Law 16:394–412
Demuth S, Doerner J (2014) Gender and sentencing in the federal courts: are women treated more leniently? Crim Justice Policy Rev 25:242–269
Dixon L, Browne K (2003) The heterogeneity of spouse abuse: a review. Aggress Violent Behav 8(1):107–130. https://doi.org/10.1016/S1359-1789(02)00104-0
Dobash RP, Dobash RE (2004) Women's violence to men in intimate relationships. Br J Criminol 44:324–349
Doerner WG, Lab SP (2012) Victimology. Elsevier, Amsterdam
EIGE (2021). What is gender-based violence? https://eige.europa.eu/gender-based-violence/what-is-gender-based-violence. Accessed 12 Nov 2021
Embry R, Lyons PM (2012) Sex-based sentencing: sentencing discrepancies between male and female sex offenders. Fem Criminol 7:146–162
Franklin C, Fearn N (2008) Gender, race, and formal court decision-making outcomes: chivalry/paternalism conflict theory or gender conflict? J Crim Just 36:279–290
Freiburger T (2010) The effects of gender, family status, and race on sentencing decisions. Behav Sci Law 28:378–395
Freiburger T (2011) The impact of gender, offense type, and family role on the decision to incarcerate. Soc Justice Res 24:143–167
Freiburger T, Hilinski C (2013) An examination of the interactions of race and gender on sentencing decisions using a trichotomous dependent variable. Crime Delinq 59:59–86
Fridel E (2019) Leniency for lethal ladies: using the actor–partner interdependence model to examine gender-based sentencing disparities. Homicide Stud 23:319–343
Gartner R, Jung M (2014) Sex, gender and homicide, contemporary trends and patterns. In: Gartner R, McCarthy B (eds) The Oxford handbook of gender, sex and crime. Oxford University Press, Oxford, pp 424–447
Gaub J, Holtfreter K (2015) New directions in intersections, inequality, and sentencing. Women Crim Just 25:298–312
Gehring KS (2018) A direct test of pathways theory. Fem Criminol 13:115–137
Gelsthorpe L (2004) Female offending, a theoretical overview. In: McIvor G (ed) Women who offend. Jessica Kingsley Publishers, London, pp 13–37
Gelsthorpe L, Larrauri E (2014) Gender and crime in Europe. In: Body-Gendrot S, Hough M et al (eds) The Routledge handbook of European criminology. Routledge, London, pp 188–203
Goethals J, Maes E, Klinckhamers P (1997) Sex/gender-based decision-making in the criminal justice system as a possible (additional) explanation for the underrepresentation of women in official criminal statistics – a review of international literature. Int J Comp Appl Crim Just 21: 207–240
Goldstein DA, Cantos AL, Brenner LH, Verborg RJ, Kosson DS (2016) Perpetrator type moderates the relationship between severity of intimate partner violence and recidivism. Crim Just Behav 43(7):879–898. https://doi.org/10.1177/0093854815616841
Goldweber A, Broidy LM, Cauffman E (2009) Interdisciplinary perspectives on persistent female offending: a review of theory and research. In: Savage J (ed) The development of persistent criminality. Oxford University Press, Oxford, pp 205–230

Goulette N, Wooldredge J, Frank J, Travis L III (2015) From initial appearance to sentencing: do female defendants experience disparate treatment? J Crim Just 43:406–417
Gracia E, Merlo J (2016) Intimate partner violence against women and the Nordic paradox. Soc Sci Med 157:27–30
Grant JM, Mottet LA, Tanis J (2011) Injustice at every turn: a report of the national transgender discrimination survey. National Center for Transgender Equality and National Gay and Lesbian Task Force, Washington
Griffin T, Wooldredge J (2006) Sex based disparities in felony dispositions before versus after sentencing reform in Ohio. Criminology 44:893–923
Gruhl J, Welch S, Spohn C (1984) Women as criminal defendants: a test for paternalism. Polit Res Q 37:456–467
Hagan J, Nagel I (1983) Gender and crime: offense patterns and criminal court sanctions. Univ Chic Press J 4:91–144
Hassett-Walker C, Lateano T, di Benedetto M (2014) Do female sex offenders receive preferential treatment in criminal charging and sentencing? Just Syst J 35:62–86
Hawkins Anderson S (2012) Girls in the juvenile justice system: the causes and correlates of girls' involvement. In: Miller S, Leve LD, Kerig PK (eds) Delinquent girls, contexts, relationships and adaptation. Springer, New York, pp 41–54
Hedderman C (2004) The 'Criminogenic' needs of women offenders. In: McIvor G (ed) Women who offend. Jessica Kingsley Publishers, London, pp 82–98
Heidensohn F (1985) Women and crime. Macmillan, London
Heidensohn F (1991) Women and crime in Europe. In: Heidensohn F, Farrell M (eds) Crime in Europe. Routledge, London, pp 55–71
Heidensohn F (2012) The future of feminist criminology. Crime Media Cult 8:123–134
Heidensohn F, Silvestri M (2012) Gender and crime. In: Maguire M, Morgan R, Reiner R (eds) The Oxford handbook of criminology. Oxford University Press, Oxford, pp 336–369
Heimer K, De Coster S (2011) The gendering of violent delinquency. In: Cullen FT, Agnew R (eds) Criminological theory: past to present, essential readings. Oxford University Press, Oxford, pp 348–356
Hilinski-Rosick CM (2016) The cycle of intimate partner violence. In: Freiburger TL, Marcum CD (eds) Women in the criminal justice system, tracking the journey of females and crime. CRC Press, Boca Raton, pp 47–66
Hilliard T, Neidermeyer PE (2018) The gendering of fraud: an international investigation. J Financ Crime 25:811–837
Holtfreter K (2014) White-collar and corporate crime. In: Gartner R, McCarthy B (eds) The Oxford handbook of gender, sex and crime. Oxford University Press, Oxford, pp 490–507
Hunnicut G, Broidy LM (2004) Liberation and economic marginalization: a reformulation and test of (formerly?) Competing models. J Res Crime Delinq 41:130–155
Jones DW (2008) Understanding criminal behaviour, psychosocial approach to criminality. Routledge, London
Klein D (2009) Etiologija kriminaliteta žena. In: Ignjatović Đ (ed) Teorije u kriminologiji. Pravni fakultet Univerziteta u Beogradu, Beograd, pp 372–387
Koons-Witt B (2002) The effect of gender on the decision to incarcerate before and after the introduction of sentencing guidelines. Criminology 40:297–327
Korkmaz S (2021) Youth intimate partner violence. In: Devaney J et al (eds) The Routledge international handbook of domestic violence and abuse. Routledge, New York, pp 155–170
Kuehnle K, Sullivan A (2003) Gay and lesbian victimization: reporting factors in domestic violence and bias incidents. Crim Justice Behav 30:85–96
Leiber MJ, Peck JH (2015) Race, gender, crime severity, and decision making in the juvenile justice system. Crime Delinq 61:771–797
Loinaz I (2014) Typologies, risk and recidivism in partner-violent men with the B-SAFER: a pilot study. Psychol Crime Law 20(2):183–198. https://doi.org/10.1080/1068316X.2013.770854

Lukić N (2019a) Nasilnički kriminalitet žena. In: Ignjatović Đ (ed) Kaznena reakcija u Srbiji, IX deo. Pravni fakultet Univerziteta u Beogradu, Beograd, pp 327–348
Lukić N (2019b) Kriminalitet maloletnica u Beogradu – studija o identifikaciji podgrupa. Crim 3: 257–277
Lydon J, Carrington K et al (2015) Coming out of concrete closets: a report on Black & Pink's National LGBTQ Prisoner Survey. Black and Pink, Dorchester
Lynch MJ (2016) Class, race, gender and criminology: structured choices and the life course. In: Milovanovic D, Schwartz MD (eds) Race, gender and class in criminology. Routledge, London, pp 3–28
Lysova A (2014) The level and dynamics of female crime in Russia. Sociol Res 53:3–12
Males M (2010) Have girls gone wild? In: Chesney-Lind M, Jones N (eds) Fighting for girls, new perspectives on gender and violence. State University of New York Press, Albany, pp 13–32
Malloch M, McIvor G (2012) Women, punishment and social justice: human rights and penal practices. Routledge Frontiers of Criminal Justice, London
Marcus-Mendoza S (2016) Incarcerated women in the United States. In: Freiburger TL, Marcum CD (eds) Women in the criminal justice system, tracking the journey of females and crime. CRC Press, Boca Raton, pp 209–222
Marsh I et al (2006) Theories of crime. Routledge, New York
Messerschmidt JW (2009) Muškost i teorijska kriminologija. In: Ignjatović Đ (ed) Teorije u kriminologiji. Pravni fakultet Univerziteta u Beogradu, Beograd, pp 435–438
Messerschmidt JW (2011) Masculinities and crime. In: Cullen FT, Agnew R (eds) Criminological theory: past to present. Oxford University Press, Oxford, pp 357–368
Miller J (2014) Doing crime as doing gender, masculinities, femininities and crime. In: Gartner R, McCarthy B (eds) The Oxford handbook of gender, sex and crime. Oxford University Press, Oxford, pp 19–39
Moffit TE et al (2004) Sex differences in antisocial behaviour, conduct disorder, delinquency and violence in the Dunedin Longitudinal Study. Cambridge University Press, Cambridge
Mogul JL, Richie A, Whitlock K (2011) Queer (in)justice: the criminalization of LGBT people in the United States. Beacon Press, Boston
Naffin N (2016) Theorizing about female crime. In: Mukherjee SK, Scutt JA (eds) Women and crime. Routledge, New York, pp 70–91
Nagel IH, Johnson BL (1994) The role of gender in a structured sentencing system: equal treatment, policy choices, and the sentencing of female offenders under the United States sentencing guidelines. J Crim Law Criminol 85:181–221
Nixon J, Humphreys C (2010) Marshalling the evidence: using intersectionality in the domestic violence frame. Soc Polit 17:137–158
Nowacki JS (2019) Gender equality and sentencing outcomes: an examination of state courts. Crim Justice Policy Rev: 1–23
O'Hara CL (1998) Children without childhood: a feminist intervention strategy utilizing systems theory and restorative justice in treating female adolescent offenders. Women Ther 20:85–101
Oskarsson S, Strand S (2021) Police perceptions of victims of intimate partner violence in same-sex relationships. In: Shackelford TK (ed) The SAGE handbook of domestic violence. SAGE, London, pp 352–367
Pattavina A, Hirschel D, Buzawa E, Faggiani D, Bentley H (2007) A comparison of the police response to heterosexual versus same-sex intimate partner violence. Violence Against Women 13:374–394
Peterman LM, Dixon CG (2003) Domestic violence between same-sex partners: implications for counseling. J Couns Dev 81:40–47
Petersson J, Strand SJM (2020) Family-only perpetrators of intimate partner violence: a systematic review. Trauma Violence Abuse 21(2):367–381. https://doi.org/10.1177/1524838018770410

Petersson J (2020) Identifying risk for recidivism among partner violent men reported to the Swedish police. Mid Sweden University, Sundsvall

Phoenix O (2018) Introducing a gender-sensitive approach to pre-trial assessment and probation: evaluation of an innovation in Kenya. Prob J. J Community Crim Just 65:184–200

Portnoy J et al (2014) Biological perspectives on sex differences in crime and antisocial behaviour. In: Gartner R, McCarthy B (eds) The Oxford handbook of gender, sex and crime. Oxford University Press, Oxford, pp 260–285

Prison Reform Trust (2017) Why focus on reducing women's imprisonment? Publications Prison Reform Trust, London

Putkonen H et al (2011) Gender differences in homicide offender's criminal career, substance abuse and mental health care. A nationwide register-based study of Finnish homicide offenders. Crim Behav Ment Health 21:51–62

Reckdenwald A, Parker KF (2008) The influence of gender inequality and marginalization on types of female offending. Homicide Stud 12:208–226

Robertson CB, Burton DL (2010) An exploration of differences in childhood maltreatment between violent and non-violent male delinquents. J Child Adolesc Trauma 3:319–329

Rodriguez F, Curry T, Lee G (2006) Gender differences in criminal sentencing: do effects vary across violent, property, and drug offenses? Soc Sci Q 87:318–339

Romain DM, Freiburger TL (2016) Chivalry revisited: gender, race/ethnicity, and offense type on domestic violence charge reduction. Fem Criminol 11:191–222

Rope O, Sheahan F (2018) Global prison trends. Penal Reform International and Thailand Institute of Justice, London and Bangkok

Russell T et al (2020) A gendered-comparative exploration of women's and men's pathways to prison in Thailand. Aust N Z J Criminol 53:536–562

Ryan J (2016) Transgender issues in the criminal justice system. https://www.lag.org.uk/article/202050/transgender-issues-in-the-criminal-justice-system. Accessed 12 Nov 2021

Schwartz J (2013) A "New" female offender or increasing social control of women's behaviour? Cross-national evidence. Fem Stud 39:809–810

Siegel LJ, Welsh BC (2011) Juvenile delinquency, the core. Wadsworth, Cengage Learning, Belmont

Simpson S (1989) Feminist theory, crime and justice. Criminology 27:605–631

Smart C (1995) Law, crime and sexuality, essays in feminism. Sage, London

Sokoloff NJ, Dupont I (2005) Domestic violence at the intersections of race, class, and gender. Violence Against Women 11:38–64

Spohn C, Beichner D (2000) Is preferential treatment of female offenders a thing of the past? A multisite study of gender, race, and imprisonment. Crim Justice Policy Rev 11:149–184

Steffensmeier D et al (2006) Gender gap trends for violent crimes, 1980 to 2003. Fem Criminol 1: 72–98

Sutherland EH, Cressey DR (1978) Criminology. J.B. Lippincott Company, Philadelphia

Sylvers P et al (2009) Biological factors and the development of persistent criminality. In: Savage J (ed) The development of persistent criminality. Oxford University Press, Oxford, pp 141–162

Tasca M, Cho A, Spohn C, Rodriguez N (2019) The role of parental status and involvement in sentence length decisions: a comparison of men and women sentenced to prison. Crime Delinq 65:1899–1924

Thijssen J, de Ruiter C (2011) Identifying subtypes of spousal assaulters using the B-SAFER. J Interpers Violence 26(7):1307–1321

Tran TD, Nguyen H, Fisher J (2016) Attitudes towards intimate partner violence against women among women and men in 39 low- and middle-income countries. PLoS One 11(11). https://doi.org/10.1371/journal.pone.0167438

Wang T (2021) Mismatched liberation theory: a comparative method to explain increasing female crime share in the United Sates. Fem Criminol:1–36

Williams SL, McKelvey DK, Frieze HI (2014) Intimate-partner violence. In: Gartner R, McCarthy B (eds) The Oxford handbook of gender, sex and crime. Oxford University Press, Oxford, pp 362–378

World Health Organization (2021) Violence against women prevalence estimates, 2018. World Health Organization, Geneva

Part III

Gender in a Private Context

Gender Equality in the Different Fields of Private Law

15

Amalia Blandino, Gabriele Carapezza Figlia, Letizia Coppo, Snežana Dabić Nikićević, and Katarina Dolović Bojić

Contents

Authors are listed in alphabetical order. Amalia Blandino authored Sect. 15.4, Letizia Coppo and Gabriele Carapezza Figlia authored Sect. 15.3. Sections 15.1, 15.2 and 15.5 are written by Snežana Dabić Nikićević and Katarina Dolović Bojić.

A. Blandino (✉)
University of Cadiz, Faculty of Law, Private Law, Cadiz, Spain
e-mail: amalia.blandino@uca.es

G. Carapezza Figlia · L. Coppo
LUMSA, Faculty of Law, Palermo, Italy
e-mail: g.carapezzafiglia@lumsa.it; letizia.coppo@unito.it

S. Dabić Nikićević · K. Dolović Bojić
University of Belgrade, Faculty of Law, Civil Law, Belgrade, Serbia
e-mail: snezana.dabic@ius.bg.ac.rs; k.dolovic@ius.bg.ac.rs

D. Vujadinović et al. (eds.), *Gender-Competent Legal Education*, Springer Textbooks in Law, https://doi.org/10.1007/978-3-031-14360-1_15

Abstract

In the field of private law, gender inequality takes many different shapes. It may at times be easily noticed from the text of the legal rules, for instance, when certain legal rights are reserved for members of a certain gender (i.e. independency to enter a marriage) or when they are available to both genders but in a discriminatory manner (i.e. men inherit twice as much as women). However, in many legal systems equality is guaranteed by law, but inequality still appears in practice. This may be seen from the fact that, on average, land assets are much more often owned by men or that a higher percentage of men run a business. Various social factors may induce gender inequality, like stereotypical division of gender roles in society (i.e. men as breadwinners and women as caregivers) or the persistence of patriarchal customs and practices (i.e. women should renounce their inheritance rights in favour of male inheritors). The consequences of such factors may also be felt in the field of tort law, especially when it comes to damages suffered by women performing unpaid domestic work or indirect damages suffered by women who have to provide the "informal support" for the person who suffered serious bodily harm that resulted in a situation of dependency. Finally, in the field of contract law, the most difficult tasks seem to be to reconcile the prohibition of discrimination with the freedom of contract and to determine the most suitable legal consequence in case of discrimination.

15.1 Introduction

Despite the evolution of human awareness and the efforts made to prevent gender discrimination, especially in the last few decades, in the field of private law we may still encounter numerous examples of gender inequality. It appears in many different shapes. Sometimes gender inequality is quite obvious: when certain legal rights, such as inheritance rights, are regulated in such a manner which leads to a direct discrimination on the basis of gender. Sometimes the traces of discrimination may be seen from the very language used by the legal system: like the standard of *pater familias* or the "reasonable man". However, it should be noted that most legal systems today actually do have a satisfactory legal framework for achieving formal gender equality. And a source of gender inequality is not so much in the legal norms but in their application or, on the contrary, in the lack of application. The crux of the problem seems to lie in the mentality of people, their tradition and the persistence of patriarchal customs and practices which often affect the capacity of women to enjoy their rights.[1] It is often socially expected, especially in developing countries, that women should not use the opportunity to enjoy certain rights even when they are provided by the law. Furthermore, even though the situation has improved over the last decades,[2] women are on average still much more engaged when it comes to housekeeping, childcare and other caring responsibilities.[3] This yields unequal opportunities for men and women because these women cannot be as economically active and engaged outside the family environment as men can. Therefore, they sometimes have limited opportunities and resources to invest in their career and generate income.

The direct results of such stereotypical views of the role of women in society may be seen in the field of proprietary relations. As will be explained in the first section of this chapter, men are, in general, in a better position than women when it comes to enjoyment of property rights and access to land and other assets and financial services. The focus will also be given to the problem of acquisition and division of

---

[1] Quintanilla (2011), p. 17.

[2] Women today can make a choice between keeping a house and raising children on the one hand, or investing in a career on the other hand. Women often manage to achieve both. Nowadays, men more and more support women to work, because women's careers could provide a higher standard of living for the whole family. Sigel (1996), pp. 116, 163.

[3] According to Gender, Institutions and Development Database (GID-DB) from 2019, only in 2/180 countries in the world women enjoy the same legal rights and decision-making abilities and responsibilities within the household as men. However, even in these 2 countries female to male ratio of average time spent on unpaid domestic, care and volunteer work in a 24-h period is to the detriment of women (more than 3:1 and almost 2:1). Also, 42% of the population in these 2 countries (strongly) agrees that "when a mother works for pay, the children suffer". See more in https://stats.oecd.org/Index.aspx?DataSetCode=GIDDB2019 Gender, Institutions and Development Database (GID-DB) 2019 (oecd.org), 15th April 2021; According to statistics conducted in certain legal systems, women spend 4.5 h a day doing housework. See "Rodna analiza sa predlogom indikatora" (2020), http://upisnepokretnosti.rs/Files/00071/Rodna-analiza-sa-predlogom-indikatora.pdf, p. 5. "*According to studies across diverse countries, nearly 90 per cent of the time spent on household food preparation is women's time, which limits their ability to generate income, engage in public life or merely recharge.*" UN Women (2018), p. 6, https://www.unwomen.org/en/digital-library/publications/2018/2/towards-a-gender-responsive-implementation-of-the-un-convention-to-combat-desertification; "*Women are two times more than men engaged in activities relates to child care and 4.3 times more engaged in housework.*" Blagojević and Bobić Hughson (2014), p. 517. Some authors write about the so-called care economy, which means activities that contribute to the well-being of others—cooking, washing, ironing, children care... Women are burdened more than men by these activities for which they don't get paid. Đurić Kuzmanović and Milinović (2014), pp. 198, 202; Šobot (2014), p. 500; On the division of household responsibilities see also OECD (2021). It is an interesting fact that the Constitution of Ireland contains such stereotypical view of the role of women in society. Art. 42 reads: "*In particular, the State recognises that by her life within the home, woman gives to the State a support without which the common good cannot be achieved. The State shall, therefore, endeavour to ensure that mothers shall not be obliged by economic necessity to engage in labour to the neglect of their duties in the home.*"

marital property since it is the terrain on which one may clearly evidence gender discrimination.

As far as contract law is concerned, one of the most difficult tasks is to reconcile the principle of party autonomy and freedom of contract with the prohibition of discrimination, including gender discrimination, since not every unequal treatment, even though based on the typical risk factors (gender, religion and the like) amounts to discrimination. The goal is, therefore, to identify where the threshold beyond which unequal treatment results into discrimination should be fixed. Or in other words, what are the parameters that must be followed to distinguish unequal treatment, which can be legitimate if based on reasonable grounds, from discrimination, which is on the contrary prohibited.

Finally, when it comes to tort law, a general concern is whether gender roles and stereotypes are of any relevance when it comes to claims for damages and their insurance. The attention will firstly be given to the problem of compensation for pecuniary and non-pecuniary damage suffered by the victim and its connection to the problem of gender inequality. The second part is dedicated to the analysis of an action for compensation for the damage actually suffered as a result of direct or indirect discrimination on the grounds of gender. And finally in the last part, a question is raised whether the use of sex as a factor in the calculation of premiums for the purposes of insurance should be considered as a form of gender discrimination.

A more thorough analysis on these issues has also the purpose to clarify why it is important to reconsider private law from a gender equality perspective and why gender competent private law should be introduced into a legal studies' curriculum. Importantly, it should be done as it would lead to a better understanding of the causes of gender inequality in practice, a changed view of the traditional gender roles in society and, subsequently, an appropriate way of how it could be prevented.

Learning Goals

- Students can recognise the difference between formal and substantive gender equality
- Students can analyse and explain which social factors contribute to gender inequality
- Students master the ability to reconcile important principles governing Private Law with the principle of non-discrimination
- Students can understand the importance of gender mainstreaming of Private law in all its dimensions, as well as in creating and implementing laws.

15.2 Gender Equality and Proprietary Relations

15.2.1 Introduction

Women property rights are still highly circumscribed in many countries.[4] Some legal systems even today do not grant women equal rights as men when it comes to obtaining, keeping or controlling property. But even when women do have the same legal rights as men, the application of such legal norms could in practice still lead to the unenviable position of women: laws are sometimes ignored or weakly enforced. Thus, women are often unable to claim their rights in the face of social and economic pressures.[5] Therefore, the first part of the "Gender Equality and Proprietary Relations" section will be dedicated to the explanation of how the legal capacity of men and women may differ with respect to acquisition and enjoyment of (property) rights.

The amount of assets women can own and control may highly be impacted by the regimes regulating property in marriage or extramarital union,[6] not only during the marriage or extramarital union but also in cases of divorce/separation. Thus, they shape the bargaining power a woman has within her household.[7] Therefore, the second section will be dedicated to the analysis of the impact of specific marital regime implemented in a legal system on spouses' property rights, especially the acquisition and division of property acquired during marriage or extramarital union.

Finally, in the last two sections attention will be given to the question of how legal norms, but also stereotypical expectations and the division of gender roles in society, may have an impact on gender equality with respect to the access to land and other immovable assets and access to other assets and financial services.[8]

---

[4] Rao (2015), p. 6.

[5] Rao (2015), p. 6.

[6] Bearing in mind that many legal systems actually provide for the same legal regime when it comes to both regulation of property acquired during marriage and extramarital union, what is mentioned hereafter for married couples and their property regimes can also be applied to non-married partnerships (between men and women).

[7] The World Bank (2011), p. 160.

[8] When it comes to inequality between partners and its legal consequences, especially with respect to proprietary relations, an interesting observation, unfortunately not much theoretically elaborated, may be made: that the same examples of inequality may also be found between partners in the same sex partnerships (in legal systems where these partnerships are legally regulated). Namely, traditional patterns of behavior may also have a huge impact on the distribution of power between partners in the same sex partnerships and therefore, may subsequently lead to inequality between them.

15.2.2 Legal Capacity of Men and Women

Until just a few decades ago, the status of men and women in almost all legal systems in the world differed in terms of their legal capacity. The same range of rights was not available to women as to men.[9] This applied not only to civil rights but also political rights. In some cases women could not be the owners of immovable property, they were often excluded from the right to inherit, in marriage all acquired property belonged to the husband, women did not have the right to vote, to act as politicians, become judges, etc. Daughters were under the patronage of the father, and married women under their husband's patronage. Even when they could own real estate, the estate was managed by the husband and all the fruits of labour belonged to him. Likewise, they often could not conclude any contract on their own, without the permission of the husband.[10]

Although the situation is far better today, discrimination between men and women still exists.[11] It can be seen even from the rules that apply in some (usually developing) countries.[12] As explained, in such systems, women's legal capacities may be reduced once they marry in such a manner that a husband's permission must be obtained when applying for a passport, entering a contract, or appearing in court.[13]

However, inequality can be seen even more in practice, despite the legal guarantee of equality. As explained, "regardless of equal inheritance rights, custom and tradition usually win out, leaving many women and girls landless".[14] In many countries even today, it is a matter of custom that a sister should renounce her right to inherit in favour of her brother(s),[15] or that the immovable property is more often bequeathed to male descendants.[16] One of the reasons for this discriminatory practice is the belief that the property inherited by a woman will inevitably become

---

[9]See for instance Sagny (2006), p. 235; Gerhard (2020).

[10]Mate (2006), pp. 448–449; Cowie (2009); Pavlović (2014), pp. 233–234.

[11]According to Gender, Institutions and Development Database (GID-DB) from 2019, only in 45/180 countries widows and daughters enjoy the same rights as widowers and sons to inherit land and non-land assets. That means that in 135/180 women suffer some sort of discrimination (either in such way that customary, religious or traditional laws discriminate against women's inheritance rights, or in a way that not all groups of women have the same rights, or even in a way that widows and/or daughters do not enjoy the same rights as widowers and sons to inherit land and/or non-land assets).

[12]This is for instance the case with countries that apply Sharia Law: in Saudi Arabia women do not have the same rights as men; the husband is the head of the household and the woman must obey him; women inherit half as much as men. OECD (2019a), pp. 2–4; See also Zarrouki (2018), pp. 6–16. In Albania the Kanun code establishes that a widow may manage land if her sons are minors. If she has no children, her in-laws will take the land and she will return to her family. OECD (2019b), p. 6.

[13]World Developement Report (2012), p. 160.

[14]Toktas and O'Neil (2013), p. 27.

[15]Bordia Das (2008), p. 282.

[16]Toktas and O'Neil (2013), p. 27.

the property of her husband or her in-laws and will thus be lost to another family.[17] Also, women often forego their right to inherit because they fear social judgment.[18] Moreover, even when women do inherit property, control of their property remains in the hands of male family members.[19] In some legal systems the law allows that only one spouse be registered as the owner of the real estate even though it was acquired in marriage.[20] In practice it is usually the husband, which gives him the opportunity/power to undertake all legal transactions related to that real estate, from its acquisition to its subsequent disposal (encumbrance or alienation).

15.2.3 Marital Property

Gender inequality may also appear as a result of the application of a marital regime implemented in a certain legal system. Roughly speaking, there are several marital regimes which regulate the question of property ownership during the marriage (or extramarital union).

Firstly, the so-called "separation of property regime", which means that spouses maintain separate ownership of any property they acquire during the course of a marriage. Even though this regime may be suitable for women entrepreneurs, it is considered as disadvantageous for most women, due to the fact that non-monetised contributions (such as housekeeping, childcare and other caregiving duties) are usually not recognised upon divorce or in the case of widowhood.[21]

Secondly, so-called "customary regimes"[22] wherein the problem of gender inequality is even more apparent. The reason lies in the fact that in such regimes men traditionally administer marital property and therefore have full control over the assets during marriage. Furthermore, non-monetised contributions are not being recognised. And finally, in some cases women even lose the property they brought into the marriage upon divorce.[23]

Thirdly, the so-called "community of property regime". Legal systems which implemented such a regime seem to give better protection to women, especially in

---

[17] OECD (2019c), p. 4.

[18] There is a stigma attached to women who choose to pursue their legal rights as they are often seen as "taking away" what should belong to the brother. OECD (2019d), pp. 3–4.

[19] Toktas and O'Neil (2013), p. 27. The tradition obliges women to register bought or inherited land in the name of their husband or another close male relative. OECD (2019e), p. 4.

[20] Art. 176 of the Serbian Family Law, *Official Gazette RS, No. 18/2005, 72/2011 and 6/2015;* Art. 289 of the Montenegrin Family Law, *Official Gazette RCG, No. 1/2007 and Official Gazette CG, No. 53/2016 and 76/2020.*

[21] Rao (2015), p 6. "*Of the 35 countries whose laws on separate ownership of property were surveyed, only 7 recognized non-monetary contributions*". World Development Report (2012), p. 162.

[22] These regimes are the default in only four countries in Africa—Botswana, Burundi, Nigeria, and Swaziland. World Development Report (2012), p. 162.

[23] World Development Report (2012), p. 162.

the case of divorce or widowhood, since all property acquired during the marriage is jointly owned, except for the inherited property or the property received as a gift. The benefits are also in the fact that it implicitly recognises non-monetized contributions to the household.[24] However, even in such legal systems gender inequality exists. For instance, in some countries women are still being deprived of control when it comes to the administration of the joint marital property which is in the hands of husbands during the marriage.[25] The inability to control property may lead to the inability to build or retain wealth, which then may lead to the inability to access the formal financial sector.[26] Also, in some legal systems,[27] the law provides for a possibility of rebutting the assumption that spouses' shares are equal after the division of marital property and the "superiority" of men can easily be noticed in the case of divorce: it is much easier for men to prove that their contribution to the enlargement of marital property is bigger, since on average they earn more than women. As already mentioned, women are usually much more engaged when it comes to housekeeping and caring for children[28] and therefore, more inclined to leave their jobs or work part-time.[29] But even when they work full time, they are usually not in a position to accept any additional engagements that might bring them extra money. The lack of time may also lead to, for instance, missing the chance for personal and professional development which might otherwise lead to a better job position or a higher pay. On the other hand, women's engagement around the house and children allows men to work and develop undisturbed and consequently earn more and reduces the cost of housekeeping and babysitting. Even though the courts take in consideration the non-monetised contribution to the enlargement of the marital property (i.e. housekeeping, childcare, etc.), it is still much less valued than the direct contribution.[30] The division of marital property also leads to the

[24]World Development Report (2012), p. 162.

[25]That is the case in 10 of the 43 countries surveyed that have had community property as the default regime over the past 50 years. World Development Report (2012), p. 162.

[26]Rao (2015), p. 6.

[27]This is the case, for instance, with Serbian or Montenegrin legal systems. See Art. 180 of the Serbian Family Law, "*Sl. glasnik RS", br. 18/2005, 72/2011 - dr. zakon i 6/2015*and Art. 294 of the Montenegrin Family Law, *"Sl. list RCG", br. 1/2007 i "Sl. list CG", br. 53/2016 i 76/2020.*

[28]"*According to recent data from some 90 countries, women devote on average roughly three times more hours a day to unpaid care and domestic work than men, limiting the time available for paid work, education and leisure and further reinforcing gender-based socioeconomic disadvantages.*" Report of the Secretary-General (2019), p. 11.

[29]"*Women are more likely to work on a part-time basis across all Member States.*" "*Young adults make up a significant proportion of part-time workers, with 40 % of women and 24 % of men working on a part-time basis in the age bracket 15-24, 30 % of women and 6 % of men in the age bracket 25-49, and 34 % of women and 9 % of men in the age bracket 50-64*". This is the statistics for the European countries for 2012. See European Institute for Gender Equality (EIGE) (2014), pp. 21–24.

[30]Manji (2018), pp. 53–54. For instance, statistics show that women in Serbia spend on average 4.5 h a day doing housework, whereas men only 2 h a day. It has been calculated that for this

inconvenient question of where women and children will eventually live, as custody over children is usually given to the mother.[31]

Finally, it should be mentioned that in some countries each couple may opt for one among multiple regimes that are available to them.[32] However, even though women theoretically have the option to choose the regime that offers them the most protection, for instance the community property regime, the use of that option has been very limited in practice and most couples opt for the default regime even though it may not be as protective for women.[33]

All aforementioned information raises another question of what type of rules are more advantageous for women in case of division of marital property: the rigid or flexible rules. Some authors take as an example the Swiss system, as a rigid one, and the English system, as a flexible one.[34]

Example

Swiss Civil Code prescribes four "property masses"—the wife's matrimonial and non-matrimonial property and the husband's matrimonial and non-matrimonial property.[35] The Code also prescribes what belongs to the spouse's marital property (primarily the spouse's income, compensation for inability to work . . .) on one hand[36] and what is non-marital property of the spouse (things for personal use, assets that the spouse acquired before marriage or assets inherited or acquired with no fees during marriage) on the other hand.[37] The most complicated part of the Swiss system is determining the contribution of one property to another (for example, something was bought with money from marital property and became a part of the separate property), after which each spouse's marital property is divided in half, and each spouse receives one half of each.

As a complete contrast to such a rigid and complicated Swiss system is the English system in which the court makes a decision, taking into account criteria, such as financial resources of the parties, their respective contributions, their needs, the age of each party, the duration of the marriage etc.[38] ◄

amount of work women should earn €138 per month, that is €1650 per year. Republički zavod za statistiku, Žene i muškarci u Srbiji, 2017.

[31]The institute that aims to protect women and underage children is so-called *habitatio* and it allows a mother to live with underage children after divorce in an apartment/house owned by the other spouse until the child reaches adulthood.

[32]World Development Report (2012), p. 162.

[33]World Development Report (2012), p. 162.

[34]Bock (2008), pp. 289–303.

[35]Bock (2008), p. 291; Art. 196, 197 and 198 Swiss Civil Code.

[36]Art. 197 Swiss Civil Code.

[37]Art. 198 Swiss Civil Code.

[38]Bock (2008), p. 293.

In the end of this section, it should be mentioned that some legal systems prescribe a legal fiction that, in the case where only one spouse is registered as the owner of a real estate acquired during the marriage, even though the real estate is jointly acquired in marriage, it will be considered as if both spouses have been registered (both are considered as owners).[39] The legal fiction has been created to protect women since it was usually the husband who was registered as the owner. However, the fiction created many problems in practice.[40] Namely, in cases where the husband concluded some legal transaction related to that real estate all by himself, which means without the permission or even the knowledge of his wife, the courts had to choose whether to protect the wife's property rights, on one hand, or the third party's rights, on the other hand, since the third party usually had no idea that the real estate also belongs to the seller's wife (the unregistered spouse).

15.2.4 Access to Land and Other Immovable Assets

When it comes to the ownership and other rights on immovables, there are still significant gaps between men and women which leads to an overall weaker economical standing of women, bearing in mind that land assets (and real estate in general) are an important collateral and economical resource.[41] According to the Gender, Institutions and Development Database (GID-DB) from 2019, only in 37 of 180 countries in the world do women and men have the same legal rights and secure access to land assets. However, even in these countries the percentage of women among the total number of agricultural holders is much less than the percentage of men.[42] Furthermore, women farm holders have significantly smaller farms and of lower quality than men farm holders.[43] This is especially the case when it comes to rural areas. Even though women are perceived as a driving force for the maintenance, conservation and development of these areas, they also represent "an invisible

---

[39] Art. 176 of the Serbian Family Law, *Official Gazette RS, No. 18/2005, 72/2011 and 6/2015;* Art. 289 of the Montenegrin Family Law, *Official Gazette RCG, No. 1/2007 and Official Gazette CG, No. 53/2016 and 76/2020.*

[40] See more in Dabić and Dolović Bojić (2019), pp. 407–436.

[41] Rao (2015), p. 6. Povlakić and Mezetović Međić (2018), p. 45.

[42] See https://stats.oecd.org/Index.aspx?DataSetCode=GIDDB2019. As an example of a major gender inequality with respect to land rights see Bicchieri and Ayala (2017). On the share of women among owners or rights-bearers of agricultural land see also Food and Agriculture Organization of the United Nations (FAO), (2021) http://www.fao.org/sustainable-development-goals/indicators/5a1/en/.

[43] According to European Institute for Gender Equality (EIGE), 71% of EU farms with livestock are run by male farm holders, and only 27% by female farm holders (the remainder belongs to legal persons). In 2013, women represented 24% of EU farm holders in organic farming, and they occupied 13% of the EU area devoted to organic farming. See https://eige.europa.eu/gender-mainstreaming/policy-areas/agriculture-and-rural-development (EIGE 2021). "Rural women and girls 25 years after Beijing: critical agents of positive change", FAO, IFAD and WFP (2020), p. 15, http://www.fao.org/3/cb1638en/CB1638EN.pdf, 5 July 2021.

force"—it is much more often a case that they assist their husband and other self-employed men with performing unpaid or unrecognised agriculture work, such as raising crops, taking care of domestic animals and producing agricultural products, than that they themselves hold property rights to land or farms.[44] As explained, the main reason lies in the fact that, even when formal laws and policies are gender sensitive, they may be disregarded in rural and indigenous communities that rely on traditional, unwritten customary practices rather than on written codified law.[45] Additionally, the registration of land is usually under men's name as they are considered the managers and heads of household.[46] However, it is also a result of the default marital regime in some legal systems—separation of property—'which usually discriminates against women by failing to recognise the wives' contribution to the formation of marital property through domestic labour or child-rearing and other caregiving duties.[47]

15.2.5 Access to Other Assets and Financial Services

The fact that, in comparison to men, a smaller percentage of women own immovable property, which is an important collateral, represents also a barrier in accessing credit to start or expand their business.[48] Therefore, it is not a surprising fact that globally there are much more male owned businesses than female owned businesses. Furthermore, female owned businesses are smaller in comparison to male owned businesses, measured by the employment and turnover.[49] Other reasons that have been identified as potential constraints on women's enterprises are[50] firstly, the continuing pay gap between women and men, which may restrict the financial resources available to women for the creation and growth of business. Secondly, the occupational segregation, both horizontal and vertical: women more often than their male counterparts work part-time, in a quite narrow range of occupations and

---

[44] Some research show that more than 80% of rural women in the European Union are so-called "helping spouses"—they assist or participate in the farm business without being a business partner in the formal sense. See Quintanilla (2011), pp. 7 and 9. OECD (2019f), p. 7.

As reported by the Secretary-General in 2009. "*Women constitute up to 70 per cent of the agricultural labour force, but most do not own or control any land. Rural women own less than 10 per cent of property in the developed world, and 2 per cent in the developing world. It is estimated that women in Africa receive less than 10 per cent of all credit going to small farmers and only 1 per cent of the total credit going to the agricultural sector.*" See Report of the Secretary-General 2009, para 4.

[45] "Rural women and girls 25 years after Beijing: critical agents of positive change", FAO, IFAD and WFP (2020), p. 16, http://www.fao.org/3/cb1638en/CB1638EN.pdfhttp://www.fao.org/3/cb1638en/CB1638EN.pdf, 5 July 2021; OECD (2019d), p. 7; OECD (2019g), p. 7.

[46] OECD (2019b), p. 6; OECD (2019h), p. 8.

[47] Rao (2015), p. 6.

[48] OECD (2019i), p. 7.

[49] Amin (2010), p. 1. OECD (2019d), p. 8.

[50] Carter (2006), pp. 41–47.

face barriers in entering senior management and higher paid occupations, which altogether leads to less work experience and less variety of work experience. Finally, women experience significant challenges between balancing work and life (i.e. pregnancy, childbirth, childcare and other caring responsibilities), which can have a negative impact on their business and in general restrict women's business ownership opportunities.

It should be mentioned that, as opposed to regular financial resources (i.e. bank loans), microcredit is much more available to women. However, it does not solve the problem of gender inequality when it comes to the access to financial resources. Firstly, it is shown that in some countries (e.g. Bangladesh) in many cases women do not really control the use of the funds they obtain—since women have easier access to microcredit, men take advantage of the situation to obtain funds.[51] Secondly, even though microfinance can support female entrepreneurship by providing easier access to finance, some studies show that the lending rate is still low and that women are rather more penalised than men in their access to microcredit, which cannot be explained by their personal differences or differences in projects. Thirdly, as explained, microfinance institutions, as traditional banking institutions, appear to be more interested in the credit relationship and the likelihood of loan repayment than in the type of business they are financing, which means that they do not really promote female enterprise beyond credit and do nothing to stop women staying with traditional activities.[52]

A problem of gender inequality may also appear in a slightly different guise and even less apparent. Namely, it is not so rare a case that the husband invests money, movable or immovable property or legal rights that are in the regime of joint ownership into the company shares.[53] In such cases the question arises whether these company shares only belong to the spouse who invested in them or whether they are in the regime of joint ownership (which means that shares also belong to the wife who is not a member of the company as well). The problem becomes more amplified in case they get divorced. A divorce is usually followed by a division of the property and determination of each spouse's contribution to the joint property during their marriage. If one of the spouses (usually the husband) is a company member and, therefore, a shareholder, one major dilemma is how it should be decided if a spouse (usually the wife) who is not a company member requests that its contribution to the acquisition of the company share be determined.

Example

In a situation where a husband has invested jointly owned property into the company shares the Serbian highest court has decided in the following manner: "*A spouse who does not have the status of a founder may claim against his spouse*

[51] Brana (2013), p. 3.

[52] Brana (2013), p. 16.

[53] Manji (2018), p. 55.

with the status of a company founder only reimbursement of his contribution to the acquisition of the joint property which had been, without his consent, invested as the founding contribution of the other spouse in the newly formed company."[54] ◀

15.3 The Impact of Gender on Contract Law: When Party Autonomy Meets the Prohibition of Discrimination

15.3.1 Introductory Remarks

Slawson once wrote that the «male bias» of our society has not entailed significant consequences on contract law.[55] Such assumption opened the way to a lively debate that could be actualised in the following question: does gender have an impact on contracts and contracting?

The question is double-faced: on the one hand, it could be dealt with from a multi-disciplinary perspective, at the borderline between law and neighbouring sciences like anthropology or sociology, by investigating if and to what extent contract law is born gendered and how it could be rewritten in a gender-neutral way; on the other hand, it can be dealt with through a more positive-law-focused approach, by analysing how rules of contract law can prevent gender-based discriminations.

The first topic has been widely explored by feminist legal theories,[56] which argue in a nutshell that, at least in the western legal tradition, even contract law bears a strong male imprinting.[57] Several traces of this may be found in the very language used by legal systems to describe contract doctrines:[58] perhaps the most evident example is the fact that the standard of diligence or efforts required to the parties in the performance of obligations is the one of 'the good family father'[59] or the one of

[54] See the Decision of the Supreme Court of Serbia, Rev. 1556/06 on 22. November 2007.

[55] Letter from W. David Slawson, Professor of Law, University of Southern California, to Mary Joe Frug, Professor of Law, New England School of Law 1–2, 24 June 1988, quoted by Frug (1992), p. 1029.

[56] See Chap. 2 above. For an overview of the feminist approach to the law, see, from different perspectives, Menkel-Meadow (1996); Chamallas (2013); Bartlett (1990), p. 829.

[57] Threedy (1999), pp. 1247–1265; moreover, see Dalton (1984), p. 997.

[58] Moreover, a gendered reading reveals what 'Law & Gender' studies have pointed out with reference to legislation in general: on the whole, contract law results into the prevalence of rationality over intuition and senses-based knowledge, of objectivity over subjectivity, of abstraction over contextualization, and of hierarchy-focused decision making over consensus-building or compromise-oriented processes. In other words, contract law as well results into the prevalence of qualities that, according to anthropologists, tend to be typical of the male gender over qualities that tend to be typical of the female gender. See Olsen (1998), pp. 691–707.

[59] See e.g. Italian Civil code, art. 1176.

the 'reasonable man'.[60] In the view of the mentioned theories, the reason lies in the fact that contract law was developed in its main rules and doctrines in a time when women neither had access to contracting nor could be members of the legal profession or legal academia.[61] Contracting was restricted, given that women were under the guardianship of their fathers or husbands and contracts were limited to the market sphere, being instead excluded from the domain of familial relationships.

The second topic—how rules of contract law can prevent gender-based discriminations—is in constant evolution especially at a European level and is closely intertwined with wide-ranging issues like the need to reshape the relationship between production, competition and solidarity and to reconcile party autonomy or freedom of contract with the goal of an equal access to the goods and services offered on the market.[62]

In this very analysis of the impact that cultural stereotypes and preconceptions have on the dynamics affecting the contractual relationship, namely on the selection of the other contracting party and the choice of certain contract conditions, lies the core of every gender-oriented analysis of contract law. Therefore, it will be the object of the following section.

15.3.2 The Prohibition of Contractual Discrimination and Its Sources

The prohibition of discrimination is a principle rooted both in the *acquis commun* (i.e. in the legal traditions of each Member States) and in the communitarian *acquis* (i.e. the in the legal rules elaborated by European institutions). First of all, it must be remarked that non-discrimination belongs to the constitutional traditions of almost all the Member States,[63] if not directly, under the umbrella of the principle of equality, and, if not expressly, through the interpretation of Constitutional Courts and the doctrines developed by Constitutional scholarship.

Example

Art. 3 of the Italian Constitution, in declaring that all citizens are equal before the law, without any distinction based on sex, race, language, religion, political views, personal and social conditions, has been interpreted as imposing on the legislator the duty to treat equally situations that are reasonably equal and differently situations that are reasonably different; Art. 28(2) of Cyprus Constitution provides that 'Every person shall enjoy all the rights and liberties provided

[60] See Epstein (1973), pp. 643–666.

[61] See Threedy (1999), who suggests that women have resolved the dichotomy between market and non-market by 'bringing traditional nonmarket "women's labor" to the market, and by bringing the market home'.

[62] See Carapezza Figlia (2018), pp. 1 ff.

[63] Apparently, there are one current and one former Member States that do not provide protection against discrimination at a Constitutional level: Denmark and the United Kingdom.

for in this Constitution without any direct or indirect discrimination against any person on the ground of his community, race, religion, language, sex, political or other convictions, national or social descent, birth, colour, wealth, social class, or on any ground whatsoever, unless there is express provision to the contrary in this Constitution'; Art. 6(2) of the Bulgarian Constitution provides that 'there shall be no privileges or restriction of rights on the grounds of race, nationality, ethnic self-identity, sex, origin, religion, education, opinion, political affiliation, personal or social status or property status'; section 12(2) of the Slovakian Constitution reads that 'Fundamental rights and freedoms are guaranteed to everyone in the territory of the Slovak republic regardless of sex, race, colour of skin, language, belief and religion, political affiliation or other conviction, national or social origin, nationality or ethnic origin, property, descent or other status. No one may be harmed, preferred or discriminated against on these grounds'; Art. 91 of the Latvian Constitution provides that 'Human rights shall be realised without discrimination of any kind'; Art. 14 of the Slovenian Constitution provides that everyone shall be guaranteed equal human rights and fundamental freedoms irrespective of national origin, race, sex, language, religion, political or other conviction, material standing, birth, education, social status, disability or any other personal circumstance. ◄

This has gradually led to the acknowledgement, by European case-law and European constitutional-rank sources, of non-discrimination, in its descent from the broader principle of equality,[64] as a fundamental pillar of the Union order.

Besides its constitutional relevance, the right not to be discriminated against is also laid down by several provisions of European soft and hard law. As to soft law, chapter 3 of the Acquis Principles (Articles 3:101-3:203) is entirely devoted to the prohibition of discrimination and falls between the chapters dealing respectively with pre-contractual obligations (chapter 2) and with the conclusion of contracts (chapter 4).[65] As to hard law, the provision devoted to the prohibition of

[64] See, among others, Case C-810/79, Überschär, Judgment of 8 October 1980, ECR 2747; Case 354/95 The Queen v National Farmers' Union et al, Judgment of 17 July 1997, ECR I-4559, para 61 (1995); Case 13/94 S. v Cornwall County Council, Judgment of 30 April 1996, para 18, ECR I-2165 (1996); Case 144/04 Werner Mangold v Rüdiger Helm, Judgment of 22 November 2005.

[65] See Acquis Principles, Chapter 3, Section 1: General rules/Definitions. Article 3:101: Principle of non-discrimination in contract law. Any discrimination based on sex, racial or ethnic origin is prohibited. Article 3:102: Discrimination (1) "Discrimination" means: 1. A situation where one person is treated less favourably than another person is, has been or would be treated in a comparable situation; 2. a situation where an apparently neutral provision, criterion or practice would place persons with a particular feature at a particular disadvantage when compared with other persons; (2) Discrimination also includes 1. unwanted conduct which violates the dignity of a person and which creates an intimidating, hostile, degrading, humiliating or offensive environment, or which aims to do so (harassment); or 2. any form of unwanted physical, verbal, non-verbal, or psychical conduct of a sexual nature that violates the dignity of a person, or which aims to do so, in particular when such conduct creates an intimidating, hostile, degrading, humiliating or offensive environment (sexual harassment). (3) Any instruction to discriminate also amounts to

discrimination in general is Article 13 of the Treaty Establishing the European Communities (now Article 19 of the Treaty on the Functioning of the European Union), as introduced in 1997 by the Treaty of Amsterdam.

15.3.3 The Foundation of the Principle and the Structure of the Discrimination Test

The above-illustrated normative framework highlights the twofold role played by the principle of equality: on one side, it is a fundamental right of individuals, on the other side, it is an objective limit to the legislative power in a broad sense that also includes transactional autonomy. The direct applicability of the principle within private relationships casts light on the core issue: the prohibition of discrimination is a limit to party autonomy and, more specifically, to freedom of contract.

This latter, like the right to non-discrimination, is a value that is protected at a constitutional level by the Member States and must be considered, as well, a pillar of the European Union order. Thus, it is necessary to strike a balance between the two. The only way to reconcile the freedom of parties to choose their contracting partner according to their preferences and to determine the content of the relationship in line with their interests is to assume that not every unequal treatment, even though based on the typical risk factors (gender, religion, and the like) amounts to a prohibited discrimination.

That is why the first approach to the discrimination test—the *tertium comparationis* method—has been abandoned both by the Court of Justice of the European Union[66] and by the European Court of Human Rights.[67] According to that

discrimination. Article 3:103: Exception. Unequal treatment which is justified by a legitimate aim does not amount to discrimination if the means used to achieve that aim are appropriate and necessary. Section 2: Remedies. Article 3:201: Remedies. (1) A person who is discriminated against on the grounds of sex, ethnic or racial origin in relation to contracts that provide access to, or supply goods or services which are available to the public, including housing, is entitled to compensation. (2) Where appropriate, the discriminated person is entitled to other remedies which are suitable to undo the consequences of the discriminating act, or to prevent further discrimination. Article 3:202: Content of the remedies. (1) Compensation under Art. 3:201(1) may include damages for pecuniary and nonpecuniary losses. (2) The amount of any damages for non-pecuniary losses, and remedies granted under Art. 3:201(2), must be proportionate to the injury; the deterrent effect of remedies may be taken into account. Article 3:203: Burden of proof. (1) If a person who considers himself or herself discriminated against on one of the grounds mentioned in Art. 3:201(1) establishes, before a court or another competent authority, facts from which it may be presumed that there has been such discrimination, it falls on the other party to prove that there has been no breach of the principle of non-discrimination. (2) Paragraph (1) does not apply to proceedings in which it is for the court or another competent authority to investigate the facts of the case.

[66] Case 177/88 Dekker, Judgment of 8 November 1990, ECR 3941 (1990); Case 32/93 Webb, Judgment of 14 July 1994, ECR I-3567 (1994). See also, Case 13/94 S. and Cornwall County Council n 73 above, I-2165, para 22; Case 117/01 K.B., Judgment of 7 January 2004, ECR I-541 (2004).

[67] See, e.g., Eur. Court H.R., Karlheinz Schmidt v Germany, Judgment of 18 July 1994, para 24; Eur. Court H.R., Petrovic v Austria, Judgment of 27 March 1998, para 30; Eur. Court H.R.,

approach, for the purpose of ascertaining discrimination, it was enough to compare the way in which the alleged discriminated person is treated, the way in which other people are treated in the same situation and the way in which the discriminated person would be treated if there was no prejudice against him/her. But, that way, the concept of discrimination ended up being reduced to that of unequal treatment.

The problem is, instead, to identify where the threshold beyond which unequal treatment results into discrimination should be fixed. In other words, what are the parameters that must be followed to distinguish unequal treatment, which could be *per se* legitimate, from discrimination, which is on the contrary prohibited (see the example at the end of this section).

As European case-law suggests,[68] the criteria for the discrimination test should be, in a nutshell, the following: after an unequal treatment has been detected, what should be assessed is whether such inequality has an objective and reasonable justification, whether it pursues a legitimate aim and whether the means used to pursue such aim are proportional to the aim itself. If the answer to one of the questions is negative, then the unequal treatment falls into the scope of the prohibition of discrimination.

From the mentioned criteria it can be drawn that the discrimination test is double-phased. The first step is to ascertain whether there has been an unequal treatment (based on risk factors) at all, according to the *tertium comparationis* method. The next step is an assessment of whether such unequal treatment is reasonable and justified and complies with the principle of proportionality. This principle is another pillar of the Community order and a key element in the balancing test undertaken by the European Court of Human Rights whenever it is called upon to decide on a restriction by the Contracting States to one of the fundamental rights or freedoms protected by the Convention.

It is easy to figure that, this way, the problematic focus of the discrimination test moves to the identification of what can justify unequal treatment. The answer implies the existence of a hierarchy of values to be balanced with the right to non-discrimination and such hierarchy should be committed to the whim of the legislators or the courts but inferred from the constitutional axiology.

An example, taken from real case-law,[69] could be useful to clarify the point, even though it deals more specifically with sexual orientation, rather than gender itself.

Example

In 2014 Mr. Lee, a gay activist advocating same-sex marriage, went to its trusted bakery in Belfast to order a cake and have it customised with the slogan 'Support Gay Marriage'. A few days after having placed its order and received the payment

Niedzwiecki v Germany, Judgment of 25 October 2005, para 32; Eur. Court H.R., Si Amer v France, Judgment of 29 October 2009, para 39, all available at www.echr.coe.int.

[68] See n. 13 and n. 14 above.

[69] Lee v Ashers Baking Company Ltd [2018] UKSC 49, on which see Periello (2018), p. 639; Fitzsimons (2016), pp. 66–67.

receipt, Mr. Lee received a phone call from the bakery informing him that the order had been cancelled and refunded because the owners were devout Christians who believed gay marriage to be a sin and intended to run their business in compliance with their religious beliefs. Feeling outraged, Mr. Lee sued the bakery on the ground that the refusal to perform the contract amounted to a discriminatory conduct. In 2018, the Supreme Court ruled that there had been no discrimination, mainly because the bakers' conduct was justified on the ground that a person cannot be forced to convey a message which is against his/her religious belief. If we stood stick to the *tertium comparationis* method, we should argue that the bakers' conduct is discriminatory simply because they treat gays and people supporting gay marriage differently from the other customers; but if we overcome that approach, we may (though the answer is not so undisputed) conclude that the unequal treatment is justified by freedom of religion and is therefore reasonable and compliant with the general prohibition of discrimination. ◀

Besides being helpful for marking the line between justified treatment and discrimination, the mentioned case is interesting because it demonstrates that the prohibition of discrimination, like the other fundamental principles, has a horizontal effect. According to the horizontal effect doctrine, developed by the Court of Justice,[70] individuals are entitled to rely on the direct effect rules contained in the Treaties conferring individual rights even in claims brought against another individual before a national court. This means that the violation of the prohibition at issue can be claimed by an individual even when it was perpetrated by another individual, rather than by the State.[71]

15.3.4 The Scope of the Prohibition of Contractual Discrimination

Given that the prohibition of discrimination is a limit to party autonomy, and more specifically to freedom of contract, scholars have always been reluctant in advocating its application to all contractual relationships, regardless of the type of contract and the qualities of the parties involved.

In particular, it has been often claimed that the scope of the prohibition should be restricted to contractual offers made to the public.[72] This latter solution matches with the minimum threshold of protection imposed by European legislation, where Directive 2004/113 addresses the prohibition of unjustified direct and indirect discrimination on the grounds of sex in the access to and supply of goods and services to 'all persons who provide goods and services, which are available to the

[70] On the development of the doctrine at issue, see, for all, Walkila (2016).

[71] See e.g. Court of Justice, judgment of 19 April 2016, case C-441/14, Dansk Industri (DI), acting on behalf of Ajos A/S v. Estate of Karsten Eigil Rasmussen [GC].

[72] On the topic, see, in particular, Pinto Oliveira and McCrorie (2008).

public' and are 'offered outside the area of private and family life', or the areas of media and education.[73]

In support of the view that the prohibition at issue should apply only to offers to the public it is usually argued that only in those cases discrimination would be capable of undermining market efficiency and the fundamental right to personal dignity of the discriminated individuals, i.e. of those who have been excluded from the access to the goods and services offered. Moreover, it has been observed that an exception to the general principle that contractual choices are unquestionable would be justified only in offers to the public, because in that case discrimination would affect an entire class of people.

As to the first argument, it can be easily rebutted by observing that the foundation of non-discrimination principle does not lie in a mercantile logic such as the one advocated by the opinion at issue, as such a logic would be inconsistent with the constitutional values involved in the principle of equality. Human dignity is equally affected in discrimination through offers to the public and in discrimination through individual offers.

As to the second argument, one can object that the 'mass effect' of discrimination may be produced also in case of individual offers, whenever the offeror makes systematically discriminatory choices while negotiating with potential contracting parties. Furthermore, the refusal to conclude contracts with persons belonging to a certain category may hinder or even prevent access to goods and services, also in the case of individual negotiations.

As to the need of preserving freedom of contract, this goal must be reached regardless of the way in which the contract has been negotiated. The need to adjust the application of the prohibition at issue to accommodate it with freedom of contract should depend upon teleological and systematic evaluations and not merely upon a procedural approach focused on contract formation.[74] In other words, it cannot be upheld in absolute terms that non-discrimination only applies to offers to the public. It must be acknowledged that, within different practical contexts, the effect of the prohibition varies depending on the different status of the interests at play and the extent to which they are protected by the system.[75]

The deeper the impact of a contract is on the personal sphere of the contracting parties, the wider should their margin of appreciation be. Such margin should be full when the pre-contractual negotiations pertain to the area of 'private and family life', such as in cases involving the lending of a holiday home to a member of the family or the rent of a room in a private residence.

[73]The Directive has been taken as a model also by non-member States, such as Iceland, Liechtenstein, the FYR of Macedonia, Montenegro, Norway and Turkey. For an overview of the different solutions adopted by the Member States in the implementation of the Directive, see Burri and McColgan (2009). Furthermore, see Timmer and Senden (2016), pp. 67 ff.

[74]Carapezza Figlia (2018), p. 104.

[75]Ibidem, p. 105.

Example

As an example of the first situation, one could mention, besides the already illustrated bakery case,[76] the owner of a private home who refuses to rent it to an unmarried woman with child on the grounds of the stereotype that women have lower income and therefore are not reliable payers.[77] The second situation would instead occur, for instance, if the contract of lease contained an express term prohibiting the subletting of the house to women. ◀

Besides those cases, the guidelines for scaling the application of the non-discrimination principle should remain the ones above illustrated.

15.3.5 Possible Remedies for Contractual Discrimination

Discrimination may entitle the victim to different remedies. This would depend on the stage of the contractual relationship in which the unequal treatment took place and on whether such treatment consisted of the upstream refusal by one party to conclude the contract with the other or resulted in the provision of discriminatory terms[78] (see the example at the end of Sect. 15.3.4 above). When the discriminatory conduct takes place in the negotiations stage and results into the refusal by one of the parties to conclude the contract at all, or even to enter the precontractual dealings, the injunction to cease the discriminatory treatment may result into the obligation for the other party to negotiate the contract with the discriminated party. In case the other party fails to comply with such an obligation, damages would be awarded following the rules on precontractual liability. Damages will then be limited to the so-called 'negative interest' of the victim. Normally, they will cover the expenses made by the latter relying on the forthcoming conclusion of the contract and the chances that the victim has lost of engaging negotiations with other parties.

Dealing with precontractual discrimination, the most controversial issue concerning the possible remedies available to the victim is whether the latter is

[76] Lee v Ashers Baking Company Ltd, *supra*.

[77] Case-law on the issue is lacking poor, as discrimination in the field renting of private houses renting discrimination is more frequently based frequent on different the basis of other risk factors, namely such as race and religion, and furthermore it is not so easy for the victim of discrimination to prove that gender was actually the actual reason why for the other party had refused refusal to conclude the contract. Nevertheless, the practical relevance of was gender, but we can infer that the problem can be inferred is quite frequent in practice from other sources: in particular from the findings of e.g. a Belgian study undertaken carried out in 2006, which showed found that a significant large number of landlords was is strongly prejudiced against the idea of having single women or unmarried mothers in their own property. Some of the persons interviewed proved to be deeply influenced by the stereotype that women are less suitable than not as good as men at handling the practical aspects related to the management of properties of maintaining a property. On the topic, see, more in general, Ringelheim and Bernard (2013).

[78] See Carapezza Figlia (2018), pp. 113 ff.

entitled to claim for specific performance, i.e. to obtain from the court a judgment producing the same effects as the contract which the other party has refused to conclude for discriminatory reasons.

Undoubtedly, such a remedy would grant the discriminated party a higher protection, as it would place such party in the same situation in which it would have found himself/herself had he/she not been discriminated against. The problem is that the remedy of specific performance can apply only when there is upstream an obligation to be performed. In the case at issue, the only obligation that arises from the negotiations is the one not to discriminate against the other party, while there is no obligation to conclude the contract. Such objection appears to be irrefutable and leads to exclude specific performance from the range of the possible remedies, unless there are special provisions imposing on certain parties an obligation to contract with all offerors.

The same result as specific performance could be reached, outside the area of contractual remedies, through the rules on tort liability and, namely, through the so-called compensation in kind. According to that rule, the victim is entitled to claim for the elimination of the damage or the replacement of the damaged good, instead of claiming for the monetary equivalent, provided that such activities are materially possible and, at least in some systems, not excessively burdensome for the tortfeasor.[79]

Courts have not yet dealt with the issue, but the latter solution should be rejected as well, for several reasons.[80] First, compensation in kind is aimed at restoring the situation as it was prior to the loss suffered. When applied to discrimination cases, it would not simply restore the *status quo ante* but create a new legal relationship. Secondly, compensation in kind and the creation of a new legal relationship are effects that, procedurally speaking, follow from two different types of judgments: compensation is imposed through an order which needs to be enforced, whereas the creation of a new legal relationship is the automatic effect of a constitutive judgment.

Given the ability of constitutive judgments to interfere directly, without the intermediation of enforcement procedures, on private relationships, normally civil law courts have the power to issue them only in the cases expressly provided by the law.

Example

For instance, in Italy, the discriminated party could obtain a judgment standing for the contract that the other party has refused to conclude, when the gender-based discriminatory conduct is attributable to providers of services that are available to the public and are excluded from the scope of private and family life. In fact, Art. 28 of *Decreto legislativo* 25 July 1998 no 286, implementing the already mentioned Council Directive 2004/113/CE of 13 December 2004,

[79] See, e.g., art. 2058 of the Italian Civil code.

[80] See Carapezza Figlia (2018), pp. 115–116.

provides the courts with the power to adopt 'any measure that is adequate for removing the effects of discrimination'. In that case, however, constitutive relief is possible only to the extent that the goods or services are still available and the terms of the refused contract were sufficiently specific. ◀

When, instead, the unequal treatment is laid down in the contractual regulation, like in the case of clauses through which one party undertakes the obligation not to negotiate and conclude contracts with people belonging to a certain gender or clauses that apply more onerous conditions to them, the first remedy available is the invalidity of the contract. The grounds for voidness are either the infringement of a mandatory provision, when the prohibition of discrimination is embodied in a specific legislative rule, or the inconsistency with public policy. In this case, equality of treatment is simply a general principle covered by the Constitution or other constitutional-ranked sources at the European level.[81]

In line with the general trend towards the prevalence of remedies that preserve the contractual bound over remedies that completely neutralise it, upheld by European legislation and shared by the legal traditions of the Member States,[82] partial voidness will apply. Consequently, the discriminatory clauses will be severed from the contract, while the rest of it will remain unaffected. In case the clauses at issue were such as to apply more onerous conditions, they are likely not to be severed entirely but rather to be adjusted or supplemented by the competent courts so that their discriminatory effect is neutralised.

Example

Think of a clause contained in a lease contract that imposes on the lessee the prohibition of subletting the apartment to transgenders.[83] Such a clause would be declared void, on the grounds that it discriminates against contracting parties for their gender, and it would be entirely severed from the contract. The practical consequence of it is that the lessee would be free to sublet the apartment to whoever he/she wishes, including transgenders. ◀

[81] Namely art. 14 of the European Convention on Human Rights (ECHR), art. 19 of the Treaty on the Functioning of the European Union (TFUE) and art. 21 of the Charter of Fundamental Rights of the European Union (CFREU). To this extent, the Court of Justice of the European Union has considered the prohibition of discrimination as a 'general principle of Community Law' since Case C-810/79 Überschär, Judgment of 8 October 1980, ECR 2747. On the topic, see, for all, Bell (2003); Berger (2008), p. 864. From a gender-perspective, see the already mentioned study Gender equality law in Europe, How are EU rules transposed into national law in 2016?

[82] See, e.g., the Directive on Unfair Terms in Consumer Contracts and, as to the interpretation of the contract, art. 4:5 of the Unidroit Principles ('all terms to be given effect').

[83] Similar cases, where discrimination did not concern transgender but homosexual couples, are the following ones, decided by the European Court of Human Rights: ECHR, Karner v. Austria, 24 July 2003; ECHR, Kozak v. Poland, 2 March 2010.

Example

In a Belgian case,[84] a transgender had been refused access to a tour of Jordan, run according to a room-sharing model, unless he agreed to pay an extra fee for a single room. The Belgian civil court found the contract discriminatory and therefore ordered the operator to enrol the claimant without the additional fee. Moreover, the Court awarded compensation to the transgender.[85] ◄

The remedy of voidness can be accumulated with the one of compensation, provided that the discriminated party succeeds in proving that it suffered some damages, whether patrimonial or personal, as a direct consequence of the unequal treatment. In order to discourage discrimination on a more general scale, the special rules adopted by some systems award to the victim punitive damages. In addition, in some cases, the victim is entitled to claim for an injunction through which the court orders the party to make the unequal treatment cease.[86]

15.4 Other Areas of Gender-Sensitive Private Law[87]

15.4.1 Gender Equality in the Field of Tort Liability

The effectiveness of the principle of equality requires a re-reading of tort law from a gender perspective. The question is whether gender roles and stereotypes are relevant for claims for damages and their insurance.[88] Our vision will focus on the current landscape of tort liability, which allows us to consider the recourse to traditional standards of diligence that attribute the ideal model of conduct to men as being superseded. This is the case of the rule of the *"good father of the family"* in civil law countries. Indeed, the diligence of the *bonus pater familias* is still in force in some legislations, such as the Spanish Civil Code, but the courts interpret it in the sense of *"reasonable person"*. In common law countries, the standard of care has been measured through the *"reasonable man"*, a rule that has later been transformed into the seemingly more inclusive *"reasonable person standard"*. This rule is an example of a supposedly neutral rule that was, in reality, permeated by the male perspective and notions of the masculine ideal.[89]

[84] Civil Court in Antwerp (31 May 2017), Nieuw Juridisch Weekblad, 2018, p. 450, with P. Borghs's case note.

[85] On the topic, see, more in general, Van den Brink and Dunne (2018).

[86] See, e.g., art. 28 of Italian *Decreto legislativo* 1 September 2011 n. 150. For an overview of the remedies provided by the legislation of the Balkans, see Reich et al. (2014), pp. 83–105.

[87] This section has been translated with the translation service of the University Research Institute for Sustainable Social Development (INDESS).

[88] Finley (1989), Vol. 1, p. 41.

[89] Finley (1989), pp. 57–58.

The ultimate aim of tort law is that the tortfeasor compensates the person who has suffered damages. These damages can be pecuniary or non-pecuniary. In pecuniary damages, compensation includes the material losses suffered as a consequence of the harmful event, i.e., consequential damage and the profits lost due to the same, i.e., loss of earnings. Just as the compensation of consequential damage does not raise relevant questions from a gender perspective, the compensation of loss of earnings suggests certain aspects of interest worth reflecting on. Also, from the point of view of gender, it is interesting to analyse the compensation of non-pecuniary damage and the most relevant questions raised by the compensation of aesthetic damage.[90]

15.4.1.1 Loss of Earnings for Loss of Wages or Other Professional Income

In general, loss of profit is considered the frustrated gain or profit not obtained due to a harmful act or omission. This item of damage consists of the increase in assets that, with a certain probability, was expected given the normal course of circumstances, The obtaining of which however, is frustrated as a consequence of the tortfeasor's harmful act or omission. In regard to loss of profit, there are various questions and practical problems that arise.

First of all, there are difficulties related to the proof of the damage itself and its quantification. As a general rule, this difficulty tends to be more notorious in cases where it is the woman who suffers the effective loss of earnings as a result of the harmful event, insofar as it prevents her, either temporarily or permanently, from carrying out her activities. This is the case, for example, in cases where the victim of the harmful event carries out a productive activity but her remuneration is not fixed or stable. This circumstance, especially in the current situation of economic crisis, mainly affects the female population as it is women who, to a greater extent, suffer from the precariousness and temporary nature of the labour market. A negative factor when assessing loss of earnings due to loss of wages or other professional income.[91] The fundamental problem arises because the loss of earnings requires a judgement of probability as to the outcome so that there is relative certainty as to the gain that would have been obtained in the absence of damage. Thus, when the income from work or professional activity is not regular or is not subject to a fixed criterion, it will be difficult to prove the income that the woman ceased to obtain as a result of the harmful event. Undoubtedly, this difficulty in proving loss of earnings will affect, to a greater or lesser extent, the result of the claim for compensation.

A very similar situation arises in the case of domestic work or the employment relationship of domestic workers since in many countries, these services are very rarely standardised or regularised ("undeclared labour").Thus, it would be quite complicated to prove the performance of such activities and the income derived from them. Hence, in the cases described above, the woman is at a clear disadvantage

[90] Mesa Marrero (2014), pp. 281–308.

[91] https://ec.europa.eu/eurostat/web/lfs/data/database.

since the reparation of the financial consequences of the harmful event will almost always be incomplete.[92]

15.4.1.2 Compensation for Damages Suffered by Women Performing Unpaid Domestic Work

Traditionally, it has been women who have taken care of domestic tasks. The incorporation of women into the world of paid work has highlighted the replacement cost that this incorporation entails and the opportunity cost faced by those who decide to stay at home and take care of domestic work.[93] When, for example, a woman who works exclusively at home, as a consequence of a certain accident, suffers significant bodily injuries that prevent her from carrying out her usual domestic activities, the question arises as to whether it is appropriate to compensate for the pecuniary damage caused (apart from the biological and psychological damage in itself considered). In these cases, there is a tendency to think that if the woman's activity does not generate economic income, she does not suffer any pecuniary damage that should be compensated. However, for the victim, the fact of not being able to devote herself to the work she was doing in her home before suffering the injuries constitutes a loss that must be compensated.[94] Resolution 75-7 (Principle 5) of the Committee of Ministers of the Council of Europe, of 14 March 1975, has pronounced in this sense, stating that "for the victim, the fact of no longer being able to carry out the work he was doing in his home before the injurious event constitutes a loss which gives rise to the right to compensation, even if he has not been replaced by another person for this work".

Therefore, even if the work of a housewife is not a productive activity in economic terms, it is nowadays accepted that the injured party is entitled to compensation for the pecuniary damage suffered, to the extent that the injuries prevent her, temporarily or permanently, from engaging in her usual occupation. The accident that leaves the housewife injured and unable to carry out her tasks entails the destruction of a workforce with a pecuniary value, regardless of whether or not actual expenditure has been made to replace those tasks. In the quantification of the damage, however, the salary of a person replacing the injured housewife may be used.

Example

A is a housewife who is seriously injured in a traffic accident and is therefore unable to carry out any domestic work for a considerable period. If A hires domestic help, the salary of the hired person will constitute a pecuniary loss. Even if A does not hire anyone and his family and friends take over the domestic

---

[92] Mesa Marrero (2014), p. 287.

[93] Del Olmo García (2013) (www.indret.com).

[94] Karner and Oliphantn (2012).

chores, A will have suffered a pecuniary loss. A's work had an economic value, and its interruption represents a compensable loss, which must be recognised. ◀

Also, concerning the housewife, the question arises as to what the economic valuation of the damages should be if the victim, in addition to her dedication to work in the home, had effective possibilities of returning to work. Due to the tort attributable to a third party, suffers a situation of temporary or permanent incapacity, which not only prevents her from devoting herself to her usual activities, but also frustrates her professional reintegration. In these cases, the damage suffered cannot technically be classified as loss of earnings. Yet it should not be ignored that the harmful event causes damage insofar as it frustrates the possibilities of professional reintegration and, consequently, deprives the victim of the capacity to obtain earnings. In such cases, we are faced with what doctrine and case law described as *"loss of opportunity"*, which means the loss by the victim of an opportunity linked to a right or a specific expectation, which prevents the possibility of a future event that could be beneficial to him from taking place. Thus, the certainty of the loss of generating a profit constitutes a compensable pecuniary loss, provided that the necessary causal link between the harmful event and the lost opportunity is accredited, which must undoubtedly be assessed according to the specific circumstances of each case.[95]

15.4.1.3 Compensation for Dependency Situations

There are other cases in which the woman is not the direct victim of the harmful event but suffers indirectly from its consequences. This is the case, for example, when a family member suffers serious bodily harm that results in a situation of dependency. Social reality shows that the care of the dependent person is usually carried out within the family, and it is the woman who, in most cases, assumes this vital role, dedicating her time and efforts to the care and attention of the family member.[96] Thus, it is mainly women who provide the *"informal support"* for the dependent person. Evidently, this circumstance has a negative impact on their prospects of accessing the labour market and prevents or at least makes it very difficult for women to continue to carry out their work or professional activity as they did before the injury, which leads to an inevitable loss or reduction in income.

In such cases, we are dealing with an indirect loss of earnings, since the woman loses her income, either due to the loss of her job or the necessary reduction in working hours or due to the neglect of her business, provided that it can be established that this circumstance derives from the demanding dedication involved in caring for the dependent person. In order to quantify this detriment to assets that are indirectly caused by the harmful event, it will be necessary to make a comparison between the assets situation that actually exists after the event and the situation that would foreseeably have existed if the event had not occurred.

[95] Mesa Marrero (2014), p. 290.

[96] https://ec.europa.eu/eurostat/cache/infographs/womenmen/bloc-3d.html?lang=en.

However, if, in general, the proof of loss of earnings is subject to restrictive criteria, there is no doubt that in the case of indirect loss of earnings, the courts tend to be even more demanding when assessing whether the causal link that must necessarily exist between the loss of earnings and the damaging event that caused it is accredited or not.[97]

15.4.1.4 Non-pecuniary Damage

In addition to the purely pecuniary damage, another type of damage can occur that derives fundamentally from the injury to the personality rights: the so-called moral damage. Its main function is to compensate for the physical or psychological damage that the victim suffers as a consequence of the loss or deterioration of any of his essential goods or rights (life, bodily or mental integrity, dignity, liberty and honour, among others). The aim is to compensate for physical or psychological harm that affects the basic goods and rights of the person considered in itself, regardless of its link to gender. In this sense, the case of *Carvalho Pinto de Sousa Morais v. Portugal, 25 July 2017*[98] is relevant, in which the national court had reduced the compensation awarded to a 50-year-old woman who, following failed surgery, was unable to have sexual intercourse, partly on the basis of age and gender stereotypes. In particular, the court based its reasoning on the fact that the claimant, due to her age, was no longer sexually active.[99] The ECtHR highlights "the contrast between the applicant's case and the approach taken in two judgments which concerned allegations of medical malpractice by two male patients who were fifty-five and fifty-nine years old respectively". As stated in the judgment, "the Supreme Court of Justice found in those cases that the fact that the men were no longer able to have normal sexual relations had affected their self-esteem and caused "tremendous shock" and "strong mental shock"." and "severe mental trauma". The ECtHR emphasises that "the domestic courts took into consideration the fact that the men could not have sexual relations and how that had affected them, regardless of their age". Contrary to the applicant's case, "the Supreme Court of Justice did not take into account whether the plaintiffs already had children or not, or look at any other factors". The ECtHR decided that the Supreme Administrative Court's reasoning led to a difference of treatment of the applicant based on her sex and age, amounting to a breach of Article 14 in conjunction with Article 8.

---

[97] Mesa Marrero (2014), pp. 287–294.

[98] App. No. 17484/15, *Case of* OF Carvalho Pinto de Sousa Morais v. Portugal (ECtHR, 25 July 2017).

[99] The Supreme Administrative Court relied on the fact that the applicant "[had been] already fifty years old at the time of the surgery and had two children, that is, an age when sexuality [was] not as important as in younger years, its significance diminishing with age" (paragraph 16). The EctHR notes that "the question at issue here is not considerations of age or sex as such, but rather the assumption that sexuality is not as important for a fifty-yearold woman and mother of two children as for someone of a younger age. That assumption reflects a traditional idea of female sexuality as being essentially linked to child-bearing purposes and thus ignores its physical and psychological relevance for the self-fulfilment of women as people".

However, this does not prevent that in certain cases, due to the nature of the property or right injured, the victim of non-pecuniary damage is much more frequently a woman. This occurs, for example, in cases of violence against women, aggression against sexual freedom and, in general, in all those cases in which a woman's dignity is harmed, such as when she suffers discriminatory treatment because of her gender (for example, rape, forced prostitution, forced conception or abortion, genital mutilation, sexual harassment or unwanted touching, among others).

In another order of things, but also within the category of non-pecuniary damage, reference must be made to a personal injury of singular importance: aesthetic damage. In general, this type of damage is identified with the physical irregularity or external, visible and permanent bodily alteration that pejoratively alters the person's external appearance. Moreover, there is no doubt that the modification of that external appearance due to defects or bodily sequelae has harmful consequences, to a greater or lesser extent, for the person who suffers them. Concerning the aesthetic damage, it is debatable whether the sex of the injured person should be taken into account as a parameter for measuring the intensity of the aesthetic damage. Some argue that sex should not be excluded as an additional element that could be considered when assessing the incidence and intensity of the aesthetic harm in each case. To this end, it is argued that there are surely some sequelae that cause more significant harm to a woman than to a man, and others that have a more negative effect on the image of a man than on that of a woman. It is not a question of introducing a discriminatory factor to favour victims of a particular sex, but rather of the judicial body being able to weigh up all the circumstances that influence the specific case when assessing and adequately measuring the true extent of the aesthetic damage caused to the person who suffers it. This happens, for example, in cases of injuries and sequelae that affect the image of the person as a consequence of undergoing cosmetic surgery treatments and operations. Precisely, in this area of non-medical or non-curative medicine, case law shows that the victims of injuries are mainly women. Although in recent years there have been more and more men, the after-effects have, in many cases, an important anti-aesthetic impact, which the courts usually take into consideration when weighing up all the data that determine the intensity of the aesthetic damage.[100]

15.4.2 Compensation for Damages as a Legal Remedy for the Victim of Gender-Based Discrimination in the Provision of Goods and Services

This section will deal with damages as a legal remedy that the law makes available to the victim of gender discrimination, in the field of the supply of goods and services. Article 8.2 of Directive 2004/113/EC of 13 December 2004 *implementing the*

[100] Mesa Marrero (2014), pp. 298–301.

principle of equal treatment between men and women in the access to and supply of goods and services imposes on the Member States the obligation to introduce

> "such measures as are necessary to ensure real and effective compensation or reparation, as the Member States so determine, for the loss and damage sustained by a person injured as a result of discrimination within the meaning of this Directive, in a way which is dissuasive and proportionate to the damage suffered" and that "the fixing of a prior upper limit shall not restrict such compensation or reparation".

This is an action for compensation available to the victim of discrimination in the field of the supply of goods and services to claim compensation for the damage actually suffered as a result of discrimination, whether direct or indirect, on the grounds of sex. It is not only a matter of ensuring the indemnity of the victim of gender discrimination, but the ultimate aim must be to deter future discriminatory conduct.

As far as the criterion of imputation is concerned, this is a purely objective liability, as the rule does not require the discriminating person to have the intention to discriminate, nor that the discriminatory conduct be culpable. It is only necessary for a situation to arise in which, directly or indirectly, there is discriminatory treatment on the grounds of sex. In any case, the obligation to compensate will only arise if there is damage as a consequence of the discriminatory conduct, as this is an essential element for the application of the rules on civil liability. As to the content and scope of compensation, it is clear that all damages actually suffered by the victim of discrimination are compensable, both pecuniary damages and non-pecuniary or non-pecuniary damages, although the latter are the most characteristic of this type of situation. Although both must be proven, there is no doubt that the burden of proof is more rigorous when compensation is sought for the pecuniary damages actually caused by the discriminatory conduct or practice. When it comes to compensation for non-pecuniary damage, which tends to occur in most discrimination cases, the most complicated issue for the judicial body is the quantification of this damage (for example, it is difficult to assess the psychological harm caused as a result of discriminatory conduct).

This balancing test must enable the court to award the victim compensation that is, in any event, proportionate to the harm suffered. Under the case-law of the ECJ, such proportionality is interpreted as meaning that the compensation awarded to the injured party as a result of the discrimination must, in any event, be adequate so as to ensure that the victim is guaranteed compensation, which makes it possible to make full reparation for the damage actually suffered.[101] Moreover, Member States are prohibited from limiting, *a priori*, the maximum amount of compensation to which the person discriminated against would be entitled. The judge or competent authority

[101] Case C-407/14, María Auxiliadora Arjona Camacho v. Securitas Seguridad España SA. (ECJ 17 December 2015).

may fix the amount of compensation without having to take into account tables or scales. Consequently, the victim of discriminatory conduct has the possibility to bring an action for compensation for all the damage he or she has actually suffered as a result of the unlawful conduct.

15.4.3 The Use of Sex as a Factor in the Calculation of Premiums for the Purposes of Insurance

When taking out insurance policies, insurance companies usually set premiums based on, among other things, the sex of the insured. This is a statistical differentiation, as gender is used as an indicator of the probability that the risk being insured against will be realised. Insofar as statistics show that women in Europe live on average 5.5 years longer than men (2018 data),[102] that women generate more medical expenses and that more men drivers than women are involved in road accidents, women pay higher premiums for health and survival insurance, and men pay higher premiums for premature death insurance and compulsory motor insurance.[103] The Proposal for a Council Directive 2003/0265 *implementing the principle of equal treatment between women and men in the access to and supply of goods and services* provided for an absolute ban on the use of sex as a factor in the calculation of premiums and benefits in insurance and equivalent financial services. In response to the critical reaction from the insurance market and some Member States, the final version of Directive 2004/113/EC empowers Member State governments to permit proportionate differences in individuals' premiums where the use of sex is a determining factor, and to inform the Commission thereof (Art. 5.2). To ensure that differentiation is not arbitrary, it uses sex as a conditional calculation factor based on relevant and accurate actuarial and statistical data. It also sets another limit, which consists of prohibiting costs related to pregnancy and maternity from leading to an increase in the premiums paid by women (Art. 5.3). Finally, the Court of Justice of the European Union has declared that Article 5(2) of Directive 2004/113 is invalid, with effect from 21 December 2012, because it is contrary to the objective of equal treatment between women and men as set out in Directive 2004/113.[104]

---

[102] https://ec.europa.eu/eurostat/web/products-eurostat-news/-/edn-20200930-1.

[103] Aguilera Rull (2014), pp. 17–18.

[104] Case C-236/09, Association belge des Consommateurs Test-Achats ASBL, Yann van Vugt, Charles Basselier v. Council of Ministers (ECJ 1 March 2011).

15.5 Conclusion

It seems indisputable that on a global level a lot has been done to prevent and eliminate gender inequality, especially in the last decades. As explained, most legal systems today do not contain legal norms which would *prima facie* be accountable as a source of gender inequality. Furthermore, prohibition of discrimination is even explicitly guaranteed by the constitutions and laws of many countries. However, despite the satisfactory legal framework for achieving gender equality, certain life circumstances and social factors may still induce gender inequality. Having this in mind, it seems that the road to gender equality in the field of private law goes beyond the mere adoption of legal rules. Legal systems need to ensure the application of such legal rules. Moreover, legal systems should find a way to promote gender equality in all areas of life and try to change the stereotypical way of thinking and the division of men's and women's jobs and responsibilities: for instance, men should be encouraged to take parental leave; men and women should be equally paid for the same job; women entrepreneurship should be encouraged, etc. Such actions could, in general, create a solid ground for a better financial position of women, an increase in their assets, a better creditworthiness, a better position in case of divorce, and an overall higher degree of independence—which may have a huge influence on the freedom of women to use the rights guaranteed by law, as well. In line with this, efforts should also be made that the housekeeping, childcare and other caring responsibilities be valued in a more adequate way, throughout the whole private law regulations, bearing in mind that it impacts women's (as the most usual caring person) ability to generate income, women's position in marital or extramarital union, women's position in case of any damage suffered and the like. Finally, it seems important to mention that some principles of private law may interfere with the idea of achieving absolute gender equality. This is especially the case with parties' freedom of contract and the solution lies in finding the right criteria for making a distinction between the concepts of (seemingly) unequal treatment, which should be allowed, and discrimination, which should be avoided and sanctioned.

Questions

1. Do legal rules in your legal system or their application (or the lack of application) create legal grounds for gender inequality when it comes to the legal capacity of men and women?
2. What kind of marital regime is implemented in your legal system and how does it affect spouses' ownership and control of property acquired during marriage (acquisition and division)?
3. If one spouse invests jointly owned property into a company, what may the other spouse claim?
4. Under what conditions unequal treatment of individuals belonging to different genders can be qualified as discrimination?

(continued)

5. Does the prohibition of discrimination apply outside the area of contracts made through offers to the public?
6. What are the possible forms of gender-based contractual discrimination and their remedies?
7. Based on the regulations on civil liability in your legal system, determine whether it uses standards of care that attribute to men the ideal model of conduct (such as the rules of the "good father of the family" or "the reasonable man").
8. As a result of an accident, a woman who works exclusively in her home suffers a significant bodily injury that prevents her from carrying out her normal domestic activities. Is compensation payable in respect of the pecuniary damage caused?
9. Is compensation for non-pecuniary damage, which is intended to compensate for the physical or psychological harm that the victim suffers due to the loss or impairment of any of his or her essential goods or rights linked to gender?
10. When taking out insurance, can insurance companies set premiums based on the sex of the insured?

References

Aguilera Rull A (2014) Primas distintas en función del sexo en la contratación de seguros: ¿método neutral de cálculo de riesgos o discriminación? In: Marrero CM, Pineda CG (eds) Mujeres, contratos y empresa desde la igualdad de género. Tirant lo Blanch, Valencia, pp 17–36

Amin M (2010) Gender and firm-size: evidence from Africa. Econ Bull 30:663–668

Bartlett K (1990) Feminist legal methods. Harv Law Rev 103:829–888

Bell M (2003) The right to equality and non-discrimination. In: Hervey T, Kenner J (eds) Economic and social rights under the EU charter of fundamental rights. A legal perspective. Hart, London, pp 91–110

Berger VA (2008) Privatrechtlicher Diskriminierungsschutz als Grundsatz im Gemeinsamen Referenzrahmen für Europäisches Vertragsrecht. Eur Rev Priv Law 16:843–870

Bicchieri M, Ayala A (2017) Legal pluralism, women's land rights and gender equality in Mozambique, harmonizing statutory and customary law. Food and Agriculture Organization of the United Nations, Roma

Blagojević M, Bobic Hughson M (2014) Towards new understanding of change in gender relations at the micro level: Serbian case. https://www.academia.edu/11710228/TOWARDS_NEW_UNDERSTANDING_OF_CHANGE_IN_GENDER_RELATIONS_AT_THE_MICRO_LEVEL_SERBIAN_CASE. Accessed 7 Dec 2021

Bock A-F (2008) Dividing the assets upon the dissolution of a marriage: a comparison of legal systems which apply a hard and fast rule and systems with a discretionary approach to the division of the assets. In: Boele-Woelki K, Sverdrup T (eds) European challenges in contemporary family law. Intersentia, Antwerpen, pp 289–303

Bordia Das M (2008) What money can't buy: getting implementation right for MDG3 in South Asia. In: Buviníc M, Morrison AR, Waafas Ofosu-Amaah A, Sjöblom M (eds) Equality for

women, where do we stand on millennium development goal 3? The World Bank, Washington, pp 261–291
Brana S (2013) "Microcredit: an answer to the gender problem in funding?", Small Business Economics, June 2013. https://www.researchgate.net/publication/226218614_Microcredit_An_answer_to_the_gender_problem_in_funding
Burri S, McColgan A (2009) Sex discrimination in the access to and supply of goods and services and the transposition of Directive 2004/113/EC. http://www.gender.sachsen-anhalt.de/uploads/tx_nwcitavilist/files/European%20(3).pdf. Accessed 7 Dec 2021
Carapezza Figlia G (2018) The prohibition of discrimination as a limit on contractual autonomy. Italian Law J 4:91–117
Carter S (2006) Women's business ownership: recent research and policy developments. https://www.researchgate.net/publication/253378610_WOMEN'S_BUSINESS_OWNERSHIP_RECENT_RESEARCH_AND_POLICY_DEVELOPMENTS. Accessed 7 Dec 2021
Chamallas M (2013) Introduction to feminist legal theory. Aspen Law and Business, New York
Cowie A (2009) A history of married women's real property rights. Aust J Gend Law 6:1–21
Dabić S, Dolović Bojić K (2019) Raspolaganje jednog (van)bračnog druga nepokretnošću u zajedničkoj svojini. Pravo i privreda 7–9:407–436
Dalton C (1984) An essay in the deconstruction of contract doctrine. Yale Law J 94:997–1116
Del Olmo García P (2013) Housekeeping capacity and tort law in Europe. Indret 4:1–54
Đurić Kuzmanović T, Milinović J (2014) Gender and economy: household, market, state and gender budgeting. Collection of Matica Srpska for Social Sciences. 3, 2014, Novi Sad
EIGE (2014) Gender equality and economic independence: part-time work and self-employment review of the implementation of the Beijing Platform for Action in the EU Member States. https://eige.europa.eu/publications/gender-equality-and-economic-independence-part-time-work-and-self-employment-report. Accessed 7 Dec 2021
EIGE. Agriculture and rural development, https://eige.europa.eu/gender-mainstreaming/policy-areas/agriculture-and-rural-development. Accessed 7 Dec 2021
Epstein AL (1973) The reasonable man revisited: some problems in the anthropology of law. Law Soc Rev 7:643–666
FAO. Sustainable development goals. http://www.fao.org/sustainable-development-goals/indicators/5a1/en/. Accessed 7 Dec 2021
FAO, IFAD and WFP (2020) Rural women and girls 25 years after Beijing: critical agents of positive change. http://www.fao.org/3/cb1638en/CB1638EN.pdf. Accessed 7 Dec 2021
Finley L (1989) A break in the silence: including women's issues in a torts course. Yale J Law Fem 1:41–73
Fitzsimons E (2016) A recipe for disaster? When religious rights and equality collide through the prism of the Ashers Bakery Case. Hibernian Law J 15:66–67
Frug MJ (1992) Rescuing impossibility doctrine: a postmodern feminist analysis of contract law. Univ Pa Law Rev 140:1029–1046
Gender, Institutions and Development Database (GID-DB) (2019). https://stats.oecd.org/Index.aspx?DataSetCode=GIDDB2019. Accessed 7 Dec 2021
Gerhard U (2020) Civil law, a tool of masculine domination. https://ehne.fr/en/encyclopedia/themes/gender-and-europe/civil-law-a-tool-masculine-domination/civil-law-a-tool-masculine-domination#sommaire-women-s-rights-in-various-legal-systems. Accessed 7 Dec 2021
Karner E, Oliphantn K (2012) Loss of housekeeping capacity. tort and insurance law, vol 28. De Gruyter, Alphen aan den Rijn
Manji A (2018) Land law, great debates in gender and law. In: Auchmuty R (ed) Great debates in gender and law. Palgrave, London, pp 49–57
Mate M (2006) Landholding and property rights. In: Schaus M (ed) Women and gender in medieval Europe – an encyclopedia. Routledge, New York
Menkel-Meadow C (1996) Women's way of knowing law: feminist legal epistemology, pedagogy and jurisprudence. In: Golberger N, Tarule JM, Clinchy BM, Belenky MF (eds) Knowledge,

difference and power: essays inspired by women's ways of knowing. Basic Books, New York, pp 61–85
Mesa Marrero C (2014) El derecho de daños desde una perspectiva de género. In: Marrero CM, Pineda CG (eds) Mujeres, contratos y empresa desde la igualdad de género. Tirant lo Blanch, Valencia, pp 967–982
OECD (2019a) Social Institutions & Gender Index (SIGI) - a detailed profile for Saudi Arabia. https://www.genderindex.org/wp-content/uploads/files/datasheets/2019/SA.pdf. Accessed 7 Dec 2021
OECD (2019b) Social Institutions & Gender Index (SIGI) - a detailed profile for Albania. https://www.genderindex.org/wp-content/uploads/files/datasheets/2019/AL.pdf. Accessed 7 Dec 2021
OECD (2019c) Social Institutions & Gender Index (SIGI) - a detailed profile for North Macedonia. https://www.genderindex.org/wp-content/uploads/files/datasheets/2019/MK.pdf. Accessed 7 Dec 2021
OECD (2019d) Social Institutions & Gender Index (SIGI) - a detailed profile for Kosovo. https://www.genderindex.org/wp-content/uploads/files/datasheets/2019/XK.pdf. Accessed 7 Dec 2021
OECD (2019e) Social Institutions & Gender Index (SIGI) - a detailed profile for Serbia. https://www.genderindex.org/wp-content/uploads/files/datasheets/2019/RS.pdf. Accessed 7 Dec 2021
OECD (2019f) Social Institutions & Gender Index (SIGI) - a detailed profile for Croatia. https://www.genderindex.org/wp-content/uploads/files/datasheets/2019/HR.pdf. Accessed 7 Dec 2021
OECD (2019g) Social Institutions & Gender Index (SIGI) - a detailed profile for Bosnia and Herzegovina. https://www.genderindex.org/wp-content/uploads/files/datasheets/2019/BA.pdf. Accessed 7 Dec 2021
OECD (2019h) Social Institutions & Gender Index (SIGI) - a detailed profile for Bulgaria. https://www.genderindex.org/wp-content/uploads/files/datasheets/2019/BG.pdf. Accessed 7 Dec 2021
OECD (2019i) Social Institutions & Gender Index (SIGI) - a detailed profile for Ukraine. https://www.genderindex.org/wp-content/uploads/files/datasheets/2019/UA.pdf. Accessed 7 Dec 2021
OECD. Social Institutions & Gender Index (SIGI) - Countries/Territories in Europe. https://www.genderindex.org/country-profiles/?region=europe. Accessed 7 Dec 2021
Olsen FE (1998) The sex of law. In: Kairys D (ed) The politics of law: a progressive critique. Basic Books, New York, pp 691–707
Pavlović Đ (2014) O obveznostima i ugovorima uopšte. Pravni fakultet Univerziteta u Beogradu, Beograd
Povlakić M, Mezetović Međić S (2018) Uređenje imovinskih odnosa bračnih I vanbračnih partnera na nekretninama I rodna ravnopravnost, Zbornik radova Imovinskopravni aspekti porodičnih odnosa. https://www.google.de/url?sa=t&rct=j&q=&esrc=s&source=web&cd=&ved=2ahUKEwjvj9791dH0AhW6hf0HHX2CD1wQFnoECAIQAQ&url=https%3A%2F%2Fpf.unmo.ba%2Fsystems%2Ffile_download.ashx%3Fpg%3D4511%26ver%3D1. Accessed 7 Dec 2021
Periello LE (2018) Discrimination based on sexual orientation and religious freedom in European contract law. Italian Law J 4:639–664
Pinto Oliveira MN, McCrorie B (2008) Anti-discrimination rules in European contract law. In: Grundmann S (ed) Constitutional values and European contract law. De Gruyter, Alphen aan den Rijn, p 115
Quintanilla C (2011) Rural women in Europe. http://semantic-pace.net/tools/pdf.aspx?doc=aHR0cDovL2Fzc2VtYmx5LmNvZS5pbnQvbncveG1sL1hSZWYvWDJILURXLWV4dHIuYXNwP2ZpbGVpZD0xMjYwNyZsYW5nPUVO&xsl=aHR0cDovL2Fzc2VtYmx5LmNvZS5pbnQvbncveG1sL3hzbC1mby9QZGYvWFJlZi1XRC1BVC1YTUwyUERGLnhzbA==&xsltparams=ZmlsZWlkPTEyNjA3. Accessed 7 Dec 2021
Rao S (2015) Gender and financial inclusion through the post. https://www.unwomen.org/-/media/headquarters/attachments/sections/library/publications/2015/discussion-paper-gender-and-financial-inclusion-through-the-post.pdf?la=en&vs=3008. Accessed 7 Dec 2021

Reich N, Jessel-Holst C, Josipović T, Dollani N (2014) Autonomy and antidiscrimination in private law - the experience of the Western Balkans, SEELS Network, Civil Law Forum for South East Europe, Skopje, 2014, pp 83–105
Ringelheim J, Bernard N (2013) Discrimination in housing. European Commission, Directorate-General for Justice, Brussels
Rodna analiza sa predlogom indikatora (2020). http://upisnepokretnosti.rs/Files/00071/Rodna-analiza-sa-predlogom-indikatora.pdf. Accessed 7 Dec 2021
Sagny M (2006) Eastern Europe. In: Schaus M (ed) Women and gender in medieval Europe. Routledge, New York
Sigel RS (1996) Ambition & accommodation, how women view gender relations. University of Chicago, Chicago
Šobot A (2014) Economic activity of middle – aged women in Serbia as relevant gender equality issue. Zbornik Matice srpske za drustvene nauke 148:499–510
The World Bank (2011) World development report 2012, Gender equality and development. https://openknowledge.worldbank.org/handle/10986/4391. Accessed 7 Dec 2021
Threedy DL (1999) Feminists & contract doctrine. Indiana Law Rev 32:1247–1265
Timmer A, Senden L (2016) Gender equality law in Europe. How are EU rules transposed into national law in 2016? European Commission, Brussels
Toktas S, O'Neil ML (2013) How do women receive inheritance? The processes of Turkish women's inclusion and exclusion from property. Asian Women 29:25–50
UN Women (2009) Report of the Secretary-General, Improvement of the situation of women in rural areas. https://www.unwomen.org/en/docs/2009/7/situation-of-rural-women-report-2009-a-64-190. Accessed 7 Dec 2021
UN Women (2017) Republički zavod za statistiku, Žene i muškarci u Srbiji, 2017. https://publikacije.stat.gov.rs/G2017/Pdf/G20176008.pdf. Accessed 7 Dec 2021
UN Women (2018) Towards a Gender-responsive Implementation of the United Nations Convention to Combat Desertification. https://www.unwomen.org/-/media/headquarters/attachments/sections/library/publications/2018/towards-a-gender-responsive-implementation-of-un-convention-to-combat-desertification-en.pdf?la=en&vs=3803. Accessed 7 Dec 2021
United Nations Economic and Social Council (2019) Report of the Secretary-General, Special edition: progress towards the Sustainable Development Goals. https://unstats.un.org/sdgs/files/report/2019/secretary-general-sdg-report-2019%2D%2DEN.pdf. Accessed 7 Dec 2021
United Nations Economic and Social Council (2019) Report of the Secretary-General, Special edition: progress towards the sustainable development goals. https://unstats.un.org/sdgs/files/report/2019/secretary-general-sdg-report-2019%2D%2DEN.pdf. Accessed 7 Dec 2021
Van den Brink M, Dunne P (2018) Trans and intersex equality rights in Europe – a comparative analysis. European Commission, Directorate-General for Justice and Consumers, Brussels
Walkila S-HI (2016) Horizontal effect of fundamental rights in EU law. Europa Law Publishing, Amsterdam
Zarrouki A (2018) Equality between men and women in the Islamic law of inheritance (trans: El Balti B). https://papers.ssrn.com/sol3/papers.cfm?abstract_id=3327773. Accessed 7 Dec 2021

Gender Competent Family Law

16

Ivana Barać, Amalia Blandino, Letizia Coppo, Giampaolo Frezza, Uros Novaković, Fuensanta Rabadán, and Zara Saeidzadeh

Contents

Authors are listed in alphabetical order. Ivana Barać and Uros Novaković authored Sect. 16.8, Amalia Blandino authored Sect. 16.3. Letizia Coppo and Giampaolo Frezza wrote Sect. 16.4, Fuensanta Rabadán wrote Sects. 16.5 and 16.6 and Sects. 16.1, 16.2, 16.9 as well as the abstract were written by Zara Saeidzadeh.

I. Barać
University of Belgrade, Faculty of Law, Civil Law, Belgrade, Serbia
e-mail: ivana.barac@ius.bg.ac.rs

A. Blandino (✉) · F. Rabadán
University of Cadiz, Faculty of Law, Private Law, Cadiz, Spain
e-mail: amalia.blandino@uca.es; fuensanta.rabadan@uca.es

L. Coppo · G. Frezza
LUMSA, Faculty of Law, Palermo, Italy
e-mail: letizia.coppo@unito.it; frezza@lumsa.it

U. Novaković
University of Belgrade, Faculty of Law, Private Law, Belgrade, Serbia
e-mail: uros.novakovic@ius.bg.ac.rs

Z. Saeidzadeh
Örebro University, School of Humanities, Education and Social Sciences, Örebro, Sweden
e-mail: zara.saeidzadeh@oru.se

D. Vujadinović et al. (eds.), *Gender-Competent Legal Education*, Springer Textbooks in Law, https://doi.org/10.1007/978-3-031-14360-1_16

Abstract

This chapter discusses the construction of family and family law as central tenets of gender equality projects in law and society. It begins with a review of the evolution of family institution from the traditional nuclear to the models that are not constituted through either heteronormativity or marriage contract. Hence, it draws on LGBTQIA+ family formations including parenthood and intimate partnership. Furthermore, the chapter elaborates on the development of gender equality in family law and marriage contract in various social settings through an intersectional analysis of rights and responsibilities of partners, parents, and children. The chapter also explores domestic violence as a matter of gender equality in family law. It discusses how legal protection and prevention of domestic violence in family law can reduce harmful effects on family members, who are the victims of violence directly or affected by domestic violence as witnesses.

16.1 Introduction

This chapter introduces the institution of family as one of the most important sites where gender and power relations define individual and collective practices. Feminist theoretical perspectives on the construction of egalitarian family based on gender equality are covered in this chapter. Therefore, it elaborates on the following key concepts: patriarchy and patriarchal dividend, gender binary system, male privilege/authority, dual family model, marriage contract, commodification, the concept of care, marriage property regimes, non-heteronormative parenting, reproductive autonomy, childcare, and co-responsibility as well as domestic violence.

Learning Goals

- The first learning objective of this chapter is to explain how feminists' critical views on traditional family practices and gender inequalities within family law and society have led to important legal and policy changes overall. The main learning objective is to understand the difference between traditional family and family laws on one hand and the egalitarian family and family laws, on the other. Feminists have disrupted the institution of family as a safe and stable place for women where women's lives are constrained by multiple forms of violence and discrimination, particularly domestic violence. Thus, feminists' approaches in debunking patriarchy and male authority have not only contributed to the recognition of women's unpaid work in family, but also women's participation in labour market. As a result, domestic violence has been challenged in its form of women's economic dependence.
- The second objective of this chapter is to analyse marriage contract through a gender perspective, an analysis that problematises unequal power relations and gender inequalities within marriage as a social and a legal practice. Issues of same-sex and gender non-binary marriage are discussed according to the International and European Human Rights Conventions drawing on the right to marry and choose one's family. Furthermore, the legal and social implications of marriage contract such as filiation, property, alimony and spousal maintenance and divorce are discussed within substantive and procedural law.
- The third objective of this chapter is to present how an egalitarian family model can be realised through acknowledging equal rights and responsibilities based on gender, sexuality, (dis)ability, nationality, race, ethnicity, age and religion, all of which needs legal recognition. The chapter argues that family is not constituted by a heterosexual married couple who are assigned specific gendered roles. Moreover, parenting is not defined on the basis of biology, nor is it established on a binary understanding of gender. The development of assisted reproductive technology has advanced family formation insofar as to make it possible for single persons, same-sex couples and trans persons to become parents.

16.2 Family from a Gender Perspective: Evolution and the Current Situation

The construction of family and relationships within family have great impacts on how laws, such as family law, regulate family and family relations. In the study of gender perspective on family law, it is important to consider the evolution of the concept of family from a traditionally grounded, model male-dominated (by husband or father), to a gender-equality-based model. This section will focus on the development of gender equality in family law and policies as well as how these developments can be improved for a more gender equal family in contemporary societies.

The traditional nuclear structure of family consisting of a man and a woman with children who live together has changed due to development of an urban industrial and highly mobile society across time. This has also led to the isolation of nuclear family, and the growth of companionship different from traditional family. One of the structural changes which has been associated with industrialisation has been the separation of home and work activities.

A traditional model of family justifies the dominance of men over women and the oppression of children by parents. On this construction of family, discriminatory family laws become a way to reinforce the patriarchal male domination and parental oppression by portraying them as lawful. However, laws and policies have undergone changes throughout history differently in different societies. More egalitarian family laws have been developed to account for plurality and diversity of the ways through which human relations are shaped and family institution is formed in contemporary societies.

Example

The success of the "One million signatures" campaign of the women's movement in Morocco since 1992 led to the Moroccan's family law reform which took place in 2004. This was the landmark for reducing men's dominant position within the family providing equal rights for women and children. ◄

Family in modern industrialised societies has been changing more rapidly since the end of World War Two. By focusing on changes in the process of family formation in several modern industrialised countries, it is argued that the increase of women's participation in labour market and the rise of women's earning power and capital investment have been the most critical factors in the process of the evolution of family structure.[1]

During the last decades of twentieth century, the traditional family has been replaced by a multitude of understandings of what constitutes a family. This is due to a number of factors, including, the increased rate of divorces, participation of

[1] Blossfeld and Kiernan (2019).

women in paid labour force and the growth of female headed households.[2] The structure of family in many European countries has altered throughout the century due to the developments of gender relations and deconstruction of essentialist gender roles in society.

Nowadays, in many societies, marriage contract is not necessarily the basis of forming a family. Male authority in the family has gradually disappeared, and same-sex couples' cohabitation and marriage are legally recognised in many European countries such as Andorra, Austria, Croatia, Cyprus, Greece, Denmark, Sweden, Finland, Iceland, Norway, Ireland, Italy, Spain, Slovenia, Switzerland, Portugal, the Netherlands, Malta, Liechtenstein, Luxembourg, Germany, and France. In these countries, same-sex social and legal visibility are allegedly entered the family systems. The Nordic countries have been the pioneer in adopting legal recognition of same-sex marriage and parenthood in comparison with other European countries.[3]

In contrast to the patriarchal family model, today we find a family model in which mothers and fathers exercise their rights and responsibilities over their children on equal terms, whether in the framework of a marital relationship or a de facto union. We also find same-sex families, single-parent families, etc. The emergence of new family models is the result of a gradual process in which, among other factors, the demands of feminist movements and LGBTQIA+ groups, and the recognition in international and national legal texts of the principle of equality and non-discrimination on the grounds of sex, sexual orientation or gender identity, have played a decisive role. Among the international texts, we can cite, for example, the Convention on the Elimination of All Forms of Discrimination Against Women, of 18 December 1979, in particular, Articles 5 b) and 16.1, which establish the obligation of States Parties to take appropriate measures to eliminate discrimination against women in matters relating to marriage, family and rights and responsibilities over children. We can also cite the Principles on the Application of International Human Rights Law in relation to Sexual Orientation and Gender Identity ("Yogyakarta Principles"), of 26 March 2007, which in its Principle 24 recognises the right of everyone to found a family, regardless of sexual orientation or gender identity, and the obligation of States to take the necessary legislative and other measures to ensure the right to found a family, including through access to adoption or assisted procreation, without discrimination on the basis of sexual orientation or gender identity. However, these principles are not a treaty and therefore do not constitute a binding norm for States that have signed up to them but are intended to guide the application of international human rights law to protect LGBTQIA+ persons.

Gender competent family law and policies are the major site for promotion of gender equality in many countries since the structure of the traditional/mainstream family law is based on patriarchal dividend and gender binary system that values and privileges men.

---

[2] Nelson (1997).

[3] Digoix (2020).

Gender equality happens through changes in gender and gender relations. In the Nordic countries, gender equality policies started to develop in the 1880s regulating the lives of women in the family and public realm. The central issue of women's movements in all the Nordic countries in 1905 was the reform of marriage law through which they demanded to repeal a husband's authority in marriage and also to grant women economic independence.[4] Thus, all the Nordic countries united to establish the Scandinavian law committee with the aim of enhancing gender equality in the Nordic countries through harmonization of marriage law in 1909.[5] The outcome of the committee brought about reforms concerning the liberal formation and dissolution of marriage in 1913 and gender equality legal effects of marriage in 1918.[6]

The Nordic countries marriage law reform presented a family model that is structured as a dual breadwinner model. In this model, the work of women at home is legally recognised as contributing to family maintenance. At the same time, eugenic ideologies were used in Nordic countries to introduce marriage impediments for people of old age, people with a lot of children, people who are mentally challenged, immigrants and those with deaf-muteness.[7]

Family policy in Nordic countries emphasises on the link between gendered division of labour, unpaid work and gender equality in labour market which supports women's employment and values care work. The Nordic model recognises individualism while emphasising on the collective responsibility for family care by combining family and work obligations with childcare which is both free and of a good quality. This approach is explained as defamilisation.

► **Definition** Defamilisation is a concept that is used in refer to welfare states relationship with family and work force. Therefore, Defamilisation describes the Nordic countries' approach to gender equality policy by which family and work obligations are combined with high quality and affordable childcare institutions.[8] Defamilisation indicates the division of labour between the family, market and the state. In other words, the family goes public.[9]

The Swedish welfare state, as part of the Nordic model of gender equality, emphasises equality for all through universal benefits.[10] In the 1960s, a shift from the nuclear family to the individual family member took place in Sweden as the women's role as both mothers and workers became part of family policy discourse.[11]

---

[4]Melby et al. (2006), pp. 651–661.

[5]Melby et al. (2006), pp. 651–661.

[6]Ibid.

[7]Ibid. See also: Mattila (2019).

[8]Sandin (2012), p. 61.

[9]Sümer (2014), pp. 59–69.

[10]Esping-Andersen (1990), pp. 92–123.

[11]Sümer (2014), pp. 59–69.

Sweden has taken up a more progressive approach with regard to family policy in comparison with many other countries in the world. For example, women were allowed to divorce their partners without any particular reason in 1974 and women were granted the right to abortion until the18th week of pregnancy without providing reasons in 1975. However, when it comes to LGBTQIA+, Sweden, among other Nordic countries, has a long way to go. For example, assisted reproduction with donated sperm has been legal for same-sex couples in Sweden since 2005[12] and for single people since 2016.[13] However, egg donation is only legal for opposite sex couples, which forbids gay men in Sweden to receive egg donation. Before 2013,[14] not only were trans people unable to freeze and save gem cells before gender affirming treatment, but they were also forced to sterilisation prior to the legal gender transition in Sweden.[15]

Granting family rights to LGBTQIA+ people in Europe has been contested since early 2000. As a result, same-sex partnership and civil union are deemed legal in many European countries. Whereas same-sex marriage is not yet legalized in most of Europe. For example, Switzerland has just passed a legislation same-sex marriage through a referendum in 2021. Legal recognition of parenthood rights is still limited in some European countries such as Spain, Italy and Serbia. Moreover, very few countries have granted equal parenting rights to trans and queer couples. For example, Norway introduced a gender-neutral Marriage Law in 2009 replacing the law on Registered Partnership that was introduced in 1993.[16] The new law gives lesbian, gay and heterosexual couples equal marriage and parenting rights however, it does not recognize trans parenthood.[17] It took until 2019 for Swedish law to finally recognise trans parenthood, which allows trans people to be acknowledged on their children's documents. Furthermore, trans men who give birth are recognised as fathers and trans women are recognised as mothers.

Legal change and development of gender equal family polices benefit from applying intersectional analysis and conceptualisation of multiple inequality grounds. Social divisions of sexuality a long with discrimination based on 'race', class, ethnicity, age, (dis)ability and religion must be taken into account in approaching gender equality family policies. "Directives on gender equality at EU level have a material scope that extends from equal pay, equal treatment in employment and self-employment to pregnancy protection, parental leave, access to services and social rights".[18]

[12] Assisterad befruktning och föräldraskap: Lagutskottets betänkande 2004/05:LU25.

[13] Assisterad befruktning för ensamstående kvinnor: Socialutskottets betänkande 2015/16:SoU3.

[14] Lag (1972:119) om fastställande av. könstillhörighet i vissa fall.

[15] Lag (1999:332) om ersättning till steriliserade i vissa fall.

[16] Frantzen (2011), p. 273.

[17] Hollekim et al. (2012), pp. 15–30.

[18] Kantola and Nousiainen (2009), pp. 459–477.

16.3 Gender and Marriage Perspectives[19]

16.3.1 Discrimination Against Married Women: Evolution to the Present Situation

The family founded on marriage has historically been the traditional family model, influenced by European religious, cultural, political and philosophical traditions. In this patriarchal family, the husband was the head of the family and had the power to decide on all matters relating to married life, and the upbringing and education of minor children, given his status as the sole holder of parental authority. In the name of good family governance, the husband had the power of control over his wife; this included the power to prevent her from engaging in any extramarital activities that were seen as incompatible with her family duties. In this sense, the codifications considered the husband to be the head of the marital community who should therefore decide family matters. The wife was responsible for the care of family members and management of the household, in a division of roles governed by the principles of inequality and submission. This resulted in a marriage, in which the woman suffered discrimination, due to her status as a wife, against her husband. Married women lacked capacity and autonomy insofar as they owed obedience and submission to their husbands. Women were under the legal guardianship of their fathers until marriage, and then the husband took over as legal guardian of his wife. Women suffered a substantial limitation of their capacity, so married women constituted a different and inferior status to their husbands. Through marriage, the woman became entitled to take her husband's name and, more importantly, achieve his family status. Married women were also subject to marital authority in the area of the property. The wife appears to have been almost a 'possession' of the husband because of his legal guardianship over her.[20] Marital authority thus took the form of a set of prerogatives granted to the husband, his spouse and concerning his property.

As we can see, the marriage regulation reflected the gender roles attributed to spouses. In this sense, discrimination against women was particularly intense for married women, i.e. in their position within marriage. The unmarried woman, subjected to the power of the family, found herself in an even worse situation when she decided to marry. The new marital status, instead of bringing her new levels of freedom or recognition of her rights, caused her to fall into a situation of profound inequality and discrimination. More seriously, however, many of the above restrictions persisted in the legal systems of Western European societies well into the twentieth century.

It is interesting to mention that, at least since 1825, the year William Thompson published his attack on the 'white slave code' of marriage, feminists have criticised marriage on the grounds that it was not a valid contract. Specifically, marriage is

[19] This section has been translated with the translation service of the University Research Institute for Sustainable Social Development (INDESS).

[20] Sörgjerd (2012), p. 30.

criticised as being called a contract, when it is an institution in which one of the parties, the husband, has exercised the power of a slave owner over his wife, making it far removed from a contractual relationship.[21]

Around the time of the two world wars, marriage underwent an evolution in European countries: from a traditional model based on the husband's priority, to one founded on the equality of reciprocal rights and duties between the spouses. However, in some countries, such as Sweden, the change was introduced in 1920[22] and others, such as Spain, from 1981 onwards.[23]

Thus, the wife's submission to the marital authority in fixing the place of residence, the acquisition of nationality[24] or the imposition of the husband's surname disappeared.[25] Regarding the spouses' relationship with their children, equality between the spouses was expressed by placing husband and wife on par as legal guardians of their joint children. The husband's power in the administration and disposition of property also disappeared. The normative evolution towards marital equality resulted in suppressing of the wife's unilateral duties, replacing them with reciprocal rights and duties of respect and protection between the spouses. The idea of marriage as a joint project, based on equality, to which each spouse contributed according to his or her capacity, was central in European legislation. Since the various reforms that have modified family law, the dignity and moral and legal equality of the spouses has been assumed as a fundamental pillar of the system, so that it is difficult to defend any limitation of the rights of the individual on the grounds of marriage.

16.3.2 The Right to Marry and Form a Family

By way of introduction, we may note that marriage is a legal bond, created voluntarily, between two persons who—depending on the acceptance of same-sex

---

[21] Pateman (1997), p. 154.

[22] Karlsson Sjögren (2011).

[23] In the Spanish legal system, the Law of 13 May 1981 brought about the expected institutional change in this area.

[24] Article 9.1 of the Convention on the Elimination of All Forms of Discrimination against Women declares that 'States Parties shall grant women equal rights with men to acquire, change or retain their nationality. They shall ensure in particular that neither marriage to an alien nor change of nationality by the husband during marriage shall automatically change the nationality of the wife, render her stateless or force upon her the nationality of the husband'.

[25] In App. No. 29865/1996, *Case of Ünal Tekeli v. Turkey* (ECtHR, 16 November 2004), para. 66, App. No. 7971/2007, *Case of Leventoglu Abdulkadiroglu v. Turkey* (ECtHR, 28 May 2013), para. 22 and App. No. 38249/09, *Case of Tanbay Tüten v. Turkey* (ECtHR, 10 December 2013), para. 28, among others, the Courts found a discrimination on the grounds of sex that authorities had refused to allow the applicants to bear only their own surname after their marriage, whereas Turkish law allowed married men to bear their own surname.

marriage by national laws—may or may not be of the same sex and who usually, but not necessarily, live together.[26]

Formal or de jure family relationships represent a typical situation under Article 8 of the Convention for the Protection of Human Rights and Fundamental Freedoms ('the Convention'),[27] which recognises the right to private and family life. The European Court of Human Rights has emphasised, in this regard, that 'whatever else the word 'family' may mean, it must, at any rate, include the relationship that arises from a lawful and genuine marriage'.[28] Article 12 of the Convention states that '[m]en and women of marriageable age have the right to marry and to find a family, according to the national laws governing the exercise of this right'.[29] From the inclusion of the formula 'according to the national laws governing the exercise of this right', it is evident that Article 12 of the Convention does not guarantee an unlimited right. "The national legislature has been left a certain margin for subjecting the right laid-down exercise in Article 12 to certain conditions, regulating the legal consequences of marriage and laying down provisions concerning the resulting family ties".[30] The limitations ensuing from national law must not restrict or reduce the right to marry in such a way or to such an extent that the very essence of the right is impaired.[31]

Article 12 autonomously safeguards two rights: the right to marry and the right to found a family. The former is essentially 'a right to form a legal relationship, to acquire a status'.[32] The right to found a family, conceived in the light of Article 12,

[26] Almeida (2015), p. 117.

[27] The Convention was adopted by the Council of Europe on 4 November 1950.

[28] App. Nos. 9214/80; 9473/81; and 9474/81, *Case of Abdulaziz, Cabales and Balkandali v. The United Kingdom* (ECtHR, 28 May 1985), para. 62.

[29] Article 9 of the Charter of Fundamental Rights of the European Union (2000) expresses itself in similar terms: 'The right to marry and the right to found a family shall be guaranteed in accordance with the national laws governing the exercise of these rights'. Furthermore, Article 23.2 of the International Covenant on Civil and Politican Right (1966) reads as follows: 'The right of men and women of marriageable age to marry and to found a family shall be recognized'. Finally, it is worth mentioning Article 16 of the Convention on the Elimination of All Forms of Discrimination against Women (1979). This article states the following: '1. States Parties shall take all appropriate measures to eliminate discrimination against women in all matters relating to marriage and family relations and in particular shall ensure, on a basis of equality of men and women: (a) The same right to enter into marriage; (b) The same right freely to choose a spouse and to enter into marriage only with their free and full consent [. . .]'.

[30] Van Dijk (2006), p. 842.

[31] App. No. 11329/1985, *Case of F. v. Switzerland* (ECtHR, 18 December 1987), para. 32 and App. No. 30141/04, *Case of Schalk and Kopf v. Austria* (ECtHR, 24 June 2010), para. 49.

[32] App. No. 7114/75, *Case of A. S. Hamer against The United Kingdom* (ECtHR, 13 December 1979), para. 58.

presupposes the existence of marriage (couples living together outside marriage, on the other hand, deserve protection under Article 8).[33]

The right to marry is protected even where there is no intention or possibility of procreation.[34] The right to found a family entails the right of a married couple to procreate and have children, although this does not mean that the person must enjoy the real possibility of procreation. Thus, it is considered that the inability of a couple to conceive or raise a child cannot *per se* deprive them of the right to marry.[35]

Article 12 does not distinguish between the right to marry and the right to remarry.[36] Thus, ensuring the right to remarry for divorced persons in cases where the contracting state recognises the possibility of dissolving the marriage bond through a divorce.

The essential effect of marriage is to give birth to a marital status, which gives rise to a series of relationships and duties that develop within the framework of a community. Marriage creates a legal relationship reflected in the personal sphere and the property of each of the spouses.

16.3.3 Personal Aspects (Equal Rights and Duties of the Spouses)

"The ECtHR has held that marriage continues to be characterised by a corpus of rights and obligations that differentiate it markedly from the situation of a man and woman who cohabit".[37] The principle of equality governs all these rights and duties arising from the marriage. The legislation describes the rights and duties of spouses, which they have in the same way without discrimination on the grounds of sex. The recognition of equality and equal rights between husband and wife is one of the significant democratic achievements that is now an irreversible part of our legal culture.

Article 12 is inspired by Article 16 of the Universal Declaration of Human Rights, which is expressed in broader terms, adding that spouses 'are entitled to equal rights as to marriage, during marriage and at its dissolution'.[38] This reference to the equality of spouses was included in 1984 in Protocol no. 7 to the Convention for

[33]European Court of Human Rights, *Guide on Article 12 of the European Convention on Human Rights. Right to marry*, First edition—31 December 2020, 5 (https://www.echr.coe.int/Documents/Guide_Art_12_ENG.pdf).

[34]App. No. 7114/75, *Case of A. S. Hamer against The United Kingdom* (ECtHR, 13 December 1979), para. 58.

[35]App. No. 28957/95, *Case of C. Goodwin v. The United Kingdom* (ECtHR, 11 July 2002), para. 98.

[36]App. No. 11329/1985, *Case of F. v. Switzerland* (ECtHR, 18 December 1987), para. 33.

[37]App. No. 27110/95, *Case of J. O. Nylund v. Finland* (ECtHR, 29 June 1999), para. 8 and App. No. 11089/84, *Case of Lindsay v. the United Kingdom* (ECtHR, 11 November 1986), para. 181.

[38]In the same terms, Article 16.1.c) of the Convention on the Elimination of All Forms of Discrimination against Women guarantees 'The same rights and responsibilities during marriage and at its dissolution'.

the Protection of Human Rights and Fundamental Freedoms. Article 5 of this Protocol, under the title of 'Equality between spouses', states that '[s]pouses shall enjoy equality of rights and responsibilities of a private law character between them, and in their relations with their children, as to marriage, during marriage and in the event of its dissolutions', and adds that '[t]his Article shall not prevent States from taking such measures as are necessary in the interest of the children'.

Spouses are equal before the law in duties and rights. In this regard, Article 16.1. g) of the Convention on the Elimination of All Forms of Discrimination against Women specifies that 'States Parties shall ensure, on a basis of equality of men and women, the same personal rights as husband and wife, including the right to choose a family name, a profession and an occupation'. This equality means that decisions affecting the family may be taken by one or the other. If such decisions are agreed upon, it is irrelevant who makes them. Otherwise, no opinion will be predominant, but judicial intervention will be necessary. On this premise, the logical conclusion must be that the duties and rights imposed on marriage are reciprocal.

It should be noted that a married woman's unilateral decision to terminate her pregnancy voluntarily is not a breach of any marital duty.[39]

16.3.4 Patrimonial Aspects (Management of Marital Property)

If we said earlier that the principle of the husband's authority and the corresponding submission of the wife was evident in the personal sphere, the same was true in the property sphere, where the husband had the initiative. With marriage, the woman lost the capacity to dispose of her property and contractually bind herself without her husband's consent. This power of domination is transferred from the father to the husband. The husband's power over the wife's property took precedence, restricting her capacity to act. The husband administered the marital property, represented the wife, and allowed her to act in the course of business. Traditional law required the husband's permission for the wife to perform various acts. In addition to that, married women could not engage in trade without a marriage license. An example of the secondary role of the wife was the dowry, which compensated the husband who was obliged to feed her.

Today, the marginalisation of the married woman concerning the administration and disposal of marital property has been abolished.[40] In the legislation of the majority of the countries, the management of the matrimonial property is no longer

[39] The *European Court of Human Rights*, in App. No. 8675/15, *Case of G. Boso c. Italy* (ECtHR, 5 September 2002), in a case where the applicant complained that the legislation on the termination of pregnancy had prevented him from founding a family, found that the termination of the wife's pregnancy was in conformity with Article 12 of the Convention.

[40] Article 16.1.h) of the Convention on the Elimination of All Forms of Discrimination against Women recognises 'The same rights for both spouses in respect of the ownership, acquisition, management, administration, enjoyment and disposition of property, whether free of charge or for a valuable consideration'.

attributed to the husband but is rightly divided between the two spouses. Nevertheless, a high percentage of women continue to carry out domestic chores, either exclusively or in combination with outside work.

The life partnership that originates with marriage requires a response from the legal system to several questions that affect both the spouses' financial relations and those with third parties. It is necessary to provide a legal answer to a number of questions, such as how to contribute to the burdens generated by marriage, the organisation of the powers of management, organisation or disposition between the spouses, the organisation of their assets and the relationship between their asset's liability towards third parties. It is the principle of equality between spouses that inspires the normative response to all these questions. Thus, there is no longer forced representation of one spouse by the other, and, on the other hand, the spouses can relate financially to each other and third parties in the same way as they did before marriage since marriage does not restrict legal capacity.

About the specific property regimes applicable to the spouses (usually community or separation of property), community property regimes, in which there is a common property for both spouses, constitute an equitable system in the event of an economic imbalance between the two spouses, as was the case when the woman married and devoted herself exclusively to housework. The entry of women into the labour market, and changes in gender roles, have led to separate property regimes being the most suitable to guarantee the total capacity and equality of the spouses. Separation of property systems can be unfair to the spouse—up to now, it has always been the woman—who, having no or minimal initial assets, has collaborated in the development and increase of the other spouse's assets.

16.3.5 Non Binary Marriage

The traditional understanding of marriage is a union between persons of different biological sexes. The transformations that social evolution has brought to the institution of marriage have destroyed the dogma that marriage can only occur between a man and a woman. The opposition to same-sex marriage inevitably reflects a desire to maintain a difference between sexual roles on which traditional marriage is founded.[41]

The wording of Article 12 of the Convention seems to imply that the holders of the right to marry are two persons of different sexes. On the other hand, Article 9 CFR contains no mention of the sex of the spouses, omitting any express literal reference to the man or the woman.

[41] Herring (2019), p. 106.

Initially, the ECtHR rejected the right of trans individuals to marry people of the same biological sex.[42] The starting point was that Article 12 of the Convention enshrines the traditional concept of marriage as being between a man and a woman.[43] However, some European States recognised marriage between a transsexual and a person of the same biological sex. A new stage in recognition of the right to marry for transsexuals was opened in the Case of *Goodwin v. The UK*, 11 July 2002,[44] with the acceptance that the inability to procreate cannot, *per se*, be regarded as an obstacle to marriage and, consequently, with the recognition of the transsexual's right to marry. It should be noted that the Yogyakarta Principles plus 10 (2017) state that "no status, such as marriage (...) may be invoked as such to prevent the legal recognition of a person's gender identity" (principle 3).

As far as homosexually oriented persons are concerned, while societal developments have profoundly changed the institution of marriage since adopting the Convention, there is no consensus in Europe on same-sex marriage. The ECtHR has held that the Convention does not oblige the Contracting States to grant same-sex couples access to marriage,[45] marriage being widely accepted as conferring a particular status and special rights on those who enter it.[46] For the ECtHR, the protection of marriage constitutes, in principle, a fundamental and legitimate reason which may justify a difference in treatment between married and unmarried couples.[47] Thus, States have a certain margin of appreciation to treat differently married and unmarried couples, particularly in matters falling within the realm of social and fiscal policy such as taxation, pensions and social security.[48] These conclusions are valid despite the gradual evolution of States in this area, as more and more countries allow couples of the same sex to marry;[49] others offer legal

[42] App. No. 9532/81, *Case of Rees v. The United Kingdom* (ECtHR, 17 October 1986), paras. 49–50 and App. No. 10843/84, *Case of Cossey v. The United Kingdom* (ECtHR, 27 September 1990), para. 43.

[43] In App. Nos. 22885/1993 and 23390/1994, *Case of Sheffield and Horsham v. The United Kingdom* (ECtHR, 30 July 1998), para. 66, the Court recalls that the right to marry guaranteed by Article 12 refers to the traditional marriage between persons of opposite biological sex.

[44] App. No. 28957/95, *Case of C. Goodwin v. The United Kingdom* (ECtHR, 11 July 2002), para. 98, 100–104.

[45] App. No. 30141/04, *Case of Schalk and Kopf v. Austria* (ECtHR, 24 June 2010), para. 63 and 101, App. No. 37359/09, *Case of Hämäläinen v. Finland* (ECtHR, 16 July 2014), para. 71 and 102 and App. Nos. 26431/12; 26742/12; 44057/12 and 60088/12, *Case of Orlandi and Others v. Italy* (ECtHR, 14 December 2017), para. 192, among others.

[46] App. No. 13378/2005, *Case of Burden and Burden v. The United Kingdom* (ECtHR, 12 December 2006), para. 59 and *Şerife Yiğit v. Turkey* (ECtHR, 2 November 2010), para. 72.

[47] App. No. 34615/97, *Case of F. Quintana Zapata v. Spain* (ECtHR, 4 March 1998).

[48] See, *mutatis mutandis*, *Burden*, cited above, para. 65.

[49] Currently 16 European countries legally recognise same-sex marriages: Austria, Belgium, Denmark, Finland, France, Germany, Iceland, Ireland, Luxembourg, Malta, Netherlands, Norway, Portugal, Spain, Sweden and the United Kingdom.

protection to stable same-sex unions outside the institution of marriage (civil partnerships).[50]

16.4 Gender Perspective and Divorce/Separation

16.4.1 The Impact of Gender on the Temporary or Final Break-Up of the Marital Relationship

The temporary or final break-up of the marital relationship is perhaps one of the fields in which the contribution of gender studies to legal studies is more evident and more significant. The reason lies, on one side, in the close connection between the impact of divorce on the spouses' patrimonial and personal conditions and the cultural and professional roles that society traditionally allocates to each gender, on the other side, in the link between the approach towards marriage and divorce and the features that are inherently typical of each gender, female, male or trans.[51]

Although the regime of separation and divorce takes different shades in each legal system, we could argue that, at least in all countries belonging to the Western legal tradition, it is aimed at granting equal treatment to the spouses, not only from a formal but also from a substantive viewpoint.

The core of such a regime is the attempt to remedy the imbalances that the establishment, regulation, suspension and interruption of the marital relationship have created between the spouses as a product of factors like their mutual attitudes towards negotiation and litigation, their respective degree of commitment to family life, their propensity to form another family and their chance of doing so, their way of balancing the care of the family with their personal and professional ambitions.

16.4.2 Gender Equality and the Grounds for Separation/Divorce

The legislative and judicial tactics to reach such goal have faced deep transformations over the years, along with the evolution of the societal perception of genders. The first and more elementary step towards equality has been granting both spouses the right to obtain separation and divorce on the same grounds and without the need of the other spouse's consent.[52]

Gradually, most legal systems have moved from a fault-based separation and divorce to a non-fault model in which separation and divorce can be granted to each

[50]Fourteen European countries recognise some form of same-sex civil union, namely Andorra, Croatia, Cyprus, the Czech Republic, Estonia, Greece, Hungary, Italy, Liechtenstein, Monaco, Montenegro, San Marino, Slovenia and Switzerland.

[51]For a general overview of the main sociological implications, see Leopold (2018).

[52]See Boele-Woelki et al. (2004). The law should permit both divorce by mutual consent and divorce without consent of one of the spouses.

of the spouses upon the mere allegation of an 'irretrievable breakdown' of the marital relationship. This solution mirrors the *acquis commun* and is the one adopted by the Principles of European Family Law.[53]

Some legislations still list the typical grounds of divorce, among which scientific progress forced to add the change of gender by one of the spouses, but such grounds simply coexist with the 'irretrievable breakdown' allegation, rather than replacing it.[54]

Moreover, in the majority of legal systems fault is still a relevant element but to other effects, such as succession rights of the separated or divorced spouse, welfare-linked rights and the existence and quantification of maintenance.[55] Though, the very concept of fault has been evolutionary construed by courts: case-law is now set on the view that fault cannot be automatically inferred from the mere infidelity of one of the spouses, while it occurs only when this latter's behaviour was such as to violate the other spouse's dignity.[56]

16.4.3 Gender Equality and the Consequences of Separation/Divorce: The Distribution of Marital Property

The second tactic for promoting formal equality between the spouses in facing the criticalities of the marital relationship deals with the consequences of, rather than the grounds for, separation or divorce. In other words, the goal of gender equality requires an accurate assessment and management of the rules on the division of marital property and assets between the spouses and on the allocation of financial resources, usually labelled as maintenance.

As far as the distribution of marital property is concerned, in a time when women were considered the weaker sex, most legislations attempted to remedy the inequality by establishing as a default rule the community of goods. In a nutshell, the purpose of such regime is to avoid that one of the spouses—historically speaking,

[53] Principles of European Family Law Regarding Divorce and Maintenance Between Former Spouses, above, Chapter I.

[54] See, e.g. the French Civil code, which provides four types of divorce: divorce by mutual consent, divorce by acceptance of the principle of the marital breakdown, divorce for irretrievable alteration of the marital relationship, and divorce for fault (arts 229 ff.); and the Italian Statute No. 898 of 1970, which provides that divorce can be claimed by one of the spouses when the spiritual and material community between them cannot be maintained or rebuilt (art. 1) due to one of the circumstances listed thereafter in art. 3, among which the conviction of one of the spouses for certain criminal offences, the serious mental illness of one of the spouses, the prior separation, the fact that one of the spouses remarried abroad; the failure to consume the marriage and the change of sex by one of the spouses.

[55] Ruggeri et al. (2019).

[56] See, in particular, Italian case law: ex multis Corte di Cassazione, 15 settembre 2011, No. 18853, Famiglia, persone, successioni, 2012, 94, which clarified that the spouse can be liable for adultery and therefore bear the duty to compensate the other spouse only when his conduct was such as to infringe the other spouse's dignity or undermine his/her health.

the husband—is the sole owner of matrimonial property just because he is the only one who is entitled to work and therefore the only one who can afford to purchase assets.

In fact, the community regime entails that an ideal half of every goods, including e.g. earned qualifying periods for pension, that is purchased during the marriage, even by only one of the spouses, belongs to the other spouse. This means, on one side, that the consent of both spouses is needed to transfer the ownership of matrimonial property, and, on the other side, that such property will be equally divided between the spouses upon divorce.

Not every system solved the problem of gender equality through the community of goods. In some of them there is no pre-fixed default regime, but courts have the power to distribute martial property between former spouses in the way that is more adequate for mitigating the economic or financial imbalances caused by divorce, even if such distribution turns out to be disproportional and even if it involves the spouses' personal property.[57]

A glance at practice reveals that, following the evolution of women's role in society, especially from the viewpoint of working ability, nowadays couples tend to opt for the separation of goods, according to which each spouse remains the owner of the goods that he/she purchased in his/her name and with his/her own resources, or for other conventional regimes, rather than keeping the default one.[58]

16.4.4 Gender Equality and the Consequences of Separation/Divorce: Maintenance

As far as financial consequences of the marital break-up are concerned, the goal of gender equality needs to be reached through the regulation of after-separation or after-divorce maintenance.

In this domain as well, legislation and above all case-law are in constant evolution. The original trend was to award to the spouse who would have found itself in a detrimental position after divorce a periodical allowance. Both the decision to award the allowance and the calculation of its amount used to depend upon three parameters: the compensative criterion, the punitive criterion and the hardship criterion.

---

[57] For instance, this is the case of the English system, where the first and foremost technique for regulating the consequences of the martial break-up is the distribution of property between the former spouses through the so-called property adjustment orders. See Matrimonial Causes Act 1973, Part II, as amended by the Matrimonial and Family Proceedings Act 1984 and by the Welfare Reform and Pensions Act 1999.

[58] Besides practice, in some States community of goods is not the default regime anymore. For instance, in Germany the default regime is *Zugewinngemeinschaft*, according to which each spouse remains the owner of the goods he purchased prior to and during the marital relationship (see § 1363 and § 1378 BGB).

Compensation referred to the need of rewarding the spouse that sacrificed his—but most of the time, her—professional and personal ambitions for the care of the family and the family home; the punishment referred to the need of sanctioning the spouse who was responsible for the end of the marital relationship; and hardship referred to the need of providing the weaker spouse with enough resources to live by.

One of the most controversial issues has always been the establishment of the threshold of that "live by" concept. In a first phase, most systems tended to hold that the periodical allowance should be such as to grant the spouse the same standard of living that he—but most of the time, she—used to enjoy in the wedlock.[59]

In close connection with this aspect, the duration of the periodical allowance tended to be equalled to the weaker spouse's life. Such approach, though, is reasonable only to the extent that the weaker spouse has no chance of rebalancing its position otherwise, for instance by finding a job on its own.

Absent this, the approach risks to result into a discrimination of the stronger gender. In fact, on one hand, the weaker spouse may be encouraged to behave opportunistically, relying on the fact that he/she would always benefit of maintenance even if he/she makes no effort to become financially independent; on the other hand, the duration of the periodical obligation to pay the allowance creates a further tie between the spouses, which is a tie of economic dependence, thus never allowing the spouses to start their new life.

For those reasons, the courts' and the legislators' approach has gradually changed and moved towards the so-called 'clean break philosophy', which has been variously interpreted by the legal systems.[60] In some of them, it meant the residuality of maintenance and the prevalence of other remedies, such as property adjustment or pension sharing mechanisms;[61] in some others it meant the payment of a lump-sum maintenance rather than of a periodical allowance or the limitation of the duration of maintenance.[62]

---

[59] In particular, the use of the "standard of living" criterion rather than the "economic independence" criterion has been heatedly debated by Italian case-law: for an overview, see Terlizzi (2018).

[60] See nn 46–47. In Italy, see e.g., Corte di Cassazione 10 May 2017 no 11504, Famiglia e diritto, 636 (2017).

[61] This is the solution adopted by the Family Law (Scotland) Act 1985, on which Fotheringham (2019), p. 601; Mair et al. (2016). Scottish legislation is perceived as a model of efficiency and predictability both by Scottish family law experts and practitioners and by English jurists. See, for all the Proposal by Baroness Deech: Divorce (Financial Provision) Bill [HL] (HL Bill 21 of 2016–17).

[62] Principles of European Family Law Regarding Divorce and Maintenance Between Former Spouses, above, Principle 2:8 Limitation in time. The competent authority should grant maintenance for a limited period, but exceptionally may do so without time limit. Principle 2:9 Termination of the maintenance obligation. (1) The maintenance obligation should cease if the creditor spouse remarries or establishes a long-term relationship. (2) After its cessation according to paragraph 1 the maintenance obligation does not revive if the new marriage or long-term relationship ends. (3) The maintenance obligation should cease upon the death of either the creditor or the debtor spouse. On the French system, see Bidaud-Garon (2019), pp. 581–600.

▶ **Definition** The 'clean break' can be defined as the approach to the regulation of the consequences following a divorce that aims at terminating the situation of economic dependence of one spouse from the other within a reasonable time after the end of the marital relationship.

The underlying idea is that the weaker spouse should be encouraged to become financially independent as soon as possible and break the ties with the other spouse (and also with the court, as all the remedies that do not imply an ongoing obligation are not subject to judicial revision).

Such new approaches have raised several gender-based objections and concerns, above all among family law attorneys and experts.[63] First, it has been observed that economic independence upon divorce, or within a short time from that, neither grants gender equality nor the rebalancing of the spouses' positions, as women continue to be awarded lower salaries. Secondly, the 'clean-break philosophy' often does not take into account the fact that the women who have waived their career for the care of the family face significant difficulties in re-entering the labour market and in finding a job capable of providing them with an adequate salary on the basis of the compensative criterion.

The mentioned risks require a careful assessment of the circumstances through a case-by-case approach and a reasonable application of general principles. An efficient and rather fair model is offered, on those grounds, by the Scottish legislation.

Example

The Family Law (Scotland) Act 1985, section 9.1, lists the principles that courts must follow in selecting the most adequate financial order to regulate the consequences of divorce. Those principles are: (a) the fair sharing of matrimonial property; (b) the balancing principle, according to which fair account should be taken of any economic advantage derived by either party from contributions by the other, and of any economic disadvantage suffered by either party in the interests of the other party or of the family; (c) the fair sharing of the burden of childcare; (d) the readjustment principle, according to which a party who has been dependent to a substantial degree on the financial support of the other party should be awarded such financial provision as is reasonable to enable him/her to adjust, over a period of not more than 3 years from the date of the decree of divorce, to the loss of that support on divorce; (e) the relief from financial hardship, according to which a party who at the time of the divorce seems likely to suffer serious financial hardship as a result of the divorce should be awarded such financial provision as is reasonable to relieve him/her of hardship over a reasonable period. ◀

[63] See Schumm and Abbotts (2017), p. 1116.

Along with the advent of the "clean-break philosophy", the courts have gradually abandoned the 'standard of living' criterion in favour of a mixture between a compensative criterion and the readjustment principle.[64] On this view, one could claim that nowadays, maintenance orders should be aimed at granting the spouse who has waived his/her personal or professional ambitions for the family enough resources to adjust to the new situation and find a job in line with the path that had concretely been undertaken and then interrupted with the marriage.

One of the strengths of the latter approach lies in its gender neutrality. The concrete assessment of the circumstances of the case and of the effective degree to which the spouses committed themselves to the marital life allows courts to overcome the binary male-female antithesis and focus on the personal features behind the genders. This flexible approach could be particularly helpful when separation and divorce proceedings involve trans-genders or same-sex couples.[65]

16.4.5 From Gender Equality to Party Autonomy: The Recognition of Divorce Agreements

Another step in the evolution of the relationship between gender and the marital break-up has been the legal recognition and enforcement of pre-nuptial or post-nuptial agreements regulating the consequences of separation and divorce.[66] The underlying idea is that equality should lead to autonomy: the marital relationship is a place where the spouses share the same chance of personal growth and development so that the shaping of their living-together as well as their breaking up should be committed to them.

This presupposes that the spouses really are on equal footing when negotiating the agreement. In order to grant such substantive equality, courts tend to be particularly careful in applying those contract law doctrines that are aimed at the protection of weaker parties, such as moral duress, fraud and, from a common law perspective, unconscionability.

A fundamental upstream tool for granting such substantive equality between the parties would undoubtedly be the use of trained facilitators, like mediators or

[64] See, e.g., the evolution of Italian case law, on which Terlizzi (2018), p. 449.

[65] For an in-depth analysis, see Kim and Edward (2018), pp. 384–398.

[66] Principles of European Family Law Regarding Divorce and Maintenance Between Former Spouses, above, Principle 2:10 Maintenance agreement. (1) Spouses should be permitted to make an agreement about maintenance after divorce. The agreement may concern the extent, performance, duration and termination of the maintenance obligation and the possible renouncement of the claim to maintenance. (2) Such an agreement should be in writing. (3) Notwithstanding paragraph 1, the competent authority should at least scrutinise the validity of the maintenance agreement.

negotiators, with special skills and experience in the different approaches to negotiations that are typical of each gender.[67]

16.5 Gender Perspective and Unmarried Couples

The increased sensitivity of the law to those relationships in which the parties live together as a couple in an enduring relationship without being married or otherwise related,[68] mainly known as cohabitations or *more uxorio* partnerships or *de facto* unions, can be considered as a milestone in the path towards gender equality.[69] In fact, the formal and substantive equality of the spouses, which is the pillar of modern family law, would be severely undermined if marriage was the only possible choice for a couple that wished to build up a family without having their children labelled and treated as illegitimate or simply share a life together without being outlaw.

A prejudice still exists, deeply rooted in certain social or geographical or religious contexts, against cohabitation and affects mostly women, who are sometimes educated by their families in the belief that marriage is the key to a full self-realization, one of the paramount goals in life and an absolute must in case of pregnancy. But, nowadays, this is only a social prejudice, by no means supported by the law. In fact, European legal orderings have gradually removed all those obstacles that could lead couples to consider marriage as the only real alternative.

Ordinary and constitutional case-law of the various legal systems has started acknowledging cohabitation—provided that it was effective, of a significant duration and based on affection, not merely on a sexual intercourse[70]—as a community in which human beings can express their personality and around which revolve interests worthy of protection. This has allowed courts to acknowledge, for instance, the right of the surviving cohabitant to replace the other in the lease for the family

[67] See Menkel-Meadow (2012); and, focused on a more specific topic, Feigenbaum (2015), p. 245.

[68] This definition is drawn from Principle 5:1 of the Principles of European Family Law regarding the property, maintenance and succession rights of couples in *de facto* unions, available at http://ceflonline.net/wp-content/uploads/English-De-Facto.pdf. Not every legal system defines the concept of cohabitation. For a definition, see, e.g., Art 515-8 of the French Civil Code, according to which a *concubinage* is a factual union characterized by common life with the character of stability and continuity, between two persons of the opposite or same sex, living as a couple; and Art 1, section 35, of legge 20 maggio 2016 no 76 (so-called legge Cirinnà), according to which cohabitants (*conviventi di fatto*) are two persons, having reached the majority of age, that are bound on regular basis by a couple relationship of mutual moral and patrimonial assistance, without being related or married to each other.

[69] From a non-European perspective, see Song and Lai (2020), pp. 53–80.

[70] See Hiekel et al. (2014), pp. 391–410.

home and to extend to cohabitants the rules on civil liability for protecting them against the tortuous infringement of their relationship by third parties.[71]

In the meantime, pushed by case-law and a pressing social need, legislation has begun extending to cohabitants certain public law privileges granted to spouses, namely, the right to visit the ill partner in the hospital or in prison, the possibility to adopt children or to resort to medically assisted reproduction and access organs donation.[72] The more significant step of such legislative evolution has been the reforms of family and succession law towards the acknowledgement of the full equality between children born within a marital relationship and children born outside it and the full equalization of their legal position.

While all systems have dealt with non-marital filiation, not all of them have enacted a specific and comprehensive regulation of the relationship between cohabitants. This can be easily explained and justified considering that one of the possible reasons behind the choice of cohabitation instead of marriage is the will to prevent the relationship from being regulated by the State or equalled to marriage or the will to self-regulate it.[73] The European Commission on Family law attempted to provide a comprehensive set of principles, but such principles are not binding and they have not been followed by every Member State.[74]

Generally speaking, the regulation of such aspects as the distribution and management of the couple's property and assets and the contribution to the family *ménage* is committed to the cohabitants' agreement. For some of those aspects, like post-cohabitation maintenance, such agreement can be just the primary source of regulation, meaning that, if the cohabitants did not provide anything, there will be specific legal provisions applicable; for some other aspects, like property

[71] For instance, since the early 1990s, Italian courts have held that in case of death of a cohabitant caused by the tortuous conduct of a third person, the surviving cohabitant is entitled to claim for the compensation of the damage caused by the wrongdoer, under the general rules on civil liability (Art 2043 Italian civil code), even if the law does not provide him/her with any right of maintenance towards the other partner, on the grounds that the *more uxorio* relationship, though unregulated by the law, is considered by the legal ordering as an interest worthy of protection. See Corte di Cassazione 10 March 1994, n. 2322, Giurisprudenza italiana, 1995, I, p. 1370. Cohabitation is protected by the Italian Constitution as one of the groups in which human personality is expressed: see, for all, Corte Costituzionale 8 February 1977 no 556, Giurisprudenza italiana, 1980, I, p. 346; Corte Costituzionale 7 April 1988 no 404, Foro italiano, 1988, I, c. 2515; Corte Costituzionale 13 May 1998 no 166, Giustizia civile, I, p. 1759.

[72] For an overview of the complete framework of national legislations on *more uxorio* relationships, see the country reports available on the Commission on European Family Law (CEFL) website: http://ceflonline.net/informal-relationships-reports-by-jurisdiction. For a comprehensive analysis of the topic.

[73] Other reasons might be the will not simply to avoid external regulation but to self-regulate the relationship; or just the need to wait a certain time before marriage, in which case cohabitation becomes a sort of preliminary stage of the marital relationship; or the fact that one or both cohabitants are married with somebody else and do not want to end their prior relationships; or even the mistrust in the institution of marriage. On the topic, see Mol (2016), pp. 98–113.

[74] Principles of European Family Law regarding the property, maintenance and succession rights of couples in *de facto* unions, above.

distribution, it can be the only source of regulation, meaning that, absent it, there are no provisions applicable, neither *ad hoc* rules nor the ones devoted to the marital relationship.

This could raise a double problem: on one side, the possible substantive inequality of the cohabitants can result into an imbalance of bargaining power during the negotiation of the cohabitation agreement and therefore lead to an undue prevarication of the stronger party over the weaker one. On the other side, the lack of equalizing default provisions like the ones concerning the community or the separation of goods can enhance the risk for the weaker party to be placed in a worse position than the one prior to the beginning of cohabitation in case the relationship comes to an end.

As far as the first problem is concerned, where no specific legislation exists, the only form of protection available to the weaker party is the one provided by general contract law, namely the rules on the defects of consent; but the concepts of duress, mistake, fraud and lack of capacity seem to be unsuitable, as their application requirements are too narrow for including simple gender-related weaknesses.

As to the second problem, when an agreement between the parties is formed, in the absence of specific provisions, the only form of protection will be the validity test of the contract on the grounds of its compliance with mandatory provisions, public policy, and in the Italian system also morals. When there is no agreement between the parties and there are no default provisions, the forms of protection available will have to be drawn from outside the scope of family law. Namely, one should look at: (a) contract law, when the criticalities concern the purchase of goods by one of the cohabitants with money partially belonging to the other or the relationship with creditors or the restitution of the family house exclusively owned by one of the cohabitants; (b) property law, when the criticalities concern the management, sale or division of property jointly purchased by the cohabitants; (c) restitution law for unjust enrichment or liberalities when it is a matter of the mutual contribution of cohabitants to the cohabitation project.

16.6 Gender Perspective and Establishment/Contestation of Parenthood[75]

The impact of the gender perspective on filiation covers a wide range of issues, but to go into each of them in detail would go beyond the scope of this textbook, so we will focus on those that we consider being the most salient.

[75]This section has been translated with the translation service of the University Research Institute for Sustainable Social Development (INDESS).

16.6.1 Filiation Rights

As we have pointed out, the patriarchal family placed the father, as the head of the family, in a privileged position. One manifestation of this hegemonic position was the preference in the assignment of the paternal surname over the maternal surname when legally determining the son or daughter's filiation. Even if a person's maternal and paternal filiation had been determined, the father's surname was assigned or, if both the maternal and paternal surname could be given, the paternal surname came first. The establishment of an egalitarian family model implies recognising the same rights and responsibilities for the mother and the father in relation to their children; therefore, the continuation in the national legislation of the preference of the paternal surname would be contrary to this egalitarian model. In this regard, the European Court of Human Rights (ECtHR) has ruled in the Case of *Cusan and Fazzo v. Italy* that the Italian legislation imposing the assignment of the paternal surname to children and making it impossible for parents to choose freely and consensually between the paternal and maternal surname was contrary to Article 14 (prohibition of discrimination) in relation to Article 8 (right to respect for private and family life) of the European Convention on Human Rights.[76]

16.6.2 Adoption

Principle 24 of the Yogyakarta Principles requires States to take the necessary measures to ensure the right to find a family, including through access to adoption, without discrimination based on sexual orientation or gender identity. It also includes the obligation to take the necessary measures to ensure that the best interests of the child shall be a primary consideration in all decisions concerning children undertaken by courts and other institutions and that the sexual orientation or gender identity of any family member or other person may not be considered incompatible with such best interests.

On the other hand, the ECtHR has not affirmed the existence of a right to adopt. However, it has affirmed that the selection processes or the examination of future adoptive parents' suitability should not be influenced by discriminatory considerations or stereotypes based on the sexual orientation of those applying for adoption. In this respect, the ECtHR has ruled in the *Case Fretté v. France* that there was no discrimination in the selection process on the grounds of the applicant's sexual orientation.[77] However, this judgment has several dissenting opinions which maintain that the applicant's homosexuality conditioned the refusal to the adoption.

---

[76] App. No. 77/07, Case of Cusan and Fazzo v. Italia (ECtHR, 7 January 2014), para. 62, 66 and 67.

[77] App. No. 36515/1997, Case of Fretté v. France (ECtHR, 26 February 2002), para. 42 and 43.

In the Case of *E.B. v. France*, the ECtHR considered that there was a discrimination in the selection process on the grounds of the sexual orientation of the applicant.[78] However, this judgment has several dissenting opinions which argue that the refusal was based on the child's welfare because of the applicant's partner's lack of involvement in the adoption process.

16.6.3 Paternity Investigation and Filiation Proceedings

On the other hand, paternity claims arise as a right of the child in cases where the father has abdicated his responsibility to prevent the mother from being the only one obliged to bear the burden of raising the child.[79] However, at the same time, paternity claims are also a right of the man who wants to assume his responsibility for the child's care and maintenance. Besides, it should be taken into account that these claims involve a variety of rights, such as the mother's right to privacy, the child's right to privacy and the father's right to family.

16.6.4 Filiation and Transgender

Many legal questions arise in relation to the paternity or maternity of transgender persons, for example, does a trans-woman have to stay the father? Can she become a mother of the child? And vice-versa. The answer to these questions will depend on whether the change of gender, as well as its possible rectification in the registry, took place before or after the determination of parentage.[80]

16.6.5 Assisted Procreation

Regarding medically assisted reproduction, which includes assisted reproductive technology, the advances that have taken place in this field have favoured the emergence of new family models, insofar as they make it possible for single people without a partner and same-sex couples to become mothers or fathers.

In particular, assisted procreation with an anonymous sperm donor intervention allows a woman to become a single mother without any responsibility for the biological father. This procedure is also used by female couples who wish to become mothers. In some legislation, the motherhood of both women is legally recognised.[81]

---

[78] App. No. 43546/2002, Case of E.B. v. France (ECtHR, 22 January 2008), para. 96, 97 and 98.

[79] Vivas Tesón (1999), p. 373.

[80] For a more detailed study of the issue, see Jarufe Contreras (2016).

[81] For example, in the Spanish law about assisted procreation, but just when both women are married (see Article 7.3 of Ley 14/2006, de 26 de mayo, sobre técnicas de reproducción humana asistida).

However, in others, only the legal motherhood of the woman who gestates and gives birth to the baby after undergoing this procedure is recognised.[82] The latter situation poses some legal problems, especially when the couple breaks up, for the woman who has no legal link to the child but has also acted as a mother.

On the other hand, using assisted procreation, surrogacy allows men who wish to become parents alone, male couples and couples in which one of the partners is unable to gestate to become parents. Through surrogacy, one or two people (intended parents) enter into a contract with a woman (surrogate mother) who agrees to undergo this procedure to become pregnant (with her genetic material, that of the intended parents or that of a donor) and give birth to a child who will be given to the intended parents.[83] However, surrogacy is an illegal practice in most countries, for example, in Spain, Germany or Sweden.[84] The regulation of surrogacy is widely controversial, with voices for and against it.

The arguments in favour are very varied, among them, it is argued that no legalisation of this procedure would prevent biological parenthood through assisted procreation for men who want to be single fathers and male couples, as opposed to single women and female or heterosexual couples. This sector argues also that a law that guarantees the surrogate mother's rights would not infringe on her rights but would represent a decision in the exercise of her reproductive autonomy.[85] Among those who defend it, some argue that it should be free of charge to avoid the commodification of women.[86] On the contrary, others argue that the surrogate mother should receive financial compensation as is done in other procedures of assisted procreation, for example, egg and sperm donation.[87]

The sector against surrogacy argues, among other reasons, that surrogacy violates women's rights, that it contributes to their commodification, as it turns according to their opinion women's bodies into objects (as happens e.g. in prostitution), and to their exploitation, considering that most surrogate mothers tend to be women with few economic resources and living in countries with more income inequality. Furthermore, they argue that in its altruistic version, it contributes to devaluing pregnancy and childbirth, as has happened with other roles traditionally played by women (housework or raising children).[88]

The ECtHR has ruled on surrogacy in several judgments. In all of these judgments, the ECtHR has ruled about the problem concerning children born through surrogacy abroad whose filiation is intended to be registered in the country

---

[82] For example, the Spanish law about assisted procreation (see above) recognizes the maternity of both women when they are married but it says nothing when they are a couple of facto.

[83] Rodríguez Ruíz (2017), p. 259; Souto Galván (2006), pp. 182–183.

[84] As example, see Spanish law about assisted procreation (Article 10 of Ley 14/2006, de 26 de mayo, sobre técnicas de reproducción humana asistida).

[85] Rodríguez Ruiz (2017), pp. 267–268; Igareda González (2020), p. 87.

[86] Souto Galván (2006), p. 195.

[87] Igareda González (2020), p. 83.

[88] Rodríguez Ruiz (2017), p. 261.

of origin of the intended parents, where this procedure is prohibited.[89] However, in these judgments, the ECtHR has not ruled on whether it is appropriate to legalise this practice, leaving this issue to each State's power.[90]

Finally, access to assisted procreation has also allowed women to delay motherhood, for example, by the procedure of egg cryopreservation. This reality finds voices for and against it. On one hand, assisted procreation allows women to decide, in the exercise of their reproductive autonomy, to delay motherhood to focus on their working careers. On the other hand, defending the benefits of these procedures and technology for women in the labour market implies imposing on them the parameters of a typically male work model where pregnancy, childbirth and child-rearing are not contemplated, instead of establishing measures that allow women to balance their work and family lives, and to establish an egalitarian model where child-rearing is also part of the work and family life of men.[91]

To conclude, regarding filiation, assisted procreation has favoured new models of family, but also creates some controversial issues that are unresolved or arises different opinions for and against. One of the most problematic issues is surrogacy. Some argue that a protective law for the surrogate mother is in accordance with women reproductive autonomy. On the contrary, others argue that surrogacy violates women's rights and contributes to their commodification.

16.7 Gender Perspective and Parental Responsibility, Child Custody and Child Support[92]

An androcentric society's construction was possible by relying on a specific family model as the most basic form of social organisation. A family was a social group encompassed by different people, goods, and resources, under the father's power, as the family's head. Thus, in Ancient Rome, the *pater familias* exercised power over his wife, children, slaves, and property. This patriarchal family model persists over the centuries. Although it underwent some variations, its essence remained the same: the male's hegemonic role in the public sphere was transferred to the family, so the father made the family sphere decisions, also concerning his children. Woman remained in the domestic sphere, in their role as wife and mother, under the decisions of the husband/father.[93]

---

[89] App. Nos. 65192/11 and 65941/11, Case of Menesson and Labassee v. France (ECtHR, 26 June 2014). App. No. 25358/12, Case of Paradiso and Campanelli v. Italy (ECtHR, January 2017). App. No. 906372014, Case of Foulon and Bouvet v. France (ECtHR, 21 July 2016). App.11288/2018, Case of D v. France (ECtHR, 16 July 2020).

[90] Igareda González (2020), p. 78.

[91] Álvarez Medina (2017), pp. 158–160.

[92] This section has been translated with the translation service of the University Research Institute for Sustainable Social Development (INDESS).

[93] Moraga García (2014), pp. 480–481.

With industrialisation (nineteenth century), the dichotomy between public/masculine and private/feminine became more acute. A rural way of life, where the family produced its resources and all family members contributed to its support, including the children as labourers from a very young age, is abandoned. With industrialisation, production was transferred to factories and family resources to its support had to be found outside the home, and this task fell to the father, who had to go out to work.[94] Although the majority of women remained at home, some women also started to work in factories and to access the labour market but keeping their household and childcare obligations.[95] Besides, children's rights began to emerge. Children started not to be considered as labour force, and the idea of woman as the best suited to care for young children prevailed, following child protection's footsteps.[96] As husband and father, the man was responsible for the family's economic support. The woman was responsible for the care of the children and the home without losing the father's hegemonic role within the family. This patriarchal model was what the codification movement of the nineteenth century took up and regulated, giving it legal backing. For this reason, in the nineteenth-century civil codes, the father had attributed authority and decision-making power over the children, with the mother occupying a secondary or subsidiary role, even though the mother carried out the functions of upbringing, care, and education of the children in practice.[97] The father maintained his authority over the children after the divorce to the mother's detriment (as we will see below). Even widowed woman continued in this subsidiary position, transferring decision-making power over the children to another male member of the family (the grandfather, an older brother or the woman's new husband).[98]

On the contrary, European codes nowadays establish the equality of father and mother in exercising their rights, duties and responsibilities towards their children. Following the example of the Spanish Civil Code, contrary to its original wording, the current Article 154 states:

> "Unemancipated sons and daughters are under their parents' parental authority. Parental authority, as parental responsibility, shall always be exercised in the interests of the sons and daughters, following their personality, and with respect for their rights and their physical and mental integrity".

In the Spanish Civil Code, parental authority is now a concept stripped of the old authority or hegemonic power of the father and configured as a responsibility, a function exercised for the benefit of the children and on equal terms by the parents,[99]

---

[94] Esquembre Valdés (2006), p. 42; Moraga García (2014), p. 481; Avilés Hernández (2019), p. 201.

[95] Esquembre Valdés (2006), p. 43.

[96] Moraga García (2014), p. 481; Avilés Hernández (2019), p. 201.

[97] Moraga García (2014), p. 481.

[98] Moraga García (2014), p. 482. Avilés Hernández (2019), p. 200.

[99] Verdera Izquierdo (2014), p. 457.

whether they are married or an unmarried couple, and whether they are of different or the same sex. Other examples of parental co-responsibility can be found in Article 316 of the Italian Civil Code.

This principle of co-responsibility can also be found in international law. Thus, the Convention on the Elimination of All Forms of Discrimination against Women (CEDAW), 18 December 1979, establishes in Article 5 b) that States Parties shall take all appropriate measures to ensure "the recognition of the common responsibility of men and women in the upbringing and development of their children, it being understood that the interest of the children is the primordial consideration in all cases". Moreover, Article 16.1 (d) and (f) of CEDAW establishes that States Parties shall ensure, on a basis of equality of men and women, the same rights and responsibilities as parents, irrespective of their marital status, in matters relating to their children; and with regard to guardianship, wardship, trusteeship and adoption of children; in all these cases, the interests of the children shall be paramount. Furthermore, in the United Nations Convention on the Rights of the Child of 20 November 1988, Article 18.1 says that "States Parties shall use their best efforts to ensure recognition of the principle that both parents have common responsibilities for the upbringing and development of the child. Parents or, as the case may be, legal guardians shall have the primary responsibility for the upbringing and development of the child. The bests interest of the child will be their basic concern". Including the principle of co-responsibility in the Convention on the Rights of the Child makes it possible to sustain its relationship with the children's welfare. However, the latter must guide the exercise of this co-responsibility. Besides, it should be taken into account that Article 3.1 of the Convention on the Rights of the Child states that in all actions concerning children, the best interest of the child shall be a primary consideration. Nevertheless, as we shall see below, the interest of the child, being an indeterminate concept, can also be used to perpetuate gender inequalities.[100] In this sense, the General Comment No. 14 (2013) of the Committee on the Rights of the Children highlights in paragraph 34 that "the flexibility of the concept of the child's best interests allows it to be responsive to the situation of individual children and to evolve knowledge about child development. However, it may also leave room for manipulation; the concept of the child's best interests has been abused (. . .) by parents to defend their own interests in custody disputes."[101]

The evolution from a patriarchal family towards a model in which father and mother exercise their parental responsibility on equal terms has occurred gradually. The demands of feminist movements have undoubtedly played a fundamental role in

[100] Choudhry et al. (2010), p. 9; Rodríguez Ruiz (2017), p. 51.

[101] See General Comment No.14 (2013) on the right of the child to have his or her best interests taken as a primary consideration (art. 3, para. 1) of the Committee on the Rights of the Children. The Committee on the Rights of the Child monitors implementation of the Convention on the Rights of the Child by its State parties. https://www.ohchr.org/en/hrbodies/crc/pages/crcindex.aspx

this change. Both national and international legal texts have gradually taken up and covered the principle of equality and non-discrimination on the grounds of sex, which consequently must also be reflected in the regulation of parental responsibility. Likewise, the prohibition of discrimination on the grounds of sexual orientation or gender identity and the progressive recognition of LGTBQIA+ groups' rights regarding marriage, adoption, and access to assisted reproduction techniques have led to other family models being contemplated.

However, despite the formal recognition of equality in the exercise of parental responsibility, gender roles or stereotypes continue to weigh heavily in children's upbringing, care, and education, giving rise to material inequality situations. It happens because women have entered the labour market and the public sphere, but men have not entered the domestic sphere or have done so late, incompletely and unequally.[102] For this reason, it is still mainly women who take maternity leave, leave of absence and reduced working hours to care for their children.[103] Balancing between work and family life is still seen as particularly difficult for women, as they are who mainly carry the burden of domestic life. Thus, it has been argued that in practice, the current family model presents characteristics of an egalitarian system but also with roles and elements typical of the patriarchal family.[104] It shows that there is still a long way to go in terms of material equality. Therefore, positive and inclusive actions are required to remove these obstacles, but without falling into the trap of paternalism so that, far from promoting equality, the measures adopted perpetuate these inequalities or gender stereotypes. Moreover, following a gender perspective is no longer enough to adopt measures focused on a single aspect or area; instead, it requires cross-sectional actions that remove these gender inequalities or stereotypes, involving different areas (legal, social, educational, etc.) in a connected way.

On the other hand, inequality in children's care and responsibilities has been particularly evident in divorce cases or lack of parents' cohabitation. The conception of the family and the roles that its members play within it have conditioned the consequences of the cohabitation break-up in parental responsibilities.[105]

Thus, initially, considering that the father had a preferential role in decision-making about the children during the marital cohabitation, he was granted custody of the children with the divorce or the cohabitation break-up. The divorced or separated mother did not cohabitate, did not participate in decision-making and could even lose the right to interact with her children.[106]

[102] Moraga García (2014), p. 482.

[103] Wallbank (2010), pp. 107–110; Moraga García (2014), p. 483.

[104] Collier (2010), pp. 128–129.

[105] Avilés Hernández (2019), p. 198.

[106] Moraga García (2014), p. 482; Avilés Hernández (2019), p. 200.

Gradually, the balance has shifted child's custody towards the mother since, as we have seen above, under the influence of child protection measures, the idea that it is in the child's best interests to remain in the mother's care is gaining ground.[107] The father is responsible for the payment of maintenance and has visiting rights. The father's role as breadwinner and the mother as carer, with the dissociation between public/male and private/female, continues in these cases of the parents' cohabitation break-up.

This scheme is maintained, although the legal texts regulate the figure of custody in an egalitarian manner, without leaning towards the father or the mother, but rather towards the parent who is more apt to take care of the child. It is because the choice of the most suitable parent following the principle of the welfare of the child means that in this difficult choice, judges opt for the parent who, until before the break-up, had been carrying out the tasks of raising and caring for the children, i.e. mostly the mother.[108] This sole custody system means that in practice, the mother continues to bear a more significant burden in the children's care and education, which worsens when the father neglects his responsibilities, for example, when he fails to pay child support. On the other hand, fathers argued that this model of custody prevents them from having a fluid relationship with their children and even from participating in making important decisions regarding their education or health when the figure of custody also includes or involves these parental responsibilities and also places an excessive financial burden on them (payment of alimony, moving out of the family home).[109] At this point the debate on joint or shared custody arises.[110]

Joint custody appears as an egalitarian model favouring co-responsibility after the break-up of the parents' cohabitation. Joint custody would make it possible to distribute the burden of parenting between the parents and favour a fluid relationship between the children and both parents after the break-up of cohabitation, all of this to benefit the child's well-being.[111]

However, this type of custody is subject to criticism. According to a critical voice,[112] the implementation of this regime in legal texts does not correct the inequalities between fathers and mothers in the care of children but rather maintains them to the detriment of women. Specifically, this opinion maintains that, even though the family model has changed a great deal and men are increasingly involved in childcare, childrearing's burden continues to fall mainly on women. If the father

[107] Avilés Hernández (2019), pp. 201–202.

[108] Vivas Tesón (1999), p. 339; Verdera Izquierdo (2014), p. 459; Rodríguez Ruiz (2017), p. 44.

[109] Wallbank (2010), pp. 95–96.

[110] We will use both terms as synonyms, although in some legal system they can involve some differences. Furthermore, joint and shared custody has different meanings in the diverse legal system and can involve cohabitation, care and making decisions concerning children. In any case, the model of joint or shared custody arises in relation to the debate about exercising parental rights and responsibilities on equality after the parents' cohabitation break-up. We will try to use these terms in a broad sense that encompasses their different meanings.

[111] Verdera Izquierdo (2014), p. 459.

[112] Moraga García (2014), pp. 479–485, 489–491.

was not involved in childcare before the break-up, shared custody would not correct this inequality. For this reason, this critical voice considers that shared custody should not be regulated in legal texts as a preferential system, nor should it be granted automatically by the courts. According to this opinion, before opting for this regime, the dedication that the parents have had during their cohabitation should be taken into account, so that shared custody should be chosen when both parents have been involved in the care of their children in a similar way. This critical view also considers that in those societies (for example, in Swedish) in which structural changes have been carried out to remove the obstacles that prevented the consolidation of an egalitarian family model (free childcare from the age of zero, rationalisation of work schedules to favour the balance with family life, parental leave for both parents under equal conditions, and so forth), this system of custody would be viable. But not in societies where the family model in practice is far from equal because the necessary conditions are not in place. The most critical voices against shared custody argue that it is a sexist and patriarchal demand. They believe that most fathers' rights movements that demand it are trying to maintain or recover the hegemonic position they had within the patriarchal family and get rid of their economic burdens; they argue that there is no genuine interest in sharing children's upbringing.[113]

Regardless of these views, there is no doubt that joint custody encourages co-responsibility and is in accordance with Articles 5 b) and 16.1 (d) and (f) of the CEDAW, as well as Article 18.1 of the Convention on the Rights of the Child, mentioned above. Let it be supposed that it is understood to be in the children's best interests that both parents participate in their care and upbringing during cohabitation; in that case, there is no reason to argue otherwise when they cease to cohabit. In this regard, Article 16.1(d) of CEDAW says that States Parties shall ensure, based on equality of men and women, the same rights and responsibilities as parents "irrespective of their marital status", but also adds "in all cases, the interests of the children shall be paramount". Therefore, the children's interests should guide this principle of co-responsibility, also when the parents do not live together.

In this sense, physical joint custody (cohabitation and care) favours co-responsibility. However, this system will not always be possible, for example, when the parents' homes are far apart, and in this case, other models that favour co-responsibility should be chosen. Thus, physical custody may be attributed to one of the parents with an extensive visiting regime for the non-residential parent, establishing the duty of both parents to contribute to the financial support of the child and also co-responsibility in legal custody, parental responsibility or parental authority (depending on the terminology of each legal system), i.e., the possibility of intervening in decision-making on important issues relating to the education, health, etc., of the child.

In the case of a shared custody model or other co-responsibility models over the children, the welfare of the children must be taken into account. Moreover,

[113] Moraga García (2014), pp. 482, 489–490.

according to Article 3.1 of the Convention on the Rights of the Child the best interest of the child shall be a primary consideration ahead of parents' interests. Nevertheless, the child's interests may not be used as an excuse to perpetuate situations of inequality, in one sense or another. In other words, it must be avoided that in the name of the welfare of the child, a system of sole or shared custody is chosen, not because the situation makes it advisable, but because of the maintenance of beliefs or stereotypes based on gender roles (for example, parents' sexual orientation, fathers are not suitable to care for young children, labour women are not good mothers, boys should be cared for by fathers and girls by mothers, among others). As noted above, this requires examining, among other issues, the relationship that the parents have had concerning the child and the relationship of the parents to each other before cohabitation break-up.[114] Therefore, joint custody would not be viable when violence has been exercised against the child and when one of the parents has exercised violence against the other. This raises all the problems related to gender violence, which we will not dwell on here since it is the subject of study in section 7, but on which it should be noted that it will have to be borne in mind when determining the system of custody, visitation rights or relationship with the non-residential parent and the exercise of parental responsibility.

To conclude, gradually, the patriarchal family has given way to a family model in which parents have equal rights and responsibilities over their children, in legal texts. After parents' cohabitation break-up, this situation of equal rights and responsibilities must be maintained in accordance with the child's interest. In this sense, shared custody arises as a system that favours co-responsibility after parents' break-up. However, despite the legal recognition of equality, gender roles and stereotypes continue to weigh heavily in the family, so that mothers are the main carers of children in practice. Because of that, it is required to remove stereotypes through actions that favour an equalitarian model of family in which both parents share their responsibilities over their children. In any case, child's interest has to be the primordial consideration and must not be used to perpetuate gender roles.

16.8 Gender Perspective and Domestic Violence

For a long time, domestic violence was regarded as a question pertaining to the private sphere of one's life and was understood to be a rare occurrence and unusual behaviour.[115] It was only after the actions of feminist movement conducted in the 1970s, that domestic violence was identified as a human's right issue. Such a conclusion was deduced from the fact that domestic violence against women was "global, systematic and rooted in power imbalances and structural inequalities between men and women."[116] Legal scholars maintain that there are two different

[114] Vivas Tesón (1999), p. 340; Wallbank (2010), p. 95; Rodríguez Ruiz (2017), p. 47.

[115] Petrušić and Konstantinović-Vilić (2010), p. 10.

[116] Choudhry (2010), p. 145.

schools of thought in regard to domestic violence. The first, feminist approach, considers domestic violence to be a result of power imbalances between women and men and the individual characteristics of the perpetrator, while the second school of thought considers domestic violence to be the result of emotional power imbalances in family relations caused by different factors and influences (unemployment, poverty, mid-life crises, alcoholism, etc.).[117]

Nevertheless, the understanding commonly accepted by authors is multi-layered, as it explains domestic violence to be a result of the deeply rooted roles assigned to women and men and of different socio-economic, social, cultural and psychological factors. For example, if we consider the everlasting cultural definition of gender roles and the belief in the inherent superiority of men on one side and women's economic dependence on men on the other, it can be deduced that women can feel trapped in their position.[118] Domestic violence and its causes have become an issue of both international and domestic legal concern.[119] As previously stated, it can also be deduced from the WHO's Report which concludes that globally, most violence against women is perpetrated by the current or former husband or intimate partner and that more than 641 million women aged 15 or older have been subjected to intimate partner violence.[120] With that in mind, it does not come as a surprise that the international community has enacted several international instruments related to the elimination of violence against women and in turn domestic violence.[121] Hence, the previously mentioned Convention on the Elimination of All Forms of Discrimination against Women takes an important place in bringing the female half of humanity into the focus of human rights concerns. Activities were also conducted on a regional level, as the Council of Europe has, in 1950, adopted the European

[117] Draškić (2008), p. 344.

[118] Schuler et al. (1996), pp. 1729–1742.

[119] Schuler et al. (1996), pp. 1729–1742.

[120] "Violence Against Women Prevalence Estimates, 2018, Executive Summary", World Health Organization on behalf of the United Nations Inter-Agency Working Group on Violence Against Women Estimation and Data (VAW-IAWGED), accessed April 20 2021, https://www.who.int/publications/i/item/9789240022256, VI.

[121] The General Assembly of the United Nations adopted the Declaration on the Elimination of Violence against Women with the resolution 48/104 of 20 December 1993, accessed April 20, 2021, https://www.ohchr.org/Documents/ProfessionalInterest/eliminationvaw.pdf. The Declaration urged Member States to exercise due diligence to prevent, investigate and, in accordance with national legislation, punish acts of violence against women, whether those acts are perpetrated by the State or by private persons.

The said Declaration led to the adoption of the Bejing Declaration and Platform for Action adopted at the 16th plenary meeting of the Fourth World Conference on Women, on 15 September 1995, accessed April 20, 2021, https://www.un.org/womenwatch/daw/beijing/pdf/BDPfA%20E.pdf.

The General Assembly of the United Nations, on its 58th session on 22 December 2003 adopted the General Assembly Resolution 58/147 on elimination of domestic violence against women, accessed 20 April 2021, https://undocs.org/en/A/RES/58/147. The said resolution stipulated that that domestic violence is of public concern and required States to take serious action to protect victims and prevent domestic violence.

Convention of Human Rights (ECHR).[122] Although the ECHR does not specifically deal with the question of domestic violence it cannot be denied that it has "proved itself to be much more effective than other such instruments in ensuring State compliance with the human rights norms it represents."[123] In that respect, the European Court of Human Rights (ECtHR), aimed to achieve the rightful implementation of the ECHR in case of any breach of rights set thereto, has relatively recently had the chance to apply the ECHR to the issue of domestic violence. To be precise, it was first in *Kontrová v Slovakia*[124] that the ECtHR underlined the duty to take positive action to prevent a risk to a victim of domestic violence.[125] In *Bevacqua and another v Bulgaria*[126] the Court has, for the "first time recognised that a failure to protect a woman and her child from violence and harassment can constitute a violation of Article 8 of the Convention and urged the State to intervene where women face situations of violence in the private sphere."[127] Finally, in *Opuz v. Turkey*,[128] the Court held for the first time that domestic violence in the case at hand was gender-based[129] and that it "affected mainly women and that the general and discriminatory judicial passivity in Turkey created a climate that was conducive to domestic violence."[130] Aside from the ECHR, it is important to underline that the COE has adopted the Convention on preventing and combating violence against women and domestic violence in 2011[131] (also known as the Istanbul Convention) which is the first legally binding instrument in Europe aimed to combat gender-based violence. According to the provisions of Istanbul Convention, the state is obliged to "prevent all forms of violence against women, take actions aimed to protect the those who experience it and prosecute perpetrators, and to promote equality between women and men prevent violence against women by encouraging mutual respect or non-violent conflict resolution and questioning gender stereotypes."[132]

---

[122] European Convention on Human Rights as amended by Protocols Nos. 11 and 14 supplemented by Protocols Nos. 1, 4, 6, 7, 12, 13 and 16, accessed on 20 April 2021, https://www.echr.coe.int/documents/convention_eng.pdf.

[123] Choudhry (2010), p. 147. That does not come as a surprise if we bear in mind that the ECHR guarantees amongst other, the right to life (Art. 2), prohibition of torture and inhuman or degrading treatment or punishment (Art. 3) and the right to respect for private and family life (Art. 8).

[124] App. No. 7510/04 Case of Kontrová v Slovakia (ECtHR, 31 May 2007).

[125] App. No. 7510/04 Case of Kontrová v Slovakia (ECtHR, 31 May 2007), para. 49.

[126] App. No. 71127/01 Case of Bevacqua and S. v Bulgaria (12 June 2008).

[127] App. No. 71127/01 Case of Bevacqua and S. v Bulgaria (12 June 2008), para. 65.

[128] App. No. 33401/02 Case of Opuz v. Turkey (9 June 2009).

[129] App. No. 33401/02 Case of Opuz v. Turkey (9 June 2009), para. 200.

[130] App. No. 33401/02 Case of Opuz v. Turkey (9 June 2009), para. 198.

[131] The Council of Europe Convention on preventing and combating violence against women and domestic violence, adopted on 11 May 2011, accessed on 20 April 2021, https://www.coe.int/en/web/conventions/full-list/-/conventions/rms/090000168008482e.

[132] "What is the Istanbul Convention? Who is it for? Why is it important?" Publication of the European Commission, accessed on 17 June 2021, https://ec.europa.eu/justice/saynostopvaw/downloads/materials/pdf/istanbul-convention-leaflet-online.pdf.

It is important to note that domestic violence leads to grave consequences on the overall well-being of victims. Domestic violence can lead to unwanted pregnancies, STDs, miscarriages, depression, anxiety, low self-esteem, eating disorders and even to most fatal consequences such as suicide and intimate femicides[133] (gender-based murder of women and girls).[134] It should be stressed that one study testifies that in 2018 there were 147 cases of femicide in Germany, 139 in the United Kingdom and 121 in France![135]

As previously mentioned, most violence against women is perpetrated by the current or former husband or intimate partner. As a result, domestic violence has its deteriorating effects on the regulation of divorce/separation, especially when the said relationship includes children. It is not unusual that women often remain part of a destructive and unhealthy relationships mainly because they feel "helpless to leave the abusive partner"[136] and because "their alternatives are limited if they do not have economical and personal resources to make a satisfactory exit."[137] Accordingly, victims of domestic violence often opt to ignore the problem, adjust to the needs of the perpetrator and to remain silent on this issue. There are a variety of reasons which define the victim's decision not to report domestic violence. These reasons generally relate to the victim's feeling of shame to report the wrongdoing, understanding that the act of domestic violence was a rare occurrence which will not be repeated and a lack of trust towards the authorities. Moreover, authors argue that "there are some groups of women which are not even aware of the fact that they too are intitled to a life without domestic violence, such as Roma women, handicapped women, women in villages, etc."[138]

---

[133] Mršević (2014), p. 87. See also "Understanding and addressing violence against women", World Health Organization, 2012, accessed June 17 2021, https://apps.who.int/iris/bitstream/handle/10665/77421/WHO_RHR_12.38_eng.pdf;jsessio.

[134] "Domestic Violence against Women and Girls", United Nation's Children Fund, Innocenti Research Center, Florence, No. 6, 2000, accessed April 20, 2021, https://www.unicef-irc.org/publications/pdf/digest6e.pdf, p. 19.

It has been evaluated that a total of 50,000 deaths worldwide in 2017 were the deaths of women and girls resulting from intentional homicide perpetrated by an intimate partner or other family member. "Global Study on Homicide, Executive Summary", United Nations Office on Drugs and Crime, United Nations (2019), accessed April 20, 2021, https://www.unodc.org/documents/data-and-analysis/gsh/Booklet1.pdf, p.14.

[135] Statista Research Department, accessed on June 17, 2021, https://www.statista.com/statistics/1096116/femicide-in-europe-in-2018/#stat; Yllö, Bogard (1988), cited by Baber and Allen (1992), p. 52. Gelles, Conte, cited by Baber and Allen (1992), p. 52. See Mršević (2014), p. 51. In that respect Choudhry argues that "the individual interests of a parent victim of domestic violence could easily be overridden by the interests of the child, if those interests are threatened by choices made by that parent – choices which can range from a failure to leave an abusive relationship or to co-operate in action taken against the perpetrator." Mullender (1995); Hester et al. (2000), new edn 2007, p. 153. Choudhry (2010), p. 147.

[136] Yllö, Bogard (1988), cited by Baber and Allen (1992), p. 52.

[137] Gelles, Conte, cited by Baber and Allen (1992), p. 52.

[138] See Mršević (2014), p. 51.

The problem becomes even more severe if the said relationship includes children. It is not unusual that a victim remains part of an abusive relationship in order to protect the life and well-being of her/his offspring, seeing that a different scenario could potentially result in a tragic manner for both the victim and the child.[139] Since victims fear not only for their life, but more importantly for the life of their children they usually decide to do nothing on the subject matter, as they see no other possibility but to accept the position they are in. Such fear is indeed justified if we bear in mind that domestic violence has its serious implications on children as well. Better said, a study shows that at least 750,000 children a year witness domestic violence. Moreover, children who have experienced domestic violence are more likely to suffer from emotional trauma and mental health difficulties in adult life.[140]

The question of domestic violence is indeed recognised as a problem affecting women and children's fundamental human rights globally. It can nevertheless be argued that the existing system of international human rights fails to "adequately reflect and respond to the experiences and needs of women."[141] It is hence required to firstly address and adjust the existing understanding of the patriarchal division of sex roles and instead not only promote but also achieve material gender equality in every area of contemporary family life. Secondly, both the international and national systems ought to undergo a systematic change which will put more focus on the prevention of domestic violence and on rising awareness on harmful effects of domestic violence. Moreover, actions ought to be taken in order to create more reliable surroundings for the victims which would in turn lead to the increase of their trust in the authorities and to their willingness to report an act of domestic violence and to seek protection. Such behaviours would lead to the decrease of the rate of domestic violence and would pave the way towards a more balanced society.

16.9 Conclusion

Family law and family policies are the major site for the promotion of gender equality in many countries because unequal power relations and gendered practices are codified through family law reinforcing patriarchal structure and male domination. The backbone of family law in many countries is based on the patriarchal dividend and a heterosexual gender binary system that values heterosexual relations and enhances men's privilege.

Family as an interconnection between private and public spheres, is where various forms of violence and discrimination take place. Therefore, women's

[139] In that respect Choudhry argues that "the individual interests of a parent victim of domestic violence could easily be overridden by the interests of the child, if those interests are threatened by choices made by that parent – choices which can range from a failure to leave an abusive relationship or to co-operate in action taken against the perpetrator."

[140] Mullender (1995); Hester et al. (2000); new edn. 2007, cited by Choudhry (2010), p. 153.

[141] Choudhry (2010), p. 147.

movements have globally aimed to struggle for gender equality in family laws and policies by disrupting the institution of family that is based on patriarchal system, unequal power relations and gender inequalities. Hence, feminists have questioned family as a safe and stable place for women by advocating for family law reforms. The development of family laws has focused on equal power relations among family members including intimate partners (current and ex-partners), children, parents, and extended family members. Moreover, structural inequalities and violence in family, especially violence against women has been problematised through intersectional analysis of multiple inequality grounds i.e., sexuality, age, class, race, ethnicity, nationality, (dis)ability for over 70 years at international and national levels around the world.

The chapter's first key point is a critical examination of family as an institution where unequal gender roles are introduced through marriage law. What constitutes a family and to that extent what defines parenthood is based on the social and legal systems' perspective on gender. Thus, gender equality family laws and policies aim to promote a form of family that is based on sexual and gender diversity.

The second key point of the chapter is discussed through critical analysis of marriage and laws surrounding marriage related issues such as property, maintenance, divorce, parenthood, and child support. In this regard, gender equality law and policy development move towards equality of rights between partners. The life partnership that originates with marriage and ends with divorce requires a response from the legal system to several questions that affect both the spouses' financial relations and those with third parties.

The third key point that the chapter discusses is on the best interests of the child in family, which is also based on equal treatments of parents not only from a formal but also from a substantive viewpoint. In this sense, shared custody arises as a system that favours co-responsibility after parents' break-up. However, despite the legal recognition of equality, gender roles and stereotypes continue to weigh heavily in the family, so that mothers are the main carers of children in practice. Because of that, it is required to remove stereotypes through actions that favour an equalitarian model of family in where both parents share their responsibilities over their children in practice.

Domestic violence is the fourth important key point in this chapter as a gendered matter in family law. It was only after the actions of feminist movement conducted in the 1970s that domestic violence was identified as legal issue. Domestic violence against women is a crystal-clear result of systemic violence and structural inequalities imbued with unequal power relations in family. Moreover, domestic violence is not only based on gender oppression, but also oppression based on sexuality, race, class, ethnicity, religion, nationality and age.

Questions

1. **Understanding family formation:** The objective of this exercise is to understand the ways in which gender-equal family is constituted through the process of developing family equality law and policies.
   Analyse family law in your country by investigating how family is constructed with regards to gender and sexuality, then examine how gender division of labor is handled? Do gender roles define person's rights and responsibilities in family? Could you identify unequal power relations between the members of family? In what ways? How would you make changes to the current gender dynamics?
2. **Marriage and gender perspectives:**
   Analyse the evolution that the regulation of marriage has had in your country's legal system. Point out the most significative changes that have taken place from a patriarchal model to an egalitarian model. Point out those aspects that are still pending in the achievement of an egalitarian model.
3. **Parental responsibilities and child custody:**
   How has the regulation of parental responsibility and/or custody evolved in your country's legal system? What have been the most significant changes that have taken place from a patriarchal model to an egalitarian model in your country's legal system? What aspects are still pending in the achieve-ment of an egalitarian model in your country's legal system?

References

Almeida S (2015) Familia a la luz del Convenio Europeo de Derechos Humanos. Juruá, Lisboa

Álvarez Medina S (2017) La autonomía reproductiva. Relaciones de género, filiación y justicia. Revista jurídica Universidad Autónoma de Madrid 35:145–170

Avilés Hernández M (2019) Cambios históricos en el sistema de custodia preferente: hacia un derecho de familia occidental caracterizado por el cuidado compartido de los hijos tras la ruptura conyugal. La Razón Histórica 44:197–208

Baber K, Allen K (1992) Women and families, feminist reconstructions. Guilford Press, New York

Bidaud-Garon C (2019) Compensatory allowance after divorce in French law: La prestation Compensatoire. Houst J Int Law 41:581–600

Blossfeld HP, Kiernan K (2019) The new role of women: family formation in modern societies. Routledge, London

Boele-Woelki K, Pintens W, Ferrand F et al (2004) Principles of European family law regarding divorce and maintenance between former spouses. Intersentia, Antwerp-Oxford

Choudhry S (2010) Mandatory prosecution and arrest as a form of compliance with due diligence duties in domestic violence – the gender implications. In: Wallbank J, Choudhry S, Herring J (eds) Rights, gender and family law. Routledge, Oxon, pp 144–169

Choudhry S, Herring J, Wallbank J (2010) Welfare, rights, care and gender in family law. In: Wallbank J, Choudhry S, Herring J (eds) Rights, gender and family law. Routledge, Oxon, pp 1–25

Collier R (2010) Fatherhood, law and father's rights: rethinking the relationship between gender and welfare. In: Wallbank J, Choudhry S, Herring J (eds) Rights, gender and family law. Routledge, Oxon, pp 119–143
Council of Europe (2011) Convention on preventing and combating violence against women and domestic violence. https://rm.coe.int/168008482e. Accessed 24 Nov 2021
Digoix M (2020) Same-sex families and legal recognition in Europe. Springer, London
Draškić M (2008) Nasilje u porodici: Prva presuda Vrhovnog suda Srbije. The annals of Faculty of Law in Belgrade. Belgrade Law Rev 56(2):341–351
Esping-Andersen G (1990) 4 the three political economies of the welfare state. Int J Sociol 20:92–123
Esquembre Valdés MM (2006) Género y ciudadanía, mujeres y Constitución. Feminismo/s 8:35–51
European Commission. What is the Istanbul Convention? Who is it for? Why is it important?" Publication of the European Commission. https://ec.europa.eu/justice/saynostopvaw/downloads/materials/pdf/istanbul-convention-leaflet-online.pdf. Accessed 24 Nov 2021
Feigenbaum J (2015) Bargaining in the shadow of the "law"? – the case of same-sex divorce. Harv Negot Law Rev 20:245
Fotheringham JM (2019) Spousal maintenance in Scots family law. Houst J Int Law 41:601–627
Frantzen T (2011) Norway. Am Univ J Gend Soc Pol Law 19:273
Herring J (2019) Family law. Pearson, New York
Hester M, Pearson C, Harwin N (2000) Making an impact: children and domestic violence. Jessica Kingsley Publishers, London
Hiekel N, Liefbroer AC, Poortman A-R (2014) Understanding diversity in the meaning of cohabitation across Europe. Eur J Popul 30:391–410
Hollekim R, Slaatten H, Anderssen N (2012) A nationwide study of Norwegian beliefs about same-sex marriage and lesbian and gay parenthood. Sex Res Soc Policy 9:15–30
Igareda González N (2020) La gestación por sustitución: una investigación sobre género, derecho y reproducción humana. In: Espuny Tomás MJ, Vallés Muñío D, Velo I, Fabregat E (eds) La investigación en derecho con perspectiva de género. Dykinson, Madrid, pp 77–87
Jarufe Contreras D (2016) Algunas notas jurídicas sobre transexualidad y filiación. https://www.thefamilywatch.org/wpcontent/uploads/escrito-juridico-13.pdf. Accessed 3 Sep 2021
Kantola J, Nousiainen K (2009) Institutionalizing intersectionality in Europe: introducing the theme. Int Fem J Polit 11:459–477
Karlsson Sjögren Å (2011) Matrimony, property and power: marriage settlements in Sweden 1870–1920. Scand J Hist 36:443–461. https://doi.org/10.1080/03468755.2011.599932
Kim SA, Edward S (2018) Gender in the context of same-sex divorce and relationship dissolution. Fam Court Rev 56:384–398
Leopold T (2018) Gender differences in the consequences of divorce: a study of multiple outcomes. Springer, Amsterdam
Mair J, Mordaunt E, Wasoff F (2016) Built to last: The Family Law (Scotland) Act 1985–30 years of financial provision on divorce. https://eprints.gla.ac.uk/117617/1/117617.pdf. Accessed 24 Nov 2021
Mattila M (2019) An Unholy Union? Eugenic feminism in the Nordic countries, ca. 1890–1940
Melby K, Pylkkänen A, Rosenbeck B, Wetterberg CC (2006) The Nordic model of marriage. Women's Hist Rev 15:651–661
Menkel-Meadow C (2012) Women in dispute resolution: parties, lawyers and dispute resolvers – what difference does 'Gender Difference' make? https://heinonline.org/HOL/LandingPage?handle=hein.journals/disput18&div=28&id=&page=. Accessed 24 Nov 2021
Mol C (2016) Reasons for regulating informal relationships: a comparison of nine European jurisdictions. Utrecht Law Rev 12:98–113
Moraga García MA (2014) Igualdad y custodia compartida. In: Valencianes C (ed) Igualdad y democracia: el género como categoría de análisis jurídico. Litolema, Valencia, pp 477–491
Mršević N (2014) Ka društvu bez nasilja. Institut društvenih nauka, Belgrade
Mullender A (1995) Children living with domestic violence: putting men's abuse of women on the childcare agenda. Whiting and Birch, London

Nelson HL (ed) (1997) Feminism and families. Psychology Press
Pateman C (1997) The sexual contract. Polity Press, Oxford
Petrušić N, Konstantinović-Vilić S (2010) Porodičnopravna zaštita od nasilja u porodici u pravosudnoj praksi Srbije. Autonomni ženski centar, Ženski istraživački centar za edukaciju i komunikaciju, Belgrade
Rodríguez Ruiz B (2017) Género y Constitución. Mujeres y varones en el orden constitucional español. Editorial Juruá, Lisboa
Ruggeri L, Kunda I, Winkler S (2019) Family property and succession in EU Member States – national reports on the collected data. https://www.euro-family.eu/documenti/news/psefs_e_book_compressed.pdf. Accessed 24 Nov 2021
Sandin B et al (2012) Situating child consumption: rethinking values and notions of children, childhood and consumption. Nordic Academic Press, Central Lund
Schuler SR, Hashemi SM, Riley AP, Akhter S (1996) Credit programs, patriarchy and men's violence against women in rural Bangladesh. Soc Sci Med 12:1729–1742
Schumm R, Abbotts C (2017) Spousal maintenance and gender inequality. Family Law:1116–1118
Song J, Lai W (2020) Cohabitation and gender equality. China Rev 20:53–80
Sörgjerd C (2012) Reconstructing marriage. Intersentia, Cambridge
Souto Galván B (2006) Dilemas éticos sobre la reproducción humana. Feminismo/s 8:181–195
Sümer S (2014) The Nordic approach to work and care: challenges on the way to inclusive citizenship. Tidsskrift for kjønnsforskning 38:59–69
Terlizzi G (2018) 'Ties that bind': maintenance order after divorce in Italy. Italian Law J 4:449–476
United Nation's Children Fund (2000) Domestic violence against women and girls. https://www.unicef-irc.org/publications/pdf/digest6e.pdf. Accessed 24 Nov 2021
United Nations (2019) Global study on homicide, executive summary. https://www.unodc.org/documents/data-and-analysis/gsh/Booklet1.pdf. Accessed 24 Nov 2021
Van Dijk P (2006) The right to marry and to found a family. In: van Dijk P, van Hoof F, van Rijn A, Zwaak L (eds) Theory and practice of the European Convention on Human Rights. Intersentia, Cambridge, pp 837–850
Verdera Izquierdo B (2014) El ejercicio de la patria potestad en igualdad de condiciones. Valoración de la custodia compartida. In: Mesa Marrero C, Grau Pineda C (eds) Mujeres, contratos y empresa desde la igualdad de género. Tirant lo Blanch, Valencia, pp 453–480
Vivas Tesón I (1999) La situación de la mujer en el derecho civil, Tomo III. In: Mujer e Igualdad: la norma y su aplicación. Instituto Andaluz de la Mujer, Sevilla, pp 299–398
Wallbank J (2010) (En)gendering the fusion of rights and responsibilities in the law of contact. In: Wallbank J, Choudhry S, Herring J (eds) Rights, gender and family law. Routledge, Oxon, pp 93–118
WHO (2012) Understanding and addressing violence against women. https://apps.who.int/iris/bitstream/handle/10665/77421/WHO_RHR_12.38_eng.pdf;jsessio. Accessed 24 Nov 2021
WHO (2018) Violence against women prevalence estimates, 2018: executive summary. https://www.who.int/publications/i/item/9789240026681. Accessed 24 Nov 2021

Labour Law and Gender

17

Thais Guerrero Padrón, Ljubinka Kovačević, and Mª Isabel Ribes Moreno

Contents

Authors are listed in alphabetical order. Thais Guerrero Padrón authored Sects. 17.3 and 17.4, Ljubinka Kovačević wrote Sects. 17.1, 17.2, 17.7 and 17.8; Sects. 17.5 and 17.6 are written by Mª Isabel Ribes Moreno.

T. G. Padrón · Mª I. Ribes Moreno (✉)
University of Cadiz, School of Labour Sciences, Cadiz, Spain
e-mail: thais.guerrero@uca.es; isabel.ribes@uca.es

L. Kovačević
University of Belgrade, Faculty of Law, Belgrade, Serbia
e-mail: ljubinka@ius.bg.ac.rs

D. Vujadinović et al. (eds.), *Gender-Competent Legal Education*, Springer Textbooks in Law, https://doi.org/10.1007/978-3-031-14360-1_17

Abstract

The chapter presents an overview of key labour law institutions, aiming at discussing the importance of the gender perspective in labour law. Therefore, the introductory section of the chapter will put this issue into the context of historical and conceptual framework genesis of regulating employment relationships. These issues are connected with the legal subordination and economic dependence of employees, which produce the need to create and implement norms that protect employees, as a weaker party to the employment relationship. This includes the limitation of employers' (managerial, normative and disciplinary) prerogatives, in order to create the conditions for effective enjoyment of the right of jobseekers and employees for protection against gender-based discrimination. The labour law is, in this regard, traditionally conceived according to the model of a male worker, who is employed on the basis of a standard employment contract (open-ended full time employment contract). This then results in a failure to recognise or provide sufficient consideration of the specific needs that women have as participants in the labour market. The use of the feminist method, which included the understanding of gender as an analytical category in the field of labour law, opened up a new set of labour law issues. For example, in easing the ban on women working in physically demanding jobs, and the conceptualisation of the need to reconcile the professional and family duties of employees.. On the other hand, contemporary labour law, when creating conditions for achieving gender equality, is aimed primarily at women's empowerment in the world of work. Persisting with this approach can lead to an oversimplified understanding of the principle of gender equality, ignoring the special needs of men in the world of work, as well as ignoring the importance of their role for consistent implementation of the principle of gender equality and women's empowerment. The second section of the chapter will provide analysis of gender-based discrimination during the hiring process. Other sections will cover the risk of gender-based discrimination regarding rights, obligations and duties deriving from employment relationship, labour law measures to encourage improvements in the occupational safety and health, work-life balance for parents and caregivers, sexual harassment at work and promotion of gender equality in collective labour law.

17.1 Introduction

The employment relationship, as the central institute of labour law, is connected with the idea that an employee exclusively or predominantly makes a living by working on behalf and under prerogatives of an employer. This is because an employer, in addition to the *de facto* authority, manifested in economic dominance, also has the legally recognized managerial, normative and disciplinary prerogatives. Labour law allows for this deviation from the principle of equality of the parties to a contract because employers could not organise their activities without issuing orders and instructions, supervising employees and imposing disciplinary sanctions. Legal subordination and economic dependence of employees, however, produce the need to create and implement norms that can prevent abuse of employer's prerogatives and protect employees, as a weaker party to the employment relationship. In that sense, the history of labour law can be seen as a process of gradual limitation of the employer's prerogatives, in order to create the conditions for effective enjoyment of labour rights—including the right of jobseekers and employees to protection against discrimination. This is why the principle of equality and the principle of non-discrimination appear as basic principles of contemporary labour law.

An important segment of protection for jobseekers and employees from discrimination is their protection from gender-based discrimination. The labour law is, in this regard, traditionally conceived according to the *model of a male worker who is employed on the basis of a standard (open-ended full time) employment contract.* This results in a failure to recognise or provide sufficient consideration of the specific needs that women have as participants in the labour market. This is further reflected in the field of social security law,[1] which is built on the *male breadwinner model,* where the female takes care of (young and old) family members who are dependents. Thus, marriage and motherhood emerge as an alternative to paid work for an employer.[2] This approach survived after the Second World War, even after the lifting of the ban on employment of married women, which existed in certain countries and certain work environments.[3] This further means that unequal treatment of men and women in the world of work was based, above all, on the inequality that existed between them in the family and society. Since the power that men had in the family and society facilitated their domination in the world of work and *vice versa.*[4] Resulting in a labour law that contributed to the legal invisibility of women, as well as to the legitimisation of the patriarchal concept of work.[5] The period following the end of World War II was marked by the intensive inclusion of women in the labour market in Europe and North America. However, the labour legislation traditionally regulated only a few marginalised "women's" labour issues, primarily *maternity*

[1] See Chap. 10.

[2] Lyonette (2013), pp. 198–203.

[3] Deakin (2005), p. 57.

[4] Pascall (1997), pp. 30–31.

[5] Hunter (1991), p. 320.

protection and special protection of women due to their weak constitution. Biological differences between men and women were considered to be the key reason for making qualitative differences between male and female workers.[6] Although the legislative intervention in the area of maternity protection was an improvement, given the period of labour exploitation that preceded the adoption of protective labour legislation, some of these solutions eventually led to a "legal blockade" of women's opportunities to work and earn, under the same conditions as men.[7] This practice is also referred to as *'benign discrimination'*.

► **Definition** "Benign discrimination" is, above all, related to the ban on night work of women in industry and the ban on employing women in physically demanding jobs, such as jobs performed underground, underwater or in construction.

Apart from these issues, and, later, the issue of equal pay for men and women for equal work, (national and international) labour legislation, as a rule, did not take into account experiences typical for female workers. Nor did it identify the specific consequences that the seemingly neutral labour law rules or practices had on them. Also, the tension between the professional and family duties of female workers has traditionally been considered a natural and inevitable consequence of women's participation in the labour market, which is why the legislation lacked instruments aimed at facilitating the reconciliation of these duties.[8]

When it comes to labour law as a scientific discipline, sex or gender, as a rule, are not considered important analytical categories. This was reflected in the content of labour law textbooks, in which issues related to the position of female workers were often ignored, or only mentioned in several footnotes. The best case scenario would be one or two lessons discussing the issue, but only in terms of typical women's labour law topics.[9] In the 1980s, social sciences started applying a *feminist method*,[10] which influenced the conceptualisation of the need to reconcile the professional and family duties of employees.[11] As a result, a new set of labour law issues was opened up such as re-examining the tendency to make employment relationships more flexible from a gender perspective. However, this coincided with the establishment in the 1980s of a dominant neoliberal strategy of economic development. Consequently, a number of non-standard employment contracts emerged as well as new forms of work. Many of these new forms of work were extremely precarious, where women were disproportionately more represented than men.[12] In addition to the changes that have taken place in the family structure and the affirmation of the new

[6]Kollonay-Lehoczky (2017), p. 359.

[7]*Ibid.*

[8]Conaghan (2017), p. 94.

[9]Hunter (1991), pp. 307–308.

[10]Conaghan (2017), p. 100.

[11]Marry (2012), pp. 342–343.

[12]Fredman (2004), p. 299.

concept of a *dual breadwinner model*,[13] new gender-sensitive issues have emerged. However, modern legal systems do not recognise all of these changes and some are waiting to be recognised by the lawmakers and social partners (trade unions, employers and employers' organisations). Since some of these changes are perceived as accidental, i.e. as part of the social context in which labour law is created, applied and interpreted. Finally, we should not lose sight of the fact that contemporary labour law, when creating conditions for achieving gender equality, is aimed primarily at women's empowerment in the world of work. This approach is justified, given that female workers are more likely to face unfavourable treatment and are more likely to be discriminated against than men. However, persisting with this approach can lead to an oversimplified understanding of the principles of gender equality, *ignoring the special needs of men in the world of work, as well as ignoring the importance of their role for consistent application of the principle of gender equality and women's empowerment.*[14] Therefore, in order to eliminate gender-based discrimination from the world of work, the special needs of men needs to be taken into account, in addition to the needs of female workers. This applies pressure on men to accept and abide by gender stereotypes in the world of work, including the stereotype that measures concerning the reconciliation of professional and family duties of employees should only be addressed to women. As well as to the stereotype that male workers do not need special protection in the workplace.[15] On the contrary, labour law should strive for the equal treatment of all genders, especially regarding participation in family duties, through fair rules on family related leave.

Learning Goals

- The chapter is designed to create a framework for understanding the gender perspectives on key labour law institutions and their re-evaluation on the basis of gender equality principle.
- The chapter tends to stimulate students to critical thinking and cooperative learning in order to better conceive the need, challenges and obstacles for effective implementation of gender equality principle in the world of work.
- Students should be able to use the gender equality principle as a basis for re-evaluating applicable sources of law and legal concepts and theories, as well as existing legal problems regarding the status of women, persons with

(continued)

[13]Certain authors, instead of the dual breadwinner model, cite the *adult-worker model family*, which presumes that all adult family members participate in the labour market. On the other hand, there are authors who, having in mind the low wages earned by female workers, primarily due to their part-time work or work on the basis of some other non-standard employment contract, use the term *one-and-a-half earner model* to denote this new family model. Acc. to Lewis (2001), pp. 152–169.

[14]International Labour Office (2013), pp. 2–3.

[15]Resolution concerning gender equality at the heart of decent work, adopted by the General Conference of the International Labour Organization at its 98th Session on 17 June 2009, para. 6.

family duties and non-binary people in the world of work. This is followed by the review of the capacity of legal instruments to ensure gender equality in the labour market.

17.2 Gender-Based Discrimination During the Hiring Process

17.2.1 Access to Employment and Occupational Segregation

The need for economic security is one of the basic needs of every human being. It can be satisfied by entering into employment relationships, where the worker, in addition to procuring means of subsistence, gets the opportunity to develop his/her personality, by working for the employer. For the employer, the purpose of employment is to recruit workers who are expected to perform their tasks to the best of their abilities. This further means that an employer's freedom of enterprise, freedom of contract, as well as responsibility to ensure proper functioning of the organisation, allow for significant freedom in choosing co-workers. Including prerogatives to manage the hiring process, to establish the job requirements and to select the person for the job. In that sense, one of the basic duties of an employer is to respect the dignity of the candidates and treat them in accordance with the skills and abilities crucial for their performance, and not based on *prejudices and stereotypes related to their sex/gender*.[16] Stereotypes above all concern physical capabilities, but are not limited to them. However, we must not lose sight of the so-called *statistical stereotypes* that have influenced the institution of the (male) sex, as a special requirement for certain jobs, only because the physical capabilities of an average woman are less than the physical capabilities of an average man.[17] This regularly leads to *occupational segregation*, in terms of giving preference to workers of one sex when hiring for certain jobs. We should also have in mind that even though women graduate from university in greater percentages than men, they are, in general, more likely to get a job in lower-paying sectors. Despite their higher education, they also represent a smaller portion of the total number of employees in more attractive advanced-career sectors.[18] On the other hand, men are underrepresented in the areas of education (which is true for primary and secondary school but not higher education) for health care and social protection. In this regard, we should bear in mind that work in female dominated fields is often paid less than work

[16] Fenwick and Hervey (1995), p. 446.

[17] Holzleithner (2017), p. 38.

[18] Across the EU, in 2016, the employment rate for women was 65.3% compared to 76.8% for men. In the same year, women represented 3/4 of workers who pursue paid work on a part-time basis (22% of those women worked less then 20 h a week) and they tend to work in lower-paying sectors and at more junior levels than men. Acc. to: Eurofound (2020), p. 13; European Group on Ethics in Science and New Technologies (2019), p. 32.

in male dominated fields, regardless of the level of education and experience of workers.[19] This practice exists in almost all European countries, with the consequences of segregation differing from one country to another. In this regard, one should take into account that many women work in modestly paid, insecure jobs,[20] often without a legal basis and that many female workers encounter the '*glass ceiling*' phenomenon.

▶ **Definition** The metaphor '*glass ceiling*' refers to invisible barriers that prevent persons of a certain gender (typically women) from rising beyond a certain level in a job hierarchy.

On the other hand, for most women, working for an employer is accompanied by unpaid work in the household, i.e. housework and child care (and not only childcare by mothers, but also grandmothers in raising grandchildren) and care for family members dependent on assistance from others. This *double working engagement of women* represents a great challenge for female workers and their employers, as well as for society as a whole. Especially because the culture of capitalism does not value such tasks as taking care of family members.[21]

The risk of gender-based discrimination is first and foremost, expressed in terms of *establishing job requirements*. As these conditions must be *directly related to a specific job*, direct gender discrimination will only exist if gender is required for a job where it is not necessary for successful performance of duties.

Example

The decision of the editorial staff of an all-male fishing magazine, not to hire a woman for the position of a journalist, due to the belief that she would be uncomfortable and unhappy to work in an all-male work environment (UK Equality Act/2010/Code of Practice on Employment, para. 3.14). ◀

On the other hand, indirect discrimination is established by seemingly neutral provisions, criteria or practices. The application of which puts job seekers of one gender at a disadvantage compared to other workers, as is the case with prescribing certain physical characteristics as job requirements (height, weight or Body Mass Index, strength and other conditions that are impossible or much harder for women to meet), although they are not necessary for successful performance of duties. The general prohibition of establishing personal characteristics as special requirements for employment is not to be confused with the permissible differentiation between jobseekers by sex/gender. In these situations, the prohibition of differentiation could jeopardise the proper functioning of the organisation because for the jobs in

[19] Müller (2019), pp. 20–21.
[20] Auvergnon (2008), pp. 13–14.
[21] Grgurev (2014), p. 136.

question, sex is a *genuine and determining occupational requirement*. Reasons of professional necessity that in exceptional cases justify sex as a special requirement for employment can be numerous, starting with *authenticity*, which allows an employer to hire only persons of a specific sex due to their physical appearance. Such is the case with models hired to present a collection of men's or women's clothing, theatre, ballet or opera artists, as well as models in painting and photographic studios.[22] Sex can also be determined as a special requirement for *reasons of decency*, in jobs that involve physical contact of an employee with employer's clients (concerning certain social and cultural expectations).[23] Furthermore, sex may be established as a special employment requirement when prescribed by the *nature of the institution* in which the work is to be performed, such as penitentiaries, or institutions in which persons requiring special care or supervision are housed, if they are exclusively male or exclusively female. In addition, sex can be specified as a special requirement if the worker is expected to work or live in the household of the employer or the employer's client, which includes intensive contact with certain persons and access to intimate details of their lives. In this regard, it is necessary to assess in each case whether a job requires an employee of a certain sex, so that the permitted exception wouldn't lead to the widespread exclusion of women/men from certain professional fields. This was confirmed in the case law of the European Court of Justice (ECJ).

Example

Unjustified exclusion of women from all military tasks involving the use of weapons, resulting in women only being hired for military health service jobs and military orchestras can be deemed as widespread exclusion of women from this professional field, as ECJ confirmed in Case C-285/98, *Tanja Kreil* v *Bundesrepublik Deutschland*, (ECJ 11 January 2000), para 27. ◄

[22]Nevertheless, artistic freedom enables employers in these businesses to entrust certain female acting, opera or ballet roles to women, or men, if the director of the play decides to abandon the conventional approach.

[23]For example, in the early 1980s, the European Court of Justice confirmed that societal expectations regarding decency and privacy (more precisely, the specific quality of the relationship established between a patient and a midwife, i.e. the sensitivity of a patient who had just given birth) justify exclusive training and hiring of women for midwifery—Case C-165/82, *Commission* v *UK* (ECJ 8 November 1983), para. 18. In the following decades, access to this profession was provided to men both in the United Kingdom, as the country against which the aforementioned proceeding was initiated, and in all other EU Member States, which underlined the importance of the obligation to periodically review the legitimacy of excluding persons of a certain sex from certain professions. Barnard (2012), p. 365.

The Court has also confirmed in a number of judgments (e.g. with regard to the work of police officers and the marines)[24] that EU Member States enjoy the discretion to exclude certain professional activities from the scope of secondary anti-discrimination legislation in the EU. This prerogative is, however, limited by the requirement that the exclusion concerns only certain activities and the obligation that states periodically review the legitimacy of the exclusions, as they may become illegal after a period of time. The same view is found in the standards of the Council of Europe and the jurisprudence of the European Court of Human Rights, which has repeatedly concluded that banning the employment of women in public companies because they have not served in the military, which is only allowed for men, represents discrimination of the right to respect for private and family life.[25]

On the other hand, the small number of women engaged in physically demanding occupations can be explained by the fact that *physical ability tests* are often designed with male workers (and dominant ethnicity) in mind—as a kind of a "universal worker", against whom the abilities of all workers are evaluated.[26] Gender-based discrimination should also be prevented in further stages of the hiring process. This especially goes for the *interviews with the candidates*, conducted by the employer (or the hiring committee) and, of course, for the *selection decision* itself. In practice, women are often asked about family planning. This is however, difficult to prove in anti-discrimination proceedings e.g. in Greece, Hungary, Germany, Croatia and the Czech Republic, especially because many female workers decide not to initiate proceedings against employers due to the economic pressure to ensure subsistence from employment.[27] Further, due to the fear of victimisation when applying for other jobs. Oversight of the employment process is, therefore, very important, especially via the participation of the labour inspectorate. However, some countries try to prevent the use of the off-limits questions in interviews by having trade union or works councils representatives present. Furthermore, in some legal systems there is a rule stating that a candidate has the right not to answer the employer's off-limits questions and that their actions will not be considered illegal.[28] Moreover, in some

[24] See: Case C-222/84, *Marguerite Johnston* v *Chief Constable of the Royal Ulster Constabulary* (ECJ 15 May 1986); Case C-273/97, *Angela Maria Sirdar* v. *The Army Board and Secretary of State for Defence* (ECJ 26 October 1999).

[25] The court qualified the dismissal of a worker as discrimination against the enjoyment of the right to respect for private and family life, due to the fact that such a drastic measure, as dismissal for being a female, violates the worker's self-esteem and, consequently, her private and family life, especially bearing in mind the possibility to work in future jobs she specializes in, since she had passed the professional exam for work in the public sector. App. No. 61960/08, *Case of Emel Boyraz v. Turkey* (EctHR 2 December 2014). See: App. No. 30733/08, Case *of Hülya Ebru Demirel* v. Turkey (EctHR 19 June 2018).

[26] Holzleithner (2017), p. 18.

[27] Masselot et al. (2012), pp. 13–14.

[28] See: French Labour Code (*Code du travail*/2018/, Art. L1225-2), Slovenian Law on Employment Relations (*Zakon o delovnih razmerjih*, Uradni list, št. 21/13, 78/13, 47/15, 33/16, 52/16, 15/17, 22/19, 81/19, 203/20, Art. 29, para. 2); Croatian Labour Law (*Zakon o radu*, Narodne novine, No. 93/14, 127/17, 98/19, Art. 25). The European Committee of Social Rights has not directly

legal systems, candidates have the right to provide false answers to the employer's off-limits questions, which cannot be considered a violation of the principle of good faith. The employer, therefore, cannot claim that he was misled about the essential characteristics of the contracting party, and accordingly, cannot seek the annulment of the employment contract.[29] The same solution is provided by the ILO standards, which prohibits the possibility of disciplinary punishment of an employee (including dismissal, as the most severe of the disciplinary measures) who gave a false answer to a question not directly related to the performance of duties. Unless there are exceptional reasons that justify the collection of sensitive personal data.[30]

17.2.2 Positive Action Measures

Protecting the right to equal access to employment does not only mean banning the exclusion of women or men from the labour market. Implementing *programs should also be done, which can help workers return to the world of work or improve their position in the labour market after a career break due to family duties* (e.g. by refreshing their knowledge and acquiring skills needed to adapt to innovations in technology or science that have occurred in the meantime).[31] In addition, states are obliged, through employment services, to implement measures to employ vulnerable categories of workers who encounter problems during professional reintegration (e.g. victims of domestic violence, Roma people and workers from other marginalised groups). This includes the obligation of public employment services to ensure equal access of their services for all genders. Further, employment and self-employment of the underrepresented gender must be encouraged with the inclusion of a larger number of persons of the underrepresented gender in certain active employment policy measures. Also, public employment services are obliged to prevent the publishing of advertisements where conditions are related to sex/gender. Thus, the prohibition of advertisements with discriminatory content, includes an obligation for *gender-neutral advertising of vacancies.* This can be done by omitting from the advertisement illustrations suggesting that a job should be performed by a worker of a specific sex. Employers should also refrain from using terms that imply preference for candidates of a certain sex and gender in the wording of job titles, such as for stewardesses, firemen etc. It is considered good practice to clearly state in the advertisement that persons of both sexes may apply for the job, either by explicitly stating this by announcing the job title is open for both genders, or by

---

formulated such a requirement as a condition for the effective application of Article 20 of the Revised European Social Charter, but its practice shows that it positively rates national regulations that explicitly prohibit questions on pregnancy, adoption or family planning. Kollonay-Lehoczky (2017), p. 368.

[29] Radé (1997), p. 128.

[30] Protection of workers' personal data. An ILO code of practice, point 6.8. in connection with points 6.5–6.7.

[31] Kollonay-Lehoczky (2017), p. 366.

marking it "m/f". However, with regard to the third gender, it can be argued that presented labels in advertisements could lead to discrimination against non-binary people. Therefore, preference should be given to the existing gender-neutral advertising, or to advertisements indicating that the advertised jobs are available for m/f/x.[32] This rule may be derogated for positive action measures, provided that the advertisement indicates the reason for the different treatment.

When it comes to *positive action measures*, the state must intervene in order to facilitate employment of workers who have traditionally faced unfavourable treatment, as well as groups of workers who would not be able to improve their position in the labour market without these measures. The content of positive action measures can vary widely, from providing support and encouraging workers from these groups to apply for jobs, over assisting them to gain experience and improve their skills, to employment quotas.[33] International instruments for the protection of human rights and fundamental freedoms, including CEDAW (Article 4), confirm the possibility of introducing positive action measures and the same applies to EU law.[34] Public authorities in certain countries reaffirm the obligation to give priority to recruiting candidates of the under-represented sex. The underepresented sex may have difficulty finding and retaining employment in certain jobs due to prejudices and stereotypes related to the roles and abilities of members of different sexes. For example, there is a 30%, quota for female cadets in military and police academies, or for training women for police and military jobs, which is reflected in the employment of women in the security sector. These measures can also be introduced in favour of men, as is the case for kinder garden jobs in the Nordic countries, which is traditionally a female-dominated sector, due to the association of child care being a woman's job.[35] In this regard, it should be noted that the implementation of these measures raises delicate legal issues. European countries share a negative experience with the implementation of quotas for employment of women, as evidenced by the judgment in the *Kalanke* case. The ECJ found the measure that allows, in case of

[32] KU Leuven (2016), p. 56.

[33] This is particularly evident when giving preference to candidates of the under-represented sex in the field of higher education, because the number of full professors at higher education institutions in EU Member States is far beneath the expected, given the gender structure of graduates at universities (European Commission. 2019. *She figures*, Luxembourg: Publications Office of the European Union, 115). However, implementation of quotas in this field is accompanied by serious dilemmas regarding their justification, bearing in the importance of the merit system. Wallon et al. (2015), p. 42.

[34] See: Treaty on the Functioning of the EU, Art. 157, para. 4; Charter of Fundamental Rights of the EU, Art. 23, para. 2; Directive 2006/54/EC, Art. 3; Costello and Davies (2006), pp. 1600–1601.

[35] In addition to these stereotypes (and stigmatization of men who choose to pursue this career), the authors cite low earnings of pre-school teachers as an important factor in the low representation of men in the field of preschool education. On the other hand, pedagogical and psychological research shows that the contact of young children with pre-school teachers of both sexes have significant psychological value for children, which is why they need to be provided with a more diverse educational environment, in which teachers will mirror the gender differences in society, as well as ethnicity, social origin, etc. International Labour Office (2013), p. 15.

lower representation of women in work environments, automatic and unconditional advantage in employment and advancement to women compared to men with the same abilities, to be illegal. Such measures, in the opinion of the ECJ, went beyond the legal instruments for promotion of equal opportunities for men and women because it replaced that goal (promotion of equal opportunities) with the outcome (equal representation) that should result from equal opportunities.[36] That position has, since the *Badeck* judgment, been nuanced and, to some extent, abandoned in favour of the position on the *conditional nature of positive action measures*. Namely, the ECJ's new approach to this issue implies that quotas can be applied under two conditions: (a) that women are not automatically and unconditionally given preference when female and male job candidates have the same qualifications; (b) that the employer makes an objective assessment of the candidates' abilities, with the possibility of taking into account the specific personal circumstances of each candidate.[37] The second condition implies, more precisely, a *saving (hardship) clause*, which allows, in the process of selection, deviation from preferential treatment of women, if there are reasons of greater "legal weight" on the side of the male candidate, e.g. if he is a war veteran. The ECJ stated that the measures of positive action consisting of strict (automatically and unconditionally applicable) quotas in the selection stage are unacceptable. The further development of jurisprudence has confirmed the position that these measures can be applied only if, during the consideration of the submitted applications and verification of the abilities of the candidates, two or more candidates with the best qualifications have been selected. If their (best) qualifications are equal, the female candidate should be given preference over the male candidate. Conversely, if the male candidate has better qualifications, the female candidate cannot be given preference over the male candidate.[38] On the other hand, in the *Marschall* and *Abrahamsson* cases, the EU Court of Justice concluded that the provisions favouring women, without taking into account the specificities of the relevant qualifications of male candidates, which were better, does not constitute a legal exception to the prohibition of discrimination.[39]

17.3 Equal Treatment at Work

Indeed, the right to equal opportunities and equal treatment is a fundamental principle of EU law, of particular relevance in the field of employment and occupation. Article 157 (3) of the Treaty on the Functioning of the EU provides a specific

[36] Case C-450/93, *Eckhard Kalanke* v *Freie Hansestadt Bremen* (ECJ 17 October 1995), paras. 22–23.

[37] Case C-158/97, *Georg Badeck et al.* v *Landesanwalt beim Staatsgerichtshof des Landes Hessen* (ECJ 28 March 2000), para 23.

[38] Hießl (2012), p. 51.

[39] See: Case C-409/95, *Hellmut Marschall* v *Land Nordrhein-Westfalen* (ECJ 11 November 1997); Case C-407/98, *Katarina Abrahamsson and Leif Anderson* v *Elisabet Fogelqvist* (ECJ 6 July 2000).

legal basis for the adoption of measures to ensure the application of this principle—including the principle of equal pay for equal work or work of equal value. In addition, Articles 21 and 23 of the Charter of Fundamental Rights of the European Union also prohibits "any discrimination on grounds of sex" and enshrines the right to "equal treatment between men and women in all areas, including employment, work and pay".

In fact, Directive 2006/54 and its interpretation by the ECJ, is the reference in this area, without prejudice to other international and national legal instruments. It contains specific provisions to implement the principle of equal opportunities and equal treatment of men and women regarding access to employment, promotion and vocational training, working conditions, in particular pay, and occupational social security schemes (Article 1).

The Directive includes mechanisms to ensure the effective application of the principle of equal treatment to all persons who consider themselves wronged by failure to apply that to them. It comprises measures "to ensure real and effective compensation or reparation for the loss and damage sustained by a person injured as a result of discrimination on grounds of sex, in any case dissuasive and proportionate measures to the damage suffered".[40] A relevant instrument of defence is the reversal of the burden of proof which allows potential victims of discrimination, on grounds of sex, to present "before a court or other competent authority, facts from which it may be presumed that there has been direct or indirect discrimination". In this case, the respondent has the burden "to prove that there has been no breach of the principle of equal treatment".[41] (Articles 18 and 19).

17.3.1 Working Conditions and Promotion

The principle of equal treatment means the absence of direct or indirect discrimination on grounds of sex "in the public or private sectors, including public bodies, in relation to employment and working conditions, including dismissals as well as pay as provided for in Article 141 TEC –currently Article 157 TFEU–" (Article 14 (1) (c) of the Directive 2006/54).

The expression "working conditions" is broad and includes, among others, remuneration, classification in a salary group, recognition of previous periods of service, entitlement to leave, additional payments and overtime supplements. It is clear from the case-law of the ECJ that "unfavourable treatment of a woman related to pregnancy or maternity constitutes direct discrimination on grounds of sex. Indeed, only women can become pregnant, so that any less favourable treatment based on pregnancy or maternity constitutes direct discrimination on grounds of sex and, as such, is not justifiable".[42] For instance, "a woman who is deprived of the

[40] Art. 18 of Directive 2006/54.

[41] Art. 19 of Directive 2006/54.

[42] Case C-284/02, *Land Brandenburg v Ursula Sass* (ECJ 18 November 2004), paras. 35–36.

right to an annual assessment of her performance and, therefore, of the opportunity of qualifying for promotion as a result of absence on account of maternity leave, is discriminated against on grounds of her pregnancy and her maternity leave. Such conduct constitutes discrimination based directly on grounds of sex".[43]

The consequences of maternity on working conditions may represent a handicap for women. The same occurs for working women and men when exercising rights to paternity and/or adoption leave. To this respect, Directive 2006/54 contains particular provisions in terms of protection of the woman's biological condition during pregnancy and maternity. Further, it contains measures aimed to guarantee working conditions of male and female workers when taking paternity or maternity leave. In this way, women on maternity leave and working men and women exercising the rights to paternity and/or adoption leave, are entitled, after the end of said-leave period, to return to their job or to an equivalent post, on terms and conditions which are no less favourable to them. Further, they will be able to benefit from any improvement in working conditions to which they should have been entitled during their absence (Arts. 15 and 16 of Directive 2006/54).

The aim is "to avoid the loss or diminution of rights arising from an employment relationship, acquired or in the process of being acquired, to which the worker is entitled when he/she starts maternity leave or parental/adoption leave, and to ensure that, at the end of such leave, he/she is in the same situation as he/she was in before the leave".[44] A relevant concept in this respect is "rights acquired or in the process of being acquired". Related to a parental leave, the ECJ has established that this concept covers "all the rights and benefits, whether in cash or in kind, derived directly or indirectly from the employment relationship, which the worker is entitled to claim from the employer at the date on which parental leave starts Directorate-General for Justice (European Commission)".[45] We can consider that this may be applied to maternity leave.

To summarise, maternity leave and paternity/adoption leave may not entail the loss of employment rights for the beneficiary. As long as the employment relationship persists, the worker who is on such leave must continue to have the same working conditions that apply to workers who derive from this employment relationship.

Example

For instance, in a case of salary promotion where the entire period of maternity leave is not taken into account in the calculation of the qualifying period for

[43]Case C-136/95, *Caisse nationale d'assurance vieillesse des travailleurs salariés (CNAVTS) v Evelyne Thibault* (ECJ 30 April 1998), para. 32.

[44]Case C-537/07, *Evangelina Gómez-Limón Sánchez-Camacho v Instituto Nacional de la Seguridad Social (INSS), Tesorería General de la Seguridad Social (TGSS) and Alcampo SA.* (ECJ 16 July 2009), para. 39, and Case C-116/08, *Christel Meerts contra Proost NV* (ECJ 22 October 2009), para. 39.

[45]Case C-116/08, cited, para. 43.

classification in a higher salary grade, there is a clear disadvantage. Only the first 8 weeks of maternity leave were taken into account, but not the subsequent 12 weeks, to the detriment of the worker. There is a difference in treatment compared to other workers—men and women—who move up the pay scale without this type of maternity-related limitation.[46] ◀

17.3.2 The Principle of Equal Pay of Men and Women and Gender Pay Gap

The principle of equal pay for equal work or work of equal value for men and women constitutes an essential part of the *acquis* which has been extensively developed in the case-law of the ECJ. The principle is laid down in Art. 157 TFEU (previously Art. 141 TEC and before that Art. 119 TEEC) and developed by Directive 2006/54.

Several questions arise. Firstly, the concept of "pay". From the *Defrenne I* judgment, the case-law has developed a very broad concept of pay within the meaning of Art. 119 TECC, "that comprises any consideration, whether in cash or in kind, whether immediate or future, provided that the worker receives it, albeit indirectly, in respect of his employment from his employer."[47] "The fact that certain benefits are paid after the end of the employment does not prevent them from being paid within the meaning of the aforementioned Article".[48] This is the concept set out in the current Art. 157 TFEU, which includes a wide variety of benefits according to the case-law, for instance:

- "The rail travel facilities granted in kind by the employer to the retired employee or his dependants directly or indirectly in respect of his employment";[49]
- Compensation awarded to a worker for unfair dismissal, insofar as it is paid by virtue of his employment relationship. It occurs when such compensation comprises, on the one hand, the part of the remuneration that the worker would have received if he had not been dismissed and, on the other hand, compensation for the damages caused by the dismissal, i.e. due to the expenses incurred and the loss of earnings.[50]
- The benefits of the occupational pension scheme based on an agreement between the employer and the works council which supplements the social benefits paid

[46] Case C-284/02, cited.

[47] Case 80/70, *Gabrielle Defrenne v Belgian State* (ECJ 25 May 1971).

[48] Case 12/81, *Eileen Garland v British Rail Engineering Limited* (ECJ 9 February 1982), para. 5, and Case C-109/91, *Gerardus Cornelis Ten Oever contra Stichting Bedrijfspensioenfonds voor het Glazenwassers- en Schoonmaakbedrijf* (ECJ 6 October 1993), para. 8, para. 10.

[49] Case 12/81, cited, paras. 7–9.

[50] Case C-167/97, *Regina v Secretary of State for Employment, ex parte Nicole Seymour-Smith and Laura Perez* (ECJ 9 February 1999), paras. 26–28.

under generally applicable national legislation, which are fully financed by the employer and received by the employee by virtue of his or her employment relationship.[51]

Secondly, the meaning of "same work" and "work of equal value" under the principle of equal pay.

Art. 4 of Directive 2006/54 states that "for the same work or for work to which equal value is attributed, direct and indirect discrimination on grounds of sex with regard to all aspects and conditions of remuneration shall be eliminated. In particular, where a job classification system is used for determining pay, it shall be based on the same criteria for both men and women and so drawn up as to exclude any discrimination on grounds of sex".

On the one hand, the ECJ has identified the following criteria for determining when it is "the same work" for the purposes of applying the principle of equal pay: (1) the nature of the work or tasks performed, (2) the training requirements for its exercise, and (3) the working conditions under which it is carry out. These criteria apply even when different groups of workers, who do not have the same professional qualifications for their occupation, perform an apparently identical activity. For example, the special training factor may objectively justify a pay difference between workers performing the same work, where the employer demonstrates that it is for the performance of specific tasks entrusted to the employee.[52]

On the other hand, the concept of "work of equal value" is linked to job classification systems and is a source of retributive discrimination. It has been questioned whether a classification system is compatible with the principle of equal pay, when it is based on criteria that favours one sex over the other, (e.g. based on the criteria of muscle demand or muscular effort and the heaviness of the work). The ECJ has ruled that "where a job classification system is used in determining remuneration, that system must be based on criteria which does not differ according to whether the work is carried out by a man or by a woman and must not be organised, as a whole, in such a manner that it has the practical effect of discriminating generally against workers of one sex". In addition, "even where a particular criterion, such as that of demand on the muscles, may in fact tend to favour male workers [. . .] it must, in order to determine whether or not it is discriminatory, be considered in the context of the whole job classification system, having regard to other criteria influencing rates of pay. A system is not necessarily discriminatory

[51] Case C-170/84, *Bilka - Kaufhaus GmbH contra Karin Weber von Hartz* (ECJ 13 May 1986), paras. 20–22, Case C-262/88, *Douglas Harvey Barber contra Guardian Royal Exchange Assurance Group* (ECJ 17 May 1990): the Court decided that all forms of occupational pension constituted pay for the purposes of former Article 119, and that the principle of equal treatment therefore applied to them.

[52] Case C-109/88, *Handels- og Kontorfunktionærernes Forbund I Danmark v Dansk Arbejdsgiverforening, acting on behalf of Danfoss* (ECJ 17 October 1989), para. 23.

simply because one of its criteria makes reference to attributes more characteristic of men. In order for a job classification system as a whole to be non-discriminatory (. . .) it must, however, be established in such a manner that it includes, if the nature of the tasks in question so permits, jobs to which equal value is attributed and for which other criteria are taken into account in relation to which women workers may have a particular aptitude".[53]

Lastly, the issue of "gender pay gap". This is a clear indicator of the imbalance between male and female workers in labour relations, with direct effects on women's lower pensions, leading to a higher risk of poverty for women. The causes of the gender pay gap are varied, more noticeable in the private sector than in the public sector, and in any case related to the way women work. Women tend to work part-time temporary jobs or jobs with little stability, in feminised sectors or jobs with poorer working conditions. These differences tend to worsen with age and are also affected by the career breaks that women often experience for family reasons.

A theoretical distinction is made between the adjusted and non-adjusted gender pay gap. The adjusted one takes into consideration not only the gross income of male and female workers, but also various socioeconomic and cultural factors that influence this difference. Such as differences in education and training, work experience, the productive sector in which they work, whether they are predominantly male or female jobs, duration of working time and type of activities. The non-adjusted gender pay gap, which is officially used in the UE,[54] represents an average of differences between the gross earnings of male and female workers, regardless of other socioeconomic and cultural considerations. Therefore, the gender pay gap is one of the indicators that best illustrates the differences between men and women in the labour market. It is a broader concept than equal pay for work of equal value, which reflects the average hourly wage difference between male and female employees in the economy as a whole. The gender pay gap levels vary significantly across the EU.[55]

17.3.3 Gender Equality, Flexible Employment Contracts and Flexible Working Conditions

As Directive 2006/54 states, (Recital 11), "the problem of the continuing gender-based wage differentials and marked gender segregation on the labour market," could be addressed "by means such as flexible working time arrangements, which enable both men and women to combine family and work commitments more successfully".

[53] Case C-237/85, *Gisela Rummler v Dato-Druck GmbH* (ECJ 1 July 1986), paras. 13 and 15.

[54] See Directorate-General for Justice, European Commission (2014), p. 5.

[55] In this regard, see the full report by Eurostat "Gender pay gap statistics" https://ec.europa.eu/eurostat/statistics-explained/index.php/Gender_pay_gap_statistics.

Flexibility is a necessary tool in the labour market, both for companies and employees. Companies need to increase flexible working conditions to function better in order to respond to changes in demand and remain competitive. While employees need more flexibility to reconcile work with personal and family life. A balance of interests needs to be found so that the flexibility demanded by companies, especially in working time (overtime, part-time work, flexible schedules, night work, shift work, working from home, atypical working hours, staggered working hours, etc.), does not harm the health and well-being of workers in terms of gender equality.

The EU established a basic framework for working time through the Working Time Directive 2003/88[56] and the Part-Time Work Directive 97/81.[57] The objectives of the Framework Agreement on part-time work, which was annexed to the latter, was on one hand, to "provide for the removal of discrimination against part-time workers and to improve the quality of part-time work.", On the other hand, "to facilitate the development of part-time work on a voluntary basis and to contribute to the flexible organization of working time in a manner which takes into account the needs of employers and workers" (Clause 1 of Directive 97/81). In this field, the principle of non-discrimination means, in respect of employment conditions, that "part-time workers shall not be treated in a less favourable manner than comparable full-time workers solely because they work part time, unless different treatment is justified on objective grounds." (Clause 4.1).

From a gender perspective, working time flexibility has a positive value, as more individualised working time helps employees to maintain a work-life balance. However, greater flexibility may have a negative effect on gender equality. In fact, part-time work is the framework for indirect gender discrimination to the detriment of women. Precisely because in many countries, part-time work is mostly performed by women for various reasons and is concentrated in low-paid sectors with little or no training and career opportunities, even affecting their social security rights.[58]

In order to determine the existence of indirect discrimination, the case-law carries out three successive and mutually exclusive tests. First, it determines whether there is a difference in treatment between full-time and part-time workers, by comparing the particular aspect concerned (e.g. pay). If the answer is yes, the ECJ checks, secondly, whether the difference in treatment affects significantly more women than men (a statistics test). Third, if the answer to the previous question is affirmative, the question arises whether the difference in treatment can be justified on the basis of objective factors unrelated to discrimination.[59] Finally, the absence of justification

[56]Directive 2003/88/EC of 4 November 2003 *concerning certain aspects of the organisation of working time*. OJ L 299, (2003), pp. 9–19.

[57]Directive 97/81/EC of 15 December 1997 *concerning the framework agreement on part-time work concluded by UNICE, CEEP and the ETUC*. OJ L 14, (1998), pp. 9–14.

[58]Plantenga and Remery (2010).

[59]Cases C-399/92, C-409/92, C-425/92, C-34/93, C-50/93 and C-78/93, *Stadt Lengerich v Angelika Helmig and Waltraud Schmidt v Deutsche Angestellten-Krankenkasse and Elke Herzog v Arbeiter-Samariter-Bund Landverband Hamburg eV and Dagmar Lange v Bundesknappschaft Bochum and*

will determine the existence of discrimination. Conversely, if the difference in treatment is justified, the suspicion of discrimination disappears.

For instance, "the provision of a collective agreement which allows employers to maintain a distinction as regards overall pay between two categories of workers, that is to say, those who work for a minimum number of hours per week or per month and those who perform the same type of work but do not work such a minimum number of hours, constitute discrimination against female workers vis-à-vis male workers, if in fact a much lower percentage of men work on a part-time basis than women [. . .]. In order to exclude discrimination, it must be shown that the difference in treatment between the two categories of workers is based on objectively justified factors unrelated to any discrimination on grounds of sex".[60] Regarding justifications, the ECJ has rejected employers' arguments based on economic issues. Thus, "so far as the justification based on economic grounds is concerned, it should be noted that an employer cannot justify the discrimination [. . .] solely on the ground that avoidance of such discrimination would involve increased costs".[61]

17.3.4 Gender-Based Discrimination Regarding Termination of Employment

The principle of non-discrimination on grounds of sex "is not confined to discrimination based on the fact that a person is of one or other sex. It also comprises discrimination arising from the gender reassignment of a person in so far that such discrimination is based, essentially if not exclusively, on the sex of the person concerned. Therefore, where a worker is dismissed on the ground that he or she intends to undergo, or has undergone, gender reassignment, he or she is treated unfavourably by comparison with persons of the sex to which he or she was deemed to belong before undergoing gender reassignment".[62] It may be considered a discrimination on grounds of sex, unless the employer's decision is objectively justified.

One of the reasons for dismissal is often maternity. "The risk of dismissal on grounds of sex related to maternity may have harmful effects on the physical and mental state of pregnant workers, workers who have recently given birth or workers who are breastfeeding, including the particularly serious risk of inciting a pregnant worker to voluntarily terminate her pregnancy".[63] This justifies specific protection against dismissal. Article 10 of Directive 92/85 encourages Member States to take

---

Angelika Kussfeld v Firma Detlef Bogdol GmbH and Ursula Ludewig v Kreis Segeberg (ECJ 15 December 1994), paras. 23–26.

[60] Case C-184/89, *Helga Nimz v Freie und Hansestadt Hamburg* (ECJ 7 February 1991), para. 12.

[61] Case C-243/95, *Kathleen Hill and Ann Stapleton v The Revenue Commissioners and Department of Finance* (ECJ 17 June 1998), para. 40.

[62] Case C-13/94, *P v S and Cornwall County Council* (ECJ 30 April 1996), paras. 17–21.

[63] Case C-394/96, *Mary Brown v Rentokil Ltd* (ECJ 30 June 1998), para. 18.

the necessary measures to prohibit the dismissal of pregnant workers, workers who have recently given birth and workers who are breastfeeding. This should be during the period from the beginning of pregnancy to the end of maternity leave, "save in exceptional cases not connected with their condition" (par. 1).[64]

Regarding the latter expression, the case-law has underlined that the "reasons not relating to the individual workers concerned" may be those specific to collective redundancies, i.e. economic, technical or organisational reasons, or reasons connected with the organisation or production of the undertaking. Those circumstances do not preclude the employer from providing a higher level of protection for pregnant workers, workers who have recently given birth or workers who are breastfeeding.[65]

This protection against dismissal also covers the period before maternity leave, when the dismissal is due to reasons related to a pregnancy-related illness. The employer must give written notice of the reasons justifying his decision to dismiss. In addition, workers must be protected from the consequences of unlawful dismissal.

The prohibition of dismissal of workers during pregnancy and until the end of maternity leave is not limited to the notification of dismissal but concerns other preparatory acts of dismissal. A contrary interpretation would deprive Art. 10 of Directive 92/85 of its effectiveness. The prohibition of dismissal covers, for example, the pregnancy phase of the worker. This can be seen if the employer advertises a job in a newspaper in order to start looking for a permanent replacement for her, with the clear intention of dismissing her because of her pregnancy or the birth of a child.[66]

The prohibition of dismissal provided for in Art. 10 of Directive 92/85 applies to both fixed-term and open-ended contracts. The non-renewal of a fixed-term contract when it has reached its expiry date cannot be regarded as a dismissal prohibited by that provision. Unless it is motivated by the pregnancy of the worker, in which case it would constitute direct discrimination on grounds of sex (as such unjustifiable).

The protection of women workers against discriminatory treatment, on the grounds of pregnancy, includes legal action under national law to enforce their rights in the event of dismissal. On the basis of Art. 12 of Directive 92/85, Member States must provide for measures to ensure effective and efficient judicial protection, with a real deterrent effect against the employer and, in any case, adequate in relation to the damage suffered. Thus, the ECJ has considered less favourable treatment of a woman, in relation to her pregnancy, the procedural rules that provide for an action for annulment and reinstatement as the only means of appeal against her dismissal

---

[64]Directive 92/85 of 19 October 1992, *on the introduction of measures to encourage improvements in the safety and health at work of pregnant workers and workers who have recently given birth or are breastfeeding*. OJ L 348, (1992), pp. 1–7.

[65]Case C-103/16, *Jessica Porras Guisado v Bankia SA and Others* (ECJ 22 February 2018), para. 49.

[66]Case C-460/06, *Nadine Paquay v Société d'architectes Hoet + Minne SPRL.* (ECJ 11 October 2007), para. 35.

excluding an action for damages. Whereas such an action is available to any other employee who has been dismissed.[67]

Similar protection applies in Art. 16 of Directive 2006/54, in relation to workers (men and women) exercising paternity and/or adoption leave rights, where the dismissal is due to the exercise of these rights. In particular, protection against dismissal when the worker has applied for or taken parental leave extends to the calculation of dismissal compensation. As the case-law points out, a redundancy payment paid to a worker employed for an indefinite period and on a full-time basis, calculated on the basis of the reduced salary they received while on temporary part-time parental leave, is not admissible.[68]

17.4 Labour Law Measures to Encourage Improvements in the Occupational Safety and Health

The Community Charter of the Fundamental Social Rights of Workers (1989), states that every worker must enjoy satisfactory conditions of safety and health in his working environment (par. 19). To this end, the Directive on Health and Safety at Work states that particularly sensitive risk groups must be protected against risks arising specifically from work.[69] One such group is pregnant workers, workers who have recently given birth or workers who are breastfeeding, for whom Directive 92/85 sets out the measures necessary to encourage improvements in occupational safety and health. A challenge in this area is to ensure that protective measures do not disadvantage women in the labour market and in their working conditions, nor contradict the principle of equal treatment of men and women. As regards to this principle, "the ECJ has consistently recognised the legitimacy of protecting a woman's biological condition during pregnancy and maternity and of introducing maternity protection measures as a means to achieve substantive equality".[70]

17.4.1 Occupational Risk Assessment and Prevention

Besides the maintenance of rights linked to the employment contract, including maintenance of payment and/or entitlement to an adequate allowance and protection against dismissal for reasons associated with their condition, Directive 92/85 lays down several obligations for the employer. These range from the assessment of risks according to the particular circumstances of the worker due to her pregnancy or breastfeeding, to the adoption of a series of measures to protect her from those risks

[67] Case C-63/08, *Virginie Pontin v T-Comalux SA* (ECJ 29 October 2009), para. 76.

[68] Case C-116/08, cited, para. 56.

[69] Directive 89/391 of 12 June 1989 *on the introduction of measures to encourage improvements in the safety and health of workers at work.* OJ L 183, (1989), pp. 1–8.

[70] Recital 24 of Directive 2006/54.

that cannot be eliminated or avoided. A relevant aspect is that the worker must inform the employer of her particular maternity condition, whatever stage she is in (Art. 2). It is supposed to make it possible for the employer to take the necessary measures to protect her from the point of view of occupational risk prevention. The measures are as follows:

1. A Risks Assessment
   "For all activities liable to involve a specific risk of exposure to the agents, processes or working conditions, the employer shall assess the nature, degree and duration of exposure, in the undertaking and/or establishment concerned, of pregnant workers, workers who have recently given birth or workers who are breastfeeding, either directly or by way of the protective and preventive services. It will allow to assess any risks to the safety or health and any possible effect on the pregnancy or breastfeeding of them, and decide what measures should be taken. The related workers or their representatives should be informed of the results of such assessment and of all measures to be taken concerning health and safety at work". (Art. 4 of Directive 92/85).
   The case-law has noted that "a risk assessment is a systematic examination of all aspects of work which comprises at least three phases: the first phase consists of identification of hazards (physical, chemical and biological agents; industrial processes; movements and postures; mental and physical fatigue; other physical and mental burdens). The second phase provides for identification of worker categories (pregnant workers, workers who have recently given birth or workers who are breastfeeding) which are exposed to one or several of those risks. The third phase, namely, the qualitative and quantitative risk assessment, represents the most delicate phase in the process, in that the person carrying out the assessment must be competent and take due account of relevant information . . . in applying appropriate methods in order to be able to conclude whether or not the hazard identified entails a risk situation for workers".[71]
2. Adaptation of working conditions or working time.
   If the results of the assessment referred to in Art. 4 (1) reveal a risk to the safety or health or an effect on the pregnancy or breastfeeding of the worker concerned, the employer shall take the necessary measures to ensure that, by temporarily adjusting her working conditions and/or her working hours, the exposure of that worker to such risks is avoided. (Art. 5 (1) of Directive 92/85).
3. Functional mobility.
   If the adjustment of her working conditions and/or working hours is not technically and/or objectively feasible, or cannot reasonably be required on duly substantiated grounds, the employer shall take the necessary measures to move the worker concerned to another job. (Art. 5 (2) of Directive 92/85).

[71] Case C-531/15, *Elda Otero Ramos v Servicio Galego de Saúde and Instituto Nacional de la Seguridad Social* (ECJ 19 October 2017), para. 48.

4. A leave from work.
   If moving her to another job is not technically and/or objectively feasible or cannot reasonably be required on duly substantiated grounds, the worker concerned shall be granted leave in accordance with national legislation and/or national practice for the whole of the period necessary to protect her safety or health. (Art. 5 (3) of Directive 92/85).

   In the cases referred to in Articles 5, 6 and 7, the employment rights relating to the employment contract, including the maintenance of a payment to, and/or entitlement to an adequate allowance for the workers concerned must be ensured (Art. 11 (1) of Directive 92/85).

17.4.2 Maternity Protection

The aforementioned provisions (adaptation of working conditions or working time, functional mobility or a leave from work) shall apply, mutatis mutandis, if a female worker engaged in an activity prohibited for pregnancy or breastfeeding becomes pregnant or starts breastfeeding and informs her employer thereof (Art. 5 (4) of Directive 92/85). Prohibited activities are, for example, the underground mining work or activities involving a risk of exposure to certain physical, biological and chemical agents (Art. 6 and Annex II of Directive 92/85).

In addition, pregnant workers and workers who have recently given birth or are breastfeeding are not obliged to perform night work (as defined on Directive 2003/88). It aims to strengthen their protection by establishing the principle that they are not obliged to perform night work as long as they submit a medical certificate indicating the need for such protection on the basis of their safety or health (Art. 7 of Directive 92/85). The ECJ considers that "night work may have a significant effect on the health of pregnant women, women who have recently given birth or women who are breastfeeding. The risks for those women vary with the type of work undertaken, working conditions and the individual concerned. Consequently, because of increased tiredness, some pregnant or breastfeeding women may not be able to work irregular or late shifts or work at night. In such cases, a transfer to daytime work, or a leave from work, or an extension of maternity leave (where such a transfer is not technically and/or objectively feasible or cannot reasonably be required on duly substantiated grounds) should be made possible".[72]

In cases of night work, employment rights relating to the employment contract, including the maintenance of a payment to, and/or entitlement to an adequate allowance for workers must be ensured (Art. 11 (1) of Directive 92/85).

[72] Case C-41/17, *Isabel González Castro v Mutua Umivale and Others* (ECJ 19 September 2018).

In particular, another protective provision is the right of pregnant workers to attend ante-natal examinations when they have to take place during working hours, without loss of pay (Art. 9 of Directive 92/85).

17.4.3 Protection of Workers Who Have Recently Given Birth

To complete the protection, workers are entitled to a continuous period of maternity leave of at least 14 weeks allocated before and/or after confinement. This leave must include compulsory maternity leave of at least 2 weeks allocated before and/or after confinement (Art. 8 of Directive 92/85). The case-law specifies that "maternity leave is intended, first, to protect a woman's biological condition during and after pregnancy and, second, to protect the special relationship between a woman and her child over the period which follows pregnancy and childbirth, by preventing that relationship from being disturbed by the multiple burdens which would result from the simultaneous pursuit of employment."[73] In this respect, the Court accepts that a provision, in a national collective agreement reserved to female workers and not to male workers, who bring up their child themselves, the right to leave after the expiry of statutory maternity leave. Provided that such leave is intended to protect workers in relation to the effects of pregnancy and maternity.[74]

For the provisions on maternity leave to be useful, the employment rights of workers must be guaranteed and in particular, the maintenance of adequate pay and/or the right to an adequate allowance (Art. 11(2) of Directive 92/85). The allowance shall be considered adequate, "if it guarantees an income at least equivalent to that which the worker concerned would receive in the event of a break in her activities for reasons connected with her state of health, subject to the limits laid down by national legislation" (par. 3).[75]

17.4.4 Protection of Workers Who Are Breastfeeding

"The condition of a breastfeeding woman is intimately related to maternity, and in particular to pregnancy or maternity leave, so workers who are breastfeeding must be protected on the same basis as workers who are pregnant or have recently given birth".[76]

---

[73] Case C-184/83, *Ulrich Hofmann v Barmer Ersatzkasse* (ECJ 12 July 1984), para. 25, and Case C-12/17, *Ministerul Justiţiei and Tribunalul Botoşani v Maria Dicu* (ECJ 4 October 2018), para. 34.

[74] Case C-463/19, *Syndicat CFTC du personnel de la Caisse primaire d'assurance maladie de la Moselle v Caisse primaire d'assurance maladie de la Moselle* (ECJ 18 November 2020), para. 74.

[75] Case C-411/96, *Margaret Boyle and Others v Equal Opportunities Commission* (ECJ 27 October 1998), para. 40, and Case C-167/12, *C. D. v S. T.* (ECJ 18 March 2014), para. 33.

[76] Case C-531/15, *Elda Otero Ramos v Servicio Galego de Saúde e Instituto Nacional de la Seguridad Social* (ECJ 19 October 2017), para. 59.

As stated above, during breastfeeding, the employer must carry out a risk assessment and if necessary, take measures to protect the worker by adapting working conditions and working time, or through functional mobility or, finally, through work leave.

In order to be in conformity with the requirements of Art. 4 (1) of Directive 92/85, the ECJ underlines that "the risk assessment of the work of a breastfeeding worker must include a specific assessment taking into account the individual situation of the worker in question in order to ascertain whether her health or safety or that of her child is exposed to a risk. Employers will need, for as long as those women continue to breastfeed, to review the risks regularly to ensure that such female workers are not exposed, or exposed as little as possible, to risks that could damage health or safety [. . .]. A certain number of those substances are excreted through breast milk, and the child is presumed to be particularly sensitive".[77]

17.5 Protection of Workers on Work-Life Balance for Parents and Caregivers

One of the most complex issues that affects equality between women and men both directly and indirectly is that of caring for children and family members. Traditionally, the cultural and social model of role distribution considered men to be the breadwinners, while women took care of the family, given that they were not fully incorporated into the labour market. In short, this has contributed to the construction of a gender stereotype creating unequal expectations about the role of women and men in society, attributing to women caring and nurturing tasks, although progress has been made in recent times.

Currently, women tend to assume the majority of unpaid work, with huge differences in the time spent between men and women, a fact that is clear throughout the world.[78] This is also evident in the EU Member States, with significant data emerging from Eurofound's study on *Striking a balance: reconciling work and life in the EU*, based on the European Working Conditions Survey (EWCS) as well as the European Quality of Life Survey (EQLS). The analyses show that equal sharing of work and care activities is the exception rather than the rule in all EU countries, although there are significant differences among them.[79]

It is a fact that an adequate equal treatment policy requires the protection of workers' rights to adapt working conditions to family responsibilities. In this sense, at an international and European level, rules have been drawn up to balance private and working life in order to facilitate it.

[77] Case C-531/15, cited, para. 49 and 51.

[78] Addati et al. (2018).

[79] https://www.eurofound.europa.eu/sites/default/files/ef_publication/field_ef_document/ef18065en.pdf.

Firstly, within the ILO framework, the Maternity Protection Convention, 2000 (C183) and the Workers with Family Responsibilities Convention, 1981 (C156) address these needs, giving them the importance they require. The content of C183 establishes the rights to maternity and highlights that the exercise of maternity rights cannot constitute a source of discrimination in employment. As far as C156 is concerned, the articles do not go beyond a mere programmatic exercise, given that its fundamental aim is expressed in line with other international instruments on equal opportunities and equal treatment for men and women. Both Conventions refer to different international instruments on the elimination of all forms of discrimination against women. Yet C156 mentions that the States Parties recognise that in order to achieve full equality between men and women, it is necessary to modify their traditional role in society and in the family. On this issue, the Convention offers a vision of the future, directing States to develop, as part of their national policy objectives, various aspects that seek to ensure that the exercise of work-life balance does not lead to discrimination in employment for workers (Art. 3). In line with this objective, awareness-raising policies should be formulated through education and information, as well as guidance and training for the retention of workers with family responsibilities in the labour market. One of the most ambitious objectives is to address their needs by planning local or regional communities and in turn, by developing or promoting community services, public or private, such as childcare and family assistance services and facilities. Undoubtedly, the eventual implementation of these measures would enable the exercise of work-life balance with a public service vocation.

Secondly, as far as the EU framework is concerned, the content of its normative development is more comprehensive and complex, closely related to the Institution's equality policies and in line with UN action on this issue. The EU policy "*in this area is to encourage and, if possible, adapt working conditions to family responsibilities. Protection of women within family life and in the course of their professional activities is, in the same way as for men, a principle which is widely regarded (. . .) as being the natural corollary of the equality between men and women (. . .).*"[80] Moreover, following the enactment of the European Charter of Fundamental Rights, leave periods related to childbirth and childcare have acquired a "constitutional" nature. Article 33.2 of the Charter states "*To reconcile family and professional life, everyone shall have the right to protection from dismissal for a reason connected with maternity and the right to paid maternity leave and to parental leave following the birth or adoption of a child.*"

These rights have been developed by the UE law, incorporating minimum provisions, which allow the exercise of family responsibilities and promote equal treatment as well. On the other hand, Directive 96/34/EC initially regulated work-life balance but was revised by Directive 2010/18/EU of 8 March 2010 *implementing the revised Framework Agreement on parental leave concluded by*

[80]Case C-243/95, *Hill and Stapleton v The Revenue Commissioners and Department of Finance* (ECJ 17 June 1998), para. 42.

BUSINESSEUROPE, UEAPME, CEEP and ETUC.[81] The latter directive has been repealed by Directive (EU) 2019/1158 of 20 June, *introducing appropriate measures to aim at a fair sharing of family responsibilities.*[82] Specifically, Directive (EU) 2019/1158 establishes rights that allow the exercise of care work, configured around two institutions: firstly, the figure of leaves of absence, in a broad sense, and secondly, the organisation of work with flexible working hours. These are minimum provisions, which make it possible to exercise family responsibilities, reinforcing more equal sharing, as well as to promote equal treatment, as set up in its Recitals.

Moreover, although these institutions are key elements in the development of parenting and care, their use sometimes leads to indirect discrimination against women. Thus, despite the enormous progress that has been made, there are still gaps to be filled. Consideration should be given to the fact that entering rules to eliminate or reduce gender inequality can also perpetuate their traditional gender roles and place men in a secondary position in terms of assuming family responsibilities.[83] Specifically, it is necessary to overcome the concept of conciliation to move on to other more gender-sensitive, such as co-responsibility or sharing of responsibilities. The change in terminology would clearly imply a paradigm shift and would promote far-reaching social changes.[84] Therefore, the EU's action continues, with its institutions, to make a commitment to gender equality and to develop strategies to address this issue, in accordance with Sustainable Development Goal (SDG) 5 of the UN's 2030 Agenda to achieve equality for women.

17.5.1 Maternity Leave, Assisted Reproduction Techniques and Surrogate Maternity

The relationship between parents and children as an element of reconciliation is common to maternity leave, paternity leave and parental leave. The purpose of maternity leave, its distinguish feature, is to protect not only the relationship between a woman and her child after pregnancy and childbirth, but also the biological condition of women during and after pregnancy and her physical recovery.[85] Accordingly, the ECJ has argued in its rulings the differences between maternity leave and parental leave.

[81] OJ L 68, 18.3.2010, 13–20.

[82] OJ L 188, 12.7.2019, 79–93.

[83] Cases C-476/99, *H. Lommers v Minister van Landbouw, Natuurbeheer en Visserij* (ECJ 19 March 2002) para. 41 and C-104/09, *Pedro Manuel Roca Alvarez v Sesa Start España ETT, S.A* (ECJ 30 September 2010) para. 36. See: Cabeza Pereiro and Ballester Pastor (2015), pp. 116–121.

[84] Ballester Pastor (2011), pp. 17–18.

[85] This interpretation derived to the Case C-184/83, *Hofmann,* cited. has been partially questioned in the Opinion of advocate general Bobek, delivered on 9 July 2020, Case C-463/19, *Syndicat CFTC du personnel de la Caisse primaire d'assurance maladie de la Moselle v Caisse primaire d'assurance maladie de Moselle,* para. 38–80.

Maternity leave is a right

▶ **Definition** "*intended to protect a woman's biological condition and the special relationship between a woman and her child over the period which follows pregnancy and childbirth, by preventing that relationship from being disturbed by the multiple burdens which would result from the simultaneous pursuit of employment.*"[86]

Furthermore, parental leave

▶ **Definition** is a right "*. . . granted to parents to enable them to take care of their child (. . .) until the child has reached a given age.*"[87]

Notwithstanding, certain problems have arisen regarding the consideration that should be given to attempting maternity through assisted reproduction techniques, such as in vitro fertilisation and/or hormonal treatments. Currently in modern society, women have been delaying the age of maternity, among other factors, to consolidate their employment situation.[88] This fact, together with the evolution of family models, has developed fertility treatments, as they are used by women with difficulties in conceiving, those who experience motherhood alone and homosexual couples.

Nevertheless, this social change has not been received within a legislative framework and reservations are expressed about the extension of the Directive 92/85 to the protection of women under fertility treatments. Consequently, "*an employee who undergoes an in vitro fertilisation procedure is not a 'pregnant worker' for the purposes of the first part of Article 2(a) of Directive 92/85/EEC, if, at the time at which she was given notice of termination of employment, her ova had been fertilised in a laboratory but had not yet been transferred to her body.*"[89]

On the other hand, Directive 2019/1158 does not include leaves to facilitate fertility treatments which, in addition to being financially costly, might also require the temporary absence from work. Indeed, the legislation has not provided a solution for women undergoing fertility treatments, only protecting them against possible actions contrary to the principle of equality under the Directive 2006/54/EC. Furthermore, it should be borne in mind that fertility treatments involve hormone treatment which may cause the woman a discomfort incompatible with her work. Accordingly, if women need to rely on the common rules of the sick-leave scheme to undergo to in vitro fertilization (IVF) treatments, this fact could lead to dismissal, given that illness is not a cause of discrimination prohibited by EU directives. In any

---

[86]Case C-519/03, *Commission v Luxembourg* (ECJ 14 April 2005), para. 32, and Case C-315/14, *Estrella Rodríguez Sánchez v Consum Sociedad Cooperativa Valenciana* (ECJ 16 June 2016), para. 44.

[87]Case C-519/03 and Case C-315/14, *ut supra*.

[88]The 2018 Fertility Survey of the Spanish National Institute of Statistics reveals a direct link between these two factors. https://www.ine.es/prensa/ef_2018_d.pdf.

[89]Opinion of advocate general Ruiz-Jarabo Colomer, delivered on 27 November 2007, Case C-506/06, *Sabine Mayr v Bäckerei und Konditorei Gerhard Flöckner OHGayr*, para. 48.

case, as the CJEU has ruled,[90] this situation would be discrimination on grounds of sex, as it is only women who can suffer this type of sick leave. Therefore, protection for pregnancy should at least be extended to those cases in which undergoing fertility treatments is the immediate step prior to becoming pregnant, by facilitating reconciliation and reinforcing the guarantees against possible discriminatory treatment.

Another new phenomenon are surrogacy techniques with two common types. Firstly,

Example

when a heterosexual couple, male homosexual couple, or a single male parent find a surrogate mother to be artificially inseminated with the husband's, one of the intended fathers or an anonymous donor sperm. ◄

These are the traditional cases where the surrogate is also the biological mother of the child. Notwithstanding, by the popularising of IVF, it allowed women to fertilise healthy eggs in a laboratory and have them implanted in another woman. This is known as a gestational surrogate, when the mother will not be genetically related to the child and setting up a second type of surrogacy.

Example

A couple (heterosexual or not), or a single parent could find a surrogate mother to be artificially inseminated with her egg (from the intended mother or from an anonymous donor's) and/or his sperm (from the intended father or an anonymous donor's). ◄

All the aforementioned examples illustrate non-biological reproductive techniques that have raised a complex legal issue as to whether they fit within the framework of Directive 92/85. First of all, the question arises as to whether, if the intended mother (or mothers in homosexual couples), meaning the one who does not carry the baby, would be entitled to maternity leave. In principle, the ECJ refused to grant protection under that directive to an intended mother who, although she had not given birth to her child, was breastfeeding the baby.[91] The Court argued the Directive (Art. 14) could not apply to the case, since its purpose is to protect pregnant workers, after childbirth or during breastfeeding for reasons of occupational health. Notwithstanding, the Advocate General's (AG) Opinion offers a wider scope in "*Directive 92/85 and framed in its historical context. In the early 1990s the practice of surrogacy was not as widespread as it is today. It is thus not surprising that the normative structure of Directive 92/85 is based on an approach which takes biological motherhood as the norm.*" For this reason, AG considers that intended

[90] Case C-506/06, *Sabine Mayr v Bäckerei und Konditorei Gerhard Flöckner OHGayr* (ECJ 26 February 2008), para. 55.

[91] Case C-167/12, *C. D. v S. T.*, (ECJ 18 March 2014).

mothers deserve the same consideration as the biological mother, if she assumes custody immediately after the birth: "*In the same way as a woman who herself has given birth to a child, an intended mother has in her care an infant for whose best interests she is responsible.*"[92] No differences can be made "*precisely because she herself was not pregnant, she is faced with the challenge of bonding with that child, integrating it into the family and adjusting to her role as a mother.*"[93] This way was also stressed by the Court, rejecting the possible application of maternity leave for surrogate mothers, considering that the refusal did not constitute discrimination on grounds of sex under Directive 2006/54 (Arts. 4 and 14).[94] In sum, these new reproductive techniques are not covered by Directive 2006/54 and can only be redirected to the provisions of Directive 2019/1158. On the other hand, it is a need for reform of Directive 92/85, considering since where surrogacy is legal, maternity leave (Art. 8) would have to be distributed between the surrogate and the intended mothers, if both are workers.

Nevertheless, the protection of the child's rights must be considered and not be reduced, therefore, the intended mother should not have her leave limited and should enjoy it in full, which would not be the case for the leave of the biological mother who only has to protect her physical recovery by not sharing the care of the baby.

Consequently, it would be necessary to consider whether the aforementioned Directives need to be revised with this approach, to guarantee the rights of those who use assisted reproductive technologies. In order to avoid a possible lack of protection of their parental rights.

17.5.2 Paternity, Parental and Carers Leave

The formula for work-life balance has traditionally focused around leave. To this end, successive EU Directives have developed an increasingly broad and co-responsible right to share responsibilities. In this regard, the new Directive (EU) 2019/1158 introduces significant changes thereby contributing to gender equality.

Firstly, the regulation of paternity leave represents an extraordinary step forward, as it incorporates a new instrument which complements the maternity leave provided for in Directive 92/85/EEC.[95] The Directive provides that on the birth of a child, the

---

[92] Opinion of advocate general Kokott, delivered on 26 September 2013, Case C-167/12, *C. D. v S. T.*, para. 46.

[93] Opinion of advocate general Kokott, *ut supra.*

[94] Case C-363/12, *Z. v A Government department and The Board of management of a community school* (ECJ 18 March 2014).

[95] Proposal for a Directive of the European Parliament and of the Council amending Council Directive 92/85/EEC on the introduction of measures to encourage improvements in the safety and health at work of pregnant workers and workers who have recently given birth or are breastfeeding. Brussels, 3.10.2008, COM (2008) 637 final. Initially, the possibility to reform Directive 92/85, at consolidating co-responsibility by incorporating exclusive paternity leave into

parent—or an equivalent second parent if recognised by national law—shall be entitled to ten working days of paternity leave. This entitlement shall be taken as provided for in national transposing legislation partly before or only after the birth of the child or by flexible arrangements. It shall be granted without any link to marital or family status, in order to avoid discrimination, and shall not be subject to seniority or previous periods of employment. The financial compensation with the exercise of the right has to be granted. The States should set a level for the payment or allowance at least equivalent to the level of national sick pay. Additionally, it has a reinforced protection, in the same terms that provided for maternity, in accordance with the provisions of Directive 54/2006 (Art. 16 on parental leave and adoption).

On the other hand, the parental leave has been improved and, while maintaining its duration at 4 months individually attributed, its partial non-transferability has been increased to 2 months. What is worthy of criticism is the failure to promote more decisively "*the balanced participation of women and men in professional/ public life and in private/family life is (...) a key area for gender equality and is essential for the development of society*".[96] Nonetheless, the inclusion of an entitlement to remuneration or a financial benefit may encourage men, who usually have higher salaries, to take parental leave. The leave must be requested with a period of notice and may be conditional to a period of work qualification or to a length of service qualification of less than 1 year. For the purpose of calculating, the qualifying period shall be taken into account for the sum of successive fixed-term contracts with the same employer. The employer may, for productive circumstances, postpone the leave, in which case the employer must provide written justification. However, the Directive proposes that in these cases a flexible formula for exercising the right may be chosen.

Carers' leave is a new instrument, intended to allow individual workers to meet the needs of their family members by granting them 5 working days a year. The Directive provides that Member States may make the exercise of this leave, conditional upon adequate justification. Finally, all these measures are accompanied by the maintenance of the right already provided for in Directive 2010/18 to leave on grounds of force majeure, the purpose of which is to be able to attend to urgent family reasons, understood as cases of illness or accident, which require the immediate presence of the worker.

All rights are reinforced in the Directive to avoid discrimination on the grounds of their exercise (Art. 11). Labour rights will be guaranteed (Art. 10), as well as protecting against dismissal for this reason and, along these lines, reversing the burden of proof, which will fall on the employer who has dismissed the worker (Art. 12). All measures represent a substantial change towards equality. Further, they contribute to increased opportunities for men and women with caring responsibilities to remain in the labour force and, at the same time, reinforcing the co-responsibility.

---

the Directive was raised. Notwithstanding, it was quite controversial, and has not been finally implemented.

[96] App. no. 30078/06, *Case Konstantin Markin v. Russia* (ECtHR 22 March 2012), para. 35.

Notwithstanding those positive strides, challenges remain in increasing the non-transferability of leaves to encourage co-responsibility, ensuring similar duration to paternity and maternity leave, preventing women from making more intensive use of this right.

17.5.3 Flexible Working Arrangements

Finally, it should be noted that the Directive (EU) 2019/1158 provides a significant contribution to a real work-life balance, by improving the right to flexible working arrangements. In this respect, the wording of the rules on flexitime have modernised and improved the content of Directive 2010/18. The current Directive includes the definition of flexible working arrangements in Article 3.1 (f) and devotes a single provision (Article 9) to regulate it—clarifying some questions on the exercise of the right in recitals 34–36.

The measures are outlined as follows: Firstly, it is shaped as a genuine right that is ensured to workers with children up to a certain age, which shall be at least 8 years. The same entitlement is also given to carers. Therefore, the Directive represents an important step forward for equality, not only for the extension of the entitlement, but also in the transposition methods that must be adopted in relation to the previous Directive. Indeed, the wording stipulates that the Member States shall take the necessary measures to ensure that workers have the right to flexible working time. The obligation now does not rely on transposition methods, such as collective agreements, but imposes compliance on the State. Consequently, the current Directive corrects the nature of the previous Directive as an open standard.[97] Thus, it avoids the possibility that the right becomes an empty shell by limiting the provisions to a reduction in working hours.

Secondly, it is an obligation of result, where employers are required to consider and comply with requests for flexible working time, which is different from *taking into consideration* what was previously provided for. If the request cannot be accommodated, the employer must provide adequate justification for the refusal or postponement of the request.

Thirdly, this right is independent, unrelated to other forms of leave, such as parental or maternity leave. The right to request is set up independently and can be exercised at any time within the period established by national law. Therefore, the entitlement is enhanced and differs to the regulation under the Clause 6(1) of the revised Framework Agreement, "*which relates to situations in which a worker returns to work following 'parental leave', cannot be interpreted as also covering a situation in which a worker returns from 'maternity leave' within the meaning of Directive 92/85.*"[98]

---

[97] Case C-366/18, *José Manuel Ortiz Mesonero v UTE Luz Madrid Centro* (ECJ 18 September 2019), para. 48.

[98] Case C-351/14, cited, para. 48.

Lastly, the Directive provides for flexibility, meaning different possibilities to adjust the working patterns. Furthermore, the Directive suggests a range of possibilities such as "the use of remote working arrangements, flexible working schedules, or reduced working hours."[99] On the one hand, the exercise of the right may be subject to reasonable limitations and to certain requirements, such as a period of length qualification or a length of service (not exceeding 6 months). And explicitly targeting that "in successive fixed-term contracts with the same employer, the sum of those contracts shall be taken into account for the purpose of calculating the qualifying period."[100] On the other hand, the worker has the right to adapt the duration of the leave to his or her needs, even returning to the original working pattern before the end of the agreed period justifying a change of circumstances.[101]

In short, it is the development of a new approach to the right to a work-life balance, which contributes to keeping carers and family members, usually women, in the workplace. Thereby strengthening their position in the labour market.

17.6 Gender-Based Harassment, Sexual Harassment and Other Forms of Gender-Based Violence at Work

Violence takes on different forms in the workplace: aggressions—which can be physical, psychological or both at the same time, tensions and/or different forms of harassment. Sexual harassment at work began when women entered the labour market, although it was not recognised as a problem until 1970.[102] Harassment can come from colleagues, bosses and even third parties outside the organisation and can take place in the workplace or even outside, in person or through digital devices.[103]

Although it is a fact that both men and women can be subject to harassment, statistics prove that harassment is mostly suffered by women.[104] The reason for this

[99] Directive (EU) 2019/1158 of the European Parliament and of the Council of 20 June 2019, recital (34) and Art. 3.1 (f).

[100] Directive (EU) 2019/1158, Art. 9.4.

[101] In these cases, the employer shall consider and respond the request, taking into account the circumstances, Directive (EU) 2019/1158, Art. 9.3. In this respect, the circumstances must be taken into account without disproportionate requirements which otherwise would be discriminatory, Case C-116/06, *Sari Kiiski contra Tampereen kaupunki* (ECJ 20 September 2007).

[102] See: Rubenstein (1988), p. 2.

[103] Surprisingly sexual harassment is worse in top management categories. Approximately 75% of women have experienced sexual harassment, the percentage is a 74% of those in the professional occupational category. Vid. https://fra.europa.eu/sites/default/files/fra-2014-vaw-survey-at-a-glance-oct14_en.pdf.

[104] There are many reasons for this, listed in this chapter, e.g.: their situation in the labour market is inferior to that of men—lower salaries in similar or same jobs—greater temporality in women's contracts and also due to the difficulty of access to higher level positions and/or the assignment of less qualified tasks that justify their professional hierarchical subordination. The ILO express in a

is that sexual harassment is linked to unequal power relations, based on gender stereotypes.

▶ **Definition** Gender is the roles or stereotypes socially constructed based on the characteristics of woman or men

As the Istanbul Convention set out

> "shall mean the socially constructed roles, behaviours, activities and attributes that a given society considers appropriate for women and men."[105]

The concept of gender therefore encompasses sexual diversity, since the individuals can have a biological sexual identity that does not correspond to their gender identity. Sexual harassment is thus connected to the concept of gender, understanding such conduct as part of the structure of domination over gender identity or sexual orientation.

In 1958 the ILO approved the Convention no. 111 on discrimination in employment and occupation. While the C111 was not intended to regulate issues of violence or harassment in the workplace, sexual harassment was considered as a particular form of discrimination on grounds of sex. Understanding it was a violation of the right to equal opportunities between persons of both sexes.[106] The ILO addressed that sexual harassment significantly affected women's employment and career prospects, has a negative impact on health and safety at work, and also on the dignity in the workplace.

The European Union began to tackle this issue in 1986, when the European Parliament, in its Resolution of 11 July,[107] urged the Member States to achieve a legal definition of sexual harassment at work and worked out the needed solutions. Nevertheless, the Rubenstein Report,[108] carried out in 1987 on behalf of the Commission, conducted an in-depth study on the subject and deemed necessary the adoption of a directive specifically to cover this area. The Report resulted in the Council Resolution of 29 May 1990 and Commission Recommendation 92/131/ EEC of 27 November 1991 on the protection of the dignity of women and men at work, the annex to which contains a code of practice on sexual harassment.[109]

worksheet that in the European Union, 40–50% of women have reported some form of sexual harassment at the workplace.

[105] Article 3. (c) of Council of Europe Convention on preventing and combating violence against women and domestic violence (Istanbul Convention).

[106] The ILO Committee of Experts condemned sexual harassment under the provisions of the Discrimination (Employment and Occupation) Convention, 1958 (No. 111).

[107] European Parliament's Resolution on Violence against Women (1986) Doc. A2-44/86, OJ C 176, 14.07.1986, 73–83.

[108] See: Rubenstein (1988), p. 2.

[109] OJ C 157, 27.06.1990, 3–4 and OJ L 49, 24.02.1992, 1–8, respectively.

Consequently, sexual harassment was the starting point for establishing a regulation about harassment in the European Union.

The Directive 2002/73/EC of the European Parliament and of the Council of 23 September 2002, now recast in Directive 2006/54/EC of the European Parliament and of the Council of 5 July 2006, on the implementation of the principle of equal opportunities and equal treatment of men and women in matters of employment and occupation (Arts. 2.1.(c) and (d) y 2.2. (a)), was the first binding legislation introducing important issues regarding sexual harassment and harassment based on sex in the framework of the European Union.

The EU has not developed a general normative instrument on harassment, but its action has been based on the principle of non-discrimination. Thus, in addition to the above, other equality directives prohibit "harassment" as discriminatory behaviour regarding race, ethnic origin, disability, religion, age or sexual orientation. These issues are covered by the Council Directive 2000/43/EC of 29 June 2000, implementing the principle of equal treatment between persons irrespective of racial or ethnic origin (Art. 2.3) and Council Directive 2000/78/EC of 27 November 2000, establishing a general framework for equal treatment in employment and occupation (Arts. 2.2 and 2.3).[110] Finally, Directive 2010/41/EU of the European Parliament and of the Council on the application of the principle of equal treatment between men and women engaged in an activity in a self-employed capacity and repealing Council Directive 86/613/EEC, includes the prohibition of harassment and sexual harassment in the relationships between the self-employed worker and third parties (Art. 3 (c) and (d)).[111]

Lastly, with the adoption of the resolution of 11 September 2018 on measures to prevent and combat mobbing and sexual harassment at workplaces, in public spaces, and political life in the EU (2018/2055(INI)), the European Parliament called on the Commission to submit a proposal for a directive to tackle all forms of violence against women and girls and gender-based violence (Recommendation 17). In addition, the urgent need for standards on violence and harassment at work was reiterated, which should have provided a legislative framework (Recommendation 25). On 5 March 2020, the European Commission presented its Gender Equality Strategy 2020–2025, including measures against harassment at work.[112]

---

[110] OJ L 180, 19.07.2000, 22–26 and OJ L 303, 2.12.2000,16–22, respectively.

[111] OJ L 180, 15.7.2010, 1–6.

[112] The situation is different with regard to members of the administration in the EU framework. Indeed, the European Civil Service Law affecting civil servants and EU agents has specific rules directly addressing harassment in general and gender-based harassment, which has been the subject of attention at the European Court of Justice. See: Council Regulation (EC, Euratom) No 723/2004 of 22 March 2004 amending the Staff Regulations of officials of the European Communities and the Conditions of Employment of other servants of the European Communities (OJ L 124, 27.04.2004, 1–118), Council Decision of 24 September 2004 concerning the Staff Regulations of the European Defence Agency, 2004/676/EC, (OJ L 310, 7.10.1994, 64–71).

Ultimately, the recently adopted ILO Convention C190 (C190 in short) on violence and harassment is a milestone as the first binding international convention on this issue.[113] The importance of C190 is due to the fact that it offers an innovative and complete treatment of harassment at work. Measures that should be taken to prevent and address it are also spelled out and gender-based harassment is specifically addressed.[114] The C190 entered into force on 25 June 2021, but regarding the EU States it must be highlighted that the Convention covers matters which fall within the competence of the EU, such as health and safety at work, equality and non-discrimination. Consequently, the European Commission proposed a Council Decision to authorise the Member States to ratify the Convention No. 190, which has not yet been adopted by the Council.[115]

17.6.1 Gender-Based Harassment in the Workplace

The C190 set out an all-inclusive definition of violence and harassment at the workplace

> "*a range of unacceptable behaviours and practices, or threats thereof, whether a single occurrence or repeated, that aim at, result in, or are likely to result in physical, psychological, sexual or economic harm, and includes gender-based violence and harassment.*"[116]

Nevertheless, in accordance with the Convention, the States may provide in their national law single or separate concepts if necessary.

Considering that violence and harassment in the world of work can constitute a human rights violation or abuse, contrary to decent work, the Convention eliminates the need for the repetitive actions or the intentional nature of harassment, as is set out in many national laws. Additionally, the Convention admits that violent or harassing behaviour may be intentional (or not) when causing harm, and when the behaviour is likely to cause harm even if they do actually not cause it.

Moreover, C190 refers to sex or gender as a cause of harassment, expressly mentioning this type of discrimination as a specific and distinct modality, although included in the general definition. The Convention introduces as a priority objective the achievement of real gender equality, giving a singular treatment to workplace violence with a gender perspective as a cause of discriminatory violence at work.

---

[113] Together with the ILO Violence and Harassment Recommendation, 2019 (No. 206).

[114] International Labour Organization (2016): https://www.ilo.org/wcmsp5/groups/public/%2D%2D-dgreports/%2D%2D-gender/documents/meetingdocument/wcms_522932.pdf.

[115] Proposal for a Council Decision authorising Member States to ratify, in the interest of the European Union, the Violence and Harassment Convention, 2019 (No. 190) of the International Labour Organization, Brussels 22.1.2020, COM(2020) 24 final.

[116] Article 1.1.(a).

This treatment of violence and harassment with a gender perspective is an important differentiating factor, as the concept of gender goes beyond that of sex and allows for more effective protection against harassment. The C190 states that violence and harassment at work must be tackled with an inclusive and integrated approach that considers causes and risk factors (such as gender stereotypes and the abuse of gender-based power relations) or intersections with other causes of discrimination (race, age, disability, etc.), that may give rise to multiple discrimination.

17.6.2 Sexual and Sexist Harassment and Cyber-Bullying

As provided in the Convention, gender-based violence and harassment is

> "*violence and harassment directed at persons because of their sex or gender, or affecting persons of a particular sex or gender disproportionately, and includes sexual harassment.*"[117]

Jointly introducing the terms "gender" with "sex" constitutes a significant step forward in the regulation. Notwithstanding, the Convention does not differentiate between sexual harassment and harassment on grounds of sex or gender, even though it states that gender harassment includes both behaviours.

Thus, the C190 stated that sexual harassment is covered by gender-based harassment. This is because sexual harassment is a behaviour of a sexual, verbal, non-verbal or physical nature that creates an intimidating, humiliating, degrading or an offensive environment. In this particular regard, sexual harassment is not based exclusively on the satisfaction of a sexual desire, but on the consolidation of a gender stereotype, in which the one who is the active subject comes to materialise his or her position of prevalence within the sexual stereotype, confirming that sexual harassment is a variety of gender harassment. Gender-based harassment may be perpetrated by different individuals, including colleagues, supervisors, subordinates and third parties. Consequently, it may be "*'vertical' of a subordinate by a superior or vice versa, peer-group ('horizontal') harassment or harassment of a mixed type.*"[118]

Notwithstanding, the Directive 54/2006/EC establishes definitions that need to take into account this issue.[119] Firstly, in accordance with its provisions, harassment on grounds of sex is defined as

[117] Article 1.1.(b).

[118] European Parliament resolution of 20 September 2001 on harassment at the workplace (2001/2339(INI)), point 6. OJ C 77 E, 28.3.2002, 138–141.

[119] Holtmaat (2011), pp. 4–13.

▶ **Definition** "*unwanted conduct related to the sex of a person [that] occurs with the purpose or effect of violating the dignity of a person, and of creating an intimidating, hostile, degrading, humiliating or offensive environment.*"[120]

Harassment on grounds of sex refers to discriminatory behaviour on the basis of a person's sex, however, the explicit recognition of gender in Convention 190 allows for a more appropriate interpretation to be consolidated.[121]

Example

Hence, gender-based harassment is, for example, when a worker (male, female or LGBTQIA+) suffers harassment for taking on childcare duties ◀

The reference to gender broadens the framework of protection. Thus, in the above example, not only those women who have taken on a feminised role, such as caregiving, but also all those who do not act in accordance with their traditional gender roles, would be protected from violence or harassment. For example, men (or LGBTQIA+ persons) who care for their children. In this way, protection from discriminatory harassment is improved for anyone affected by gender role prejudice.

Sexual harassment, which is also included in C190 but not defined, is the form of gender-based harassment most frequently studied in scientific literature. The sexual harassment could be manifested as a "conduct used explicitly or implicitly as a basis for a decision which affects a person's job"[122] a so-called *quid pro quo*, or as conducts "that creates an intimidating, hostile or humiliating working environment for the recipient",[123] called a hostile work environment. According to the definition of Directive 2000/54, sexual harassment is

▶ **Definition** "*where any form of unwanted verbal, non-verbal or physical conduct of a sexual nature occurs, with the purpose or effect of violating the dignity of a person, in particular when creating an intimidating, hostile, degrading, humiliating or offensive environment.*"[124]

Hence, the elements which manifest themselves as identifiers of conduct under the Directive are threefold. Firstly, the conduct may be verbal, non-verbal or physical; secondly, it must be of a sexual nature; and thirdly, it must reflect an intention or purpose to offend against a person's dignity. However, the definition in the Directive is flawed in that it appears to require a manifest refusal on the part of

[120] Article 2.1.(c).

[121] More appropriately worded than in the anti-discrimination directives, which speak of harassment without reference to gender.

[122] *Brief n°2: Sexual harassment in the world of work*, https://www.ilo.org/wcmsp5/groups/public/%2D%2D-dgreports/%2D%2D-gender/documents/briefingnote/wcms_738115.pdf.

[123] *Brief n°2: Sexual harassment in the world of work, ut supra.*

[124] Article 2.1.(d).

the victim of harassment. In this regard, the CJEU, in one of the few rulings that dealt with this issue, taking a stance against this interpretation, considering that "*victims do not have to prove that such conduct is unwelcome in order for it to qualify as sexual harassment, since that criterion needs to be fulfilled only where the facts complained of relate solely to the mere manifestation of sexual interest*".[125]

Nonetheless, it should be noted that C190 introduces a more protective legal regime for gender-based violence and harassment than that contained in the Directives, which even improves on what the Convention itself provides for violence or harassment in general.[126] Indeed, in the case of gender-based violence and harassment, as stated in Article 1.1.(b), the mere existence of the conduct constitutes harassment, even if it is not intentional, or when the behaviour is likely to cause harm even but does actually not cause it. Consequently, the Member States have to define these conducts in their laws.

Another important fact to highlight is the scope of application of the Convention (Article 3), considering that harassment may occur at work, but also in other related situations, thus expanding the application to the "world of work". This includes situations that happen at work and rest places, but also in accommodation provided by the employer, during commuting, at social or training events and on the way to and from work.

Example

Explicit or sexual jokes, unwanted comments, physical contacts, exhibition of explicit pictures, sexual assaults. ◀

However, the key point that we need to emphasise is that the Convention incorporates situations of violence and harassment through work-related communications, including those enabled by information and communication technologies. This paragraph would introduce cyberbullying, as a form of harassment, a situation encountered increasingly often at work. The addition of cyberbullying is an important step forward in protecting against this silent scourge that allows for different and increasingly imaginative forms of violence and harassment, both sexual and gender-based cyberbullying.

Example

Emails, text messages, telephone calls, dissemination of real or simulated digital content of a sexual or non-sexual nature, which are unreasonable or vexatious to the worker. ◀

[125] Case T-549/93, *D v Commission of the European Communities* (ECJ 26 January 1995). Sexual harassment court cases can only be found in the ECJ regarding EU civil servants and officers.

[126] See: Lousada Arochena (2019), pp. 61–63.

The European Parliament, in its Resolution of 11 September 2018,[127] had identified cyberbullying as an emerging problem, calling for a review of EU regulations to combat harassment (Recommendation 21).

17.6.3 Measures Provided in Convention 190 ILO

The Convention establishes different measures to guarantee the prevention and elimination of the violence and harassment at work. States shall adopt laws and regulations defining and prohibiting these behaviours in the workplace (with special care to gender-based violence and harassment).

In any case, the States should bear in mind the right to equality and non-discrimination in employment and occupation, considering the fact that some groups are more vulnerable and disproportionately affected by these issues. At the same time, the adoption of the measures need a collaboration between the Governments, employers and workers and their organisations, identifying the most exposed sectors and occupations, including any kind of work arrangements and the informal economy workers. The laws and regulations need to give effective protection to all affected groups.

The Convention also obliges Member States to follow up and monitor legislation in this area. They will also have to establish complaint mechanisms with specific procedures and sanctions, witness protection measures, privacy protection to the persons involved, and legal, social, medical and administrative assistance services for victims and complainants, always taking gender considerations into account. Hence, the C190 introduces the requirement for the States to set up measures for the protection for victims and against retaliation,[128] and guarantee that workers have the right to remove themselves without reprisal when harassment at work may affect their safety. Finally, it will ensure that the labour inspectorate has the power to act in such cases. Therefore, should be established

> "*an effective access to gender-responsive, safe and effective complaint and dispute resolution mechanisms, support, services and remedies*"[129]

and urges States indeed to recognise the effects of domestic violence in order to mitigate its impact on the world of work.

---

[127] European Parliament resolution of 11 September 2018 on measures to prevent and combat mobbing and sexual harassment at workplace, in public spaces, and political life in the EU (2018/2055(INI)), OJ C 433, 23.12.2019, 31–41.

[128] Even the Recommendation is a non-binding guideline, it sets out more specific measures to address gender-based violence and harassment, as well as practical measures to mitigate the impact of domestic violence in the world of work, such as: providing temporary leave for victims, flexible working hours, including domestic violence in workplace risk assessment and raising awareness of the effects of domestic violence.

[129] Article 10 (e).

Moreover, the employers have specific duties, together with the workers' representatives, controlling the prevention of violence and harassment in the "world of work", devoting particular attention to the gender perspective. And, if it is reasonably practicable, they shall, firstly, adopt and implement an adequate policy. Secondly, they have to identify, evaluate, prevent and control the risk of violence and harassment at work, taking into account these risks in the management of occupational safety and health. Lastly, they shall give information and training about the risks and prevention measures of the workplace.

Finally, the C190 includes the obligation to ensure guidance, resources and training or other tools not only in general but also on gender-based violence and harassment at work to the employers, workers and their organisations, including awareness-raising campaigns (Article 11).

In short, we believe that the EU needs to tackle this problem firmly and should move forward and complete the regulation with a Directive. From our point of view more resolute action is required against harassment. Otherwise, some states may not ratify or accomplish the content of the C190 and thus fail to comply with its objectives and provisions.

17.7 Gender Perspective in Collective Labour Law

Labour law was developed with a collective vision, where an employee was viewed as an integral part or member of a group of workers.[130] By recognising collective freedoms and rights, such as freedom of association, the right to collective bargaining, the right to strike and the right to participation (in decision-making, management, and ownership), workers can be adequately represented in relations with their employer, can express their views, and take industrial action. Thus, it can rightly be said that, at a collective level, labour law creates equality which, due to legal subordination, can never be reached and achieved in full at the individual level.[131] Furthermore, the collective dimension of labour law is not only manifested through the collective rights, but is in reality almost always subtly present when exercising rights deriving from an individual employment relationship.[132] This unequivocally confirms that individual and collective employment relationships are complementary, which, when it comes to gender equality, is manifested primarily through the fact that *collective agreements are powerful tools for achieving gender equality in the world of work*. This is because the normative part of the collective agreement can regulate gender issues, as well as because all the working conditions that are otherwise regulated by this part of the collective agreement, can be reviewed from a gender perspective (pay, working hours, health and safety).[133]

[130] Adam (2005), p. 9.

[131] Supiot (2007), pp. 124–125.

[132] Supiot (1990), p. 488.

[133] International Labour Office (2007), p. 70; Blackett and Sheppard (2017), p. 669.

The same applies to the re-examination, from a gender perspective, of the criteria for the selection of candidates for employment, conditions for advancement and other issues where we have to consider the special needs that workers of a certain sex/gender. As well as workers with family duties connecting the exercise of their rights or with the taking on of certain obligations deriving from an individual employment relationship. In addition, the role of law as an instrument for achieving social change related to implementation of the principle of gender equality is rather limited.[134]

Gender issues, however, are rarely regulated by collective agreements. An important reason for this is that *women are under-represented in trade unions*, although ILO Conventions no. 87 and 98 acknowledged the right to form trade unions without discrimination. Although many national trade union confederations in European countries have women's sections, we can see that a modest number of female workers are trade union members, or members of trade union committees that participate in negotiations with employers, or members of trade union governing bodies that make important decisions.[135] There can be many reasons for this, from the burden of family duties not leaving them with enough time to participate in trade union activities, professional segregation and insufficient determination and training of women to participate in trade union activities, to gender stereotypes and the fact that trade unions are insufficiently sensitive, due to male dominance in membership and leadership, to the needs of their female members.[136] Effective implementation of the principle of gender equality, therefore, presupposes developing a culture of tolerance in work environments, as well as in sensitising workers and employers to issues related to ensuring gender equality. Especially because trade unions have a crucial role (and responsibility) in identifying and combating gender-based discrimination in the workplace, by organising trainings on how to protect against discrimination, and by providing protection, assistance and support to members who feel discriminated against.[137]

[134] However, we should not lose sight of the fact that greater prospects for promoting gender equality through social dialogue exist precisely in countries with a solid legal framework for combating gender-based discrimination, as well as legislative incentives to regulate gender issues at a company or sectoral level, as is the case, for example, in France and Spain. Briskin and Muller (2011), pp. 8–9.

[135] This is also true for trade unions in EU Member States where women make up about 40% of members, but, despite solid representation in membership, occupy on average only 5–20% of seats in union bodies, with a particularly modest number in higher status bodies, as opposed to secretariats or working groups whose members are appointed on the basis of expertise, in which the representation of women is somewhat higher. Acc. to Briskin and Muller (2011), p. 12.

[136] International Labour Office (2007), p. 70.

[137] It is therefore not surprising that the European Committee of Social Rights, in evaluating the harmonization of national legislation and practice with Revised European Social Charter regularly asks the contracting parties for information on forms of trade union participation in this area, in order to create conditions for effective exercise of the rights of workers who believe they have been discriminated against. Kollonay-Lehoczky (2017), p. 376.

In addition to strengthening the role of trade unions, it is necessary to strengthen the role of *employers and employers' organisations* in this area. This is especially true for overcoming cultural, social and economic barriers that make it impossible or difficult for women to become managers and employers. Which is why employers' associations need to encourage women's self-employment, keeping gender-sensitive statistics, and adopting gender equality action plans, codes of conduct and other instruments relevant to the promotion of gender equality.[138]

In addition to the aforementioned, the social partners play their role in achieving gender equality through strengthening *the (bipartite and tripartite) social dialogue on gender issues*, because social change would not be possible without the participation of stakeholders in the process.[139] Even more so because women are under-represented not only in membership and the governing bodies of trade unions, but also in tripartite governing bodies and, particularly, in the governing bodies of employers' associations. Although it cannot be reliably claimed that greater representation of women at these levels necessarily contributes to better representation of their interests in the social dialogue.[140] But even with that reservation, there is a need for collective labour law to become gender sensitive. This requirement also applies to the European social dialogue, which is why we need to mention the Framework of actions on gender equality (2005), in which the European social partners (ETUC, Business Europe, UEAPME and CEEP) called on national social partners to commit to reviewing gender roles, achieving greater participation of women in decision-making, reconciling work and family duties of employees and overcoming the gender pay gap. However, when it comes to international framework agreements, gender equality is, as a rule, mentioned only as a part of the commitment of the contracting parties to the application of standards contained in eight fundamental conventions of the ILO, including Conventions nos. 100 and 111.[141]

Also, we should mention the importance of works councils and other (non)-institutional forms of employees' participation in decision-making for the effective application of the principle of gender equality, as evidenced by the provisions of the Directive 2009/38/EC on the establishment of a European Works Council. The European Works Council represents a form of participation of employees in multinational companies operating at the EU level, whose composition should reflect as much as possible the composition of employees in the company, both quantitatively and qualitatively. The latter implies a proportional representation of employees by gender,[142] while in a number of cases, European works councils signed statements,

[138] International Labour Office (2007), pp. 67–68.

[139] Supiot (1990), p. 60. This has also been confirmed at the level of the International Labour Organization (2009), p. 2.

[140] Briskin and Muller (2011), p. 8.

[141] In accordance with The ILO Declaration on Fundamental Principles and Rights at Work (1998), along with Conventions nos. 100 and 111, fundamental conventions of the ILO are Conventions regulating abolition of forced labour (nos. 29 and 105), freedom of association (nos. 87 and 98) and child labour (nos. 138 and 182).

[142] Directive 2009/38/EC, Art. 6, para. 2, point b).

together with central management of multinational companies, dedicated to gender issues.[143]

17.8 Conclusion

Despite the positive changes in labour legislation related to the adoption of anti-discrimination regulations and the proper and complete identification and regulation of certain issues in light of the special needs and risks that are particularly inherent to female workers, certain problems remain unresolved. This is particularly true of occupational segregation, which reduces women's ability to compete in the labour market on "equal footing" with men and makes it difficult to effectively enforce anti-discrimination legislation. This is accompanied by the "glass ceiling" phenomenon, especially since it is manifested not only in the obstacles that women encounter during career advancement, but also in the lack of their participation in organisation and management.[144] Finally, we should take note of the trend of increased hiring of female workers in jobs that pay less and are less secure, since many women work part-time or on the basis of other non-standard employment contracts or in new forms of work. In that context, *gender competent labour law* should be designed to create a framework for understanding gender perspectives on key labour law institutions and their re-evaluation on the basis of gender equality principle. This is followed by the review of the capacity of legal instruments to ensure gender equality in the labour market. This is because labour law rules that were adopted as a result of social recognition of the need to acknowledge, overcome or at least mitigate the particular problems faced by female workers in the labour market are insufficient to achieve equality. This is especially true, having in mind the impact of the changes that have taken place in recent years in society and in the world of work, starting with *technological changes*, which affect workers differently in different parts of the world. But also in different industries, economic activities and territorial units within the same country, with deepening inequalities among members of society, including gender inequality.[145] In addition, there are *climate changes* that are having harmful effects on businesses, although they can create opportunities for new jobs. Furthermore, the world of work is affected by *demographic changes*, especially the tendencies of population aging and increased life expectancy, which emphasise the need for rising institutional assistance as well as engagement of both genders in the care for the elderly. Also, there is a need for maintaining the working capacity (and work motivation) of older workers, as well as the need to enable young workers to gain work experience and advance in their careers. Also, the tendencies of *intensive international migration* must be taken into account, which can have a

[143] Briskin and Muller (2011), p. 6.

[144] Pascall (1997), pp. 30–31 and 50–51.

[145] Philip et al. (2020), p. 153. The World Economic Forum estimates that 57% of workers needing to move to new jobs in the next decade will be female (World Economic Forum 2018, p. 13).

positive impact on the world of work. However, this can also lead to the establishment of various statuses for migrant workers, some of which are very precarious because employment will depend on their country of origin, the length of stay in the host country, the type of residence permit or work permit, and, in some cases, their occupation and legal status, which may also prove to be especial unfavourable for women and can lead to intersectional discrimination.[146] Finally, we should look at the recent *changes in the world of work*, which can be summed up in these three words: *job quality erosion*.[147] This feature of the modern world of work, implies the widespread practice of outsourcing, the emergence of new forms of work, some of which are extremely precarious. This series is continued by the widespread informal economy, as well as the underdevelopment and degradation of social dialogue. Taken together, these changes shed new light on the problem of gender inequality in the world of work, which has a devastating effect on social cohesion and deepens the poverty pit, while increasing social stratification.

Questions

1. Please state whether sex can be determined as an occupational requirement for employment if certain working tasks are performed in a foreign country where, due to specific national cultural circumstances, women would not be able to perform them successfully.
2. Please explain whether a general ban on women's night work in industry can be qualified as exception to prohibition of discrimination or whether this qualification is only suitable during an employee's pregnancy.
3. In the context of Directive 92/85: Why does a pregnant worker have to inform her employer of her condition? And what are the consequences of failing to do so?
4. The employer has terminated the employment relationship at the end of the probationary period. It so happened that the employee was pregnant, a fact of which the employer was unaware. Analyse this peculiar situation from the perspective of gender discrimination
5. A female worker was dismissed due to repeated absences from work. It appears that she was undergoing fertility treatment at the time of her dismissal, a fact unknown to the company. There is no evidence that she was pregnant as a result of the treatment. Assess this case in light of Art. 10(1) of Directive 92/85 by consulting the Opinion of the Advocate General in Case C-103/16.
6. Read the opinion of the Advocate General in case C-463/19. Do you consider that the Directive 92/85 should be reformed to include paternity

(continued)

[146] Fudge (2014), p. 36.

[147] Philip et al. (2020), p. 154.

leave? State if the Directive 2019/1158 confers enough rights to contribute to the objective of equality promoted by the EU.

7. Read the Antidiscrimination Directives and compare their scope with the ILO C190 scope. Do you think they need an update?
8. Considering cyberharassment, what are the measures that the worker can take in accordance with the provisions of ILO C190? What are the measures that have been implemented in your country regarding this issue?
9. In your view, which mechanisms may foster gender diversity in membership and the governing bodies of trade unions, tripartite governing bodies and governing bodies of employers' associations?
10. Analyse the evolution that the regulation of gender equality at work has had in the legal system of your country. What are the most important changes that have taken place from a failure to provide sufficient consideration of the specific needs of female workers—to women's empowerment in the world of work? Does contemporary labour law in your country ignore the special needs of men in the world of work, and the importance of their role for consistent application of the principle of gender equality?

References

Adam P (2005) L'individualisation du droit du travail: Essai sur la réhabilitation juridique du salarié-individu. L.G.D.J, Paris

Addati L, Cattaneo U, Esquivel V, Valarino I (2018) Care work and care jobs for the future of decent work. International Labour Office, Geneva. https://www.ilo.org/wcmsp5/groups/public/%2D%2D-dgreports/%2D%2D-dcomm/%2D%2D-publ/documents/publication/wcms_633135.pdf

Auvergnon P (2008) Les logiques du droit social confrontées aux évolutions des rapports de genre. In: Auvergnon P (ed) Genre et droit social. Presses universitaires de Bordeaux, Bordeaux, pp 9–36

Ballester Pastor MA (2011) Conciliación y corresponsabilidad en la Unión Europea. In: Cabeza Pereiro J, Fernández Docampo B (eds) Conciliación de la Vida Familiar y Laboral y Corresponsabilidad entre Sexos. Tirant lo blanch, Valencia, pp 17–50

Barnard C (2012) EU employment law. Oxford University Press, Oxford

Blackett A, Sheppard C (2017) Collective bargaining and equality: making connections. In: Lansky M, Ghosh J, Méda D, Rani U (eds) Women, gender and work. Vol. 2: Social choices and inequalities. International Labour Office, Geneva, pp 657–669

Briskin L, Muller A (2011) Promoting gender equality through social dialogue: global trends and persistent obstacles - working paper no. 34. International Labour Office, Geneva

Cabeza Pereiro J, Ballester Pastor MA (2015) Retos, expectativas y decepciones del derecho a la conciliación de responsabilidades. In: Cruz Villalón J, Garrido Pérez E, Ferradans Caramés C (eds) Tutela y promoción de la plena integración de la mujer en el trabajo. Consejo Andaluz de Relaciones Laborales, Sevilla, pp 116–121

Conaghan J (2017) Labour law and feminist method. Int J Comp Labour Law 33:93–114

Costello C, Davies G (2006) The case of the Court of Justice in the field of sex equality since 2000. Common Mark Law Rev 43:1567–1616
Deakin S (2005) Social rights in a globalized economy. In: Alston P (ed) Labour rights as human rights. Oxford University Press, New York, pp 25–60
Eurofound (2020) Gender equality at work - European Working Conditions Survey 2015 series. Publications Office of the European Union, Luxembourg, p 2020
European Commission (2014) Tackling the gender pay gap in the European Union. https://op.europa.eu/en/publication-detail/-/publication/12106bd8-f56c-4c42-80ee-f80fd3e035d5. Last accessed 20 Sept 2021
European Group on Ethics in Science and New Technologies (2019) Future of work, future of society. Publications Office of the European Union, Luxembourg
Fenwick H, Hervey TK (1995) Sex equality in the single market: new directions for the European Court of Justice. Common Mark Law Rev 32:443–470
Fredman S (2004) Women at work: the broken promise of flexicurity. Ind Law J 33:299–319
Fudge J (2014) Making claims for migrant workers: human rights and citizenship. Citizensh Stud 18:29–45. https://doi.org/10.1080/13621025.2014.865894
Grgurev I (2014) Diskriminacija trudnih radnica: Kako uspješno pomiriti trudnoću sa zahtjevima tržišta. In: Potočnjak Ž, Grgurev I, Grgić A (eds) Perspektive antidiskriminacijskog prava. Sveučilište u Zagrebu – Pravni fakultet, Zagreb, pp 133–152
Hieβl C (2012) Basics on European social law. Linde, Wien
Holtmaat R (2011) Sexual harassment and harassment on the ground of sex in EU law: a conceptual clarification. Eur Gend Equality Law Rev 2:4–13
Holzleithner E (2017) Gender equality and physical requirements in employment. Eur Equality Law Rev 1:13–22
Hunter R (1991) Representing gender in legal analysis: a case/book study in labour law. Melb Univ Law Rev 18(2):305–328
International Labour Office (2007) ABC of women workers' rights and gender equality. International Labour Office, Geneva
International Labour Office (2013) Men and masculinities: promoting gender equality in the world of work. International Labour Office, Geneva
International Labour Organization (2009) Social dialogue at work: voices and choices for women and men. International Labour Office, Geneva
International Labour Organization (2016) Meeting of experts on violence against women and men in the world of work (MEVWM/2016), Background paper for discussion at the meeting of experts on violence against women and men in the world of work. International Labour Office, Geneva
Kollonay-Lehoczky C (2017) Article 20 – The right to equal opportunities and equal treatment in matters of employment and occupation without discrimination on the ground of sex. In: Bruun N, Lörcher K, Schömann I, Clauwaert S (eds) The European Social Charter and the employment relation. Hart, Oxford, pp 358–380
KU Leuven (2016) How does one find her? KU Leuven Gender Action Plan. Interim Report. KU Leuven Diversity Office, Leuven
Lewis J (2001) The decline of the male breadwinner model: implications for work and care. Soc Polit 8:152–169. https://doi.org/10.1093/sp/8.2.152
Lousada Arochena F (2019) El Convenio 190 de la Organización Internacional del Trabajo sobre la violencia y el acoso en el trabajo. Revista de derecho social 88:55–74
Lyonette C (2013) The sexual division of labour. In: Evans M, Williams CH (eds) Gender: the key concepts. Routledge, London, pp 198–203
Marry C (2012) Genre. In: Bevort A, Jobert A, Lallement M, Mias A (eds) Dictionnaire du travail. Quadriage/PUF, Paris, pp 341–347
Masselot A, Caracciollo Di Torella E, Burri S (2012) Fighting discrimination on the grounds of pregnancy, maternity and parenthood: the application of EU and national law in practice in 33 European countries. European network of legal experts in the field of gender equality, Brussels

Müller T (2019) She works hard for the money: tackling low pay in sectors dominated by women – evidence from health and social care. ETUI aisbl, Brussels
Pascall G (1997) Social policy: a new feminist analysis. Routledge, London
Philip K, Lieuw-Kie-Song M, Tsukamoto M, Overbeck A (2020) Employment matters too much to society to leave to markets alone. Professionalità studi 1:152–177
Plantenga J, Remery C (2010) Flexible working time arrangements and gender equality: a comparative review of 30 European countries. Publications Office of the European Union, Luxembourg
Radé C (1997) Droit du travail et responsabilité civile. L.G.D.J, Paris
Rubenstein M (1988) The dignity of women at work, a report on the problem of sexual harassment in the member states of the European Communities. Commission of the European Communities, Brussels
Supiot A (1990) Pourqoi un droit du travail? Droit social 6:485–492
Supiot A (2007) Critique du droit du travail. Presses Universitaires de France, Paris
Timmer A (2016) Gender stereotyping in the case law of the EU Court of Justice. Eur Equality Law Rev 1:37–46
Wallon G, Bendiscioli S, Garfinkel MS (2015) Exploring quotas in academia. Robert Bosch Stiftung, Heidelberg
World Economic Forum (2018) Insight report - towards a reskilling revolution. A future of jobs for all. http://www3.weforum.org/docs/WEF_FOW_Reskilling_Revolution.pdf. Last accessed 20 Sept 2021

Further Reading

Bittman M, Folbre N (2004) Family time. The social organization of care. Routledge, London
Caracciolo di Torella E, Masselot A (2010) Reconciling work and family life in EU law and policy. Palgrave-Macmillan, London
Caracciolo di Torella E, Masselot A (2021) Caring responsibilities in European law and policy: who cares? Routledge, London
Clarke JA (2011) Beyond equality? Against the universal turn in workplace protection. Indiana Law J 86:1220–1287
International Labour Office (2018) Report V (1), Ending violence and harassment against women and men in the world of work. International Labour Office, Geneva
Méndez LM, Serrani L (2015) Work-life balance and the economic crisis: some insights from the perspective of comparative law, vol I. Cambridge Scholars Publisher, Cambridge

Integrating Gender Equality in Economics and Management 18

Lydia Bares Lopez, Francesca Costanza, Manuela Ortega Gil, and Sofia Strid

Contents

Authors are listed in alphabetical order. Although all the authors agreed on the contents of the chapter, Sect. 18.5 (and the related sections) is to be attributed to Francesca Costanza, who also coordinated the writing, Sect. 18.2 is attributable to Sofia Strid, Sects. 18.3 and 18.4 to Manuela Ortega Gil, Sect. 18.6 to Lydia Bares Lopez. Finally, Sect. 18.1 and 18.7 result from the joint efforts of all the authors.

L. Bares Lopez · M. Ortega Gil
University of Cadiz, Faculty of Law, General Economics, Cadiz, Spain
e-mail: lydia.bares@uca.es; manuela.ortega@uca.es

F. Costanza (✉)
LUMSA University Rome, Department of Law, Palermo, Italy
e-mail: f.costanza1@lumsa.it

S. Strid
School of Humanities, Education and Social Sciences, Unit of Gender Studies and Sociology, Örebro University, Örebro, Sweden

Department of Sociology and Work Science, Gothenburg University, Gothenburg, Sweden
e-mail: sofia.strid@gu.se

D. Vujadinović et al. (eds.), *Gender-Competent Legal Education*, Springer Textbooks in Law, https://doi.org/10.1007/978-3-031-14360-1_18

Abstract

This chapter deals with gender economics, gender and management, and gender and innovation. After introducing the general concept of feminist economics and its critique of mainstream economics, this chapter explains the meaning of gender indicators, gender parity, gender equality, and gender mainstreaming. It further investigates the factors causing inequalities in the labour market. Gender is afterwards addressed from a managerial perspective, embracing a multidimensional notion of performance, and considering both the management of private and public organisations. Finally, the topic gender and innovation is deepened by explaining the importance of intellectual property rights, as well as the poor visibility of women inventors in society.

18.1 Introduction

Gender equality is a complex topic, with important ramifications in economy and society. Within this chapter, an overview of key gender concepts and issues within the economic and management disciplines is discussed. In reviewing these key concepts and issues, this chapter conveys the importance of both teaching and studying gender competent economics. This chapter starts with a general section on feminist economics, conceptualised as an economics focused approach on what is needed to produce a gender equal society. It introduces different feminist critiques of mainstream economics and the idea(l)s of *homo economicus*, exploring the role of gender and intersecting inequalities in the history of economic thinking. In turn, this illustrates how macroeconomic policy both produces and reproduces differential opportunities for women, men and further genders.

The following section devoted to introducing gender indicators from an economic perspective. This distinguishes gender parity, gender equality, and gender mainstreaming indicators, pointing out key databases to extract and analyse them, and the importance of doing so. The chapter then considers gender in the labour market, investigating the factors responsible for causing inequalities in opportunity distribution and wages. Therefore, a focus on gender and management faces gender equality and its relevance in modern management, embracing a multidimensional notion of performance and considering both private and public management aspects. Finally, this chapter addresses gender and innovation by explaining the importance of intellectual property rights (patents), and the poor visibility of women inventors in society.

Learning Goals

Students will learn about and gain a basic understanding of

The key concepts in gender economics and feminist critique of mainstream economics

The meaning and function of gender indicators from the economic and innovation perspectives

Key concepts and tools in gender and management

18.2 Feminist Economics

Feminist economics has predominantly developed over the last 30 years, in particular with the emergence of the International Association for Feminist Economics and the journal *Feminist Economics* (Taylor and Francis). Its roots are significantly older, building on the USA and British political economy movements and social (welfare) reforms as their philosophical and political underpinnings. These include, in particular, John Stuart Mill, Harriet Taylor Mill, and Millicent Fawcett, writing about, and campaigning for, women's and workers' rights.[1]

Feminist economics is, in its most basic definition, the critical study of (mainstream) economics with a focus on gender inclusive economics and economic policy analysis. It calls for an inclusive critical inquiry, not only in terms of topics, but also in terms of who studies the topics, and what truths are taken for granted. It explores the influence of gender on economics, and conversely, the influence of economics on gender. Feminist economics adds a gendered eye to the field of (mainstream) economics; scrutinising and developing it, often to include what mainstream economics historically has considered "feminine" topics or "women's issues". It focuses on how different economic structures enable and reproduce gender regimes by privileging men's interests over the interests of women.[2] A crucial outcome of gender economics, and putting it into practice, is the potential to address and contribute towards the solution to some of the most pressing contemporary social, economic, and environmental concerns. Namely, the environmental and economic inequality crises, where (a) feminist practices of degrowth with care at the centre constitute a foundation for economic, ecological and social sustainability, and (b) broadening economic practices with the inclusion of gendered and intersectional perspectives. This enables a complete and accurate understanding of economic phenomena, patterns and mechanisms to reduce economic inequality. Two major

[1] Becchio (2019).

[2] Boehnert (2019).

concerns are the gendered division of labour in the market economy and the gender distribution of unpaid work within the household, in the interrelation of the two.[3]

The word economics comes from the Greek 'oikonomia', meaning 'household management'. The contemporary meaning of the term has however expanded, or narrowed, from a feminist point of view, to exclude the productions outside of the market and to include only the public production, distribution and consumption of goods and services: to study the market at the expense of the household. A key feature of feminist economics is therefore to bring the household perspective, particularly including the provision of care and unpaid work/domestic labour, back into gender analysis of economics, and to show the interrelation between the "private" and the "public". It simultaneously highlights the problems posed by a "unitary" conceptualisation of the household.[4] In making this a focus, feminist economics seeks to challenge notions of "work" and "production" based solely on public production, as contrasted to 'private' production and manufacturing, rethinking the status of the different sorts of activities that occur within our economy.

Looking at the division of unpaid work and time use patterns, these are strikingly gendered: women, on average, carry out substantially more unpaid work than men, including food management, cleaning, ironing, laundry and care work. National time use surveys show that in Ireland, Italy and Portugal, women carry out more than 70% of unpaid work. In the more (often regarded) gender equal countries of the North, women are still doing almost two-thirds of such unpaid work.[5]

Gender is consequently strongly related to unpaid work, both historically and in contemporary discourse and data: the amount of time people invest in unpaid *versus* paid work; the distribution of unpaid work time between different tasks, and the patterns of unpaid care work are largely determined by a person's gender. Despite a shift from women as workers in the private to women as workers in the public, occasionally referred to a shift from private patriarchy to public patriarchy,[6] women continue to bear the responsibility for, and spend more time, than men on unpaid housework and unpaid care work, regardless of their employment status. Further, women's spare time and volunteer activities are more likely to be related to family than are men's.[7] Women often work double shifts; a first shift paid outside of their home, and a second shift of unpaid domestic work. This is often referred to as women's double burden.[8] While this work remains unpaid and undervalued, it is crucial to the economy; keeping current workers and consumers alive and healthy, raising new generations of workers and consumers, and producing a value in itself. Therefore, not only is the gendered division of unpaid work a problem in itself, it also has a bearing on the labour market and women' participation therein; the two

[3] Waring (1988) and Crompton (2006).

[4] Agarwal (1997).

[5] OECD (2021). OECD.Stat. Employment: Time spent in paid and unpaid work, by sex.

[6] Walby (1990), pp. 91–104.

[7] Chesley and Flood (2017).

[8] Vaananen et al. (2004) and Himmelweit (2002).

'markets', the domestic/private and the public, are interrelated. In exploring how mainstream economics, including economic statistics and economic policy, would have to change in order to attribute a value to the contributions of women, some of the pioneering feminist criticism deconstructed the very basis and rational for 'modern' economics.[9]

18.2.1 Gender and the 'Economic Man'

Fundamentally, it has been argued that since modern economics is based on the notion of the "economic man", it is necessarily ideologically and politically loaded towards normalising the work and life experiences of men. Economics subsequently ignores the experiences of women, as well as those of men who do not fit the norm.[10] Introduced in the 1800s by John Stuart Mill, the concept of the 'economic man', or '*homo economicus*' was perceived as an economic actor "who inevitably does that by which he (sic) may obtain the greatest amount of necessaries, conveniences, and luxuries, with the smallest quantity of labour and physical self-denial with which they can be obtained".[11] Hence, the argument follows that the political economy removes all human desires, emotions, and 'irrationalities', except those that assist in the pursuit of wealth.

There has been extensive critique of the idea(l)s of *homo economicus*, including from within mainstream economics itself; human behaviour is irrational, and economic actors are neither always fully informed when making economic decisions, nor do they always act in their own self-interest. Despite such critique, the assumption, and ideal, of a rational economic man remains in both microeconomic and macroeconomic models in some of the most influential contemporary work (e.g., Piketty)[12] and everyday thinking.[13]

Whilst it is self-evident what this typical 'economic man' does: he works; earns an income; engages in market transactions and spends money on the consumption of goods. Contemporaneously it is equally clear what he does not: he does not do unpaid housework chores, and he does not have caring responsibilities. Hence, economic models based on the 'economic man' cannot incorporate, recognise or demonstrate gendered or intersectional inequalities. Without such recognition and visibility of multiple and complex gendered inequalities, policies to reduce them are bound to fail.[14]

The notion and idea of the economic man is not necessarily a figuration in the interests of men either; in building on *homo economicus*, the traditional economic

---

[9] Waring (1988) and Bjørnholt and McKay (2014).

[10] Nelson and Ferber (2003).

[11] Mill (2007).

[12] Piketty (2014).

[13] Morgan (2009).

[14] Strid et al. (2013).

models provide both an incomplete and inaccurate model of what affects men's lives too. Men's existence is not disconnected from, but rather depends on, the performance of unpaid work and the production and use of care. Further, men are not only the recipients of such work and care, indeed, some men are directly involved in these activities too. Finally, the notion of *homo economicus* fails to recognise the existence of further genders. The conclusions, from the perspective of feminist economics and from a gender perspective more broadly, are that a wider concept of what constitutes both the economy and gender are required. The very existence of the current system, under mainstream economics and economic theory, depends on activities outside of its empirical and theoretical scope[15] and by economic actors beyond the gender binary.

Feminist economics is therefore a necessarily comprehensive academic field, encompassing a wide range of areas aiming to add nuance and complexity to an already established field. Key areas of study within feminist economics go beyond the care economy and unpaid work (e.g. caring labour, time-use surveys, household expenditures, same-sex and lone mother families, sexuality and reproduction, and family and social policy). For example, the journal *Feminist Economics*, the international scholarly journal of the International Association for Feminist Economics (IAFFE), published by Taylor and Frances, includes articles on a wide range of topics, including:

- environmental economics (e.g., the economic effects of national or local environmental policy, the costs and benefits of alternative environmental policies, and global warming);[16]
- feminist theory and economics (including e.g., methods and argument, the history of thought, and feminist theories);
- labour markets (including e.g., stratification, employment and labour force participation, wage outcomes, wage gaps, wage discrimination, firm performance, labour market policies, informal labour, and time stress; land, agriculture and rural development);
- LGBTQIA+ economic issues; income poverty and capability deprivations (including e.g., income, poverty and capability deprivations, migration, microfinance, rights/international human rights and national, capabilities-based evaluations of outcomes, including index measures);
- assets, education, conflict/warfare, environmental degradation and climate crisis;
- and macroeconomics contexts (including e.g., crises, trade structure, financialisaton, gender budgeting, macroeconomics policies and outcomes, gender mainstreaming, and international institutions).

[15]Bjørnholt and McKay (2014).

[16]Feminist economics' interactions with ecological economics is an emerging academic field, with potential analytical synergies using degrowth and placing the care society at the center of analysis (Dengler and Strunk 2017).

Just as there are multiple linkages and interrelations between unpaid work and the conventional macroeconomy per se, these fields of study are also interlinked, suggesting to feminist economists that it is necessary to expand the boundary of conventional macroeconomics to incorporate unpaid work.
Returning to the key feature of unpaid work and the macro level, there is much empirical work and efforts to integrate unpaid work into macro policies, in particular, efforts to interrogate and understand the impacts and effects of macroeconomic policy on both paid and unpaid work, and on the relation between them. Unpaid work raises the overall well-being of the economy; it entails the productive use of human labour, and through the caring and rearing of children, unpaid work contributes to the formation of human capital. While unpaid work is excluded from, and falls outside of, the national income accounts and GDP measurements, it falls within the general production boundary. Further, various mainstream experts view unpaid work as either "care" or "work". The near global unequal distribution of work between men and women implies a violation of the basic human rights of women, with unpaid care work having an enormous impact on women's poverty and capacity to exercise their rights, and the exclusion of women's experiences and some men's experiences of work reflect the dominance of patriarchal values, bringing male bias into macroeconomics.

18.2.2 Gendering for Objectivity

The manifesto of feminist economics, Ferber and Nelson's *Beyond Economic Man: Feminist Theory and Economics*,[17] argued the very discipline of economics needed to free itself from both the dominance of men and from the bias of masculinity in economics. Further, and perhaps somewhat counter-intuitive to much feminist work, Ferber and Nelson raised questions regarding the discipline, not because economics is too objective, *but because it is not objective enough*. This epistemological critique firstly raised an empirical knowledge concern and discussed the extent to which gender influenced both the range of subjects studied by economists, and secondly, a methodological concern by questioning the very ways in which scholars have conducted their studies.

To summarise the main lines of critique of conventional/mainstream economics: (1) the majority men, or the norm group of men and their interests and concerns underlie economists' concentration on markets, as opposed to household activities; (2) the emphasis on individual choice necessarily renders social and economic inequalities invisible, and their constraints/limitations on choice unrecognised; and (3) the focus on cis men's interests has biased the definition and boundaries of the discipline; its central assumptions, its choice and acceptance of methods, and its results. To move forward, it is important to note that the objective of feminist economics is not to reject mainstream economic theory or economic practices, but

[17] Ferber and Nelson (1993).

rather to broaden them with the inclusion of gendered and intersectional perspectives, thereby enabling a fuller, and more accurate, understanding of economic phenomena, patterns, and mechanisms.

18.3 Indicators of Gender from the Economic Perspective

Indicators are essential for the study and analysis of social phenomena. Currently, there is no official definition of an indicator by any national or international body, although based on the contributions of different organisations and authors such as Bauer[18] or Land,[19] it can be defined as an instrument that provides a measure of a concept, phenomenon, problem, or social fact. Indicators can be divided into qualitative or quantitative, simple, or synthetic (if it includes several components).

The combined set of indicators is called an index. Indices help to measure complex phenomena that have different dimensions and need a set of indicators to reflect a more complete reality of the analysed phenomenon. Both indicators and indices are used for the research and visualisation of social problems and phenomena, to follow changes over time.

A gender indicator, therefore, serves to measure the state of women compared to men in different dimensions of people's lives, related to gender equality in a region.

▶ **Definition** Gender indicators could be grouped into three dimensions:

Gender equality: the European Institute for Gender Equality (EIGE)[20] defines it as "Equal rights, responsibilities and opportunities of women and men and girls and boys". It is an indicator of sustainable development.

Gender parity: it can be focused as "the equal contribution of women and men to every dimension of life, whether private or public".[21] It is also related to the terms gender balance, parity, parity democracy.

Gender mainstreaming: it involves the integration of a gender perspective into all public policy making process, regulatory measures, and spending programmes, with a view to promoting equality between women and men, and combatting discrimination. Gender mainstreaming contains two dimensions: equal representation of men and women, and gender perspective in the content of policies.[22]

[18]Bauer (1966).
[19]Land (1971).
[20]EIGE (2020).
[21]Ibid.
[22]Ibid.

18.3.1 Main Indicators of Gender Equality

The complexity of the gender equality concept has led to the creation of composite indicators of different dimensions. Among them, the following stand out:

Gender Equality Index (GEI): is used to measure the progress of gender equality in the EU. It is a tool that supports policy makers in designing more effective gender equality measures, by allowing meaningful comparisons between different gender equality domains.[23] It is based on six domains (work, money, knowledge, time, power, health), two additional domains (violence and intersecting inequalities) and 14 subdomains and 31 indicators.[24] For example, GEI of EU in 2020 edition is 67.9 out of 100 points (work = 72.2, money = 80.6, knowledge = 63.6, time = 65.7, power = 53.5, health = 88.0).

Gender Parity Index (GPI): introduced by UNESCO to measure the access to education for men and women (ratio of female to male values at a given stage of education). A GPI close to one indicates parity between the genders, below 0.97 indicates a disparity in favour of males, and above 1.03 indicates a disparity in favour of females.[25] For example, the gender parity index (GPI) of the world in 2019 was 1.131 in the school enrolment, tertiary (gross), 0.986 in school enrolment, primary and secondary (gross) and 0.981 in school enrolment, primary (gross).

Gender Inequality Index (GII): is released by the UNDP and "*measures the human development costs of gender inequality*".[26] Thus, the higher the GII value, the more disparities between females and males and more loss to human development. The country with the lowest value in 2019 was Switzerland with 0.025. The country with the highest value, the highest inequality, of the 189 countries analysed was Yemen with 0.795 It includes three aspects: reproductive health, empowerment, and economic status. In turn, this is demonstrated through the following five indicators:

Reproductive health: *maternal mortality ratio* and *adolescent birth rate*. In 2017, the country with the highest maternal mortality ratio was South Sudan with 1150 per 100,000 live births. Between 2015–2020, Niger was the country with the highest adolescent birth rate, at 186.5 births per 1000 women ages 15–19.

Empowerment: *female and male population with at least secondary education and Female* and *male shares of parliamentary seats*. In 2019, the country with the highest percentage share of seats in parliament held by women was Rwanda with 55.7%.

Economic status: *female and male labour force participation rates*. In 2019, the country with the highest force participation rate was Singapore with 1.041.

---

[23] EIGE (2013).

[24] Papadimitriou et al. (2020).

[25] Richie et al. (2020).

[26] http://hdr.undp.org/en/content/download-data.

Global Gender Gap Index:[27] was presented in 2006 by World Economic Forum (WEF). In the Global Gender Gap Report (2021), the highest ranking countries in terms of equality are Iceland (89.2) followed by Finland (86.1) and Norway (84.9). This index is founded on three basics: "First, on measuring gaps rather than levels. Second, it captures gaps in outcomes variables rather than gaps in means or input variables. Third, it ranks countries according to gender equality rather than women's empowerment".[28] It measures one important aspect of gender equality; the relative gaps between women and men across a large set of countries, and covering four key areas (Economic Participation and Opportunity, Educational Attainment, Health and Survival, and Political Empowerment).[29] These four dimensions are composed of the following indicators:

1. Five indicators of Economic Participation and Opportunity: labour force participation rate; wage equality for similar work; estimated earned income; legislators, senior officials, and managers; professional and technical workers,
2. Four indicators of Educational Attainment: literacy rate; enrolment in primary education; enrolment in secondary education; enrolment in tertiary education.
3. Two indicators of Health and survival: sex ratio at birth and healthy life expectancy (years).
4. Three indicators of Political Empowerment: women in parliament, women in ministerial positions and years with female/male head of state (last 50).

The main sources of data collecting gender indicators at international, European, and national level are: World Bank (WB),[30] United Nations (UN),[31] United Nations Educational, Scientific and Cultural Organization (UNESCO),[32] European Statistics (Eurostat),[33] European Institute for Gender Equality (EIGE),[34] United Nations Development Programme (UNDP),[35] UNESCO.[36]

18.3.2 Sustainable Development Goals and Gender Equality

The General Assembly of United Nations approved the Agenda for Sustainable Development in September 2015. This agenda includes 17 Sustainable Development

[27] https://data.humdata.org/dataset/global-gender-gap-index-world-economic-forum.

[28] Hausmann et al. (2006), p. 5.

[29] Ibid.

[30] https://www.worldbank.org/en/data/datatopics/gender.

[31] https://www.unwomen.org/es/how-we-work/gender-parity-in-the-united-nations.

[32] https://en.unesco.org/genderequality.

[33] https://ec.europa.eu/eurostat/web/main/data/database.

[34] https://eige.europa.eu/gender-statistics/dgs.

[35] http://hdr.undp.org/en/content/download-data.

[36] http://data.un.org/.

Goals (SDGs) of universal application that govern the efforts of countries to achieve a sustainable world by 2030 (1. No poverty; 2. Zero Hunger; 3. Good health and Well-being; 4. Quality Education; 5. Gender Equality; 6. Clear Water and Sanitation; 7. Affordable and Clear Energy; 8. Decent Work and Economic Growth; 9. Industry, Innovation and infrastructure; 10. Reduce Inequalities; 11. Sustainable Cities and Communities; 12. Responsible Consumption and Production; 13. Climate Action; 14. Life Below Water; 15. Life on Land; 16. Peace, Justice and Strong Institution; 17. Partnerships for the Goals). These goals are designed to achieve a sustainable future for all and to combat the challenges facing the Earth.

The European Statistics collect indicators to measure the fulfilment of Goal 5 from the aforementioned Sustainable Development Goals (SDGs), namely, to "Achieve gender equality and empower all women and girls". Such indicators are:

- Physical and sexual violence to women.
- Gender pay gap in unadjusted form.
- Gender employment gap.
- Inactive population due to caring responsibilities.
- Seats held by women in national parliaments and governments.
- Positions held by women in senior management positions.
- Early leavers from education and training.
- Tertiary educational attainment.
- Employment rates of recent graduates.

18.4 Gender in the Labour Market

The labour market is characterised by demands for goods and services, the productivity of workers and the cost of labour, and a supply represented by the labour force comprising all persons fulfilling the requirements for inclusion among the employed (civilian employment plus the armed forces) or the unemployed.[37] The labour market is diverse and segmented, mainly by age, sex, education and training, and citizenship. Many studies show that gender inequality exists. According to Eurostat, the gender employment gap in the European Union is considerable (EU-28 average 11.4%), highlighting significant differences between Member States; ranging from 1.6% of the population in Lithuania, to 20.7% in Malta (Fig. 18.1).

The main factors causing inequal feminist socioeconomics in work and employment are:

- persistent gender division of domestic and care work;
- interplay of workplace and household power relations shapes good/bad job segmentation;
- gendered wage practices target first and second earners;

[37] OECD (2021).

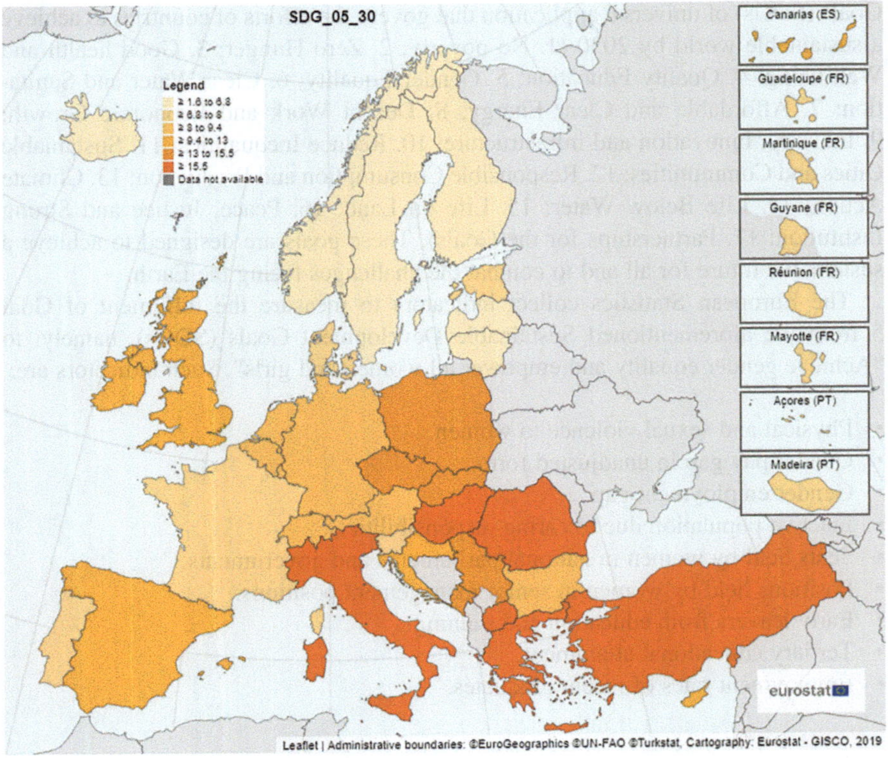

Fig. 18.1 Gender employment gap EU 2019 (Source: Eurostat, 2019)

- economic cycles (booms and busts) have gendered employment effects;
- occupational sex segregation, including feminised part-time work, influences the accompanying job design, career tracks and wage value; jobs associated with women ('women's work') are undervalued;
- sex discrimination by employers, co-workers and customers is shaped by powerful stereotypes about motherhood, and
- different standards and gendered models of family support provision.[38]

There remains a significant gender gap caused, among many factors, by occupational segregation, differences in academic specialisation, difficulty in balancing work and household responsibilities, and wage discrimination.[39] In addition, the labour market is immersed in a process of transformation caused by the introduction of the digital world into everyday life. This was accelerated by the Covid-19 pandemic; during the year 2020, teleworking and online work patterns increased considerably.

[38]Grimshaw et al. (2017), p. 6.

[39]Schanzenbach and Nunn (2017).

The study by Frey and Osborne[40] indicates that the process of digitalisation of the labour market is expected to take place in two waves. It is thought the first wave is currently underway; workers in transportation and logistics occupations, office and administrative support workers, as well as labour in production occupation, will be substituted by computer capital. This stage is to be followed by a "technological plateau" before entering the second wave. This second wave depends on the capacity of the engineering bottlenecks related to creative and social intelligence, encompassing the generalist occupations specialised in the human aspect, and specialist occupations involving the development of novel ideas and artifacts.[41] Against this background, educational attainment remains a key to improve employability and labour market outcomes.[42]

In turn, the digitalisation process can improve gender equality. The characteristics of the tasks currently performed by women, the robotisation of domestic tasks, teleworking, and social skills will open new opportunities for female employment.[43] The jobs held by women require high nonroutine manual or social skills, and this creates bottlenecks to digitalisation and automation. This opportunity will depend on the entry of women into jobs benefitting most from digitalisation (management, science, technology, engineering, mathematics, and entrepreneurship) in roles where they are currently in the minority, shown by recent data on the gender gap.[44]

In 2015, although globally women were more educated than men on the average, their chances of rising to leadership positions were exceptionally low and their labour force and wages were lower than those of men.[45] However, women had increased their participation in professional and technical occupations and controlled 64% of household spending.

In 2019, the European Union showed significant differences in employment (10.4 percentage points), labour force participation rate[46] (10.8 percentage points) and unemployment rate (−0.4 percentage points) between men and women.[47] According to literature, *age, education*, or *household financial situation*, as well as *economic, social and demographic characteristics*, influence labour supply behaviour. In poor households, the economic pressure to contribute to household income is more pronounced for both women and men.[48]

---

[40]Frey and Osborne (2017).

[41]Țițan et al. (2014).

[42]European Commission (2020).

[43]Krieger-Boden and Sorgner (2018).

[44]Frey and Osborne (2017) and Sorgner et al. (2017).

[45]World Economic Forum (2016).

[46]"This indicator is broken down by age group and it is measured as a percentage of each age group" (OECD 2021). Labour force participation rate = labour forcetotal working age population (15–64)

[47]OECD (2021).

[48]Eberharter (2001).

There are different approaches to women *labour force participation* and *family structure and household.* A study of the Japanese society by Sasaki[49] shows that married women who share the burden of household work with their parents, or in-laws, are more likely to participate in the labour force. Another study illustrated that the wife's labour supply is inversely related to the quality of the couple's relationship.[50]

The relationship between women's education and work outside from home has also been investigated, concluding that women's bargaining power increases when women are more educated relative to their spouses. Correspondingly, as women's bargaining power increases, they participate more in the labour market.[51]

18.5 Gender and Management

Gender equality is a relevant topic in modern management, since the real-life application of gendered policies at any societal level requires a joint effort of many actors (belonging both to private and public sectors), and the development of new awareness, tools, and skills.

For public and private organisations, incorporating the gender perspective in managerial processes means to acknowledge the contribution of gender diversity in affecting leadership styles at any hierarchy level,[52] and in influencing decision-making processes, information systems and accountability towards civil society.[53] However, in treating gender and management issues, it is important to consider their intersectionality with other life categories such as class, age, education, sexual orientation.[54]

Table 18.1 summarises the main features of the Gender and Management analysis conducted in this chapter. Each category of organisation (private and public) can be read in light of gender-related criteria.

Noticeably, private and public actors share a common gender-related scope, the realisation of gender equality. In pursuing this scope, each hold specific roles and responsibilities. The economic role played by private organisations makes them potential catalysts of sustainable development.[55] In contrast, public organisations, through incentives and regulations, oversee sustainable (including gender-related) policy making and implementation at the national and local level. Both spheres are addressed by referring to the Corporate Social Responsibility (or CSR) framework, considered valuable for its breadth and being comprehensive. In addition, the public

---

[49] Sasaki (2002).

[50] Mazzocco et al. (2014).

[51] Moeeni (2021).

[52] Bàez et al. (2018), Guy and Newman (2004) and Yang et al. (2019).

[53] Nadeem et al. (2020).

[54] Crenshaw (1989) and Flynn et al. (1994).

[55] Apostolopoulos et al. (2018).

Table 18.1 Features of the Gender and Management analysis (Source: own elaboration)

Gender and management topics	Private organisations	Public organisations
Gender-related scope	Gender equality	Gender equality
Gender-related roles and responsibilities	Catalysts of sustainable development	Sustainable policy making and implementation at a national and local level
Theoretical framework/s	Corporate social responsibility	Corporate social responsibility Public management and administration
Key dimensions of performance	Economic, social and environmental	Input, output, outcome. Spreadable in economic, social and environmental terms
Managerial concepts and tools	Entrepreneurial formula, social strategy CSR standards, codes of ethics and conduct, social reports, integrated reports	Management upward, outward and downward Gender-responsive public budgets

sphere also considered Public Management and Administration theories and applications.

The fact that this chapter addresses gender and management by considering private and public institutions separately, is not only to facilitate discussion and chapter readability, but also to remark sectoral specificities. However, public and private worlds are not to be intended as "institutional islands"; they continuously communicate, reinforce each other and present overlapping areas. Moreover, the public value management approach[56] is coherent with the sustainability framework and the descending accountability efforts towards several categories of stakeholders.[57]

Significantly, since the end of the twentieth century, the areas of "contamination" between public and private sectors management have been growing. Indeed, the traditional notion of public institutions, bureaucratic in nature and founded on legal power, has been criticised for its resistance to change.[58] This notion has been surpassed by: (a) the New Public Management paradigm (or NPM), which postulates the necessity to apply to the public sector tools and techniques from the private one;[59] and (b) the New Public Governance paradigm (or NPG) which emphasised the contribution of public-private cooperation to deliver value to citizens.[60]

[56] Moore (1995).

[57] Leuenberger (2006).

[58] Hughes (2003).

[59] Hood (1991).

[60] Rhodes (1996).

In both public and private organisations, the translation of gender mainstreaming in effective actions implies the adoption of a multidimensional notion of performance. As far as private actors are concerned, CSR business models represent the translation of the sustainability paradigm at a micro-level and the acceptance of an articulated finalism that, in line with the triple bottom line approach,[61] strives for satisfying balanced results along the economic, social, and environmental dimensions.

In the Public Management and Administration sphere, in conjunction with the affirmation of New Public Governance and Public Value Management paradigms[62] the performance notion runs through the entire public value chain and encloses the consideration of inputs, outputs, outcomes. In turn, such measures could be read according to a sustainability lens to highlight social policies, economic policies, and environmental policies.

In the following two sections, public and private managerial concepts and tools will be deepened. In "Gender and Corporate Social Responsibility", gender diversity and responsiveness will be analysed as part of a virtuous company's social strategy, able to contribute to other performance dimensions. In "Gender and Public Management and Administration", the gender mainstreaming approach within public organisations will consider processes of gendered performance management at both top and street management level, and illustrate the role of gender responsive public balance sheets.

18.5.1 Gender and Corporate Social Responsibility

In recent history, Corporate Social Responsibility has been gaining momentum between scholars and policy makers. It was even included in institutional agendas, particularly after the publication of the CSR Green Book[63] and the European Commission Directive on CSR.[64] Such initiatives attempted "to promote a consensus for CSR implementation through debate groups and the participation of diverse social actors".[65]

There is no unique definition of Corporate Social Responsibility, or CSR (see the contribution of Garrica and Melè for a review).[66] However, for the scopes of this chapter, CSR can be understood as:

[61] Elkington (1997) and Tullberg (2012).

[62] Stoker (2006).

[63] European Commission (2001).

[64] European Commission (2002).

[65] Celma et al. (2014).

[66] Garrica and Melè (2004).

Definition A company's commitment to be accountable for the impacts of its activity "minimizing or eliminating any harmful effects and maximizing its long-run beneficial impact on society".[67]

Furthermore, CSR concept postulates that "companies integrate social and environmental concerns in their business operations and in their interaction with their stakeholders on a voluntary basis".[68]

Company activity embeddedness in social system is part of its own entrepreneurial formula,[69] which is valid when "oriented toward simultaneously pursuing success on the competitive, social, and economic levels".[70] Thus, beside ethical reasons for Corporate Social Responsibility, it can also be intended as a strategic lever source of competitive advantage,[71] boosting company reputation within employees,[72] purchase intentions[73] and consumer awareness or attitudes.[74]

Corporate Social Responsibility can be articulated into two areas of study; internal and external CSR. The former concerns inside operations and includes employees related activities. The latter regards other stakeholders such as customers, business partners, community, environment.[75]

Corporate social responsibility is strictly related to sustainable development; a socioeconomic concept implying the satisfaction of actual needs, bearing in mind the necessities required for future generations.[76] Sustainable development is a broad concept based on three key elements: economic growth; environmental protection, and social inclusion. The sustainable development in practice entails the active role of entrepreneurship,[77] and, from a managerial perspective, a "triple bottom line" approach[78] postulating for companies the joint pursuits of economic, environmental, and social performances.[79] Consequently, profit maximisation as the unique company objective[80] is replaced by the consideration of multiple stakeholder interests in corporate activities.[81]

---

[67] Mohr et al. (2001).

[68] European Commission (2001).

[69] Coda (2012).

[70] Ibid., p. 73.

[71] Porter and Kramer (2006).

[72] Turban and Greening (2017).

[73] Luo and Bhattacharya (2009).

[74] Bhattacharya and Sen (2004).

[75] Arrive and Feng (2018) and Skudiene and Auruskeviciene (2012).

[76] World Commission on Environment and Development (1987).

[77] Apostolopoulos et al. (2018).

[78] Elkington (1997).

[79] Tullberg (2012).

[80] Friedman (1970).

[81] Freeman (1984).

In this regard, CSR accountability routes to Environment, Social and Governance (ESG); to integrate social and environmental sustainability with governance and long-term corporate vision.[82] Public awareness regarding ESG principles has converged to the formulation of ESG ratings, "evaluations of a company based on a comparative assessment of their quality, standard or performance on environmental, social or governance issues".[83]

More specifically, sustainability values are to be included within the vision and "can be addressed during strategic decision-making process and as part of the organisation's corporate, business and functional level strategies".[84]

Given the above reasoning, gender equality and responsiveness can be intended as part of a virtuous company's social strategy, being able to contribute to other performance dimensions. There are three relevant managerial aspects of gender perspective's inclusion in CSR: gender diversity in companies' boards; the organisational welfare, and the Corporate Social Responsibility tools (such as standards, codes of ethics and reports).

18.5.1.1 Gender Diversity in Companies' Boards

The first indicator of gender diversity within organisations can be envisaged within the board of directors, due to the board's role in company goal setting, including CSR policies and strategies.[85] Specifically, boards may integrate socially and environmentally responsible behaviour in the strategic planning process.[86] Frequently, in homogeneous boards, the decision-making is faster due to convergent opinions and a more fluid communication.[87] Notwithstanding, in heterogeneous groups, many points of view and skills are taken into consideration to deal with complex problems.[88]

Various scientific contributions highlight the positive impact of boards' gender diversity on environmental issues; the voluntary disclosure of greenhouse gas,[89] risks of climate change[90] and carbon reduction initiative.[91] According to the study of De Masi and colleagues,[92] three is a minimum number of female directors required on company boards, to stimulate the disclosure of ESG information, ameliorate ESG

[82]Gennari (2018).

[83]SustainAbility (2018), p. 4.

[84]Bonn and Fisher (2011).

[85]Mason and Simmons (2014).

[86]Galbreath (2018) and Michelon and Parbonetti (2012).

[87]Earley and Mosakowski (2000).

[88]Pletzer et al. (2015).

[89]Liao et al. (2015).

[90]Ben-Amar et al. (2017).

[91]Haque (2017).

[92]De Masi et al. (2021).

score and to encourage the highest contribution of women to governance performance. Indeed, "women's contribution is visible when the critical mass, identified as three women on boards, is reached, after which the voices of women are heard, and their impact becomes discernible".[93]

Valls Martínez, Cervantes and Rambaud[94] frame such propensity in five theoretical streams:

1. the social role theory: the fact that women act according to gender roles and social expectations influences their management style. This results in more empathetic and participative leadership,[95] able to handle CSR and stakeholders' expectations;
2. the resource dependency theory: according to this theoretical perspective, facing social and environmental issues requires board diversity to intercept many kinds of environmental resources;[96]
3. the legitimacy theory: legitimacy occurs when stakeholders accept a company as a corporate subject characterised by moral citizenship.[97] In this regard, a diverse board structure can contribute to legitimacy, witnessing sensibility towards women's potential and equal opportunities;[98]
4. the agency theory: in companies where it is possible to distinguish ownership and control,[99] there are information asymmetries making managers (the agents) to behave contrary to the principals' interests (i.e., the shareholders). A diverse board composition can play a role in corporate governance, whereas higher representation of women is likely to mitigate agency costs, due to their tendency to transparency and accountability;[100]
   (a) the stakeholder theory: CSR helps a company to comply with stakeholders' expectations.[101] Gender diversity contributes to this scope by allowing women moral reasoning of women in meeting stakeholder needs,[102]
   (b) the stakeholder agency theory:[103] this theory combines agency theory and stakeholder theory, assigning to the board a twofold role; as principals for managers, while contemporaneously playing the role of agents according to the stakeholders' perspective.[104]

---

[93]Ibid., p. 1866.

[94]Valls Martínez et al. (2020).

[95]Eagly et al. (2003).

[96]Pfeffer (1972).

[97]Scherer and Palazzo (2007).

[98]Gennari (2018).

[99]Jensen and Meckling (1976).

[100]Adams and Ferreira (2009).

[101]Freeman (1984).

[102]Francoeur et al. (2019).

[103]See also the business law chapter of this book for the legal provisions.

[104]Hill and Jones (1992).

18.5.1.2 The Organisational Welfare

As far as organisational welfare policies are concerned, the use of organisational welfare indicators (for example regarding the balancing of working and private lives) is instrumental to the satisfaction of internal stakeholders (workers), whose needs are to be satisfied to improve their sense of belonging.[105]

Indeed, company performances may be affected by work-family conflicts, arising whenever individuals handle these two life domains.[106] Organisations can be family-friendly by implementing solutions such as childcare assistance and flexible working hours.[107]

According to Pulejo,[108] such initiatives contain the ability to make workers feel a sense of company belonging. This is achieved through the reconciliation of family and work responsibilities as they are more effective when implemented in a systemic way, when:

(a) the organisational culture evaluates work on the basis of intrinsic quality instead of time, whereas family commitments do not penalise professional development paths;
(b) the sensitivity to reconciliation issues is widespread at all hierarchical levels,
(c) the family-friendly company policies are clearly communicated and incentivised.

18.5.1.3 Corporate Social Responsibility Tools

In this subsection the key tools fostering the implementation of corporate social responsibility (CSR) within companies are described. CSR should go "over and above their legal obligations towards society and the environment", however "certain regulatory measures create an environment more conducive to enterprises voluntarily meeting their social responsibility".[109]

The EU Commission acknowledges the key role of international guidelines and principles, such as the ISO 26000 Guidance Standard on Social Responsibility, the OECD Guidelines for Multinational Enterprises, and the United Nations Guiding Principles on Business and Human Rights.[110]

"According to these principles and guidelines, CSR at least covers human rights, labour and employment practices (such as training, diversity, gender equality and employee health and well-being), environmental issues (such as biodiversity,

[105] Pulejo (2011).
[106] Eby et al. (2005) and Somech and Drach-Zahavy (2007).
[107] Perry-Smith and Blum (2000).
[108] Pulejo (2011), p. 60.
[109] European Commission (2011).
[110] Ibid.

climate change, resource efficiency, life-cycle assessment and pollution prevention), and combating bribery and corruption".[111]

However, CSR standards do not automatically affect CSR effectiveness. They are relevant for a symbolic and signalling effect,[112] thus contributing to external legitimacy without implementing substantial commitment to CSR in organisations.[113] As remarked by Testa and colleagues,[114] CSR company internalisation depends on a series of "hard" and "soft" factors, whereas CSR standards are part of the hard determinants, together with other formal structures and routines (technology, accounting and management systems, etc...). Among the soft determinants to CSR, there are the citizenship behaviours of managers, the employees' commitment and a leadership based on good examples.[115] Other important tools helping CSR implementation at a company level are codes of ethics and conducts. CSR reports published together with financial information started to be elaborated after multiple corporate scandals in the 1990s.[116] Company nonfinancial information can be issued through social reports (or sustainability reports). These can consist of stand-alone reports, dealing with sustainability aspects and disclosing the organisational interrelations within the natural and social environment.[117] However, these reports have been criticised for their lack of a holistic view of performance, since they do not link social and environmental performance with financial information.[118] For these reasons, they must be replaced by integrated reports; corporate disclosure reports combining information regarding financial and non-financial performance.[119]

18.5.2 Gender and Public Management and Administration

In this section, the gender mainstreaming approach within public organisations considers processes of gendered performance management at both top and street management level. This illustrates the role of public balance sheets in disclosing the socioeconomic impact of gender related policies' implementation, and the potential impact of non-gendered policies on gender related issues.

As aforementioned, we assume a multi-dimensional definition of performance, based on the distinction between inputs (resource consumed), outputs (amount of goods and services produced), and outcomes (long-term socioeconomic impacts). Such an approach is coherent with the evolution of Public Management and

---

[111] Ibid.

[112] Iatridis et al. (2016) and Toppinen et al. (2015).

[113] Testa et al. (2018b).

[114] Testa et al. (2018a).

[115] Ibid., pp. 853–854.

[116] Valls Martínez et al. (2020).

[117] Dierkes and Peterson (1997) and Gray (2006).

[118] Adams and Simmet (2011).

[119] Eccles and Saltzman (2011).

Administration theory and practice, whereas the traditional bureaucratic control on inputs has been overpassed by managerial and governance-based models. Such models are more focused on public results, namely, outputs and outcomes.[120] According to Moore,[121] public managers are responsible for creating public value; a key evaluative criterion within a performance-based perspective. Moore distinguishes three public management tasks: managing upward; downward, and outward, implying specific behavioural features:[122]

Managing upward; it takes place when public top managers interact with their principals, their elected political leadership. In this sphere, public performance could benefit from more gender-representative organisations, as women managers appear to be more participatory, interactional, flexible,[123] and increase or at least maintain managerial resources and legitimacy.[124] Managing outward; is based on the managers' interactions within the networked character of public programs, with organisational success based on the capacity to keep links with the community. Both men and women managers make use of such networks, with males excelling in informal connections and females privileging formal networking.[125] Managing downward; is the classic, hierarchical public management mechanism, characterised by the managers' interactions with subordinate line managers. Here, female managers may struggle for authority, due to an image of organisational leadership mostly associated to masculine terms for executive positions,[126] unbalanced domestic responsibilities,[127] and the underestimation of emotional labour skills.[128] As a result, females in middle or top-level management positions are rarer than ones occupying street-level positions.[129]

In this context, public balance sheets, or public budgets, can help in promoting gender equality, by representing governmental statements of priorities in expenditures and revenues. We adopt the definition of "gender responsive budget" provided by Rubin and Bartle,[130] as a "government budget that explicitly integrates gender into any or all parts of the decision-making process regarding resource allocation and revenue generation".[131] The budgeting initiatives enclosing the gender perspective function at the level of national or subnational government.[132] The

[120] Stoker (2006).
[121] Moore (1995).
[122] Meier et al. (2006).
[123] Rosener (1990).
[124] Duerst-Lahti and Johnson (1990) and Stivers (2002).
[125] Powell (1993) and Smeltzer and Fann (1989).
[126] Guy (1992) and Stivers (2002).
[127] Ibid.
[128] Guy and Newman (2004).
[129] Meier et al. (2006).
[130] Rubin and Bartle (2005).
[131] Ibid., p. 259.
[132] Budlender and Hewitt (2002).

use of gender responsive public budgets started to be encouraged since the "Convention on the Elimination of All Forms of Discrimination against Women".[133] The aims of the Convention were confirmed by the United Nations' Fourth World Conference on Women, pushing governments to "incorporate a gender perspective into the design, development, adoption and execution of all budgetary processes as appropriate in or to promote equitable, effective and appropriate resource allocation and establish adequate budgetary allocations to support gender equality".[134] Later, the "European pact for gender equality"[135] prescribed to include the gender view into public policies' monitoring and evaluation at the European level, including the Union's public budgeting processes. Furthermore, the document encourages peripheral initiatives, promoting gender responsive budgets at a local level and the exchange of best practices.[136]

Public budgets are made of financial aggregates, and do not distinguish gender-specific issues or impacts.[137] However, a budget is only apparently gender neutral, ignoring this fact denotes "gender blindness" about the unintended impacts of budget policies, able to affect both revenue and expenditure.[138]

Some countries (e.g., France, Germany, Italy, and Spain in the context of the European Union)[139] have undertaken initiatives to create gender-responsive budgets, both at national and/or sub-national levels. These practices share some common traits; they all require the decision-makers' awareness on gender inequities, and the relevance of budget policies to mitigate them. Acceptance of these initiatives also requires consideration of the roles of the political environment and social values.[140]

Furthermore, efficiency and equity can find a balance in the adoption of gender-equity objectives for the definition of performance measures.[141] The gender perspective can be integrated in any step of the budget cycle, from preparation to evaluation, as reported by Rubin and Bartle.[142] Specifically, the authors suggest that in the first stage of public budgeting processes (budget preparation), gender-specific policies and priorities can be inserted.[143] In the next stage (budget approval), possible gender-responsive actions are, for example, the creation of gender guidelines in allocating resources and the inclusion of gender outcomes in fiscal notes.[144]

---

[133] United Nations (1979).

[134] United Nations (1995).

[135] Council of the European Union (2006).

[136] Pulejo (2011).

[137] Ibid., p. 260.

[138] Elson (1999) and Barnett and Grown (2004).

[139] Budlender and Hewitt (2002).

[140] Rubin and Bartle (2005).

[141] Ibid., p. 269.

[142] Ibid., p. 264.

[143] Ibid., p. 264.

[144] Ibid., p. 264.

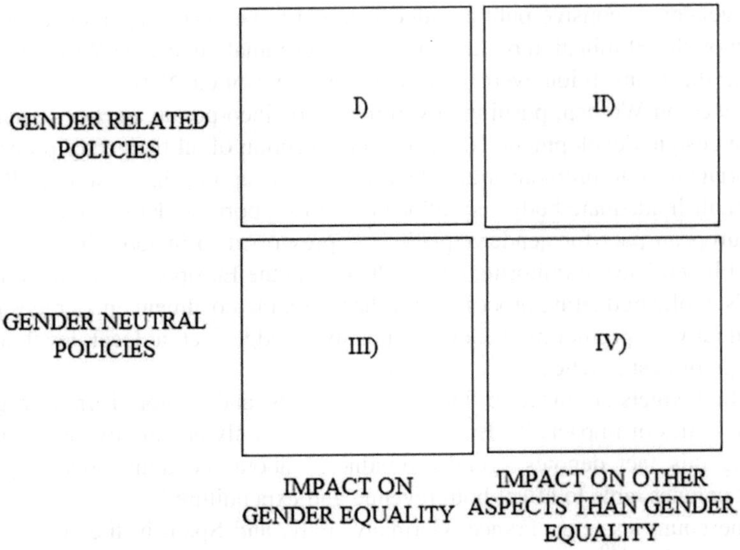

Fig. 18.2 Gender related and neutral policies' impacts (Source: own elaboration)

At budget execution, departments could be provided with specific guidelines (for spending, outsourcing, procurement, grant disbursement), whilst gender goals are implemented at a staff level.[145] The final stage of budget audit and evaluation could incorporate the gender perspective, for example, carrying out auditing activities about expenditures, outputs, outcomes, as well as compliance with gender-related goals and guidelines.[146]

Gender-related budgeting requires measuring the impacts of policy making on gender equality. The measuring/evaluation activity should regard all government functions, including seemingly gender-neutral expenditures. Indeed, direct and indirect policy impacts should be considered; one policy targeting a specific segment of population could have indirect (desired or undesired) effects on other segments, and vice versa.

Figure 18.2 proposes a bidimensional matrix to be intended as a general framework for policy analysis. The potential policy packages can be separated into two main categories: gender related policies, explicitly targeting gender inequality (and eventual intersections); and (apparently) gender neutral policies. Each category can affect gender equality and/or other aspects. Thereafter, it is possible to estimate the impact of gender policies on gender inequalities (quadrant I), on other aspects (quadrant II), the impact of gender-neutral policies on gender inequalities (quadrant III) and on other aspects than gender equality (quadrant IV). Gender-responsive budgets should disclose, at least, what is included in quadrants I and III.

---

[145] Ibid., p. 264.

[146] Ibid., p. 264.

Notwithstanding, they do not require new formats of balance sheets, but their adaptations should be read according to "gender lenses" in any existing budget format. For example, line-item budgets (organised by objects of expenditure), could separately indicate the percentage of wages/salaries or contracts to women and/or firms owned by women.[147] In contrast for performance-based budgets, where expenditures are articulated in performance objects, tasks, outputs, and outcomes, the budget document could contain the performance measures capturing gender goals.[148]

18.6 Gender and Innovation

The overall aim of this section of this chapter is to analyse the importance of intellectual property rights (patents) and the poor visibility of women inventors in society.

18.6.1 General Concepts from an Economic Angle

Innovation is a key piece in the economic development of countries. According to the Oslo Manual,[149] an innovation is "a new or improved product or process (or combination thereof) that differs significantly from the unit's previous products or processes and that has been made available to potential users (product) or brought into use by the unit (process)". A large number of innovations can be protected through intellectual property (IP) rights.

IP is defined as "creations of the mind, such as inventions; literary and artistic works; designs; and symbols, names and images used in commerce".[150] Intellectual property is divided into two groups, "industrial property" and "copyright".

Industrial property includes "inventions in all fields of human endeavour, industrial designs, trademarks, service marks and commercial names and designations" (World Intellectual Property Organization or WIPO). According to WIPO, an invention is "a new solution to a specific technical problem in the field of technology".[151]

"A patent is a legal title that gives inventors the right, for a limited period (usually 20 years), to prevent others from making, using or selling their invention without their permission in the countries for which the patent has been granted".[152]

[147] Ibid., p. 269.

[148] Ibid., p. 269.

[149] OECD and Eurostat (2018).

[150] World Intellectual Property Organization. "What Is Intellectual Property (IP)?"

[151] World Intellectual Property Organization. "Innovation and Intellectual Property".

[152] European Patent Office, "Glossary".

18.6.2 The Gender Patenting Gap

Gender disparity still exists, despite many excellent intentions and activities. Even though female undergraduate and graduate students outnumber male students in many countries, there are few female full professors. Gender disparities in employment, wages, financing, satisfaction, and patenting still exist.[153]

Many studies have attempted to examine women's involvement in science, technology, and innovation, primarily utilising statistics from patent filings and scientific publications. By methodically assigning gender to the names of inventors and authors from 14 countries, Frietsch et al.[154] explored gender-specific patterns in patenting and academic publication. The findings revealed significant disparities in female engagement across countries, with the higher-performing countries showing minimal increase in this area over the study period (1991–2005).

There are several studies that focused their attention in the second country with the most patents in the world; the United States of America.

Murray and Graham[155] used bibliometric data and semi-structured interviews to investigate the origination and maintenance of the gender gap in commercial science between 1975 and 2005 in the U.S. Women constituted 56 of a possible 148 life science faculty members (38% of the population), with 34 male (29%) and 22 female (73%) active during 2 years. According to their findings, key determinants of gender stratification in commercial science can be traced back to "when early buyers in the market activated traditional cultural stereotypes of women in science and business and showed an initial gender bias in the opportunities available to women life scientists". Homophily in mentoring and networks, among other factors, reinforced these traits through generations. While the study's findings were limited in their generalisability, they did agree that the lack of a supporting network for the patenting procedure was the most important factor in shifting gender prejudice.

Whittington and Smith-Doerr[156] looked into gender differences in commercial engagement for both industrial and university life scientists. Their findings revealed that, despite women's lower participation in patenting, the quality and impact of female patents were comparable to male patents, suggesting commercial science may be missing out on opportunities to generate value by failing to address disparities in patenting support. In a later study, Whittington and Smith-Doerr[157] examined detailed data from a sample of academic and industrial life scientists working in the United States. This highlighted the role of organisational settings in influencing gender disparities, suggesting that less bureaucratic and horizontal work relations might favour better female participation.

---

[153] Larivière et al. (2013).

[154] Frietsch et al. (2009).

[155] Murray and Graham (2007).

[156] Whittington and Smith-Doerr (2005).

[157] Whittington and Smith-Doerr (2008).

In their statistical study on the U.S. 2003 National Survey of College Graduates, Hunt et al.[158] explained the gender gap in terms of women's underrepresentation in engineering, development, and design occupations.

Sugimoto et al.[159] used 4.6 million utility patents issued by the United States Patent and Trade Office (USPTO) between 1976 and 2013. They found that the female-to-male ratio of patenting activity increased from 2.7% to 10.8% during that period, with female patentees primarily originating from academic institutions.

However, there are few studies analysing the gender patenting gap in Europe and Ibero-America.

Busolt and Kugele[160] conveyed that female participation ranged from 5% to 25% in European Union Member States, with a significant disparity between female academic production and patent output, indicating that women inventors' potential is underutilised.

For the period 1990–2006, Morales and Sifontes[161] investigated gender differences in patenting activity in eight Latin American countries: Argentina, Brazil, Mexico, Colombia, Cuba, Peru, Chile, and Venezuela. According to data from the United States Patent and Trademark Office (USPTO), female inventors account for 20% of all patents. The countries with the most gender inequality are Peru, Mexico, and Uruguay. Finally, chemistry and metallurgy are two technological disciplines with a higher female presence.

Carvalho, Bares and Silva[162] studied the female involvement in patent applications in 23 Ibero-American countries. The findings showed that even in more active economies like Portugal and Spain, women's participation in patent applications does not reach 30%.

Figure 18.3 shows the evolution of share women inventors in the period 2004–2018. Despite an encouraging record high of 17% of applications coming from female inventors in 2018, the numbers demonstrate that a large gender disparity still exists (Fig. 18.3). According to Hosler,[163] gender equality in invention was more than 75 years away.

18.7 Conclusion

The chapter has attempted to shed light on gender equality from an economic and managerial perspective. Feminist economics has been conceptualised and framed in comparison with mainstream economics, showing how macroeconomic policy produces and reproduces differential opportunities for women and men and further

[158] Hunt et al. (2013).

[159] Sugimoto et al. (2015).

[160] Busolt and Kugele (2009).

[161] Morales and Sifontes (2014).

[162] Carvalho et al. (2020).

[163] Hosler (2018).

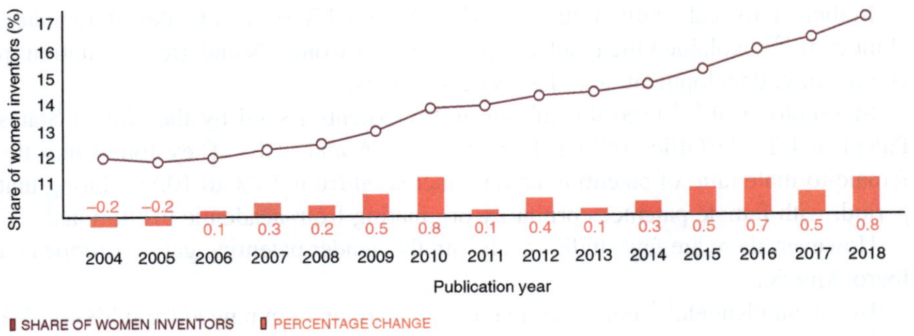

Fig. 18.3 Evolution of share of women inventors (2014–2018) [Source: World Intellectual Property Organization (World Intellectual Property Organization. Figures are rising but gender gap persists)]

genders. From raising political critique on the division of private and public, theoretical critique of the notion of 'economic man', to human rights-based critique towards the unequal division of unpaid care work, feminist economics has developed to become an academic field and institutionalised discipline in its own right. The main lines of critique of mainstream economics include: (1) majority men, or the norm group of men and their interests and concerns, underlie economists' concentration on markets, consequently leaving women's household activities and unpaid care work unrecognised; (2) the emphasis on individual choice and autonomy, rendering social and economic inequalities and their constraints/limitations on choice unrecognised; and (3) the focus on (some) men's interests has created bias in the definition and boundaries of the discipline, its central assumptions, its choice and acceptance of methods, and its results. This bias, produces theories and knowledge that have excluded the knowledge and experiences of women, may therefore not be valid. As it has been argued in the chapter, a main conclusion is that a focus on gender economics, and putting it into practice, has the potential to address and contribute to the solution to some of the most pressing contemporary social, economic, and environmental concerns.

The main gender indicators, their sources and databases have been presented in order to provide the necessary tools for students to learn how to analyse data from a gender perspective. These indicators have shown that the Baltic countries are the most gender equal. The functioning of the labour market has also been analysed from a gender perspective and the consequences that digitalisation can have on gender equality have been indicated.

Gender mainstreaming was identified as a relevant approach for promoting gender equality and combatting discrimination. It consists of the integration of gender perspective into policy making, real-life facets and manifestations. Key features of gender mainstreaming are women's equal representation in any societal aspect, and the inclusion of gendered issue within policy contents. However, alongside regulations and principle's statements, what matters is how they can be put into practice.

Thus, managerial concepts and tools used to operationalise gender mainstreaming within both private and public sectors are considered, adopting Corporate Social Responsibility as a general framework. For educational reasons, public and private actors gendered policies' design and implementation have been treated separately. However, it has been recognized that these two worlds are interrelated; the put-in-action of gender mainstreaming requires the adoption of a multidimensional notion of performance, not just focused on financial results, but also on environmental and social ones. Consequently, the profile of gender responsive companies is identified, characterised by female directors and/or organisational welfare systems fostering the balance between work and family life.

Codes of ethics, sustainability reports, gender-responsive policy design and public budgeting are described as valuable managerial tools for triggering gender equality in organisations. However, their effectiveness is not fully realisable without educational interventions aimed at stimulating motivational forces, going beyond the mere rule-compliance logic.

Finally, gender inequality in Science, Technology, and Innovation should be the focus of public policies, being better equipped to access up-to-date regional data on the evolution of gender inequalities, and the outcomes of current and previous attempts to minimise them. Offering financial aid with patenting fees, promoting women's participation in STEM fields, and enhancing business networking are just a few of policy ideas.[164]

Questions

1. What are the main lines of feminist critique of mainstream economics?
2. What is homo economicus?
3. Describe the gendered division of labour in the market economy and how the market economy could be reconsidered from a gender perspective?
4. Identify three European countries whose gender indicators show greater equality between men and women. Justify your answer.
5. Select three gender indicators related to the labour market in European countries and analyse their 2020 values.
6. What are the main factors causing feminist socioeconomic inequalities in work and employment?
7. What is Corporate Social Responsibility? How is gender related to it?
8. How is it possible to incorporate the gender perspective into public budgets?
9. Based on your own opinion, what are the main causes of the gender patenting gap?
10. How many female inventors do you know? What are their inventions?

[164] Milli et al. (2016).

References

Adams RB, Ferreira D (2009) Women in the boardroom and their impact on governance and performance. J Financ Econ 94:291–309. https://doi.org/10.1016/j.jfineco.2008.10.007

Adams S, Simmet R (2011) Integrated reporting: an opportunity for Australia's not-for-profit sector. Aust Account Rev 58:292–301. https://doi.org/10.1111/j.1835-2561.2011.00143.x

Agarwal B (1997) Bargaining' and gender relations: within and beyond the household. Fem Econ 3: 1–51. https://doi.org/10.1080/135457097338799

Apostolopoulos N, Al-Dajani H, Holt D et al (2018) Entrepreneurship and the sustainable development goals. Contemp Issues Entrep Res 8:1–7

Arrive JT, Feng M (2018) Corporate social responsibility disclosure: evidence from BRICS nations. Corp Soc Responsib Environ Manag 25:920–927. https://doi.org/10.1002/csr.1508

Bàez AB, Bàez-Garcìa AJ, Flores-Munoz F et al (2018) Gender diversity, corporate governance and firm behavior: the challenge of emotional management. Eur Res Manag Bus Econ 24:121–129. https://doi.org/10.1016/j.iedeen.2018.07.001

Barnett K, Grown C (2004) Gender impacts of government revenue collection—the case of taxation. Commonwealth Secretariat, London

Bauer RA (1966) Social indicators and sample surveys. Public Opin Q 30:339–352

Becchio G (2019) A history of feminist and gender economics. Routledge, London

Ben-Amar W, Chang M, McIlkenny P (2017) Board gender diversity and corporate response to sustainability initiatives: evidence from the Carbon Disclosure Project. J Bus Ethics 142:369–383. https://doi.org/10.1007/s10551-015-2759-1

Bhattacharya CB, Sen S (2004) Doing better at doing good: when, why, and how consumers respond to corporate social initiatives. Calif Manag Rev 47:9–24. https://doi.org/10.2307/41166284

Bjørnholt M, McKay A (2014) Counting on Marilyn Waring: new advances in feminist economics. Demeter Press, Toronto

Boehnert J (2019) Anthropocene economics and design: heterodox economics for design transitions. She Ji: J Des Econ Innov 4:355–374. https://doi.org/10.1016/j.sheji.2018.10.002

Bonn I, Fisher J (2011) Sustainability: the missing ingredient in strategy. J Bus Strateg 32:5–14. https://doi.org/10.1108/02756661111100274

Celma D, Martínez-Garcia E, Coenders G (2014) Corporate social responsibility in human resource management: an analysis of common practices and their determinants in Spain. Corp Soc Respon Environ Manag 21:82–99. https://doi.org/10.1002/csr.1301

Chesley N, Flood S (2017) Signs of change? At-home and breadwinner parents' housework and child-care time. J Marriage Fam 79:511–534. https://doi.org/10.1111/jomf.12376

Coda V (2012) The evaluation of the entrepreneurial formula. Eur Manag Rev 9:63–74

Council of the European Union (2006) Presidency conclusions of the Brussels European Council, 23/24 March 2006, 7775/1/06 REV 1. Annex II, European pact for gender equality. https://data.consilium.europa.eu/doc/document/ST-7775-2006-REV-1/en/pdf. Accessed 29 Oct 2021

Crenshaw K (1989) Demarginalizing the intersection of race and sex: a black feminist critique of antidiscrimination doctrine, feminist theory and antiracist politics. Univ Chic Leg Forum 1989: 139–167

Crompton R (2006) Employment and the family: the reconfiguration of work and family life in contemporary societies. Cambridge University Press, Cambridge

De Masi S, Słomka-Gołębiowska A, Becagli C, Paci A (2021) Toward sustainable corporate behavior: the effect of the critical mass of female directors on environmental, social, and governance disclosure. Bus Strateg Environ 30:1865–1878. https://doi.org/10.1002/bse.2721

Budlender D, Hewitt G (2002) Gender budgets make more cents: country studies and good practices. Commonwealth Secretariat, London

Dierkes M, Peterson A (1997) The usefulness and use of social reporting information. Acc Organ Soc 10:29–34. https://doi.org/10.1016/0361-3682(85)90029-7

Duerst-Lahti G, Johnson CM (1990) Gender and style in bureaucracy. Women Polit 10:67–120

Eagly AH, Johannesen-Schmidt MC, van Engen ML (2003) Transformational, transactional, and laissez-faire leadership styles: a meta-analysis comparing women and men. Psychol Bull 129: 569–591. https://doi.org/10.1037/0033-2909.129.4.569

Earley CP, Mosakowski E (2000) Creating hybrid team cultures: an empirical test of transnational team functioning. Acad Manag J 43:26–49

Eberharter V (2001) Gender roles, labour market participation and household income position. Struct Chang Econ Dyn 12:235–246. https://doi.org/10.1016/S0954-349X(01)00021-2

Eby LT, Casper WJ, Lockwood A et al (2005) Work and family research in IO/OB: content analysis and review of the literature (1980-2002). J Vocat Behav 66:124–197. https://doi.org/10.1016/j.jvb.2003.11.003

Eccles RG, Saltzman D (2011) Achieving sustainability through integrated reporting. Stanf Soc Innov Rev 9:57–61

EIGE (2013) Gender equality index: main findings. European Institute for Gender Equality, Vilnius

EIGE (2020) Glossary & thesaurus. European Institute for Gender Equality, Vilnius. https://eige.europa.eu/thesaurus/terms/1195. Accessed 29 Oct 2021

Elkington J (1997) Cannibals with forks: the triple bottom line of 21th century business. Capstone Publishing, Oxford

Elson D (1999) Gender-neutral, gender-blind, or gender-sensitive budgets? Changing the conceptual framework to include women's empowerment and the economy of care. Gender Budget Initiative Background Papers. Commonwealth Secretariat, London

European Commission (2001) Green paper – promoting a European framework for corporate social responsibility. https://ec.europa.eu/transparency/regdoc/rep/1/2001/EN/1-2001-366-EN-1-0.Pdf. Accessed 29 Oct 2021

European Commission (2002) Communication from the Commission concerning corporate social responsibility: a business contribution to sustainable development. https://op.europa.eu/en/publication-detail/-/publication/6e2c6d26-d1f6-48a3-9a78-f0ff2dc21aad/language-en. Accessed 29 Oct 2021

European Commission (2011) A renewed EU strategy 2011–14 for corporate social responsibility. https://eur-lex.europa.eu/legal-content/EN/TXT/?uri=CELEX%3A52011DC0681. Accessed 29 Oct 2021

European Commission (2020) Proposal for a Joint Employment Report 2021: text proposed by the European Commission on 18 November 2020 for adoption by the EPSCO Council. European Union, Brussels

European Patent Office. Glossary. https://www.epo.org/service-support/glossary.html. Accessed 29 October 2021.

Ferber MA, Nelson JA (1993) Beyond economic man: feminist theory and economics. Chicago University Press, Chicago

Flynn J, Slovic P, Mertz CK (1994) Gender, race, and perception of environmental health risks. Risk Anal 14:1101–1108. https://doi.org/10.1111/j.1539-6924.1994.tb00082.x

Francoeur C, Labelle R, Balti S et al (2019) To what extent do gender diverse boards enhance corporate social performance? J Bus Ethics 155:343–357. https://doi.org/10.1007/s10551-017-3529-z

Freeman ER (1984) Strategic management: a stakeholder approach. Cambridge University Press, Cambridge

Frey CB, Osborne MA (2017) The future of employment: how susceptible are jobs to computerisation? Technol Forecast Soc Chang 114:254–280. https://doi.org/10.1007/s10551-017-3529-z

Friedman M (1970) A Friedman doctrine. https://graphics8.nytimes.com/packages/pdf/business/miltonfriedman1970.pdf. Accessed 29 Oct 2021

Galbreath J (2018) Do boards of directors influence corporate sustainable development? An attention-based analysis. Bus Strateg Environ 27:742–756. https://doi.org/10.1002/bse.2028

Garrica E, Melè D (2004) Corporate social responsibility theories: mapping the territory. J Bus Ethics 53:51–71. https://doi.org/10.1023/B:BUSI.0000039399.90587.34

Gennari F (2018) Gender balance on boards and corporate sustainability for the 2030 agenda. Afr J Bus Manag 12:343–356. https://doi.org/10.5897/AJBM2018.8553

Gray R (2006) Social, environmental and sustainability reporting and organizational value creation. Whose value? Whose creation? Account Audit Account J 19:793–819. https://doi.org/10.1108/09513570610709872

Grimshaw D, Fagan C, Hebson G, Tavora I (2017) A new labour market segmentation approach for analysing inequalities: introduction and overview. In: Grimshaw D, Fagan C, Hebson G, Tavora I (eds) Making work more equal. Manchester University Press, Manchester, pp 1–32

Guy ME (1992) Women and men of the states: public administrators at the state level. M.E. Sharpe, New York

Guy ME, Newman MA (2004) Women's and men's jobs: sex segregation and emotional labor. Public Adm Rev 64:289–298

Haque F (2017) The effects of board characteristics and sustainable compensation policy on carbon performance of UK firms. Br Account Rev 49:347–364. https://doi.org/10.1016/j.bar.2017.01.001

Hausmann R, Tyson L, Zahidi S (2006) The Global Gender Gap Report 2006. http://www3.weforum.org/docs/WEF_GenderGap_Report_2006.pdf. Accessed 29 Oct 2021

Hill CWL, Jones T (1992) Stakeholder-agency theory. J Manag Stud 29:131–154

Himmelweit S (2002) Making visible the hidden economy: the case for gender-impact analysis of economic policy. Fem Econ 8:49–70. https://doi.org/10.1080/13545700110104864

Hood C (1991) A public management for all seasons? Public Adm 69:3–19. https://doi.org/10.1111/j.1467-9299.1991.tb00779.x

Hosler L (2018) From the USPTO: mind the gap – the USPTO' s efforts to narrow the gender gap in patenting and innovation. Technol Innov 19:759–762. https://doi.org/10.21300/19.4.2018.759

Hughes OE (2003) Public management and administration. an introduction. MacMillan, London

Iatridis K, Kuznetsov A, Whyman PB (2016) SMEs and certified management standards: the effect of motives and timing on implementation and commitment. Bus Ethics Q 26:67–94. https://doi.org/10.1017/beq.2016.9

Jensen MC, Meckling WH (1976) Theory of the firm: managerial behavior, agency costs, and ownership structure. J Financ Econ 3:305–360. https://doi.org/10.1016/0304-405X(76)90026-X

Krieger-Boden C, Sorgner A (2018) Labor market opportunities for women in the digital age. Econ Discuss Papers 18:1–8

Land KC (1971) On the definition of social indicators. Am Sociol 6:322–325

Leuenberger D (2006) Sustainable development in public administration: a match with practice. Public Works Manag Policy 10:195–201. https://doi.org/10.1177/1087724X06287496

Liao L, Luo L, Tang Q (2015) Gender diversity, board independence, environmental committee and greenhouse gas disclosure. Br Account Rev 47:409–424. https://doi.org/10.1016/j.bar.2014.01.002

Luo X, Bhattacharya CB (2009) The debate over doing good: corporate social performance, strategic marketing levers, and firm-idiosyncratic risk. J Mark 73:198–213

Mason C, Simmons J (2014) Embedding corporate social responsibility in corporate governance: a stakeholder systems approach. J Bus Ethics 119:77–86. https://doi.org/10.1007/s10551-012-1615-9

Mazzocco M, Ruiz C, Yamaguchi S (2014) Labor supply and household dynamics. Am Econ Rev 104:354–359. https://doi.org/10.1257/aer.104.5.354

Meier KJ, O'Toole LJ Jr, Goerdel HT (2006) Management activity and program performance: gender as management capital. Public Adm Rev, 24–36. https://doi.org/10.1111/j.1540-6210.2006.00553.x

Michelon G, Parbonetti A (2012) The effect of corporate governance on sustainability disclosure. J Manag Gov 16:477–509. https://doi.org/10.1007/s10997-010-9160-3

Mill JS (2007) On the definition of political economy. In: Hausman DM (ed) The philosophy of economics. An anthology. Cambridge University Press, Cambridge, pp 41–58

Milli J, Gault B, Williams-Baron E, Xia J, Berlan M (2016) The gender patenting gap. Institute for Womens Policy Research, Washington. https://www.research.uky.edu/uploads/iwpr-gender-patenting-gap. Accessed 29 Oct 2021

Moeeni S (2021) Married women's labor force participation and intra-household bargaining power. Empir Econ 60:1411–1448. https://doi.org/10.1007/s00181-019-01800-7

Mohr LA, Webb DJ, Harris KE (2001) Do consumers expect companies to be socially responsible? The impact of corporate social responsibility on buying behavior. J Consum Aff 35:45–72. https://doi.org/10.1111/j.1745-6606.2001.tb00102.x

Moore MH (1995) Creating public value. Harvard University Press, Cambridge

Morgan MS (2009) Economic man as model man: ideal types, idealization and caricatures. J Hist Econ Thinking 28:1–27. https://doi.org/10.1080/10427710500509763

Nadeem M, Gyapong E, Ahmed A (2020) Board gender diversity and environmental, social, and economic value creation: does family ownership matter? Bus Strateg Environ 29:1268–1284. https://doi.org/10.1002/bse.2432

Nelson JA, Ferber MA (2003) Introduction – 'Beyond economic man', ten years later. In: Nelson JA, Ferber MA (eds) Feminist economics today: beyond economic man. University of Chicago Press, Chicago, pp 1–14

OECD. Labour force participation rate (indicator). https://www.oecd-ilibrary.org/employment/labour-force-participation-rate/indicator/english_8a801325-en. Accessed 29 Oct 2021

OECD and Eurostat (2018) Oslo Manual 2018: Guidelines for Collecting, Reporting and Using Data on Innovation, 4th Edition. The Measurement of Scientific, Technological and Innovation Activities. doi:10.1787/9789264304604-en. Accessed 29 Oct 2021

Papadimitriou E, Norlén H, Del Sorbo M (2020) JRC Statistical Audit of the 2020 Gender Equality Index. LU: Publications Office of the European Union. https://publications.jrc.ec.europa.eu/repository/handle/JRC122232. Accessed 29 Oct 2021

Perry-Smith JE, Blum TC (2000) Work-family human resource bundles and perceived organizational performance. Acad Manag J 43:1107–1117

Pfeffer J (1972) Size and composition of corporate boards of directors: the organization and its environment. Adm Sci Q 17:218–228

Piketty T (2014) Capital in the twenty-first century (trans: Goldhammer A). Belknap Press, Cambridge

Pletzer JL, Nikolova R, Kedzior KK et al (2015) Does gender matter? Female representation on corporate boards and firm financial performance - a meta-analysis. PLOS ONE 10:1–20. https://doi.org/10.1371/journal.pone.0130005

Porter ME, Kramer MR (2006) Strategy and society: the link between competitive advantage and corporate social responsibility. Harv Bus Rev 84:78–92

Pulejo L (2011) La gender equality nell'economia dell'azienda. Strategie e strumenti di mainstreaming di genere per lo sviluppo sostenibile. FrancoAngeli, Milano

Rhodes RAW (1996) The new governance: governing without government. Polit Stud 44:652–667. https://doi.org/10.1111/j.1467-9248.1996.tb01747.x

Richie C, Courtney Lamendola C et al (2020) Gender Parity Index: the status of women's representation in the suffrage centennial. Represent Women Parity for women in politics. Takoma Park: RepresentWomen. https://www.representwomen.org/gender_parity_index. Accessed 5 Mar 2021

Rosener JB (1990) Ways women lead. Harv Bus Rev 68:119–125

Rubin MM, Bartle JR (2005) Integrating gender into government budgets: a new perspective. Public Adm Rev 65:259–227. https://doi.org/10.1111/j.1540-6210.2005.00452.x

Sasaki M (2002) The causal effect of family structure on labor force participation among Japanese married women. J Hum Resour 37:429–440

Schanzenbach DW, Nunn R (2017) The 51%: driving growth through women's economic participation. Brookings, Washington

Scherer AG, Palazzo G (2007) Towards a political conception of corporate responsibility. Acad Manag Rev 32:1096–1120

Skudiene V, Auruskeviciene V (2012) The contribution of corporate social responsibility to internal employee motivation. Baltic J Manag 7:49–67. https://doi.org/10.1108/17465261211197421

Smeltzer LR, Fann GL (1989) Gender differences in external networks of small business owner/managers. J Small Bus Manag 27:25–32

Somech A, Drach-Zahavy A (2007) Strategies for coping with work–family conflict: the distinctive relationships of gender role ideology. J Occup Health Psychol 12:1–19. https://doi.org/10.1037/1076-8998.12.1.1

Sorgner A, Bode E, Krieger-Boden C (2017) The effects of digitalization for gender equality in the G20 economies, women 20 study. Kiel Institute for the World Economy, Kiel. https://www.ifw-kiel.de/pub/e-books/digital_women-final_report.pdf. Accessed 29 Oct 2021

Stivers C (2002) Gender images in public administration: legitimacy and the administrative state. Sage, Thousand Oaks

Stoker G (2006) Public value management a new narrative for networked governance? Am Rev Public Adm 36:41–57. https://doi.org/10.1177/0275074005282583

Strid S, Walby S, Armstrong J (2013) Intersectionality and multiple inequalities. Soc Polit Int Stud Gend State Soc 20(4):558–581. https://doi.org/10.1093/sp/jxt019

SustainAbility (2018) Rate the raters 2018: ratings revisited. SustainAbility, New York

Testa F, Boiral O, Heras-Saizarbitoria I (2018a) Improving CSR performance by hard and soft means: the role of organizational citizenship behaviours and the internalization of CSR standards. Corp Soc Respon Environ Manag 25:853–865. https://doi.org/10.1002/csr.1502

Testa F, Olivier Boiral O et al (2018b) Internalization of environmental practices and institutional complexity: can stakeholders pressures encourage greenwashing? J Bus Ethics 147:287–307. https://doi.org/10.1007/s10551-015-2960-2

Ţiţan E, Andreea Burciu A, Manea D et al (2014) From traditional to digital: the labour market demands and education expectations in an EU context. Proc Econ Financ 10:269–274. https://doi.org/10.1016/S2212-5671(14)00302-5

Toppinen A, Virtanen A, Mayer A et al (2015) Standardizing social responsibility via ISO 26000: empirical insights from the forest industry. Sustain Dev 23:153–166. https://doi.org/10.1002/sd.1579

Tullberg J (2012) Triple bottom line - a vaulting ambition? Bus Ethics 21:310–324. https://doi.org/10.1111/j.1467-8608.2012.01656.x

Turban DB, Greening DW (2017) Corporate social performance and organizational attractiveness to prospective employees. Acad Manag J 40:658–672

United Nations (1995) Report of the fourth world conference on women. https://www.un.org/womenwatch/daw/beijing/pdf/Beijing%20full%20report%20E.pdf. Accessed 29 Oct 2021

United Nations (1979) Convention on the Elimination of All Forms of Discrimination against Women New York, 18 December 1979. https://www.ohchr.org/sites/default/files/cedaw.pdf. Accessed 29 Oct 2021

Vaananen A, Kevin MV, Ala-Mursula L et al (2004) The double burden of and negative spillover between paid and domestic work: associations with health among men and women. Women Health 40:1–18. https://doi.org/10.1300/J013v40n03_01

Valls Martínez MC, Cervantes PAM, Rambaud SC (2020) Women on corporate boards and sustainable development in the American and European markets: is there a limit to gender policies? Corp Soc Respon Environ Manag 27:2642–2656. https://doi.org/10.1002/csr.1989

Walby S (1990) From private to public patriarchy: the periodisation of British history. Women's Stud Int Forum 13:91–104. https://doi.org/10.1016/0277-5395(90)90076-A

Waring M (1988) If women counted: a new feminist economics. Harper & Row, San Francisco

World Commission on Environment and Development (1987) Our common future. Oxford University Press, Oxford
World Economic Forum (2016) The Industry Gender Gap: women and work in the fourth industrial revolution. World Economic Forum, Geneva
World Intellectual Property Organization. What is intellectual property (IP)? https://www.wipo.int/about-ip/en/. Accessed 29 Oct 2021
Yang P, Riepe J, Moser K et al (2019) Women directors, firm performance, and firm risk: a causal perspective. Leadersh Q 30:1–15. https://doi.org/10.1016/j.leaqua.2019.05.004

Further Reading

Bearfield DA (2009) Equity at the intersection: public administration and the study of gender. Public Adm Rev, 383–386. https://doi.org/10.1111/j.1540-6210.2009.01985.x.
Behson SJ (2005) The relative contribution of formal and informal organizational work-family support. J Vocat Behav 66:487–500. https://doi.org/10.1016/j.jvb.2004.02.004
Bericat E (2012) The European gender equality index: conceptual and analytical issues. Soc Indic Res 108:1–28. https://doi.org/10.1007/s11205-011-9872-z
Busolt U, Kugele K (2009) The gender innovation and research productivity gap in Europe. Int J Innov Sustain Dev 4:109–122. https://doi.org/10.1504/IJISD.2009.028066
Carvalho DS, Bares L, Kelyane S (2020) The gender patenting gap: a study on the Iberoamerican countries. J Data Inf Sci 5:116–128. https://doi.org/10.2478/jdis-2020-0025
Dengler C, Strunk B (2017) The monetized economy versus care and the environment: degrowth perspectives on reconciling an antagonism, feminist economics. Fem Econ 24:160–183. https://doi.org/10.1080/13545701.2017.1383620
Frietsch R, Haller I, Funken-Vrohlings M et al (2009) Gender-specific patterns in patenting and publishing. Res Policy 38:590–599. https://doi.org/10.1016/j.respol.2009.01.019
Goetz AM (1992) Gender and administration. Ids Bull 22:6–17
Hunt J, Garant J-P, Herman H et al (2013) Why are women underrepresented amongst patentees? Res Policy 42:831–843. https://doi.org/10.1016/j.respol.2012.11.004
Klasen S (2019) What explains uneven female labor force participation levels and trends in developing countries? World Bank Res Obs 34:161–197. https://doi.org/10.1093/wbro/lkz005
Larivière V, Chaoqun N, Gingras Y et al (2013) Bibliometrics: global gender disparities in science. Nature 504:211–213
Maier KJ, Mastracci SH, Wilson K (2006) Gender and emotional labor in public organizations: an empirical examination of the link to performance. Public Adm Rev, 899–909. https://doi.org/10.1111/j.1540-6210.2006.00657.x
Morales RM, Sifontes DA (2014) Innovative activity by gender in Latin America: a patent study. Revista Brasileira de Inovacao 13:163–185
Murray F, Graham L (2007) Buying science and selling science: gender differences in the market for commercial science. Ind Corp Chang 16:657–689. https://doi.org/10.1093/icc/dtm021
Portillo S, DeHart-Davis L (2009) Gender and organizational rule abidance. Public Adm Rev, 339–347. https://doi.org/10.1111/j.1540-6210.2008.01978.x
Powell GN (1993) Women and men in management. Sage, Newbury Park
Sevilla A (2020) Gender economics: an assessment. Oxf Rev Econ Policy 36:725–742. https://doi.org/10.1093/oxrep/graa054

Sugimoto CR, Ni C, West JD et al (2015) The academic advantage: gender disparities in patenting. PLoS One 10:1–10. https://doi.org/10.1371/journal.pone.0128000
Whittington KB, Smith-Doerr L (2005) Gender and commercial science: women's patenting in the life sciences. J Technol Transf 30:355–370. https://doi.org/10.1007/s10961-005-2581-5
Whittington K-B, Smith-Doerr L (2008) Women inventors in context: disparities in patenting across academia and industry. Gend Soc 22:194–218. https://doi.org/10.1177/0891243207313928
World Bank (2016) World Development Indicators 2016. World Bank Publications, Washington

Gender, Business and the Law

19

Mareike Fröhlich, Tatjana Jevremović Petrović, and Jelena Lepetić

Contents

Authors are listed in alphabetical order. All authors worked jointly on the content of this chapter, in particular Mareike Fröhlich authored Sect. 19.2 and 19.5, Tatjana Jevremović Petrović wrote Sect. 19.4 and Jelena Lepetić authored Sect. 19.4. All authors jointly have written Sect. 19.1 and 19.6.

M. Fröhlich (✉)
Saarland University, Faculty of Law, Europa-Institut, Saarbrücken, Germany
e-mail: froehlich@europainstitut.de

T. Jevremović Petrović · J. Lepetić
University of Belgrade, Faculty of Law, Civil Law Department, Belgrade, Serbia
e-mail: tatjana.jp@ius.bg.ac.rs; jelena.lepetic@ius.bg.ac.rs

D. Vujadinović et al. (eds.), *Gender-Competent Legal Education*, Springer Textbooks in Law, https://doi.org/10.1007/978-3-031-14360-1_19

Abstract

This chapter deals with gender equality in business law. For some time now, gender diversity has played an important role in the composition of dispute resolution bodies, boards of directors and supervisory boards, forcing the companies concerned to take action. The underlying initiatives of the EU regarding gender quotas in companies, as described in the chapter, are beginning to have an effect, as developments in the banking and financial sector also show. Although the European internal market and its fundamental freedoms do not have a direct impact, the European Union is strongly committed to the protection of gender equality, the economic empowerment of women as well as female entrepreneurship. This chapter explains in detail how forms of enterprises, financing options, education and networking can support women to become entrepreneurs and play a crucial role in business decision-making. Finally, the chapter describes the impact of international trade and investment agreements in this field. Gender mainstreaming now takes place in all recent trade agreements and opens up new opportunities for women. Although investment agreements secure and support foreign investments, which are needed to improve the welfare of states and their citizens, they also could undermine the promotion of gender equality in the investor state. These new changes could jeopardise the investment as national rules will be legally obliged to be changed.

19.1 Introduction

The Gender Equality Strategy 2020–2025 in Europe is setting up its goal to make a progress in gender equality in Europe.[1] Various specific actions in realisation of equal position in society and economy are dealt with in numerous areas of business law. They include a better gender equal business environment, encouragement of gender-smart funding and financing, as well as improvement of balanced business decision-making, in particular in boards of companies. There are many reasons why business law and its numerous areas affect gender equality, but economic consequences seem to be the greatest area impacted. The World Economic Forum stated in its report in 2022 that gender gaps in comparison to the dimension of educational attainment, health, survival and political empowerment, the economic participation and opportunities of women is regressing. According to this report, 151 years would be needed to achieve gender parity in the field of economic participation since women are still underrepresented in the labour market, especially

[1] European Commission, Communication from the Commission to the European Parliament, the Council, the European Economic and Social Committee and the Committee of the Regions, *A Union of Equality: Gender Equality Strategy 2020-2025*, March 2020.

at the seniority level. Moreover, they face inequality in financial terms in regards to wage and income as well as to the access to financial investments like credits, land or other financial products. These are all the resources which are needed to start a business.[2] These various reasons indicate why better business opportunities and encouragement in various aspects of business decision-making and involvement will also improve equality between genders in many other areas outside business law.

We will start our overview with discussing what impact the European internal market has on gender equality. Thereafter, we will address gender equality in business decision making. Gender perspective in relation to decision making has become an important issue in business law. There are two areas regarding decision making in business law in which gender needs to be considered: the selection and appointment of directors and arbitrators. Rules on transparency of gender representation in board of directors and transparency of their remuneration are also important issues from the gender perspective which shall be analysed in the following sections. We will also address gender issues in the context of trade and investment. Finally, this chapter will offer valuable insights into recent incentives in encouragement of gender sensible entrepreneurship.

We will focus on existing, proposed or envisaged legal provisions, which could promote and improve gender equality in business law. Therefore, EU law will be specifically addressed. In addition to this, various bilateral agreements in the context of trade and investments will also be taken into account.

Learning Goals

- Students should learn the role of women and LGBTQIA+ people as well as non-binary persons in the process of decision-making in business law. Besides the status quo of gender equality for the participation in corporate board of directors and board of arbitrators, different solution should be understood by students.
- The awareness of students regarding the involvement of women, LGBTQIA+ and non-binary persons in business law, especially in the banking and financing sector, will be raised. Students will recognize the importance of female entrepreneurship and its influence on the welfare of a state.
- Connecting to this, students should understand the impact of the EU internal market and its market freedoms on the improvement of gender equality in the European Union. In this context, they will also be enabled to analyse how trade and investment agreements will improve gender equality in trade, business and investment.

[2] World Economic Forum (2022).

19.2 Fostering of Gender Diversity in the EU Internal Market

This section aims to shed light on the impact of the EU internal market on gender equality. Although no direct rights arise from the market freedoms, other implications can be derived from the regulations concerning the internal market.

19.2.1 Fundamental Freedoms and Gender Rights

The development of the EU Internal Market (before Common Market) was one of the main goals since the establishment of the European Economic Community in 1957, as it is still stated in Art. 3 TEU, that "the Union shall establish an internal market." This internal market is defined in Art. 26 TFEU:

> 1. The internal market shall comprise an area without internal frontiers in which the free movement of goods, persons, services and capital is ensured in accordance with the provisions of the Treaties.

Said fundamental freedoms guarantee the free movement in all EU Member States, without any frontiers or other restrictions. Mainly, they address the Member States but individuals can also refer to them since they grant individual subjective rights to each single citizen. This direct effect was elaborated by the ECJ and gives the basis for the application of the market freedoms in the case of a cross-border situation.[3]

Art. 3 TEU says that the internal market "shall combat social exclusion and discrimination, and shall promote social justice and protection, equality between women and men, [. . .]". In this context, especially the free movement of persons, meaning the free movement of workers (Art. 45 TFEU) and the freedom of establishment (Art. 49 TFEU) could be of interest since gender-related restrictions could be connected to the person. Despite that, also restrictions for the free movement of goods (Art. 34 TFEU), services (Art. 56 TFEU) as well as capital and payments (Art. 63 TFEU) can show gender aspects. The free movement of workers prohibits the different treatment of workers based on their nationality in the field of employment, remuneration and other conditions of work and employment. The right of establishment should guarantee that foreigners, companies and firms according to Art. 54 TFEU, are treated like nationals when establishing any branch, agency or subsidiary, as well as other forms of primary establishment. The same applies to the performance of services, so that the same rules should be applied in regards to nationals. Keeping this in mind, for the application of all freedoms, a cross-border element needs to be realised without which, the scope of application is not opened.

Nevertheless, the market freedoms are not constructed in such a way that they grant individual rights because of unequal treatment based on gender. The market

[3]Case 26/62, *Van Gend and Loos*, (ECJ 5 February 1963), para. 3, 24 ff.

freedoms are rather aimed at discrimination or restrictions on the basis of different origin or nationality. This is laid down in Art. 18 TFEU:

> Within the scope of application of the Treaties, and without prejudice to any special provisions contained therein, any discrimination on grounds of nationality shall be prohibited.

There has to be either an unequal treatment because of the nationality/origin or a restriction which has the same effect.[4] An unequal treatment between women and men or a discrimination based on gender is not protected by the fundamental freedoms directly, but falls under the scope of the Charta of Fundamental Rights, explicitly Art. 20, 21 and 23.[5] This will be considered in the justification to limit excessive justifications of restrictions on fundamental freedoms and has to be respected by the Member States when they apply the market freedoms, since they are bound by the fundamental rights according to Art. 51 (1) CFR. Consequently, the market freedoms have no direct effect to support gender equality but do indirectly apply the fundamental rights on gender equality in the Charta of Fundamental Rights.

19.2.2 Indirect Influence of the Internal Market

Nevertheless, the internal market provides that all EU citizens (thus including women or non-binary persons) should participate in it to the same extent. In this regard, the EU-wide market access opened new possibilities for women to take part in economic life or in the labour market. This has led to an internal migration (migration from one EU member state to another), which is also taken up by women, especially since there is a greater need for jobs which are traditionally practiced more by women, such as in the healthcare system. The internal migration in 2020 inside the EU amounts to 1.4 million people, where most of the migrants come from Romania, Bulgaria and Italy.[6] This shows the importance of the internal market, with its freedom of workers and service suppliers, for enhancing the employment of women. The fundamental freedoms and its secondary law do not only protect the working individual themself but also the accompanying family members. In this regard, the regulation and directive on the freedom of movement for workers within the Union,[7] as well as the regulation on the coordination of social

[4] Case 8/74, *Dassonville*, (ECJ 11 July 1974).

[5] See Chap. 8 in this volume.

[6] European Union (2021).

[7] Regulation No. 492/2011 on freedom of movement for workers within the Union, OJ L 141 (2011), pp. 1–12; Directive No. 2004/38/EC on the right of citizens of the Union and their family members to move and reside freely within the territory of the Member States, OJ L 158 (2004), p. 77–123.

security systems, have also included family members in the scope of protection. Moreover, there have been various decisions by the European Court of Justice in Luxembourg which have had an indirect effect on the internal market and the promotion of gender equality. There were two types of decisions. The first category is regulating the offer of a product or service. In this context, the decisions rule that producers of goods or service provider need to gender-mainstream their products so that no differences, either in payment or use, for men and women occur. This led the European-wide market to products and services with gender-neutral characteristics. The second category directs to working conditions and the access to the labour market due to regulations with gender characteristics. This hinders the participation in the internal market and make it less attractive. The harmonisation of standards, conditions and regulations in the context of the internal markets asks and allows a gender-mainstreaming, which is not based directly on the protection of the fundamental freedoms but on the Charter of Fundamental Rights, or secondary law, seen in the mentioned directives/regulations.[8] This can be considered as an indirect effect of the EU internal market on gender equality.

Example

Case: Unisex insurance tariffs

One EU directive prohibited the use of sex as a factor in the calculation of insurance tariffs or other related financial services. This directive also provided an exemption in case the use of sex is a determining factor in the assessment of risk, based on relevant and accurate actuarial and statistical data. This was questioned by a Belgium court in a preliminary procedure. The court ruled "such a provision, which enables the Member States in question to maintain without temporal limitations an exemption from the rule of unisex premiums and benefits, works against the achievement of the objective of equal treatment between men and women [...] and is incompatible with Articles 21 and 23 of the Charter [of Fundamental Rights].[9] After this decision all new insurance tariffs were designed in a gender-neutral way. This shows exemplarily how the European Court of Justice successfully influenced the gender-mainstreaming of products and services in all Member States. ◀

[8]Case C-41/17, González Casto v Mutua Umivale, Prosegur Espana SL, INSS, (ECJ 19 September 2018; Case C-347/12, Caisse nationale des prestations familiales v Wiering (ECJ 8 Mai 2014).

[9]Case C-236/09, Association belge des Consommateurs Test-Achats ASBL, Yann van Vugt, Charles Basselier v Conseil des ministres (ECJ 1 March 2011), para. 32.

19.3 Gender and Decision-Making in Business Law

Gender perspective in relation to decision making is important not only in economic but also in the political, cultural and social sphere. Nevertheless, only the economic decision-making, with regards to the board of directors and arbitral tribunals, interferes directly with business law. Namely, the process of selection and appointment of directors (including both private and public sector) and arbitrators need to be addressed from the gender perspective. However, the former raises higher attention of both legislators and academics, especially in the EU. Finally, transparency of gender representation in corporate boards as well as transparency of remuneration of directors are important mechanisms for improving gender equality.

19.3.1 Gender Diversity in Arbitration

Parties may choose whether the dispute will be resolved by one or more arbitrators and how they will be appointed.[10] In general, they are free to choose any person having capacity to act as arbitrator to be their arbitrator.[11] Party autonomy is the main characteristics of selection of arbitral tribunal.[12] The parties alone choose an arbitrator or arbitrators for a particular dispute directly or through a previously determined third party in an *ad hoc* arbitration which they organise while they rely on an arbitral institution in case of institutional arbitration.[13] The principle of party autonomy is limited by the request of independence and impartiality of arbitrators whilst the limitation regarding appointment process is manifested through the rule of equality of parties and their right to a fair trial.[14] Requirement of minimum qualifications and more controversial requirements regarding nationality and religion may be added to previously mentioned limitations.[15] However, none of these requirements is connected to gender.[16] Yet statistics about the appointment of arbitrators, which included gender, became an important indicator for assessment of roll of females in arbitration.

Under-representation of women in international arbitration is a well-known issue in the arbitration community. However, the situation regarding both the number of women arbitrators and the level of transparency of these numbers is improving over years.

---

[10] Lew et al. (2003), pp. 223–224.

[11] Ibid.

[12] Born (2021), p. 1764.

[13] Gaillard and Savage (1999), 451.

[14] Ibid., pp. 464–465.

[15] Born (2021), p. 1783.

[16] Interestingly, requirement of "commercial man" was a part of older forms of arbitration agreements in England. Cf. Born in (2021), p. 1886. ICC Rules uses the term "President" instead of "Chairman" which was used in 1998 version of the Rules. Verbist et al. (2015), p. 15.

Example

For example, women were 6.9% of 160 arbitrators appointed by parties and 19.8% of 162 arbitrator appointees selected by London Court of International Arbitration (LCIA) in 2014 while other institutions, including International Chamber of Commerce (ICC) and German Institution of Arbitration (DIS), did not even maintain such statistics in that time.[17] Later on, gender statistics became available in ICC International Court of Arbitration and DIS, while the proportion of women arbitrators (appointed or confirmed) in ICC arbitral tribunals reached 23.4% in 2020 and exceeded 20% in DIS in 2020.[18] Also, the number of females increased to 33% of all arbitrator appointments in LCIA in 2020, while 45% of all arbitrators were selected by LCIA.[19] ◄

In general, institutions usually lead in selecting female arbitrators when compared with parties and co-arbitrators. This is expected since institutions take into consideration their own reputation on the long run while parties and co-arbitrators think mostly on the actual case when selecting arbitrators or chairs.[20] However, institutions should not only appoint women to meet or improve their statistics on the detriment of party preferences.[21] Both parties and institutions, i.e., anyone who makes an appointment, or a list of potential candidates, should consider equal representation of women in arbitration.[22]

The statistics shows that improvement is still needed. However, the range of potential mechanisms to foster gender equality is quite limited due to the nature of the arbitration. The main reasons to foster gender equality in arbitration are ethical.[23] "Leaking pipe" is an often-mentioned phenomenon associated to under-representation of women in business law, including arbitration, since the number of women entering professional carriers compared to the number of women reaching top levels are much lower.[24] Also, a vicious cycle of appointing experienced arbitrators and women arbitrators lacking experience results in low number of women appointed as arbitrators by parties.[25] In 2015, arbitration community members drew up a pledge in order to increase the number of women appointed as

[17] Greenwood and Baker (2015), pp. 416–417.

[18] See ICC Dispute Resolution 2020 Statistics. 2021. https://iccwbo.org/publication/icc-dispute-resolution-statistics-2020/. Accessed 13 October 2021; DIS statistics. https://www.disarb.org/en/networks-young-talent/gender-champion. Accessed 23 April 2021.

[19] LCIA statistics. https://www.lcia.org/lcia/reports.aspx. Accessed 13 October 2021.

[20] Van Haersolte-Van Hof (2015), p. 648.

[21] Khambata (2015), p. 636.

[22] See Greenwood (2017), p. 104.

[23] Van Haersolte-Van Hof (2015), p. 641.

[24] See Greenwood and Baker (2012), pp. 656–657.

[25] Seraglini (2015), p. 595.

arbitrators.[26] The pledge includes various measures for achieving gender equality in arbitration: fair representation of women in committees, governing bodies and conference panels on arbitration, fair representation in lists of potential arbitrators or tribunal chairs considered by parties and councils, fair representation in rosters and lists of potential candidates for arbitrators maintained by states, arbitral institutions and national committees, appointment of women when possible, the disclosure of gender statistics and finally providing mentorship for women.

As opposed to under-representation of women in corporate boardrooms, quotas are generally not considered a proper mechanism for ensuring fair representation of women in arbitration. Such intrusive mechanisms would diminish the attractiveness of arbitration as a dispute resolution mechanism which is based on party autonomy.[27] However, there are proposals to introduce quota requirements for appointing bodies under the treaties with regards to investment treaty arbitration.[28] In this type of arbitration, 5.63% of appointed arbitrators in 2012 were women in the concluded International Centre for Settlement of Investment Disputes (ICSID) cases, which remained almost the same in 2014.[29] Nevertheless, according to the newest ICSID statistics, women were 31% of appointed arbitrators, conciliators and *ad hoc* committee members in cases registered and administered by ICSID in the fiscal year 2021.[30] Widening the roll of institutions, in a process of appointing the arbitrators by moving it further from parties to institutions, is another intrusive mechanism to enhance equal representation of women in arbitrations.[31] Although it is less intrusive than mandatory quotas, it would have negative effects regarding party autonomy and lead to the decrease of the attractiveness of arbitration.

19.3.2 Gender Diversity in Corporate Boards

Board composition, including nomination and appointment of directors, is a classical topic of corporate governance and company law.

► **Definition** Corporate governance is a part of company (corporate) law which is believed to be best described in the 1992 Cadbury Report as: "the system by which companies are directed and controlled."[32]

---

[26] See more on equal representation in Arbitration Pledge: http://www.arbitrationpledge.com/about-the-pledge. Accessed 23 April 2021.

[27] See also Seraglini (2015), p. 606.

[28] Van Harten (2012), p. 2.

[29] Greenwood and Baker (2015), p. 415.

[30] See ICSID. The ICSID Caseload—statistics. Issue 2021-2. https://icsid.worldbank.org/resources/publications/icsid-caseload-statistics. Accessed 13 October 2021.

[31] See Seraglini (2015), p. 607.

[32] See Hopt (2013), pp. 10, 16; Report of the Committee on the Financial Aspects of Corporate Governance. 1992. https://ecgi.global/code/cadbury-report-financial-aspects-corporate-governance. Accessed 23 April 2021. (Sir Adrian Cadbury was the Chairman of the Committee), para. 2.5

Therefore, board diversity is also a part of corporate governance in relation to board composition. Finally, the issue of remuneration of board members and particularly the disclosure of remuneration policy is also a topic of corporate governance which needs to be analysed from the gender perspective.

In the EU, gender perspective regarding board composition appeared as an important issue of the corporate governance in 2011 when the European Commission issued a "Green paper – EU corporate governance framework", in which it emphasised economic rationales for fostering gender diversity.[33] Furthermore, the European Commission advocated for an increase of transparency of board diversity policy in its "Action plan: European company law and corporate governance – a modern legal framework for more engaged shareholders and sustainable companies".[34]

There are various measures which may be applied for enhancing gender equality in corporate boardrooms. Some of them are proposed outside of the corporate governance framework such as public procurement or state aid rules.[35] After recognising gender under-representation in corporate boardrooms as a relevant issue of business law, there is still an open question of measures in the framework of business law which should be adopted for reaching gender balance. Namely, it is disputed whether the rules should be prescribed by law or whether it is better to leave them in the realm of soft law. Furthermore, it is important to determine which companies and which board positions should be comprehended by these rules.

19.3.2.1 Setting the Scene

The average share of women in boards of the largest listed companies registered in the EU (shares of these companies are traded on the stock exchange) was 8.5% in 2003, 11.9% in 2010, 23.9% in 2016, where it reached 30% on 23 November 2020.[36] The best results were achieved in France where women made up 45.1% of board members in the largest listed companies in 2020. This is in stark contrast to eleven Member States which did not make significant effort for the underrepresented sex.[37] Furthermore, in 2020 only 20.1% of the executives, 32.6 of non-executives (32.2% of non-executive excluding employee representatives) and only 7.4% of

[33] See European Commission. Green paper – the EU corporate governance framework. COM (2011) 164 final. 2011, pp. 5–7.

[34] See European Commission. Communication from the Commission to the European Parliament, the Council, the European Economic and Social Committee and the Committee of the Regions. Action plan: European company law and corporate governance—a modern legal framework for more engaged shareholders and sustainable companies. COM/2012/0740 final. 2012. pp. 5–6. On shareholder activism in general see Lepetić (2018), pp. 106 et seq.

[35] See Szydło (2015), pp. 97, 113–114.

[36] See European Commission. Gender equality on corporate boards, Fact sheet. 2016, pp. 1–2; European Commission. Report on gender equality in the EU. 2021, p. 36; EIGE—Gender statistic database. last updated on 23 November 2020. https://eige.europa.eu/gender-statistics/dgs/browse/wmidm. Accessed 23 April 2021.

[37] European Commission. Report on gender equality in the EU. 2021, p. 36.

CEOs were women.[38] Although the progress is evident, gender balance has still not been reached.

General reasons for gender imbalances in corporate boardrooms are a result of "traditional gender roles, the division of labour, women's and men's educational choices, and women's concentration in few occupational sectors."[39] On the one hand, "double burden" embodied in work and domestic responsibilities is not a specificity relating to the position of directors, while, on the other hand, continuity and mobility needed for leadership position such as membership in the corporate boardrooms, which may be incompatible with maternity leave, are specific limiting factors affecting the opportunities for women to be appointed or reappointed as members of boards.[40]

From the perspective of the company and its shareholders, it is quite doubtful whether gender diversity in company boards should be fostered since there is no clear link between board diversity and corporate performance. Furthermore, if this link exists it is still doubtful whether the effect of the increased diversity on corporate performance is positive or negative.[41] Even if board diversity has positive effects on the performance of the company, the costs relating to delays in decision-making in heterogeneous boards may annul them.[42] Nevertheless, embracing an idea without clear evidence should not become a benchmark in company law, since similar circumstances as those regarding gender diversity followed the concept of independent directors which became widely popular and accepted.[43] Finally, even when gender diversity is fully accepted as an idea, it is not easy to define what level of diversity is desirable in company boards.[44] Therefore, finding the proper solution is challenging.

Bearing in mind all the uncertainties related to the economic rationales, one should turn to other possible reasons for fostering gender balance in corporate boards. Compared to better financial performance of the company and maximisation of shareholders' wealth, improved corporate governance, decision-making as well as better use of human resources, which did not persuade companies to take actions regarding gender imbalance, the fundamental right of equality between men and

[38] EIGE—Gender statistic database.

[39] European Commission. Gender balance in business leadership: a contribution to smart, sustainable and inclusive growth. Communication from the Commission to the European Parliament, the Council, the European Economic and Social Committee and the Committee of the Regions. 2012. COM (2012) 615 final, p. 9.

[40] See Choudhury (2014), p. 540.

[41] See the results of various research presented in Leszczyńska (2018), pp. 41–42.

[42] Szydło (2015), pp. 102–103.

[43] Enriques et al. (2017), p. 96.

[44] McCahery and Vermeulen (2014), p. 138.

women and ethical reasons are more suitable justifications for promoting gender equality in corporate boardrooms.[45]

Actions regarding participation of women in decision-making bodies were recommended back in 1984, when the Council adopted the Recommendation 84/635/EEC on the promotion of positive action for women.[46] Since then however, rules on improving gender balance in corporate boardrooms have still not been adopted in the EU. The adoption of Recommendation 96/694/EC on the balanced participation of women and men in the decision-making process followed in 1996.[47] Both of them exceed the framework of business law, since actions were needed not only in the economic, but also political, social and cultural sphere. Afterwards, "Woman on the board pledge for Europe" was launched in 2011 when listed companies were encouraged to voluntary increase the number of women in their boards.[48] However, only 24 companies signed it after a year.[49] In its resolution on women and business leadership in 2011, the European Parliament urged companies to reach the threshold of 30% membership of women in boards by 2015 and 40% by 2020.[50] Furthermore, the European Parliament recalled for reaching these targets and legislation on quotas in the resolution on equality of women and men in the European Union in 2011.[51] Finally, the European Commission reached the conclusion that the under-representation of women required concrete legal action. The proposal for a Directive on improving the gender balance among non-executive directors of companies listed in stock exchanges and related measures was published in 2012.[52] At the beginning of 2012, women made up only 15% of non-executive

[45] See Choudhury (2014), pp. 516–517; Szydło (2015), pp. 101–102, 104. Moreover, the justification may be social market economy and democracy in the framework of EU law. See Szydło (2014), pp. 168–169.

[46] Council Recommendation 84/635/EEC of 13 December 1984 on the promotion of positive action for women, OJ L 331, 19.12.1984, pp. 34–35.

[47] Council Recommendation 96/694/EC on the balanced participation of women and men in the decision-making process, OJ L 319 (1996), pp. 11–15.

[48] European Commission. Press Release IP/11/242. EU Justice Commissioner Viviane Reding meets European business leaders to push for more women in boardrooms; See more European Commission. Press Release IP/12/1205. Women on Boards: Commission proposes 40% objective. https://ec.europa.eu/commission/presscorner/detail/en/IP_12_1205. Accessed 23 April 2021.

[49] European Commission, Commission staff working document, Impact assessment on costs and benefits of improving the gender balance in the boards of companies listed on stock exchanges, accompanying the document proposal for a Directive of the European Parliament and of the council on improving the gender balance among non-executive directors of companies listed on stock exchanges and related measures. 2012. SWD (2012) 348 final, p. 6 (further referred to as: Impact Assessment, 2012).

[50] European Parliament. Resolution on women and business leadership of 6 July 2011. (2010/2115 (INI)).

[51] European Parliament. Resolution on equality between women and men in the European Union—2011 of 13 March 2012. (2011/2244(INI)).

[52] Proposal for a Directive of the European Parliament and of the Council on improving the gender balance among non-executive directors of companies listed in stock exchanges and related measures. COM (2012) 614 final, 2012/0299 (COD). 2012.

board members and on average 13.7% of board members in largest listed companies in Member States.[53] Nevertheless, the national parliaments of five Member States and one of the two chambers of the parliament of one more Member State declared that the proposal for Directive did not comply with the principle of subsidiarity.[54] Although the Directive Proposal was redrafted later on, its destiny is still uncertain.[55]

19.3.2.2 Possible Solutions

Measures undertaken to improve gender balance may be divided according to the level of their intrusion to company law. One of the least intrusive and most popular measures is creating the pool of candidates of under-represented gender, which may facilitate the selection of board members of under-represented gender in general. Although this practice may not prevent the so-called "gender matching heuristic"—matching the gender of departing and incoming member of the board (which is, for example, present in the board of directors in public companies in the U.S.), it will increase the probability of the selection of women.[56] Moreover, this may prevent the appointment of the same candidates in various companies. This phenomenon, recognised as the result of imposing mandatory quotas, is called the "golden skirts".[57] Moreover, one interesting study found that directors appointed their family members, since the number of directors with the same surname increased as a result of quota legislation in Norway.[58] Nevertheless, in order to widen the pool, the candidates who do not have experience in relation to corporate boardrooms should also be included.[59] Promoting gender equality in corporate boards by the EU institutions, programmes of training and mentoring of candidates as well as rewarding companies with best results are additional helpful mechanisms for reaching gender equality in corporate boardrooms.[60] More intrusive mechanisms are establishing the policy on diversity in boardrooms and disclosure of statistics regarding the diversity, which should only be imposed on listed companies.[61] Also, rules regarding the transparency of the process of selection of candidates and disclosure of information related to gender representation are important measures for fostering gender balanced representation in boards of directors. Selection of board

---

[53] See the 2012 Directive Proposal, recital 10.

[54] See the Report of the Presidency to Permanent Representatives Committee/Council. 9496/17, 2012/0299 (COD). 2017, p. 2.

[55] See redrafted proposal for a Directive on improving the gender balance among directors of companies listed on stock exchanges, and related measures, annexed to Report of the Presidency to Permanent Representatives Committee/Council. 9496/17, 2012/0299 (COD). 2017.

[56] See Tinsley et al. (2017), pp. 161, 181, 183.

[57] See Choudhury (2014), p. 535.

[58] Lee (2013), p. 1490.

[59] This was one of the recommendations of Lord Davies of Abersoch who reviewed the situation of female representation on boards upon request of UK government and made 10 recommendation in 2011. See Choudhury (2014), pp. 514–515.

[60] See Szydło (2015), pp. 113–114.

[61] Those are also recommendations given by Lord Davies. See Choudhury (2014), p. 515.

members is a question of company law which often leaves freedom to companies to regulate it by providing only default rules.[62] Lack of transparency has a negative effect not only on the candidates for board but also on investors who may be left without enough information to make decisions.[63] Finally, the most intrusive measures are so-called quotas. However, this measure is widely accepted for enhancing gender equality in corporate boards across Europe.

Quotas may be mandatory or voluntary. On the one hand, quotas are mandatory when non-compliance leads to sanctions, while on the other hand they are voluntary when failing to meet quota requirements is not followed by sanctions. While voluntary quotas may be imposed by corporate governance codes and principles (soft law), mandatory quotas may be prescribed only by law.

Example

1. The state recognised for its quota regulation and followed by others in Europe is Norway. Norwegian Law on gender balance requiring 40% of each sex on boards of public limited liability companies, state-owned and inter-municipal companies was adopted back in 2003.[64] Sanctions for non-compliance with mandatory quotas requirement may be forced liquidation as the most severe sanction and de-listing, voidance of the nomination, fines, etc.
2. The impact of gender equality at the corporate level is well evidenced by the legislative interventions that have profoundly affected corporate governance in Italy since 2011, similar to other EU countries.[65] Due to the law on the12th July 2011, Italy introduced significant changes to the Italian Consolidated Text of the provisions on financial intermediation (*breviter*, hereinafter, t.u.f.), in order to protect gender equality in access to the administrative and control bodies of listed companies in regulated markets and public companies.[66] Italy,

[62] Impact Assessment, 2012, p. 33.

[63] Explanatory memorandum of the proposal for a Directive of the European Parliament and of the Council on improving the gender balance among non-executive directors of companies listed in stock exchanges and related measures. COM(2012) 614 final, 2012/0299 (COD). 2012, p. 3 (further referred to as: Explanatory memorandum, 2012).

[64] See Seierstad and Huse (2017), p. 25; Senden and Visser (2013), p. 23.

[65] The following example of Italian legislation is a contribution by Dr. Carlo Petta, professor of business and law at LUMSA University in Parlemo.

[66] In 2011 in Italy the percentage ratio between men and women in top management was, respectively, 93 and 7, but also in other European countries the situation was similar. On the verge, Morera (2015), p. 531, reports that the European average stood at a ratio of 88 to 12, recording data that are much more favorable to gender balance in some countries such as Sweden. For an overall assessment of the impact of the relevant measures see European Commission. Staff Working Document. 2019, 2019 Report on equality between women and men in the EU, https://data.consilium.europa.eu/doc/document/ST-7263-2019-INIT/en/pdf. Accessed 23 April 2021. The accompanying report to the law that proposal led to law no. 120 of 2011 underlined the need to provide a corrective to the situation of chronic imbalance in the representation of genders in the top positions of listed companies since—it can be read in the same report—the presence of both genders

with Art. 147-ter, paragraph 1-ter, t.u.f. (rule governing the election and composition of the board of directors) and Art. 148, paragraph 1-bis, t.u.f. (on the composition of the supervisory bodies), has imposed the obligation for companies with listed shares and for those under public control to introduce specific clauses in the respective statutes regarding the composition of both the administrative and control bodies, such as to ensure the presence—in the original version of the provisions—of at least one third of the members belonging to the less represented gender. As can be seen immediately, the prescription refers in a neutral way to any hypothesis of under-representation related to gender and concerns both the board of directors and the supervisory body. In the original version of the provision, the reserved quota was equal to one third and had to be respected for at least three consecutive mandates: it was believed that the 9-year period was appropriate to try to achieve the goal of gender balance that was set for us with the legislation in question. Recent amendments to the t.u.f. between 2019 and 2020, however, affected both of these parameters, reshaping the minimum reserved quota from one third to two fifths and extending the provisional time regime (which would otherwise have expired in 2022) of this allocation criterion to six mandates. The extension was deemed necessary, because, in the face of some positive results resulting from the fulfilment of these obligations, it was not possible to obtain the sort of "automatism" desired in the percentage of representativeness between genders. This would have made it possible to eliminate the need for the mandatory percentage of subjects of different genders present in the companies concerned. The control over compliance with the reserve quotas is delegated to the Italian Financial Market Supervisory Authority (Consob) which, in the event of a violation, can warn the company concerned to adapt to the allocation criterion within 4 months. In the event of non-compliance, Consob applies an administrative sanction from € 100,000.00 to € 1,000,000.00 (in the case of the board of directors) or from € 20,000.00 to € 200,000.00 (in the case of the board of statutory auditors), setting a new fulfilment deadline of 3 months. In the event of further non-compliance, the members elected in the body would lose their office and would need to be replaced. Replacement would be on the basis of the lists previously formed by the company itself for the cases of replacement of the members during the term of office, given that these lists must also comply with the provisions on gender quotas. The impact of these measures in Italy has been particularly positive. The proportion of women on boards of the largest publicly listed companies in Italy has grown from 4.5% in 2010 to 38.4% in 2020. ◀

within companies is a value to be to defend and to concretize, because it allows the achievement of balance by exploiting the complementarity of male and female sensibilities.

19.3.2.3 Type of Companies and Board Positions

Rules on the structure of the organs and management of companies are not harmonised by EU company law. Nevertheless, the level of harmonisation regarding rules on public limited liability companies is the highest. Binding rules regarding gender interfere with company law and internal structures of companies. Therefore, the opposition to binding rules in the EU must be expected. It is generally accepted that listed companies should be obliged by mandatory rules since they are most visible and economically powerful, with a large number of employees, which may increase general awareness of the problem of under-representation of women in corporate boards. Apart from listing, other criteria such as market capitalisation and number of employees are also considered acceptable when deciding which companies should be obliged by special requirements.[67] Still, not all listed companies should be obliged by mandatory quotas regulation. Small and medium listed companies should be excluded, as well as large but not listed companies, not only because of the interference with freedom to conduct business but also due to a possible increase of costs regarding recruiting directors (who are often family members in SMEs), as well as costs following disclosure.[68]

Boards may be one-tier or two-tier boards depending on whether the supervision and management functions are divided.[69] Also, there are three groups of directors—executive, non-executive, as well as non-executive and independent.[70] Gender diversity should be improved regardless of the type of implemented board system. Nevertheless, non-executive board positions are considered more suitable for greater interference compared to executive directors, probably because a company's performance is less dependent on these directors.

Besides listed companies, state-owned enterprises are also recognised as being suitable for setting an example on improving gender equality. The state should contribute to board diversity in state-owned enterprises and establish a transparent board nomination process according to 2015 OECD Guidelines on corporate governance of state-owned enterprises.[71] Also, board member qualifications and the selection process including board diversity policy should be reported.[72] Contributing to board diversity in state-owned enterprises may be manifested as setting targets or quotas for women in senior management, maintaining a database of qualified candidates as well as disclosure measures.[73]

[67] Impact assessment, 2012, p. 35.

[68] Ibid., pp. 35–36.

[69] See Grundmann (2012), p. 255.

[70] See ibid., pp. 256–257.

[71] OECD Guidelines on corporate governance of state-owned enterprises. 2015, p. 20, Guideline F.2.

[72] Ibid., p. 24, Guideline A.5.

[73] Ibid., pp. 39–40.

19.3.2.4 EU Directive Proposal

In the newest report on gender equality, the Commission announced that it is still committed to its proposal from 2012 whereas the adoption of that proposal is on its agenda in the Gender Equality Strategy 2020–2025.[74] The 2012 EU Directive Proposal provides for the objectives in relation to non-executive directors in listed companies excluding small and medium companies. If the number of non-executive positions in boards of these companies held by under-represented sex (the 2012 EU Directive Proposal refers to under-represented sex and not gender) is less than 40%, the said percentage should be attained by the beginning of 2020 or in case of public undertakings, by the beginning of 2018 through the use of comparative analysis of qualifications of candidates and pre-established clear and neutral criteria.[75] Measures prescribed by the Directive Proposal comprehend administrative, management and supervisory boards. They should be imposed regardless of whether the system of board structure is a one-tier, two-tier or mixed and whether the companies may choose the preferred model. Two exceptions from the requirements are permitted if a Member State provides for the following: firstly if under-represented sex holds less than 10% of workforce in the listed company and secondly if listed companies can show that at least one third of all director positions (executive and non-executive) is held by under-represented sex.

Furthermore, listed companies should undertake individual commitments to ensure gender-balanced representation among executive directors.[76] Finally, companies shall provide information regarding gender representation and measures undertaken to achieve required objectives to the national authorities and publish them on their websites. When requirements imposed by the Directive Proposal or by the companies themselves are not met, reasons for not reaching the objectives, individual commitments and the description of measures which the company adopted or plans to adopt should also be disclosed. Examples of possible sanctions for breach of the national rules adopted in accordance with the Directive Proposal are administrative fines and nullity or annulment declared by the judicial body of the appointment, or the election of a non-executive director.[77] Rules of the proposal are minimum harmonisation rules which means that Member States may adopt more favourable measures for under-represented sex but cannot exceed the limits of unjustified discrimination or hindering the functioning of the internal market.[78]

In the selection process, priority is given to the candidate of under-represented sex if that candidate is equally qualified as the candidate of the other sex regarding

---

[74] European Commission. Report on gender equality in the EU. 2021, p. 40; European Commission. Communication from the Commission to the European Parliament, the Council, the European Economic and Social Committee and the Committee of the Regions. A union of Equality: Gender Equality Strategy 2020–2025. 2020, COM (2020) 152 final, p. 13.

[75] See the 2012 EU Directive Proposal, art. 4 (1).

[76] See the 2012 EU Directive Proposal, art. 5 (1).

[77] See the 2012 EU Directive Proposal, art. 6 (2).

[78] See the 2012 EU Directive Proposal, art. 7.

suitability, competence and professional performance, with the exception of when the balance is tilted in favour of the other candidate after the objective assessment of all criteria specific to individual candidates.[79] Unsuccessful candidates may request the disclosure of qualification criteria, the objective comparative assessment and consideration tilting the balance in favour of the selected candidate. Burden of proof that the rule on priority is not breached lies with the company when unsuccessful candidate establishes facts from which it may be presumed that the candidate of the under-represented sex was equally qualified as the appointed one.[80]

Quotas in the EU Directive Proposal are positive measures or positive action[81] which favours "access by members of certain categories of people, in this particular case, women, to rights which they are guaranteed, to the same extent as members of other categories, in this particular case, men."[82] Positive measures have to apply to the underrepresented sex though candidates need to be equally qualified.[83] The quota rule in the narrower meaning refers to the requirement to meet certain percentage of seats in the board until the expiry of the deadline regardless of the qualification.[84] Therefore, the term quota is not completely adequate when referring to the measures prescribed by the 2012 Directive Proposal, which sets requirement of equal qualification of candidates and does not impose a clear sanction for non-compliance with the quota requirement.[85] The 2012 Directive Proposal sets rules regarding recruiting and preferential treatment procedure and not the obligation to meet quotas followed by sanctions in case of non-compliance.[86] Namely, the sanction does not refer to not meeting quotas but to the situations when the criteria for attaining quotas are not met.[87] For example, it is not possible to meet quota requirements when candidates of under-represented sex do not apply for the position or when they are not equally qualified as the candidate of other sex. Finally, this measure is temporal.[88]

Positive action in the 2012 Directive Proposal is based on Article 157(3) TFEU regarding measures to ensure equal opportunities and equal treatment of men and women in employment and occupation.[89] Since the occupation has broader meaning than employment, non-executive members of the board may be included in that

[79] See the 2012 EU Directive Proposal, art. 4 (3).

[80] See the 2012 EU Directive Proposal, art. 4 (5).

[81] Masselot and Maymont (2014), p. 7; Benito Sánchez (2015), p. 16.

[82] Vasiljević and Sunko (2017), p. 29.

[83] Also, they should not be automatic but should include saving clause and be proportional. Masselot and Maymont (2014), p. 9.

[84] Ibid., p. 9.

[85] Havelková (2018), p. 12.

[86] Senden and Visser (2013), p. 33.

[87] Masselot and Maymont (2014), p. 10. However, others believe that the 2012 Directive Proposal provides for compulsory quotas. See Szydło (2015), p. 110.

[88] Masselot and Maymont (2014), p. 20.

[89] See the 2012 EU Directive Proposal, recital 1.

framework.[90] However, it is disputed whether the director should be considered as a worker. According to the CJEU *Danosa* decision, executive board members may be considered workers, yet the situation is less clear regarding non-executive members of the board.[91]

Measures provided in the Directive Proposal restrict freedom to conduct business, right to property as well as a company's freedom of contract regarding the other contractual party.[92] The restrictions are justified and in accordance with the principle of proportionality.[93] Nevertheless, there are arguments that quotas, if they are mandatory, are not compatible with the principle of proportionality.[94] Moreover, there are arguments that measures proposed in the 2012 Directive Proposal are not in accordance with the principle of subsidiarity since there was not enough time to assess whether national measures were effective and whether EU action is therefore needed.[95]

19.3.2.5 Transparency on Gender Representation in Board of Directors

Generally, financial information and reports related to that information are a natural part of interests of company law since directors are responsible for drafting and publishing them. Besides material, non-financial information may also be included in the management report. Although information regarding diversity policy is non-financial, it is a corporate governance issue in the EU law which must be included in the corporate governance statement of listed companies.[96] The corporate governance statement is a section of the management report.[97] This statement should contain a description of diversity policy regarding gender, amongst others, which is applied in relation to administrative, management and supervisory bodies. It should also contain the objectives of that policy, information regarding its implementation and results in the reporting period. Finally, when the policy is not applied, the statement should provide an explanation. The reason for including the diversity

[90] See Havelková (2018), pp. 19–20.

[91] See Masselot and Maymont (2014), p. 9; Case C-232/09, *Dita Danosa v LKB Līzings SIA* (ECJ 11 November 2010), para. 51. The decision leaves space to consider non-executive directors to be workers as well since they may be removed without justification and they receive remuneration for their services. Senden and Visser (2013), p. 29.

[92] See Explanatory memorandum. 2012, p. 6. See O'Connor (2015), pp. 144–150.

[93] See Impact assessment, 2012, 30.

[94] See Szydło (2015), pp. 97, 110.

[95] Ibid., p. 112.

[96] See Directive 2013/34/EU of the European Parliament and of the Council of 26 June 2013 on the annual financial statements, consolidated financial statements and related reports of certain types of undertakings, amending Directive 2006/43/EC of the European Parliament and of the Council and repealing Council Directives 78/660/EEC and 83/349/EEC. OJ L 182 (2013), pp. 19–76, art. 20 (1) (g) after being amended by Directive 2014/95/EU of the European Parliament and of the Council of 22 October 2014 amending Directive 2013/34/EU as regards disclosure of non-financial and diversity information by certain large undertakings and groups. OJ L 330 (2014), pp. 1–9.

[97] See possible exceptions in Directive 2013/34/EU, art. 20 (2).

policy among the disclosure requirements is to enable the so-called "group think phenomenon."[98] Furthermore, action taken to ensure gender equality in general may be mentioned in a non-financial statement which must be included in management reports of large undertakings which are public-interest entities with an average number of 500 employees.[99]

19.3.2.6 Transparency on Remuneration of Directors

Remuneration of directors in company law is usually analysed through the lens of resolving conflict of interests and protection of shareholders regardless of the gender perspective. For example, neither of the EU recommendations regarding remuneration of directors includes it.[100] Nevertheless, some general rules on transparency regarding remuneration of directors are significant from that perspective.

Fostering shareholder activism includes the shareholder right in listed companies to vote on the remuneration policy presupposing that this policy needs to be drawn up.[101] Both remuneration policy and the remuneration report, which provides for an overview of remuneration, should be publicly available on the company's website free of charge.[102] Therefore, company law creates a framework of shareholder protection regardless of the gender of directors entitled to remuneration. Yet, rules on transparency of remuneration policy and reports may have positive effects and improve gender equality. Keeping in mind that companies want to pay the best managers above average, the disclosure of directors' remuneration may result in its increase—so-called ratcheting effect.[103] Although this effect of transparency is considered negative in business law in general, it may be desirable from the gender perspective due to the increase of remuneration of directors of the otherwise underpaid gender. The disclosure of remuneration of directors is generally beneficial since companies will not risk undermining their reputation by disclosure of information that they are paying directors of under-represented gender less than the directors of other gender.

---

[98] See Directive 2014/95/EU, recital 18.

[99] See Directive 2014/95/EU, recital 7 and possible exceptions in Directive 2013/34/EU, art. 19a (1).

[100] See Commission Recommendation 2004/913/EC fostering an appropriate regime for the remuneration of directors of listed companies. OJ L 385 (2004), pp. 55–59; Commission Recommendation 2005/162/EC on the role of non-executive or supervisory directors of listed companies and on the committees of the (supervisory) board. OJ L 52 (2005), pp. 51–63; Commission Recommendation 2009/385/EC complementing Recommendations 2004/913/EC and 2005/162/EC as regards the regime for the remuneration of directors of listed companies. OJ L 120 (2009), pp. 28–31; Commission Recommendation 2009/384/EC on remuneration policies in the financial services sector. OJ L 129 (2009), pp. 22–27.

[101] Directive (EU) 2017/828 of the European Parliament and of the Council of 17 May 2017 amending Directive 2007/36/EC as regards the encouragement of long-term shareholder engagement. OJ L 132 (2017), pp. 1–25, art. 9a (1).

[102] See Directive (EU) 2017/828, Art. 9a (7) and 9b (5).

[103] See Ferrarini and Ungureanu (2020), p. 345; Bahar (2005), p. 41; Radović (2011), pp. 417–418.

Finally, the recently published new proposal for an EU Directive enhancing the equal pay through pay transparency and enforcement mechanisms is another part of the Commission's approach towards gender equality.[104] Since this proposal applies to workers, it falls within the framework of labour law, which is also important for directors who, as mentioned before, may be considered as workers.

19.4 Involvement of Women in Business Law

Keeping the above written in mind, in this part we will focus on two further areas of business law, where gender issues can be of extreme importance. These include particular insights on gender equality in banking and insurance law. We will also consider various aspects of female entrepreneurship and stress out the significance and affirmative action of the EU in this area. We will see that many important activities in this area, intended for better gender equal business environment, encouragement of gender-smart funding and financing can make a strong impact on the Gender Equality Strategy of the EU and beyond.

19.4.1 Banking and Insurance Law

Although there are many interesting points to address gender issues from the banking and insurance law perspective, we will focus on the two most important ones. Firstly, the issue of improving the gender-balance in decision-making positions, including on company boards and in politics, stays topical and is of particular importance in financial institutions. The second issue, which is of utmost importance to private parties in this area of law is based on the fundamental principle of equality between men and women and is, therefore, a focal point in equal treatment in supply and provision of financial services.

19.4.1.1 Representation of Women in Banks and Other Financial Institutions

In this section we will make a connection to the issue of gender diversity in the board of directors and other bodies of companies in various financial institutions, in particular in the banking and insurance sector. It is reported that gender diversity in boards of directors or senior executives could lead to enhanced business results,[105]

[104] Proposal for a Directive of the European Parliament and of the Council to strengthen the application of the principle of equal pay for equal work or work of equal value between men and women through pay transparency and enforcement mechanisms. 2021. COM (2021) 93 final 2021/0050 (COD), p. 3.

[105] In one of the first empirical studies on the influence of board diversity (including not only women, but also national minorities) to company's business performance, performed by Cartes, Simkins and Simpson, it was examined whether board diversity is associated with improved financial value of the firm. Their findings are that there is a significant positive relationship between gender diversity on the board of directors and firm value. See Carter et al. (2003), pp. 33–53.

including superior financial performance and better corporate governance. For further information on that point, refer to Sect. 19.3.2. Nevertheless, there are additional motives and drives to introduce gender diversity on boards of financial institutions. According to first specific theoretical researches on this issue, it has been concluded that gender diversity on boards of financial institutions could also improve risk management oversight, which is of particular importance in financial institutions.[106] This conclusion relies on behavioural economic studies, according to which women tend to be more conservative in risk-taking than man. It is not only heterogeneity, but experience, talents, perspectives and background that can lead women to a better decision-making.[107] Risk identification and adjustment to the existing risks could be improved with more cautious approach with female board members, tending to hold stricter levels of capital to risks evaluated. Also, female involvement in the boards with a tendency of stronger monitoring could improve risk oversight.[108] This could lead to a conclusion that gender diversity may reduce bank risk-taking and ultimately reduce financial distress and improve its performance.[109]

One of the empirical studies, undertaken in the past, was performed on the sample of 461 large banks from OECD countries and showed that women's participation in boardrooms had a positive impact on return equity and operation income ratio, while their participation had negative effect in risk management.[110] Nevertheless, further empirical studies could improve and be valuable to back-up these conclusions and influence prospective legal provisions on these matters.[111]

The current situation shows an inadequate proportion of women in boards of directors of banks and other financial institutions.

Example

The Deloitte Centre for Financial Services points out that in 2019, the proportion of women in leadership roles within financial services firms was 21.9%. ◀

The most important legal basis for female inclusion and fairer gender balance (including third gender) on boards of companies was until recently being covered by anti-discriminatory laws, particularly included in labour law.[112] Such formal equality in boards of financial institutions proved to not be satisfactory and was further

[106] Johnson (2017), pp. 327–376.

[107] Ibid., pp. 354–355.

[108] Ibid., pp. 360–362.

[109] Cardillo et al. (2021).

[110] Gulamhussen and Santos (2010).

[111] On the positive impact of gender diversity to better monitoring of bank managers and lower agency costs see recent studies which particularly focus on the impact of gender diversity in European bank boards on the probability and size of public bailouts. Cardillo et al. (2021).

[112] It should be mentioned that first academic studies on the topic were dealing mostly with employment inequality within banks and other financial institutions, but were also pointing to the inequality of appointment at the managerial level. See, as an example, Egan (1982), pp. 20–31.

promoted by affirmative action and specific legislation. Steps forward were made in some jurisdictions, and usually included public disclosure on diversity issues. Further, there are jurisdictions involving financial institutions, in particularly in Europe (such Norway, followed by EU Member States Belgium, France, Italy, Germany, Austria and Portugal), as well as the US, where California was the first state to include obligatory female representation, that are introducing obligatory gender diversity in companies in general.[113] An additional "soft law" approach is fostering gender balance through self-regulation and voluntary devotion to these social goals. It is, nevertheless, important to include all benefits and evaluate possible negative side effects which are specifically related to financial institutions to more general efforts, in particularly those of the European Commission to further improve gender balance on corporate boards.

19.4.1.2 Financial Services: Equal Treatment

Our next focus in this section lies on the supply and provision of financial services. It was already discussed in Sect. 19.2 that the internal market provides that all EU citizens (thus also women or the third gender) should participate in it to the same extent. It was also mentioned that principles of non-discrimination and equal treatment on the internal market also apply to financial services. Therefore, access to and supply of financial services must be considered starting from the principle of equal treatment between men and women.

This issue was expressly covered by the EU Council Directive 2004/113/EC of 13 December 2004 implementing the principle of equal treatment between men and women in the access to and supply of goods and services.[114] The directive is based on the fundamental principle of equality between men and women and has for its task the implementation of this principle in various areas, in particular in the access to and supply of goods and services. Its application is related to both direct and indirect discrimination to persons providing goods and services, available to the public and offered outside the area of private and family life. Its provisions provide for minimum standards and requirements that offer the possibility to Member States to improve and provide for more favourable provisions in relation to equal treatment in this field, including affirmative action.

Financial services fall within the scope of this directive and are of the utmost importance in the banking and insurance sector. Provisions of this directive, seen in the insurance sector, are applicable to various insurances and pensions which are private, voluntary and separate from the employment relationship, while employment and occupation fall under specific anti-discrimination provisions.[115]

---

[113] For further insight see Deloitte Centre for Financial Services (2019); as well as EIGE (2020).

[114] Council Directive 2004/113/EC of 13 December 2004 implementing the principle of equal treatment between men and women in the access to and supply of goods and services. OJ L 373 (2004), pp. 37–43.

[115] See recital 15 and art. 3 para. 4 of Directive 2004/113/EC.

Starting from the fundamental principle of equal treatment, Directive 2004/113/EC prevents difference in treatment based on the person's sex while selecting a contractual partner. Differences in treatment may be justified only by a legitimate aim, when means are appropriate and necessary, including a promotion of gender equality. Therefore, in the provision of banking and insurance services it is prohibited to discriminate contractual partners on the basis of their sex. It is particularly stressed that less favourable treatment of women based on pregnancy and maternity must be considered as a form of direct discrimination.[116] Also, in the insurance sector all costs related to risks of pregnancy and maternity must not be attributed to one sex only and must not result in differences between individual premiums and benefits.

Particular attention was paid to the use of actuarial factors in the insurance sector. It is specifically underlined that the use of actuarial factors, related to sex in all new contracts, should not result in differences when calculating premiums and benefits of consumers of insurance and other related financial services. At the time of the adoption of the directive, differences between sex in calculating insurance premiums were widespread, and it was left to the Member States to introduce a transitional period in their abolition, at the latest by the 21st of December 2007.

The initial wording of the directive allowed derogation from this provision by allowing that risk assessment may be based on differences between sexes. This derogation was permitted only if justified by actuarial and statistical data on which differences were based, but they also were to be compiled, regularly updated and published.[117] At that time, risk assessment based on differences between sexes was particularly used by insurers in life insurances. As already mentioned in Sect. 19.2.2, this derogation was found to be invalid in the Court of Justice of the EU ruling on the Test-Achats (C-236/09).[118] It was found that such provision "[. . .]works against the achievement of the objective of equal treatment between men and women . . . and is incompatible with Articles 21 and 23 of the Charter (of Fundamental Rights)".[119] It was therefore decided that starting from 21 December 2012 in all new agreements in the insurance sector *unisex tariff* must be applied without further derogations. After this ruling, special guidelines on the application of Council Directive 2004/113/EC to insurance were adopted.[120] They specified that gender status or information cannot be used on an individual level, but could be used in internal pricing and reserving, reinsurance pricing and for marketing and advertising purposes. Also, even though gender cannot be a basis for a different insurance policy, other risk factors (health status, family history) connected to physiological differences between

[116] See recital 20 and art. 4 of Directive 2004/113/EC.

[117] Art. 5 of Directive 2004/113/EC.

[118] Case (C-236/09), *Test-Achats* (ECJ March 2011).

[119] Ibid., para. 32.

[120] European Commission. Guidelines on the application of Council Directive 2004/113/EC to insurance, in the light of the judgment of the Court of Justice of the European Union in Case C-236/09 (Test-Achats). OJ C 11 (2012), pp. 1–11.

men and women can be taken into account. Finally, unisex tariff involves not only cases of direct but also indirect discrimination.

Example

According to the guidelines, "A woman with a family history of breast cancer will generally pay and additional risk premium compared to a woman who has no such family history, because it is a key factor for a woman's risk of developing this disease. There is however no reason to apply such additional premium to a man with the same family history, because the probability that he will suffer from breast cancer is very low."[121] ◀

19.4.2 Regulatory Framework for Female Entrepreneurship

Women's entrepreneurship is an important topic that is increasingly being discussed. Encouraging entrepreneurship in general, as well as some of its specific forms, has an extremely important place both at the national and at the supranational level.[122]

The last decades have been especially marked by the awareness that particular attention needs to be paid to some specific forms of entrepreneurship, which shows not only great economic potential but also has great social significance. Women's entrepreneurship is an example of such a special form of entrepreneurship. It is not only important for economic growth and development, but also has a particular significance for strengthening and recognizing the social position of women.

In this part we, therefore, intend to present an overview of the legal framework for promotion and support of female entrepreneurship which was addressed by the EU and drawn to its particular attention. The most important part of the EU legal framework for promotion and support of female entrepreneurship is based on the Small Business Act for Europe and Entrepreneurship 2020 Action Plan. As we will see further on, the EU action also includes various important support mechanisms. The most important one includes the launching of the Europe-wide online platform WEgate, designed to unite all initiatives supporting women entrepreneurship. Also, the Enterprise Europe Network (EEN) is a women entrepreneurship group on Facebook, gathering partner organisations and various interested parties from EU Member states. Its main task also is to connect women entrepreneurs to business and support networks and activities and to offer services in access to market, funding or cooperation. Finally, encouragement of business angels and other funding

[121] European Commission. Guidelines on the application of Council Directive 2004/113/EC to insurance, in the light of the judgment of the Court of Justice of the European Union in Case C-236/09 (Test-Achats). OJ C 11 (2012), pp. 1–11.

[122] Some parts in this section are taken from research on the legal framework of female entrepreneurship by Jevremović Petrović (2019), pp. 36–57.

possibilities stay in focus to promote women entrepreneurship. This issue was a particularly important policy goal of the EU and forms a part of the InvestEU project.

The EU formed the most important legal framework by adopting acts and action plans aimed at encouraging entrepreneurship in general and especially within its various specific forms, such as crafts, micro-entrepreneurial ventures, family, and women's entrepreneurship. To that end, the European Commission adopted the "Small Business Act" for Europe,[123] as well as the Entrepreneurship 2020 Action Plan.[124]

To better assess the position of women in entrepreneurship, the European Commission has undertaken empirical research and made a study that provides statistical data on women's entrepreneurship. This study includes not only the number of women entrepreneurs and their type, but also the sector in which predominant activities are carried out, age groups and educational level.[125] In addition to this, an evaluation was carried out to explore existing and encourage future promotion of women entrepreneurship based on innovation and invention.[126] Not only the ambition to carry out entrepreneurial activity, but particularly women's intellectual potential is considered to be an important contribution to competitiveness in Europe. Yet so far it has not been sufficiently used.[127] This is particularly true for women innovators or inventors who want to set up a business in the field of science and technology.

However, of all the results of the research conducted so far, the concrete steps taken by the EU and its Member states are just the beginning. It is clear that the most important task so far has been to identify the specific problems women's entrepreneurship is facing, so that mechanisms for their solution can be found.[128]

19.4.2.1 General Issues and Problems Related to Women Entrepreneurship

According to official EU statistical data, women constitute 52% of the total population, of which only a third of them in the EU are self-employed or decided to start an entrepreneurial activity.[129] According to statistical data collected in 37 European

[123] Commission of the European Communities, Communication from the Commission to the Council, the European Parliament, the European Economic and Social Committee and the Committee of the Regions. "Think Small First". A "Small Business Act" for Europe. SEC(2008) 2101, SEC(2008) 2102. 2008. COM(2008) 394 final.

[124] Communication from the Commission to the European Parliament, the Council, The European Economic and Social Committee and the Committee of the regions. Entrepreneurship 2020 Action Plan: Reigniting the entrepreneurial spirit in Europe. COM/2012/0795 final.

[125] European Commission, Directorate-General for Enterprise and Industry. Statistical Data on Women Entrepreneurs in Europe. 2014, p. 7.

[126] DG Enterprise and European Commission. Evaluation on policy: Promotion of Women Innovators and Entrepreneurship, final report.

[127] Ibid., pp. 1–2.

[128] Ibid., p. 7.

[129] Entrepreneurship 2020 Action Plan, p. 22.

countries, in 2012 women accounted for only 29% of the total number of entrepreneurs in Europe.[130] Also, only 5–15% of high-tech business ventures in the EU were owned by women.[131] This disparity is even more significant when compared to the fact that according to statistical indicators, the level of education of women in many European countries is usually higher than men.

Hence, although women constitute half of the population, women entrepreneurs—considered to be those who actively on their own or with others participate in a business venture—are in the minority.[132] Furthermore, even when they dare to take this step, they earn less, and their business venture does not develop enough, remaining mostly at the small or medium level. Areas in which women perform entrepreneurial activities usually include provision of services, in particular in the medical or educational sector. Not only are these services less paid than other activities, but they are also the areas where the potential for improvement, innovation and development is low. While the chances of a business venture failing remain high and remain mostly affected by bad market conditions.

Considering why and how to single out women's entrepreneurship has so far been the task of psychologists, and more recently of economists.[133] While for now the priority of the research has been encouraging, the decision to undertake a business venture, the second segment—whether and to what extent gender differences affect business results, has not been noticeable so far.[134]

According to recent research results, women's entrepreneurship is facing numerous obstacles, although some of them are equally present in all forms of entrepreneurship, irrespective of the sex. Typical barriers to entrepreneurship include regulatory and administrative constraints, low education levels, sparse trainings, and the lack of information. Nevertheless, a common barrier to a successful business venture is (adequate) funding. This is considered to be the major reason for the relatively low percentage of potential entrepreneurship, as only 37% of the total number of entrepreneurs in Europe choose entrepreneurship as their first choice comparing to employment.[135] Even after starting small or medium-sized entrepreneurial activities, their growth is relatively modest and hardly ever reaches the size of large companies.[136]

[130] Statistical Data on Women Entrepreneurs in Europe, p. 7.

[131] Evaluation on policy: Promotion of Women Innovators and Entrepreneurship, p. 3.

[132] Therefore, entrepreneurship does not imply only one business form of organizing economic activities. It is necessary to be understood in the wider context—as entrepreneurship including various sole entrepreneur business forms, partnerships, as well as different legal forms of companies. To be able to be considered as women's entrepreneurial ventures, the most common requirements for companies include that women have large participation in companies' capital, but also hold the position of director or board member.

[133] Minniti (2009), p. 540.

[134] Cowling (2010), p. 19.

[135] Entrepreneurship 2020 Action Plan, p. 4.

[136] Ibid.

However, there are also specific issues that can be relevant to everyone but are particularly important for women when deciding to undertake a business venture. The European Commission, for example, particularly references to lack of information, training, or education. Therefore, the significance of networking is particularly stressed upon, which can encourage business venture, and be of consequence for the dissemination of knowledge and experience. However, these factors are equally present for all forms of entrepreneurship.

Some of the problems are typical for women's entrepreneurship. An example of this is the numerous social reasons, as well as particularly noticeable problems in combining women's business ventures with their role in the family.[137] There are other reasons why women's entrepreneurship is less developed or is focused only on some areas. For example, the low presence of women in science and technology is particularly thought to stem from women's usual choices when deciding on a future profession, where typically science or technology is a "male profession", and therefore is not attractive to women.[138]

In the past decades, the EU's activities in the field of encouraging and developing women's entrepreneurship have mostly focused on understanding the problems and obstacles in that area. The same was true outside Europe, bearing in mind that female entrepreneurship is not just a European, but a world phenomenon that is given importance outside of Europe as well.[139] It is still an underdeveloped area, which so far has in mind the general policy of encouraging and developing women's entrepreneurship. Specific forms of incentives or assistance are mostly new, and their results still cannot be foreseen.[140]

19.4.2.2 Different Business Forms from a Gender Perspective

The "Small Business Act" for Europe defined ten basic framework principles that should guide the EU and Member States in promoting and encouraging small and medium-sized enterprises.[141]

> (1) Creating an environment in which entrepreneurs and family businesses can thrive and entrepreneurship is rewarded. (2) Opportunity for serious and honest entrepreneurs to get the second chance, even after bankruptcy. (3) Designing such rules that will be guided by the principle of "Think Small First". (4) Adaptation of administrative services to the needs of SMEs, especially through e-government

---

[137] See the most important challenges that the European Commission has pointed out in women's entrepreneurship. http://ec.europa.eu/growth/smes/promoting-entrepreneurship/we-work-for/women/. Accessed 23 April 2021.

[138] Evaluation on policy: Promotion of Women Innovators and Entrepreneurship, p. 3.

[139] One of the most important endeavours aimed at isolating, studying, and further encouraging women's entrepreneurship in America—the so-called The Diana project, established in 1999, is one of such examples. See Brush et al. (2010), pp. 1–2.

[140] Similar conclusions in Evaluation on policy: Promotion of Women Innovators and Entrepreneurship, p. 7.

[141] "Think Small First". A "Small Business Act" for Europe, p. 4.

and One-Stop-Shop system. (5) Adaptation of public policies to the needs of SMEs, especially the possibility of participation in public procurement and the use of state aid (6) Easier access to financing and creation of a legal and business environment that will encourage and support payments in business transactions. (7) Help SMEs to benefit more from the opportunities offered by the Single Market. (8) Promotion of education and all forms of innovation in SMEs. (9) Enable SMEs to turn the environmental challenges into opportunities. (10) Encouraging and supporting SMEs to benefit from the growth of markets.

The legislation was particularly focused on the regulation of state aid and the introduction of new organisational (European) forms of companies that would be adequate for small and medium enterprises. Other steps were also envisaged to provide more favourable tax treatment, payment regulation and other benefits particularly important in carrying out the business activities of SMEs.[142] Although the goals do not specifically highlight the encouragement of women's entrepreneurship, the specification of many of them emphasises women's entrepreneurship. They are intended to facilitate foundation of appropriate business form, as well as to be accessible for further functioning on the long term.

Even though various business forms can be addressed from the point of internal organisation and structure and its effect on the issue of gender equality, we will not further address them here. The reason is that they either fall within the scope of the composition of companies' bodies (management or supervisory boards) which we discussed in Sect. 19.3.2; or are addressed by labour law provisions. Still, some interesting research in relation to gender discrimination of minority owners and standard minority shareholders oppression mechanisms can be found in literature.[143]

19.4.2.3 Financing

If the provision of adequate funding is the most significant constraint in the development of entrepreneurship, then this is particularly true in the case of women's entrepreneurship.[144] Only 20.3% of businesses started with venture capital that belonged to female entrepreneurs.[145] Lack of financial independence, often dependence on the family, rarely exclusive ownership of real estate etc., prevents women from thinking about starting a business or developing already started businesses. That is why female entrepreneurship is typical in those areas that do not require significant, institutional, and external financing, but are based on their own savings and funds.[146]

Research studies point out numerous specifics of financing patterns, such as the fact that women's endeavours are characterised on average by lower capitalisation, a

[142] Ibid.

[143] Miller (2021), passim.

[144] Entrepreneurship 2020 Action Plan, p. 8.

[145] Evaluation on policy: Promotion of Women Innovators and Entrepreneurship, p. 2.

[146] Brush et al. (2010), p. 5.

lower ratio of debt finance and fewer opportunities to use personal funds or private equity.[147] A typical source of financing for small business—bank loans, according to many studies do not show evidence of gender-based discrimination.[148] As pointed out in Sect. 19.4.1.2 difference in treatment based on the person's sex while selecting contractual partner is forbidden. It is possible, however, that although not openly gender discriminatory, other decisive criteria are to the detriment of women's entrepreneurship: experience, business size, capital, character and scope of a business venture etc.[149]

Typical ways of financing are often inaccessible to women, which is why different mechanisms of private financing, support for the development, introduction and testing of new technologies, and loans to entrepreneurship with serious potential are increasingly desirable.[150] Therefore, some EU Member States, including Germany, but also UK, have special funding mechanisms for women, sometimes in certain special industries.[151]

During the last year the European Commission adopted "An SME Strategy for a sustainable and digital Europe" which further promotes entrepreneurship.[152] It particularly emphasised that "*...InvestEU – EU future investment funding*", a project envisaged by the European Commission, "*...could help stimulate investment in and with women and provide targeted support to extend the pipeline of investible female-led companies and funds under a gender-smart financing initiative.*" InvestEU Fund is envisaged to provide funds for various target groups, including vulnerable and specific ones. Funding should be provided not only by financial intermediaries (for example banks), but also through direct funding. Even though it is too early to make predictions of how this programme will affect female entrepreneurship, it was presumed that the number of female-led SMEs benefiting from this initiative could be tripled.[153] This project, accompanied with the already expanding projects according to Action Plan on the Capital Markets Union will benefit all market participants, and will further improve gender equality.

19.4.2.4 Education and Networking

The EU insists on connecting, networking and organising women in entrepreneurship. The Entrepreneurship 2020 Action Plan points out entrepreneurial education and training as its first pillar of action.[154] The ingrained division of occupations into

---

[147] Shaw et al. (2010), p. 187.

[148] Ibid., p. 188.

[149] Ibid.

[150] Entrepreneurship 2020 Action Plan, p. 9.

[151] See Evaluation on policy: Promotion of Women Innovators and Entrepreneurship, p. 5.

[152] Communication from the Commission to the European Parliament, the Council, the European Economic and Social Committee and the Committee of the Regions, An SME Strategy for a sustainable and digital Europe. 2020. COM(2020) 103 final.

[153] Ibid., p. 16.

[154] Entrepreneurship 2020 Action Plan, p. 5.

"male and female" and stereotypes in educational choices are important features of education in developed countries even today.[155] While typically "female" occupations are related to health care, education, administrative affairs and public relations, their presence is reduced in politics, economics, finance and also, occupations related to STEM fields.[156] Even when educated in these spheres, research in European countries indicates that women are less likely to be ready after education, or accomplishments in science, innovation and manufacturing to achieve results through entrepreneurship.[157] It is justifiably pointed out, therefore, that it is not enough just to acquire academic knowledge, but that also changes are necessary in attitude, goals, and skills, which indicate competitiveness and the ability to offer their abilities adequately.[158] Finally, education during career and for the development of personal abilities, skills etc. is important for all categories of entrepreneurs, including women.

Example

According to the Gender Equality Index 2020 provided by the European Institute for Gender Equality the lowest scores in gender inequalities are most pronounced in economic decision-making, as well as in the domain of knowledge, where gender inequalities are most pronounced in tertiary education. ◀

So far, there are extremely important initiatives at the EU level that encourage networking and organisation of women in entrepreneurship. Attention is particularly focused to mentors and business angels for women entrepreneurs. They also represent a kind of implementation of the policy of encouraging women's entrepreneurship in practice.

There are several such initiatives in Europe, the most famous of which is the European online platform for women entrepreneurs, which provides immediate practical assistance in starting commercial activities. In addition, there are numerous other European networks aimed at connecting and providing practical assistance in this area, such as the European community of women "Business Angels" and women entrepreneurs, the European network to promote women's entrepreneurship, the European network of female entrepreneurship ambassadors and the European network of mentors for women entrepreneurs.

Recently, and particularly important during the COVID-19 pandemic, the European Commission launched the Europe-wide online platform WEgate (*https://wegate.eu/*) dedicated to supporting women entrepreneurship. It is designated to unite all initiatives in this area and support starting, financing and managing of their business.

---

[155] Marques and Moreira (2019).

[156] Ibid., p. 30.

[157] Ibid.

[158] Kolin (2010), p. 125.

Providing assistance to care for children and other family members is one of the policies emphasised by the Entrepreneurship 2020 Action Plan as an important part of the Member States' strategy.[159] In response, some countries are taking special steps to provide childcare, residence and kindergarden. For example, Austria has set up regional business incubators that organise stays and childcare.[160]

Finally, the EU is taking many other steps, particularly aimed at promoting and encouraging women's entrepreneurship as a new specific subtype to which special attention is given. The EU especially insists on the necessary changes in culture concerning entrepreneurship, so that they stand out and are rewarded for the important features they have in economic growth and employment.[161] In this regard, activities that envisage awards and competitions in innovation, knowledge dissemination and other projects aimed at entrepreneurship stand out and are particularly emphasised.

19.5 Supporting Gender Equality in International Trade and Investment Agreements

Recently, gender equality has also been discussed in the context of trade and investment. In 2017, the World Bank found that discrimination against women as employees or entrepreneurs leads to a total income loss.[162] The World Trade Organisation has also responded to this with a Joint Declaration on Trade and Women's economic empowerment. This declaration expressed the "acknowledging that international trade and investment are engines of economic growth for both developing and developed countries, and that improving women's access to opportunities and removing barriers to their participation in national and international economies contributes to sustainable economic development."[163] The Informal Working Group on Trade and Gender, established in 2020, focuses on inclusive trade policies, collects data and tries to raise awareness of the issue among its members.

Trade is considered as a gamechanger which has an impact on the different roles of gender, meaning as a workforce, as producers and business owners as well as decision-makers. Especially, the lives of women can be improved by raising the number of working places for women, raising wages of women and logically the economic equality between women and men. Thus creating better jobs for women and increasing their welfare. In this context, in countries which are more open to trade, a higher level of gender equality can be found since in such countries. This may be due to a higher need for workforce and of highly skilled workers, which

---

[159] Entrepreneurship 2020 Action Plan, p. 23.

[160] See Evaluation on policy: Promotion of Women Innovators and Entrepreneurship, p. 5.

[161] Entrepreneurship 2020 Action Plan, p. 4.

[162] World Bank (2017).

[163] WTO (2017)

often cannot be met without opening new opportunities not only to men. Nevertheless, women still face discrimination concerning the integration into workforce as well as the activities as business owners. Therefore, discriminatory trade regulations, which hinder the market access of women and discriminate women-dominated industries, must be prohibited. Consequently, tariffs and nontariff barriers that are harmful to women and consumers need to be lowered and cross-border trade needs to be more attractive for women through trade facilitation as well as an easier access to finance.[164] In this regard, trade and investment agreements are considered to play a crucial role for the empowerment of women participation in trade and business.

19.5.1 Trade Agreements

Recently, the number of so-called regional trade agreements containing gender-related provisions has increased. For example, of the 305 agreements notified to the WTO that have entered into force, 83 contain explicit provisions on gender issues and another 178 contain implicit provisions.[165] As the Global Trade and Gender Arrangement between Canada, Chile and New Zealand was only recently adopted[166] and is the only exclusive agreement on gender issues, the other provisions are either found in gender chapters or elsewhere in the agreements.[167] The main actors in addressing gender issues in trade agreements are Canada and Chile, followed by the European Union, Israel, Japan, the United Kingdom and the South American countries Argentina, Brazil and Uruguay. Interestingly, many agreements that establish a customs union also contain gender-related provisions, such as the European Union, MERCOSUR, the Andean Community, COMESA, CARICOM, ECOWAS, SADC and many others. In addition, the provisions become more comprehensive if the signatory states have a higher human development level.[168]

Regulations dealing with gender issues have different forms and can be found in various places in the agreements, such as in the preamble, specific articles or chapters, but also mainly in non-specific articles and annexes. In terms of content, the provisions are also characterised by heterogeneity and deal with a wide variety of areas and connecting factors. This also applies to other subject areas and is a characteristic of bilateral agreements, as they are an expression of the interests and negotiations of the contracting parties. Nevertheless, the new deep comprehensive free trade agreements, especially those of the EU, try to apply a certain structure.

The most important gender-related provisions are those that seek cooperation as well as those that deal with specific concessions on national gender-related policies. Since the early 1980s, RTAs have included a call for the parties to cooperate with

---

[164] WTO/World Bank Group (2020).

[165] Monteiro (2021), pp. 2, 5.

[166] Global Trade and Gender Arrangement between Canada, Chile and New Zealand (2020).

[167] WTO/World Bank Group (2020).

[168] Monteiro (2021), p. 2.

each other on gender issues. It is mainly a general requirement for cooperation, which calls on the parties to consider the gender perspective in all areas of cooperation. Only the more recent agreements contain more detailed regulations and set principles for cooperation, specify different areas of cooperation or describe the forms of cooperation.

Article 13.3 of the Canada-Israel FTA:[169] Cooperation Activities

1. The Parties acknowledge the benefit of sharing their respective experiences in designing, implementing, monitoring and strengthening policies and programs to encourage women's participation in national and international economies. Accordingly, and subject to the availability of resources, the Parties shall develop programs of cooperative activities based on their mutual interests.
2. The aim of the cooperation activities will be to improve the capacity and conditions for women, including workers, businesswomen and entrepreneurs, to access and fully benefit from the opportunities created by this Agreement. These activities shall be carried out with inclusive participation of women.
3. The Parties shall encourage the involvement of their respective government institutions, businesses, labour unions, education and research organizations, other non-governmental organizations, and their representatives, as appropriate, in the cooperation activities decided upon by the Parties.
4. Areas of cooperation may include:
   (a) encouraging capacity-building and skills enhancement of women at work and in business;
   (b) promoting financial inclusion for women, including financial training, access to finance, and financial assistance;
   (c) advancing women's leadership and developing women's networks in business and trade;
   (d) developing better practices to promote gender equality within enterprises;
   (e) fostering women's representation in decision making and positions of authority in the public and private sectors, including on corporate boards;
   (f) promoting female entrepreneurship and women's participation in international trade, including by improving women's access to, and participation and leadership in, science, technology and innovation;
   (g) conducting gender-based analysis;
   (h) sharing methods and procedures for the collection of sex-disaggregated data, the use of indicators, and the analysis of gender-focused statistics related to trade; and
   (i) other issues as decided by the Parties.
5. The Parties may carry out activities in the cooperation areas set out in paragraph 4 through various means as they may decide, including workshops,

[169] Free Trade Agreement between the Government of Canada and the Government of the State of Israel (2018).

internships, collaborative research, specific exchanges of specialised technical knowledge and other activities as decided by the Parties.
6. The Trade and Gender Committee established by Article 13.4 may refer any proposed cooperation activities related to labour or labour market development to the Labour Ministerial Council established by Article 12.7 (Labour Ministerial Council) for its consideration.

Another important regulatory area is domestic gender-related policies. The agreements provide for the parties to adopt, harmonise and maintain regulations in the area of gender, labour, social and education policies. For example, the USMCA between USA, Mexico and Canada (formerly NAFTA) requires the parties to pursue policies that prevent all forms of gender discrimination in the workplace. Or for example the African regional groupings EAC and COMESA are required to have their own education and training programmes to raise awareness of gender discrimination or to strengthen women's skills. No specifications are made as to how these must be designed but most agreements contain an exemption for such issues which are excluded from the RTA as a whole or which are addressed with a differential treatment, e.g. for indigenous people and communities.

Other provisions include definitions, gender-related principles and references to other international agreements and instruments, such as CEDAW and the 1995 Beijing Declaration and Platform for Action on the rights of women and girls and their empowerment. These often confirm the implementation of the regulations there. For example in the area of corporate social responsibility in the case of the Canada-Israel RTA, which confirms in Art. 13.1 para 3 the obligations of the parties based on the OECD Guidelines for Multinational Enterprises. Furthermore, especially in the more recent RTAs, institutional arrangements have also been made. Either the general committees are used, or specific gender committees are to be formed with representatives of the parties. In addition to these committees, some RTAs also provide for national contact points and working groups. Their tasks are manifold and mainly relate to the implementation of the regulations, above all cooperation, the exchange of information and the implementation of gender policies. However, they also play a role in consultations and in cases of conflict.

A special feature of the new deep and comprehensive free trade agreements is the existence of dispute settlement provisions, so that proceedings do not necessarily have to be initiated within the framework of the Dispute Settlement Body of the WTO. However, the dispute settlement mechanism of the respective RTA, if included, can be used. Before this possibility can be considered, however, an amicable solution must be sought through consultations. Only after their failure can the dispute settlement procedures be initiated, but these are only made possible in very few RTAs on gender issues. Mostly, this is opened in connection with violations of labour rights regulations. The problem is that individuals cannot refer to the RTA, or only to a very limited extent, so that it is up to the national state to decide whether to initiate proceedings. This is regulated differently, for example, in the USMCA in Art. 23.11, which allows public submission by individuals.[170]

Example

This was done for the first time in 2021 by two Mexican women, together with various NGOs, who filed a complaint that the US was discriminating against women with its visa regime. The US issues two different visas: the H-2A for temporary seasonal agricultural workers and the H-2B for non-agricultural workers. The latter covers jobs with fewer benefits and lower pay in particular. Although the Mexican women applied several times for an H-2A visa and were sufficiently qualified for it, they were rejected. The H-2A visa is granted to 90% male workers. Both women faced sexual harassment and abuse in the workplace. An H-2A visa would help them access better jobs and working conditions. In their complaint, they saw various rights and obligations in Art. 23 USMCA violated and called on the Mexican authorities to ensure that the USA and Mexico "develop cooperative activities which address gender-related issues in the field of labour and employment, including the elimination of discrimination on the basis of sex in respect of employment, occupation, and wages" and to recommend consultation as mentioned in Art. 23.17 USMCA.[171] ◄

The extent to which gender-related provisions in free trade agreements are useful and have added value in terms of promoting gender equality in trade and supporting women's participation in trade is difficult to answer. The regulations to date are still too recent and effectiveness can only become clear in the near future. The case presented, but which is not decided yet will contribute to this, but the success or impact of gender-related provisions in RTAs must be compared comprehensively in the long term. To this end, CETA in particular provides for the exchange and analysis of methods and procedures for the collection of gender-specific trade statistics.[172]

---

[170] Chapter 23. Agreement between the United States of America, the United Mexican States, and Canada (2020).

[171] Centro de los Derechos de Migrante, inc. Amended Petition on Labor Law Matters arising in the United States submitted to the Labor Policy and Institutional Relations Unit through the General Directorate of Institutional Relations in the Secretariat of Labor and Social Welfare (STPS) United States-Mexico-Canada Agreement regarding the Failure of the U.S. Government to effectively enforce its Domestic Labor Laws and Promote the Elimination of Employment Discrimination in the H-2 Program in Violation of Chapter 23 of the United States-Mexiko-Canada Agreement (USMCA) (2021).

[172] CETA Trade and Gender Recommendation: EU-Canada Work Plan 2020-2021 (2020). Cf. UNCTAD (2020).

19.5.2 The Gender Perspective in International Investment Law and International Investment Agreements

Gender equality is undoubtedly seen as an important element for sustainable development and social welfare, nor is there any doubt that foreign investment is an important factor in achieving these goals. On the other hand, women are more affected by the impact of foreign direct investment. Although international investment law has been gender-blind for a long time, this has recently been increasingly criticised and the extent to which gender issues can also be considered has been discussed. But investments and their regulation have multiple implications for gender equality. Investments influence the labour market as well as production processes and can contribute to poverty reduction, which often affects women more. They have an impact on resource allocation and access to basic services. Investment can facilitate access to foreign exchange or influence exchange and interest rates. In addition, investment can also threaten the environment as well as the health of citizens.[173]

A major obstacle to gender mainstreaming of national regulations and changing gender policies is the obligation of states not to change the applicable national legal framework to the detriment of investors, in the future or such regulations. These are not applicable for the investor. The stabilisation clauses used for this purpose are for contracts between the investor and the host state. They are intended to minimise the risk of the investor being confronted with a situation after the investment with a change in the legal situation that results in further costs for the investor, or even makes it impossible for the investor to use his investment economically. In this case, the stabilisation clauses apply, which either declare the new regulations inapplicable or provide for financial compensation. While this does not make it impossible for states to change their regulations and for example, comply with their international obligations on gender mainstreaming, in the case of low-income countries it could lead to them having to compensate an investor with a large amount. For this reason, there is discussion about the extent to where stabilisation clauses need to be interpreted flexibly so that states that introduce a disadvantageous regulation do not have to compensate the investor for any disadvantages. Yet none of the approaches here are comprehensively convincing. The question then arises as to whether stabilisation clauses are still up-to-date or whether investors are not already sufficiently protected by the fair and equitable principle in international investment protection agreements between states.[174]

However, as uncertainties remain here as well, new ways are also proposed. In addition to the new trade and gender chapters in new deep free trade agreements and the increase of female arbitrators in arbitration panels, a gender impact assessment could be an important tool. The aim here is first to establish the current situation regarding gender policies and then to assess the potential impact on gender through

[173] Williams (2015), pp. 106 ff.

[174] Cf. Behne and Brillo (2017).

laws and measures. In this context, reference must be made to the UN Guiding Principles on Human Rights Impact Assessment of Trade and Investment Agreements, which explicitly mention gender equality as an indicator.[175] In addition, exceptions to the principles of National Treatment and Most-Favoured Nation are proposed, allowing host states to adopt regulations to promote social welfare that also affect investment. Both principles put foreign companies on an equal footing with both national companies and other foreign companies. Exceptions to this would allow the negative impacts of SMEs in low-income countries, which are often owned by women, to be mitigated as they cannot compete with foreign companies due to the national treatment principle. The same effect could be achieved by taking vulnerable groups into account in government procurement, especially women in developing countries. However, the underlying bilateral investment agreements must provide exceptions to this. The obligations of investors could also be regulated more strongly here, so that they feel obligated to non-discriminatory and equal treatment. This would be in line with the interest of companies to increase their corporate social responsibility. All proposals have a positive effect on the relationship between investment and gender, but so far, they are applied only sporadically and lack a structured approach.

19.6 Conclusion

In this chapter we pointed out that business law and its numerous areas can greatly affect gender equality. We stressed the importance of better business opportunities and encouragement in various aspects of business decision-making.

Mandatory quotas regarding composition of corporate boards and arbitral tribunals are considered controversial and unacceptable mechanism for fostering gender equality. This is especially true regarding the selection of arbitrators, keeping in mind that party autonomy is its main characteristics. Besides quotas as the most intrusive mechanisms, there are other less intrusive ones which are acceptable and should be promoted for reaching gender equality in corporate boards and arbitral tribunals. Transparency of gender representation in corporate boards and publicly available statistics regarding female arbitrators are one of them. Also, transparency of remuneration of directors represents an important mechanism for improving gender equality in corporate governance.

Many other important areas of business law have multiple implications for gender equality. Investments and entrepreneurship influence the labour market as well as production processes and can contribute to poverty reduction, which often affects women more. This is particularly true for female business ventures. Not only the ambition to carry out entrepreneurial activity but particularly women's intellectual potential is seen to be an important contribution to competitiveness in Europe. Therefore, the EU aims at promoting and encouraging women's entrepreneurship

[175] Human Rights Council (2011).

as a new specific subtype. Besides the indirect influence of the internal market, the EU, among other actors, started to gender-mainstream their international agreements, especially the trade and investment ones to safeguard that the participation in economical markets and trade are not dependent on gender.

We conclude that the attention must be called to the fact that gender equal involvement in business law can improve equality between genders in many other areas of political, economic and social life. Namely, better gender equal business environment, fostering of gender equal participation in business decision making, encouragement of gender-smart funding and further fostering of female and other sensitive groups entrepreneurship could lead to a better economic and social life of all individuals.

Questions

1. How does the EU internal market influence the gender-mainstreaming of products and services and has this an effect on the migration of workers?
2. Which mechanisms may foster gender diversity in arbitration?
3. Which mechanisms may foster gender diversity in board of directors?
4. Are mandatory quotas proper mechanism for improving gender balance in corporate boardrooms?
5. How can gender diversity on boards of financial institutions be further promoted?
6. Starting from which principle is regulated access to and supply of banking and insurance services in the EU?
7. What are the most important EU actions regarding female entrepreneurship?
8. What are specific features of gender-smart funding in entrepreneurship?
9. How can trade agreements influence the empowerment of women and support gender equality in business life?
10. Are investment agreements boosting gender equality?

References

Agreement between the United States of America, the United Mexican States, and Canada (2020). https://ustr.gov/sites/default/files/files/agreements/FTA/USMCA/Text/23%20Labor.pdf. Accessed 23 Apr 2021

Bahar R (2005) Executive compensation: is disclosure enough? https://papers.ssrn.com/sol3/papers.cfm?abstract_id=869415

Behne K, Brillo R (2017) Stabilization clauses in international investment law: beyond balancing and fair and equitable treatment. https://telc.jua.uni-halle.de/sites/default/files/BeitraegeTWR/Heft%20143.pdf. Accessed 23 Apr 2021

Benito Sánchez JC (2015) Gender imbalance within corporate governance systems in the European Union: a case for mandatory quotas. KU Leuven, Faculty of Law

Born GB (2021) International Commercial Arbitration. Kluwer Law International

Brush CG, de Bruin A, Gatewood EJ, Henry C (2010) Introduction: women entrepreneurs and growth. In: Brush CG, de Bruin A, Gatewood EJ, Henry C (eds) Women entrepreneurs and the global environment for growth: a research perspective. Edward Elgar, Cheltenham, pp 1–16

Cardillo G, Onali E, Torluccio G (2021) Does gender diversity on banks' boards matter? Evidence from public bailouts. J Corp Finan 71:101560. https://doi.org/10.1016/j.jcorpfin.2020.101560

Carter D, Simkins B, Garry Simpson W (2003) Corporate governance, board diversity, and firm value. Financ Rev 38:33–53

Centro de los Derechos de Migrante, Inc. Amended Petition on Labor Law Matters arising in the United States submitted to the Labor Policy and Institutional Relations Unit through the General Directorate of Institutional Relations in the Secretariat of Labor and Social Welfare (STPS) United States-Mexico-Canada Agreement regarding the Failure of the U.S. Government to effectively enforce its Domestic Labor Laws and Promote the Elimination of Employment Discrimination in the H-2 Program in Violation of Chapter 23 of the United States-Mexiko--Canada Agreement (USMCA) (2021). https://cdmigrante.org/wp-content/uploads/2021/03/USMCA-Amended-Peition-and-Appendices_March-23-2021_reduced.pdf. Accessed 23 Apr 2023

CETA Trade and Gender Recommendation: EU-Canada Work Plan 2020-2021 (2020). https://trade.ec.europa.eu/doclib/docs/2020/september/tradoc_158945.pdf. Accessed 23 Apr 2021

Choudhury B (2014) New rationales for women on boards. Oxf J Leg Stud 34:511–542

Cowling M (2010) Entrepreneurship, gender and job creation: European dynamics. In: Brush CG, de Bruin A, Gatewood EJ, Henry C (eds) Women entrepreneurs and the global environment for growth: a research perspective. Edward Elgar, Cheltenham, pp 19–38

Deloitte Centre for Financial Services (2019) Deloitte insights: within reach? Achieving gender equity in financial services leadership. https://www2.deloitte.com/us/en/insights/industry/financial-services/women-in-financial-services-leadership-roles.html. Accessed 17 Mar 2021

Directive No. 2004/38/EC on the right of citizens of the Union and their family members to move and reside freely within the territory of the Member States, OJ L 158 (2004), pp 77–123

Egan A (1982) Women in banking: a study in inequality. Ind Relat J 13:20–31. https://doi.org/10.1111/j.1468-2338.1982.tb00411.x

EIGE (2020) Gender Equality Index 2020: domain of power. https://eige.europa.eu/publications/gender-equality-index-2020-report/progress-gender-equality-most-notable-company-boards. Accessed 17 Mar 2021

Enriques L, Hansmann H, Kraakman R, Pargendler M (2017) The basic governance structure: minority shareholders and non-shareholder constituencies. In: Kraakman R et al (eds) The anatomy of corporate law – a comparative and functional approach. Oxford University Press, Oxford, pp 79–108

European Union (2021) Migration and migrant population statistics. https://ec.europa.eu/eurostat/statistics-explained/pdfscache/1275.pdf. Accessed 22 Apr 2021

Ferrarini G, Ungureanu MC (2020) Executive remuneration. In: Gordon JN, Ringe W-G (eds) The Oxford handbook of corporate law and governance. Oxford University Press, pp 334–362

Free Trade Agreement between the Government of Canada and the Government of the State of Israel (2018). https://www.international.gc.ca/trade-commerce/trade-agreements-accords-commerciaux/agr-acc/israel/fta-ale/text-texte/toc-tdm.aspx?lang=eng&_ga=2.25503029.962161659.1619185512-192130591.1619185512. Accessed 23 Apr 2021

Gaillard E, Savage J (eds) (1999) Fouchard Gaillard Goldman on International Commercial Arbitration. Kluwer Law International

Global Trade and Gender Arrangement between Canada, Chile and New Zealand (2020). https://www.international.gc.ca/trade-commerce/inclusive_trade-commerce_inclusif/itag-gaci/arrangement.aspx?lang=eng. Accessed 23 Apr 2021

Greenwood L (2017) Tipping the balance – diversity and inclusion in international arbitration. Arbitr Int 33:99–108

Greenwood L, Baker CM (2012) Getting a better balance on International Arbitration Tribunals. Arbitr Int 28:653–667

Greenwood L, Baker CM (2015) Is the balance getting better? An update on the issue of gender diversity in international arbitration. Arbitr Int 31:413–423

Grundmann S (2012) European company law, organization, finance and capital markets. Intersentia, Cambridge

Gulamhussen A, Santos SM (2010) Women in bank boardrooms and their influence on performance and risk-taking. https://papers.ssrn.com/sol3/papers.cfm?abstract_id=1615663. Accessed 17 Mar 2021

Havelková B (2018) Women on company boards: equality meets subsidiarity. https://jeanmonnetprogram.org/wp-content/uploads/JMWP-07-Barbara-Havelkov%C3%A1.pdf. Accessed 4 Apr 2021

Hopt KJ (2013) Comparative corporate governance: the state of the art and international regulation. In: Fleckner AM, Hopt KJ (eds) Comparative corporate governance – a functional and international analysis. Cambridge University Press, Cambridge, pp 3–101

Human Rights Council (2011) Report of the Special Rapporteur on the right to food, Olivier De Schutter, Addendum Guiding principles on human rights impact assessments of trade and investment agreements. A/HRC/19/59/Add.5. https://undocs.org/A/HRC/19/59/Add.5. Accessed 23 Apr 2021

Jevremović Petrović T (2019) Pravni okvir EU za podsticanje ženskog preduzetništva. In: Radović V (ed) Usklađivanje poslovnog prava Srbije sa pravom Evropske unije (2019). Pravni fakultet Univerziteta u Beogradu, Beograd, pp 36–57

Johnson K (2017) Banking on diversity: does gender diversity improve financial firms' risk oversight? SMU Law Rev 70:327–376

Khambata DJ (2015) Tensions between party autonomy and diversity. In: Van den Berg AJ (ed) Legitimacy: myths, realities, challenges, ICCA Congress Series, vol 18. ICCA & Kluwer Law International, pp 612–637

Kolin M (2010) Gender inequalities and the status of women in the labor market in transitional Serbia. Anthropol East Europe Rev 28:119–137

Lee F (2013) Show me the money: using the business case rationale to justify gender targets in the EU. Fordham Int Law J 36:1471–1516

Lepetić J (2018) Aktivizam akcionara. Pravo i privreda 65:105–123

Leszczyńska M (2018) Mandatory quotas for women on boards of directors un the European Union: harmful to or good for company performance? Eur Bus Organ Law Rev 19:35–61

Lew JDM, Mistelis LA et al (2003) Comparative International Commercial Arbitration. Kluwer Law International

Marques AP, Moreira HR. Women, science and entrepreneurship. How the academy can (or not) change their lives. http://repositorium.sdum.uminho.pt/bitstream/1822/23031/1/Women%2C%20Science%20and%20Entrepreneurship.pdf. Accessed 11 June 2019

Masselot A, Maymont A (2014) Balanced representation between man and women in business law: the French 'Quota' system to the test of EU legislation. CEELS Online Paper Series 3:1–25

McCahery JA, Vermeulen EPM (2014) Understanding the board of directors after the financial crisis: some lessons for Europe. J Law Soc 41:121–150

Miller MR (2021) Challenging gender discrimination in closely held firms: the hope and hazards of corporate oppression doctrine. Indiana Law Rev 54:1–36

Minniti M (2009) Gender issues in entrepreneurship. Found Trends Entrep 57:497–621. https://doi.org/10.1561/0300000021

Monteiro J-A. The evolution of gender-related provision in regional trade agreements. https://www.wto.org/english/res_e/reser_e/ersd202108_e.pdf. Accessed 23 Apr 2021

Morera U (2015) Sulle ragioni dell'equilibrio di genere negli organi delle società quotate e pubbliche. In: Studi dedicati a Mario Libertini. Giuffré, Milan

O'Connor N (2015) The impact of positive action on private law freedoms – proposed EU Directive on gender balance in the boardroom. Trinity Coll Law Rev 18:128–153

Radović V (2011) Naknada članovima uprave akcionarskog društva. Pravni fakultet Univerziteta u Beogradu, Beograd

Regulation No. 492/2011 on freedom of movement for workers within the Union, OJ L 141 (2011) pp 1–12
Seierstad C, Huse M (2017) Gender quotas on corporate boards in Norway: ten years later and lessons learned. In: Seierstad C, Gabaldon P, Mensi-Klarbach H (eds) Gender diversity in the boardroom, volume 1: The use of different quota regulation, Cham, pp 11–45
Senden L, Visser M (2013) Balancing a tightrope: the EU Directive on improving the gender balance among non-executive directors of boards of companies. Eur Gend Equality Law Rev 1: 17–33
Seraglini C (2015) Who are the arbitrators? In myths, reality and challenges. In: Van den Berg AJ (ed) Legitimacy: myths, realities, challenges, ICCA Congress Series, vol 18. ICCA & Kluwer Law International, pp 589–611
Shaw E, Carter S, Lam W (2010) An integrated view of gender, finance and entrepreneurial capital: theory, practice and policy. In: Brush CG, de Bruin A, Gatewood EJ, Henry C (eds) Women entrepreneurs and the global environment for growth: a research perspective. Edward Elgar, Cheltenham, pp 187–205
Szydło M (2014) Constitutional values underlying gender equality on the boards of companies: how should the EU put these values into practice? Int Comp Law Q 63:167–196
Szydło M (2015) Gender equality on the boards of EU companies: between economic efficiency, fundamental rights and democratic legitimisation of economic governance. Eur Law J 21:97–115
Tinsley CH, Wade JB, Main BGM, O'Reilly CA (2017) Gender diversity on U.S. corporate boards: are we running in place? ILR Rev 70:160–189
UNCTAD (2020) Gender and trade - assessing the impact of trade agreements on gender equality: Canada-EU Comprehensive Economic and Trade Agreement
Van Haersolte-Van Hof JJ (2015) Diversity in diversity. In: Van den Berg AJ (ed) Legitimacy: myths, realities, challenges, ICCA Congress Series, vol 18. ICCA & Kluwer Law International, pp 638–651
Van Harten G (2012) The (lack of) women arbitrators in investment treaty arbitration. https://papers.ssrn.com/sol3/papers.cfm?abstract_id=2005336. Accessed 21 Apr 2021
Vasiljević S, Sunko A-M (2017) EU law and gender-balanced boards: making equality effective. Croat Yearb Eur Law Policy 13:27–51
Verbist H, Schäfer E et al (2015) ICC arbitration in practice. Kluwer Law International
Williams M (2015) Gender issues and the reform of investment liberalization, IIAs and BITs. In: South Centre (ed) Investment treaties: views and experiences from developing countries. South Centre, Geneva, pp 105–123. 106 ff.
World Bank (2017) Doing Business Report 2017. https://www.doingbusiness.org/en/reports/global-reports/doing-business-2017. Accessed 23 Apr 2021
World Economic Forum (2022) Global Gender Gap Report 2022. https://www3.weforum.org/docs/WEF_GGGR_2022.pdf. Accessed 23 Apr 2021
WTO (2017) Joint declaration on trade and women's economic empowerment on the occasion of the WTO Ministerial Conference in Buenos Aires. https://www.wto.org/english/thewto_e/minist_e/mc11_e/genderdeclarationmc11_e.pdf. Accessed 23 Apr 2021
WTO/World Bank Group (2020) Women and trade – the role of trade in promoting gender equality. World Bank Publications, Washington

Further Reading

Dalmaso Marques R (2015) To diversify or not to diversify? Report on the session who are the arbitrators. In: Van den Berg AJ (ed) Legitimacy: myths, realities, challenges, ICCA Congress Series, vol 18. ICCA & Kluwer Law International, pp 579–588

Seierstad C, Gabaldon P, Mensi-Klarbach H (eds) (2017) Gender diversity in the boardroom, vol 2: Multiple approaches beyond quotas. Cham

Sinha AK, Anand P (2021) Feminist overview of international investment law – a preliminary inquiry. J Int Econ Law, 99–125, 119 et seq.

Warren E. What is a women's issue? Bankruptcy, commercial law, and other gender-neutral topics. Harvard Law School Public Law Research Paper No. 032. https://papers.ssrn.com/sol3/papers.cfm?abstract_id=310544. Accessed 17 Mar 2021

MIX
Papier aus verantwortungsvollen Quellen
Paper from responsible sources
FSC® C105338

If you have any concerns about our products,
you can contact us on
ProductSafety@springernature.com

In case Publisher is established outside the EU,
the EU authorized representative is:
Springer Nature Customer Service Center GmbH
Europaplatz 3, 69115 Heidelberg, Germany

Printed by Libri Plureos GmbH
in Hamburg, Germany